Jokhang

Gilded roofs and the Great Courtyard (Kyamra Chenmo). (1997 MF)

Cover:
The Great Temple of Lhasa, Western approach. (1985 HM)

Jokhang

Tibet's most sacred Buddhist Temple

Gyurme Dorje
Tashi Tsering
Heather Stoddard
André Alexander

Edition Hansjorg Mayer

Dedicated to the Tibetan people

The publisher would particularly like to thank his old friend, Anthony Aris for all his assistance and creative suggestions regarding this book.

First published in 2010 by Edition Hansjörg Mayer, London and Bangkok
in association with The Tibet Charitable Trust, London

Design: Hansjörg Mayer
Production: HaNaPa
Printed in Thailand by Bangkok Printing Co., Ltd.

Distributed outside the United States and Canada by
Thames & Hudson Ltd, 181A High Holborn, London WC1V 7QX

Distributed in the United States and Canada by
Thames & Hudson Inc., 500 Fifth Avenue, New York, New York 10110

ISBN: 978-500-097-692-0

Library of Congress Catalog Card number 2009934777

Contents

Introduction

Gyurme Dorje

For over one thousand three hundred years the Great Temple of Lhasa has functioned as the vital nerve centre of spiritual and economic life in Tibet. For citizens of Lhasa and Buddhist pilgrims who converge there from all quarters of the Tibetan plateau, the Great Temple (area 2,600 sq. m) is the focal point of their faith, an enduring symbol of their unique cultural heritage. Around it the old city of Lhasa developed over the centuries in a series of narrow radial roads, where commerce and barter thrive.

The Great Temple does not dominate the skyline of Lhasa in the way that the Potala rises awesomely from Red Hill (Marpori). Yet the old lanes of the city offer subtle glimpses of its high whitewashed walls, its maroo brushwood architrave, and the golden rooftop ornaments, as they reflect strong high altitude sunlight against the backdrop of a cobalt blue sky. This magnificent legacy of Tibet's first unifying king, Songtsen Gampo (b. 617)[1] has withstood successive persecutions, civil war, armed invasion, cultural revolution, and assault by armed police; and, even now, it continues to fulfil its pivotal role as the axis of the Tibetan world. Its turbulent history is the history of the Tibetan capital itself.

The building actually has several names. The formal name is Rasa Trulnang ("emanational temple of Rasa"), and to most Tibetans it is known simply as the Tsuglakhang (Skt. *vihāra*), which, in the Tibetan context, translates as "Great Temple" or "Grand Temple". Outside Tibet, it is commonly known as the Jokhang ("chapel of Jowo Śākyamuni"), after the name of its Central Inner Sanctum, and in Chinese it is called Dazhao Si ("monastery of great distinction").

Early Historical Sources

The earliest historical records that refer to the foundation of the Great Temple are the royal edicts promulgated along with the epigraphic inscriptions of King Trisong Detsen and King Senalek Jingyon, which date from the late eighth and early ninth centuries.[2] No extant literary references appear to predate the *Testament Extracted from the Pillar (bka' chems ka khol ma)* and the *Collected Works of the King Concerning the Mantra Oṃ Maṇi Padme Hūṃ (Ma ṇi bka' 'bum)*, parts of which were reputedly concealed in the Great Temple, in the manner of a time capsule, by King Songtsen Gampo himself, to be retrieved and redacted in later centuries by Atiśa (982-1054) and Drubthob Ngodrub (fl. 12th century) respectively.[3]

Another important source from this period is the *Religious History entitled Honey Essence of Flowers (chos 'byung me tog snying po sbrang tsi'i bcud)*, which was composed by Nyangrel Nyima Ozer (1136-1204), an associate of Drubthob Ngodrub.[4]

The willow enclosure fronting the entrance portico to the Great Temple (p. 95). Full moon, Losar 1989 (AA)

Devotees at the entrance portico (p. 95). (1999 HS)

Aspirational prayers in the presence of Jowo Śākyamuni. (1999 HS)

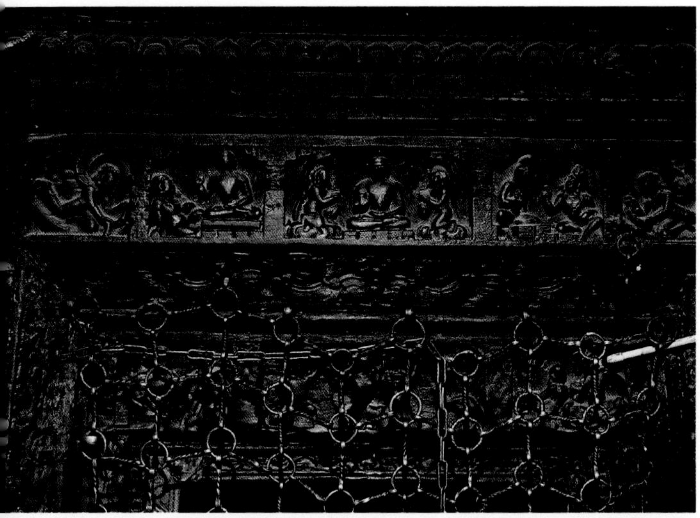

Wood carved lintels above the chapel of Maitreya. (p. 74, no. **34**, 1999 HS)

Wood carved lintels of the original Newar gateway depicting scenes from the Jātakas. (1999 HS)

Architectural Influences

These and later historical sources all attribute the original construction of the Great Temple to Newār craftsmen and artisans who were employed in Tibet, commencing in 639 or 641, by the illustrious king Songtsen Gampo.[5] The craftsmen made use of local stone, brick, adobe and timber, and, structurally, their building has successfully stood the test of time.

The king's immediate purpose was to build a temple worthy of housing the sacred images including Jowo Akṣobhyavajra *(jo bo mi bskyod rdo rje)*, Maitreya, and Tārā, which had been brought to Tibet from Nepal as the dowry of his Newār queen Bhṛkuṭīdevī. Although the existence of this queen has been disputed, owing to the paucity of Newār sources, later Tibetan chronicles do suggest that she reached Lhasa from Nepal in 632 or 634.[6] Contemporary art historians have all corroborated the Newār architectural influences, which are so prominent in the wood carvings of the Great Temple, particularly in the ancient pillars, capitals, rounded doorways and lintels of its oldest chapels.[7] The lintels display geometric patterns, animal motifs, and themes derived from Buddhist sūtras, which are all suggestive of Licchāvi origin. Even the layout of the five oldest chapels around a central atrium surmounted by a gallery on the floor above appears reminiscent of stone temples at Ellora in India and the bahals of the Kathmandu valley.

The Great Temple faces west, towards Nepal, in honour of this association with Princess Bhṛkuṭīdevī.

Certain rectangular doorways and their carvings have also been compared to those at Ajanta in South India, and it has elsewhere been suggested that the building may have initially been conceived as a royal residence. Its pentadic design-the high-ceilinged Central Inner Sanctum flanked by side-chapels and those of the north and south wings-appears to have some affinity with early Tibetan tower-fortresses *(mkhar)* at Gyama, the birthplace of King Songtsen Gampo, and Yumbu Lagang, the palace of the earliest kings.[8]

Geomantic Conceptions

Chinese influence is attested, not in the early architecture of the Great Temple, but in the legendary accounts of its geomantic importance. The Chinese princess Wencheng who reached Lhasa in 641 around the time when the construction had already begun reputedly conceived the Tibetan terrain as a "supine ogress" *(bod srin mo gan rkyal)*, who would be tamed and rendered amenable to Buddhist civilisation by the construction of geomantic temples at focal points on her limbs. The Milk Plain Lake *('o thang mtsho)* at Lhasa on which the Great Temple was founded came to be regarded as the geomantic heart of this scheme.[9] Wencheng's other contribution to the foundation of Buddhism in Tibet was the construction of Ramoche Temple in Lhasa and the installation therein of the renowned Jowo Śākyamuni image, which she had brought from China as her own dowry.[10]

The Original Construction

During the reigns of the great Buddhist kings of the Pugyal Empire (c. 633-842), the Great Temple appears to have retained its original pentadic shape. The tower of the Central Inner Sanctum occupied two storeys, while its adjacent chapels on the east wing, and those of the north and south wings, occupied a single storey on the ground and middle floors. Columns divided the structure internally into thirty-seven sections, which symbolise the thirty-seven divisions of the Vinayapiṭaka.[11] Treasures were interred within the walls and underground for the benefit of the Great Temple in future centuries.[12]

The antiquity of the top or third floor remains a matter of some speculation. However, the central chapel above the head of the Central Inner Sanctum appears to date from the royal period, as do some elements of the Chapel of the Śrīdevī Turret. On completion of the third storey, probably after the death of Bhṛkutīdevī, the Great Temple was said to symbolise the "three world systems" (Skt. *tridhātu*) of ancient Indian cosmology. Other chapels *(lha khang)* and hermitages or residential cells *(gzim khang)* on all three levels of the building were incorporated gradually into the original core structure.

The earliest images, installed during the era of King Songtsen Gampo on the ground floor, were: Dīpaṃkara Buddha in the form of Acala surrounded by his retainers (east), Amitābha (northeast), Maitreya (southeast), Mahākāruṇika (north) and Śākyamuni in the form Akṣobhyavajra (south). On the middle floor the oldest chapels appear to have been dedicated as follows, some images dating from the seventh and others from the late eighth or early ninth century: Hermitage of the King (northeast), Padmākara (southeast), Yakṣa (north), Yakṣinī (south), and Seven Generations of Past Buddhas (west).[13] On the third floor, Maitreya and his retainers were installed above the Central Inner Sanctum (east), and the Chapel of the Śrīdevī Turret (south) contained a painting of the face of Śrīdevī, reputedly drawn with the nasal blood of King Songtsen Gampo.[14] The vestibule inside the Great Acacia Gate also appears to be of great antiquity. Images of the protectors Kubera and Nanda are said to have been first installed here during the seventh century.

Guru Nangsi Zilnon (p. 77, no. **60**). (2000 GD)

Royal Patronage

Accounts of the patronage extended to the Great Temple by the powerful kings of the Pugyal Empire may be found in the aforementioned *Religious History (chos'byung)* of Nyangrel Nyima Ozer, and in later chronicles of Sakyapa, Zhalupa, and Kagyupa provenance. These include the *Religious History (chos 'byung)* of Buton Rinchendrub (1290-1364), the *Red Annals (deb ther dmar po)* of Tshalpa Kunga Dorje (1309-64), the *Clear Mirror of Royal Genealogies (rgyal rabs gsal ba'i me long),* which was composed by Sonam Gyaltsen (1312-75), the *Blue Annals (deb ther sngon po)* of Go Lotsāwa Zhonupel (1392-1481), and the *Scholars' Banquet (mkhas pa'i dga'ston)* of Pawo Tsuklak Tsengwa (1504-66).[15]

After the death of King Songtsen Gampo (circa 650), the image of Jowo Śākyamuni was taken from Ramoche and concealed in a secret compartment in the south wing of the Great Temple. This action was undertaken ostensibly to pre-empt the statue's removal by an invading Chinese army, but more probably to prevent its destruction by hostile non-Buddhist factions.[16] Then, as if to explain its present location, later narratives recount that the image of Akṣobhyavajra was removed from the Southern Inner Sanctum by the retreating Chinese forces and carried as far as Cholung where it was abandoned before being installed within Ramoche.

The images of Acala and his retainers remained undisturbed within the Central Inner Sanctum of the Great Temple until circa 710 when the Chinese Princess Jincheng reached Lhasa and became the consort of prince Me Aktsom. Through elemental divination, she is said to have retrieved Jowo Śākyamuni from its place of concealment in the south wing and installed this image on the central plinth, placing Acala immediately to its rear.

Chapel of the Seven Generations of Past Buddhas (p. 76, no. **51**). (2000 GD)

Over the century which followed, the powerful kings Me Aktsom (r. 713–755), Trisong Detsen (r. 755-797), Senalek Jingyon (r. 804-815) and

Townspeople prostrating outside the entrance portico (p. 95). (1997 MF)

Ralpachen (r. 815-836) constructed further chapels within the Great Temple, including those dedicated to Siṃhanāda and Songtsen Gampo's courtiers.

They all endeavoured to fulfil the prophetic injunction of their illustrious ancestor by offering the first fruits of their own royal construction projects to the Great Temple. Among them, circa 775, King Trisong Detsen offered the first fruits of earth and timber from the construction of Samye Monastery. The clay was used for the sculpting of the renowned images of the Four Great Guardian Kings and the wood for the construction of a door that would protect the entrance to the Central Inner Sanctum.[17]

Among all these original sacred images of Indian, Newār, and Tibetan origin dating from the royal period, only those of Jowo Śākyamuni and Songtsen Gampo now survive. The others have been damaged and destroyed as recently as the Cultural Revolution, and have been replaced by new replicas.

The extent of the original courtyard in front of the Great Temple during the royal period is uncertain, although its construction is attributed to Senalek Jingyon. The Wood Enclosure *(shing-rva)* is also said to have existed at that time, probably in a rudimentary and undeveloped form. It was here in 842 that the tantric master Lhalung Palgyi Dorje assassinated the apostate king Langdarma before fleeing to Amdo, in consequence of which it became known as the Death Enclosure *(shi-rva)*.[18] The name Wood Enclosure appears to date from the inauguration of the Great Prayer Festival in the fifteenth century.

During the persecution instigated by the Bon ministers of Langdarma some sacred images were interred, incinerated or cast into the Kyichu River, the Great Temple was closed and its Great Acacia Gate desecrated.[19] Yet, the building and its principal images somehow survived the indignities of this anti-Buddhist persecution, providing a link of continuity between the early and later phases of Buddhist expansion in Tibet. The four silver Sibling Maitreya images of the south wing were actually sculpted by Utpala of Kashmir during this period.[20]

As for the early paintings, historical sources such as the *Scholars' Banquet (mkhas pa'i dga'ston)* and later inventories *(dkar chag)* of the Great Temple attribute certain murals to the hand of King Songtsen Gampo himself, including the five buddhas of the northwest wall, the Prajñāpāramitā and narrative scenes of the southwest wall, and the Śrīdevī mural of the middle floor.[21] Yet, none of these survive in their original forms.[22] The earliest extant paintings, found in the Chapel of the Countenance, are reckoned to date from the eleventh or twelfth century.[23]

Daily assembly within the Main Hall. (p. 77, no. **55**) (2000 GD)

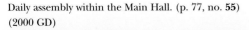

Kadampa Restorations

The next phase of development coincided with the restoration of monastic Buddhism in Central Tibet during the late-tenth century when Lu-me Tsultrim Nyingpo returned from Amdo to Central Tibet *circa* 978, having obtained the full monastic ordination from the successors of Lachen Gongpa Rabsel.[24] He reinstated the observance of monastic disciple, according to Śāntarakṣita's "Lower" Tibetan Vinaya lineage *(smad 'dul)*, and sculpted an image of Khasarpaṇi, which was then transported from Dribda Lhakhang and placed within the Chapel of the Four Sibling Maitreyas on the south wing.[25]

Later, in the mid-eleventh century, when the renowned Bengali master Atiśa was invited to teach in Lhasa, he is said to have extracted a text entitled *bka' 'chems bka' 'khol ma*, the testament of King Songtsen Gampo, which had been concealed alongside the Leaf Pillar.

Around 1076, Zangkar Lotsāwa enlarged the Central Inner Sanctum by constructing a projecting bay *(glo 'bur)* to its rear (east). He then moved the small images of the retainers of Acala to the top floor and installed in their place a large image of Vairocana Buddha in the form Hīmamahāsāgara *(thub pa gangs can mtsho)* along with an impressive retinue of standing bodhisattvas and gatekeepers, all of which he himself had sculpted. The Newār image of Maitreya Chokhor which had formerly occupied the central chapel of the top floor was reportedly brought downstairs and installed within the southeast chapel of the ground floor at this time.[26] Zangkar Lotsāwa also transformed the gallery of the east wing on the middle floor into the Chapel of the Countenance *(zhal ras khang)* and sculpted the image of Bathing Maitreya on the north wing of the ground floor.[27]

Hīmamahāsāgara, in the Central Inner Sanctum (p. 73). (1997 HS)

Kagyupa Restorations

The decades which followed this extension of the Central Inner Sanctum witnessed increasing factional conflicts among the holders of the "Lower" Tibetan Vinaya lineage, who were the successors of Lu-me. The Great Temple was neglected for a time, and it grew dilapidated.[28]

Fortunately, lineage-holders of the nascent Kagyu tradition assumed responsibility for its renovation at this juncture. In 1160, Gompa Tsultrim Nyingpo (1116-69), the nephew of Gampopa, took up residence and constructed an inner pilgrims' walkway around the Great Temple. He also commissioned murals in the Chapel of the Countenance on the first floor. A three-panelled mural on the southeast inner wall of this chapel, reflecting both Pāla and Tibetan styles, is still preserved to this day.[29]

Newly sculpted images in the Chapel of Lama Zhang (p. 82. no. **82**). (2000GD)

The Era of the Tshalpa Tripon

One of Gompa Tsultrim Nyingpo's foremost students, Zhang Yudrakpa of Tshal Gungtang (1122-93) subsequently took up residence in the middle floor of the Great Temple, and he installed the highly revered black stone image of "frog-faced" Rematī in the Śrīdevī Turret, having reputedly extracted it as treasure from Jakhar Rock in Gungtang. With the assistance of Nyingma masters such as Drogon Namka Pelwa (fl. early 13th century), Zhikpo Dudtsi (1143-99), and Taton Jo-ye (1163-1230), he constructed and maintained the Great Temple's flood-dykes on the north bank of the Kyichu.[30]

His successors who upheld the Tshalpa Kagyu lineage continued to maintain the Great Temple until the fifteenth century, assuming the official title *Tshalpa Tripon*. In 1310, they raised the gilded roofs that had been offered by kings of Yartse in NW Nepal above the ancient chapels of Jowo Śākyamuni and Mahākāruṇika.[31] They sculpted the images of King Songtsen

Gilded cīvaṃcīvaka figure on the temple roof (p. 88). (1991 US)

Gampo and his queens which once graced the Hermitage of the King on the middle floor; and they commissioned sacred images of Mañjuśrīghoṣa and Vajrapāṇi, which were placed to the right and left of Mahākāruṇika in the Northern Inner Sanctum.

Among these sacristans Gewabum (fl. early 13th century) is known to have renovated the flood-dykes and restored the damaged outer walls of the Great Temple.[32] Ga-de Zangpo (fl. late 13th century), who was respected as an emanation of the Tshalpa protector Gonpo Jarok, decorated the four groups of long columns which support the skylight of the Main Hall, and plastered five of the short transverse columns. He also commissioned the Fourth Tulku Godru to sculpt a radiantly peaceful image of the protectress Śrīdevī, which was then installed in the Chapel of the Śrīdevī Turret.

Monlam Dorje (fl. early 14th century) completed his predecessor's reconstruction of the slate gallery and skylight. He extended the twelve long columns, strengthened the bases of the sixteen short columns and enlarged the inner walkway. In addition, he commissioned statues of King Songtsen Gampo and his queens, which were placed on a stone platform outside the northeast chapel, and those of the king with his three foremost queens, three foremost ministers, and the crown prince Gungri Gungtsen, which once rested on a similar platform along the south wing.[33]

The latter's son, Kunga Dorje, who held the rank of *Tshalpa Tripon* for twenty-eight years, is better known for having composed the influential historical text known as the *Red Annals (deb ther dmar po)* between 1346 and 1363. He restored the offering lamps of the Central Inner Sanctum and engaged Phakpa Sangye Rinchen to repaint the murals of the Maṇi Wheel Chapel.[34] One of his successors, a later *Tshalpa Tripon* named Tashi, also constructed the Chapel of the Conqueror Śākyamuni on the third floor.[35]

The lineage of the Tshalpa Kagyu order continued to function independently until the fifteenth century when, under the influence of Tsongkhapa, it was absorbed by the Gelugpa who maintain its transmissions at the present day.[36]

Lama Zhang Yudrakpa (p. 70). (2000 GD)

Mahākāruṇika (p. 70). (2000 GD)

Gilded roofs surmounting the chapels of Jowo Śākyamuni and Mahākāruṇika (p. 87). (2000 AA)

Anniversary of the Mountain Hermitage of Śrīdevī[37]

On the thirteenth, fourteenth and fifteenth days of the tenth lunar month, a special ceremony known as Pelha Ridra *(dpal lha ri gra)* is performed in honour of the foremost protectress of the Great Temple, Śrīdevī *(dpal ldan lha mo)* in the wrathful form of Rematī. Once a year, before dawn on the thirteenth day, the wrathful image of Rematī, which had first been installed in the Chapel of the Śrīdevī Turret by Zhang Yudrakpa, would be taken onto the open roof by the monks of Meru. The image would be placed alongside the rooftop incense burner and prayer-flag mast. Ablutions would then be performed, the image regilded and refurbished with new ornaments and brocade robes.

On the fourteenth day a torma exorcism *(gtor rgyag)* would be performed in the presence of the cabinet ministers and important citizens of Lhasa, while finely dressed ladies of noble birth *(dpal gsol ma)* sing hymns in praise of the protectress. The image would be carried around the skylight gallery of the top floor, re-enacting Śrīdevī's circumambulation of Mt Sumeru. Hence the original name of the ceremony: *dpal lha ri rab or dpal lha ri khrod*. The sacristans and the townspeople would take turns offering money and alms – an offering known as Pelha Duchang *(dPal lha dus chang)*. Finally prayer flags and various offerings would be scattered and taken home by those attending the service. That night the image would be taken downstairs and placed in the Central Inner Sanctum, facing Jowo Śākyamuni.

On the following morning, the monks of Meru would perform *torma* exorcisms *(gtor rgyag)* at strategic points in the four directions of the city, and the image of Rematī would be carried shoulder-high by one of their number around the Barkor Jangchub Jonlam Street in great procession. En route, offerings would be made by officials, citizens and foreign envoys, following which Rematī would be escorted back to the Chapel of the Śrīdevī Turret.

Sakya Hegemony

The period during which the successive *Tshalpa Tripon* actively maintained the Great Temple largely coincided with the Sakya and Phagmodru administrations in Tibet (1235-1478). The former, though documented in

Fine costumes and jewelry on view during the Great Prayer Festival. (1943 TS)

Massed drums of the Namgyal Monastery during the Great Prayer Festival. (film stills 1943 TS)

Procession of the cavalry commanders in Mongolian dress *(yaso)* during the Great Prayer Festival.

Procession of the aristocrats during the Great Prayer Festival.

the *Red Annals* and the *Blue Annals*, is presented in greater detail in the *Royal Genealogy of Sakya (sa skya'i rgyal rabs)* by Jamgon Amnye Zhab (1597-1662).

The monastery of Sakya had been founded in 1073 by Khon Konchok Gyalpo, and nurtured by his successors in the familial line: Sachen Kunga Nyingpo (1092-1158), Sonam Tsemo (1142-82), Drakpa Gyaltsen (1147-1206), and Sakya Paṇḍita Kunga Gyaltsen (1182-1251). The last named forged an alliance with Godan Qan, the Mongol successor of Genghiz Qan in 1244, ensuring that Tibet would avoid the disastrous fate of the Tangut (Xixia) kingdom, and that the tradition of Sakya would become pre-eminent.[38] He commissioned the Stūpa of Scrutiny *(brtag pa'i mchod rten)*, a replica of which still stands in the north wing of Great Temple. It formerly contained a terracotta relic made by the hand of Songtsen Gampo. His nephew Drogon Chogyal Phakpa (1235-80) later donated the Lotus Heap Stūpa *(mchod rten padma spungs pa)*, which once graced the south wing.

The chief minister *(dpon chen)* Shākya Zangpo (fl. late 13th century), who exercised political control from the then capital of Tibet at Sakya, commissioned an ornate silver throne for Jowo Śākyamuni. His successors had the Great Acacia Gate restored and new chapels constructed on the top floor. Among them, the chief minister Wangchuk Tsondru in 1340 sculpted images of the Five Buddhas *(rgyal ba rigs lnga)* which were installed in the chapel surmounting the Central Inner Sanctum on the top floor. He also commissioned clay images of Śākyamuni Buddha, flanked by the Sixteen Elders in their distinctive bas relief grottoes, which were installed in the Chapel of the Sixteen Elders *(gnas bcu lha khang)* on the west wing of the top floor.

Until recent times, Sakya liturgies have been performed daily by monks from Gongkar Shedrubling in the Chapel of Offerings *(mchod sgrom lha khang)* on the ground floor of the Great Temple.[39] As if to commemorate this period of Sakya influence, images of the original Sakya lineage-holders were installed and venerated in the south wing of the Main Hall: Virūpa, Kunga Nyingpo, Sonam Tsemo, Drakpa Gyaltsen, Sakya Paṇḍita, and Chogyal Phakpa.[40]

Phagmodru Dynasty

Accounts of the kings *(gong ma)* of Phagmodru, who ruled Tibet from 1350-1478, are found in the aforementioned *Blue Annals* and *Scholars' Banquet,* as well as in Riwoche Pontsang's 15th century *Religious History of Lhorong (lho rong chos 'byung)*.[41] The political events surrounding the foundation of the dynasty are also documented in the testament of Tai Situ Jangchub Gyaltsen (1302-64), entitled *Meaningful to Behold (mthong ba don ldan)*.[42]

The successive kings of Phagmodru had their capital at Neudong on the outskirts of Tsetang in Southern Tibet, but nonetheless they continued to maintain the chapels of the Great Temple in Lhasa, offering support to the *Tshalpa Tripon.* In general, they were great patrons of the Kagyu school, and as a mark of Kagyu influence on the development of the Great Temple during this period, images depicting Marpa, Milarepa, Gampopa, Phagmodrupa and Zhang Yudrakpa were installed and venerated in the north wing of the ground floor. The Central Inner Sanctum also contained a revered yak-horn through which Milarepa had reputedly imparted his renowned songs of spiritual realisation *(gsung mgur)* to Rechung Dorjedrak.[43] Best known among the Phagmodru kings was Drakpa Gyaltsen (r. 1409-34), the patron of Tsongkhapa, who restored the Main Hall with its twelve long columns and enlarged the Great Courtyard (*khyams rva chen mo*), where the inaugural Great Prayer Festival was held in 1409.[44] The Chapel of the Three Approaches to Liberation *(rnam thar sgo gsum gyi lha khang)*, which adjoins the Great Courtyard was commissioned in his lifetime, apparently to fulfil the last wishes of the Chinese Emperor Yongle (r. 1403-24).

Prior to 1409 Tsongkhapa donated new brocade costumes for the images of the various chapels in the Great Temple, and sponsored their "face-gilding" *(zhal gser)* and "eye-opening" ceremonies *(spyan dbye)*. He personally offered a golden head-dress and silver alms' bowl *(bhikṣupatra)* to the most sacred image of Jowo Śākyamuni, as well as a silver head-dress to the revered image of Mahākāruṇika in the Northern Inner Sanctum. He is also said to have discovered as treasure *(gter ma)* the famous silver wine flask *('khrung ban)* of King Songtsen Gampo, which is still kept in the main chapel on the west wing of the middle floor.[45]

Massed drums during the Great Prayer Festival.

The Great Prayer Festival

It could be argued that the institution of the Great Prayer Festival of Lhasa *(lha sa'i smon lam chen mo)* by Tsongkhapa in 1409, more than any other factor, planted the seeds for the combined spiritual and temporal dominion of the Dalai Lamas, who came to rule Tibet from 1642 until 1959. This act was Tsongkhapa's supreme contribution to the legacy of the ancient king Songtsen Gampo. It skilfully associated his order with the enduring symbol of Tibet's national identity, and ensured that the Great Temple would be well maintained for centuries to come by the monks of the three large monasteries, which are in close proximity to the capital. The festival was initially introduced to commemorate the miracle performed by Śākyamuni Buddha at Śrāvastī in North India, an event associated in Tibetan tradition with the first month of the lunar calendar. This month is consequently known as the "month of miracles" *(cho 'phrul zla ba)* and it is believed that the impact of any mantra-recitation or prayer made during this month will by multiplied one hundred thousand times.

Military procession during the Great Prayer Festival.

Preparations for the festival would begin on the third day of the month, following the observance of Tibetan New Year *(lo gsar)* on the first and second days. The best description of the Great Prayer Festival is the remarkable eyewitness account of the late Hugh Richardson, based on observations made between 1936 and 1950, and published in *Ceremonies of the Lhasa*. Originally it seems that the Great Courtyard constructed by King Drakpa Gyaltsen was sufficiently large, along with the Wood Enclosure, to hold all participating monks from neighbouring monasteries, probably four or five thousand in number. However, in recent centuries the number of monks had swollen to approximately twenty thousand, filling the corridors, the western portico, the Debating Courtyard to the south, and the Barkor Jangchub Jonlam Street which surrounds the Great Temple complex. Secular and quasi-military ceremonies were subsequently integrated with the Great Prayer Festival in the seventeenth century by the Fifth Dalai Lama, in recognition of the Mongol military role in bringing his administration to power. The following account follows Richardson:

Dungchen horns blown by monks from the Namgyal Monastery outside the Great Temple.

On the third day of the first lunar month, preparations were made for the festival. A large prayer flag *(dga' ldan dar lcog)* would be erected in the northeast corner of the Barkor Jangchub Jonlam Street, after which the Lhasa magistrates, who had an office in the Great Temple and the two senior monastic proctors of Drepung Monastery would be received at the Potala Palace and given advice concerning the conduct of the festival. Authority of

Gathering of the cavalry commanders and aristocrats during the Great Prayer Festival. (1943 TS)

Large drums of exorcism.

Procession of cavalry commanders.

the city of Lhasa would then be handed over by the magistrates to the monastic proctors for the next three weeks. Monks from Drepung, Sera and Ganden then started to congregate in the vicinity of the Great Temple and the monastic police *(dob dob)* imposed their draconian rule on the townspeople, with the power to penalise or levy taxes *('khrol 'dzin)* on anyone infringing the by-laws which had to be observed throughout the month. These bylaws concerned household cleanliness, attire, public order, domestic animals, and commercial activity.

The actual Great Prayer Festival would commence on the fourth day when the assembled monks would struggle to take their seats, and from the following day onwards three sessions of prayer would be held, one before dawn, one in the mid-morning and a third in the afternoon. The government assumed responsibility for the great expense of providing food, drink and monetary offerings to the monastic congregation, supplemented by endowments received from Tibetan aristocrats, traders and foreign envoys; and there were offices in the annex of the Great Temple responsible for both storage and distribution.[46] Four enormous cauldrons, which had been offered by the Fifth Dalai Lama and the regent Sangye Gyatso, were stored in a large tea kitchen *(rung khang chen mo)*, located south of the Wood Enclosure. Later, when these proved to be insufficient, the Thirteenth Dalai Lama brought six prefabricated iron cauldrons from India, and converted an outbuilding on the southwest wing into a water storeroom *(tshogs chu gsog khang)*.[47]

The main event occurred on the fifteenth day of the month, coinciding with the full moon and the actual commemoration of the Miracle of Śrāvastī. On this day the Dalai Lama would take his seat in the Great Courtyard and then move in procession to his throne in the Debating Courtyard to expound the inner meaning of the miracle. That evening large pyramidal *torma* offerings *(bco lnga mchod pa)*, elaborately sculpted of barley dough, butter and wood, would be erected in the Barkor Jangchub Jonlam Street by the monastic communities of the city and by rival aristocratic families with a keen sense of competition.[48] At nightfall the Dalai Lama would enter the Barkor and select the winner of this competition, after which the non-monastic populace would crowd in to receive their share of the offerings and engage in nightlong revelry.

On the following day the cabinet ministers would host a reception and banquet *(bla ma dga' ston)* for the incumbent Throneholder of Ganden Monastery, who is the Head of the Gelugpa school, along with the other monastic preceptors. The venue for this was the Hall Overpowering the Three World-Systems *(gzim chung khams gsum gzil gnon)*, which has a window overlooking the Western Portico.

Sometime between the nineteenth and twenty-first days of the lunar month, the Dalai Lama would preside over an incense offering to Śrīdevī *(dpal lha'i gzab gsol)*, which was performed in the Chapel of the Śrīdevī Turret on the top floor of the Great Temple. The ceremonies held on the days that followed would then assume a strikingly military character, symbolising the former reliance of the Fifth Dalai Lama on the military might of Gushi Qan of the Oirat Mongols.

On the twenty-second day, a camp would be set up for the commanders *(ya sor)* of the two cavalry wings, dressed in ancient Mongol military garb which was normally stored in the Great Temple. The troops would be presented for review by the cabinet ministers on the plain at Drabchi to the north of the city, after which presents were distributed to the commanders.

Then, on the twenty-fourth day, the monastic proctors of Drepung would return local authority of the city to the Lhasa magistrates. The cavalry would be joined by the Zhol infantry *(gzim sbyong pa)*, singing martial paeans. Two large *torma* offerings designated for exorcism *(smon lam gtor rgyag)* would then be carried in procession from the West Gate and the Debating Courtyard into the Barkor Jangchub Jonlam Street, escorted by monks from Namgyal Monastery and Ngakpa College of Drepung respectively. Once in the Barkor, the State Oracle *(gnas chung chos skyong)* would ignite the *torma* by firing an arrow, and antiquated cannons would be fired into the mountainside south of the Kyichu River. The Dalai Lama would witness this ceremony of exorcism from the Corner Window, overlooking the west facade of the annex.

Finally, on the twenty-fifth day, the silver image of Maitreya would be carried in procession *(byams pa gdan 'dren)* from its chapel on the south wing of the Great Temple around the Barkor Street. The procession was headed by the Throneholder of Ganden Monastery, accompanied by monks from the city monasteries of Meru and Zhi-de. An offering scarf would be presented to Maitreya by the State Oracle, after which foot races and horse races were held. The entire spectacle, which concludes the Great Prayer Festival, would be witnessed by the Dalai Lama from the Zurchong Window of the southwest wing.

In 1986 and 1987 the Great Prayer Festival was once again held in the Great Temple, under the supervision of the late Tenth Paṇchen Lama, following a hiatus of more than twenty years. The monks of Ganden, Drepung and Sera were once again permitted to congregate, along with some 10,000 pilgrims from East Tibet. The replica image of Maitreya was escorted around the Barkor Street with great pageantry, and the ancient *torma* exorcism ceremony *(gtor rgyag)* was held, as in the past, on the fifteenth day of the lunar month. A colourful glossy brochure describing the event was even published by the Tibet Tourism Bureau. However, following widespread civil unrest in late 1987 and 1988, during which the Great Temple was assaulted by armed police and martial law was declared throughout the region, the authorities decided to cancel the event, fearful of the impact that large gatherings would have on political consciousness and anti-Chinese sentiment.[49] Since then until now, the Great Prayer Festival of Lhasa has been in a state of abeyance.

Procession of Maitreya during the 25th day of the Great Prayer Festival.

Monks of the Namgyal Monastery bearing censers.

Thangtong Gyalpo

During the mid-fifteenth century, the multitalented Thangtong Gyalpo (1385-64), a renowned engineer, playwright, sculptor, and Buddhist master who had founded his own unique spiritual lineage, frequently visited the Great Temple in Lhasa. On one occasion in 1437, he offered a golden alms' bowl to Jowo Śākyamuni in order to avert a potentially disastrous famine. It was his student, Dungkar Drukdrak, who sculpted the celebrated images of King Songtsen Gampo *(nga 'dra ma)*, flanked by his queens, which grace the main chapel on the west wing of the middle floor.[50] In consequence of these events, a sculpted self-portrait of Thangtong Gyalpo was also installed in the north wing of the ground floor.[51]

The Southern Debating Courtyard during the Great Prayer Festival.

Kagyu Dominance

In 1435 the power of the Phagmodru kings began to wane when Prince Norbu Zangpo of the Rinpung fiefdom seized control of the province of Tsang. His son Donyo Dorje decisively defeated the forces of King Rinchen Dorje in 1478, bringing an effective end to the dynasty.[52] From then until

Munīndra in the Main Hall (p. 77, no. **58**). (2000) GD)

Lhazang Maitreya in the Main Hall (p. 77, no. **57**). (1999 HS)

1565, the fiefs of Rinpung effectively ruled Central Tibet and Tsang, ensuring through their patronage that the Karma Kagyu school could effectively continue to rival the influence of the newly emergent Gelug order.

In 1497 the Seventh Karmapa Chodrak Gyatso founded the temple of Karma Cho-de at Thosa Nagma in Lhasa, and the following year, the forces of Rinpung occupied the city, offering spiritual authority to Zhamarpa Chodrak Zangpo, a partisan of the Karma Kagyu. He immediately prohibited the Gelug monks of Sera and Drepung from attending the Great Prayer Festival, a restriction which was maintained until 1518. During this period, the monks of Sangphu and its affiliated monasteries conducted regular ceremonies at the Great Temple, and the influence of the *Tshalpa Tripon,* who had become increasingly affiliated to the Gelugpa, began to decline. Later Gelug sources suggest that the condition of the Great Temple itself degenerated during this period of curtailment on their activities, but the Kagyu chronicles of Dakla Gampo Monastery which could be expected to present these events in a somewhat different light have rarely been studied.[53]

Contributions of the Early Dalai Lamas

In 1518, the Second Dalai Lama Gendun Gyatso (1476-1542) managed to reinstate the Great Prayer Festival, with the support of King Chenga Ngagi Wangpo of Phagmodru (r. 1514-64) who still nominally ruled Tibet during the period of Rinpung influence. The monks of Sera, Drepung, and Ganden once again were permitted to converge on the Great Temple during the first month of the year. In the lifetime of his successor the Third Dalai Lama Sonam Gyatso (1543-88) much of Central Tibet came under the authority of the kings of Tsang, who vigorously espoused the Karma Kagyu order. At this time, the Gelug school focussed its attention eastwards, establishing a number of new monasteries in Kham, and forging close links with Altan Qan of the Qosot Mongols. It was on a visit to Mongolia that Sonam Gyatso first became known under the Mongol title "Dalai Lama". Back in Lhasa, he offered a gold canopy to the image of Jowo Śākyamuni, and, in 1562, he repaired the flood-dykes on the north bank of the Kyichu.[54] Thereafter, following his injunction, the combined monks of the three major Gelug monasteries would repair the dykes each year, at the conclusion of the Great Prayer Festival. A statue depicting the Third Dalai Lama was placed above the entrance to the Northern Inner Sanctum by Miwang Pholha Tashi Tobgye in the eighteenth century. His reincarnation, the Fourth Dalai Lama Yonten Gyatso (1589-1616) was born into the royal family of Altan Qan, and, as such, was the only Dalai Lama to have not been Tibetan. In the Great Temple, he added bas-relief engravings to the throne-back and aureole of Jowo Śākyamuni.[55]

Civil War

In 1565 the power of Rinpung was usurped by Karma Tseten, a partisan of the Karma Kagyu tradition, who established the hegemony of the *Tsangpa Depa* in Central, Southern and Western Tibet with his capital at Samdrubtse (modern Zhigatse). He and his successors opposed the rising strength of the Gelugpa, and conducted military campaigns against Lhasa in 1605 and again in 1618. During this civil war, the Karma Kagyu and Gelug factions each had their proxy Mongol armies. The events of this period and its aftermath are covered in predominantly Gelug sources, such as the *Song of the Queen of Spring (dpyid kyi rgyal mo'i glu dbyangs)* composed by the Fifth Dalai Lama (1617-82), and the *Yellow Beryl (baiḍūrya ser po)* of Sangye Gyatso (16531703).[56]

In 1621, the Gelugpa installed images of Padmākara, King Trisong Detsen, and Śāntarakṣita in the Svāstika Alcove *(gYung drung sbug)* of the Great Temple as a spiritual means of ensuring victory and repelling the Mongol forces of Tsangpa Depa Phuntsok Namgyal (r. 1611-21). Following a decisive battle in which the Mongol allies of the Gelug faction defeated those loyal to Karma Phuntsok Namgyal, the authority of the Gelugpa was then restored in the Lhasa area. The governor of the Lower Kyichu region, who had estates at Ganden Khangsar, formally assumed the guardianship of the Great Temple, and from this time onwards the building was supervised by the successive generations of senior sacristans *(dkon gnyer dpon)*, who had their office on the top floor of the annex.

During the civil war, armed monks of Sera and Drepung had plundered the Karma Cho-de temple and removed a large precious silver image of Śākyamuni, which was then installed in the Chapel of the King of the Śākyas on the middle floor of the Great Temple.[57] The war came to an abrupt end in 1642 when the last *Tsangpa Depa,* Karma Tenkyong, was slain at Zhigatse by the Mongol forces of Gushi Qan Tendzin Chogyal.

Restorations of the Fifth Dalai Lama

Following the conclusion of the civil war, power passed initially to Gushi Qan, and then to the Fifth Dalai Lama Ngawang Lobzang Gyatso who imposed his combined spiritual and temporal authority throughout Central Tibet and Tsang. Mongol armies with varying degrees of success then sought to unify the Kham and Amdo regions under his rule. In this way, the administration of the Dalai Lamas *(sde pa gzhung)* came to rule a substantial area of the Tibetan plateau from 1642 until 1951. With the assistance of his regents, the Fifth Dalai Lama forged a "patron-priest" relationship, on the earlier Sakya model, first with Mongol princes, and later with the new Manchu emperor of China.

The Great Temple benefited from this largesse. Silver images of the Eight Medicine Buddhas were installed in the Chapel of the Eight Medicine Buddhas on the top floor to fulfil the dying wishes of Gushi Qan. Then the older chapels were restored, and the gilded roof, throne-back, and pillars of the Central Inner Sanctum were refurbished. The gallery was tiled with gilded copper, and a canopy of gilded copper was raised above the image of Mahākāruṇika (north wing), while gilded roofs were erected above the images of Four Sibling Maitreyas (south wing) and King Songtsen Gampo (west wing). On the roof of the Great Temple, the south-eastern turret until very recently contained a mask and stuffed image of wrathful Rematī, which had been made by the hand of the Fifth Dalai Lama. Storerooms adjoining the inner walkway were converted into chapels, and in 1648 the walls of the Great Courtyard and inner walkway were painted with exquisite murals illustrating historical figures and scenes from the *Avadānakalpalatā* and the *Bhadrakalpikasūtra.* The murals of the north wing depicted Tsongkhapa flanked by Nyingma, Kadam and Gelug lineage holders, those of the east wing depicted Tsongkhapa and his retainers, those of the south wing depicted Śākyamuni, flanked by his retainers, and those of the west wing depicted Sangye Gyatso with Gushi Qan and their retainers.[58] The names of the artisans who participated in this endeavour were inscribed on a plaque, which can still be seen to the rear of Jowo Śākyamuni.[59]

On completion of this project, the Fifth Dalai Lama composed an important inventory of the Great Temple and its contents, entitled *Crystal Mirror (lha ldan sprul pa'i gtsug lag khang gi dkar chag shel dkar me long).* Though brief in content, it appears to have been the first comprehensive

The Main Hall (p. 77, no. **55**). (1999 HS)

Chapel of Munīndra and his retainers, Middle Floor (p. 80, no. **66**). (2000) GD)

An offering maṇḍala on the altar before Jowo Śākyamuni (p. 71, no. **29**). (2000 GD)

Assembled monks at a Great Congregation ceremony in the Sungchora courtyard. (1943 TS)

description of all the chapels of the Great Temple since the earlier historical accounts of its original foundation.[60] The inventory was translated into German in 1915 by A. Grunwedel under the title "Die Tempel von Lhasa: Gedicht der ersten Dalai Lama, fur Pilger bestimmt".

The Great Congregation[61]

The ceremony of the Great Congregation *(tshogs mchod chen mo)* was inaugurated in 1682 by the regent Sangye Gyatso (1653-1703) to commemorate the death anniversary of the Fifth Dalai Lama. Prayers would be held in the Great Temple over a twelve day period, commencing on the nineteenth day of the second lunar month.[62] Senior ranking figures of the three main Gelug monasteries officiated. The highlight was the service commemorating the actual anniversary, which would be held on the twenty-fifth day of the month. In later centuries, the ceremony was extended to include the "official" death anniversaries of subsequent Dalai Lamas. On the twenty-ninth, a day on which liturgies are generally dedicated to the protector deities, a ritual thread-cross exorcism would be performed for the benefit of the Dalai Lama or his incumbent regent. The thread-cross was dedicated to the protector deity Pehar *(rgyal po rtsed mdos)* and designed to expel the negative influence of bewitching demons *('gong)* by ritual means. To this end, two "scapegoats" *(glud 'gong rgyal po)* representing these negative forces would be ritually expelled from the Lugong Gate in the west wing of the Great Temple annex, along with the thread-crosses. Each year two individuals from Phenyul and Zhol, of the same age as the ruler, or sharing his same birth sign, would be selected for this role. Various preparations were held in the week leading up to this event.

Then, on the morning of the twenty-ninth, a dough effigy of the ruler would be made, as a substitute for his long life and prosperity. That afternoon, to the accompaniment of black-hat dancers, the two "scapegoats" would rush out through the Lugong Gate, clad in goatskins and with black painted faces. Successfully challenged by the black-hat dancers, they would be expelled along with their effigies to the south and north of the Great Temple by four masked figures, representing the acolytes *('ging)* of Pehar. Then, two ritual thread-crosses would be escorted in procession, simultaneously from the Great Temple and Ramoche, to be ignited by the State Oracle. The "scapegoats" would be transported across the Kyichu from where they would ride to Samye to place the effigies in the temple of Pehar.

Finally on the thirtieth day of the month, sacred objects and banners, including a long scroll made by the regent Sangye Gyatso, were taken from the Palace Treasury on the middle floor of the Great Temple to be carried around the Barkor Jangchub Jonlam Street by selected monks from the three large monasteries. This particular ceremony was known as the "golden procession of the Great Congregation" *(tshogs mchod ser spreng)*. The monks would follow the outer circuit *(gling bskor)* around the city, as far as the Turquoise to Zhol, below the Potala. This was the signal for enormous applique tangkas to be unfurled from the south facade of the White Palace, and ritual dances to be held in the environs of the Potala. Later that day all the sacred objects would be returned to the safety of the Palace Treasury.

Contributions of the Later Dalai Lamas

Later Dalai Lamas continued to honour the ancient legacy of King Songtsen Gampo through their patronage of restoration and reconstruction projects in the Great Temple. In the early eighteenth century, the libertine Sixth

Dalai Lama Tshangyang Gyatso (b. 1683) and his regent Sangye Gyatso furnished the top floor with new images and bejewelled ornaments, as well as the gilded emblems of the thousand-spoked wheel flanked by male and female deer, which surmount all four walls.[63] Even Lhazang Qan, slayer of the regent Sangye Gyatso, commissioned a red bronze image of Maitreya for the Main Hall.[64]

In 1732, during the reign of the Seventh Dalai Lama Kelzang Gyatso (1708-57), Miwang Pholha Sonam Tobgye commissioned the three-dimensional white sandalwood palaces *(vimāna)* of Guhyasamāja, Cakrasaṃvara and Vajrabhairava, which once graced the Chapel of the Three-dimensional Maṇḍalas on the top floor of the Great Temple. Four years later, in 1736 he also donated an eight metre gilded copper image of Maitreya to the Main Hall.[65] Other large images were also installed in this central atrium: a four metre gilded copper image of Maitreya that had been commissioned by Barzhib Chukhorwa, an impressive Mahākāruṇika, which was commissioned by Doring Ngodrub Rabten in 1774, and an image of Munīndra, surrounded by the Thousand Buddhas, which had been commissioned by Gazhigung Paṇḍita.

Meanwhile, in 1756, the Seventh Dalai Lama commissioned the three-dimensional maṇḍala and silver cast images, which were once venerated in the Amitāyus Chapel of the top floor. On the political side, he restructured the cabinet of ministers *(bka' shag)* into a form which persisted into the twentieth century, in recognition of which, a throne that he had used was kept in the cabinet office on the middle floor until recent times.[66]

Starting in 1783, his successor, the Eighth Dalai Lama Jampal Gyatso (1758-1804) and the regent Ngawang Tsultrim of Tshemonling (1721-91) initiated a project which would renovate all the chapels adjoining the inner walkway, restoring their doors and window frames. They also restored the murals of the Main Hall, the upper floors, and the Great Courtyard, and rebuilt the South Gate and the Rear Gate.[67] Similarly, from 1842-44, the Eleventh Dalai Lama Khedrub Gyatso (1838-55) and the regent Ngawang Jampal Tsultrim of Tshemonling (1792-1855) refurbished all the images of the Great Temple. They commissioned ten thousand offering bowls and installed two hundred hand-turned maṇi wheels in the inner walkway. The entire north wing of the building overlooking the inner walkway, and its outer annex, were also reconstructed during this period.[68]

The advent of the twentieth century saw the city of Lhasa thrown into turmoil by the arrival of the Younghusband expeditionary force from British India and the Manchu forces of the warlord Zhao Erfeng, who sought to incorporate much of Eastern Tibet within a new Chinese province. In 1912 while Chinese and Tibetan forces fought within the city of Lhasa, artillery damaged the Great Temple, puncturing its gilded copper roofs. However, the Chinese forces were soon expelled from Lhasa following the demise of the Qing Dynasty, and the Thirteenth Dalai Lama Thubten Gyatso (1876-1933) was able to restore national sovereignty.

In the first decade of his independent rule, the damaged roofs, ornaments and galleries of the Great Temple were repaired. Then, from 1920 to 1922, the chapels and their sacred images were all refurbished, while the murals of the Great Courtyard and inner walkway were restored by skilled artists of the Zurchong School.[69] During this period, the hand-turned maṇi wheels of the inner walkway were also refurbished, and the large thousand-spoked wheel and victory turrets, which still overlook the west wing, were donated by the incumbent Changkya Qutuqtu of Gonlung in Amdo.[70]

The Thirteenth Dalai Lama was mindful of the sectarian divisions of

King Songysen Gampo (p. 77). (1995 AA)

Offering lamps in the Great Courtyard (p. 90). (1995 AA)

Consecrated water. (1995 HS)

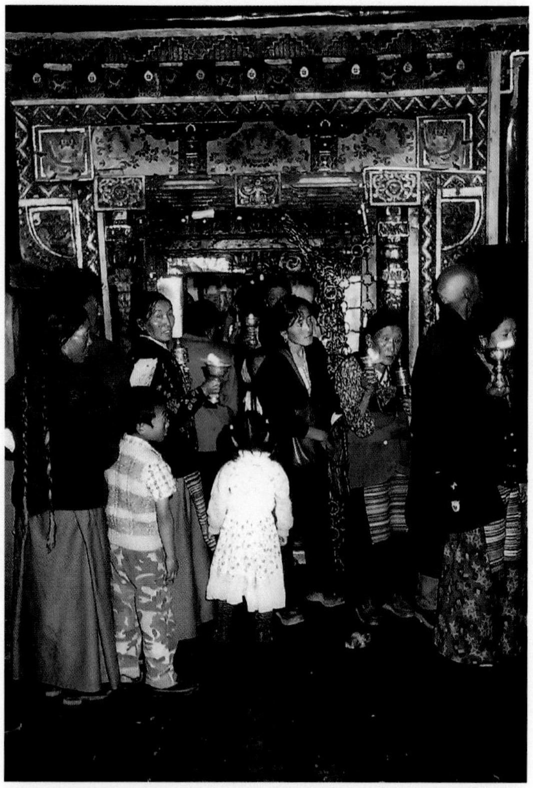

Pilgrims at the Inner Sanctum (p. 72, no. **29**). (1999 HS)

the past that had resulted in great misfortunes for Tibet. He therefore commissioned an image of Guru Saroruhavajra (Za-hor-ma) and within its heart he placed a remarkable representative image of Padmasambhava called Thongdrol Chenmo, which had been extracted as treasure by his mentor, Sogyal Lerab Lingpa (1856-1926).[71] At the same time, following the latter's advice, he installed images of the Peaceful and Wrathful Aspects of Guru Padmsambhava *(gu ru zhi drag)* and the ḍākinī Siṃhavaktrā, surrounded by a thousand miniature images of Padmasambhava, in a chapel to the east of the inner walkway. Then, to fulfil another prophecy of Chokgyur Dechen Zhigpo Lingpa (1829-70), a renowned treasure-finder of the Nyingma school, he requested the Fifteenth Karmapa (1871-1922) to sculpt an image of the protectress Tashi Tseringma. The image was duly installed in the Chapel of the Five Sisters of Longlife *(tshe ring mched lnga)* on the Great Temple roof, and propitiated thereafter by monks from Tsurphu Monastery on a regular basis.[72]

Inventories and Pilgrimage Guides

Although official records listing the contents of the Great Temple *(rten deb)* and documenting its transfer from one senior sacristan to the next *(sprod deb)* were meticulously kept, such documents were never published. If any of these manuscripts somehow survived the recent Cultural Revolution, contemporary scholars hope that they may one day be made available for research through the Lhasa archives.[73] An informative inventory documenting the restorations of the successive Dalai Lamas was also written during this period by the Thirteenth Dalai Lama himself, under the title *Pool of the Milk Plain Lake Giving Rise to Hundreds of Thousands of Faith-Inspiring Phenomena (dkar chags dad snang 'bum phrag 'char ba'i 'o thang mtsho'i rdzing bu)*.[74] From earliest times the sacred temples of Lhasa have attracted pilgrims from all regions of the Tibetan plateau. Many would make their way there on foot over several months and, in some cases, more than a year, prostrating their entire body length as they went in order to generate merit. The focal point of these pilgrimages would be the image of Jowo Śākyamuni in the Central Inner Sanctum of the Great Temple, lying at the heart of the grand geomantic scheme. In Tibetan literature there are biographical accounts of important Buddhist teachers who have experienced visions and received revelatory instructions in the presence of Jowo Śākyamuni; and there are many references to devout pilgrims of humble background who could converse with the image.[75]

The genre of the pilgrimage guide *(gnas yig)*, describing the sacred Buddhist sites of the Tibetan plateau and their spiritual significance, is almost as old as the act of pilgrimage itself. Among these works, there are two particularly wide-ranging guides, written for the aid of itinerant pilgrims from East Tibet in relatively recent times, which include descriptions of the Great Temple. In 1892 the great eclectic master Jamyang Khyentse Wangpo (1820-92) composed an *Abridged Inventory to the Sacred Places and Objects of Utsang (dBus gtsang gi gnas rten rags rim gyi mtshan byang mdor bsdus dad pa'i sa bon)*, documenting his final pilgrimage to the central regions. The work has been translated into English and it also formed the basis for Keith Dowman's *Power Places of Central Tibet.* Later, in 1920, Situ Chokyi Gyatso (1880-1925) of Katok Monastery composed his more detailed *Travelogue of A Journey through Utsang in the Land of Snows entitled Necklace of Moon Crystal (gangs-ljongs dBus-gtsang gnas-bskor lam-yig nor-bu zla-shel-gyi se-mo-do)*.[76]

During the lifetime of the Thirteenth Dalai Lama, the Great Temple was also visited by a number of foreign observers, including Sarat Chandra Das,

Perceval Landon, G.T. Tsybikov, Austin Waddell, and E.H.C. Walsh, the last two of whom attempted to draw ground plans of the building.[77]

Restorations of the Fourteenth Dalai Lama

Following the death of the Thirteenth Dalai Lama in 1933, his successor – the present Fourteenth Dalai Lama Tendzin Gyatso – was discovered in Amdo and eventually brought to Lhasa. Here, in the Great Temple, he was ordained as a novice and later as a full-fledged Buddhist monk. In 1948, the palace of the top floor, known as the Pinnacle of Ganden, was renovated, its bay window extended and surmounted by a new gilded copper roof and spire. Foreign observers who commented on or photographed the Great Temple during this period included Giuseppe Tucci, Henrich Harrer and Lowell Thomas Jr.[78]

Three years later, in 1951, Chinese forces reached Lhasa and the Seventeen Point Agreement, renouncing national sovereignty, was forcefully imposed on the Tibetan people. In 1954, a number of charitable projects were initiated in order to eliminate the potentially negative impact of an obstacle year *(keg lo)*. At that time, the Great Temple was once again refurbished. The most sacred images received "face-gilding" and "eye-opening" ceremonies, the Sunlight Apartment *(gzim chung nyi 'od)* of the top floor, where the senior Geshe Lharampa would be seated during the Great Prayer Festival, was renovated, and a new apartment for His Holiness' attendants, known as the Corner Apartment (*zur 'phyongs gzim chung*) was constructed.

However, the effect of these charitable actions was diminished by the acknowledged failure of certain sectarian cabinet ministers in 1956 to commission an image of Padmasambhava in the charismatic form Nangsi Zilnon, which would have fulfilled a prophecy of the late Dzongsar Khyense Rinpoche for the well-being of Tibet.[79] A few foreigners from sympathetic Communist countries were permitted to visit Central Tibet prior to the suppression of the uprising in 1959. Among them, the Czech travellers V. Sis and J. Vanis photographed the interior of the Great Temple between 1953 and 1955.[80]

After a sojourn in India during 1956-7, coinciding with the Buddha Jayanti celebrations, His Holiness returned to Lhasa and began to prepare for his own Geshe Lharampa examinations, which were eventually held in the Great Temple in early 1959, shortly before he was forced into exile.[81]

Cultural Revolution

During the Cultural Revolution (1966-76), unprecedented destruction was inflicted on the Great Temple. Even before that, a military canteen had been erected inside the Main Hall, and a recreation area for the Youth League had been established inside the Great Courtyard. Now, the external edifice of the building was damaged, its wealth of precious offerings plundered, and its library incinerated. According to the late Mrs R.D. Taring, the fires burned for three long weeks.[82] Almost all the renowned sacred images of the Great Temple were destroyed. Some of these had originated during the eras of the Yarlung kings and the *Tshalpa Tripon,* and had great historical importance. They included Mahākāruṇika, Tsongkhapa, Maitreya, Four Sibling Maitreyas, Eight Medicine Buddhas, the Eight Manifestations of Padmasambhava, the Peaceful and Wrathful Aspects of Śrīdevī, the large Maitreyas and Tārā. A pigsty was constructed within the Great Courtyard, and even some chapels were used as latrines. Young

Aspirational prayers. (1995 HS)

The flagstone patio (p. 90). (2000 GD)

Red guards occupy the Great Courtyard. (All 1966 TD)

Book burning during the Cultural Revolution.

Tibetans were executed in cold blood within the courtyard.[83]

Reports of this destruction reached the West and the exiled Tibetan communities of India, where they were received with horror and outrage. Such incidents provided a catalyst for the serious efforts that were subsequently made in India and the West to publish endangered Tibetan texts and document the country's artistic heritage. In 1977, in the aftermath of the Cultural Revolution, the late Hugh Richardson broke new ground by publishing a description of the chapels of the Great Temple in English. The article was based on his own personal observations, on the ground plans prepared by Zurkhang Wangchuk Gelek, and a number of textual sources, including the aforementioned *Crystal Mirror Inventory* by the Fifth Dalai Lama.[84] This pioneering work inspired Taring Dzaku Jigme to prepare detailed maps and an inventory to the chapels and offices of the Great Temple *(lha sa gstug lag khang gi sa bkra dang dkar chag)* in English, while exiled at Rajpur in India. Mr Taring was well qualified for this task, having worked for eighteen years in the Palace Treasury *(bla phyag)*. He also constructed a three-dimensional model of the Great Temple, which is still housed in the museum attached to the Tibetan Library of Works and Archives in Dharamsala. Equally inspired by Richardson and motivated by the need to document the artefacts of the Great Temple and its desecration during the Cultural Revolution, in 1982, Zhakabpa Wangchuk Kalden published a more detailed description of its chapels and offices in Tibetan language, working from his base at Kalimpong. His crucial text, which is translated into English in Part One of this book, included floor plans, historical background and important literary references *(lha ldan ra sa 'phrul snang gtsug lag khang gi dkar chag)*.

Recent Reconstruction

Following the rise to power of Deng Xiaopeng, in 1979 the Chinese central government authorised the TAR Cultural Relics Bureau to begin restoration of the Great Temple, and the complex was reopened to the public in 1982. Over the decades which followed the building was repaired, electricity was introduced, the north wing was butressed with new columns to prevent further subsidence, and clay replicas were made by master artist Yeshe Sherab and his apprentices to replace the sacred images that had been destroyed in the most important chapels. During this reconstruction the partition walls of many chapels were deconstructed and thinly rebuilt after their ancient treasures had been extracted. The ancient murals of the north and northeast walls of the middle floor wall were removed in 1986, and have only recently been replaced, while those of the south and south-east wings of the same floor were dismantled and replaced between 1991 and 1993. Former government offices contained in the outer annex of the Great Temple were rebuilt as residential units for monks. Contemporary art historians, Roberto Vitali, Heather Stoddard and Amy Heller also visited Lhasa where they were able to study the surviving murals and wood carvings, and to observe the techniques of conservation and restoration, which continued into the late 1990s.[85] The Tibet Heritage Fund also initiated an architectural survey of the site between 1996 and 2000, with the participation of Minyak Chokyi Gyaltsen, André Alexander and others. Eventually, in 2000 the Great Temple of Lhasa was listed among the ensemble of cultural relics, alongside the Potala Palace, as a UNESCO world heritage site.

The most recent on-going renovations (undertaken since 2004) have been designed to strengthen the columns in the Great Courtyard, and it is envisaged that restoration of the historically important courtyard murals will inevitably follow.

During this period, new works have appeared in Tibetan and in Chinese. In 1980 photographs of the Great Temple were published in Beijing, and an illustrated coffee table book followed.[86] In 1982, Chapel Tseten Phuntsok published his *Rough Guide to the Great Temple of Lhasa (lha sa gstug lag khang gi lo rgyus rags bshad)*. A synopsis of this account is also reproduced in Shenyen Tsultrim's *Inventory of Lhasa Monasteries (lha sa'i dgon tho),* which was published in 2001, along with a useful chronological table. The *Crystal Mirror Inventory* of the Fifth Dalai Lama was republished in a convenient pocket edition the following year. Then in 2005 Nyima Tsering's informative *Abbreviated Guide to the Great Temple of Lhasa (lha ldan gtsug lgag khang gi gnas mndor bsdus)* was published. All these works are currently for sale in the bookshop of the Great Temple.

Since 1984, the Great Temple has also become a focal point for foreign travellers and tourists, who have come to appreciate its historical importance, its art, its sanctity, and the acrid atmosphere generated by palls of smoke that rise from its butter-lamps, constantly replenished by the flow of pilgrims and devotees. Among the modern guidebooks, utilised by overseas visitors and pilgrims, that include a description and plans of the Great Temple, are Stephen Bachelor's *The Tibet Guide,* Victor Chen's *Tibet Handbook,* and my Footprint *Tibet Handbook.*

Mao's portrait over the entrance of the Great Temple.

Regular Ceremonies at the Great Temple

In addition to the daily prayers and frequent *zhabs rten* ceremonies that are sponsored by private individuals, large gatherings of pilgrims will throng through the gates of the Great Temple on certain important days of the lunar calendar. On the fifteenth day of the fourth lunar month, the enlightenment of Śākyamuni Buddha is commemorated, on the fifteenth day of the fifth lunar month the Universal Incense Offering *('dzam gling spyi bsangs)* is held on the Great Temple roof to commemorate Padmasambhava's subjugation of negative forces at Samye during the eighth century. On the fourth day of the sixth lunar month, the anniversary of the First Turning of the Doctrinal Wheel *(chos bskor dus chen)* is commemorated. Formerly, the wine flask of King Songtsen Gampo *('khrungs ban)* would be taken from its locker on this day, and the first fruits of the chang poured from it would be offered by cabinet ministers and government officials. Then, on the twenty-second day of the eighth lunar month, the anniversary of the Buddha's descent from Tuṣita *(lha babs dus chen)* is commemorated, once again attracting large numbers of the public.[87] Towards the end of the year, on an auspicious day, a consecratory ceremony *(rab gnas)* is also held as a means of repurifying the environment within the Great Temple in advance of the coming year.

The destruction of roof decorations and sacred images.

The Great Temple as a Unique National Symbol

It is true to say that all Tibetans have had a stake in the Great Temple. Throughout its long history the Great Temple has continued to symbolise the unique cultural heritage and national identity of Tibet. The kings of the Yarlung period, the great spiritual teachers of the Nyingma, Kadam, Kagyu, Sakya and Gelug lineages, and even adherents of Bon have all contributed to its development in one way or another, fulfilling the admonitions of its royal founder, Songtsen Gampo.

Although there is no overt Bon presence in the Great Temple at the

Reconstruction of the 1980s. (1987 HMS)

present day, prior to its desecration during the Cultural Revolution, on the middle floor of the annex, behind the Great Ceremonial Hall *(evaṃ phun tshogs 'dod 'khyil)*, there was formerly a chapel dedicated to the Bon protectress Sigyalma. Then, adjoining the private residence of the regent or prime minister *(gzim chung snang srid kyi nyi 'od)* on the same floor, there was a small dark chamber where the good luck sacraments of the Bon tradition would be housed. On the roof of the annex, overlooking this residence, there was also a sacred turret *(rten mkhar)* dedicated to the Bon protectress Sigyalma, where Bon practitioners from Kyormolung were officially invited each new year to replenish sacred juniper branches, thread-cross *(mdos)* symbols and prayer flags.[88]

Among the various Buddhist traditions, the contribution of the Nyingmapa to the Great Temple's development is fundamental, including as it does, the original construction by King Songtsen Gampo and its subsequent patronage by the kings of the Pugyal Empire. Images of Padamsambhava dating from diverse periods of Tibetan history can be found on the stone platform outside the northeast chapel, in the Svāstika Alcove, in the Main Hall, in the southeast chapel of the middle floor, and in the rear chapels accessed from the inner walkway. Statues of other historical figures associated with the Nyingma tradition such as Thangtong Gyalpo and Zhikpo Dudtsi are also found in the Main Hall.

Furthermore, the southwest chapels of the middle floor contains images of the protector Cimara and the Five Kingly Aspects of Pehar (*rgyal po sku lnga*), which were commissioned by Pema Wangchuk, the Fifth Rigdzin of Dorje Drak Monastery during the eighteenth century. Nine monks from Dorje Drak formerly conducted liturgies in these chapels on a regular basis.[89]

The highly revered spiritual brethren *(dge bshes)* of the Kadampa period, who followed the renunciate example of Jowoje Atiśa, were instrumental in reclaiming the Great Temple in the tenth century following its desecration and decline during the years when the empire disintegrated. Atiśa himself, with the assistance of Lhasa Nyonma, is said to have extracted King Songtsen Gampo's testament from the Leaf Pillar, and individuals of the calibre of Lu-me Tsultrim Sherab are known to have resided in the Great Temple. However, the greatest contribution of the Kadampa is recognised to be Zangkar Lotsāwa's enlargement of the Central Inner Sanctum in the late eleventh century.[90]

The contribution of the Sakya hierarchs *(gong ma)* and chief ministers *(dpon chen)* to the development of the Great Temple has already been noted. Sakya Paṇḍita and Chogyal Phakpa both offered stūpas which were consecrated in the Main Hall. Similarly, the Kagyu school, including the successive *Tshalpa Tripon,* actively maintained the Great Temple from the twelfth century through to the sixteenth. In the southwestern turret on the roof, there is a restored image of the protectress Tashi Tseringma, which had originally been sculpted by the Fifteenth Karmapa and installed by the Thirteenth Dalai Lama. The images of the four peripheral protectresses in this group were commissioned by the present Dalai Lama in the early 1950s. In consequence of all these contributions, statues of the foremost Sakya and Kagyu lineage-holders are found in the Main Hall of the Great Temple.

Under the influence of the early and later Dalai Lamas, regular Prayer Festival ceremonies were reinstated, and the Great Temple was renovated on several occasions between 1642 and 1954. The images of Tsongkhapa and his foremost students, which grace the Main Hall, the exquisite murals of the inner walkway and Great Courtyard, and the palatial chambers of the annex all bear witness to these endeavours.

Ongoing Dynamic of the Great Temple

Despite the unresolved political and social issues arising from over-centralised Chinese administration, the Great Temple continues to attract pilgrims from diverse regions of the plateau, recognisable by their distinctive dress, coiffure, dialect, and language. Overseas pilgrims espousing the various traditions of Tibetan Buddhism, and other forms of Buddhism, also come to pay their respects and make offerings in the presence of the image of Jowo Śākyamuni. More recently, large parties of Chinese visitors, including Buddhist pilgrims have also been converging on the temple, which has become a focal point for their own spiritual renaissance. The names of the dead and the living are still inscribed in gold on red paper at the request of devout pilgrims, to be incinerated as an act of purification, in the golden butter lamp of the Central Inner Sanctum. The resident monks of the Great Temple, supplemented by others from neighbouring monasteries, still continue to congregate for the observance of important Buddhist anniversaries.

Offering lamps in the Great Courtyard (p. 90). (1999 HS)

The Present Work

At the beginning of this book His Holiness the Dalai Lama's recounts early reminiscences of the Great Temple of Lhasa, during the 1940s and 1950s. In Part 1, I offer a translation of Zhakabpa Wangchuk Deden's authoritative *Inventory to the Great Temple,* augmenting this detailed text and the floor plans of the building with the commentary and well-informed observations of contemporary scholars and resident monks. In Part 2, Tashi Tsering has compiled a number of extracts from original and rarely studied sources, illustrating the significance of the central image of Jowo Śākyamuni in Tibetan life. Sonam Tsering and I translated the Tibetan version into English. In Part 3, Heather Stoddard draws upon the early historical writing of Nyangral Nyima Ozer and the biographies of Tsongkhapa, to highlight two pivotal events – the geomantic origins of the Great Temple and the inauguration of the Great Prayer Festival, concluding with a first-hand account of her rediscovery of ancient murals in the Chapel of the Countenance. Part 4, by Andre Alexander, offers a fascinating insight into the intricate architectural features of the building which reflect an undeniable Indian influence. Part 5 documents 108 bronze images, stored within the precincts of the Great Temple.

Formal debates of Buddhist logic, Monlam Chenmo. (1986 CB)

Acknowledgements

In early March 2000, I travelled to India with the encouragement and support of Hansjorg Mayer to interview HH Dalai Lama and certain other Tibetan exiles who had had close associations with the Great Temple of Lhasa. His Holiness graciously made time in his daunting schedule to record his early reminiscences of the events and ceremonies that he witnessed there during the 1940s and 1950s. The account of this interview reveals with considerable frankness the intimate dreams and feelings of devotion, trepidation, joy and regret that he experienced during those turbulent years. I am indebted to those who facilitated my stay in Dharamsala at that time: to K. Y. Takla and her staff at the Office of Tibet in London, to Venerable Norbu Donden and Tendzin Geche of the Private Office, to Thupten Sampel of the Department of Information, and of course to my publisher Hansjorg Mayer, whose enthusiasm for Tibetan culture is well known. Tashi Tsering, director of the Amnye Machen Institute, provided a number of literary reference materials, including the key *Inventory* by W. D. Zhakabpa, on which the first part of this book is based.

Others India-based Tibetans who helped elucidate the plans and layout of the Great Temple include senior figures such as Tutop Ngawang Narkyid (now retired) and the late R. D. Taring whose husband Jigme Taring had prepared two and three dimensional plans of the building during the 1960s. Among the younger generation, I had detailed discussions with one former sacristan of the temple, venerable Ngawang Yonten, and with Chung Tsering of the Education Department, the venerable Phuntsok and the venerable Lobzang Sherab, who had all served as monks in the Great Temple during the 1980s.

In Lhasa, where I have had the good fortune to travel annually since 1985, my research was facilitated by venerable Tubten Rinchen and venerable Tendzin Chopel, both senior incumbent lamas of the Great Temple, and by the many caretaker monks who actively maintain the complex at the present time. Other friends have also assisted on the ground over many years. They include Samten, Karma, Martin Landy and Louise Panton, who accompanied me through the chapels and annexes of the Great Temple while I was researching this particular project.

Thanks to Sonam Tsering, my co-translater of Tashi Tsering's chapter and to Martin Boord for the index.

The gilded roof of Jowo Śākyamuni (centre), flanked by those of Mahākāruṇika (left) and Four Sibling Maitreyas (right), (p. 87). (1994 AA)

Spectators overlooking the Great Courtyard during the Great Prayer Festival. (1921 RL)

Personal Reminiscences of the Great Temple by His Holiness the Dalai Lama

Interviewed at Thekchen Choling by Gyurme Dorje
2.30 p.m. 9th March, 2000

Q: Does Your Holiness have any special recollection of past visits to the Great Temple of Lhasa, during the Great Prayer Festival (smon lam chen mo), or on other occasions?

A: I personally have a stronger impression of some of the images. Foremost among them of course is Jowo Śākymuni, the main image of Buddha Śākyamuni. When I received ordination as a novice monk the ceremony was held in the presence of this image in the Central Inner Sanctum (Jokhang), and then when I received the full-fledged monastic ordination, the ceremonies also took place in the presence of this same image. As a monk, therefore, I have a special empathy with this image on account of these events.

Another impressive image was that of Mahākāruṇika in the form Rangjon Ngaden, with one thousand arms and one thousand eyes. After I reached India, just before the Cultural Revolution and shortly before this renowned Mahākāruṇika image was destroyed, one night I had a very clear dream in which I approached the original statue inside the Great Temple. I looked at the image, which was almost winking to indicate that I should draw near. With deep emotion and faith, and a close feeling of empathy, I approached and embraced that image, as you would a person. Then, immediately it started reciting a verse and I also followed in accompaniment.

The words of the verse were:
brtson gru brtsam pa'i brtson 'grus kyis/
brten sbro le lo ma mchis shing/
stobs dang ldan pa'i lus sems kyis/
brtson 'grus pha rol phyin rdzogs shog.

This is a short prayer dedicated to Maitreya Buddha, which translates as: *Establishing a steadfast vitality and avoiding laziness by means of continuous perseverance, may the perfection of perseverance be perfected with powerful body and mind!*

The main point of the verse is the admonishment to maintain one's courage, resolve or determination. Shortly thereafter, the image of Mahākāruṇika was destroyed, so I had the thought that this dream may indeed have been relevant!

Then on a few other occasions, I also very clearly dreamt of the main image of Jowo Śākyamuni.

The next image that I recall is the likeness of King Songtsen Gampo on the first floor. It has a very beautiful face, and whenever I passed through the Great Temple, whenever I saw that statue, I always had mixed emotions: partly of faith, since we Tibetans believe that Songtsen Gampo was a manifestation of Avalokiteśvara, and partly of nationalistic sentiment because he

Large torma offerings being paraded through a crowd as part of the ceremonies of the 'Offerings of the Fifteenth Day' of the Great Prayer Festival. (1921 RL)

Monks seated in a courtyard of the Jokhang during the Great Prayer Festival. (1921 RL)

The assembled monks of Namgyal Tratsang, outside the Main Entrance (p. 95). (1937 HR)

had been the first king or emperor of unified Tibet. We Tibetans still revere him as the ancient leader who united the kingdoms of Zhangzhung and Tibet. So, from one side there was a nationalistic sentiment, and from the other a devout Buddhist emotion. So complicated! Then, there was a statue of the venerable Tsongkhapa, with regard to which I may also have had mixed feelings. Tsongkhapa was a great spiritual teacher and a great scholar. Yet, of course, he was born in Amdo, and I am also from Amdo! [laughter]. We Amdowa people are like that!

Then of course, in my own time, in the mid 1950s, a new image of Guru Gyagarma, an aspect of Padmasambhava, was constructed in the main hall. On this matter, I have great regrets. When Dzongsar Khyentse Rinpoche arrived in Lhasa from Kham, following the civil unrest that occurred there in 1956, he came to see me, asking for the oral transmission *(lung)* of some short text. At that time, as a spiritual means of protecting the security of Tibet, he made a prophetic declaration that the Tibetan Government should construct an image of Padmasambhava in the wrathful form Guru Nangsi Zilnon at the centre of main hall of the Great Temple, with four stūpas – one in each of the four directions of the Jowo Śākyamuni. Unfortunately, as you know, some of the five cabinet ministers of the day had a sectarian attitude and were disinclined to accept the advice of a great master of the eclectic tradition of Kham-particularly regarding Nyingmapa icons. So, the construction of the image and the four stūpas did not materialise. No one paid proper attention to this. Instead of the prophesised image of Padmasambhava in the form Guru Nangsi Zilnon, they installed a smaller image in the form known as Guru Gyagarma.

Afterwards, when some officials reported this to Dzongsar Khyentse Rinpoche, he commented – I heard this not directly but through a third person – "A regrettable mistake has been made! Now the Dalai Lama with some of his entourage will have to go to India!" So, on account of that malpractice on the part of certain government ministers, I still have some regret. Even if some of them were sceptical of the prophetic instruction, they could still have resolved to construct the recommended image and stūpas alongside Jowo Śākyamuni, and the problem would not have arisen. However, at that time, they did not even bother! So that is one sad story.

Then, in front of the image of Jowo Śākyamuni there was an emblematic vajra sceptre. In the summer of 1958 I received a report from the monastic officials who supervise the Great Temple, stating that some sacred bone relics *(rin srel)* had emerged of their own accord from the mantra core of the image through the vajra sceptre. Some of these relics had already been brought to Norbulingka. At that time, we were very sceptical. We thought that the senior sacristan *(dkon gnyer dpon)* was responsible! We were always making jokes at his expense since his behaviour was somewhat strange! So we thought that that strange person might do something strange! We were very sceptical. Therefore one day, I sent Mr Phala [Thubten Oten], the home minister to the Great Temple. He had all the sacred bone relics that had appeared there cleared away, and then he placed a

Troops of the cavalry commander during the Great Prayer Festival. (1937 HR)

Monks and military attendants during the Great Prayer Festival. (1937 HR)

The assembled monks of Namgyal Tratsang, outside the Main Entrance (p. 95). (1937 HR)

Cavalry Commanders prostrate to HH Dalai Lama, outside the Great Temple. (1937 HR)

sealed cloth bag in front of the vajra sceptre so that no one could tamper with it. Then, after two days, I myself visited the Great Temple, and opened the bag. It was full of sacred relics! Very strange! That was my own direct experience.

Q: *So, was this a sign?*

A: I'm not sure! The image of Jowo Śākyamuni is not a living being in the ordinary sense of that term, but around that time, the normally unrestricted blessings which it confers on people who come to make offerings and pray in its presence were about to change. Shortly thereafter, restrictions were imposed on all these activities, as if the Jowo image was itself placed under house arrest! Then, subsequently during the Cultural Revolution, the main hall of the Great Temple was converted into a slaughterhouse for pigs. So the emergence of the sacred relics from the mantra core of the image could have reflected a change in mood, indicating that soon everything was about to change for the worse.

Lastly, there was another statue of Padmsambhava, one which had been commissioned by the Thirteenth Dalai Lama, and which was destroyed during the Cultural Revolution. In its mantra core my predecessor had inserted a small representative image *(sku tshab)* of Padmasambhava which had been unearthed as a relic of sacred treasure *(gter ma)* by Terton Sogyal Lerab Lingpa, and offered to him, with the instruction that it should be inserted within the mantra core of his newly constructed Padmasambhava. More recently, in the early 1980s, that small representative image was eventually brought from Tibet to Nepal, where it came into the hands of the late Dilgo Khyentse Rinpoche. Rinpoche entrusted a special envoy to bring that small image to me, and I still keep it in my room.

Q: *Are there any particularly strong memories that still come to mind concerning the Great Prayer Festival (smon lam chen mo)?*

A: My special recollection of the Great Prayer Festival is one of fear! I was very afraid! I was most anxious that I would not be able to recite by heart the prayers that I had to recite. These days, in Dharamsala, I participate in the reconstituted Great Prayer Festival with full concentration. In Tibet, there was no concentration of prayer, but a concentration of fear! Anxiety! My only concern was that I could recite the prayers without mistake. I had not much idea about the meditational side of things! When I first participated, I was. I think, seven or eight years old. So several other young monks had learned the prayers by heart, and on the actual day I was so frightened that while reciting the initial prayer I could not see any of the congregation, or anything at all! I blindly recited the prayers, and then after a few minutes I noticed some pigeons moving around the courtyard. That was after a few minutes! At the beginning I could see nothing. I was so afraid! So that was a real blessing! A punishment! Later I thought that that sensation of fear was so ridiculous, so useless! This was supposed to be a Prayer Festival. Prayer implies some kind of happy mood. But fear, anxiety, and hatred spoil the prayers. So therefore, here, nowadays, I don't care whether I can recite the verses without error or not. I often recite the scriptures by heart as much as I can. Then, if I have

doubts, I look at the printed page! I have come to think that the meaning of these prayers is more important than just reciting their verses by heart without mistake. So that was my strongest memory of the Great Prayer Festival. And as soon a session of prayer would come to an end, I experienced great relief!

I have other memories, particularly of the fifteenth day of the Great Prayer Festival. In the evening when the large *torma* offerings are erected outside the Great Temple and the congregation circumambulates the Barkor Jangchub Jonlam Street, I recall that there were many splendid offerings and beautiful butter sculptures. There was a strong sense of competition, along with the playing of the military band. So I very much enjoyed that!

Q: *Competition in what sense? Between the monasteries?*

A: There were several monasteries participating in the Great Prayer Festival, but the cabinet ministers and senior aristocratic families also used to engage in rivalry when sponsoring large butter sculptures. The poorest of those families, I recall, was the Doring family! The minister of the Doring family who held the rank of Dedril *(bde dril)* was addicted to opium. His family at that time was therefore in a state in decline. So the sculpture constructed in the name of his family was usually of very poor quality! Then, I think, there was also a strong sense of competition between the Upper Tantric College *(rgyud stod)* and the Lower Tantric College *(rgyud smad)*. I do think so!

The atmosphere at that time was very special. I was not much aware of it then, but nowadays I realise that the Jowo Śākyamuni image is the most sacred of all statues in Tibet.

The Great Prayer Festival, which had been originally instituted by the venerable Tsongkhapa, eventually, over time, became the largest congregation of monks and the biggest venue for debate in Tibet. This is how it came to be regarded as the prime location for the examination of all the great scholars of the Gelugpa tradition. This was the time of the year when those seeking the rank of Geshe Lharampa *(dge bshes lha rams pa)* could take their examinations. When this custom began, I do not know. Firstly, I think Tibetans never record dates clearly, and secondly my own knowledge of history is very poor!

So, the whole day had a scholastic programme. The early morning session was taken up with prayer, followed by a debate based on the *Exposition of Valid Cognition (Pramāṇavārttika)*. Then, at noon, the discussion focused on the *Ornament of Emergent Realisation (Abhisamayālaækāra)* and the *Introduction to Madhyamaka (Madhyamakāvatāra)*. Finally, the evening was devoted to the *Treasury of Buddhist Phenomenology (Abhidharmakośa)* and the *Root Discourse of Monastic Discipline (Vinayamūlasūtra)*. Among these, the evening session was the longest! And all those who had already attained the rank of *geshe* came to take part in the dialectics. Almost all the scholars of the Gelugpa tradition participated. At the very least, I think, four or five thousand monks gathered together, and in the centre of that assembly, there was just one individual person debating. In the whole hall there was complete silence. The atmosphere was one of great dignity, serenity and

Procession of the Nechung Oracle in the Barkhor. (1939 HR)

Ceremonial drums outside the Great Temple. (1937 HR)

sanctity. But for outsiders or newcomers it would have been difficult for their noses to stand the atmosphere because there was a very strong pungent smell of rancid butter, even in the open courtyard! The smell even reached that far!

And then, in the Chapel of the Śrīdevī Turret *(dpal lha lcog)*, there were thousands of rats! You could also smell the rats! The sacristans even fed grain to the rats, and I never saw any cats around! In some of the darker chapels, containing images of wrathful deities, I used to be very frightened.

As for the inscription behind Jowo Śākyamuni, we never documented it. No one paid any attention to it, apart from certain foreign visitors. Wasn't it Harrer, or Prince Peter of Greece, who carried out some research? We never gave it our attention. There was also an ancient manuscript in the chapel above the image of Jowo Śākyamuni to which we didn't pay much attention. I heard it was a sacred manuscript, but do not know what it was.

Then, there is the small statue of the emanational goat on the north wing of the ground floor, with which I had some feeling of empathy. It was supposed to symbolise the sacred goat, which according to legend had helped build the Great Temple in ancient times.

There was also a black-painted spot where the butter lamps were kept. People used to say it connected down to the subterranean Milk Plain Lake *('o thang mtsho)* upon which the Great Temple was originally constructed, and that you could hear the sound of aquatic birds there. Once I even put my ear to this spot and listened, but heard no sound. Yet, some say that occasionally people can hear this sound.

Q: *Are there particular memories of the time when Your Holiness took the examination at the Great Temple, or are they similar to those you already described in connection with the congregation at the Great Prayer Festival?*

A: I recall reciting many prayers before the examinations and feeling much calmer. Of course I had another kind of anxiety as to whether my final examinations would be successful or not. A little anxiety, but deep inside I was confident that I would still be the Dalai Lama! So even if I didn't pass the examinations, something would turn out all right!

There is an actual experience I had when some great scholars started debating. I could not figure out, at first, the direction in which they were leading the debate, because they could take it into complicated and contradictory areas. When some of these great scholars started debating, I had more anxiety. But once they reached their conclusion, I would appreciate that we had indeed arrived at the main point! Then, on the occasion of my first examination at Drepung Monastery, I was deeply moved. I cried for more than one minute while reciting the prayers to Buddha and all the great Indian lineage-holders – those authors of those texts we had studied. Such prayers are generally recited in a very beautiful way, with the simple monk's yellow hat, not the long-eared paṇḍita hat, held out in the hands, and at the end of each verse an obeisance is made. So while reciting the verses, the hat is held out and at the end of each verse you touch your

Exorcism ceremony outside the Great Temple (p. 20). (1937 HR)

The Ging dancers drive out the Lugong Scapegoat (p. 20). (1940 HS)

Raising the *torma* of exorcism during the Great Congregation (p. 20). (1946? HR)

forehead to the hat as a sign of homage. While I was making this recitation, I really felt the presence of all those ancient Indian masters, like Nāgārjuna and Āryāsaṅga. I was deeply moved! At that time in Drepung, and also at the final examinations in the Great Temple, all Tibetans and I had the sense that this was an important occasion. The whole atmosphere in the city at that time was extremely tense. The rooftop of every building occupied by the Chinese military was sandbagged. There was a lot of tension, so while from one perspective, it was a very joyful and happy occasion for all, there was also an aspect of fear and tension. Very good for meditation on impermanence! The next day what would happen? Nobody knew. Impermanence had become very real. Yet it was a source of joy in spite of that difficult situation. At last I had this opportunity to take the final examinations in the presence of thousands of great scholars and senior monks.

I noticed that after the examinations, while I was happy, my two tutors and the assistant tutors who had prepare me for that occasion were extremely happy, saying that the examinations had gone wonderfully well. Of course my knowledge compared to those great scholars was nothing, but they all said I had great potential. For example, one extremely great scholar who was a monastic preceptor of Drepung Monastery, *Gyen* Jampa Gyaltsen, made a comment after witnessing my first examination in Drepung that if the Dalai Lama could study full-time as ordinary monks do, then he would become an unparalleled scholar. So that means that at that time I had not reached that level! That was very true!

Earlier, after I returned to Tibet from the Buddha Jayanti celebrations in India in 1956, I reached Lhasa in February 1957. Soon after, we decided that my final examinations would be held in 1959. So now that the date for the final examinations had been decided, I began to concentrate fully on my studies, from March 57 through to March 59, for two years. My assistant tutor *(bsan zhabs)* in Madhyamaka and dialectics, a Mongolian scholar from Sera Monastery, subsequently told me that if I had studied each of the *Five Basic Texts (po ti lnga)* for one year with the same effort, studying for a further three years, I would become an excellent scholar! So that was his way of indicating that at that time I was not an excellent scholar! Such was my "empty aspiration!" He and I resolved that after the final examination we would review some of the important texts. However, this plan was interrupted by the events of 10 March 1959. There were explosions. One of my great regrets was that he could not come to India.

After I reached India in April 1959, I began to study once again the *Ornament of Emergent Realisation,* the *Exposition of Valid Cognition,* and the *Introduction to Madhyamaka.* And I have continued to study Madhyamaka over the last forty years, from 1960 until the present. Over the last forty years I have continued to study as much as I could. So, now, if I were to take the examinations, I would do quite well!

Q: *Your Holiness, Tibetan people in general have a very special sense of devotion when they think of Jowo Rinpoche and the Great Temple. There are those who will prostrate their entire body length across the entire*

Crowd control during the Great Prayer Festival (p. 15). (1937 HR)

Tibetan plateau in order to make offerings to Jowo Śākyamuni in Lhasa. Can you explain the basis for this strong devotion that the people have?

A: Of course there are some scriptures stating that even if you see a buddha statue while your mind is still dominated by anger and other dissonant mental states, or if you have no special devotion but see the image by chance, the imprint of that experience can enable you eventually to see limitless buddhas. So our devotion is founded on the basis of such faith.

We believe that the image of Jowo Śākyamuni was constructed in India, where it was blessed by Lord Buddha in person and subsequently taken to China, from where it reached Lhasa. Whether that is all true or not, I do not know. But, in this regard, there is one strange fact that my junior tutor Trijang Rinpoche once told me. Once someone came to Lhasa from Kongpo Bonri to meet Trijang Rinpoche, and while in Lhasa he visited the Great Temple. However, on entering the Central Inner Sanctum where the image of Jowo Śākyamuni is housed, he could not see the statue, except for its plinth! He was most upset because he had failed to see the buddha image, which everyone else can see. So he asked Trijang Rinpoche what he had done to have had such a bad residue of past karma! This actually happened in Tibet in our generation. How strange! At the same time, I have heard no reports of Chinese communists who have no faith at all not seeing the image! Then again, there are many anecdotes of individuals who have actually conversed with Jowo Śākyamuni.

Q: *There seem to be many accounts in Tibetan literature and in the oral tradition of people who have conversed with Jowo Śākyamuni, or of making special prayers in his presence.*

A: The Fifth Dalai Lama in his Secret Visions *(gSang ba rgya can)* on many occasions received teachings from celebrated teachers of the past whose forms appeared to emerge from the images of Kyirong Jowo and Phakpa Wati, the two renowned "sibling" images of Avalokiteśvara, as he used to call them. When he saw these statues, on certain occasions, visions appeared from their heart. To such people these images are living – but to us they are not alive.

Strange events such as this do occur. For example, *Gyen* Yeshe Donden passed away last year. In 1959 he remained behind in Tibet when I left. Then, I think in a monastery or prison or somewhere, one day he dreamt that he met me and that I actually gave him some kind of instruction, telling him not to remain there, but to leave Tibet forthwith! He had confidence in that dream and, following it, finally escaped.

There was another Tibetan, who in the late 1980s came from Tibet and stayed on in India. On one occasion he decided to return home, either for family reasons, or to see his birthplace. He first came to Dharamsala, hoping to see me, but at that time I was not free, so he could not have an audience. That night he had a dream in which the Dalai Lama instructed him to go to Tibet for ten months and then return to India. There would be no problem! He followed this advice exactly, and later when I met him he told me that although he could not meet me

Foot soldiery on the roof of the Great Temple, during the Great Prayer Festival (p. 15). (1936 SC)

Government officials in the corridor of the Annex, with foot soldier guards above. (1936 SC)

personally prior to his departure, I had appeared to him in a dream and given him instructions, which he had followed. From my side, I was unaware of it all! Therefore, it appears that some people are susceptible to such subtle spiritual influences.

To some, the image of Jowo Śākyamuni is just a statue. Nothing! Just as some Chinese used to say to the Tibetans, "Since you have so much devotion for these statues, if you are hungry, perhaps they will feed you!" For some, it is almost like that! From their point of view the Jowo is just a statue. In their view, nothing happens to those who disparage it, and it itself does not feed the devotee. But to some people with a different background, a different residue of past actions, and in some cases, a different sort of mentality, these images are real, and can confer blessings. Such people consider the Jowo image to be very sacred for this reason.

Actually, a true practitioner, a true follower of Buddha, should not make such distinctions, regarding an old statue as more precious and a new statue as less sacred. That's wrong! There should be no difference between an image made of gold and an image made of clay. Yet this statement is only relatively true! For, on one level, some of these old images do have distinctions owing to the fact that their original blessing was conferred by great spiritual teachers of the past, so that they have a greater repository of spiritual energy than those that are newly constructed. Some sacred places inhabited by accomplished meditators also retain a particular resonance, and on reaching them, without explanation, you may have some special feeling whereas in some more beautiful environments, that kind of feeling may be absent.

The cavalry of the commanders ride past the Great Temple. (1937 HR)

Prayer ceremonies in the Great Courtyard (p. 90). (1922 WR)

Part 1

Zhakabpa's Inventory to the Great Temple of Lhasa

Gyurme Dorje

Ceiling panels of the Central Inner sanctum. (1996 AA)

The Construction of the Great Temple

Wood carved panel above the lintel of the entrance to the Hermitage of the Religious King (p. 82, no. **80**). (2000 HS)

Second floor gallery of the Main Hall (p. 82). (2000 GD)

The Tibetan religious king Songtsen Gampo, who is revered in Tibet as a human incarnation of the bodhisattva Mahākāruṇika, took as one of his queens Bhṛkuṭīdevī *(bal bza' khri btsun)*, the daughter of King Aṃśuvarman, founder of the Thakuri Dynasty in neighbouring Nepal. Aṃśuvarman, a contemporary of Songtsen Gampo's father King Namri Songtsen, had inaugurated his own calendrical era in 576, but his successor Udayadeva was overthrown in 624. The latter's son and rightful heir Narendradeva, a devotee of Matsyendranāth, sought refuge in Tibet until the restoration of his rule in 641, and the princess Bhṛkuṭīdevī is said to have reached Lhasa during that period (circa 632-634), bringing a dowry of precious jewels and sacred images.[91] Foremost among these were: the statue of Akṣobhyavajra *(jo bo mi bskyod rdo rje)*, depicting the Buddha the size of an eight-year-old, which is revered for having been consecrated by Śākyamuni Buddha himself; the statue of Maitreya in the Gesture of Teaching the Sacred Doctrine (*byams pa chos 'khor*), which had been consecrated by Buddha Kāśyapa; and the sandalwood statue of "speaking" Tārā *(sgrol ma gsung byon)*.

Later King Songtsen Gampo invaded the Sino-Tibetan borderlands and married Wen-cheng Kon-jo, the daughter of the Chinese Emperor Taizong of the Tang dynasty.[92] The Chinese title *baowang* ("jewel king") was subsequently bestowed upon the king by Emperor Gaozong. Princess Wencheng came to Tibet, bringing as her dowry the statue of Jowo Śākyamuni which depicts the Buddha the size of a twelve-year old, and which had also been consecrated by the Buddha himself, along with treatises on medicine and divination, and many gifts of exquisite brocade silk. The princess is known to have remained in Lhasa until her death circa 680-1.

Following these marital alliances, Songtsen Gampo subsequently married Litigmik, daughter of King Limigkya of Zhangzhung, Ruyongza Gyalmotsun who was the daughter of a Tangut potentate, and Mongza Tricham, daughter of a minister from Tolung Mong.

In Lhasa, the Newār princess Bhṛkuṭīdevī constructed on Red Hill (Marpori) an unrivalled palatial mansion commensurate with the King's military conquests.[93] Subsequently, each of the queens expressed to the king their wish to build a temple to hold the sacred images, which they had brought to Tibet as their respective dowries. According to tradition, the Chinese princess was then invited to survey a site suitable for the construction of the Newāri princess's temple. Wen-cheng Kon-jo inspected the site by means of the divination techniques expounded in the Portang scrolls,[94] and her prognosis suggested that it would be auspicious if the Milk Plain Lake of the Lower Kyichu valley *(skyid shod 'o thang mtsho)* was reclaimed and a temple constructed above it. However the Newār princess doubted the prognosis, thinking that Wen-cheng Kon-jo's advice seemed inauspicious, and she appealed to the king. The king prayed to his meditational deity, and consequently received a prophetic declaration that accorded with the suggestion of the Chinese princess.

Thereupon, beams were secured across the small Milk Plain Lake, and the lake was filled in with earth that had been transported by goats, enabling the construction of the Great Temple to begin. According to legend, gods and demons persistently demolished by night the edifice raised by human

Lintel above the entrance to the Central Inner Sanctum (p. 72, no. **29**). (1996 HS)

Entrance to the Hermitage of the Religious King (p. 82, no. **80**). (2000 GD)

beings during the day. The king and his two foreign queens, therefore, resolved to remain in retreat at the Palace of Nyangdren Phabongkha to propitiate the sublime bodhisattva Mahākāruṇika. Eventually they received a prophecy that, from the standpoint of geomancy, the Tibetan terrain appeared to assume the form of a supine ogress. Before the construction of the Great Temple could be completed, it would be necessary to suppress the geomantic focal points on her body. If "frontier taming" temples, "further taming" temples and "district controlling" temples were erected along with their appropriate representative images at these focal points, the king's wishes would be effortlessly accomplished.

In compliance with this prophecy, four "frontier taming" temples *(mtha' 'dul lha khang bzhi)* and subsidiary temples were built: the Migyur Lhakhang at Maldro Katshel in Uru, along with its subsidiary Sengshang Girti Lhakhang; the Tradruk Tashi Jamnyom Lhakhang at Yarlung in Yoru, along with its subsidiary Tsenthang Yu'i Lhakhang; the Tsangdram Gegye Lhakhang in Tsang, along with its subsidiary Gedrung Lhakhang; and the Drompagyang Drime Namdak Lhakhang in Ngamring, along with its subsidiary Dre Lhakhang.

Four "further taming" temples *(yang 'dul lha khang bzhi)* were also constructed: Kongpo Buchu Lhakhang on the "tiger's head" in the east; Lhodrak Khomthing Tergyi Lhakhang on the "dragon's crest" in the south; Tshalrik Sherab Me'i Lhakhang on the "red bird's spine" in the west; and To Traduntse Lhakhang on the "turtle's brow" in the north Finally, four "district controlling" temples *(ru gnon lha khang bzhi)* were built: Tshangpa Lungzhon Lhakhang, Den Longthang Dolma Lhakhang, Mangyul Jamtrin Gegye Lhakhang, and Lhodruk Paro Kyerchu Lhakhang.[95] Along with all these buildings, the appropriate representative images were also constructed. In this way, the Great Temple came to form the centre of a grand geomantic scheme whereby temples were erected in three successive rings of four on the body of the "supine ogress" which is Tibet (i.e. on her shoulders and hips, elbows and knees, and hands and feet).[96]

Based on the calculation of King Songtsen Gampo's birth in 617 (fire ox year),[97] the Milk Plain Lake was filled and the foundations of the Great Temple laid upon it in 639 (earth pig year) when the king was in his twenty-third year. The foundations of the stone walls were actually secured at the centre of the Milk Plain Lake, a power place perceived as the core or axis of a stone stūpa, the very fabric of which is said to have materialised from the self-manifesting pristine cognition of buddha-mind. On each of its four sides long beams of water-resistant wood were secured. In order to prevent the timbers from being eroded by water, they were coated with mud provided by serpentine water spirits *(klu)*. A moulding of bronze was applied to the ends of each timber, and the cavities were filled with molten bronze. Upon this secure foundation, the lake was filled, utilising earth that had been transported by a goat.

The Great Temple was then constructed by Tibetan corvée labourers and skilled craftsmen working in clay, stone and wood, who were revered as emanations of the king. One day when the Newār princess Bhṛkuṭīdevī arrived at the lake-side to draw water, a female servant peered through the gate of the Great Temple while she was drawing water, and saw a carpenter wearing a silk turban, emblematic of royalty. She laughed loudly, saying, "He is a veritable emanation!" The king is said to have been distracted by this, and his axe slipped, accidentally cutting the noses of the hundred lions that decorate the beam-ends. His chisel also slipped, piercing a hundred gashes, and his saw slipped, chipping the edges of a hundred pillars.[98]

Once the main chapels of the ground floor had been constructed, Bhṛkuṭīdevī summoned skilled Newāri artisans and Tibetan corvée labourers to complete the construction of the first and second floors. The original layout appears to have had a Newār model, although traditional accounts also claim the building to have been modelled on Vikramaśīla Monastery in India.[99] When the top floor was finally completed after the death of Bhṛkuṭīdevī, the Great Temple was said to symbolise the three buddha-bodies *(sku gsum)* or three world-systems *(khams gsum)*. A distinctive Newār influence is clearly discernible in the original rounded door-frames of the main chapels of the ground and first floors, while Indian influences can be seen in the rectangular doorways of the south and north wings.[100]

The Great Temple was then named "Great Emanational Temple of Ra-sa, place of the goat" *(ra sa 'phrul snang gi gtsug lag khang)*, firstly because the earth had been transported by an emanational goat, and secondly because a particularly wonderful temple resembling an optical illusion had been constructed there once the lake had been filled. Others, too, described the building as "an apparitional Great Temple giving rise to four delights" *(dga' bzhi 'phrul snang gi gtsug lag khang)*. Firstly, it delighted Buddhists since its four gates were fashioned in the style of a celestial palace *(vimāna)*, secondly it delighted Bonpos since its walls were fashioned in the design of a svāstika, thirdly it delighted mantrins since its pillars were fashioned in the design of a ritual dagger, and fourthly it delighted the populace because its joists and beams were fashioned in the design of a lattice *(mig mang)*. The building had four gates: one in each of its four walls, and thirty-seven pillars, symbolic of the thirty-seven sections of the Vinaya. The main gate faced west towards Nepal because the Newār princess Bhṛkuṭīdevī had commissioned its construction.[101]

Once the building had been constructed, sacred images were brought there from the Red Palace, and the primary images were installed in a pentadic arrangement, comprising five main chapels within the square hall. An image of Dīpaṃkara Buddha in the form Acala *(rgyal ba mi 'khrug pa)* was installed in the Central Inner Sanctum, along with his eight retainers. Images of Amitābha with his eight retainers were installed in the chapel to the right, and Maitreya in the Gesture of Teaching the Sacred Doctrine *(byams pa chos 'khor)* in the chapel to the left. Mahākāruṇika in the form Rangjon Ngaden, which had been fashioned as a likeness of King Songtsen Gampo himself, was installed with its retinue in the Northern Inner Sanctum, and Śākyamuni in the form Akṣobhyavajra *(jo bo mi bskyod rdo rje)*, which had been the dowry of Bhṛkuṭīdevī, in the Southern Inner Sanctum. The original name Rasa ('place of the goat') was then altered to Lhasa ('place of the deity') following the temple's consecration.

The installation of these images was commemorated with an inconceivable array of butter lamps and [lavish] offering utensils. The serpentine kings *(Nāgarāja)* Nanda and Upananda are said to have arrived there, saying, "Build an image of us since we will protect the temple!" The ten-headed ogre Daśagrīva of Laṅkā also arrived, saying, "Build an image of me because I will protect this temple from the dangers of fire!" The sylvan spirit Kubera arrived, saying, "Build an image of me because I will protect this temple from the dangers of all four elements!" Then, the protectress Śrīdevī appeared and said, "Build an image of me because I will protect this temple from the dangers of humans and non-humans!" Images of all these protector deities were therefore constructed in accordance with their respective wishes. Then, the king concealed many treasures within the temple for the future

Confession Buddhas of the Skylight Gallery (p. 82). (2000 GD)

Entrance to the Northern Inner Sanctum (p. 68, no. **16**). (1999 HS)

"The emanational goat" (p. 76, no. **45**). (2000 GD)

The Great Acacia Gate (p. 66 and 90, no. **1**). (1999 HS)

well being of his subjects. Adjacent to the Vase Pillar *(ka ba bum pa can)* he concealed treasures of the sacred doctrine. At the Leaf Pillar *(ka ba shing lo can)* he concealed the *Testament of the King (rgyal po'i bka' chems)* and alongside it a treasure of gold. Adjacent to the Snake's Head Pillar *(ka ba sbrul sgo can)*, he concealed a treasure of wrathful mantras and sorcery. Adjacent to the Lion Pillar *(ka ba seng mgo can)*, he concealed a treasure concerning animal husbandry. Then, the king had a jewel called Ratnadeva inserted into a casket of banded chalcedony *(gzi)*, which was wrapped in fine brocade silk and concealed underneath an image of Jambhala. He had a jewel called Taksha Dewa wrapped in snakeskin and concealed in the chapel dedicated to serpentine water spirits *(klu khang)*. He had a monk's alms' bowl, which was fashioned of beryl, filled with various edibles and concealed it in the chapel dedicated to sylvan mountain spirits *(gnod sbyin gyi khang pa)*. Then in order to facilitate the future restoration of the building, he had a large container filled with gold, silver and other precious metals, which he then concealed underneath this great maṇḍala.

Furthermore, in order that timely rain might fall, that the harvest might be abundant, and that armed forces might not invade from the borders, the king concealed gold, silver, and jewels, wrapped in containers of brocade silk, in those chapels dedicated to the serpentine water spirits and the sylvan mountain spirits, and throughout the inner circumambulatory walkway of the temple. He then disclosed the various benefits which would accrue from venerating, paying homage, making offerings and cirumambulating this "divine place" *(lha sa)*, and those which would arise in consequence of seeing, hearing, and recollecting it. He also explained the advantages of restoring the outer dykes that protected the temple from the nearby Kyichu River, and of venerating the sacred receptacles of offering within its chapels. His son, the crown prince Gungsong Gungtsen (r. 641-5), inscribed this edict, which was concealed as a treasure within the chapel of the sylvan mountain spirits, with a prayer that worthy and fortunate individuals might discover it in the future. In this way the aspirations of the king and his queens were fulfilled. When the edict was rediscovered, the following pronouncements made by the king concerning the Great Temple became universally known throughout Tibet:[102]

> Whenever the Tibetan people are without confidence,
> And incited by malevolent forces,
> If they have faith in the emanational attributes of King Songtsen,
> Paying homage to his lotus feet,
> There is no doubt that they will achieve a genuine result
> In their accumulation of the provision of merit
> Through acts of homage, circumambulations, offerings, and so forth!

Specifically, concerning the advantages of seeing the Great Temple and its sacred images, scriptures and stūpas, which are respectively symbolic of buddha-body, speech and mind, the king himself declared, "If the Great Temple is seen once, entrance to rebirth in inferior realms will be cut off. If seen twice, one will acquire the body of a god or human, and attain release from rebirth in cyclic existence. If it is seen thrice, the three poisons will be pacified right where they are, and one will attain the three buddha-bodies."

As for the advantages of hearing about the Great Temple, he said, "If word of the Great Temple reaches even the ears of an animal, that creature will reach the pathway that leads to release from the sufferings of cyclic existence. If gods or humans hear of the Great Temple, they will attain release from rebirth in cyclic existence!"

On the advantages of recalling the Great Temple, he said, "One who recalls the enlightened attributes of the meditational deities [depicted within it] can purify the obscurations of five thousand aeons, and is capable of comprehending the profound implications of the uncreated reality of all things".

On the advantages of paying homage to the Great Temple, he said, "One who prostrates before the Great Temple will come to have an excellent physique, with a golden-like lustrous complexion that is beautiful to behold, speech that is pleasant to hear, words worthy of retention, and a great charisma, delighting gods and humans. Such a person will associate with buddhas and bodhisattvas, acquire great resources, be reborn in the higher realms of cyclic existence, and swiftly attain the level of nirvāṇa."

On the advantages of offering butter lamps in the Great Temple, he said," One will become like a lamp in the world, endowed simultaneously with the pure vision of divine clairvoyance and eyes of flesh. One will comprehend both virtuous and nonvirtuous doctrines, dispel the darkness of fundamental ignorance, and attain the light of discriminative awareness. In this way, one will avoid rebirth in deluded states, possess great resources, be reborn in the higher realms of cyclic existence, and swiftly attain the level of nirvāṇa".

Finally, the king mentioned the inestimable advantages of offering gold to gild the images of the Great Temple and of circumambulating them, "Negative acts such as the ten non-virtuous actions will be purified, diseases, demonic possession, obstacles and so forth will be pacified, the lifespan will be prolonged, one's purpose will be fulfilled, throughout the succession of one's lives one will acquire an excellent physical body, with the good fortune to practice the sacred doctrine, and finally one will attain the level of the buddhas".

Decorative pillar outside the Central Inner Sanctum. (1999 HS)

Decorative lintel of the Central Inner Sanctum. (1999 HS)

Later Phases of Restoration and Extension

After the death of King Songtsen Gampo and his queens, during the reign of the king's grandson Mangsong Mangtsen, some historical accounts suggest there was an armed invasion from China.[103] In accordance with the testament of his royal grandfather, Mangsong Mangtsen had the image of Jowo Śākyamuni taken from the Ramoche temple, which had been built by the Chinese Princess, and concealed within the Southern Inner Sanctum of the Great Temple, which had a round entrance. The gate was then plastered over and a painting of Mañjuśrīghoṣa superimposed. When the Chinese forces reached Lhasa, they burned the Red Palace, and mistaking the image of Akṣobhyavajra *(jo bo mi bskyod rdo rje)* which was the principal image of the temple for Jowo Śākyamuni, they carried it off a day's march. However, the weight of the statue increased, forcing them to abandon it at Cholung, unable as they were to carry it further. An emanational army then emerged from the navel of the image of Ucchūṣmakrodha, which guards the entrance to the Amitābha Chapel, and expelled the Chinese forces to their own domain. The image of Akṣobhyavajra was brought back from Cholung and installed in the Ramoche temple that had been built by the Chinese Princess Wencheng.

Subsequently in the early eighth century, the Chinese princess Jin-cheng Kon-jo, who was the queen of the Tibetan king Tride Tsukten, also known as Me Aktsom, began to search for the image of Jowo Śākyamuni which had been the dowry of her relative Wen-cheng Kon-jo. Learning of its whereabouts through secret divination, she extracted the image from the Southern Inner Sanctum with its round entrance, and had it installed as the principal representative image within the Central Inner Sanctum (Jokhang). In this way, it is explained that the locations of the two Jowo images were interchanged.

The excellent tradition of making offerings in the Great Temple was continuously maintained during the later reigns of the great Tibetan kings Trisong Detsen, Mune Tsenpo, Senalek Jungyon, and Tri Relpachen. Senalek Jingyon is said to have cleared an area for the construction of an outer courtyard and Tri Relpachen built the Meru and Karu temples to the rear. Nonetheless, on account of the feeble merit of the Tibetans in general, during the reign of Langdarma Udumtsen, around 838 (earth pig year), a demon consumed the heart of the king and he instigated a persecution of Buddhism.[104] During that period, the two Jowo images, Maitreya in the Gesture of Teaching the Sacred Doctrine *(byams pa chos 'khor)* and other sacred objects were buried underground, some images, scriptures and stūpas were cast into the Kyichu River, some were burned, and others were pierced by weapons.[105] The Main Gate of the Great Temple was plastered over, and desecrated with a painting depicting a venerable Buddhist monk drinking wine. Inside the courtyard a knackers' yard was set up for the slaughtering of goats and sheep. However, in 842 (water dog year), the evil king was slain and liberated from subsequent rebirth in evil existences by Lhalung Palgyi Dorje, an actual student of Padmasambhava, who resided at the Yerpa hermitage, in accordance with an exhortation of the protectress Śrīdevī.[106]

Ucchūṣmakrodha (p. 71, no. **25**). (2000 GD)

Extant murals from the Chapel of the Countenance (p. 79, no. **79**). (1991 US)

The Great Temple was gradually reopened by Langdarma's two sons, Namde Osung and Ngadak Yumten. The images that had been buried were reinstated on their respective thrones, and the custom of making continuous offerings was partly reinstated. However, the wishes of the princes were not fulfilled on account of civil insurrection, and a long period of political decline ensued.

Still later, when the peerless Jowoje Dīpaṃkara Atiśa (982-1054) was residing at Nyethang, he visited Lhasa to see the images of Jowo Śākyamuni in the Great Temple. While contemplating the inventory of the Great Temple, as had been predicted by a mad ḍākinī of Lhasa,[107] he extracted a scriptural treasure entitled *The Testament of the King (rgyal po'i bka' chems ka 'khol ma)* from the Leaf Pillar *(ka ba shing lo can)*. Consequently Atiśa performed unsurpassed acts of veneration in the Great Temple.

During the first sexagenary year cycle, Zangkar Lotsāwa Phakpa Sherab enlarged the Central Inner Sanctum, and modified the Chapel of the Countenance above.[108] He constructed many representative objects of buddha-body, speech and mind, including the image of Vairocana Buddha in the form Hīmamahāsāgara *(thub pa gangs can mtsho)* with his retinue which graces the Central Inner Sanctum, and the image of "Bathing" Maitreya (*byams pa 'khrus mdzad*), which was installed in the north wing.

Then, in 1160 (iron dragon year of the third cycle), when Gompa Tshultrim Nyingpo (1116-69) arrived in Lhasa, he thought it would be impossible to repair the great damage which had been inflicted on the chapels of the Great Temple during the aforementioned period of factionalism and civil insurrection.[109] However, in a dream, the lord Gampopa appeared to him and said, "Will you have the courage to make me secure?" It is said that tear-drops actually manifested at the eyes of the Jowo Śākyamuni image at that time. Therefore, Gompa stayed on in Lhasa and carried out an excellent restoration of the Great Temple, renovating, in particular, the murals of the Chapel of the Countenance on the first floor, and building the inner pilgrims' walkway *(bar 'khor/ nang 'khor)*.[110]

Shortly thereafter, Zhang Yudrakpa, also known as Zhang Tsondru Drak, was entrusted with the maintenance of the Great Temple. His successors were the incumbents of Tshalpa *(tshal pa'i sde pa)* who successively maintained the chapels.[111]

Lumen, the son of King Anantamul of Yartse, nowadays in NW Nepal, who was an unblemished descendent of the Tibetan religious kings, donated the gilded roof *(rgya phibs)*, which can still be seen above the image of Jowo Śākyamuni. Later, King Putimul of Yartse and the minister Palden Drakpa jointly donated the gilded roof, positioned above the image of Mahākāruṇika.[112]

Then, in order that the flooding waters of the Kyichu River might not inflict harm in summer on the city of Lhasa and above all on the Great Temple, a stone dyke was constructed through the miraculous powers of Drogon Namkha Pelwa, the son of the great treasure-finder Nyangral Nyima Ozer (1136-1204). Zhikpo Dudtsi (1143-99) subsequently renovated this river dyke on approximately four occasions, at which times he also restored and venerated the chapels of the Great Temple. Taton Jo-ye (1163-1230), the student of Zhikpo Dudtsi, also attended upon the two images of Śākyamuni for six years.[113] *Lha-rje* Gewabum attended to the repairs of the river dyke, and restored the damaged outer walls of the Great Temple, thereby performing an unsurpassed act of offering.

The Vase Pillar (p. 71, no. **27**). (1999 HS)

The Leaf Pillar (p. 74, no. **33**). (1999 HS)

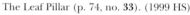

Entrance to the Chapel of Maitreya (p. 74, no. **34**). (2000 GD)

The Vase Pillar (p. 71, no. **27**). (2000 GD)

The chief ministers who governed Tibet during the Sakya period of administration, headed by Śākya Zangpo, gradually restored the Acacia Gate of the Great Temple and constructed new rooftop chapels. During the fourteenth century, Monlam Dorje, the son of Ga-de Zangpo Do-de of Tshal Gungthang, completed the slate gallery *(rdza'i gYab 'khor ma)* of the first floor, along with the skylight *(thog gseng)* and windows *(lcags khra)* overlooking the Main Hall (*dkyil 'khor mthil*). He extended the twelve great pillars, the bases of the sixteen smaller pillars, and the corridor of the inner pilgrims' walkway.[114]

When Phakpa Sangye Rinchen, the spiritual son of Drogon Donyo Zhakpa visited Lhasa, Tshalpa Kunga Dorje, author of the *Red Annals*, sought the ordinations of a renunciate and full-fledged monk from him, and was given the name Gewei Lodro. At Tshalpa's request, he became a benefactor of the Great Temple, restoring the offering lamps of the Central Inner Sanctum, and repainting the murals of the Maṇi Wheel Chapel *(skor khang)* with his own hand.[115]

Around the turn of the fifteenth century, while Tsongkhapa Lobzang Drakpa (1357-1419), founder of the Gelugpa school of Tibetan Buddhism, was passing a summer rain retreat at Choding, he received a prediction from the bodhisattva Mañjughoṣa that, if he were to restore the image of Jowo Śākyamuni at Lhasa, along with its Great Temple and other sacred images, and institute a Great Prayer Festival, the precious teaching of the Buddha would flourish in all directions, and all sentient beings of the six realms would benefit.

Although the Great Temple, which had been constructed by the King Songtsen Gampo, had been the recipient of immeasurable acts of offering and veneration, owing to the deteriorating merit of living beings its chapels had gradually become dilapidated and ruined. Beggars were residing in some of the chapels, lighting fires and placing food, torn clothing, and personal utensils on the sacred images. Unable to bear these actions, Tsongkhapa purposefully encouraged some of his attendants to prepare a banquet by the banks of the Kyichu River. The beggars were invited and fed, after which Tsongkhapa admonished them repeatedly not to light fires in the chapels or place used clothing on the images. Finally, the governor of the Lhasa area, Depa Neupa, removed all their possessions from the Great Temple and sealed the gates.[116]

Advised and motivated by Tsongkhapa, Drakpa Gyaltsen, who was the king (*gong ma*) of Tibet, set about repairing and restoring the Great Temple and its sacred contents, with the aid of Neu Namka Zangpo, his nephew, retainers and relatives. In 1409 (earth ox year of the first cycle), the Great Courtyard *(khyams rva chen mo)* in front of the Acacia Gate was enlarged. A stone quarry at Nyangser Menri was excavated, and the flagstones of the courtyard were restored, using natural paving stones of different shapes and colours. The twelve pillars extending to the skylight roof of the Main Hall *(dkyil 'khor mthil)*, with its vajra-parapet, were also restored.[117] The building was then offered to Tsongkhapa and his students, and all the material resources that could be found were amassed to facilitate the inaugural Great Prayer Festival.[118]

That same year Tsongkhapa propagated the Buddhist teachings in all directions. In order that the good auspices might permeate the world, both in the short and long term, he offered a golden headdress to the image of Jowo Śākyamuni and thereby transformed the image from one depicting the Buddha-body of Emanation into one depicting the Buddha-body of Perfect Resource. He offered a silver alms' bowl, to be placed in the lap of the image.[119]

Assembled monks and spectators in the Great Courtyard. (1986 CB)

The monastic body during the Great Prayer Festival. (1986 CB)

In addition, he offered a silver head-dress to the image of the bodhisattva Mahākāruṇika in the form Rangjon Ngaden, and, alongside the image of the first floor depicting King Songtsen Gampo, he placed the king's own silver wine flask *('khrung ban)* with its "horse-head" stopper *(rta mgo ma)* – an object which he himself had unearthed as a treasure by the banks of the Kyichu river. He painted the faces of the images with gold *(zhal gser)*, performed "eye-opening" ceremonies *(spyan dbye)*, donated costumes to all of the images within the Great Temple, and presented an exquisite cloud-mass of offerings that were beyond imagination.

Chenga Sonam Gyaltsen of Phagmodru, King Drakpa Gyaltsen, and other royal patrons then inaugurated the annual custom of the auspicious Great Prayer Festival during the Month of Miracles, starting on the first day of the month and continuing up to the sixteenth day of the month. On these occasions, divine and human offerings, conjoined with profound and extensive acts of veneration, were made to ten thousand monks of the monastic community.[120]

So it was that Tsongkhapa himself remarks in the *Prayer from his Secret Biography (rJe thams cad mkhyen pa'i gsang ba'i rnam thar gsol 'debs)*, "After I had consecrated as [sacraments of] supreme bliss a hundred wondrous, auspicious and diverse offerings, during the month of great miracles at the pilgrimage site of Chokhor Lhasa, the conquerors of the ten directions and their sons were delighted".

In 1437 (fire snake year of the seventh sexagenary cycle), when there was a natural disaster in Tibet caused by poor harvest, the accomplished master Thangtong Gyalpo went begging for gold. He made an alms bowl fashioned of one hundred and twenty-seven srang of gold, which he then filled with various grains and offered to Jowo Śākyamuni. A timely rain fell in consequence of his prayers. The harvest and cattle thrived, and the country was protected from the fears of famine.[121]

Later, during the lifetime of Norbu Zangpo and Donyo Dorje of Rinpung, the local governor of Lhasa Nang-tse was executed in the lower Kyichu valley, along with his nephew. The mighty forces of Rinpung used this incident as a pretext to attack Lhasa in 1498 (earth horse year of the eighth cycle). The senior magistrate of the city Nelpa'i Sakyong Ngagi Wangpo and his relatives were all detained at Kyormolung, and the Rinpungpa confiscated their estates *(gzhis ka sne'u)* and possessions. From then until 1518 *(earth tiger)*, for a period of twenty years the monks of Sera and Drepung were not permitted to hold the Great Prayer Festival and Zhamarpa Chodrak Zangpo held sway in the city. Consequent on this decline in the fortunes of the Gelugpa school, partisans such as Sumpa Khenpo claim the Great Temple fell into a state of disrepair, the continuity of offerings was interrupted, and maintenance of the building deteriorated.[122]

In these circumstances, the *yogin* Drakpa Tha-ye, following the advice of his spiritual teacher, went to pay his respects to the two images of Jowo Śākyamuni in Lhasa. The courtyard of the Great Temple was constantly filled with pilgrims and vagrants, and he stayed there among them incognito. A certain Trulzhik Sangsampa also happened to be living there in the guise of a beggar. At first he did not recognise Drakpa Tha-ye, but eventually did so, and they entered into a dialogue. One day when Donyo Dorje and his retainers came to pay their respects to the image of Jowo Śākyamuni, they heard word that the venerable Drakpa Tha-ye was living among the beggars. The official Awarpa was sent to question him, and later, the official's secretary Yungpaba went to meet him, carrying items for a feast-offering ceremony and some special presents. Later, Donyo Dorje summoned him to Dekyiling in

Bellows-shaped stone of the Vestibule (p. 66, no. **3**). (1996 AA)

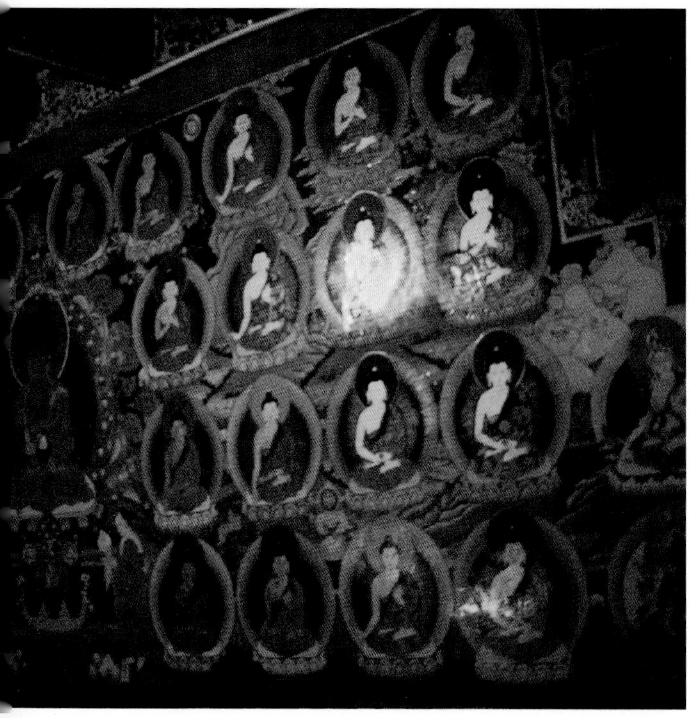

Mural depicting the Five Buddhas (p. 66, no. **5**). (2000 GD)

Lhasa, where they held a long discussion, in consequence of which he imbued the ruler with a more positive perspective. One can learn from his entreaty that great damage had been inflicted on the Great Temple.[123] During that period of Rinpung dominance, when the properties of the landowners of the lower Kyichu valley were confiscated and the Prayer Festival was observed for nineteen years only by a few monks from Sangphu and other adjacent monasteries of the Kagyu and Sakya traditions, Tsongkhapa's legacy is said to have suffered. Devout patrons grew disillusioned when they observed the misconduct of the assembly of monks. Regular donations were interrupted, and the "cloud-mass" of offerings traditionally presented to the image of Jowo Śākyamuni was made in name alone. Subsequently, when the Second Dalai Lama Gendun Gyatso (1476-1542) sought to restore these traditions and offering ceremonies, he explained his purpose to the then king of Tibet, Ngagi Wangchuk Tashi Drakpa Gyaltsen, undaunted by the scale of the material resources and arduous efforts that would be required. The king was well disposed to the idea, and so it was that, commencing from 1518 (earth tiger year of the ninth year cycle), the Dalai Lama presided over the Great Prayer Festival. One and a half thousand monks from Drepung and three hundred monks from Sera congregated in accordance with the former custom. A "cloud-mass" of offerings was presented in the Great Temple, the monks were served in the proper manner, and prayers were dedicated for the flourishing of the Buddhist teachings, and the spiritual and temporal well-being of all living beings.[124]

In 1562 (water dog year of the ninth cycle), when excessively heavy rainfall threatened to flood the city of Lhasa and the Great Temple, the dykes of the Kyichu River and particularly the dyke that protects Jowo Śākyamuni were repaired on the advice of the Third Dalai Lama Sonam Gyatso. From the following year onwards, after the completion of the Great Prayer Festival, a custom was introduced whereby the combined monks of the three major Gelugpa monasteries would carry stones to repair the Jowo's dyke. In this way the current of the Kyichu River was diverted to the south, the city and the Great Temple were protected from the fear of floods, and a canopy of refined gold was offered, above the head of the image of Jowo Śākyamuni.[125]

As for the throne of Jowo Śākyamuni, during the late 13th century, an exiled Mongol prince named Hulau, a descendant of Genghiz Qan, had arrived in Tibet to receive teachings on the sacred doctrine from Buton Rinchendrub at Zhalu and Lodro Gyaltsen at Sakya. He had offered a large amount of pure white silver, with the intention of making a new throne for the image of Jowo Śākyamuni in the Great Temple. The chief minister Śākya Zangpo had personally taken charge of this project, and an ornate throne of white silver had been made, supported by a lion, elephant, horse and peacock.

Later, the King of Jang, Sonam Rabten commissioned extraordinary works of arts, including a pillar with the motif of a rising dragon, a pillar adorned with precious jewels, and a two-storey silver Chinese-style gilded roof *(rgya phibs)* which was erected above the Central Inner Sanctum. The Fourth Dalai Lama Yonten Gyatso (1589-1616), in the course of restoring the throne-back of the Jowo image, offered a bas-relief engraving depicting the twelve deeds of Śākyamuni Buddha, which was fastened to the throne-back (*rgyab yol*), along with silver-moulded images of the Sixteen Elders *(gnas brtan bcu drug)* which were added to the middle ring of the aureole *('od skor bar ma)*, and gold-moulded images of the spiritual teachers of the aural lineage of Ganden, which were added to the inner ring of the aureole *('od skor nang ma)*.[126]

In 1621 (iron bird year of the tenth cycle), during the civil war, more than two thousand Mongol troops led by Lhatsun Lobzang Tendzin and Guru Hortheji reached Lhasa. On the first day of the seventh month the Mongol forces launched a surprise attack on the Tsang military camps near Lhasa, while the army of the *Tsang to Depa* Phuntshok Namgyal was away at Kyangthang Gang. A terrifying battle ensued, and most of the Tsangpa soldiers were slain. At that time, the Fourth Paṇchen Lama Lobzang Chogyen who was residing at Drepung immediately went to mediate on the battlefield. The lives of many thousands of troops were spared on account of his appeal, while the opposing Tsangpa and Mongol forces made offerings in common to the Paṇchen Lama.[127] Starting from then, the responsibility for maintaining the offering ceremonies in the Great Temple, and replenishing the offering lamps and food offerings, was assumed by the Ganden Khangsar estate, maintained by the governor of the lower Kyichu area, Jeri Taktsewa.[128]

Following the decisive intervention of Gushi Qan in the Tibetan civil war, an administration combining spiritual and temporal authority was inaugurated by the Fifth Dalai Lama Ngawang Lobzang Gyatso in Lhasa. He and his successive regents: Sonam Chopel, Lobzang Thutob, Lobzang Jinpa, and Sangye Gyatso restored the earlier "patron-priest" model relationship, in consequence of which the gilded roof of the Central Inner Sanctum was restored and the slates of the gallery *(mda'gYab)* were replaced with tiles of gilded copper. A new gilded roof was erected above the image of Four Sibling Maitreyas *(byams pa mched bzhi)* on the south wing, and the old gilded roof above the image of King Songtsen (*chos rgyal nga 'dra ma*) on the middle floor was renovated.

In the Central Inner Sanctum six gold bas-reliefs depicting the lion, elephant, horse, peacock, *cīvaṃcīvaka,* and athlete motifs *(khri drug 'gyogs)* were newly commissioned and fastened to the throne back. The gilded roof, the actual lion throne, and the pillars were all refurbished. Silver-plated objects were gilded, and the throne-back was ornamented with diverse kinds of priceless jewels, including Dakmema's turquoise head ornaments, and covered with scenes representing the divine assembly of the medicine buddha, Vaiḍūryaprabhārāja.

A canopy of gilded copper was also placed immediately above the image of Mahākāruṇika in the form Rangjon Ngaden. On the surface of the canopy where it adjoined the throne-back, maṇḍalas were inscribed, depicting *Avalokiteśvara According to the Tradition of the King (spyan ras gzigs rgyal po lugs),* and *'Gro 'dul yid bzhin nor bu,* according to the treasures of Nyangrel Nyima Ozer *(nyang gter 'gro 'dul yid bzhin nor bu),* with those of *'Gro ba kun sgrol and 'Khor ba dbyings sgrol* recognisably to the right and left.

On the rear side of the throne of Jowo Śākyamuni the names of the artists and those who supervised this grand renovation project were clearly inscribed. They include the foremost Newār coppersmiths Master Siṃha and Amarasiṃha, and the Tibetan craftsmen Tashi Gonpo, the Newār craftsman Dhanaśīla, the Tibetan craftsmen Namse and Norbu Tshering, the skilled carpenters Nesar Jamyang Khyentse and Tsekha Chokyong, and the skilled calligraphers Jamyang Wangpo from Gyantse and Ngawang Phuntsok.

Many chapels of the lower and upper storeys were restored, and many rooms on the roof and in the inner pilgrims' walkway were converted into chapels. Representative images were constructed, and the Great Courtyard (*khyams ra chen mo*) with its eight long pillars and its portico was expanded to cover an area of one hundred and twenty pillars.[129] Murals depicting the deeds of Śākyamuni Buddha, according to the *Avadānakalpalatā,* and images

Gilded roof of the Palace of the Dalai Lamas (p. 105). (1990 US)

Chapel of the Four Sibling Maitreyas (p. 75, no. **44**). (2000 GD)

Aspects of Tārā, mural in the southern wing of the Middle Floor (p. 80). (2000 GD)

Confession Buddhas of the skylight gallery (p. 82). (2000 GD)

of the thousand buddhas of the *Bhadrakalpikasūtra* were painted in the Great Courtyard and on the outer and inner walls of the inner walkway by skilled artists: Taklung Palgon, Kalden from Lhasa, Lobzang from Drongtse, Sangak Kharpa who was the foremost exponent of the mKhyen lugs style, Umdze Tsunchung, and Zhang Go-kye. Throughout the three floors of the Great Temple they restored old lacquerwork and paintwork; and within the Great Courtyard they renovated the long and short swags *(dra ba dra phyed)* suspended from the rafters, which were made of the finest silk material, as well as the silk pendants *(phan)* draped from the long columns, and the small silk pouches of scented offering flowers *(phye phur)*.

The Sixth Dalai Lama Tsangyang Gyatso and the regent Sangye Gyatso subsequently formed their own patron-priest relationship. Consequently, they embellished the Great Temple with a matchless array of gilded copper artefacts, including the images, swags and ornate brackets of the upper gallery *(mda'gYab steng)*, immediately below the gilded roofs, as well as the thousand-spoked wheels flanked by male and female deer, the parapets and gable ornaments on all four sides of the roof.[130]

During the late eighteenth century, the Eighth Dalai Lama Jampal Gyatso and Ngawang Tshultrim, the first regent from Tshemonling formed their own priest-patron relationship. From 1783 (water hare year of the thirteenth cycle) onwards, they began to restore the murals of the Great Temple and its faded paintwork. They renovated the chapels on the south and north wings of the inner pilgrims' walkway, which had been damaged and neglected, and restored the gates, windows and metal railings. At the same time, they demarcated a boundary between the sacred chapels and the "profane" public toilet facilities *(spyi gcod)* contained in the outer annex; and supervised the rebuilding of the doors of the South Gate and the Rear Gate with their outer vestibules *(phyir khyams)*. The old wooden structures of the building were repainted; while the old murals of the upper floors, the Main Hall *(dkyil 'khor mthil)*, the Great Courtyard and the great throne located in the Debating Courtyard *(gsung chos ra)* were properly conserved and repainted. Finally, a room for storing planks of wood used as offering platforms *(kun bzang mchod sprin khang)* was constructed off the courtyard, facilitating access from the Secret Gate *(gsang sgo)* to the inner pilgrims' walkway during the Great Prayer Festival.[131]

During the nineteenth century, the Eleventh Dalai Lama Khedrub Gyatso and Ngawang Jampal Tshultrim, the second regent from Tshemonling, formed their particular patron-priest relationship, on the basis of which, from 1842 (water tiger year of the fourteenth cycle) until 1844 (wood snake year), they restored the Great Temple, along with Ramoche and the Potala Palace. During that period, elaborate offerings were made, the faces of all the representative images within the Great Temple were regilded *(zhal gser)*, and eye-opening ceremonies *(spyan dbye)* were performed. Embellishments were added to the upper and lower storeys, ten thousand offering bowls were newly commissioned, and some two hundred hand-turned maṇi wheels were installed along the inner walls of the inner pilgrims' walkway.

Images of buddhas and bodhisattvas were painted on the capitals of the long pillars supporting the courtyard, and those of all the pillars of the skylight gallery *(mthong khor)* and the portico *(sgo 'phyor)*. A gatehouse with gilded windows was also constructed. Finally, extensive construction work was undertaken on the north wing of the inner pilgrims' walkway, extending upwards through the storeroom of the Palace Treasury *(bzo khang byang gling khang mo che)* as far as the public toilet facilities on the rooftop, along with their connecting ramp.[132]

Subsequently the political situation deteriorated. The Manchu Emperor, utilising the patron-priest relationship as a pretext, forced the Tibetan government to accept the presence of his two representatives *(amban)* in Lhasa, one of whom had an executive role and the other a subsidiary role. Many Chinese traders then arrived in their wake and took up residence in the vicinity of the Great Temple. Incited by the hostile forward policy of the Manchus, which was to devour Tibet, a large Chinese army under the authority of the Amban Lien-yu and General Chung-yin invaded Tibet in 1911. In 1912 (water mouse year of the fifteenth cycle) for almost a whole year, the Chinese and Tibetan forces fought within the city of Lhasa, resulting in the destruction of virtually one third of the city. Artillery and fires destroyed much of the Great Temple, and its gilded-copper roofs were punctured with bullet holes.

Following the collapse of the Qing Dynasty and the assumption of genuine political power by the Thirteenth Dalai Lama Thubten Gyatso, a team was appointed to supervise the restoration of the entire Great Temple complex and its consecrated images that had been subjected to the utmost devastation. These included Lachak Khenchung Kelzang Ludrub, Lazha Gabu Tashi Phuntsok, Leja Lhanyer Tsedrung Sharchi Drakpa Chogyal, Tsipa Dekharwa Tsewang Rabten, Shochanang Jinpa Tharchin, and Jangpa Kelzang. The Dalai Lama repeatedly visited the Great Temple in person to inspect their progress. In 1913 (water ox year of the fifteenth cycle) the punctured holes of the roofs, galleries, victory turrets, spire, and the ornaments attached to the potentilla architrave *(spen rgyan)* were repaired and gilded by Dojo Palkhyil, Tsedongpa, and others, working under the supervision of the skilled coppersmiths Udrung Tsering, Gyaltsen, and Tshakpa Jampa. Rust was removed from all remaining parts of the structure.

Further restoration work was undertaken on the outer and inner walls of the inner pilgrims' walkway and the courtyards *(khyams ra)* from 1920 (iron monkey) to 1922 (water dog), starting from the Acacia Gate *(seng ldeng sgo mo che)*. This project was carried out by skilled stonemasons such as Drungtok Phutung Chenpo, Sonam Dorje, Uchen Chime Tobgyal, Karma Tsering, and Nying-nye, while the murals were restored by highly skilled artists such as Drungtok Dorje Tsewang, Zedong Kelzang, and Sertul Umdze Kelzang Norbu. Without damaging the ancient paintings, they traced the line drawings in red vermilion on white paper of finest quality *(skyem shog)*, and applied the pigments in the prescribed manner. In this way, the original murals were exactly and painstakingly restored, the captions were inscribed in gold, while the mantras of retention (*dhāraṇī*) and aspirational prayers were elegantly embossed in Rañjanā and Vartula scripts, or in Hor-yig, forming horizontal bands on a frieze of gold foil. These inscriptions and the captions which accompanied the representative images and scenes from the *Avadānakalpalatā*, as well as the mantras of retention and aspirational prayers based on the *Collected Works* of the Fifth Dalai Lama, were all executed by the calligrapher Nyeltrul Tendzin Trin-le Ozer who was an assistant tutor of the Dalai Lama from Deyangling College at Drepung. Even the cotton and hide coverings of the hand-turned maṇi wheels in the pilgrims' walkway were replaced, painted, and covered in gold foil.

In short, all the paintwork and murals of the inner chapels and the outer residences were restored, and all the major and minor images, foremost among them the two images of Jowo Śākyamuni, had their faces painted with refined gold, new "eye-opening" ceremonies were held, and their blue-coloured crowns, ear-rings, necklaces, and robes were all refurbished. The canopies within the chapels of all three storeys, and the old brocade

Crocodile gargoyle and gilded copper snow lion (pp. 88-89). (2009 LG)

Roof embelishments (p. 88). (1996 AA)

Lion faced and human faced cornice (p. 82). (1996 AA)

Chapel of the Graduated Path, Middle Floor (p. 80, no. **65**). (2000 GD)

Murals outside the Chapel of the Religious King, Middle Floor (p. 81, no. **74**). (2000 GD)

hangings in the skylight gallery *(mthong 'khor)* of the Great Courtyard *(khyams ra chen mo)*, and those suspended from the long pillars were replaced with equally exquisite materials. Finally, in order that the murals of the outer and inner walls of the pilgrims' walkway and its courtyard might not be defaced by handprints, a wooden frame with wire netting was fitted to the walls. In this way, the shrines and images of the Great Temple were refurbished. Such acts of restoration illustrate how the Thirteenth Dalai Lama was most gracious.[133]

In 1921 (iron bird year), the Changkya Qutuqtu of Amdo and all the other spiritual teachers and monks of Gonlung Monastery jointly presented a thousand-spoked wheel motif in gilded copper, one and a half times the size of a man, flanked by two deer facing one another to the right and left. This was positioned directly above the window *(rab gsal)* of the Khamsum Zilnon Residence, along with two very large gilded-copper victory turrets, more than twice the size of a man, which were positioned to the right and left of the deer, above the potentilla architrave.

Some years later, the Fourteenth Dalai Lama Tendzin Gyatso was enthroned and ordained as a renunciate monk in the Great Temple. It was here that he received the academic title Geshe Lharampa *(dge bshes lha ram pa)*. Later, during His Holiness' "year of obstacles" *(dgung keg)*, the Tibetan government implemented several construction projects and plans designed to promote acts of charitable service. Among these, in 1954, a special supervisor was appointed to oversee the restoration of the Great Temple and its offering ceremonies. The faces of all the most important representative images, including Jowo Śākyamuni were gilded; "eye-opening" ceremonies were performed, while robes and lamps were offered. All the damage that had been inflicted on the inner chapels and the administrative outer annex was repaired.

The bay window from which His Holiness would view the congregations in the Great Courtyard below *(tshogs gzigs gnang yul)*, which is on the south side of his Palace *(gzim chung dga' ldan yangs rtse)* was also extended. This facilitated the construction of a gilded copper roof and a spire above the window, along with the Sunlight Apartment *(gzim chung nyi 'od)* and its verandah which extends from east to west (*shar nub yug sbrel 'gag*). All these projects were carefully and faithfully supervised by the responsible government offices, and by the Chief Sacristan *(dkon gnyer dpon)*, the Sacristan of the Top Floor *(rtse mo'i dkon gnyer)*, and the sacristans of the individual chapels.

It is impossible to estimate all the sacraments offered to Jowo Śākyamuni and other important images over the centuries by the successive Dalai Lamas, regents, spiritual teachers, officials, and devout farmers, nomads, businessmen, and artisans from all the three provinces of Tibet, not to mention the donations presented by government ministers, incarnate lamas, and patrons from China, Mongolia, Nepal, Bhutan, and Ladakh. Such sacraments included crown ornaments of pure gold decorated with clusters of precious gems, ear-rings, necklaces, garlands, robes, gold and silver alms' bowls, maṇḍalas, pewter water-offering bowls, butter lamps, drink-offering bowls, thousand-spoked wheels, flower vases, the seven royal insignia *(rgyal srid sna bdun)*, the eight auspicious symbols *(rtags brgyad)*, the eight sacraments of accomplishment *(rdzas brgyad)*, and symbols of the five sensory attributes *('dod yon sna lnga)*. Even this description resembles a mere drop of water in an ocean. For the great cloud-mass of offerings which were made devoutly, faithfully and joyfully by government officers and private individuals is indescribable, representing the quintessence of their wealth.

All such offerings were made with the pure aspiration that all sentient beings might come to possess the eight leisures and ten favourable conditions for Buddhist practice.

Following the Chinese Communist occupation of Tibet, an unprecedented destruction was inflicted on the Great Temple after 1951 (earth pig year of the sixteenth cycle) when the traditional political administration of Tibet, in which both spiritual and secular affairs were combined, was forcefully replaced. Starting from then, the government's custom of making continuous offerings was abandoned, wealthy patrons set aside their customary offerings and no longer paid their respects at the shrine of Jowo Śīkyamuni out of fear of the Chinese. The Great Temple quickly degenerated. A Chinese military canteen was erected inside the main hall *(dkyil 'khor mthil)*, and a meeting hall and recreation area for the Youth League was established inside the Great Courtyard *(khyams ra chen mo)*, so that there were habitual acts of desecration.

In particular, during the Cultural Revolution (1966-76), the ignorant and impetuous Tibetan masses were coerced and incited by Chinese Red Guards to destroy the external edifice of the Great Temple and most of its sacred images of historical importance. Foremost among these destroyed images were Mahākāruṇika in the form Rangjon Ngaden, Tsongkhapa surrounded by his eight pure disciples, the Likeness of Tsongkhapa *(rje nga 'dra ma)*, Maitreya in the Gesture of Teaching the Sacred Doctrine *(byams pa chos''khor)*, the Four Maitreya Siblings *(byams pa mched bzhi)*, and the Eight Medicine Buddhas – all of which had been located in important ground floor chapels. Other major images that were destroyed included the Eight Manifestations of Padmasambhava, the likeness of King Songtsen Gampo with his queens, and the Peaceful and Wrathful Aspects of Śrīdevī from the middle and top floors, Jamchen and Guru Gyagarma from the centre of the Main Hall *(dkyil 'khor mthil)*, and the Tārā Chapel of the inner pilgrims' walkway.

The zealots bored a hole in the left knee of Jowo Śakymuni, and they carried off to China all the most important sacraments of offering, including the Jowo's body ornaments, and the bas relief carvings depicting the divine assembly of Bhaiṣajyaguru, and the spiritual teachers of the aural lineage of Ganden which had been cast in gold and fastened to the throne-back *(rgyab yol)* of Jowo Śākyamuni. Along with these they took the silver-cast bas-relief depicting the Sixteen Eders *(gnas brtan cu drug)*, the canopy of pure gold, the pillars decorated with clusters of priceless jewels, the golden butter lamps, the golden water offering bowls, the golden alms' bowl, the golden maṇḍala, and the golden wheel.

They left unprotected and unattended sacred chapels that had been venerated for centuries. A pigsty was constructed within the Great Courtyard, and a new well was excavated to provide drinking water for the pigs. Dogs and pigs were allowed to lie in a filthy condition inside the chapels, and even on the golden throne of Jowo Śākyamuni. The place was filled with the stench of faeces and urine left by dogs, pigs and human beings. Inside the Great Courtyard, the PLA shot and executed sixty-one young Tibetans on a single occasion. From time to time unforgettable reports such as these, which pierce the ears like thorns, reached the exiled community in India. If one could obtain the original sources documenting this unprecedented destruction, it would be worthwhile to make an accurate, written record of all those events.

In 1977 (fire snake year of the sixteenth cycle) when the policy of the Beijing government was slightly modified, those acts of destruction were belatedly attributed to the Gang of Four, headed by Lin Bao. Then, in 1979

Narrative scenes from the mural of the North Wing, Middle Floor (p. 82). (2000 GD)

Entrance to the Chapel of Munīndra and his retainers (p. 80, no. **66**). (2000 GD)

Guru Nangsi Zilnon (p. 77, no. **60**). (2000 GD)

Manifestations of Padmākara in the Middle Floor (p. 79, no. **61**). (2000 GD)

by way of compensation, they initiated a programme to restore certain important religious sites in Tibet under the aegis of the local branches of the Cultural Relics Bureau. The Great Temple of Lhasa was designated as a cultural relic of the first category. The building was reopened under the supervision of nine monks, and the internal and external paintwork restored. Substitute pillars were made to support the throne of Jowo Śākyamuni, while silver butter lamps and some silver offering bowls were arrayed on the altar. A new skylight *(gseng thog)* was raised above the gallery *(gnam yangs)* and vajra parapet of the main hall. Since the metal railing and altar which formerly demarcated the Main Hall had been destroyed, a temporary direct passageway was constructed from the Great Acacia Gate *(seng deng sgo mo che)* to the vestibule in front of Chapel of Jowo Śākyamuni. The pigsty and the military canteen were removed, electricity was introduced, and the exteriors and interiors of the chapels were cleaned.

Some new clay images were sculpted during this period, including a replica of Mahākāruṇika in the form Rangjon Ngaden, and the likeness of Tsongkhapa *(Je Ngadrama)*, which were placed in the appropriate chapels of the ground floor, and Songtsen Gampo with his queens, and the Peaceful and Wrathful Aspects of Śrīdevī *(dpal lha zhi drag)* which were placed in the upper storeys. These new images tragically lack the sacred consecratory cores *(gzungs 'jug)* which imbued them with their spiritual power and sanctity, and some are also said to lack the iconometric proportions and measurements prescribed in the tantras. For example, a face which was too small was transported from elsewhere and attached to the replica Maitreya image in the centre of the Main Hall. Other new replicas were subsequently constructed, including the Eight Manifestations of Padmasambhava of the middle floor and the images of the Tārā Chapel in the inner pilgrims' walkway. By 1982 most chapels had been reopened with new replica clay images, and the public were once again permitted to pay their respects to Jowo Śākyamuni.

A decision was then taken to replace the inner walls and wooden structures of the building, apparently in order to avoid the threat of subsidence in the north wing.

Over the decade that followed, a number of early murals on the north, northeast, and southeast wings of the middle floor, which had remarkably survived the Cultural Revolution, were copied and removed. The partition walls between the chapels were dismantled and rebuilt, and precious artefacts which had been inserted within them at the time of their original construction, according to Tibetan tradition, were conveniently extracted. Sensitive to this issue, an article published in China's Tibet (Spring, 1993) asserts that video recordings were made of these relics being replaced within the walls following their reconstruction.

Despite these efforts, no electric cables were inserted within the walls as a protection against fire hazards, and instead unsightly cables were laid along the outer surfaces of the walls and lintels. Access was denied to parts of the north wing until 1992, and a large wooden ramp filled the atrium of the Main Hall. Some have suggested that the subsequent restoration of the ancient wooden superstructure of the building and repainting of the walls in bright acrylic colours, which continued into 1994, arguably contravened Chinese law on the protection of cultural heritage. The legacy of the great Tibetan artists and craftsmen of the past who painstakingly renovated the chapels of the Great Temple over succeeding generations was certainly impossible to emulate. In recent years, many of the important government offices contained in the outer annex of the Great Temple were also demolished and rebuilt as residential units for monks, while the Assembly Hall of the Drepung Ngakpa College was controversially detached from the building and converted into non-monastic residential apartments.[134]

Since 2000, the Great Temple complex has been formally recognised as a UNESCO world heritage site, within the ensemble of the Potala Palace. Then, in 2004 the Great Courtyard was partly closed to the public while engineering work was carried out to strengthen its supporting columns. Access to the building during this period was provided from a ticket office located in the Debating Courtyard on the south wing. It is envisaged that the next phase of restoration will focus on the 17th century murals of the Great Courtyard.

Despite the upheavals and desecration of the past half century, the Jokhang, the Central Inner Sanctum of the Great Temple, still survives, as it did during the interregnum following the collapse of the Tibetan monarchy in the ninth century, The backdrop for a succession of key events in Tibet's turbulent history, the building even now continues to function as the focal point for pilgrims converging in Lhasa from all quarters of the Tibetan plateau. While the skyline of the city of Lhasa rapidly changes and new high-rise towers of glass and concrete begin to proliferate, the seventh century Great Temple stands apart, as the pulsating heart of the old city.

Barkor Square (p. 95). (1986 CB)

West facade of the Great Temple, with Barkor Square in the foreground (p. 95). (1986 CB)

The Chapels of the Ground Floor

The chapels of the Great Temple form a rectangle (82.5 sq.m.) three storeys high, enclosing the Main Hall *(dkyil 'khor mthil)* on all four sides. This building is surrounded on the north, east and south sides by an inner circumambulatory pathway, traditionally known as the Barkhor but nowadays also known as the Nangkhor, while to the west is the Great Courtyard *(khyams rva chen mo)* and the annex *('dab 'byar)* where private apartments and administrative offices are located. Other buildings, including the Meru Nyingba Temple adjoin the Great Temple, and the whole complex is encircled by an intermediate circumambulatory pathway, known as the Barkor, the axis from which the radial streets of the old city of Lhasa extend in all directions. An outer circumambulatory walkway known as the Lingkhor, on which pilgrims even now circumambulate the entire city of Lhasa, including the Potala Palace, forms an outer ring-road, and much of it has been incorporated into the modern road infrastructure of the city.

Chapel of the Serpent King Nanda (p. 78, no. **118**). (1996 US)

The North Wing of the Vestibule

The Great Temple is entered through the Great Acacia Gate (**1**, *seng ldeng sgo mo che*), which combines Tibetan metalwork with interesting geometric patterns reminiscent of Newāri or Kashmiri influence.[135] On the west wing, within the vestibule, one will first pass on the left (north) side, the Chapel of Kubera, leader of sylvan and water spirits (**2**, *gnod sbyin nā ga kubera'i lha khang*). This chapel contains the charismatic images of Kubera and Gandharva Pañcacīrin, which are said to have appeared in a vision to King Songtsen Gampo and were therefore constructed during his lifetime and charged with the task of protecting the building. These images are followed by others depicting Vajrapāṇi and Raudrāntaka Mahākāla, which were later constructed by Gyer Lhapa. However since most of these protectors are located behind the entrance gate, they cannot easily be described. Some images within the Chapel of Kubera have recently been reconstructed, but the chapel is noteworthy nowadays because it functions as the control room for the electricity supply for all three floors of the building.

Then, alongside a bellows-shaped stone (**3**, *rdo sbud pa can*), above which exiting pilgrims pray in the belief their wishes will be fulfilled, there is the Chapel of the Serpentine Water Spirits (**4**, *klu khang*), containing an image of Nāgarāja Nanda. This chapel was once filled with treasure-vases containing minerals *(sa bcud bum gter)*, vases dedicated to the gods *(lha bum)*, and vases dedicated to the serpentine water spirits (*klu bum*). Traditional accounts suggest that when the original Acacia Gate was replaced, it was stored within this chapel, and that a replica of one of Śākyamuni Buddha's original [Indian] monasteries is buried underneath the vestibule.

Chapel of the Spiritual Teachers (no. **6**). (2000 GD)

Chapels of the North-west Corner

Leaving the vestibule and entering the Main Hall (*dkyil 'khor mthil*), the chapels are circumambulated in a clockwise direction. On the left, adjacent to the entrance, the east-facing murals depicting the five buddhas (**5**, *pañcajina*): Vairocana, Ratnasambhava, Amitābha, Amoghasiddhi and Vajrasattva. These were originally attributed to the hand of King Songtsen Gampo, and are revered as a receptacle of buddha-body *(sku rten)*. They are now partly visible, and have not yet been renovated. The pilgrim first approaches the fifteenth century Chapel of the Spiritual Teachers (**6**, *bla ma lha khang)*, also known as the Chapel of Ganden, in which the central image depicts Tsongkhapa. The statue is surmounted by a silk canopy and flanked on the right in succession by his four disciples from U: Geshe Jamkarwa Palden Zangpo, Tokden Jangchub Senge, Neten Rinchen Gyaltsen, and Neten Zang Kyongwa, and on the left in succession by his four disciples from Do-me: Tokden Jampal Gyatso, Geshe Sherab Drakpa, Geshe Jampal Tashi, and Geshe Palkyong. Collectively these are known as the "eight pure retainers" *('khor dag pa rnam brgyad)*. The images of this chapel have been restored, apart from the central image of Tsongkhapa, which is partly original. Next to that chapel, there is an east-facing door (**7**), beyond which a staircase leads to the middle storey. Formerly it functioned as the main staircase giving access to the chapels of the upper floors, but nowadays the door is kept closed.

Chapel of Kubera (no. **2**). (1992 HMS)

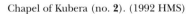

Next there is the south-facing stūpa, known as the Stūpa of Scrutiny (**8**, *brtag pa'i mchod rten*), a receptacle of buddha-mind *(thugs rten)* which was constructed by Sakya Paṇḍita Kunga Gyaltsen and contains a terracotta relic made by the hand of King Songtsen Gampo. The present stūpa is a replica of the destroyed original. To its left there appears to have been a Chapel of Amitābha (**9**, *'od dpag med lha khang*),[136] but it has not functioned as a chapel for centuries. It is now a storeroom for old and damaged offering utensils, blocked off by the wooden balustrade that runs in front of the stūpa. Also to the left of the stūpa there were once three hand-turned prayer wheels and alongside them on clay thrones were representative images (**10**) of Lochen Rinchen Zangpo, Barawa Gyaltsen Zangpo, Phagmodrupa Dorje Gyalpo, Ngaripa Senge Gyaltsen, and Yangphugpa Sangye Pelzang, which were constructed by Zhika Nelpa. Of these, replicas of the first and fourth have recently been inserted within a protective glass case, alongside a new image of Śākyamuni Buddha. The other new replicas are located further on the opposite wall (see below 43).

Chapels of the North Wing

The pilgrim will then approach the south-facing chapels of the north wing. Among these, the first, known as the Chapel of the Medicine Buddhas (**11**, *sman bla'i lha khang*) contains a central image of Bhaiṣajyaguru, flanked on the right in succession by Sunāmaparikīrtaṇa, Ratnacandrarāja, and Suvarṇabhadravimala, and on the left in succession by Aśokottama, Dharmakīrtisāgaraghoṣa, Abhijñārāja, and Śākyaketu. Collectively these are known as the eight medicine buddhas *(sman bla bde gshegs brgyad)*, and all of them have been restored.[137]

Alongside the entrance to this chapel, raised on a clay platform to the right, behind a protective glass case, there are new images of the Seventh Dalai Lama Kelzang Gyatso, and the mighty lord of yoga Milarepa (**12**). The cracked murals to their rear depicting the Potālaka Buddhafield demonstrate the inadequate restoration techniques employed in recent years. In an alcove behind the original clay platform there was once an image of Duldzin Drakpa Gyaltsen, or, according to some, Je Monlam Pelwa, who was one of the seven initial throne-holders of Ganden *('jam dbyangs gtsang pa bdun brgyud)*.

The most revered receptacle of buddha-speech *(gsung rten)* in the Great Temple is a wood-carved inscription of the Six Syllable Mantra of Avalokiteśvara, which was reputedly the first product of the Thonmi Sambhoṭa's Tibetan writing system (**13**, *bod kyi yig phud*), and its origin is attributed to the hand of King Songtsen Gampo.

Chapels of the Medicine Buddhas (p. 67, no. **11**). (2000) GD)

Śākyamuni flanked by Lochen Rinchen Zangpo and Ngaripa Sangye Gyaltsen (p. 67, no. **10**). (2000 GD)

Inscription of the Six-syllable Mantra (p. 67, no. **13**). (2000 GD)

Images of Dalai Lama VII and Milarepa (p. 67, no. **12**). (2000 GD)

Stupa of Scrutiny (no. **8**). (2000 GD)

Replica of Mahākāruṇika in the Northern Inner Sanctum (no. **16**). (2000 GD)

Entrance to the Northern Inner Sanctum (no. **16**). (2000 GD)

Formerly it was kept in front of the Chapel of the Medicine Buddhas, resting on the edge of a beam that connects the Main Hall *(dkyil 'khor mthil)* with the adjacent Chapel of Offerings *(mchod sgrom lha khang)*. Four resident monks from the Sakya monastery of Gongkar Shedrubling would continuously make offerings in the Chapel of Offerings (**14**, *mchod sgrom lha khang)* to the east of that beam, following the liturgies of the *Attainment of Sublime Mahākāruṇika which Liberates All Beings from the Three Inferior Destinies ('Phags pa thugs rje chen po ngan song kun grol gyi sgrub mchod)*, and the *Attainment of the Five Deities of Amoghapāśa (Don zhags lha lnga'i sgrub pa)*. This inscription has now been placed inside the Chapel of the Bathing Maitreya, in a niche above the entrance (see below, fig. 18). According to another tradition, the original inscription was fashioned of stone and offered by Shenpa Marutse, general of the King of Hor, as an act of atonement for his many murderous past actions.

Above the entrance to the Northern Inner Sanctum, which has a magnificent Newār door frame with a chain curtain, there was an image of the Third Dalai Lama Sonam Gyatso which had been commissioned by Zhabdrung Tashi Tobgye, the governor of the Lower Kyichu region, along with images of the Lords of the Three Enlightened Families (**15**, *rigs gsum mgon po)*. The latter have now been restored.

The main image within the Northern Inner Sanctum (**16**, *gtsang khang byang ma*) depicts the bodhisattva Mahākāruṇika in the form Rangjon Ngaden. The original image was one of only four in the Great Temple surmounted by gilded roofs, and it was revered as the first to be consecrated in the original building, and as the most sacred of all images, with the exception of Jowo Śākyamuni.

According to one legend, before King Songtsen Gampo completed the construction of the Great Temple, he prayed to his meditational deity Mahākāruṇika in order to pacify the malevolent forces that were obstructing the building. He then received a prediction that he should commission an image of Mahākāruṇika, using a body-cast *(sku 'bag)* identical in size to his own body.

The monk Ākarmatiśīla, himself revered as an emanation of the king, brought an *urāgagarbha* white sandalwood statue of Avalokiteśvara from a desert island in the Indian Ocean for insertion within the new image as a mantra core *(gzungs 'jug)*. Along with it he carried relics of Śākyamuni Buddha from Magadha, sand from the Nairañjanā River, water from the Ganges, leaves from the Bodhi Tree, and various types of soil, stone and water from the power places of ancient India. All these he offered to the king, who then summoned the Newāri sculptor Trowo, saying, "Can you make an image of Eleven-faced Mahākāruṇika modelled on my own body-cast?" "I can!" he replied.

Thereupon, the sculptor mixed together the sacred soil, stone, and water, and other sacred ingredients, among which the foremost was a fragment of *urāgagarbha* white sandalwood, into a pulverised medicinal paste, and fashioned a large mound of clay, adding the milk of a red cow and a white goat. The king laid his head against the clay as if it were a pillow, and prayed to his meditational deity, saying, "Of all the many aspects assumed by my meditational deity Avalokiteśvara, I should commission an image of eleven-faced Cintāmaṇi (i.e. Mahākāruṇika) because that form is superior." Thereupon, he had a vision of all the buddhas and bodhisattvas converging, like particles forming a ray of light, and vanishing into the mound of clay.

The king then fell asleep, thinking, "This image of my meditational deity will be endowed with blessings!" When he awoke the following morning, an image of eleven-faced Cintāmaṇi had "appeared naturally" (*rang byon*) from the clay, so there was no need for the image to be constructed by the labour of the artisans. The three primary faces of the image were white in colour and peaceful, symbolising the enlightened activity of pacification. The three faces above these were yellow in colour and ravenously wrathful, symbolising the enlightened activity of enrichment. The two faces above these were coral red in colour and delightedly wrathful, symbolising the enlightened activity of subjugation; and the two faces above those were black and terrifyingly wrathful, symbolising the enlightened activity of violent wrath. These eleven faces were surmounted by the head of Amitābha, minium red in colour, its proportions equal to those of the king's head.

The foremost pair of hands were folded together at the heart (*añjalīmudrā*), the second right hand was raised upright, the third was holding a wheel, the fourth was in the supreme gesture of generosity (*dānamudrā*), and the fifth held an image of Amitābha. Among the left hands, the second was holding a white lotus, the third a container of sacred pills, the fourth a jewel, and the fifth a bow and arrow. There was an eye depicted along with a hand-emblem in the palm of each of the other hands, making up the thousand hands of the image. As for the torso, the left breast was covered with an antelope hide, and it was adorned with all the major and minor marks, emitting an effulgence of light.[138]

Despite the fact that the image had naturally arisen, the king said that the buddha relics and the natural statue of Mahākāruṇika made of *urāgagarbha* sandalwood still had to be offered as a mantra core, whereupon a ray of light emanated from the heart of the naturally arisen image, as Mahākāruṇika replied, "Offer them!" The lower robe of the left leg raised itself above the knee and the relics and natural image of Mahākāruṇika inserted themselves naturally as a mantra core, coming to rest at the heart of the image, and assuming the function of a *jñānasattva*! Consequently, the Amitābha image tilted slightly to the left, and Mahākāruṇika's lower robe remained above knee-length!

In accordance with the king's decree, the Newār sculptor built to the right of Mahākāruṇika, images of Lokeśvara, Bhṛkuṭī, Sārasvatī, and Amṛtakuṇḍalin, while to the left he fashioned Khasarpāṇi, Tārā, Mārīcī and Hayagrīva. Once the construction of the Great Temple had been completed, Jowo Mahākāruṇika and this retinue are said to have moved from the Potala Palace of their own accord to this Northern Inner Sanctum, without requiring human effort. The king then concealed as treasure a *Doctrinal Cycle of Mahākāruṇika (Thugs rje chen po'i chos skor)* under the foot of Hayagrīva.[139]

According to another legendary account, at the time of King Songtsen Gampo's demise, the king himself, accompanied by the Newār princess Bhṛkuṭī, the Chinese princess Wen-cheng Kong-jo, the Mong princess Tricham, and his nephews, grandsons and ministers, all entered the chapel, where they received many oral instructions concerning the future revelation of these treasures.[140] The king then said, "If the citizens of Tibet wish to see me in the future, they should pray to this sublime Avalokiteśvara. It will not be different from meeting me in person!" Along with the Newār princess Bhṛkuṭī, the Chinese princess Wen-cheng Kong-jo, and the gatekeepers Amṛtakuṇḍalin and Hayagrīva, he then vanished into the heart of the Mahākāruṇika image, so that the pristine cognition of his buddha-mind actually came to reside within it.[141] For these reasons, the image became known as Rangjon Ngaden ("endowed with the five natural aspects").[142]

In 1967 (fire sheep year), during the Cultural Revolution, this image in which the pristine cognition of the buddhas actually resided, was destroyed by a mindless mob, incited by Red Guards. A fragment of one of its heads was later smuggled to India via Nepal, and inserted within the core of the main Mahākāruṇika image in the Great Temple at Dharamsala.[143] When a new replica was eventually made, one portion of the original and a fragment of the original sandalwood core which had been saved by a nun from Trazhol Court, were subsequently inserted within it, along with its mantra core, for which reason the new replica is still said to retain a great blessing. It is also considered to be slightly larger than the original, but the full extent of the image to hard to discern within its protective glass case.

The images of Mañjuśrīghoṣa and Vajrapāṇi located to the right and left of Mahākāruṇika were reputedly commissioned by the *Tshalpa Tripon*. In later centuries, a monk from Zhi-de Dratsang had responsibility for cleaning this chapel. Two of his colleagues would maintain the golden butter lamps and arrange the altar.

To the left of the Northern Inner Sanctum on a clay platform (**17**), there was a sculpted self-portrait of the accomplished master Thangtong Gyalpo, followed by images of Phadampa Sangye and Virūpa. Nowadays this platform supports new replicas depicting the same series with Phagmodrupa to the extreme left.

The next chapel is known as the Chapel of the Bathing Maitreya (**18**, *byams pa 'khrus mdzad*). Inside, above its entrance, in the niche where a replica wooden inscription of the original Six Syllable Mantra of Avalokiteśvara now rests, there were images of the Buddhas of the Three Times. Within the chapel the main image was that of the "bathing" Maitreya, which had been sculpted by Zangkar Lotsāwa Phakpa Sherab in the eleventh century, using spring water in which King Songtsen Gampo and his queens had once bathed. A sandalwood image of Mañjughoṣa which had been brought there from Goyo Lhakhang rested in the lap of this central image of Maitreya, along with a white alloy image of Amitāyus, which had once been the meditational deity of Guru Dharmakīrti of Suvarṇadvīpa. The modern replica of Maitreya still has an impressive aureole, and in front, the old image of Mañjughoṣa has been restored.

Further objects of veneration within the chapel included statues of Vajrapāṇi, Avalokiteśvara, Tsongkhapa, and White Tārā, the reliquaries of Ngok Lekpei Sherab and Tsondru Nyingpo of Ngari who sculpted some of the chapel's earliest images. It also contained a copy of the *Prajñāpāramitā in One Hundred Thousand Sections ('Bum)* which had been commissioned by the aforementioned Shenpa Marutse, as a means of confessing his negativity, and, in the centre, a stone butter lamp named Tashi Obar *(bkra shis 'od 'bar)*,

Chapel of Bathing Maitreya (no. **18**). (2000 GD)

Virūpa and Śākyaśrī. (2000 GD)

Phangmodrupa and Thangtong Gyalpo (p. 69, no. **17**). (2000 GD)

Chapel of Tsongkhapa (no. **22**). (2000 GD)

Gatekeeper Vajrapāṇi (no. **23**). (2000 GD)

Chapel of Amitābha (no. **24**). (2000 GD)

which had been offered by Tsongkhapa in person. The stone basin known as Trudo Padma Pungpa, where King Songtsen Gampo and his queens once bathed, which formerly stood outside this chapel on a clay plinth to the left (**19**), has been repositioned inside the chapel, although it is uncertain whether this is original or not.

Outside the chapel to the right, on a clay platform there is a new image of Mahākāruṇika in a glass case, flanked by statues of Śākyasrī, the great paṇḍita of Kashmir, and Lama Zhang Yudrakpa to the left, and Zhikpo Dudtsi who several times repaired the dykes that protected the Great Temple from the flooding Kyichu waters, to the right, alongside Vajrapāṇi. Zhakabpa adds that formerly, there were images of Śāntarakṣita, Padmasambhava and Kamalaśīla, which had been sculpted by the great treasure-finder Pema Lingpa (1450-1521); and a statue of Bhaiṣajyaguru, sculpted by Nelchung Ripa. These have not yet been replaced.

Chapels of the North-east Corner

Next, underneath the Chapel of Tsongkhapa, which is approached via a stone staircase with metal railings, there is the Treasury of Jowo Śākyamuni (**20**, *jo bo'i mdzod*). This chamber once housed the crown-ornaments, ear-rings, heart-ornaments, necklaces and other sacred regalia belonging to the two Jowo images of the Great Temple and Ramoche, along with gold and silver butter lamps, water offering bowls, ornate alms' bowls, offering-maṇḍalas, thousand-spoked wheels, and other precious artefacts, amassed like a pile of jewels, in the care of the Chief Sacristan *(dkon gnyer dpon)*.

In its interior recess, sometimes known as the Chapel of the Milk Plain Lake (**21**, *'o thang mtsho'i lha khang*), there are reportedly kept the sacraments of the lake *(mtsho rdzas)*, vases *(bum pa)*, treasures *(gter)*, and other objects of offering which are presented to the subterranean water spirits of Milk Plain Lake, below the foundations of the building. A stone slab within this chapel is said to give access to the subterranean lake, and officials of the Tibetan government would formerly make offerings here each year to the serpentine water spirits, as they also did at Lhamo Latso and Yamdrok Yutso. In recent times, access to this chapel was largely blocked-off by the Chapel of Tsongkhapa above, and nowadays it is always kept closed, although some reports do suggest that the hand becomes cold when inserted into a cavity in the floor of this inner chamber.

Within the Chapel of Tsongkhapa (**22**, *tsong kha pa'i lha khang*), located at the top of the stone staircase with metal railings, there is a replica image of Tsongkhapa, the original of which was said to bear a remarkable physical likeness to the master himself because it had been commissioned during his own lifetime and was handled personally by him.[144] However, there are other traditions attributing its miraculous construction to the protector deity Dharmarāja, or alternatively to a later Mongol potentate. In his autobiography, Palden Chokyong, the great monastic preceptor of Ngor Monastery, comments that the sight of this image always conferred great blessing, and that since it was permeated by the fragrance of moral discipline, beads of sweat appear would even appear upon it.[145] Zhakabpa also recalls Thubten Lobzang, a retired preceptor of Ngakpa College at Sera, saying there was a sweet fragrance of moral discipline permeating this chapel at all times, and that the complexion of the image appeared to change.

To the left of this central statue there was an image of Choje Kunga Tashi of Sakya who was the senior spiritual teacher of the Chinese Da Ming Emperor Yongle, and an image of Buton Rinchendrub, which had been sculpted by Lochen Jangchub Tsemo. To the right of the main image were other statues depicting Ngulchu Gyalse Thokme Zangpo, Dampa Sonam Gyaltsen of Sakya, Mu-se Dorje Gyaltsen, and the Third Karmapa Rangjung Dorje. These peripheral figures have also been restored and repositioned.

Chapels of the East Wing

Just beyond the stone staircase of the Chapel of Tsongkhapa, there is the replica of an image of the gatekeeper Vajrapāṇi (**23**), which had originally been made by the hand of King Songtsen Gampo. Later in the ninth century, when Buddhism was persecuted by King Langdarma Udumtsen, a rope was placed around the neck of this image, with the intention of throwing it into the Kyichu River. However, the person who pulled the rope vomited blood at that very spot and died, for which reason the apostate king is said to have ceased to dismantle the Great Temple.

Alongside Vajrapāṇi is the Chapel of Amitābha (**24**, *'od dpag lha khang*), sometimes known as the "chapel were final obstacles are dispelled" before pilgrims come to view Jowo Śākyamuni. The entrance has an original sloping and intricately carved Newār door-frame with an unpainted patina, and a chain curtain. The central image of Amitābha was sculpted by a Newār artisan, in accordance with a vision personally experienced by

Songtsen Gampo. Later, at the time when Songtsen Gampo and his queens are said to have vanished into the aforementioned image of Mahākāruṇika, immeasurable rays of light emanated, permeating the upper and lower storeys of the Great Temple. These rays of light were then reabsorbed into the images of Jowo Akṣobhyavajra, Maitreya in the Gesture of Teaching the Sacred Doctrine, Buddha Amitābha, the image of Acala known as Jowo Midro Sungjon, White Hayagrīva, Tārā, Bhaiṣajyaguru, and Ucchūṣmakrodha, whereupon these became known as the eight deities into which light rays had emanated (*'od zer 'phros pa'i lha brgyad*). This image of Buddha Amitābha, which was one of the eight, has been destroyed and a new replica, protected within a glass case, now takes its place.

In its retinue were images of the Eight Closest Bodhisattvas (*nye sras brgyad*): Avalokiteśvara, Kṣitigarbha, Nivāraṇaviṣkambhin, Ākāśagarbha, Samantabhadra, Mañjuśrīghoṣa, Vajrapāṇi and Maitreya. The hands, feet and postures of these images were all described as being slightly idiosyncratic, but they have all been replaced since the Cultural Revolution when the originals were destroyed.

Outside the entrance is a replica image of the gatekeeper Ucchūṣmakrodha (**25**), also revered as one of the eight deities into which light-rays had emanated. According to legend, when a Chinese army invaded Lhasa after the death of Songtsen Gampo, an emanational army is said to have emerged from the navel of this image and expelled the Chinese troops to their own land.[146] Alongside it, arrayed on a clay platform to the left (**26**), are smaller statues of King Songtsen Gampo and his three main queens in Chinese style, which were sculpted by the *Tshalpa Tripon* Monlam Dorje, along with Guru Saroruhavajra (Za-hor-ma). This latter statue had been commissioned by the Thirteenth Dalai Lama Thubten Gyatso and it contained a remarkable representative image of Padmasambhava called Tongdrol Chenmo, which had been extracted as treasure by the treasure-finder Sogyal.[147] Four monks would traditionally come from Meru Nyingba, which was affiliated to Nechung Monastery, to make feast-offerings in its presence every tenth and twenty-fifth day of the lunar month. Then, from 1896 (fire monkey year of the fifteenth cycle), a custom was introduced whereby on the tenth day of the monkey month of each monkey year, the Guru Saroruhavajra image would be escorted by a procession of monks to Nechung, where an elaborate tenth day festival would be held. In front of it, there is also a small image of Hayagrīva.

Adjacent to the platform, there is the Vase Pillar (**27**, *ka ba bum pa can*), in the vicinity of which doctrinal scriptures were discovered and underneath which scrolls containing the long, medium and short versions of the king's own biography were later unearthed. Some of the wood panelling on the bulbous Vase Pillar was replaced at the time when the Central Inner Sanctum was recently renovated, and its fine decorative motifs have been damaged.

At this point the pilgrim reaches the wooden floor (**28**, *pang gcal*) of the foyer in front of the Central Inner Sanctum (*gtsang khang dbus ma*), the chapel in which the image of Jowo Śākyamuni resides. To the right of the entrance, there are images of the great guardian kings of the west and north Virūpākṣa and Vaiśravaṇa, while to the left there are images of the great guardian kings of the east and south Dhṛtarāṣṭra and Virūḍhaka. The sculptures, in Chinese style, are slightly larger in size than a virile youth, with large protruding eyeballs, moustaches, beards, a manifestly haughty demeanour, and either wrathful or flirtatious facial expressions.[148]

Legend recounts that when King Trisong Detsen built Samye Monastery, the first fruits of the earth were offered to the Great Temple in Lhasa, and used to sculpt these images of the Four Great Guardian Kings, while the first fruits of the timber were also offered for the construction of the great gate at the entrance to this Central Inner Sanctum.[149] The original sculptures were destroyed during the Cultural Revolution and have since been replaced. The highly polished wooden floor of the foyer is also new – the original having been fashioned of exquisite interlocking planks of thick white and red sandalwood.

The lintel of the great gate has a three-tiered wooden arched pediment. The carved timbers of this pediment and those of the beams, capitals and gateposts were adorned and embellished with exquisite motifs depicting gods, goddesses, flowers, tress, and so forth. The original chain curtain *(a lung can)*, which pilgrims lick to cure stammering and enhance their discriminative awareness, was an exact replica of those that covered the entrances to the old chapels of Ancient India. Bells of varying sizes were attached above the chain mail, and one of these is said to have been the bell which Maudgalyāyana used to arouse his mother to recollect the guidance of Lord Buddha, and another was the bell which the treasure-finder Guru Chowang had used to encourage his own mother to recollect the recitation of the mantra OṂ MAṆI PADME HŪṂ. Above the bells was a

King Songtsen Gampo and queens with Guru Saronravajra to the rear (no. **26**). (2000 GD)

The Guardian Kings Dhṛtarāṣṭra and Virūḍhaka (no. **28**). (2000 GD)

The Guardian Kings Virūpākṣa and Vaiśravaṇa (no. **28**). (2000 GD)

yak-horn into which the venerable Milarepa (1040-1123) reputedly entered and imparted his songs *(gsung mgur)* in order to instruct his disciple Rechung Dorje Drak at Palmo Pethang. Immediately next to that, facing the west, the south and the north were a thousand miniature gilded-copper images of Amitāyus, which had been sculpted by *Shedra Kalon* Dondrub Dorje. None of these adornments can presently be seen around the chain curtain, but the magnificent carved and richly painted doorway remains.

The Central Inner Sanctum (**29**, *gtsang khang dbus ma*), otherwise known as the Jokhang, is the largest and loftiest chapel within the Great Temple. It contains the 1.5 metre high representative image of Jowo Śākyamuni which is most revered throughout Tibet. The following account of its origin accords with the *rgyal rabs gsal ba'i me long*.

Once when Lord Buddha was residing at Jetāvana, in the sanctuary of Anāthapiṇḍada, along with the four categories of his retainers *('khor rnam bzhi)*, the bodhisattva Mañjuśrī made the following prayer of supplication, "O Transcendent Lord Buddha, at the present time sentient beings actually behold your visage. They actually make offerings to you, and consequently they actually acquire merit. However when you have passed into final nirvāṇa, there will be no receptacle through which sentient beings might acquire merit. I therefore implore you to reveal an appropriate receptacle of offerings or field of merit through which all sentient beings might acquire merit in the future". Lord Buddha then smiled and emitted four rays of light from his countenance. One penetrated the great god Brahmā, one penetrated the great planetary divinity Rāhu, one penetrated Devendra śakra, and one penetrated the king of artisans Viśvakarman; so that their brilliance was enhanced.

The god Brahmā folded his hands in the *añjalī* gesture and prayed that a receptacle of the Buddha-body of Reality *(dharmakāya)* might be made of the five precious metals. Rahu prayed that a receptacle of the Buddha-body of Perfect Resource *(sambhogakāya)* in the form Vairocana Hīmamahāsāgara *(thub pa gans can mtsho)* might be made of molten sapphire and emerald. Śakra prayed that a receptacle of the Buddha-body of Emanation *(nirmāṇakāya)* might be made of many divine and human jewels. In this way, they prayed that the king of artisans, Viśvakarman, might himself be permitted to sculpt these images.

Accordingly, the symbolic receptacle of the Buddha-body of Reality was constructed in the form of a stūpa, and introduced first to the god-realms *(devaloka)* and later to Oḍḍiyāna by the ḍākinīs, where it became renowned as Intangible Glory (*dpal regs pa med pa*). The symbolic receptacle of the Buddha-body of Perfect Resource in the form Vairocana Hīmamahāsāgara was installed on an island in the great outer ocean,[150] where it acted on behalf of the living beings who resided there. Then two symbolic receptacles of the Buddha-body of Emanation were sculpted from the materials provided by Śakra. Prajāpati demonstrated the size of the images to be built, saying that the smaller image sculpted at the time when Lord Buddha was eight years old should equal the size of the throne in Lumbinī Grove, and that the larger one, sculpted at the time when Lord Buddha was twelve years old, should have its legs resting on the lower lintel of the Śrāvastī Gate and its head touching the upper lintel. The king of artisans Viśvakarman sculpted these images accordingly, in the form of the Buddha-body of Emanation, and, as such, they could not be distinguished from the actual body of the Buddha. In this way, Viśvakarman contributed to the glory of all gods and men, and Lord Buddha himself performed the consecration ceremony. Among these two images, the one representing Lord Buddha the size of a twelve-yearold remained for many years within a shrine in the god-realms.[151] Thereafter, for some centuries it was installed in Oḍḍiyāna, and then for some centuries it remained at Vajrāsana in India. During the reign of an Indian king named Dharmapāla, the Emperor of China was one Tre Nyima Dzaya (sPre nyi-ma dza-ya).[152] Although the two kings never met and never saw one another, they became friends, and exchanged gifts. On one such occasion, to commemorate the defeat of the Yāvanas, the Emperor of China sent a seamless silk cloak with a golden knot *(śrīvatsa)* motif at its heart. The Indian king in return sent this image of Jowo Śākyamuni, the size of a twelve-year-old, by boat, along with four monks to make offerings. In this way, the image is said to have reached China.

According to another Chinese chronicle, when the descendants of the Zhou Emperor *(ci'u rgyal po)* had held the capital Dong-jing *(dung tsing)* for thirty-six generations, the younger brother of the emperor became the king of Si-chen (?).[153] At that time, the image of Jowo Śākyamuni and a sandalwood image of Jowo were brought to China. Then, after many years had passed, when Wen-cheng Kon-jo, the daughter or relative of the Tang Emperor Taizong, arrived in Tibet in 641 as the consort of the Tibetan king Songtsen Gampo, she is said to have brought this image as her dowry *(rten skal)*.[154]

Jowo Śākyamuni (no. **29**). (2000 GD)

Dīpaṃkara Buddhan (no. **29**). (2000 GD)

When it first reached Tibet, this image of Jowo Śākyamuni, which could not be distinguished from the actual historical Buddha, was initially installed as the foremost receptacle of offerings in Ramoche, which had been built by the Chinese Princess. However, after King Songtsen Gampo and his two queens had vanished into the heart of the aforementioned Mahākāruṇika image, the king is said to have reemerged and offered a final testament *(mtha'tshig)*[155] to his ministers to the effect that the abodes of the two images of Śākyamuni should be interchanged in order to promote the auspicious coincidence necessary for the continuity of Tibet as a field of merit.

This injunction was not implemented, and immediately after the king's death, during the reign of his grandson *(dbon sras)* Mangsong Mangtsen, a Chinese army reportedly entered Tibet.[156] Fearing that the Jowo Śākyamuni image would be lost to China, the new king had it concealed within the mirror-shaped Southern Gate of the Great Temple behind a wall painting of Mañjughoṣa, with the result that the Chinese forces who could not recognise the actual image carried off by mistake the image of Akṣobhyavajra. After about one day's march, the weight of the Jowo Akṣobhyavajra image increased, and they were unable to escort it further, abandoning it at Cholung where it remained for many years. Meanwhile, the image of Dīpaṃkara Buddha in the form Acala *(mi 'khrugs pa)* which had been constructed during the lifetime of King Songtsen Gampo remained undisturbed within the Central Inner Sanctum. Subsequently, when Princess Jin-cheng Kong-jo arrived in Tibet as the consort of King Me Aktsom, circa 710, she began to search for the original Jowo Śākyamuni image that had been the dowry of her relative Wencheng. She eventually cognised its whereabouts through elemental divination *('byung rtsis)* and extracted it from the mirror-shaped Southern Gate. Jowo Śākyamuni was then moved into position on the throne of the Central Inner Sanctum, and has ever since remained in that position, revered as the most sacred field of merit for all living beings throughout Tibet.[157]

As for the image of Dīpaṃkara Buddha in the form Acala (*sangs rgyas mi 'khrug pa*), which had stood in lieu of the Jowo image, there had been a plan to install it in another chapel. However, it was placed on the ground immediately behind the throne of Jowo Śākyamuni after it itself was heard to proclaim, "I will not move from here!" Because the area behind the Jowo image is extremely narrow, strips of wood were fastened around the base of Acala to secure it in place. This image is also revered as one of the "eight gods into whom rays of light emanated" *('od zer 'phros pa'i lha brgyad)*, and it is additionally known by the epithet, "one which proclaimed it would not move from the presence of the Jowo" *(jo bo mi 'gro gsung byon)*.

During the eleventh century, the Central Inner Sanctum was enlarged by Zangkar Lotsāwa Phakpa Sherab.[158] As far as the images of Dīpaṃkara Buddha in the form of Acala and his eightfold retinue *(mi 'khrug pa gtso 'khor dgu)* were concerned, he kept Acala in its position behind Jowo Śākyamuni but moved the eight retainers into the chapel on the top floor, directly above the head of Śākyamuni, and immediately below the gilded roof of the Central Inner Sanctum. In their place Zangkar Lotsāwa constructed to the rear of Jowo Śākyamuni a two-storey (6 metre high) image of Vairocana Hīmamahāsāgara, flanked by twelve standing male and female bodhisattvas, and the charismatic gatekeepers Vajrapāṇi and Hayagrīva.

The Central Inner Sanctum also contained images of Maitreya, Mañjughoṣa and Tsongkhapa, which had been sculpted by Lingchak Drukpon, the reliquary of Korpon Jangchub Sempa, a gold image of the Seventh Dalai Lama Kelzang Gyatso, and a silver image of the Thirteenth Dalai Lama Thubten Gyatso. All the peripheral figures presently contained in the Jokhang are said to be replicas of recent construction.

Nowadays the main image is seated upon a three-tiered stone platform, flanked by smaller images of Maitreya and Mañjughoṣa. The headdress and ear-ornaments *(rna rgyan)* originally date from the time of Tsongkhapa, and the pearl-studded robe from that of the Da Ming emperor. Although the gold headdress itself was retrieved from a dark storeroom above the Mahākāruṇika Chapel, where it had been placed during the Cultural Revolution, most of these ornaments have been recently replaced. There is, however, one large pearl-like crown-ornament, larger than an egg, which is said to be original. Supporting the overhead canopy there are ornate silver-plated pillars with dragon motifs; and above the crown there is a silver sphere that was donated by a Mongol Qan.

In the passageways to the right and left of the main image within the Central Inner Sanctum there are vantage points from which pilgrims may view the facial expression of Jowo Śākyamuni. On the right and left knees of the image there are places where

Vairocana Hīmamahāsāgara (no. **29**). (2000 GD)

Standing bodhisattvas in the retinue of Vairocana (no. **29**). (2000 GD)

Chapel of Maitreya (no. **34**). (2000 GD)

Avalokitésvara, Dolopa and Amitāyus (no. **32**). (1996 US)

Anśa and students with the gilded mural of Dolma Darlenma to the rear (no. **32**). (2000 GD)

Guru Padmākara (no. **30**). (2000 GD)

pilgrims may touch their heads and present offering scarves, approaching via a gate and a flight of wooden steps. Formal offerings are made on the right side of the gold throne.

In the past, there was one monk from Losaling College at Drepung, who acted as the sacristan, with responsibility for keeping the chapel clean, while two other sacristan monks from Zhi-de Dratsang and two monks from Ngakpa College at Drepung had responsibility for arranging the hundreds of gold and silver butter offering lamps. The main gold butter lamp *(ser skong)*, which had originally been offered to the Central Inner Sanctum by Longdol Lama and which used to be replenished several times each day by visiting pilgrims, is said to have offered release from rebirth in lower realms of existence to those who filled it as an act of offering. This lamp in all probability no longer exists because the present golden butter lamp appears to be a replica with a stem of average length. The original had a shorter than usual stem in the form of a human figurine raising the cup upwards. There were several other gold butter lamps, including one offered by a previous Paṇchen Lama, but the most renowned and the oldest was that offered by Longdol Lama. Behind Jowo Śākyamuni, there is a copper plaque with an inscription commemorating earlier restorations of the throne-back and the aureole.[159]

The elaborately decorated high ceiling of the wooden foyer displays a marked Newār influence. At the level of the cornice there is an image of Guru Padmākara (**30**), kept alongside a maṇḍala in a glass case, immediately above the place where pilgrims make their prostrations. This image which entreats Jowo Śākyamuni not to depart for the abodes of the serpentine water spirits was constructed during the lifetime of the Seventh Dalai Lama Kelzang Gyatso, in accordance with a prophetic declaration contained in the treasures discovered by Gampopa Orgyan Dudul Lingpa. It is believed that there are serpentine water spirits behind the Jowo image, calling it downwards, and whenever sacristans contact that area with their hands they may be infected by the water spirits. Every evening a monk of the Jokhang chapel will recite prayers and offer a libation *(ser khyems)*, entreating Jowo Rinpoche not to depart for the abodes of the serpentine water spirits. To its right, there is an image of Vijaya (**31**), which had originally been commissioned by Demo Jampal Delek Gyatso of Tengyeling.

Then, continuing in a clockwise direction from the Central Inner Sanctum and its wooden foyer, the pilgrim will reach a small image of Vajrapāṇi on a clay platform, along with other images of Munīndra, Atiśa, Dromton Gyalwa Jungne, and Naktso Lotsāwa. Behind them, there is a gilded mural depicting Dolma Darlenma (**32**) who is renowned for having accepted an offering scarf from Sakya Paṇḍita.[160] The fresco is also revered as one of the "eight gods into whom rays of light emanated," and pilgrims still gild her face as an act of merit. In front of this clay platform there is the Leaf Pillar (**33**, *ka ba shing lo can)*, near which Atiśa is said to have extracted King Songtsen Gampo's testament, the *bka' 'chems ka khol ma,* from the edge of a beam.[161]

Next to the platform, there is the west-facing Chapel of Maitreya in the Gesture of Teaching the Sacred Doctrine (**34**, *byams pa chos 'khor gtso 'khor*), which has an original seventh century sloping Newār doorframe. It contained a red bronze image of Maitreya in the teaching gesture, with webbed fingers, which, according to legend, had been commissioned by King Kṛkin and consecrated by Buddha Kāśyapa. The image was brought to Tibet from Nepal as part of Princess Bhṛkuṭī's dowry, and transported on foot, "through dangerous ravines where rocks and rivers clashed together." It is renowned as one of the "eight gods into which light rays were emanated" *('od zer 'phros pa'i lha brgyad).* The present image is a replica but its finely carved aureole may be original.

To its right and left there were images of Tārā Who Protects from the Eight Fears (*sgrol ma 'jigs brgyad ma*), which were sculpted during the lifetime of King Songtsen Gampo. In the northwest corner, there is the replica of a small stove (**35**), said to replace the original stove of the Newār princess Bhṛkuṭī.[162] Even today, when the mothers of Lhasa pat this stove, they believe it will enhance the quality of their cuisine. Alongside the entrance of this chapel upon a woollen mat it is said there was once kept a splendid tiger skin, described in some sources as "Songtsen Gampo's tiger emanation."[163] However there is nothing to be seen there in recent times. Outside, guarding the entrance to this chapel, are standing images of the Indian protector deities: Brahmā and Śakra, on the left and right respectively.

Next, beyond the entrance to the chapel, seated on a clay platform (**37**), there are restored images of Four-armed Avalokiteśvara, Dolpopa Sherab Gyaltsen of Jonang (1292-1361) and Amitāyus.

Chapels of the South-east Corner

Next to the clay platform there is the Chapel of Avalokiteśvara in the form Siṃhanāda (**38**, *spyan ras gzigs seng ge sgra grogs kyi lha khang*). It contains a central image of Amitābha, flanked by six aspects of Avalokiteśvara, the nearest to the entrance, Siṃhanāda, giving the chapel its name. The others are Semnyi Ngalso and a fourfold group comprising Mahākāruṇika in union with consort and flanked by male and female offspring. Here, too, there were formerly images of the gatekeepers Brahmā and Śakra, which had been sculpted from the first fruits of the earth acquired at the time when King Ralpachen built the temple of Tashido at Onchangdo. All the existing images contained within this chapel are replicas. Outside the chapel there is a 1.5m stone column with a hole at the top, to which pilgrims press their ears in order to hear the sound of the mythical *anga* bird at the bottom of the Milk Plain Lake. However, this column is not original, and its replacement was erected in the wrong location, according to the late Tenth Paṇchen Rinpoche. The original aperture, where the *anga* bird could be heard before 1959 was plastered over and an altar erected above it. Yet visiting pilgrims still insist on placing their ears here!

To the left, there is a south-facing passageway (**39**) that leads via a stone staircase up to the middle storey of the Great Temple. Formerly this staircase was fashioned of finely worn juniper planks and only opened to give access to the Śrīdevī Turret (*dpal lha lcog*). In 1992 the original wooden steps were replaced by a new stone flight of stairs and inset within the stairwell. Nowadays this staircase serves as the main point of access for the upper floors of the Great Temple.

Continuing beyond the passageway, in the south-east corner beyond the stairs, the pilgrim reaches a north-facing chapel known as Svāstika Alcove (**40**, *gYung drung sbug*), containing replica images of Padmākara, King Trisong Detsen, and Śāntarakṣita. According to some sources the image of Śāntarakṣita was substituted by an image of Padmasambhava. These were originally sculpted in order to repel a Mongol army during the reign of *Tsang-to Depa* Phuntsok Namgyal. On the wall alongside the entrance to that chapel there is a gilden mural behind a protective lattice, depicting Bhaiṣajyaguru (**41**), regarded as one of the "eight gods into whom rays of light were emanated."

Chapels of the South Wing

The first of the chapels visited on the south wing is the North-facing Chapel (**42**, *byang gzigs lha khang*), also known as Sempa Tsokhor. Formerly it contained images of the Buddhas of the Three Times: Dīpaṃkara the buddha of the past, Śākyamuni the buddha of the present and Maitreya the buddha of the future – as well as Bodong Chok-le Namgyal and Taklung Ngawang Drakpa. This chapel was until recently used as a butter storeroom, but now it contains a series of newly sculpted meditational deities depicting the retinue of Amitāyus in *yab yum* posture, according to the tradition of Jetāri. To the left of the entrance are new images depicting the three Deities of Long life (*tshe lha rnam gsum*).

To the right of the entrance (**43**), there were formerly statues of King Songtsen Gampo and his queens, along with Mongza Tricham, Prince Gungri Gungtsen, Thonmi Sambhoṭa, Gartong Tsenyulsung, and Zhanglon Nachenpo, which were commissioned by the *Tshalpa Tripon* Monlam Dorje. These original statues have been destroyed and no effort has yet been made to replace them. Instead, there is there is a mural depicting King Songtsen Gampo and his queens, fronted by protective glass cases containing a new image of Dolchung Korpon - a former sacristan who immolated himself in the Central Inner Sanctum, followed by statues of Barawa Gyaltsen Pelzang, Yangphugpa Sangye Pelzang and a hatless Phagmodrupa.

Next, there is the north-facing Chapel of the Four Sibling Maitreyas (**44**, *byams pa mched bzhi'i lha khang*), which is one of only four in the Great Temple surmounted by a gilded roof. It contained as its centrepiece one of the four silver-cast images of Maitreya, collectively known as the four sibling Maitreyas, which had been cast by the attendant Utpala of Kashmir at the time of Langdarma, using white silver which Paṇḍita Tsultrim Nor had extracted from the stomach of a Jambhala statue in the lower storey of Meru Nyingba Temple, following his successful propitiation of Jambhala. Each year, during the Great Prayer Festival on the twenty-fifth day of the Month of Miracles, this image of Maitreya would be transported by cart around the Barkor of Lhasa in a ceremony known as the Escorting of Maitreya (*byams pa gdan 'dren*).[164] The original image was destroyed during the Cultural Revolution, and its replacement, kept inside a protective glass case, was subsequently brought to the Great Temple from Drepung Monastery.

The chapel additionally once housed an image of Mañjughoṣa which had been meditational deity of King Aṃśuvarman,[165] an image of Khasarpaṇi which had been sculpted by Lu-me and brought from Dribda Lhakhang, an eleven-faced Mahākāruṇika

Chapel of Siṃhanāda (no. **38**). (2000 GD)

Padmākara in the Svāstika Alcove (no. **40**). (2000 GD)

Stone column outside the Chapel of Siṃhanāda (no. **38**). (2000 GD)

Pilgrims listening out for mythical anga bird (no. **38**). (2000 MF)

Chapel of the Nine Aspects of Amitāyus (no. **53**). (1996 US)

Mural of Prajñāpāramita (no. **52**). (2000 GD)

Chapel of the Mirror-shaped Southern Gate (no. **48**). (2000 GD)

Secret Chamber of Concealment (no. **49**). (2000 GD)

image which had been consecrated by Kāśyapa, and a Vajrasattva image which had been sculpted during the lifetime of King Songtsen Gampo. Other images here included Mahāsahasrapramardaṇa, Mahāpratisāra, Yamāntaka, Padmāntaka, Vighnāntaka, and Black Jambhala. However, the peripheral images contained in this chapel at the present day are all newly sculpted replicas.

In front of the offering lamps, there was an image of the sacristan *Lharje* Gewabum, rebuilder of the Kyichu dykes, which he himself had personally handled.[166] Also, behind the image of Vighnāntaka, in the northeast corner, there is a half metre high gilded head of Ramo Gyawu (**45**), the legendary emanational queen of goats who transported the earth at the time when the Milk Plain Lake was reclaimed and sealed. This was renowned as a natural "multiplying image" *(sku 'phel ma)* since the head had discernibly increased in size over the centuries.[167] The present replica is still venerated by pilgrims. Formerly, two monks from Meru Dratsang acted as sacristans of this chapel.

To the left of the Chapel of the Four Sibling Maitreyas, there was formerly a stūpa known as Chorten Padma Pungpa (**46**), which contained terracotta images made by the hand of Drogon Chogyal Phakpa. Alongside it were images of the lineage holders of the Sakya school: Virūpa, Sachen Kunga Nyingpo, Jetsun Sonam Tsemo, and Jetsun Drakpa Gyaltsen. The stūpa no longer exists, but there are in its place on a newly built clay platform replica statues of the five original Sakya hierarchs, (l. to r.) Sonam Tsemo, Drakpa Gyaltsen, Kunga Nyingpo, Sakya Paṇḍita and Drogon Chogyal Phakpa (**47**).[168] The first of these appropriately sits in front of a celebrated painting of Mañjughoṣa (see below, fig. 50).

To their left is the Chapel of the Mirror-Shaped Southern Gate (**48**, *lho sgo me long can gyi lha khang)*, which contains an image of Amitābha in the guise of the Buddha-body of Perfect Resource, flanked to the left and right by the Eight Medicine Buddhas. This room is also known as the "chapel of the eight medicine buddhas" *(sman lha bde gshegs brgyad kyi lha khang)* and as the "chapel where the Jowo was concealed *(jo bo sbas sa'i lha khang)* because, in the wall behind the image of Ratnacandra (one of the eight medicine buddhas), there is a square cavity giving access to the secret chamber (**49**) where Jowo Śākyamuni had been concealed following the death of Songtsen Gampo, ostensibly to prevent its removal by a Chinese army. Outside this secret chamber, a mural of Mañjughoṣa was drawn to render its entrance invisible. Later, when the Chinese princess Jin-cheng learned of Jowo Śākyamuni's whereabouts through elemental divination, she was unable to break down the door behind the painting of Mañjughoṣa. At that time, the painting itself reputedly said, "Permit me to move aside!" Whereupon it did move aside, enabling the Jowo image to be extracted. Subsequently the painting was given the name "Mañjughoṣa who Moved Aside of his own accord" (**50**, *'jam dbyangs sku gYol ba*). Nowadays the painting is visible directly behind the aforementioned lineage-holders of Sakya.

Within the Chapel of the Seven Generations of Past Buddhas (**51**, *sangs rgyas rabs bdun gyi lha khang*) located to the left of these Sakya lineage-holders, there were images of all seven successive buddhas of the immediate past, namely: Vipaśyin, Śikhin, Viśvabhuk, Krakucchanda, Kanakamuni, Kāśyapa, and Śākyamuni. The traditional guidebooks say that six of these were fashioned of exquisite old bronze, and that the plinth of the remaining one was left empty, in consequence of which a bronze image miraculously alighted there from India! Most of the images in this chapel are now modern replicas.

Chapels of the South-west Corner

Continuing into the southwest corner, one enters an east-facing chapel or alcove (**52**). Here behind a protective wooden balustrade, there is a mural depicting Prajñāpāramitā, which once had an open eye in the forehead. This painting was originally attributed to King Songtsen Gampo, and according to one tradition, the open eye naturally appeared of its own accord after an old lady miraculously had her sight restored on praying to the image. Another tradition refers to this painting as "open-eyed Avalokiteśvara" (*mig 'byed spyan ras gzigs*). In any case, the present mural is of modern execution.

Accessed from that alcove, there is the north-facing Chapel of the Nine Aspects of Amitāyus (**53**, *tshe dpag lha du'i lha khang*) containing replica images of the nine aspects of Amitāyus. The murals of both the alcove and its inner chapel depict the Three Deities of Longevity (*tshe lha rnam gsum*).[169]

Continuing in a clockwise direction along the west wing towards the main gate, the pilgrim will next approach the east-facing Chapel of the Religious King and his Courtiers (**54**, *chos rgyal yab yum sras blon bcas kyi lha khang*). The chapel has a wonderfully carved Newār doorway and it still contains original images of Songtsen Gampo, flanked by the Newār princess Bhṛkutī, the Chinese princess Wencheng, the Mon princess Tricham,

Prince Gungri Gungtsen, and the two ministers: Thonmi Sambhoṭa who is depicted holding a book in his hand, and the governor Gar Tongtsen, holding a staff.[170] In front of the image of Songtsen, there was an intact pillar which went by the name "fulfiller of all prayers" (*smon lam btab tshad 'grub bo*). Some of the images of this chapel were preserved without damage during the Cultural Revolution, as were its offering bowls and butter lamps.

Outside, there are historically important murals depicting the foundation of the Great Temple and the events of Songtsen Gampo's reign, including the construction of the first Potala Palace. The procession of Jowo Śākyamuni from China is vividly depicted, as is the casting of Princess Wencheng's ring into the Milk Plain Lake prior to the construction. These were originally drawn during the lifetime of King Songtsen Gampo, but until their recent restoration, they were hard to discern on account of the grime and darkness.

Miwang Maitreya (no. **36**). (1996 US)

Main Hall

The Main Hall (**55**, *dkyil 'khor mthil*) from which all these chapels are accessed is two storeys high, and has three transverse sections, two supported by short columns (*ka ba thung thung*) and one by long columns (*ka ba ring bo*). Immediately inside the vestibule, there are two rows of short columns running transversely from north to south, the southernmost ones bearing painted scrolls of the Sixteen Elders. In the centre of the hall there are four groups of long columns which support the skylight, their decoration originally dating from the period of Ga-de Zangpo's restoration. Running transversely along the interior portion of the hall, in front of the Central Inner Sanctum there are twelve short columns (*ka ba thung thung*), six on either wing, which probably date from the 7th century because they are characterised by short bases and round shafts, suggesting an authentic Newār design. Five of them (three at the north end and two at the south end) were plastered, probably in the 14th century for protection or reinforcement by Ga-de Zangpo and his son.

The carved timbers of the pillars, beams, capitals and buttresses which connect the Main Hall with the upper storeys of the Great Temple are reminiscent of the carved pillars, beams and masonry of sixth century Indian vihāras, fragments of which can still be seen in museums at Sarnath, Calcutta, and Delhi.

Barzhib Maitreya (no. **59**). (1996 US)

Within the metal railing at the centre of the Main Hall, where offering ceremonies are even now performed, is a west-facing, four metre high gilded copper image of eleven-faced Mahākāruṇika (**56**), with a small gilded statue of the previous Paṇchen Lama in front. The original, commissioned in 1774 by Doring Ngodrub Rabten, was destroyed in the Cultural Revolution and later replaced with the present replica. The hall also contains three enormous images of Maitreya. Among these, the impressive eight metre high gilded copper image (**59**), which faces west, was originally commissioned by Barzhib Chukhorwa. The slightly smaller gilded copper image (**36**), which faces north within its own lattice enclosure, was originally commissioned in 1736 (fire dragon year of twelfth cycle) by Miwang Pholha Sonam Tobgye. Its mantra core contained important receptacles of offering,[171] including a ritual vase (*las bum*) which had been used by Padmasambhava at Māratika Cave in Nepal. The third was a smaller red bronze image (**57**), originally commissioned by Lhazang Qan.

Chapel of the Religious King and his Courtiers (p. 76, no. **54**). (2000 GD)

In addition, the hall contains a thirty-two digit west-facing image of Munīndra, known as *thub dbang zangs mtha' ma* (**58**), surrounded by gilded copper images of the Thousand Buddhas, which had all been originally commissioned by Gazhigung Paṇḍita.

Finally, there was a gilded copper image of Padmsambhava in the form Guru Gyagarma (**60**), fifteen times the average height, which was belatedly commissioned in 1955 (wood sheep year) following a prophetic declaration made by the previous Dzongsar Khyentse Rinpoche. The insertion of the mantra core and the consecration were performed by Minling Chung Rinpoche in accordance with the correct procedures. However, as His Holiness the Dalai Lama has indicated,[172] the actual prophecy had required the construction of a three-storied image of Padmsambhava in the form Nangsi Zilnon along with four stūpas to be built around Jowo Śākyamuni, in order to generate an auspicious coincidence for securing the well-being of Tibet and its government. Reports suggest that Dzongsar Khyentse Rinpoche was saddened by news of the improper implementation of his prophecy, provoking the further prediction that the Dalai Lama would have to leave for India along with his entourage.

Mahākāruṇika in Main Hall (no. **56**). (2000 GD)

All these central images have been destroyed and restored in the wake of the Cultural Revolution. In place of Guru Gyagarma, a six metre high west-facing image of Nangsi Zilnon now stands. It was built at the behest of His Holiness the Dalai Lama and

"Lhasa Jowo Unseen by the Nuns of Lhasa". (2000 GD))

consecrated by the late Dilgo Khyentse Rinpoche, to belatedly fulfil the prophecy of Dzongsar Khyentse. Since then, the tenth and twenty-fifth day feast-offerings have been observed in the Main Hall of the Great Temple. Immediately in front of the Nangsi Zilnon image, there is a deep well, which has been boarded over.

Resting in a glass case on a high crossbeam between the aforementioned image of Munīndra and the vestibule, a small Jowo image faces towards the Central Inner Sanctum. Omitted in Zhakabpa's plan of the Great Temple, this image is known as the 'Lhasa Jowo Unseen by the Nuns of Lhasa' (*lha sa'i jo mo lha sa jo bo ma mjal*) because the nuns and ladies of Lhasa who frequently visit the Jokhang to make offerings are unaware of its presence here.

The railed enclosure of the Main Hall once protected sealed chests containing gold and silver offering maṇḍalas and assorted offering utensils of great value, which had been presented by the Tibetan government and by Buddhist patrons from China, Tibet, and Mongolia. Among them were historically attested objects of veneration, including the helmet and armour (*khrab rmog khrab can ma*) of a general's son who had been slain in antiquity by the forces of Hor. All of these chests have been removed or destroyed.

Daily offerings were once maintained within the Main Hall by five monks from Chushur Tharpaling who would pay homage and make offerings according to the *Liturgy of the Sixteen Elders.* Such rites are maintained by the Great Temple's own resident monks at the present day. The chapels are filled with bright butter lamps, while the altars of the Main Hall, which were once covered with hundreds of brass and gold offering bowls (*'khor yug ma*), each holding eight measures (*khal*) of melted butter, are once again replete with newly fashioned offering utensils. The light from the lamps shimmers throughout the day and night, permeating the building with the fragrant scent of smoke offerings and incense. The prayers of pilgrims, the chanting of the monks and the crescendo of skull-drums, bells, cymbals, and horns resonate throughout the building.

The South Wing of the Vestibule

After completing a circumambulation of the chapels that adjoin the Main Hall, the pilgrim may then ascend to the upper storeys of the Great Temple or exit through the Great Acacia Gate. As the gate is approached on the south wing of the vestibule, one will pass the Chapel of the Serpentine King Nanda (**118**, *klu rgyal dga' ba'i lha khang*), which contains a restored image of the serpentine king Nanda, along with vases holding the charms which control the gods (*lha bum*) and serpentine water spirits (*klu bum*).

Outside the entrance to this chapel, on the floor of the vestibule, there is the aforementioned bellows-shaped stone (*rdo sbud pa can*), which points directly towards the heart of Jowo Śākyamuni in the Central Inner Sanctum when one faces east, standing above it. It also points directly above to the Chapel of the Likeness of the Religious King (*chos rgyal nga 'dra ma'i lha khang*). Underneath this bellow-shaped stone, there is reputed to be a copper amulet containing the skulls of the Four Great Guardian Kings and many gemstones. These were inserted and concealed as treasure by King Songtsen Gampo during the seventh century, in conjunction with aspirational prayers that Tibet would become endowed with all necessary material wealth and successive generations of competent spiritual teachers.[173] All pilgrims visiting the Great Temple pray here in the belief that their wishes will be fulfilled.

Then, a few steps further on, there is a chapel to the left (**119**), which is said to contain the images of Mahākala and Daśagrīva Rāvaṇa of Laṅkā, constructed in the lifetime of King Songtsen Gampo, as well as images of Hayagrīva and Lhamo Drelzhonma which were constructed later by Ge-re Lhapa. However, it is always kept locked, so its contents are uncertain.

Suspended from a beam just inside the Great Acacia Gate there is a large cracked bell(**120**), which was brought to Lhasa in 1720 (iron mouse year of the twelfth cycle) by Capuchin missionaries from Italy. Its rim bears the Latin inscription *Te Deum Laudamus.*

Mural depicting the foundation of the Great Temple (p. 77, no. **54**). (2000 GD)

The Chapels of the Middle Floor

Chapel of the Guru (no. **61**). (2000 GD)

Climbing the main staircase (**39**) in the southeast corner, adjacent to the Chapel of Avalokiteśvara in the form Siṃhanāda, the pilgrim will reach the middle storey of the Great Temple. Formerly, access to the middle storey was gained from the staircase (**7**) located behind the Stūpa of Scrutiny (*brtag pa'i mchod rten*) in the northwest corner.

Chapels of the South-east Corner

Heading directly east from the top of the stairs, the pilgrim will reach the Chapel of the Guru (**61**, *gu ru'i lha khang*), sometimes also known as the "chapel of the likeness of the guru" (*gu ru nga 'dra ma'i lha khang*) or as the "chapel of the master of the middle storey" (*bar khang slob dpon*). Within this chapel, which has an original tapering portico with exquisite wood carvings in Newāri style and a lattice gate, the centrepiece was an image of Padmākara in the form Guru Saroruhavajra (*gu ru mtsho skyes rdo rje*). Around its neck there was a great *rudrākṣa* rosary, which Padmākara had reputedly used for mantra recitation at the time when he subdued the malign gods and ogres (*lha srin*) of Tibet.[174] Flanking this image to the right and left were his foremost consorts: Mandāravā and Yeshe Tshogyal, along with images of his eight manifestations (*gu ru mtshan brgyad*), namely: Padmasambhava, Nyima Ozer, Śākya Senge, Tsokye Dorje, Loden Cho-se, Senge Dradrok, Padma Gyalpo, and Dorje Drolo. When the images of this chapel were recently restored, the sculptor experienced some difficulty because he mistakenly fashioned the replica of Dorje Drolo with the figure of a monk crushed under one of its feet. This figure was subsequently removed due to public objections and replaced by a horse or donkey figurine. Some murals have been restored within the chapel, executed in red line on a gold background, while others on the north wall are blackened.

Chapel of the Graduated Path (p. 80, no. **65**). (2000 GD)

Outside the chapel to the left there was once a hand-turned wheel containing one billion (*ther 'bum*) of the Vajra Guru mantra.[175] The wall (**62**) adjacent to the entrance, which was constructed in the eleventh century by Zangkar Lotsāwa appears to have retained its original murals until the restoration of the 1990s.[176] The new murals, proected by a metal grill, depict Padmākara surrounded by his eight manifestations. Formerly, at the second step of the staircase leading into this chapel, there was a mural depicting the protectress Śrīdevī, which was originally attributed to King Songtsen Gampo.

Corridor and staircases accessing the Middle Storey (no. **39**). (2000 GD)

A wooden gateway leads from here onto a catwalk, from which one will reach the west-facing Chapel of the Countenance (**79**, *zhal ras lha khang*). It was from here that pilgrims could once view the face of Jowo Śākyamuni from the middle floor. The original approach was walled-off by Zangkar Lotsāwa to prevent pilgrims walking above the Jowo and the chamber thus created was completely remodelled at the time when he enlarged the Central Inner Sanctum. Now, only the westernmost part of the original chamber remains, offering a view of the image below. The remaining east inner wall behind the head of Jowo Śākyamuni has a well-preserved three-panelled mural, suggesting a synthesis of Tibetan and Pāla styles, which predates the integrated Tibeto-Newār style of the 15th century. These have also been attributed to Gompa Tsultrim Nyingpo.[177]

To the left of that Chapel of the Guru, there is the Chapel of Cakrasaṃvara (**63**, *bde mchog gi lha khang*), containing replica images of Śrīcakrasaṃvara and his consort Vajravārāhī (*dpal 'khor lo bde mchog*),[178] which were reputedly made of local clay from Lhasa. To the left of this chapel, there is the stone staircase (**64**), which leads down to the ground floor and up to the Śrīdevī Turret. Traditionally it was known as a rear or "secret" entrance (*gsang sgo*) and remained closed, except on special occasions.

Chapel of the Countenance (no. **79**). (2000 GD)

Chapels of the South Wing

Then, walking to the west along the south wing of the middle storey, where the murals have recently been restored,[179] the pilgrim will reach a series of north-facing chapels. The initial murals, which are covered by multi-coloured prayer flags, depict Śrīdevī and the protector deities.

Chapel of the King of the Śākyas (no. **70**). (2000 GD)

Protector cavern of the Five Aspects of Pehar (no. **71**). (2000 GD)

Chapel of the Munīndra and his Retainers (no. **66**). (2000 GD)

Then, there is the Chapel of the Graduated Path (**65**, *lam rim lha khang*),[180] which once contained images of certain lineage teachers of the graduated path (*lam rim bla brgyud*), including Lhodrak Drubchen Namka Gyaltsen and Je Phabongkha Dechen Nyingpo. Following the Cultural Revolution, the chapel was used as a butter storeroom, but since 1992 these images have been restored. The murals depicting the lineage-holders of the graduated path are executed in red line on a gold background. Outside, continuing along the gallery, the badly restored murals depict Padmākara with his twenty-five disciples and Tsongkhapa, protected by metal grills.

The next chapel to its left[181] has a richly decorated doorway, flanked by two black lion rampants on a red background. This is the Chapel of Munīndra and his Retainers (**66**, *thub dbang gtso 'khor gyi lha khang*), the foremost image depicting Śākyamuni, flanked by his supreme pious attendants (*nyan thos mchog zung*), Śāriputra and Maudgalyāyana, and standing images of the eight closest bodhisattvas (*nye sras brgyad*) to the left and right. This chapel has recently been refurbished and reopened. In front of its entrance, there were three hand-turned maṇi wheels (**67**), said to have belonged to King Songtsen Gampo and his queens, which have not yet been replaced. A panel of restored external murals also depicts Śākyamuni Buddha.

Next there is the north-facing Chapel of Munīndra (**68**, *thub dbang gi lha khang*), which contained another central image of Munīndra, flanked by the seven other buddhas of medicine (*sman bla bde gshegs mched bdun*), and a consecrated image of Hayagrīva in the form Tamdrin Sangdrub. These have been restored, with the exception of the Hayagrīva image. On the wall outside this chapel there was formerly a mural depicting White Hayagrīva (**69**), revered as one of the "eight divine images into which light rays were emanated" (*'od zer 'phros pa'i lha brgyad*). The restored mural can still be seen on this panel, amid a group of wrathful protectors.

The last of the chapels on the south wing of the middle storey is the north-facing Chapel of the King of the Śākyas (**70**, *shāk ya'i rgyal po'i lha khang*). It contained a large silver image of Śākyamuni, which had been the centrepiece of Karma Cho-de, a temple built in 1479 (earth pig year of the eighth cycle) by the Seventh Karmapa Chodrak Gyatso at Thosa Nagma in Lhasa, and subsequently destroyed by the armed monks of Sera and Drepung monasteries.[182] Next to this silver image, there was a mask attached to the surface of a pillar, marking a place frequented by the protector Jatri Chenchik, minister of Monbuputra, the eastern kingly aspect of Pehar. The chapel contains new replica images, and the original silver image no longer exists. Outside the door, there is a poorly restored panel of murals depicting aspects of Tārā.

Chapels of the South-west Corner

Continuing into the southwest corner of the middle storey, the pilgrim will next reach the north-facing entrance to the Protector Cavern of the Five Aspects of Pehar (**71**, *sku lnga'i mgon khang phug*). The lattice doorway is bordered by a newly constructed partition wall, its panels inscribed with the auspicious Chinese motif "shou". This chapel once contained nine central and peripheral images (*gtso 'khor dgu*). The main image, one and a half metres high, depicted Hayagrīva in the form Tamdrin Sangdrub, according to the tradition of Kyergang. It was flanked by images and threadcrosses (*rten mdos*) representing the Five Kingly Aspects of Pehar (*rgyal po sku lnga*), which were commissioned by Pema Wangchuk, the Fifth Rigdzin Chenpo of Dorje Drak Monastery, to secure the well being of Tibet. Located to the right and left of the central image, these were respectively: Śrīdevī and Pehar, the kingly aspect of buddha-activities. To the right of Śrīdevī was the kingly aspect of buddha-body Monbuputra, and to its right the kingly aspect of buddha-speech Dralha Kyechik. To its right there was an image of Dutsen. Then, on the left side of King Pehar, there was the kingly aspect of buddha-attributes Shingjachen, and to its left the kingly aspect of buddha-mind Śakra, while to its left there was an image of Lutsen.

An inner recessed chamber which the pilgrim will enter through a doorway on the south wall of this chapel contained a stuffed image of the red sylvan mountain spirit Cimara (**72**, *gnod sbyin tsi'u dmar po*). Inside the protector cavern, nine monks and a vajra-master from Thubten Dorje Drak would continuously perform the rites of reparation and confession.

Nowadays, these rites are still conducted in the outer cavern, while the restored images of the protectors, including that of Hayagrīva, have all been placed within protective glass cases within the inner recessed chamber. The outer cavern remains empty, but for some restored murals depicting the confession buddhas.

Chapels of the West Wing

On the west wing of the middle storey, one will first reach the Chapel of Aśvottama (**73**, *rta mchog lha khang*), containing the restored seven precious insignia of royal dominion *(rgyal srid rin po che sna bdun)* and so named because the precious insignia of the supreme horse *(rta mchog)* faces the door.

Next to it, there is the spacious Chapel of the Religious King (**74**, *chos rgyal lha khang*), entered and exited through two east-facing doors which have preserved their original seventh century frames. This is one of the four chapels of the Great Temple which are surmounted by a gilded roof. It contains original images of the Seven Generations of Past Buddhas *(sangs rgyas rabs bdun)* which were commissioned by King Songtsen Gampo himself. In front of these there is a celebrated gilded copper likeness (*nga 'dra ma*) of the king himself, flanked by statues depicting the Newār princess Bhṛkuṭī (left) and the Chinese princess Wencheng (right). These are said to have been sculpted by a student of Thangtong Gyalpo, named Dungkar Drukdra.[183] The middle finger of the right hand of the central image, which assumes the earth-touching gesture *(bhūmisparśamudrā)* is said to contain the actual middle finger of the king. Accordingly, devout pilgrims believe that all wishes are fulfilled when they pray, touching it with their heads. The lower part of this image has survived, but it lacks the original mantra core, which was discarded during the Cultural Revolution. At that time, the gold torso was moved to a location in the east wing of the Great Temple to prevent theft, and later returned to its rightful place in the refurbished chapel. On the south wall of the chapel there are smaller images depicting the king and his foreign queens.

Behind the main images there is a series of remarkable wall-painted maṇḍalas, depicting the assemblies of Nīladaṇḍa, Hevajra and Vajrabhairava (top left); Bhaiṣajyaguru, Mahākāruṇika and Akṣobhya (bottom left); Sarvavid Vairocana (concealed behind the central image); Guhyasamāja, Cakrasaṃvara and Mahācakra Vajrapāṇi (top right); and Amitāyus, the Sixteen Elders and Avalokiteśvara in the form Mind At Rest (bottom right). These have been accurately repainted during the recent phase of restoration.

Among other artefacts on display in this chapel, there was a special gold ring which Princess Wencheng had offered to King Songtsen, which was only displayed once a year during the *dPal lha ri khrod* ceremonies.[184] The ring that is now on display is a new replica, the original having been lost or destroyed.

A cabinet resting on a wooden stand in front of the main image still contains an original silver wine flask which may well be of Scythian or Kushan origin, and which is known as *'khrungs ban rta mgo ma*. This was reputedly the wine flask used by King Songtsen Gampo himself. It had been inserted as treasure in the fissure of a rock within the Gye-re (Drakral) Ravine, and later, in the early fifteenth century, it was extracted by Tsongkhapa and presented to this chapel as an offering. The fissure is said to have subsequently assumed the shape of the wine flask. Some reports also suggest the flask has been silver plated in recent centuries. Like the ring, the wine flask appears to have been employed only once a year during the *dPal lha ri khrod* ceremonies, at which time it is said to have been filled quickly and easily by those of greater merit but slowly by those of feeble merit.

Outside the chapel, the restored murals of the west wall, protected by a metal grill, depict ancient kings and figures associated with the early phase of Buddhist propagation in Tibet.

Next, there is the Chapel of the Sages of the Six Realms (**75**, *thub pa rigs drug lha khang*), containing an image of four-armed Avalokiteśvara, flanked by the six sages. These comprise: Munīndra, sage of the god realms who holds a lute, Vemacitra, sage of the antigods, who holds a sword an shield, Śākyamuni, sage of humans who holds a alms' bowl, Śākyasiṃha, sage of animals who holds a alms' bowl full of nectar, Jvālamukha, sage of the tormented spirits who holds a jewel, and Yama Dharmarāja, sage of the hells who holds fire and water.[185] All these images are newly sculpted, as are the internal murals depicting Amitāyus in red on a cream background.

Chapels of the North-west Corner

The pilgrim will then reach a closed staircase (**76**), leading up to the top storey of the Śrīdevī Turret. Beyond it in the gallery there is a wall panel depicting Tsongkhapa, with miniature images of Padmākara and White Tārā above the shoulders. The last east-facing Chapel of the Seven Patriarchs (**77**, *nyan thos gtad rabs bdun*) once contained

King Songtsen Gampo (no. **74**). (1996 US)

Chapel of the Sages of the Six Realms (no. **75**). (2000 GD)

Chapel of the Seven Patriarchs (no. **77**). (2000 GD)

The wine flask of King Songtsen Gampo (no. **74**). (2000 GD)

a central image of Kāśyapa, flanked by Ānanda, Śāṇavāsika, Upagupta, Dhītika, Kṛṣṇa, and Sudarśana, who collectively formed the original succession of the Buddhist monastic order in ancient India. These images have been restored, and the internal murals also depict Amitāyus, executed in red line on a gold background.

Just outside, there were several large maṇi wheels (**78**), one of which has now been restored. Ten nuns from each of the main nunneries near Lhasa: Nelchungri, Garu Gon, Tshangkhung and so forth, would come in rotation to turn these wheels and perform prostrations, intoning the *Eulogy to the Twenty-one Tārās.*

The regent Sangye Gyatso. (2000 GD)

Chapels of the North Wing

Heading along the north wing of the middle storey, the pilgrim will pass three successive south-facing chapels, which were originally dedicated to yakṣa and yakṣiṇī protectors,[186] but in more recent centuries functioned as libraries and storerooms. Two of them formed the Kungarawa, and were once completely filled with woodblocks (**84**) and old manuscripts of the *Kangyur and Tengyur* (**83**). Now they contain no books since the volumes were all destroyed during the Cultural Revolution. Instead the first of these chapels houses various new images that have been presented to the Great Temple by private individuals, including the Three Deities of Longevity. Padmākara, Tārā, Mañjughoṣa and Mahākāruṇika. The second has a number of small old images that did survive the Cultural Revolution. The third (**82**) was formerly a residence of Lama Zhang Yudrakpa, and now contains finely sculpted images of Amitābha, Avalokiteśvara, and Padmākara. The seventh century frescoes of the north wing were copied and removed for restoration during the 1980s, and were replaced in the late 1990s.[187] They now depict narrative scenes illustrating early Tibetan history and the temples and palaces constructed by the early kings.

New murals of the north wing. (2000 GD)

Chapels of the North-east Corner and East Wing

Continuing into the northeast corner of the middle storey, there is a west-facing chapel, known as the Hermitage of Tsongkhapa (**81**, *rje'i zim sbug*).[188] It formerly contained images of Tsongkhapa, Hayagrīva in the form Tamdrin Yangsang, and Vajrabhairava in the form Rapelma. The last of these images was so-called because the horns of its bull-head were said to expand in size. Nowadays, the hermitage is closed, dark and empty.

Next, on the east wing, there is a chapel with a round carved wooden door that faces towards the west. This is known as the Hermitage of the Religious King (**80**, *chos rgyal zim sbug*), and it once contained the images of King Songtsen Gampo and his queens, which were sculpted during the Tshalpa era. It has undergone restoration since the late 1990s, and now contains newly sculpted images of the royal family, along with Hayagrīva and Vajrabhairava. All the original frescoes of this corner have been removed, copied and recently replaced.

Lion-faced beam-ends. (2000 GD)

Then, heading through an alcove with a north-facing door, one will reach the northern entrance to the west-facing Chapel of the Countenance (**79**, *zhal ras lha khang*),[189] Nowadays there is no access to this belvedere, which is blocked off by a wooden railing.

One thousand and twenty-eight "arrow-size" (*mda' tshad ma*) white terracotta stūpas formerly lined the skylight gallery (*mthong 'khor*) of the main hall. There were also images of the Sixteen Elders of indeterminate size, and the Four Great Guardian Kings, along with statues of Atiśa with Dromton and Ngok, Tshongpon Gelek, and Longdol Lama. Nowadays there is an impressive line of Confession Buddhas, arrayed transversely along the east wing of the skylight gallery. The beam-ends, supported by the columns which rise from the ground floor below, have carved relief images of lion faces, their noses reputedly blunted by a slipping axe[190] and there is a cornice with one hundred lion-faced figurines and a single human-faced figurine (*seng ge brgya la mi gdong gcig*).[191] These apparently date from the earliest phase of construction. Furthermore, there were also many bronze moulds for casting stūpas and small votive stūpas kept on this gallery, which offers excellent views of the images in the Main Hall below and of the skylight above.

Mani wheel of the north-west corner (no. **78**). (2000 GD)

The Śrīdevī Turret and Chapels of the Top Floor

The Śrīdevī Turret (*dpal lha lcog*) on the top floor of the Great Temple can be approached from a staircase on the northwest corner, which is generally kept closed, or from the main stone staircase on the southeast corner, which was once regarded as a rear entrance. The present description assumes that the pilgrim will reach the third floor via the northwest staircase. Passing through the east-facing door (**76**) adjacent to the Chapel of the Six Sages (**75**, *rigs drug lha khang*) on the middle storey, the pilgrim will ascend a wide wooden staircase which leads to the turret.

Chapel of the North-west Corner

Turning left and walking in a clockwise direction from the top of the stairs, there is the south-facing Chapel of the Eight Medicine Buddhas (**85**, *sman bla bde gshegs brgyad kyi lha khang*). This once contained silver images of the Eight Medicine Buddhas, which were commissioned to fulfil the dying wishes of Gushi Qan, as well as a human-size silver image of Vajrapāṇi, and two gilded copper statues of unidentified spiritual teachers.

Chapels of the North Wing

Walking along the north wing of the upper gallery, the pilgrim will then reach the south-facing Chapel of the Conqueror Śākyamuni (**86**, *rgyal ba shāk ya thub pa'i lha khang*), which was built by Tashi, a senior sacristan from the Tshalpa era. Flanking the central image were the seven other buddhas of medicine (*sman bla bde gshegs mched bdun*), surrounded by bodhisattvas and Vaiśravaṇa, chief of the sylvan spirits. There were also images of the protector Tha-ok Chokyong – an aspect of Pehar,commissioned during the time of the second regent of Tsemonling, and of wrathful Śrīdevī (*dpal lha drag mo*), which was of later construction.

During the recent restoration of the Śrīdevī Turret, a single extant folio of a gold-inscribed manuscript version of the *Kangyur,* which had originally been brought from China and had formerly been stored in the Chapel of the Śrīdevī Turret, was kept temporarily in this chapel. The folio, which was difficult to read, was inscribed with white gold lettering on extremely long Tibetan paper and it had a page reference label (*kha byang*) inscribed in Chinese script.[192]

Next, there is the south-facing Chapel of Śākyamuni and his Retainers (**87**, *ston pa gtso 'khor gsum*), who include Śāriputra and Maudgalyāyana, flanked by the eight main bodhisattvas (*nye sras brgyad*).

Beyond that, there is a sealed south-facing doorway (**88**) which formerly led to a connecting ramp which, since the time of the Eleventh Dalai Lama Khedrub Gyatso and Ngawang Jampal, the second regent of Tshemonling, had given access to the rooftop kitchen (*rtse mo'i rung khang*) and the public toilet facilities in the annex. The ramp no longer exists and the rooms of the annex beyond are now monastic quarters.[193] Bypassing that doorway, one will come to a south-facing chapel which once contained silver stūpas symbolising the eight deeds of the Buddha (**89**, *bde gshegs brgyad kyi mchod rten*) and gilded copper images of the Sixteen Elders. All the chapels of this wing are now empty and currently contain no objects of veneration.

Chapels of the North-east Corner and East Wing

Reaching the east wing of the top storey, the pilgrim will first approach the west-facing Chapel of the Great Sage (**90**, *thub chen lha khang*),[194] which once contained an image of Mahāmuni flanked by Śāriputra, Maudgalyāyana, the eight main bodhisattvas, and the two wrathful gatekeepers. Next to it, there is a chapel with a west-facing double gate, located directly above the head of Jowo Śākyamuni (**91**, *Jo bo'i dbu thod lha khang*), which acts as a conduit for the smoke from the butter lamps below. Originally, during the lifetime of King Songtsen Gampo it housed the images of Maitreya in the Gesture of Teaching the Sacred Doctrine (*byams pa chos 'khor*), replicas of which can still be seen on the ground floor.[195] Later, when Princess Jincheng had the rediscovered Jowo Śākyamuni image installed in the Central Inner Sanctum, the aforementioned image of Acala, which had been on the central plinth since the time of King Songste Gampo's grandson, was placed directly

Approach to the Chapel of the Śrīdevī Turret (no. **93**). (1991 AA)

Ceiling panel. (1991 AA)

behind the Jowo[196] The other images forming Acala's retinue (*mi 'khrug gtso 'khor*) remained in their original locations until the eleventh century when Zangkar Lotsāwa moved them into this chapel on the top floor at the time when he enlarged the Central Inner Sanctum. Later, images of the Five Buddhas (*rgyal ba rigs lnga*) commissioned by Wangtson, the chief minister (*dpon chen*) of Sakya, were also installed in this upper chapel. None of these images have survived, but the chapel does contain faded murals and many small original statues that were offered by the people and stored here after the Cultural Revolution.

Next, there is a turret-like office (**92**, *las shag dang gnyer tshang*), used by the sacristans of the top floor. It housed the wicker baskets containing the sacraments of Śrīdevī, and a clay "toad-flask"[197] which was used as a container for consecrated wine. The first fruits of the old and recent wine offerings, that had been offered to the peaceful and wrathful aspects of the protectress Śrīdevī (*dpal lha zhi drag*), were also kept here. Nowadays these rooms remain empty and unused.

Chapel of Śrīdevī (no. **96**). (1994 HMS)

Chapels of the South-east Corner and South Wing

Bypassing that office, the pilgrim now reaches a north-facing assembly hall with a skylight window (**93**, *'du khang seng gYab can*), also known as the "Chapel of the Śrīdevī Turret" (*dpal lha lcog gi lha khang*). Here, feast-offerings would be held when monks from Meru Dratshang visited the turret. On its interior wall there was a natural relief image of the protector Brahmā Śaṅkapāla (**94**), revered as a "speaking image", as well as a natural relief image of Hayagrīva. These have not survived, nor has the aforementioned gold-inscribed manuscript version of the Kangyur, which was once housed here. Nowadays the interior murals, executed in white, red and gold on black background, depict Śrīdevī, Mahākala, and Bhairava, while those of the external walls depict Six-armed Mahākala, the Fifth Dalai Lama, Sangye Gyatso, and Gushi Qan, with Rematī, Śrīdevī, and the twelve mountain goddesses (*brtan ma bcu gnyis*).

In the southeast corner of this room, there is a west-facing doorway finely carved in Newāri style (**95**) – its surrounding lintels bearing a Newāri inscription which lists the gilded copper lion-headed figurines (*tsi par/tsipata*), ornate swags, and *gañjira* spire which had been donated by the Newār business community of Lhasa. Passing through that door, which is surmounted on the roof above by a gilded-copper victory banner,[198] the pilgrim will descend a flight of steps to reach the Chapel of Śrīdevī (**96** ,*dpal ldan lha mo dung skyong ma'i lha khang*). Here, there is the sacred peaceful image of the protectress Śrīdevī – the sole mother, which is known [on occasions] to assume wrathful, alluring and resplendent demeanours and which contains within it a painting of the face of Śrīdevī, drawn with the nasal blood of King Songtsen Gampo.[199] This image, imbued with a radiance arising from the consecration of actual pristine cognition, was fashioned by the Fourth Tulku Godru, a skilled clay sculptor, around the time of *Tshalpa Tripon* Ga-de Zangpo, who was himself regarded as an emanation of the protector Gonpo Jarok. The present image is a replica, and people say that its facial expression has actually been enhanced following the restoration.

Chapel of Frog-faced Remati (no. **97**). (1994 HMS)

A recess in the north wall of this chapel gives access to an interior chamber, known as the Chapel of Frog-faced Śrīdevī (**97**, *dpal lha sbal gdong ma'i lha khang*). This contains an exquisite natural black stone image of the head of Rematī with the face of a frog (**97**), which had been extracted as treasure by Zhang Yudrakpa from the area nearby Jakhar Rock at Gungtang. The lower part of the image is stuffed. According to one tradition, the head had assumed the ugly shape of a frog in retribution for him having infringed a maternal injunction. This image appears to have survived the Cultural Revolution when its head was reputedly turned into a plaything for the children of the Barkor, and the body has been restuffed.

Formerly, four monks from Meru Dratshang would offer libations (*ljags skyems*) and conduct the rituals in the presence of these peaceful and wrathful images of Śrīdevī, and there was a single sacristan of the top floor, responsible for managing and supervising the upper and lower chapels of the turret. A strong odour of wine used to permeate these chapels where crowds of people would offer libations to the peaceful and wrathful images of Śrīdevī, and there were thousands of rats swarming around the mounds of grain that had been offered.[200] This phenomenon was once attributed to the broken commitments of the wrathful Śrīdevī; however, the rats have long since disappeared.

During the Great Prayer Festival and also on the great anniversaries of the Buddha's deeds, all the monastic and lay officials, headed by the Dalai Lama and his regent (*skyabs mgon mchod yon*), would attend the incense offering to Śrīdevī (*dpal lha gzab gsol*). At that time, the officials would don their ancient Tibetan military regalia – metal helmets, horned helmets, and armour, and file through the skylight gallery (*mthong 'khor*) of the top floor below the gilded roofs, chanting paeans in eulogy of the leader of the Dralha (*dgra lha*).

Each year from the thirteenth day of the tenth lunar month, the stuffed image of wrathful Śrīdevī would be escorted to the gallery in front of the turret, where ablutions would be performed.[201] Then, on the fourteenth day of that month *torma* offerings indicative of spiritual accomplishment were distributed to the people of Lhasa, and, in the ceremony called *dPal lha ri khrod*,[202] which re-enacts the circumambulation of Mt Sumeru by Śrīdevī, the image would be carried around the skylight gallery of the top floor. Then, on the fifteenth day the monks of Meru Dratshang would assemble and perform a *torma* exorcism rite, in which the torma for averting misfortune were deposited in the four directions of the city of Lhasa. The monks would then escort the wrathful image of Śrīdevī on the Barkor Jangchub Jonlam. Although the elaborate rites of the *dPal lha ri khrod* ceremony are not presently observed, the face of the image is still only cleansed once a year, at this point in the calendar.

On that occasion and whenever incense was offered to Śrīdevī, a group of finely dressed ladies known as Pelsolma (*dpal gsol ma*) would come to make offerings to the peaceful and wrathful images of Śrīdevī, and perform the rites of reparation and confession, intoning their prayers in a sweet melody. Formerly, the group would comprise the wives of ministers, military officers and the aristocrats, but in more recent times the nobility were represented by twenty beautiful young girls wearing pearl head-dresses, blouses, shawls and other ancient ornaments. This was a most noble and pleasing tradition.

Continuing along the south wing of the top storey, adjacent to a back door that leads into the aforementioned Chapel of the Śrīdevī Turret, there is the north-facing Chapel of the Spiritual Teacher (**98**, *bla ma lha khang*). It once contained images of Atiśa flanked by his foremost students, and the past incarnations of the First Dalai Lama Gendundrub, as well as a sandalwood model of the Jarung Khashor Stūpa in Nepal. In a box alongside the stūpa there was an extraordinary copy of the *Aṣṭasāhasrikāprajñāpāramitā*, inlaid with conch (*dung bdar bsgrigs*).

Next, there is the Chapel of the Three-dimensional Maṇḍalas (**99**, *blos blangs khang*), housing exquisitely crafted white sandalwood celestial palaces (*vimāna*) of the foremost meditational deities: Guhyasamāja, Cakrasaṃvara and Vajrabhairava. The materials were provided by Miwang Pholha Sonam Tobgye in 1732 (water mouse year of the twelfth cycle), and the faces of the deities were then sculpted by Zhok Donyo Khedrub and Phurchok Ngawang Jampa. Unfortunately neither of these chapels is functioning at the present time, but the latter does have newly sculpted images of the Thousand Buddhas.

Mural of Vajrasattva (p. 86). (1996 AA)

Chapels of the South-west Corner and West Wing

Reaching the southwest corner of the top floor, the pilgrim enters the east-facing Chapel of the Nine Aspects of Amitāyus (**100**, *tshe dpag lha dgu*), which formerly contained a three-dimensional maṇḍala and silver cast images of all the nine aspects of Amitāyus. These had been commissioned in 1756 (fire mouse year) by the Seventh Dalai Lama Kelzang Gyatso.

Next, there is the large east-facing Chapel of the Sixteen Elders (**101**, *gnas bcu lha khang*), also known as the "auspicious myriad gate chapel" (*bkra shis khri sgo*). It contained clay images of Śākyamuni Buddha, flanked by the Sixteen Elders, the layman Dharmapāla and the monk Ho-shang, each of them located in a distinctive bas relief grotto. These images had been commissioned much earlier by *dpon chen* Wangchuk Tsondru during the Sakya overlordship of Tibet (1253-1358), and were based on two models: one housed in the Imperial Palace of Dadu (modern Beijing) and another which had been brought to Yerpa by Lu-me and Drom Chungwa.

At the centre of this chapel there was a three-dimensional maṇḍala depicting the buddhas of medicine, and there were murals painted by Chinese artists, illustrating the acts which the bodhisattva Maṇibhadra performed on behalf of his spiritual teachers, including Mañjuśrīghoṣa and Maitreya, as well as the cosmic array of sentient beings described in the *Avataṃsakasūtra*. The chapel also contained other extraordinary murals and engravings, including the lineage of the Sakyapa school and the royal line of the Dzungar Mongols, while the walls of its vestibule depicted Vaiśravaṇa in the form Nam-se Trinsebma and the Four Great Guardian Kings (*rgyal chen bzhi*). However, these chapels are completely empty at the present day.

To the left of this last chapel, a double staircase (**102**) leads up to the lower gallery (*mda' yab 'og ma*) of the Great Courtyard and the Palace Treasury (*bla brang phyag mdzod*) in the annex. Behind it, another staircase (**103**) leads directly up to the gilded roofs of the Great Temple. There are newly painted murals adjacent to these recently refurbished staircases.

Monks in ceremonial dress in the Main Hall (p. 77, no. **55**). (2000 GD)

The Atrium and the Murals of the Top Gallery

At the centre of the open-roofed Śrīdevī Turret, there is the restored skylight window of the main hall, covered with wire netting (**104**). On the roof, above the capitals of the long columns which support the central atrium of the Main Hall, there is a platform where the residents of Lhasa would hoist prayer flags (**105**, *dar lcog 'dzugs yul*), and an incense burner (**106**). An east-facing staircase (**107**) also leads up to the gilded roofs from here.

As for the murals of the top gallery (*'khyams 'khor*), the south wall, beyond the entrance to the Chapel of the Śrīdevī Turret, depicts Six-armed Mahākāla, surrounded by Śrīdevī and four sylvan mountain spirits (*gnod sbyin*), followed by the Fifth Dalai Lama, Sangye Gyatso and Gushi Qan; and then by Śrīdevī in the form "protectress of the three levels of existence" (*dpal ldan srid gsum*), flanked by the two protectors called Dagmo Khordongchen and the twelve mountain goddesses (*brtan ma bcu gnyis*). Alongside this last mural, there was a "crooked pillar" (**108**, *spyan log gis 'chus pa'i ka ba*), which is said to have derived its shape when glanced at by an unidentified spiritual master, but it has now been replaced by a nondescript column. The western extremity of this south wall is covered with murals of the Buddha, drawn in black on a gold background.

The walls of the west wing depict Sukhāvatī Buddhafield, surrounded by images of Amitāyus, drawn in black on a soft tinted copper base. The walls of the north wing depict the Yulokopa buddhafield surrounded by images of Green Tārā, drawn in black on a soft green-tinted silver base. The walls of the east wing depict the Potālaka buddhafield, surrounded by images of Vajrasattva, drawn in black on a soft silver base. Lastly, beside the door of the turret, there are multicoloured paintings of the sacraments representing the peaceful and wrathful forms of Śrīdevī. Despite the recent restoration of these murals, many of them have four or five layers of paint, and the lower layers have yet to be inspected.

Monks assembled in the Main Hall before the image of Lhazang Maitreya (p. 77, no. **36**). (1994 HS)

The Gilded Roofs of the Great Temple

Ascending the aforementioned east-facing staircase (**107**) adjacent to the Chapel of the Śrīdevī Turret, the pilgrim will reach the flat rooftop of the Great Temple, where there are four gilded Chinese-style roofs (*rgya phibs*) and four corner chapels or turrets (*lcog*).

The Four Gilded Roofs

The bright sunlit roofs present a great contrast to the dark smoke-filled chapels of the Great Temple's interior. Among them, the largest gilded roof to the east surmounts the Chapel of Jowo Śākyamuni (**109**, *jo bo'i rgya phibs*). This was donated during the 14th century by Tewmul, the son of Anantamul, king of Yartse, who is regarded as a descendant of King Songtsen Gampo.[203] The gilded roof to the south surmounts the head of the Four Sibling Maitreya images (**110**, *byams pa rgya phibs*). Its golden lustre is tarnished, reputedly because it had originally been erected on the palace roof of King Gocha and then buried underground for a long period.[204] Old people say that its shape would change on account of long-term rusting. Later it was restored by the Tibetan Government (Ganden Phodrang) and repositioned above the Chapel of the Four Sibling Maitreyas. The gilded roof to the west was donated by the Tibetan government during the lifetime of the Fifth Dalai Lama, and positioned above the chapel containing the likeness of King Songtsen Gampo (**111**, *chos rgyal rgya phibs*). Lastly, the gilded roof to the north is located above the Chapel of Mahākāruṇika in the form Rangjon Ngaden (**112**, *thujs rje rgya phibs*). It was donated in the late 14th century by Pratimul, the son of king Punimul of Yartse and his minister Palden Drakpa.[205]

The Four Turrets

Within the south-eastern turret (**113**, *shar lho'i lcog*), also known as the Chapel of the Wrathful Mother Śrīdevī (*dpal lha yum drag mo'i lha khang*), there is a mask and stuffed image of Rematī, the wrathful aspect of Śrīdevī, which is said to have been made by the hand of the Fifth Dalai Lama. To its left there is a costume which was once worn by Lhalung Palgyi Dorje, who assassinated and "liberated" the apostate king Langdarma in the Wood Enclosure.[206] To the right of Rematī, there was a remarkable wooden protuberance shaped like a rhino horn, which had emerged naturally through a crack in the plaster underneath a *torma* offering box, and it was daubed with powdered gold.[207] A chilling wind emerged from a crack in the east wall of that chapel, invariably exuding a putrefying odour, which was said to have resembled the breath of a dying person. The sacristans of this corner chapel, those of the Protector Chapel of Śrīdevī below, and those of the rooftops all formerly belonged to Meru Dratshang.

Alongside the door of that chapel, there is a small prayer flag (**114**, *dar chen chung chung*), which was reputedly "hoisted at the time of good tidings" (*gtam snyan dar 'phyar*) by the regent Sonam Chopel when Donyo, the Bonpo king of Beri in Kham was slain by Gushi Qan during the 17th century. The chapel has been renovated since 1992, and is now open for rites of reparation and confession, though the small prayer flag outside the door no longer stands.

Inside the southwestern turret (**115**, *nub lho'i lcog*), there are the images and thread-crosses of the protectresses known as the Five Sisters of Longlife (*tshe ring mched lnga*). Among them, the image of Tashi Tsheringma was constructed during the lifetime of the Twelfth Dalai Lama to secure the well being of Tibet and Kham in accordance with a prophetic treasure of Chokgyur Dechen Zhigpo Lingpa.[208] The images of the other four protectresses of this group, namely Thing-gi Zhelzangma, Miyo Lobzangma, Chopen Drinzangma, and Tekar Drozangma, were constructed later. Formerly, five monks from Tshurphu Monastery would perform the continuous rites of reparation and confession in this corner chapel; but the images installed here now are all modern replicas.

Inside the north-western turret (**116**, *nub byang gi lcog*), there were vases containing charms which control the mundane gods (*lha bum*), serpentine water spirits (*klu bum*), and the sacred essence of the earth (*sa bcud bum pa*), and a stationery storeroom belonging to the Palace Treasury (*bla brang phyag mdzod*). Later, in accordance with the advice of the present Fourteenth Dalai Lama, the gilded copper images of the spiritual teachers of the graduated path (*lam rim*) were removed from the Śrīdevī Turret and installed here.

The roof-top motif of the Dharma Wheel flanked by a stag and doe (p. 88). (2009 LG)

Gilded copper parapet (p. 88). (2009 LG)

Roof-top view. (2009 LG)

Inside the north-eastern turret (**117**, *shar byang gi lcog*), which is also known as the Chapel of the Sixteen Elders (*gnas bcu lha khang*), there was once an exquisite set of the Sixteen Elders in their grottoes (*gnas bcu brag ri ma*), fashioned of medicinal clay. During the Great Congregation (*tshogs mchod chen mo*) when the supervisor of the offering-sacraments would take up residence in the rooftop Accounting Room (*rtsis khang*),[209] board meetings of the accounts chamber would be held in this corner chapel for the duration of the festival, while the archivists and assistant accountants would take up temporary residence in the area immediately below the eastern gilded-roof of the Central Inner Sanctum (i.e. the actual Jokhang). Neither the northwestern nor the northeastern turret has yet been restored.

Gilded roof of the Palace. (2009 LG)

The Roof Ornaments

Rising above these turrets of the four corners, the roof is embellished by a gilded copper spire (*gañjira*), victory banners (*dvaja*), and yak-tail poles (*rnga thugs*).[210] Ornamental bells are suspended from the gilded roofs in the four cardinal directions, encircling them on all sides. These bells are marked with the seed-syllables of the five enlightened families, and their flat copper rims are engraved with verses from the *Ratnāvalī* and the *Bodhisattvacaryāvatāra*, aspirational prayers for enlightenment and entering the path of the conquerors, as well as wish-granting prayers, verses of good auspices, and retentive mantras (*dhāraṇī*) including the *Heart Mantra of Dependent Origination*. Living creatures are roused from the sleep of fundamental ignorance and encouraged to practice the sacred doctrine by the pleasant tinkling of the bells as they sway gently in the wind.

Gilded roof of the Central Inner Sanctum (p. 87, no. **109**). (1991 US)

The Railing and Parapet

A gilded copper railing (*sgrom skyor*) completely surrounds the roof, and each of its four sides is emblazoned by a thousand-spoked golden wheel flanked by a stag and a doe who gaze intently at the wheel, freely relishing the nectar of the Buddha's sacred doctrine. *Cīvaṃcīvaka* figurines that have a human torso and bird wings, holding various musical instruments in their hands, also embellish the corners.

The original slate parapet (*rdza'i mda'gYab*) which runs around all four walls is said to have been constructed by *Lharje* Gewabum, or another *Tshalpa Tripon*, and replaced during the lifetime of the Fifth Dalai Lama by one of gilded copper. Subsequently, the regent Sangye Gyatso, under the pretext of performing virtuous acts to secure the long life of the recently deceased Dalai Lama, had the lotus-shaped gutters (*chu skyor*) forming the top rim of the gilded copper parapet inscribed with mantras of retention in Rañjanā script, wish-granting prayers, and benedictions. The rim below that was adorned with a band of ornate swags, suspended from the mouths of lion-faced figurines, and the rim below that was encircled with a band of finely crafted bas relief images, slightly larger than "arrow-size". These depicted various mundane and supramundane deities including the Buddhas of the Three Times, the Eight Medicine Buddhas, the Thirty-five Confession Buddhas, and various meditational deities (Guhyasamāja, Cakrasaṃvara, Vajrabhairava, Hevajra, Kālacakra, Khecarī, Sarvavidvairocana, Vairocana, and Vajrasattva), along with the eight main bodhisattvas, Tārā who protects from the eight fears, the Sixteen Elders, the six ornaments and two supreme masters of Ancient India, the eight manifestations and twenty-five disciples of Padmasambhava, the eighty-four accomplished masters of Ancient India, Atiśa flanked by Dromton and Ngok, the five founders of Sakya, Marpa flanked by Milarepa and Dakpo Lharje, Tsongkhapa flanked by his two foremost students, and the successive incarnations of the Dalai Lamas.

Completing this band were the protector deities Mahākāla, Śrīdevī, the Five Sisters of Longlife and the Four Great Guardian Kings. Other protector deities were also depicted in the cardinal and intermediate directions of this band: the four-faced Brahmā riding a swan, Rudra riding a garuḍa, Ṣaḍānana with six faces, Gaṇapati riding a mouse, Indra riding an elephant, Agni riding a goat, Vāyu riding a deer, Sūrya steering a chariot pulled by seven horses, Candra riding a chariot pulled by deer, Vaiśravaṇa, god of wealth, riding a lion, Jambhala riding a dragon, Jagala riding a vulture, Yama riding a buffalo, a serpentine water spirit with the body of a man and the tail of a snake, and finally the ten-headed Rāvaṇa. Underneath this frieze of relief images, each corner of the gilded copper parapet was adorned with a crocodile gargoyle (*makara*), their mouths continuously spouting water as a harbinger of non-virtuous times to come.

Decorative spires and cīvaṃcīvaka figures on the roof (p. 88). (1991 US)

The External Walls

The surfaces of the white walls below the parapet were adorned with gilded copper motifs some of which represented good auspices and others the aversion of negativity. These included the Four Great Guardian Kings, the ten powerful aspects embodied in the seed-syllable of the *Kālacakra Tantra (rnam bcu dbang ldan)*, the seven symbols of royal dominion (*rgyal srid sna bdun*), the eight auspicious symbols (*bkra shis rtags brgyad*), and the four directional animals, viz. tiger, lion, garuḍa and dragon.

At each corner of the red potentilla frieze below the parapet there was a ferocious gilded copper lion with a turquoise mane, about the size of wild yak. Devout pilgrims believed that sometimes, as a harbinger of inauspicious times, the mane would shake, and on other occasions the eyes would open and the fangs become exposed.[211]

The Internal Walls of the Rooftop

Below the parapet and the lotus-engraved beams (*padma chos brtsegs*), all four inner walls of the rooftop were covered with a magnificent series of murals depicting one thousand images of Amitāyurjñāna, executed in unheated gold on a vermilion base – vibrant, lustrous and radiant. These have now been restored.

After finally circumambulating the chapels and turrets of the rooftop, the pilgrim will then descend to the ground floor via the staircase at the northwest corner, and leave the Main Hall through the vestibule and the Great Acacia Gate.

Gilded Victory Banner on the roof of the Great Temple (p. 88). (2009 LG)

Incense offerings on the roof of the Great Temple. (1986 CB)

The Ground Floor Annex

Exiting through the Great Acacia Gate, the pilgrim will reach the Great Courtyard (*khyams ra chen mo*) of the Great Temple. The gate itself is ornamented with Derge crafted metalwork and surrounded by murals depicting Maitreya (left), Tsongkhapa (above), and Dīpaṃkara (right). The Great Courtyard takes the form of an open roofed atrium supported by eight long pillars and one hundred short pillars. Extending east from the courtyard, there is the inner walkway (*nang 'khor*), traditionally known as the "intermediate walkway" (*bar 'khor*), through which pilgrims circumambulate the Great Temple.

The Flagstone Patio

The area just below and in front of the entrance portico (*khyams ra'i sgo 'phyor*) of the Great Acacia Gate has a flagstone patio (*rdo gcal*) formed of forty-one natural paving stones, particularly fine in shape and colour. One tradition recounts that these were extracted from a large boulder, incapable of being transported by human hand, which had been shackled and dragged there by the legendary Tibetan potentate Ponpo Wang. King Songtsen decreed that the boulder should be left there for the construction of the patio. Among the flagstones, there is a large fossilised stone, known as Amolongkha (**121**).[212] An adjacent flagstone bears a footprint of the Thirteenth Dalai Lama (**122**), and this was enclosed within a wooden frame with a cover resembling a Chinese-style roof. The lustrous agate-like Amolongkha stone is still extant, while the footprint is nowadays covered by a metal case. A metal security gate nowadays restricts unauthorised access to the entrance portico and the Main Hall beyond.

Alongside the flagstones nearest to the South Gate (*lho sgo*) of the Great Temple, there were four fist-sized rocks (**123**), which Tsangnyon Heruka Sangye Gyaltsen and Unyon Kunga Zangpo are said to have deposited there in jest. The two accomplished masters then took turns at throwing stones until a stone thrown by Tsangnyon became embedded in a column (**124**) alongside the Dolma Lhakhang, and another thrown by Unyon became embedded in a column (**125**) adjacent to the butter storeroom (*mar khang*). Only the stone adjacent to the Dolma Lhakhang survived the Cultural Revolution intact, but the authorities recently substituted it, wary of the veneration it had received. The stone reputedly thrown by Unyon has also popularly been attributed to another master, named Logu, who hailed from Amdo.

The Main West Gate (p. 95, no. **197**). (1991 US)

The Great Courtyard

The Great Courtyard (**126**, *khyams ra chen mo*) which measures 1,248 square metres was constructed during the time of Tsongkhapa for the holding of the first Great Prayer Festival in 1409. Within it, the monks of the monastic community would later take their seats to perform "thousandfold offering rites" (*stong mchod*) during special government ceremonies, as well as on the fifteenth, thirtieth and eighth days of the lunar month, and at important anniversaries (*dus chen*). These monks included a group who would invariably sit within a screen-covered alcove in the northwest of the courtyard, making the "daily offerings of the courtyard" (**127**, *khyams rva rgyun mchod pa'i bzhugs sa*).[213] Once a year, during the fourth lunar month (*sa ga zla ba*), a screen would also be drawn across the south-west corner of the courtyard, and monks from the Ngakpa College at Drepung would install themselves there, performing the means for attainment and offering rites associated with Bhaiṣajyaguru.

Above all, once a year during the Great Prayer Festival (*smon lam chen mo*) and during the Great Congregation (*tshogs mched chen mo*), more than twenty thousand monks from Drepung, Sera and Ganden would assemble there, completely filling the courtyard and the inner circumambulatory walkway to its east, south and north, as well as Wood Enclosure (*shing rva*) to the south-west, and the Lower Gallery (*mda'gYab 'og*) above. Traditionally, monks from Sera would be seated to the north, those from Drepung in the centre, and those from Ganden in the south.

Wealthy benefactors, headed by officials of the Tibetan government (*Ganden Phodrang*), would amass great acts of merit, presenting "cloud-like" offerings to the Jowo images of the Great Temple and Ramoche. At such times, the assembled monks would be venerated with offerings of communal soup (*mang thug*), barley flour (*tsha gra*), and

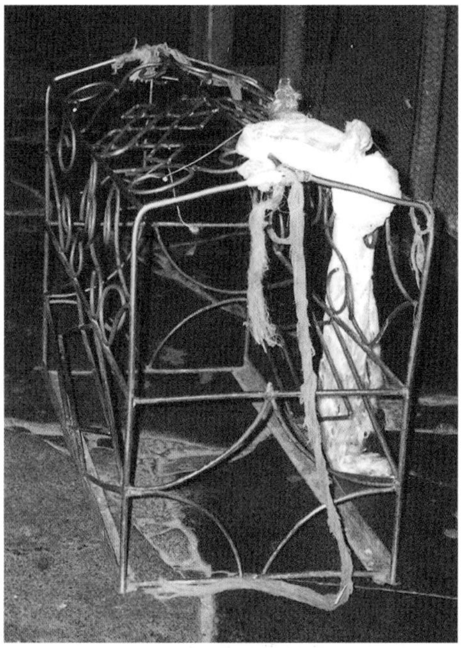

Protected footprint of the 13th Dalai Lama (no. **122**). (2000 GD)

money (*sku 'gyed*), enabling them to make aspirational prayers for the flourishing of the Buddhist teaching and for the happiness of all sentient beings. In addition, communal meals, money and other alms would also be offered to many thousands of senior citizens, disabled persons, including those who were paralysed, blind and crippled, and to the destitute, providing them with the leisure and favourable conditions required for Buddhist practice.

It was in this manifestly peaceful location that six or seven incidents occurred during the Cultural Revolution. On one occasion, sixty-one young Tibetan men and girls were killed. Thereafter a slaughterhouse for pigs was set up in the Great Courtyard, and a new well was constructed as a trough.[214]

Currently the pillars that support the Great Courtyard are being strengthened, and further renovations of the historically important murals, here and in the inner walkway, are anticipated.

Monks and devotees in the Great Courtyard adjacent to the Great Acacia Gate (p. 90, no. **126**). (1999 HS)

Chapels of the North Wing of the Great Courtyard

A doorway to the right of the alcove where daily offerings were once performed in the Great Courtyard leads into the Chapel of the Three Approaches to Liberation (**128**, *rnam thar sgo gsum gyi lha khang*). Here there were central images of the Buddhas of the Three Times, flanked by the eight main bodhisattvas, and the gatekeepers Hayagrīva and Vajrapāṇi. These had all been commissioned to fulfil the dying wishes of Emperor Yongle (*da yan rgyal po*). The chapel also contains a staircase by which the Dalai Lama would descend from his private apartments on the top floor of the annex to preside over the Great Prayer Festival and the Great Congregation, and through which he would pass on other important ceremonial occasions.

Within this chapel, there is a west-facing storeroom which also functioned as the Main Tea Room (**129**, *ja khang chen mo*) of the Palace Treasurer (*bla brang phyag mdzod*). Opposite it, there was an east-facing storeroom, known as the West Tea Room (**130**, *ja khang nub ma*). These rooms and the chapel from which they are accessed are now used exclusively for storage.

Just beyond the door, on the north side of the Great Courtyard, there is a cross-shaped stone platform (**131**) on which the great throne (*bzhugs khri chen mo*) of the Dalai Lama would be raised during the Great Prayer Festival and other ceremonial occasions. The stone platform still exists, and in recent times was used as a throne by the late Tenth Paṇchen Lama when he visited the Great Temple. On either side, there are smaller clay platforms where the venerable heads of Shartse and Jangtse colleges of Ganden would sit, as well as the acting and retired preceptors of the three great monasteries, and their Lharampa and Tshogrampa scholars (*dge bshes*). Alongside a pillar in front of the Dalai Lama's throne, there is a smaller clay platform (**132**) where the chant-master of the Great Assembly Hall of Drepung (*'bras spungs tshogs chen*) would sit during these ceremonies. All these smaller platforms have been removed.

Heading towards the inner circumambulatory walkway, on the left, there is the east-facing entrance to the Chapel of Tārā (**133**, *sgrol ma'i lha khang*). This room contains a restored image of Tārā in the form Cintāmaṇicakra, the original of which had been constructed by Nyagnyon Sewa Rinchen, and it was flanked by images of White and Green Tārā. Behind are statues of Nyagnyon and Atiśa, while, arranged in two tiers on the west wall was a full set of the Twenty-one Tārās, which had originally been commissioned by the Seventh Dalai Lama Kelzang Gyatso. On the north wall there were images of Śāntarakṣita, Padmasambhava and King Trisong Detsen, along with Tsongkhapa and his foremost students. A long stone altar stands in front of the inner gateway. This temple has now been refurbished with new replica images, and it is actively venerated at the present time.

According to legend, there once was an accomplished master named Nyagnyon Sewa Rinchen who had been born in the Nyar-ge area of Dokham. While travelling on pilgrimage to Central Tibet, from a mountain pass in Kongpo he had a vision of Tārā who had assumed a human form. He therefore collected a sack full of earth and on reaching Lhasa, he made an image of Tārā to be installed in this chapel. However the clay he had collected was only sufficient for completing the lower part of the image, and not the upper part. He considered returning to Kongpo to bring more earth, and sat one-pointedly in meditation, at which point the upper part of the image manifested of its own accord, saying, "You should not worry about going to bring more earth. I have come here!" For this reason, the original image is reported to have imbued an extremely great blessing.[215]

Pilgrims entering the Great Courtyard. (2000 GD)

Formerly, there were some thousands of mice in this chapel, sustained by the grain offerings; and five monks from Nyag-re Khangtshang at Drepung would reside there continuously, reciting the *Rite of Tārā* (*sgrol chog*). On the surface of the wall to the right of the chapel entrance, there is a flagstone with a handprint and a footprint, which according to some were those of Nyagnyon Se Gompa himself, and according to others they belonged to either Druknyon Kun-le or Longdol Lama.

The east-facing door to the left of this chapel is the North Gate (*byang sgo*) of the Great Temple. It also gives access to the storeroom for offering planks (**134**, *mchod sprin khang*), and to a staircase (**135**) that leads up to the Lower Gallery (*mda' gYab 'og*). To the west of the staircase, there is a room where twenty monks from the Ngakpa College of Sera would perform "thousandfold offering" rites (**136**, *stong mchod bzhengs pa'i bzgugs khang*), and immediately opposite is their kitchen (**137**, *rung khang*). Nowadays these rooms and the old kitchen are only used for storage. If the pilgrim exits from this alcove through a north-facing door (**138**), he will reach the northern section of the Jangchub Jonlam in the Barkor.

Chapels of the North Wing of the Inner Walkway

The rooms on the south and north wings of the inner walkway were converted into chapels during the period of the regent Sangye Gyatso, and subsequently refurbished during the era of the Eighth Dalai Lama Jampal Gyatso and Ngawang Tshultrim, the first regent of Tshemonling, at which time their doors and window frames were also renovated.

Next to the entrance to the storeroom that houses the offering planks, there were four inter-connecting south-facing chapels, the first of which (**139**) contained images of Kurukullā and Hayagrīva in the form Tamdrin Sangdrub, the second (**140**) contained images of the thousand-armed and thousand-eyed Mahākāruṇika, the third (**141**) images of Sarvavidvairocana and Vairocanābhisambodhi; and the fourth (**142**) an exquisite silver set of stūpas symbolising the eight deeds of Śākyamuni Buddha.[216] All of these chapels remain empty at the present day.

Chapels of the East Wing of the Inner Walkway

Continuing into the east wing of the inner walkway, the pilgrim will soon reach a chapel with two west-facing entrances (**143**). It contained a set of the Sixteen Elders, commissioned by Sangye Gyatso, and another exquisite set made of sandalwood, which were positioned on a platform along the north wall of the room. This chapel was only open to the public at times when a new Senior Sacristan assumed responsibility for the supervision of the Great Temple. On such occasions the Senior Sacristan and a group of four accompanying monks from Tshemonling College would perform the daily *Homage and Offering to the Sixteen Elders (gnas brtan phyag mchod)*.

Next, there is another west-facing chapel with a double door (**144**), which once contained central images of the peaceful and wrathful aspects of Guru Padmsambhava (*gu ru zhi drag*) and the ḍākinī Siṃhavaktrā, surrounded by a thousand miniature images of Padmasambhava. These were all commissioned during the lifetime of the previous Thirteenth Dalai Lama, in accordance with a prophetic declaration of Terton Sogyal concerning the security of Tibet and Kham. Although these chapels were all empty in 1991, restoration work has subsequently been undertaken in the Chapel of the Sixteen Elders and the Chapel of the Hundred Thousand Images of Padmasambhava, which are actively venerated by visiting pilgrims.

Next, the pilgrim will reach the East Gate (**145**, *shar sgo*) of the Great Temple, also known as the "Rear Gate to Sera" (*se ra ltag sgo*) because during the Great Prayer Festival and Great Congregation (*smon tshogs*), a column of monks from Sera Thegchenling would file into the Great Temple via that rear gate. The gate has undergone reconstruction following the Cultural Revolution.

The passageway behind this gate gives access to a number of other rooms. Among them, there is the kitchen with a double north-facing entrance (**146**) where noodle soup would once be prepared for monks participating in the Great Prayer Festival and the Great Congregation. It contains four very large bronze cauldrons. Another south-facing door leads from this passageway into a hall from which five further rooms are accessed. These include an east-facing storeroom (**147**) where sacred and valuable medicines would be kept, a south-facing storeroom (**148**), another south-facing storeroom (**149**) for rice husks (*'bras sog*), and two west-facing storerooms for rice (**150**) and wooden planks (**151**). Yet another south-facing storeroom (**152**), reached directly from the passageway, was used for storing pinewood planks. Nowadays, the rear kitchen still contains its large cauldrons, but is no longer in use. The area once occupied by the storerooms (**147-152**) has been

The Rear Gate to Sera (no. **145**). (1996 AA)

completely rebuilt to a new design, with the exception of storeroom 148, which remains empty.

Opposite the last mentioned storeroom (**152**), there is a north-facing door (**154**) leading into a storeroom for communal barley (*tsha grva*) which would be shared out between the monks attending the Great Prayer Festival and the Great Congregation. This storeroom is still in use today, At the very end of the passageway, there is the east-facing King's Gate (**153**, *rgyal sgo*) through which the pilgrim can gain access to Meru Nyingba Temple[217] and the eastern sector of the Barkor Jangchub Jonlam.

If the pilgrim bypasses the East Gate, and continues circumambulating the inner walkway in a clockwise direction, he will reach a west-facing door (**155**), where a staircase leads up to the Lower Gallery (*mda'gYab 'og*) and the Accounting Room (*rtsis khang*). A back door on the left leads from here into the aforementioned kitchen where noodle soup would be made, and another on the right leads into a hallway from where a south-facing door (**156**) gives access to the assembly hall used by the colleges of Nyetang and Rato during the Great Prayer Festival and the Great Congregation. Yet another door (**157**) leads from this hallway into a narrow sunlit passageway and thence into the southern sector of the Barkor Jangchub Jonlam. However, the assembly hall and the adjacent rear doorway are now inaccessible.

Chapel of Cimāra, Middle Floor (p. 80, no. **72**). (2000 GD)

Chapels of the South Wing of the Inner Walkway

Continuing into the south wing of the inner walkway, the pilgrim will pass a north-facing door, which leads into five inter-connected chapels. The first (**158**) once contained gilded copper images of the Eight Medicine Buddhas (*sman bla bde gshegs brgyad*), the second (**159**) contained images of the Sixteen Elders, the third (**160**) contained no representative objects of buddha-body, speech and mind, and it once had a back door which formerly led to an assembly hall used by the Ngakpa College of Drepung, and through which the monks of Drepung would reach the South Gate (*lha sgo*) while performing the Great *Torma* Exorcism during the Great Prayer Festival. The fourth chapel (**161**) contained images of the lineage holders of the graduated path (*lam rim bla brgyud*); and the fifth (**162**) contained eight silver stūpas representing the eight deeds of Śākyamuni Buddha (*bde gshegs brgyad kyi mchod rten*).[218] A corner of this last chapel was also dedicated to aspects of the protector deity Mahākāla, and therefore contained images of Nagpo Korsum and Trinchol Bulmi Gonpo. All these chapels are now empty.

The Great South Gate (**164**, *lho sgo chen mo*) of the Great Temple is also sometimes known as the South Gate to Ganden (*dga'ldan lho sgo*) because a row of monks from Ganden Namgyaling would file through its outer and inner portals (*rgyal sgo*) during the Great Prayer Festival and the Great Congregation. Adjacent to the South Gate, there is a west-facing storeroom with inner and outer chambers (**163**) which belonged to the Palace Treasury (*bla brang phyag mdzod*). The Committee Room of the Tibetan Cabinet is located above the inner portal of the South Gate on the middle floor. Within the gateway itself, there is an east-facing door (**165**) and a west facing door (**166**), both of which lead into disused storerooms for communal barley dispensed during the Great Prayer Festival and the Great Congregation. During the recent renovations of the Great Courtyard, access to the Great Temple was only possible through this South Gate, where a temporary ticket office had been opened.

Winter in the Debating Courtyard (p. 95, no. **168**). (1996 LH)

The Debating Courtyard

Exiting through the outer portal of the South Gate (**167**), the pilgrim will reach the Debating Courtyard (**168**, *gsung chos rva*) and the southern section of the Barkor Jangchub Jonlam. The Debating Courtyard, renovated in 1986, contains the three-tiered stone thrones used by the Dalai Lama and the Ganden Tri Rinpoche during the Great Prayer Festival and the Great Congregation, and in front there is an enormous open flagstone courtyard where the monks receiving the teachings would be seated.[219] The annual monastic examinations for the *geshe* degree would be held here.

The north, south, and east wings of the inner walkway, starting from the storeroom that houses the offering planks (*mchod sprin khang*) and continuing as far as the South Gate (*lho sgo*), an area covered by approximately forty pillars, contain some two hundred hand-turned maṇi wheels.[220] The sound of these wheels, turned by the pilgrims who circumambulate the Great Temple, still continues to rumble like thunder.

Some of the special pillars within the Great Courtyard (*khyams ra chen mo*), the Wood Enclosure (*shing rva*), and the north, east and south wings of the inner walkway have metal buttresses. There was a bizarre custom observed during the Great Prayer Festival and the Great Congregation when young servants of the aristocracy holding thick staffs

Incense offerings. (1999 HS)

Incense offerings in the Barkor Square (p. 95). (1999 HS)

The Wood Enclosure (no. **174**). (2000 GD)

would beat two of these pillars alternately with their staffs, in view of the assembly, as a way of disciplining the monks seated within the assembly and as an ostentatious display of their own bravado.

Chapels and Storerooms of the South Wing of the Great Courtyard

Continuing the clockwise circumambulation from the South Gate, the pilgrim will reach a north-facing door on the south wing of the Great Courtyard. This leads into the Main Butter Storeroom (*mar khang chen mo*) of the Palace Treasury, which has inner and outer chambers (**169-170**). The Palace Treasury would store butter here for all the offering lamps that burn daily in the upper and lower chapels of the Great Temple. Butter would also be stored for the thousands of special butter lamps to be offered during annual festivals, and for the preparation of Tibetan tea, to be offered continuously to the monks participating in the Great Prayer Festival and the Great Congregation, The butter within the storeroom would melt during the hot summer months, leaving a small pool of melted butter (**171**) in the middle. Cleaners would scoop the melted sacraments from this pool of butter with long wooden-handled copper ladles. Because the storeroom was so large, it was most important to maintain good order, so that the old butter could be dispensed before fresh butter. These storerooms are not currently in use.

The Wood Enclosure

After this storeroom, there is a north-facing doorway (**172**) giving access to the corridor of the Wood Enclosure. This is where the main ticket office of the Great Temple is located, and it is also the main exit for visiting pilgrims. Within the corridor, a double staircase (**173**) leads up to the Great Ceremonial Assembly Hall (*e vaṃ tshogs chen*) and other private apartments on the middle floor of the annex. Opposite the double staircase there is a west-facing door (**175**) leading into a kitchen larder (*rung khang gi thab chas*) used during the Great Prayer Festival and the Great Congregation. Within it, there is another storeroom (**176**) for copper tea ladles, while on the other side of the corridor, opposite the kitchen larder, there is a south-facing storeroom (**177**) for silver tea ladles. Further along the corridor, there is a very large room with a west-facing door, known as the Storeroom of the Magistrates of Lhasa (**178**, *lha sa gnyer tshang pa*). These storerooms all remain empty at the present time, except the last mentioned, which does contain a large unused kitchen range.

Then the pilgrim will enter the Wood Enclosure (*shing rva*, **174**). This courtyard seems to have been known originally as the Death Enclosure (*shi rva*) since the apostate king Langdarma was reputedly assassinated in its vicinity by Lhalung Palgyi Dorje during the ninth century. Later, it functioned as a yard for stockpiling firewood during the Great Prayer Festival, and it was later enlarged by the Tibetan Government so that its lower and upper floors (*shing rva steng shod*) could hold congregations of monks from Drepung during the Great Prayer Festival and the Great Congregation.

To the south of the Wood Enclosure, there are two passageways (**179** and **180**) leading into a large tea kitchen (**181**) for use during the Great Prayer Festival and the Great Congregation. Within it cooking cauldrons of various sizes were once kept. During the lifetime of the Fifth Dalai Lama, two very large cauldrons were donated at the insistence of the regent Lobzang Thutob, and two further large cauldrons were donated by the regent Sangye Gyatso at the time when he introduced the annual ceremony of the Great Congregation. Later still, these turned out to be insufficient as the number of participating monks increased, and following further exhortation, during the lifetime of the Thirteenth Dalai Lama, six prefabricated iron cauldrons from India were offered for this purpose. In recent times, the passageways and kitchen have been combined into a single large room, which is no longer used as a kitchen.

A west-facing door (**182**) at the far side of this erstwhile kitchen leads into a meeting room that was once used by the stewards of the wood supply and the servants of the Great Temple's monastic proctors (*dge gYog*). To the east of the kitchen, there was a staircase (**183**) leading up to the proctors' room (*zhal ngo khang*), while alongside it the west-facing door (**184**) of the oil storeroom, and next to it the west-facing door (**185**) of a tea and butter storeroom. Both the meeting room and the staircase have been dismantled, and the storerooms for oil, tea and butter no longer function as storerooms. In fact, this whole area has been incorporated into a newly designed residential unit for monks.

A south-facing gate (**186**) at the far side of the former kitchen, known as the "water gate" (*chu sgo*), leads to the lane from which water would be transported for ceremonial gatherings and to the Sabogang area of the Barkor Jangchub Jonlam. To the west of the "water gate" is an east-facing outbuilding (**187**, *gtsug lag khang 'debs sbyar khang*) which was converted into a water storeroom (*tshogs chu gsog khang*) during the time of the Thirteenth Dalai Lama. Water was once piped here from the Kyichu River in the interests of sanitation and to avoid the problem of drawing water from the Great Temple's wells during the Great Prayer Festival and the Great Congregation. Nowadays, this water storeroom has been converted into a car park. Adjacent to the "water gate" there is an east-facing wood storeroom (**188**), and next to that an east-facing public toilet (**189**).

Then, returning to the south wing of the Wood Enclosure, there are three further north-facing rooms comprising a storeroom for communal barley (**190**), and two rooms where wooden planks would be stored by the Palace Treasury (**191**/**192**). All of these storerooms still exist today.

In front of the entrance to the barley storeroom, an east-facing staircase (**193**) gives access to the Office of the Magistrates of Lhasa (*lha gnyer las khungs*) and the monastic proctors' room (*zhal ngo khang*) on the floor above. On the west wing of the Wood Enclosure, there is the Great Victory Gate (*rgyal sgo chen mo,* **194**) which leads into the large open square to the west of the Barkor, and which nowadays serves as the main exit for visitors to the Great Temple. Finally, on the north wing, there were two south-facing rooms (**195**/**196**) where pine logs and planks were once stored by the Palace Treasury, and which have now been converted into a single room for the storage of oil and rice.

Stele inscribed with the smallpox edict (no. **200**). (1991 US)

The Main West Gate, the Outer Portal, and the Barkor Square

Returning from the Wood Enclosure to the Great Courtyard, the west wing is dominated by the Main Gate (**197**, *gzim sgo lte ba*) which is also known as the "westfacing gate of the great courtyard." A vestibule (**198**) supported by two pillars (*gzim sgo phyi nang gnyis bar*) is located between this inner gateway and the outer portal (*sgo mchor gyi gzim sgo phyi ma*). It contains images of the Four Great Guardian Kings (*rgyal po chen po bzhi*), backed by 17th and 19th century frescoes of gandharva and serpentine water spirits, along with Samantabhadra's paradise and the Four Harmonious Brethren (*mthun pa spun bzhi*). Both the Main Gate and its outer portal are generally kept locked nowadays, and access to the Great Courtyard is obtained from the Wood Enclosure. Very rarely, access may also be obtained through the side door of the Lugong effigy.[221]

Then, exiting through the outer portal (**199**), which has six fluted columns, the pilgrim will reach the western sector of the Barkor Jangchub Jonlam, formerly known after its flagpole, the Juya Darchen, and which now extends into an open square.[222] Here, there is an enclosure containing Princess Wencheng's Willow Tree stump, known as the "hair of Jowo" (**200**, *jo bo'i dbu'i skra*), and two recently planted willows. In front of the stump is the pock-marked obelisk of 1794 admonishing against smallpox, and another inscriptionless stele.

Within an adjacent enclosure to the north, there is an historically important six metre obelisk (**201**) with Chinese and Tibetan inscriptions. These refer to the Peace Treaty demarcating the border between Tibet and China which was established at a Sino-Tibetan convention held at Gugu Meru in 823 (water hare year) during the reigns of the Tibetan king Tri Relpachen and the Chinese emperor Mun-zong (Tib. *Bun bu He'u tig Hang*).

View of the obelisks and Willow-tree Enclosure in the Barkor Square (nos. **200-201**). (2000 GD)

Below the outer portal (*sgo mchor*) on the south side there is a small doorway known as the side door of the Lugong effigy (**202**, *glud 'gong gsang sgo*). Each year on the twenty-ninth day of the second lunar month a *torma* in the form of the "thread-cross of the king spirits" (*rgyal po rtsed mdos*) would be ritually expelled from the Great Temple, and the ritual scapegoat known as Lugong Gyalpo would be escorted into the street through this small doorway, along with a substitute thread-cross (*glud 'gong*).[223] Behind the side door, a staircase leads up to the Dalai Lama's Palace (*bla brang steng*) and the Prime Minister's Hall of Phenomenal Existence (*srid blon gyi gzim chung snang srid*). Below the outer portal on the north side there is an alcove known as the Maṇi Wheel Jechen Chapel (**203**). This chapel no longer has a distinct entrance but an enormous Maṇi Wheel protrudes into the area in front of the outer portal, where visiting pilgrims constantly turn it. Above, the portal is surmounted by a balcony hidden by a yak-hair curtain from which dignitaries would observe ceremonies conducted in the Great Courtyard and in the square outside.

Itinerant pilgrims and citizens of Lhasa continuously make prostrations upon the natural flagstones (**209**) in front of the outer portal of the Great Courtyard. Many of the stones have been worn down to reveal a concave impression of the human body. According to Heinrich Harrer's *Seven Years in Tibet*, there was a party of Christian missionaries who resolved to return to their homeland having seen these flagstones where the hard stone had been worn down into a concave shape by centuries of prostration,

Looking out from the Great Courtyard onto the flagstone patio where townspeople daily offer their prostrations. (1996 AA)

knowing they would be unable to propagate Christianity in a country endowed with such devout and long-standing expressions of the Buddhist faith.[224] To the south of the flagstones, there is a north-facing storeroom (**210**) where communal barley was kept. Amid the crowds who throng the entrance, there are monks and lay scribes who write in gold ink on red paper the names of deceased persons or petitioners, which are then burned by pilgrims as an offering within the Central Inner Sanctum.

The North-west Corner of the Great Courtyard

Most of the rooms in the northwest corner of the Great Courtyard are storerooms supervised by the Palace Treasury, for which reason they can easily be reached from a staircase leading down from the middle floor, or from the west-facing Sheep Pen Doorway (**204**, *lug tshang gi sgo*) which leads into the open square. Formerly, when sheep destined for the abattoir were freed as an act of merit in the name of Jowo Śākyamuni and Jowo Akṣobhyavajra, they were not released into the city parks, but led through this door into the Sheep Pen for safekeeping. Nowadays the Sheep Pen is empty, although sheep and rams that have been released from the abattoir as a meritorious act are still occasionally kept outside. Inside the Sheep Pen there is also a north-facing storeroom (**205**) for communal dry meat and seasoning (*bzhes rdor yongs sha*) used in the preparation of noodle soup for monks participating in the Great Prayer Festival and the Great Congregation. Opposite it there is a storeroom (**206**) for communal butter, and, at the far end of the pen, an east-facing door (**207**) leads outside and to a north-facing storeroom (**208**) where bales of wool, including soft cashmere and coarse outer wool, were kept. All these storerooms are now empty, and the east-facing exit is kept locked.

Now the frescoes of the Great Courtyard will be described, along with the murals on the internal and external walls of the inner circumambulatory walkway, and those of the entrance vestibule or portico.

The entrance to the Great Courtyard. (1996 AA)

Laundry break. (1999 HS)

Murals of the Great Courtyard and the Inner Walkway

The Murals of the Great Courtyard

The murals adorning all four walls of the Great Courtyard were commissioned in 1648. On the walls of the north wing, behind the Great Throne, the foremost murals depict Tsongkhapa. To his right are Śāntarakṣita, King Songtsen Gampo, Atiśa, Dromton Gyalwei Jung-ne, the First Dalai Lama Gendundrub, the Second Dalai Lama Gendun Gyatso, the Third Dalai Lama Sonam Gyatso, and the protectress Rematī, while to his left are Padmasambhava, King Trisong Detsen, the Fourth Dalai Lama Yonten Gyatso, the Fifth Dalai Lama Ngawang Lobzang Gyatso, the Seventh Dalai Lama Kelzang Gyatso, and the protector Dorje Drakden.

On the east wall of the Great Courtyard, above the Great Acacia Gate, there are frescoes depicting Tsongkhapa flanked by his foremost students, with Maitreya to the right and Dīpaṃkara to the left, each of these buddhas being encircled by their parents and retinues of arhats, deities, and human disciples.

On the south wing of the Great Courtyard, the upper wall adjacent to the Great Butter Storeroom (*mar khang chen mo*) has murals depicting Śākyamuni, flanked by Śāriputra and Maudgalyāyana, with Avalokiteśvara to the right and Mañjughoṣa to the left.

On the west wing of the Great Courtyard, inside the Great Main Gate, the murals depict the assemblage known as Khamsum Wangdu, which features the regent Sangye Gyatso[225] and Gushi Qan Tendzin Chogyal, priest and patron, surrounded by their Chinese, Tibetan and Mongolian courtiers.

Mural from the Great Courtyard; depicting the regent Sangye Gyatso in conference with the Mongol Gushi Qan. (1996 AA)

The cloisters (*nang 'khor*) of the Great Courtyard are adorned on all four sides by the Thousand Buddhas of the Auspicious Aeon, each of whom is encircled by their respective parents and retinues of arhats, pious attendants, deities and human disciples.[226]

In the middle of the ceiling (*gnam pang*) supported by two columns, directly in front of the Great Acacia Gate, there were murals depicting the maṇḍala of the nine aspects of Amitāyus, embossed with unheated powdered gold. Other areas of this ceiling were decorated with the retentive mantras (*dhāraṇī*) of Kālacakra, Guhyasamāja, Cakrasaṃvara, Bhairava, the Lords of the Three Families, and other deities, inscribed in Rañjanā script. The mantras were embossed on gold leaf, and set within the petals of an eight-petalled lotus. The beams and rafters are adorned with the motif of the leaping lion.

The capitals of the eight long pillars and those of the smaller pillars of the Great Courtyard, those of the east, south and north wings of the inner walkway, and those of the portal were all renovated during the time of the second regent from Tshemonling, and are once again undergoing renovation at the present time. They depict representations of buddhas and bodhisattvas, seated in palaces of gilded copper.

The Murals of the Inner Walkway

The inner walkway, lined with prayer wheels, has murals outlined in gold on a red background, interspersed with stūpas and relief-images. Among them, the murals on the inner walls of the walkway, extending clockwise along the north-facing wall and along the east-facing wall, as far as the second east-facing projecting bay (*glo bur*) behind the Central Inner Sanctum, depict the array of buddha-fields according to the *Avataṃsaka Sūtra* and the introductory chapter of the *Prajñāpāramitā Sūtra in Eight Thousand Sections* (*Aṣṭasāhasrikāprajñāpāramitāsūtra*), as well as the buddha field of Sukhāvatī, the ten deeds of Maitreya, Thongwa Donden, and other scenes, each captioned according to their respective traditions. In the middle of the east-facing projecting bay, there are scenes depicting Śākyamuni Buddha's performance of miracles at Śrāvastī (*cho 'phrul dus chen*), flanked by Śāriputra and Maudgalyāyana, and encircled by arhats, deities and human disciples.

Then, extending clockwise along the remainder of the east wall and along the south-facing wall, the murals depict Śākyamuni Buddha's defeat of the six extremist teachers of Ancient India through miraculous power. These miracles of the Buddha are each depicted with their respective captions, starting with King Prasenajit's invitation to the Buddha and his pious attendants on the first day, and continuing through to King Bimbisāra's invitation.

Figure of a standing peaceful bodisattva from the Great Courtyard. (1996 AA)

Each of the inner walls also has a unique miniature depiction of Padmākara in the form Guru Nedogma.[227] These are the work of a skilled artist, for they are seldom encountered elsewhere.

As for the murals on the outer walls of the walkway, the wall immediately to the right of the Chapel of Tārā depicts the successive incarnations of the Dalai Lama, from the First Dalai Lama Gendundrub as far as the Seventh Dalai Lama Kelzang Gyatso, followed by a representation of the Thirteenth Dalai Lama Thubten Gyatso in the form Khamsum Wangdu, as well as the protectors Six-armed Jñānanātha, four-faced Mahākāla, Śrīdevī, and Dorje Drakden. To the left of the door of this chapel, the murals depict the Eighth Dalai Lama Jampal Gyatso and his patron, in the form known as Khamsum Wangdu, along with Śrīdevī and the sylvan mountain spirit Cimara.

The murals on the wall to the left of the entrance to the storeroom where the offering planks are housed, and along the north outer wall of the inner walkway,[228] extending clockwise as far as the first door of the Chapel of the Guru on the east wing, depict the foremost scenes on the right branch of the Wish-Granting Tree of the *Buddha's Hundred Deeds* (*Avadānakalpalatā*), including the buddha-fields of the ten directions, Śākyamuni, Kāśyapa, Kanakamuni, Krakucchanda, Viśvabhuk, and Sumānodharmadhara. These are then followed in succession by other scenes from the *Avadānakalpalatā*, starting from the narrative of Subhāṣitāgadeśin (*legs bshad 'tshol ba*) on the fifty-third branch and continuing as far as the narrative of Jimutavāhana (*sprin bzhon*) on the one hundred and eighth branch.

On the wall between the two west-facing doors of the Chapel of the Guru, the murals depict other foremost scenes from the *Avadānakalpalatā,* including Śākyamuni Buddha, flanked by Śāriputra and Maudgalyāyana, and encircled by his father Śuddhodhana, his mother Māyādevī, King Udrayana, King Bimbisāra, King Prasenajit, and the householder Anāthapiṇḍada. The murals of the upper right depict Śūra, Chogyal Gewang, Lodro Zangpo, Shongtong Dorje Gyaltsen, and the Fifth Dalai Lama, while those of the upper left depict Tsongkhapa, Chogyal Phakpa, Zhalu Chokyong Zangpo, Se Dawa Wangpo, and Nyimapel, along with the protector Śrīdevī in the form Palden Dungkyong Wangmo, and the gatekeeper Hayagrīva. Outside the Sera Rear Gate, there are murals depicting the guardian king of the north Vaiśravaṇa, and the guardian king of the east Dhṛtarāṣṭra.

Then, extending clockwise from the wall to the left of the Sera Rear Gate as far as the corner of the South Gate, the murals of the outer wall successively depict the gatekeeper Acala, Drib Dzongtsen, Sugata Śikhin (*bde gshegs gtsug tor*), Vipaśyin, the Eight Medicine Buddhas, the Five Buddhas in the guise of the emanational buddhabody, and the Sugata Siṃhanāda, along with captioned scenes from the *Avadānakalpalatā*, starting from the depiction of King Prabhāsa on the first branch and continuing as far as the narrative of "feeble merit" (*bsod nams dman pa*) on the fifty-second branch.

On the west-facing wall within the portals of the South Gate, there were frescoes depicting Drepung, Sera, Ganden, Samye, and Tradruk monasteries, along with the great guardian king of the south Virūḍhaka. On the east-facing wall within the portals of the South Gate are Virūpākṣa, the great guardian king of the west, along with scenes depicting the original Great Temple and the Potala Palace with Zhol village, and Dhānyakaṭaka Stūpa. There are also representations of King Songtsen Gampo, accompanied by his queens, the royal prince, and his ministers.

On the wall to the south of the Chapel of the Sixteen Elders, there was also an extraordinarily rare and skilfully executed miniature representation of Tārā in the form Jig-gye Nedogma (*jigs brgyad nas rdog ma*), depicted amidst trees and leaves.[229]

The wood panelling above the murals is decorated with a frieze (*gzham bu*) and ornamental swags. Along its full length the frieze carries mantras of retention inscribed in Rañjanā and Vartula scripts, as well as Hor-yig stacks, their syllables embossed on gold foil. These mantras include the *Long Retentive Mantra of Uṣṇīṣavijayā* (*gtsug tor rnam rgyal ma'i gzungs ring*), the *Hundred Syllables of the Tathāgatas* (*de bzhin gshegs pa'i yi ge brgya pa*), the *Long Retentive Mantra of Amitāyus* (*tshe gzungs ring ba*), the *Long Retentive Mantra of Mahākāruṇika* (*thugs rje chen po'i gzungs ring*), the *Immaculate Uṣṇīṣa* (*gtsug gtor dri med*), the *Secret Relics* (*gsang ba ring srel*), the *Long Retentive Mantra of the Hundred Thousand Ornaments of Enlightenment* (*byang chub rgyan 'bum gyi gzungs ring*), the *Aspirational Prayer for Endurance* (*brtan bshugs*), the *Heart Mantra of Dependent Origination* (*rten snying*), the *Retentive Mantra* of *the Three Deities of Longevity* (*tshe lha rnam gsum gyi gzungs*), the *Vajravidāraṇa* (*rdo rje rnam 'joms*), and the *Mantra of Consecration* (*supratiṣtha*).

The Inner Walkway. (1997 MF)

The Murals of the Outer Portal

Below the portal of the Great Gate (*gzhung sgo chen mo'i sgo mchor*), to the left and right, there are murals depicting the guarding kings of the four directions: Virūḍhaka, Virūpākṣa, Vaiśravaṇa, and Dhṛtarāṣṭra, surrounded by gandharvas, kumbāṇḍas, serpentine water spirits, and sylvan mountain spirits. Above these are the protector Kṣetrapāla, lord of wealth, in the guise of a monkey,[230] and the protectress Kado Sunga; while to their right and left are diagrams of geometric poetry (*kun bzang 'khor lo*).

All these murals, as mentioned above,[231] were executed during the lifetime of the Fifth Dalai Lama by the master artist Taklung Pelgon and by Kalden of Lhasa, Lobzang of Drongtse, Umdze Tsunchung, Sangak Kharwa Tshepel, and Zhang Gokye. The techniques of all these artists in draughtsmanship, design, and painting were based on the traditions of Lhodrak Menthangpa and Gongkar Khyentse. Later, when the murals were restored during the twentieth century through the kindness of the Thirteenth Dalai Lama, the master artists of the Zurchong School worthy of accepting this new commission included Drungtok Dorje Tsewang, the master gilder Kezang Norbu, Uchen Tshering Gomarwa, Zamdong Kelzang, Kethung Umdze, Tsedrung Yeshe Gyatso, and Sonam Rinchen. They and all the other skilled artists who applied their expertise in draughtsmanship, painting, and gilding to produce original creations in addition to reproductions of older works left a legacy worthy of exhibition throughout the world. Their techniques for grinding natural mineral ores, gold, silver and copper to produce completely unadulterated pigments are highly respected even now. Although great damage was inflicted on the walls of the Great Courtyard during the Cultural Revolution, some original murals from the pre-1959 period have nonetheless been preserved, alongside newly commissioned paintings.

Pilgrims in the Inner Walkway. (1999 HS)

The Middle Floor Annex: Private Apartments and Government Offices

The Vicinity of the Great Ceremonial Hall of the Middle Floor

Ascending the double staircase (**173**) which leads to the middle floor of the annex from the north-east corner of the Wood Enclosure, the pilgrim will reach the entrance to the Great Ceremonial Hall (**211**, *e vaṃ phun tshogs 'dod 'khyil*). This hall is occupied by the Dalai Lama and his entourage during the Great Prayer Festival and on other special ceremonial occasions. In addition to its main west-facing door, it also has a north-facing rear entrance (**212**). Within the hall there is a platform for the throne of the Dalai Lama, with long columns in front and a very large atrium in the centre. In recent times this hall has been used as a reception room for sculptors and those appointed to consecrate sacred images.

To the south of the hall there is a small storeroom for ceremonial food (**213**, *dkar spro khang*), which has both west and north facing entrances. A corridor leads east from here towards the south-facing Chapel of the Bon Protectress Sigyalma (**214**) and a west-facing meeting room (**215**, *tshogs khang*)[232] which once contained many ancient manuscripts, such as the *Collected Works of Lishu Tagring (Li shu stag ring gi gsung 'bum)*. These rooms are now empty, except for the Bon chapel, which no longer exists.

Passing through another door on the side of this corridor (**216**), one will reach the two back doors (**217/218**) which lead from the government offices above, down into the Debating Courtyard (*gsungs chos rva*), and a staircase (**219**) which leads up to the roof (*ya steng*). Another staircase (**220**) located in the corridor, almost opposite that door, leads down to the Storeroom of the Magistrates of Lhasa (*lha sa gnyer tshang pa*).

The Great Ceremonial Hall (no. **211**). (1996 AA)

The Vicinity of the Office of the Magistrates of Lhasa

Further along this corridor, overlooking the south side of the Wood Enclosure, one will reach another staircase (**221**) which leads up to the Foreign Reception Office on the top floor (*yar steng phyi rgyal las khungs*). Continuing along the corridor from there, one will come directly to the south-facing entrance of the Prayer Festival Administrator's Office (**222**, *spyi khyab las khungs*), which also served as an office for the chant-master of the Assembly Hall at Drepung. The room has a window, situated immediately above the Victory Gate of the Wood Enclosure.

Returning to the corridor, just to the west of the aforementioned staircase that leads up to the roof, there is a north-facing doorway (**223**), which leads south into another winding corridor. Eight different rooms adjoin this corridor, and the largest of these is the Office of the Magistrates of Lhasa (**224**, *lha sa gnyer tshang pa*), approached via a flight of two stone steps and a door-curtain on the left. An interior chamber within this office functions as a storeroom (**225**, *lha gnyer mdzod khang*) where chests of luck-bringing sacraments (*gYang sgam*) and documents were once kept. Outside the door, on the opposite side of that corridor, there is the east-facing Hermitage of Nechung Drayang Lingpa (**226**),[233] and, next to it, an east-facing public toilet (**227**), and an east-facing storeroom for ceremonial food (**228**).

Continuing to the south end of the corridor, and along the south wing of this complex, one will reach two north-facing rooms (**229/230**) which function during the Great Prayer Festival and the Great Congregation as an office for the two senior monastic proctors from Drepung and also for the two supervisors of the water supply (*chab bdag ma*). Then, continuing along the south wing of the corridor into its east wing, one will reach two west-facing rooms (**231/232**) which functioned as the offices of the bursar (*spyi so*) of Drepung Monastery and the head (*sde pa*) of Tashi Khangsar Residence at Drepung. All the rooms described in this section appear to have survived, but they no longer function as offices. The corridor once formed an open gallery overlooking the Great Kitchen (*rung khang chen mo*) on three sides, and access to the kitchen was gained from a staircase (**233**) located on the east wing of the corridor. As stated above, the kitchen and staircase have been removed, their space converted into residential units for monks.

During the Great Prayer Festival and the Great Congregation, the corridors between the Office of the Magistrates of Lhasa and the Senior Proctors' Rooms (*zhal ngo khang*) were filled each morning by monastic disciplinarians and others responsible for carrying

money and scarves offered by suppliants. In the evenings it also bustled with activity, as benefactors handed over their offerings in the presence of the security personnel of the top floor, the head of the Tashi Khangsar, the two senior monastic proctors (*zhal ngo*), and those in charge of tea supplies. Here, tea, butter, rice, barley, salt and condiments would be weighed and measured at the same time, the tally being kept by tea-makers and kitchen assistants.

The Vicinity of the Prime Minister's Apartment

Heading north from the entrance to the Great Ceremonial Hall (**211**, *e vaṃ tshogs chen phun tshogs 'dod 'khyil*), and through a north-facing doorway (**234**), one can then turn a corner to reach the Hall of Phenomenal Existence (**235**, *gzim chung snang srid*) which was formerly an official residence of the regent or prime minister.

Receptionists, security guards, and aides once blocked its entrance, but now it contains the electrical generator for the outer annex of the Great Temple. Inside this hall, which was used for ceremonial occasions, there is an inner chamber known as the Sunlight Apartment (**236**, *gzim chung snang srid nyi 'od*), where the staff of the regent or prime minister would meet. It has a south-facing window overlooking the Wood Enclosure. After the Chinese occupation of Tibet in 1952 (water dragon year), it was in this chamber that the Seventeen Point Agreement was imposed upon the Prime Minister Lobzang Tashi, and cabinet ministers such as Dekharwa (Lukhang) Tshewang Rabten and Zurkhar Wangchen Gelek by Chinese civilian and military officials. Here, too, the decision was taken to amalgamate the Tibetan armed forces with the PLA, even before the Chinese Flag had been raised above the Potala Palace.

The outer apartment also has three interior private rooms (**237/238**),[234] two of which were adjoining and once occupied as private rooms by the Dalai Lama and the regent, and the third which once functioned as a small chapel. In recent times the late Tenth Paṇchen Rinpoche would also reside here when visiting Lhasa. Nowadays, however, this complex of rooms has been converted into a kitchen, with residential quarters for monks.

Outside the entrance of the prime minister's apartment, a corridor leads north to reach the secret passageway of the Lugong (**239**), and slightly further on, a staircase (**240**) leads up to the Dalai Lama's Palace (*bla steng rgyal ba'i gzim chung*) on the top floor. Behind this staircase there is the east-facing door of the Hall Overpowering the Three World-Systems (**241**, *gzim chung khams gsum gzil gnon*), which has a window overlooking the flagstones of the square below, in the direction of the Princess' Willow Enclosure (*jo bo'i dbu skra*). This was originally an important meeting room for the regent and senior ministers of the Tibetan government,[235] and later it was where the cabinet would occasionally receive foreign dignitaries. Such proceedings would be conducted inside that chamber, behind a brocade screen. Ordinarily, the room served as a temporary storeroom for the Palace Treasury, for which reason it always had a strong aroma of fruit and medicine. Nowadays it is generally kept empty, though sometimes used, as in the past, for storing dry noodles and condiments. Three inter-connected north-facing rooms (**242/243/244**), accessed from within this chamber, were originally designated to house the chests containing the luck sacraments of the protector Gonkar Yizhin Norbu, the luck sacraments of the Bon tradition, and other sacred objects belonging to the Palace Treasury because their inner walls adjoin the prime minister's apartment (*gzim chung snang srid kyi nyi 'od*). Among these, the middle one, which once held luck sacraments of the Bon tradition, is dark and empty, while the other two (**242** and **244**) now function as a kitchen and residential quarter respectively.

Former ministerial offices of the Middle Floor. (1996 AA)

The Vicinity of the Palace Treasury

In the corner of the corridor (*gYab ' khor 'og*) to the north of the entrance to this chamber (*gzim chung khams gsum gzil gnon*), there was office space for the clerks (**245**, *jo lags nang gzan kyi las khungs*) employed by the Palace Treasury (*bla brang phyag mdzod*). Alongside the wall they would keep their dry measures and steelyards for weighing items of expenditure for use in daily offering ceremonies, and many metal keys for the various storerooms would also be suspended there from their leather straps. Following recent reconstruction, a proper office has been built in this corner. Next to this corner there is an east-facing door (**246**) that gives access to three separate storerooms and a flight of stairs leading down to the ground floor. The first of these (**247**, *gYu lo bkod*) would store dried fruit and candy, the second (**248**, *rin chen gter mdzod*) brocade, fine silk, and cotton, and the third (**249**, *dngul rkyan khang*) woollen textiles and silver ladles for use during the Great Prayer Festival and the Great Congregation. The first of these storerooms (**247**) is now a cash depository, and the second (**248**) is used for storing dry meat, while the third (**249**) is still used as a storeroom for textiles.

Descending the staircase (**250**) next to this last room, one will reach the Sheep Pen, where sheep freed in the name of Jowo Śākyamuni are kept. Immediately above the Sheep Pen, there is a large disused storeroom (**251**, *bla phyag sha khang*), in which condiments and dried meat for the Great Prayer Festival and the Great Congregation were formerly stored.

Just beyond the aforementioned clerks' seats, there is an east-facing storeroom (**252**, *lcang lo can*), now redesigned, where cotton merchandise and other important articles were once kept. Outside that room, in a south-facing corridor (**253**, *gYab 'khor 'og*) with a wooden railing, was the place where the four monastic and lay officials of the Palace Treasury would meet, and, in front, there was the seat of the secretary (*drung yig*) to the Palace Treasury. Although the officials of the Palace Treasury had no meeting room apart from this narrow corridor, the atrium in front of the corridor was open and spacious, enabling them to come and go with ease. Behind the seats of the officials of the Palace Treasury there is a small door giving access to a chamber with inner and outer rooms. The inner room (**255**, *gYang khang*) held chests containing the good luck sacraments of the wealth deities, including Vaiśravaṇa, Kubera, Jambhala, and Vasudharā, and it is said to have been piled with gemstones and precious metals including gold and silver. Whenever the rituals and means for attainment of the good luck sacraments were being performed within that room, there was a rule that, apart from the presiding vajra-master, only the officials of the Palace Treasury would be allowed to enter. The outer room was an archive (**254**, *gna' 'jog khang*), where ledgers and important contracts were kept. These rooms now serve as a vault.

Heading east, one then comes to a south-facing door, giving access to the Storeroom of the Palace Treasury (**256**, *gsol mdzod khang*) and a staircase (**257**) by which the Dalai Lama would ascend from the Chapel of the Three Approaches to Liberation (*rnam thar sgo gsum gyi lha khang*) on the ground floor, during the Great Prayer Festival and the Great Congregation. In recent times the storeroom has been converted into a kitchen. East of that was the Cashier's Room (*dngul rtsis khang*, **258**), a spacious chamber where money for use during the Great Prayer Festival would be stored and counted, but which has since been demolished.

During the Great Prayer Festival and the Great Congregation a large open-roofed enclosure of black tweed would be erected across the court in front of the Palace Treasury to hold public spectators. A cotton tent with a canopy and a wooden frame would be erected further to the west for those visiting important dignitaries, such as the cabinet ministers. The carpets and upholstery used by the cabinet were kept in a south-facing storeroom (**259**, *bka'shag gdan khang*) in the middle floor, overlooking the eight long pillars of the Great Courtyard below, while the tents and picnic canopies belonging to the Palace Treasury were stored in an adjacent north-facing room (**260**, *bla phyag gur khang*). On the floor immediately above these storerooms, the sacraments that bind the geomantic spirit lords of the soil were kept so that snow and gales might be avoided during the Great Prayer Festival and the Great Congregation. Both of these storerooms for official carpets and tents have been turned into residential quarters for monks and their present entrance is to the east.

Girls bearing offering scarves. (1997 MF)

Offices Adjoining the Lower Gallery

Proceeding clockwise around the gallery of the middle floor (*mda'gYab*) which overlooks the inner walkway, one will first reach an east-facing chamber from where the main image in the Chapel of Tārā below can be viewed. Next to it, a south-facing door (**261**) leads into the Office of the Sacristan of the Thousandfold Offerings (**262**, *stong mchod gnyer pa'i las shag*), which is situated directly above the storeroom used for holding offering planks. Slightly west of that office, there is a large "butter melting" room (**263**, *mar bzhu khang*) belonging to the Palace Treasury.[236] Further east, along the gallery, a west-facing door leads into a storeroom of the Palace Treasury, which also functioned as a tailors' workshop (**264**, *bzo khang byang gling kham mo che*). Both the office and the butter storeroom have recently been converted into residential quarters for monks, while the former workshop now serves as their kitchen.

Then, continuing along the north wing of the gallery, one will reach a south-facing door which gives access to the former Security Office (**265**, *bde 'jags las khungs*) on the west (left) and the Litigation Office (**266**, *gyod zhib las khungs*) on the east (right). The latter had in past centuries been the Land Revenue Office. The next south-facing door (**267**) gives access to the connecting ramp of the Śrīdevī Turret upstairs, and a staircase (**268**) that leads down to the public toilet facilities on the floor below. Continuing along the north wing, one will pass the south-facing door of the former Criminal Investigation Bureau (**269**, *bsher khang*). Suspended from the right and left walls alongside this door were truncheons, fetters, vices, leg-irons, pillories, and other gruesome instruments of punishment, while on the wall there was a chart documenting the scale of offences and the appropriate sentences. The final south-facing door is that of a storeroom (**270**, *mdzod khang*).[237] All these offices and the storeroom on the north wing have now been converted into residential units. Next, one will reach the east wing of the gallery where there are two main west-facing doors. The first of these (**271**) gives access to the rice granary of the Palace Treasury (**272**), a granary for crushed barley (**273**), a storeroom for mineral-based medicines (**274**), and a large room (**275**) belonging to the sacristans of the offering sacraments, where donations for presentation during the Great Congregation were stored. These too have been converted into residential quarters for monks, with the exception of the barley granary, which is now a toilet.

Within this compound there is also a staircase (**276**) leading up to the Accounting Bureau (*rtsis zhib zhib khang las khung*) and the Office of the Senior Sacristan of the Great Temple (*sku gnyer dpon*); while another staircase (**277**) leads down to the storeroom of the Palace Treasury (*bla phyag gi mdzod khag*) on the ground floor.

These stairs have been reconstructed and now face east. The second west-facing door is that of the now dysfunctional Government Chancellery (**278**, *spyi khyab rtsis khang phun tshogs bkod pa*) – an office where the revenue derived from the agricultural and dairy produce of the entire Tibetan nation was once calculated. Along its north, east and west walls, chests containing documents were stacked as high as the ceiling in alphabetical order, while on the altar the foremost images were those representing Śākyamuni Buddha, the Fifth Dalai Lama, and Sangye Gyatso. The seats of the senior accountants, accountants and their assistants were arranged according to rank, and alongside their mats there were abacuses, weights, dice, rulers and other instruments of measurement. On the pillars and tables there were many parchment scrolls, and a red silk scroll inscribed with a name list of the presiding clerks hung from one of the long pillars.

Heading clockwise, directly from the Chancellery, one reaches a north-facing staircase (**279**) that leads down to the inner walkway. Next, on the south wing of the gallery there are a series of north-facing doors. The first gave access to an outer kitchen for the cabinet (**280**, *bka' shag gsol thab*) and an inner storeroom for kitchen utensils used by the cabinet chef (**281**). The second functioned as the National Agricultural Bureau (**282**) and the third as the War Office (**283**, *dmag phog las khungs*).[238] Since the main War Office was located at Zhol, below the Potala, this room was only designated as a war office whenever the military commanders had to petition the cabinet. The next north-facing room, which belonged to the Palace Treasury, was a storeroom for offering grain (**284**). The next was a storeroom for old, non-essential cabinet archives (**285**), and the next was a rear entrance to the cabinet office (**286**). All these rooms on the south wing of the gallery have been converted into residential quarters for monks, with the exception of the kitchen utensil store (**281**) which no longer exists as a separate unit.

South-west corner of the top floor (p. 106). (1996 AA)

The Vicinity of the Cabinet Office

The main entrance to the Executive Cabinet Office, which once handled civilian and military affairs, is a south-facing door (**287**) on the ground floor, alongside the South Gate of the Great Temple. From inside that door, an east-facing wooden staircase (**288**) leads upstairs to the Office of the Cabinet Secretary (**289**, *bka' shag drung yig gi las khungs*) which has an open-roofed gallery. From here, a south-facing door leads into a narrow dimly lit waiting room (**290**) where the seats of the four junior cabinet receptionists were located. Those dark passages were once filled with officials whose duties were to remind the authorities of the various petitions that had been made.

In front of the reception desk, a south-facing door gives access to the cabinet toilets (**291**); while to its left, there is an east-facing door (**292**) flanked by two hanging leopard-skin "fly-whisk" sceptres, emblematic of courage and royal dominion. Entering through that door, one reaches the former Cabinet Secretariat (**293**, *mgron drung sgang*), a small anteroom with a single pillar and a south-facing window in the northeast corner of which were the seats of the two cabinet secretaries (*bka'drung gnyis*) and the seats of the four aides to the cabinet (*bka' mgron bzhi*). In front of the pillar is the narrow place where the Secretary from Eyul (*e pa drung yig*) would sit. Beyond this anteroom, unprotected by any special barrier, there was the actual Cabinet Office (**294**, *bka' shag lhan khang*). This room

Ven. Tubten Rinchen in the Jokhang. (1999 HS)

has a south-facing window and once had a shrine with images of Tsongkhapa, the Seventh Dalai Lama Kelzang Gyatso, and the Thirteenth Dalai Lama Thubten Gyatso. It also contained the throne of Kelzang Gyatso, adjacent to a paper-screen south-facing window. Its dark red cushion had a green head resembling the head of a horse. In front of the throne there was a flat table. Along the east wall there was a woolsack seat where the cabinet secretaries sat when they were sworn into office. In front of that were the "official" bench *(tham gdan)* and the table of the cabinet ministers. The pillar was covered with parchment scroll documents of immediate concern, while important old documents were stored in a small interior room, with one pillar and a skylight window (**295**, *bka' shag yang khang*).

Until 1951 the cabinet was responsible for executive decisions, foreign and home affairs, civilian and military matters, the economy, and the raising of tax revenue from country estates. Although it was the most senior and most important executive position to which anyone could be appointed, the office was not particularly large. Yet, for over two hundred and fifty years, this office functioned as the executive authority from which independent Tibet was securely governed, its political constitution conjoining both spiritual and secular powers.

Since 1642 (water horse year of the eleventh cycle) when political control of Tibet was assumed by the Ganden Phodrang during the reign of the Fifth Dalai Lama, there have been several individuals who have held the rank of minister. When this system was first introduced, the ministers would only form a joint committee at times when they were in Lhasa, and they each had their individual responsibilities and power bases in the provinces. Feuding ministers provoked civil unrest and caused economic hardship during the early reign of the Seventh Dalai Lama Kelzang Gyatso; and the interregnum which followed saw unlimited power exercised by a single individual during the rule of Miwang Pholha Sonam Tobgye and his son Gyurme Namgyal. These events prompted the Seventh Dalai Lama to assume formal responsibility for both spiritual and secular affairs in 1751 (iron sheep year of the thirteenth cycle). He appointed a cabinet comprising one monastic cabinet minister and three civilian cabinet ministers; and he bestowed upon these officials the seals of the cabinet (*dam phrug bde skyid ma*), along with his aspirational prayers. As if to emphasise their importance, he also appointed cabinet secretaries, cabinet aides, and security personnel. The cabinet of ministers (*bka' blon gyi shag*) which he instated in order that the political affairs of the country might be stabilised, continued to function inside Tibet until the 1950s, and even since then, it has continued to function in exile, albeit in a modern context.

The area once occupied by the cabinet offices has been completely reconstructed in recent times. A residential unit for monks is now located adjacent to the entrance (**287**), and the toilet is now entered from the top of the wooden staircase (**288**). The office of the cabinet secretary (**289**) no longer has a special function, but the reception area (**290**) along with the actual cabinet office and secretariat (**292-4**) have all been converted into residential units for monks.

The Corner Verandah (p. 106, no. **311**). (1996 LH)

The Top Floor Annex: Palace of the Dalai Lama

The Palace of the Dalai Lama

The Palace (*bla brang steng*) or Private Apartment of the Dalai Lama (*rgyal ba'i gzim chung*) is located in the northwest corner of the top floor of the annex. Ascending the aforementioned staircase (**240**) alongside the Office of the Palace Treasury on the middle floor, the pilgrim will emerge on the top floor alongside a large south-facing verandah with a black tweed screen (**296**). This is the reception area for the Palace of His Holiness the Dalai Lama. The entrance of the palace is flanked by two hanging leopard-skin "fly-whisk" sceptres, emblematic of courage and royal dominion, while to its left and right are the seats of the four security personnel (*gzim 'gag*), the senior Potala receptionist (*rtse mkhan mgron che ba*) and his assistant receptionists (*rtse mgron*). Here also are the seats of the senior lay officials: those of the *dza sag* and *tha' ji* ranks, the military paymaster (*phog dpon*), the general (*mda' dpon*), the finance minister (*rtsis dpon*), the treasurer (*phyag mdzod*), the princely aristocrats (*sras rnam pa*), the heads of all the government departments, and their clerks.

Entering the palace, His Holiness' chamber is on the left of the hallway and that of his personal attendant on the right.[239] Directly ahead is the west-facing entrance of the hall known as the Pinnacle of Ganden (**297**, *dga' ldan yang rtse*). Its atrium is supported by long columns, and it has a bay window (**298**) from which His Holiness would observe the congregations in the Great Courtyard below. In 1948 (*fire bird year*) when this apartment was renovated, a gilded copper roof was erected above the window along with a *gañjira* spire. Inside the hall, there is a shrine containing images of the Thirty-five Confession Buddhas, and in front of it two rows of seats are arranged. The higher row, situated immediately in front, comprises the seats of the Dalai Lama and those of his two tutors, while the lower row comprises the seats of the ministers, the head monastic preceptor, and the high ranking officials of the Private Office, as well as escorts (*phebs 'go*) and assistant tutors (*mtshan zhabs*). To the east of the hall, a doorway leads into two small chambers which were once used by the Dalai Lama and his personal attendant,[240] and thence into a library (**299**, *phyag dpe khang*)[241] and a private bedroom (**300**, *mtshan gzim khang*). A corridor leads west from the hall through a back door (**301**) to a private toilet (**302**, *gzim gcod*) on the north wing. All the rooms in the Palace have been preserved, although it is unclear whether its contents now match their original inventory.

West of the screen covering the entrance to the Palace there was formerly a narrow enclosure, containing the south-facing Sunlight Apartment (*gzim chung nyi 'od*). This was where the senior Lharampa Geshe would be seated during the Great Prayer Festival and where the successive fifteenth day ceremonies and prayers for longevity would be performed. However, in 1954 (wood horse year), this apartment and its enclosure were renovated from east to west. A ramp was constructed, connecting this area with an outside public toilet on the north wing (**303**), and on the west wing a new complex known as the Bright Corner Window (*gzur 'phyongs rab gsal kun gsal*) was constructed for the use of the Dalai Lama's personal attendants. It comprised three outer rooms, and two inner rooms (**304/305**), one of which had a corner window directly overlooking the flagstones of the portals below, for which reason it was known as the Corner Apartment (*zur 'phyongs gzim chung*). This is where the main bookshop, souvenir store and refreshment lounge of the Great Temple are now located.

The West Wing of the Top Floor

Rising above the window of the aforementioned Hall Overpowering the Three World-Systems (**241**, *gzim chung khams gsum gzil gnon*) on the middle floor, there are an exquisitely fashioned gilded-copper wheel with a thousand spokes (**306**), flanked by two facing deer, and the two enormous gilded-copper victory banners (**307**). These were donated to the Great Temple in 1921 (iron bird year of the fifteenth cycle) by Changkya Qutuqtu and the monastic community of Gonlung Monastery in Amdo.

Then, on the north wing of the open gallery which overlooks the prime minister's aforementioned Hall of Phenomenal Existence (*gzim chung snang srid*) on the middle floor below, there is the sacred turret (*rten mkhar*) of the Bon protectress Sigyalma (**308**), which was once adorned with juniper branches, a threadcross and a flag. Each

Looking down on the Great Courtyard, and the Palace of the Dalai Lama to the left. (1998 AA)

The Pinnacle of Ganden (no. **297**). (2000 GD)

Palace of the Dalai Lama. (2009 LG)

Snow-lion overlooking the South-west corner of the top floor. (2009 LG)

year offerings were made there, and Bon practitioners from Kyormolung in Tolung would replenish the wood, at the behest of the Office of the Magistrates of Lhasa, who have this responsibility. Next to it, there was the Workroom of the Palace Steward (**309**, *bla brang khang gnyer*), and south of the gallery overlooking the Great Ceremonial Hall (*e vaṃ tshoms chen*) of the middle floor there was a rooftop kitchen (**310**, *rtse gsol thab khang*), which still stands. The sacred turret of Sigyalma is empty, and the workroom was destroyed during the Cultural Revolution.

The South-west Corner of the Top Floor

Overlooking the Debating Courtyard (*gsung chos rva ba*), there is a chamber known as the Corner Verandah (**311**, *zur 'phyongs gzim 'gag*) on account of its large corner window. Accessed from within it, there is a small room known as the Corner Hermitage (**312**, *zur 'phyongs gzim sbug*), where, during the Great Prayer Festival, the Dalai Lama would come to witness the *torma* exorcism performed by monks from the Ngakpa College of Drepung Monastery, or the procession of Maitreya around the Great Temple, and the concomitant sporting contests: horse-races, foot-races, and weight-lifting. The murals of the Corner Verandah depicted the legendary origins of the Tibetan race; and at times other than when the Dalai Lama was visiting, the chamber would function as a studio for the best *thangka* painters of Lhasa, for which reason these artists came to be known as the Zurchongpa ("corner") School. Later, after the Chinese occupation of Tibet, Sino-Tibetan committee meetings were held here; and the rooms are now occupied by some of the seniormost monks of the Great Temple.

Occupying the west wing of this southwest corner of the top floor, and directly above the Hermitage of Nechung, there are three east-facing rooms, approached from a long corridor. The first was the Endowment Office (**313**, *thebs sbyar las khungs*), where donations for the Great Prayer Festival and the Great Congregation would be tallied. Previously it had functioned as the National Mint (*bod gzhung shog dngul las khungs*) until the mint was relocated at Drachi Logtrul. Nowadays this office is occupied by senior resident monks.

The second room on this wing was an open court (*bar 'khyams*), and the third was formerly the Foreign Reception Office (**314**, *phyi rgyal las khungs*), which had an inner recess (**315**). Finally, there is a north-facing room accessed from the same corridor, where tax revenues levied on salt, wool, and tea would be gathered (**316**). Nowadays, the foreign reception office remains empty, while the others have been converted into a single residential unit for monks.

The North Wing and Northeast Corner of the Top Floor

Ascending to the top floor of the annex from the aforementioned staircase (**268**) on the north wing of the gallery of the middle floor, which is located between the former Revenue Office (**266**, *'bab zhib las khungs*) and the Criminal Investigation Office (**269**, *bsher khang las khungs*), the pilgrim will see a ramp leading south towards the Śrīdevī Turret. To the north of this ramp, there are three rooms: the kitchen of the sacristan of the top floor (**317**, *rtse mo'i gnyer pa*) the kitchen of the monks of Meru Dratsang (**318**), and an adjacent public toilet (**319**, *spyi gcod*). This complex has now been converted into residential units for monks.

Alternatively, if one reaches the top floor of the annex via the aforementioned south-facing staircase of the east wing (**276**), which is located between the Criminal Investigation Office and the Government Chancellery (**278**, *rtsis khang*), one will come to the Accounting Bureau (**320**, *rtsis zhib zhib khang las khungs*), which was formerly established by *spyi mkhan* Palden Dondrub. This room contains an inner and an outer chamber. Next to it, there was the office of the Senior Sacristan of the Great Temple (**321**, *sku gnyer dpon gyi las shag*). East of that, there was a public toilet (**322**), and to the north, the large Treasury for Offering Sacraments (**323**, *chos rdzas sgang*) which was supervised by the sacristan of the offering sacraments and religious implements (*mchod rdzas do dam pa*). This entire complex now forms a redesigned residential unit for monks, which contains many smaller rooms than in the past.

Roof brackets. (2009 LG)

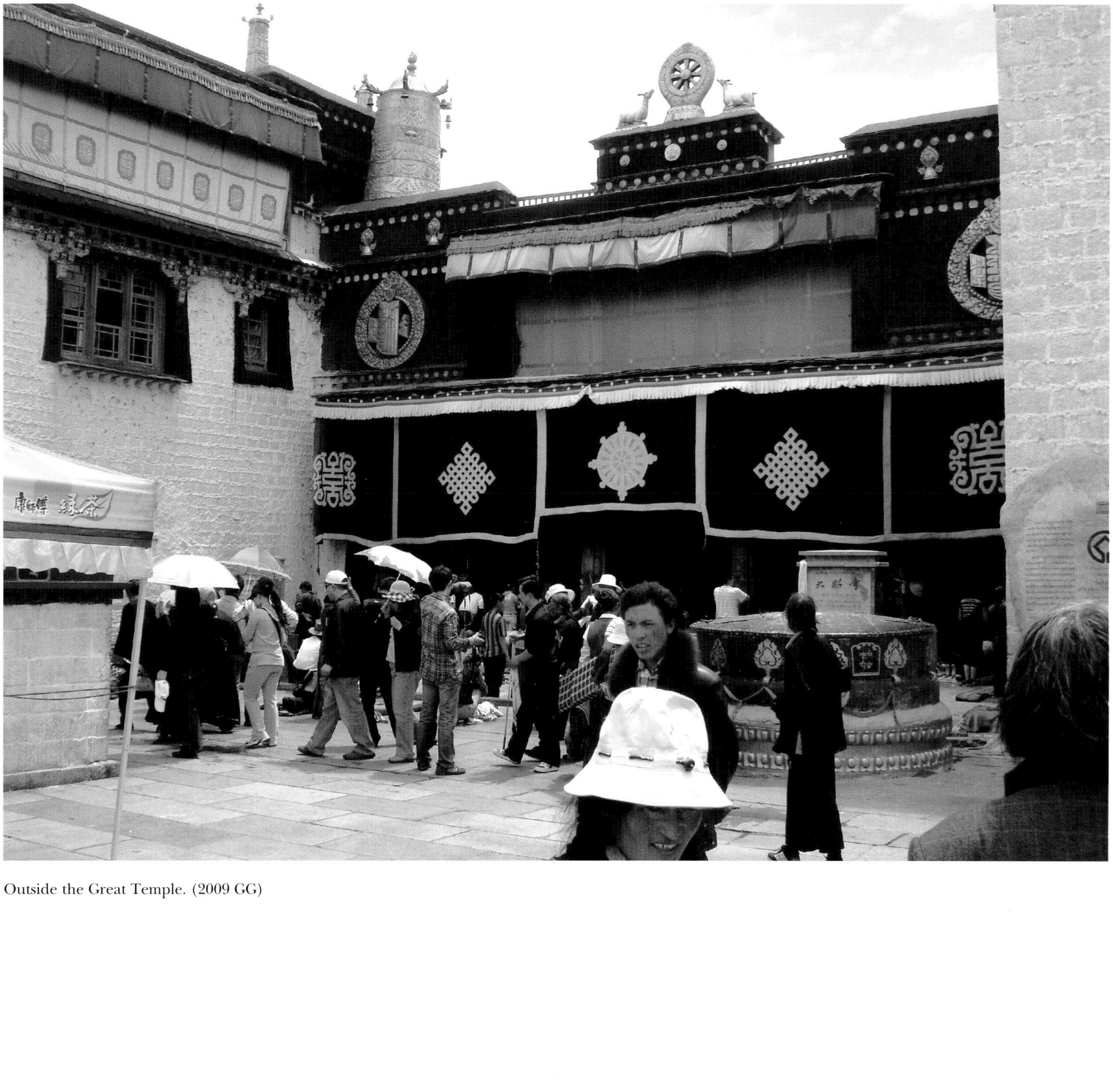

Outside the Great Temple. (2009 GG)

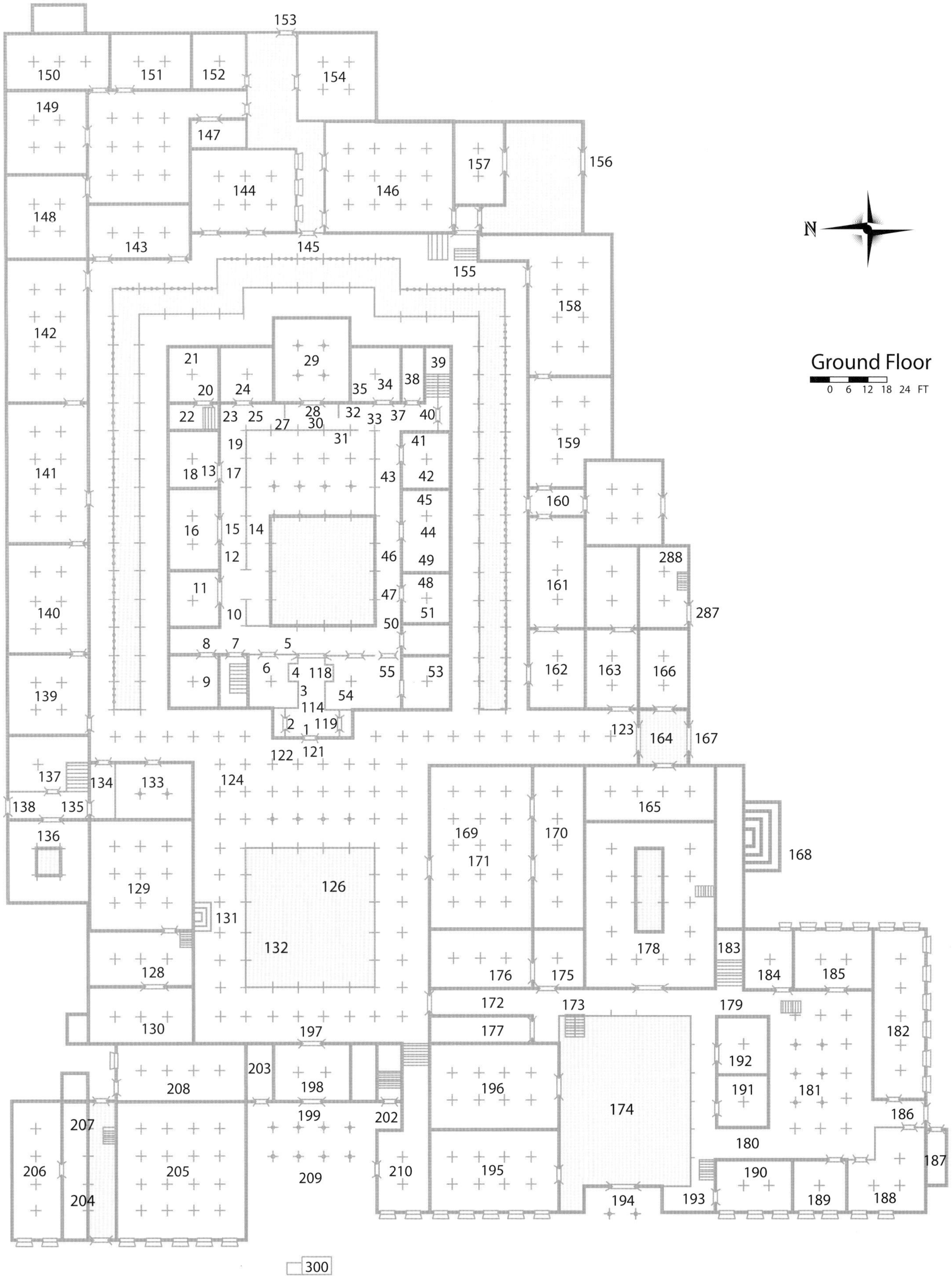
Ground Floor
0 6 12 18 24 FT
N
153
150 151 152 154
149 147
144 146 157 156
148 143 145 155
142 158
21 29 39
20 24 35 34 38
22 23 25 28 27 30 32 33 37 40
31
19 41
18 13 17 43 42 159
141 45
16 15 14 44 160
12 46 49
11 48 288
140 10 47 51 161 287
50
8 7 5
9 6 4 118 55 53 162 163 166
139 3 54
114
2 119 123 164 167
1
122 121
137 134 133 124 165
138 135
136 169 170
171 168
126
129
131 178
132
128 176 175 183 184 185
172 173 179
130 177 182
197 192
203 198 196 191 181
208
199 202 174 186
207 180
206 205 209 210 195 190 187
204 194 193 189 188
300

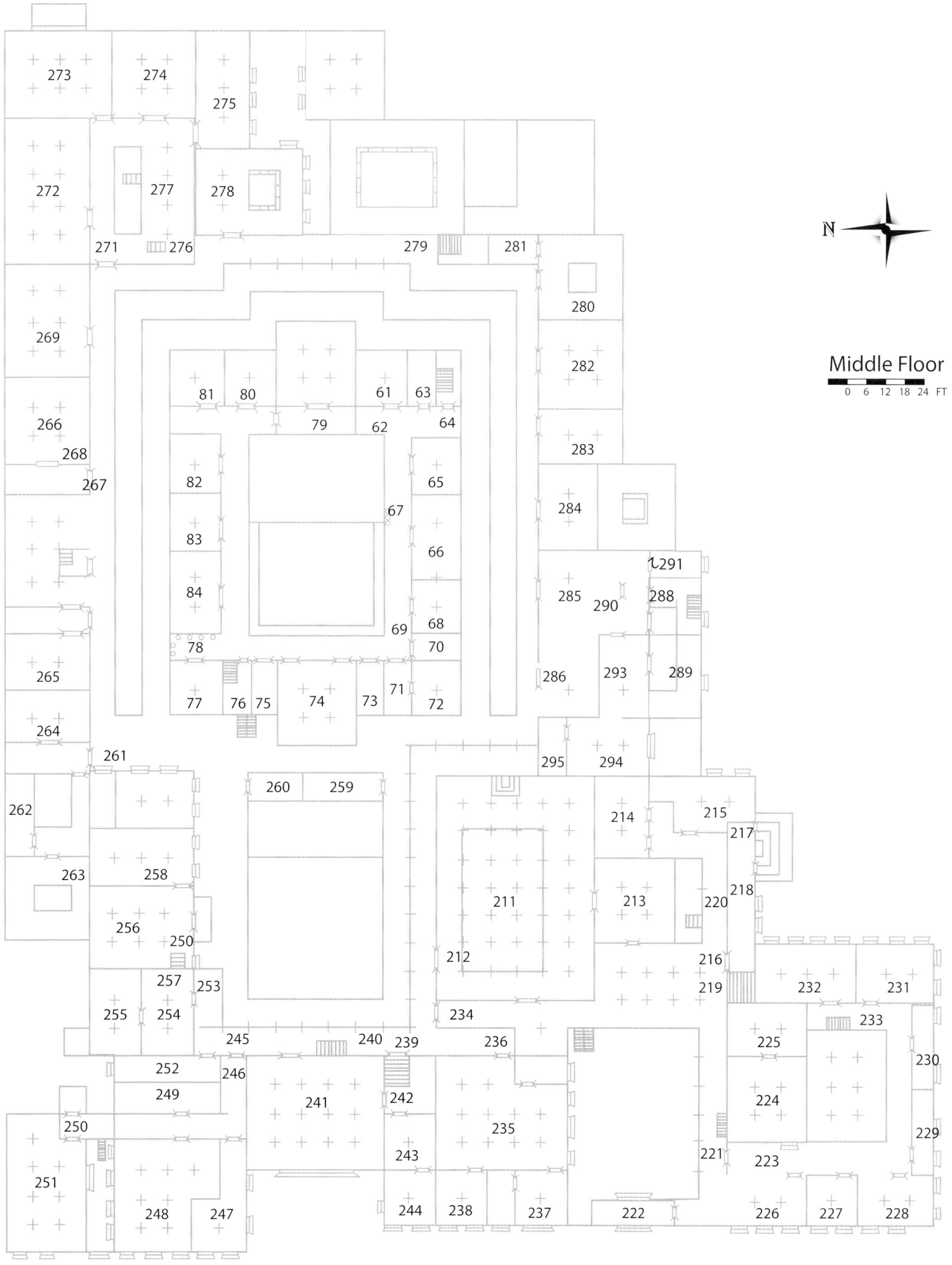
N
Middle Floor
0 6 12 18 24 FT
273
274
275
272
277
278
271
276
279
281
280
269
282
81
80
61
63
79
62
64
266
268
283
267
82
65
67
284
83
66
84
291
285
290
288
69
68
78
70
265
286
293
289
77
76
75
74
73
71
72
264
261
295
294
260
259
214
215
262
217
263
258
211
213
218
220
256
250
212
216
257
253
219
232
231
255
254
234
233
245
240
239
236
225
230
252
246
249
241
242
224
250
235
229
251
243
221
223
248
247
244
238
237
222
226
227
228

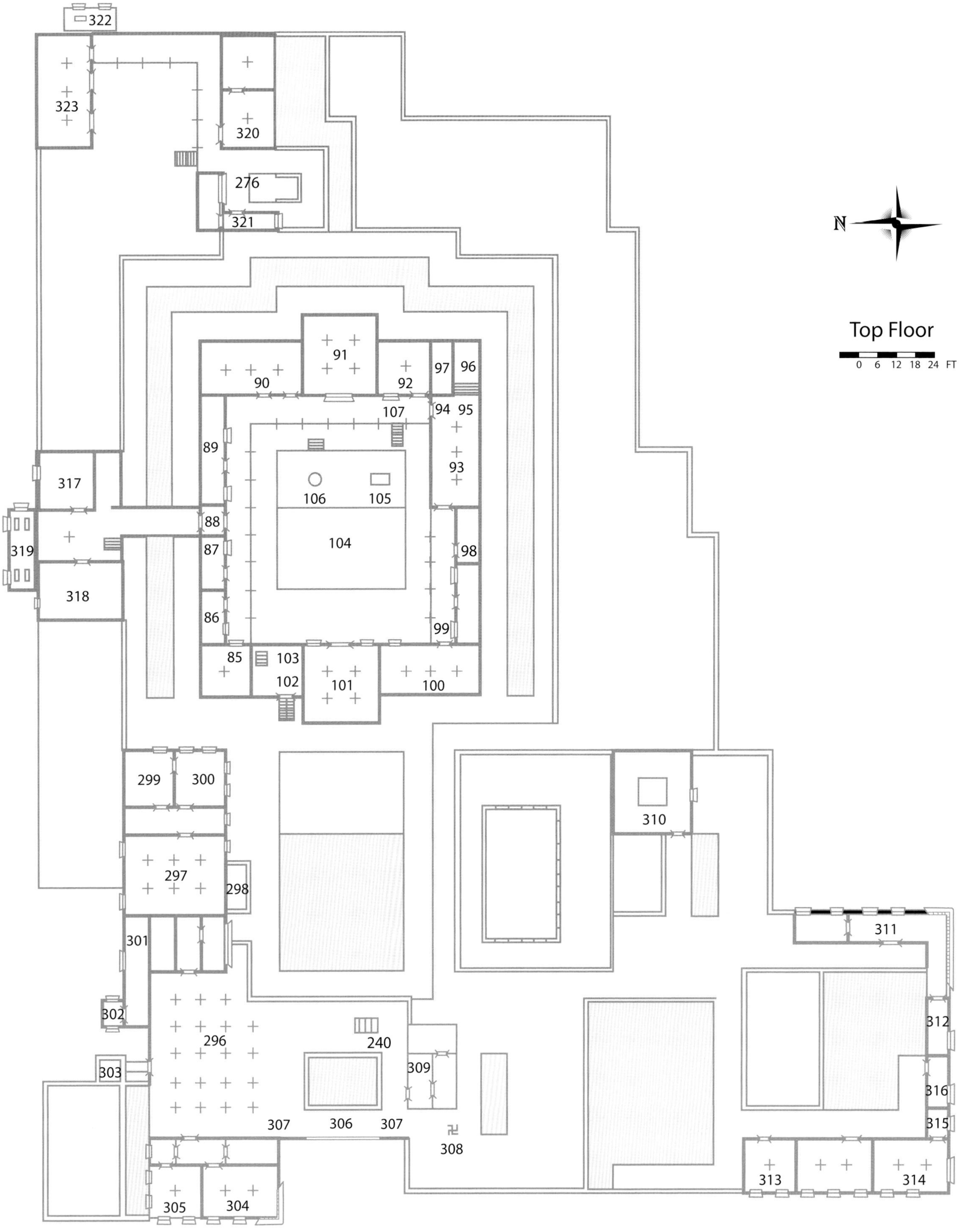

Top Floor
0 6 12 18 24 FT
N
322
323
320
276
321
91
90
92
97
96
107
94
95
89
93
106
105
317
88
104
319
87
98
318
86
99
85
103
102
101
100
299
300
310
297
298
311
301
302
296
240
312
303
309
316
307
306
307
315
308
313
314
305
304

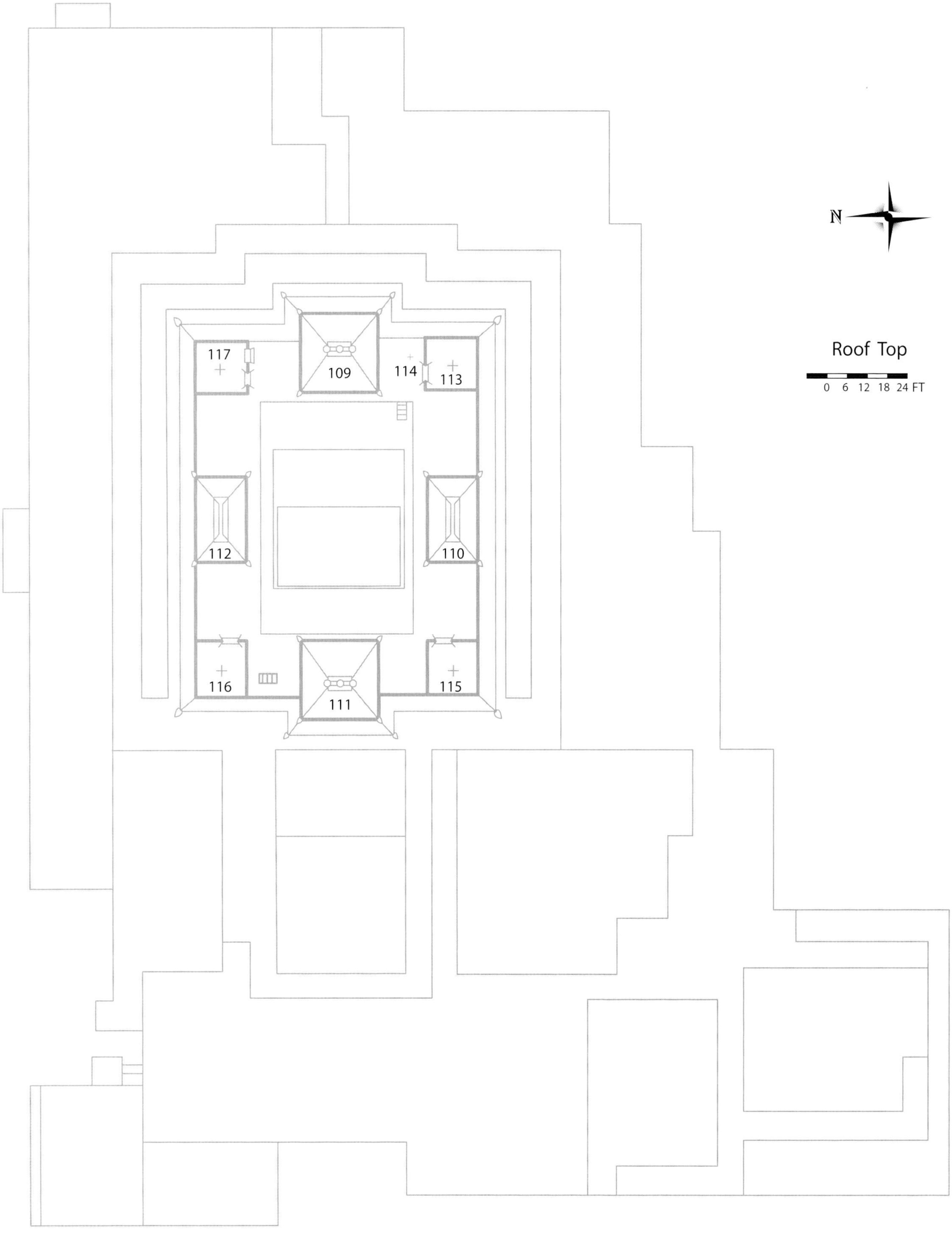
N
Roof Top
0 6 12 18 24 FT
117
109
114
113
112
110
116
111
115

Plans of the Great Temple

Plan of Ground Floor

a. Great Temple

1 Great Acacia Gate (*seng ldeng sgo mo che*)
2 Chapel of Kubera (*gnod sbyin na ga kubera'i lha khang*)
3 Bellows-shaped stone (*rdo sbud pa can*)
4 Chapel of the Serpentine Water Spirits (*klu khang*)
5 Murals of Five Buddhas (*pañcajina*)
6 Chapel of the Spiritual Teachers (*bla ma'i lha khang*)
7 Door
8 Stūpa of Scrutiny (*brtag pa'i mchod rten*)
9 Chapel of Amitābha (*'od dpag med lha khang*)
10 Restored images of Lochen Rinchen Zangpo *et al*
11 Chapel of the Medicine Buddhas (*sman bla'i lha khang*)
12 Restored images of Milarepa *et al*
13 Wood-carved inscription of the Six Syllable Mantra (*bod kyi yig phud*)
14 Chapel of Offerings (*mchod sgrom lha khang*)
15 Restored Lords of the Three Enlightened Families (*rigs gsum mgon po*)
16 Northern Inner Sanctum of Rangjon Ngaden (*gtsang khang byang ma*)
17 Restored images of Phagmodrupa *et al*
18 Chapel of the Bathing Maitreya (*byams pa 'khrus mdzad*)
19 Stone Basin (now repositioned within chapel; *'khrus rdo padma spungs pa*)
20 Treasury of Jowo Śākyamuni (*jo bo'i mdzod*)
21 Chapel of the Milk Plain Lake (*'o thang mtsho'i lha khang*)
22 Chapel of Tsongkhapa (*tsong kha pa'i lha khang*)
23 Image of Gatekeeper Vajrapāṇi
24 Chapel of Amitābha (*'od dpag lha khang*)
25 Image of Gatekeeper Ucchūṣmakrodha
26 Images of Songtsen Gampo with his queens, and Saroruhavajra (*Za-hor-ma*)
27 Vase Pillar (*ka ba bum pa can*)
28 Wooden Foyer (*pang gcal*)
29 Central Inner Sanctum or Jokhang (*gtsang khang dbus ma/ jo khang*)
30 Image of Guru Padmākara
31 Image of Vijayā
32 Mural of Dolma Darlenma
33 Leaf Pillar (*ka ba shing lo can*)
34 Chapel of Maitreya in the Gesture of Teaching the Sacred Doctrine (*byams pa chos 'khor gtso 'khor*)
35 Queen's Stove
36 Image of Maitreya commissioned by Miwang Pholha Sonam Tobgye
37 Images of Amitāyus, Dolpopa Sherab Gyaltsen, and Avalokiteśvara
38 Chapel of Siṃhanāda (*spyan ras gzigs seng ge sgra grogs kyi lha khang*)
39 Passageway/Stone Staircase
40 Svāstika Alcove (*gYung drung sbug*)
41 Mural of Bhaiṣajyaguru
42 North-facing Chapel of Sems-pa gtso-'khor (*byang gzigs lha khang*)
43 Restored images of Dolchung Korpon *et al*
44 Chapel of the Four Maitreya Siblings (*byams pa mched bzhi'i lha khang*)
45 Gilded Head of Emanational Goat (*ra mo rgya'u*)
46 Unrestored Padma spungs-pa Stūpa
47 Original hierarchs of Sakya: Sakya Paṇḍita, Chogyal Phakpa, Drakpa Gyaltsen, Kunga Nyingpo and Sonam Tsemo
48 Chapel of Mirror-Shaped South Gate (*lho sgo me long can gyi lha khang*)
49 Jowo's Concealment Chamber (*jo bo'i sbas sa*)
50 Mural of Mañjughoṣa (*'jam dpal kho gYol ma*)
51 Chapel of Seven Generations of Past Buddhas (*sangs rgyas rabs bdun gyi lha khang*)
52 Alcove of Prajñāpāramitā Mural
53 Chapel of the Nine Aspects of Amitāyus (*tshe dpag lha dgu'i lha khang*)
54 Chapel of Religious King and Courtiers (*chos rgyal yab yum sras blon bcas kyi lha khang*)
55 Main Hall (*dkyil 'khor mthil*)
56 Image of Eleven-faced Mahākāruṇika
57 Image of Maitreya commissioned by Lhazang Qan
58 Image of Munīndra, in the form Thubwang Zangthama
59 Image of Maitreya commissioned by Barzhib Chukhorwa
60 Image of Nangsi Zilnon (formerly Guru Gyagarma)
118 Chapel of the Serpentine King Nanda (*klu rgyal dga' ba'i lha khang*)
119 Chapel of Mahākāla and Daśagrīva Rāvaṇa of Laṅkā
120 Capuchin Bell

b. Ground Floor Annex

121 Amolongkha fossil in flagstone patio (*rdo gcal*)
122 Footprint of the Thirteenth Dalai Lama
123 Unrestored Four Rocks Deposited by Tsangnyon Heruka and Unyonpa
124 Embedded Stone Cast by Tsangnyon Heruka (recently removed)
125 Embedded Stone Cast by Unyonpa (lost)
126 Great Courtyard (*khyams ra chen mo*)
127 Northwest Alcove for "daily offerings of the courtyard" (*khyams rva rgyun mchod pa'i bzhugs sa*)
128 Chapel of the Three Approaches to Liberation (*rnam thar sgo gsum gyi lha khang*)
129 Main Tea Room of Palace Treasury (*bla brang phyag mdzod'i ja khang chen mo*)
130 West Tea Room (*ja khang nub ma*)
131 Stone Platform of the Great Throne (*bzhugs khri chen mo*)
132 Unrestored Platform for throne of the Drepung chant-master (*'bras spungs tshogs chen*)
133 Chapel of Tārā (*sgrol ma'i lha khang*)
134 Storeroom of Offering Planks (*mchod sprin khang*)
135 Staircase to Lower Gallery (*mda' gYab' og*)
136 Thousandfold Offering Chamber (*stong mchod bzhengs pa'i bzgugs khang*)
137 Kitchen (now used for storage)
138 North Exit to Jangchub Jonlam in Barkor
139 Chapel of Kurukullā and Hayagrīva in the form Tamdrin Sangdrub
140 Chapel of Mahākāruṇika
141 Chapel of Sarvavidvairocana and Vairocanābhisambodhi
142 Chapel of Eight Stūpas
143 Chapel of Sixteen Elders
144 Chapel of Peaceful and Wrathful Aspects of Padmsambhava (*gu ru zhi drag lha khang*)
145 East Gate (*shar sgo*) a.k.a. "Rear Gate to Sera" (*se ra ltag sgo*)
146 Prayer Festival Kitchen
147 Medicine Storeroom (now part of redesigned residential unit for monks)

148 Storeroom (now empty)
149 Rice Husk Storeroom (now part of redesigned residential unit for monks)
150 Rice Storeroom (now part of redesigned residential unit for monks)
151 Storeroom for Wooden Planks (now part of redesigned residential unit for monks)
152 Storeroom for Pinewood Planks (now part of redesigned residential unit for monks)
153 Kings Gate (*rgyal sgo*) or East Exit to Jangchub Jonlam in Barkor
154 Storeroom for Communal Barley (*rtsam bzhes pa'i grva 'jug khang*)
155 Staircase to Lower Gallery (*mda' gYab 'og*) and Accounting Room (*rtsis khang*)
156 Assembly Hall of Nyetang and Rato (*snye thang rva stod pa'i tshogs khang*)
157 South Exit to Jangchub Jonlam in Barkor
158 Chapel of Eight Medicine Buddhas (*sman bla bde gshegs brgyad*)
159 Chapel of Sixteen Elders
160 Assembly Hall of Drepung Ngakpa College (now detached and converted into housing)
161 Chapel of Lineage Holders of Graduated Path (*lam rim bla brgyud*)
162 Chapel of Eight Stūpas (*bde gshegs brgyad kyi mchod rten*)
163 Storeroom of Palace Treasury (*bla brang phyag mdzod kyi mdzod khang*)
164 Great South Gate (*lho sgo chen mo*), a.k.a. South Gate to Ganden (*dga' ldan lho sgo*)
165 Storeroom for Communal Barley (now disused)
166 Storeroom for Communal barley (now disused)
167 Outer Portal of Great South Gate
168 Debating Courtyard (*gsung chos rva*)
169 Outer Butter Storeroom of Palace Treasury (*bla phyag gi mar khang chen mo mdo*)
170 Inner Butter Storeroom of Palace Treasury (*bla phyag gi mar khang chen mo sbug*)
171 Pool of Melted Butter (*mar bzhu brdzing chung*)
172 Exit to Wood Enclosure
173 Double Staircase to Great Ceremonial Hall (*e vaṃ tshogs chen*)
174 Wood Enclosure (*shing rva chen mo*)
175 Prayer Festival Kitchen Larder door (*rung khang gi thab chas*)
176 Storeroom for Copper Tea Ladles
177 Storeroom for Silver Tea Ladles
178 Storeroom of the Magistrate of Lhasa (*lha sa gnyer tshang pa*)
179 Passageway to Great Kitchen (now converted into a residential unit)
180 Passageway to Great Kitchen (now converted into a residential unit)
181 Great Kitchen (*gsol ja'i rung khang chen mo*) (now converted into a residential unit)
182 Meeting Room (*tshogs khang*) for Wood Stewards and Servants of the Proctors
183 Staircase to Senior Proctors' Room (*zhal ngo khang*) (now demolished)
184 Oil Storeroom (*snum khang*, now converted into a residential unit)
185 Tea and Butter Storeroom (*ja mar khang*, now converted into a residential unit)
186 Water Gate (*chu sgo*), exit to Jangchub Jonlam in Barkor
187 Outbuilding (*gtsug lag khang 'debs sbyar khang*, now converted into a car park)
188 Wood Storeroom (*shing khang*)
189 Public Toilet (*spyi gcod*)
190 Storeroom for Communal Barley (*tsha grva'i rtsam khang*)
191 Plank Storeroom of Palace Treasury (*pang leb 'jug khang*)
192 Plank Storeroom of Palace Treasury (*pang leb 'jug khang*)
193 Staircase to Office of the Magistrates of Lhasa (*lha gnyer las khungs*) and the Proctors' Room (*zhal ngo khang*)
194 Great Victory Gate (*rgyal sgo chen mo*)
195 Pine Log Storeroom of Palace Treasury (*som hril 'jug khang*)
196 Pine Log Storeroom of Palace Treasury (*som hril 'jug khang*) these two rooms have been converted into a single storeroom for oil and rice
197 Main Gate (*gzim sgo lte ba*)
198 Vestibule
199 Outer Portal of Main Gate (*sgo mchor gyi gzim sgo phyi ma*)
200 Princess Wencheng 's Willow Tree stump (*jo bo'i dbu'i skra*)
201 Peace Treaty Obelisk (*rgya bod sa mtshams dbye ba'i chings rdo*)
202 Side Door of the Lugong Effigy (*glud 'gong gsang sgo*)
203 Maṇi Wheel Alcove (*ma ṇi bye chen lha khang*)
204 Sheep Pen (*lug tshang*)
205 Storeroom for Communal Dry Meat and Seasoning (*bzhes rdor yongs sha*)
206 Storeroom for Communal Butter (now empty)
207 Exit (now locked)
208 Wool Storeroom (*bal dang khul rtsid 'jug khang*)
209 Prostration Flagstones (*phyag 'tshal de bzad pa'i rdo gcal*)
210 Storeroom for Communal Barley (now empty)

Plan of the Middle Floor

a. The Great Temple

61 Chapel of the Guru (*guru'i lha khang*)
62 Unrestored Mural of Śrīdevī
63 Chapel of Cakrasaṃvara (*bde mchog gi lha khang*)
64 Stone Staircase
65 Chapel of the Graduated Path (*lam rim lha khang*)
66 Chapel of Munīndra and Retainers (*thub dbang gtso 'khor gyi lha khang*)
67 Three Hand-turned Maṇi Wheels (not yet restored)
68 Chapel of Munīndra (*thub dbang gi lha khang*)
69 Unrestored Mural of White Hayagrīva
70 Chapel of the King of the Śākyas (*shāk ya'i rgyal po'i lha khang*)
71 Protector Cavern of the Five Aspects of Pehar (*sku lnga'i mgon khang phug*)
72 Image of Cimara (*gnod sbyin tsi'u dmar po*)
73 Chapel of Aśvottama (*rta mchog lha khang*)
74 Chapel of the Religious King (*chos rgyal lha khang*)
75 Chapel of the Sages of the Six Realms (*thub pa rigs drug lha khang*)
76 Closed Staircase
77 Unrestored Chapel of the Seven Patriarchs (*nyan thos gtad rabs bdun*)
78 Unrestored Large Maṇi Wheels
79 Chapel of the Countenance (*zhal ras lha khang*)
80 Hermitage of the Religious King (*chos rgyal zim sbug*)
81 Hermitage of Tsongkhapa (*rje'i zim sbug*)
82 Hermitage of Lama Zhang (*bla ma zhang gi gzim phug*)
83 Kungarawa Woodblock Library (now lost)
84 Kungarawa Manuscript Libaray (now lost)

b. Annex

211 Great Ceremonial Hall (*e vaṃ phun tshogs 'dod 'khyil*)
212 Rear Entrance to Great Ceremonial Hall
213 Storeroom for Ceremonial Food (*dkar spro khang*), now empty
214 Unrestored Chapel of the Bon Protectress Srigyalma
215 Meeting Room (*tshogs khang*), now empty
217 Back Door (to government offices above and the Debating Courtyard below)
218 Back Door (to government offices above and the Debating Courtyard below)

219 Staircase to rooftop
220 Staircase to Storeroom of the Magistrate of Lhasa (*lha sa gnyer tshang pa*)
221 Staircase to Foreign Reception Office
222 Prayer Festival Administrator's Office (*spyi khyab las khungs*)
223 Doorway
224 Office of the Magistrates of Lhasa (*lha sa gnyer tshang pa*)
225 Inner Storeroom (*lha gnyer mdzod khang*)
226 Hermitage of Nechung Drayang Lingpa
227 Public Toilet
228 Storeroom for Ceremonial Food
229 Office of Senior Proctor from Drepung Assembly Hall
230 Office of Senior Proctor from Drepung Assembly Hall
231 Office of the Bursar (*spyi so*) of Drepung Monastery
232 Office of the Head (*sde pa*) of bKra-shis khang-gsar at Drepung
233 Demolished Staircase
234 Doorway
235 Hall of Phenomenal Existence (*gzim chung snang srid*)
236 Sunlight Apartment (*gzim chung snang srid nyi 'od*)
237 Private Room Used by Regent (now converted into residential area)
238 Chapel or Private Room of Paṇchen Lama (now converted into residential area)
239 Secret Passageway of Lugong Effigy
240 Staircase to Palace of the Dalai Lama
241 Hall Overpowering the Three World-Systems (*gzim chung khams gsum gzil gnon*)
242 Chamber containing good luck sacraments of Gonkar Yizhin Norbu (now kitchen)
243 Chamber containing good luck sacraments of the Bon tradition (now empty)
244 Chamber containing sacred objects of the Palace Treasury (now a residence)
245 Office Space for Clerks of the Palace Treasury (*bla phyag nang gzan kyi bzhugs yul*)
246 Doorway
247 Storeroom for Dried Fruit and Candy (*gYu lo bkod*), now a cashiers' office
248 Storeroom for Brocade and Fine Silk (*rin chen gter mdzod*), now a storeroom for dry meat
249 Storeroom for Textiles and Silver Ladles (*snam chas dang dngul rkyan khang*)
250 Staircase to Sheep Pen
251 Disused Storeroom for Condiments and Dried Meat (*bla phyag sha khang*)
252 Storeroom for Cotton Textiles (*lcang lo can*), now redesigned
253 Corridor of Palace Treasury
254 Vault of Palace Treasury (*gYang khang*), now a bank vault
255 Archive of Palace Treasury (*gna' 'jog khang*), now a bank vault
256 Storeroom of the Palace Treasury (*gsol mdzod khang*)
257 Staircase used by Dalai Lama
258 Prayer Festival Cashier's Room (*dngul rtsis khang*), now demolished
259 Storeroom for Cabinet Carpets and Upholstery (*bka' shag gdan khang*)
260 Storeroom for Tents and Canopies of the Palace Treasury (*bla phyag gur khang*), these last two rooms are now conjoined in a single residence, entered from the east
261 Way to storeroom of the offering planks (*mchod khri khang*)
262 Office of the Sacristan of Thousandfold Offerings (*stong mchod gnyer pa'i las shag*), now a residential unit
263 Butter Melting Room of the Palace Treasury (*mar bzhu khang*), now a residential unit
264 Storeroom of the Palace Treasury (*bzo khang byang gling kham mo che*), now a residential unit
265 Security Office (*bde 'jags las khungs*), now a residential unit
266 Litigation Office (*gyod zhib las khungs*), formerly the Land Revenue Office and now a residential unit
267 Door to Connecting Ramp
268 Staircase to public toilet
269 Criminal Investigation Bureau (*bsher khang*), now a residential unit
270 Storeroom (*mdzod khang*), now a residential unit
271 Rice Granary of the Palace Treasury, now a residential unit
273 Granary for Crushed Barley, now a toilet
274 Storeroom for Mineral-based Medicines, now a residential unit
275 Storeroom for Ritual Sacraments (*mchod rdzas 'jug khang*), now a residential unit
276 Staircase to Office of the Senior Sacristan (*sku gnyer dpon*)
277 Staircase to Storeroom of Palace Treasury
278 Government Chancellery (*spyi khyab rtsis khang phun tshogs bkod pa*), now empty
279 Staircase to inner walkway
280 Cabinet Kitchen (*bka' shag gsol thab*), now a residential unit
281 Cabinet Kitchen Utensil Room, now demolished
282 National Agricultural Bureau (*so nams las khungs*), now a residential unit
283 War Office (*dmag phog las khungs*), now a residential unit
284 Storeroom for Offering Grain (*mchod ' bru 'jug khang*), now a residential unit
285 Old Cabinet Archives (*bka' shag yig rnying 'jug khang*), now a residential unit
286 Rear Entrance to the Cabinet Office
287 Doorway, now a residential unit
288 Wooden Staircase, alongside which a toilet has now been constructed
289 Office of the Cabinet Secretary (*bka'shag drung yig gi las khungs*), now a residential unit
290 Cabinet Waiting Room (*bka' shag gi gzim chung 'gag*), now a redesigned residential unit
291 Cabinet Toilets (*bka' shag gi gzim gcod*)
292 Door to the Cabinet Rooms (*bka' shag gi gzim sgo*), now part of a redesigned residential unit
293 Cabinet Secretariat (*mgron drung sgang*), now part of a redesigned residential unit
294 Cabinet Office (*bka' shag lhan khang*), now part of a redesigned residential unit
295 Cabinet Archive (*bka' shag yang khang*), now part of a redesigned residential unit

Plan of the Top Floor

a. The Great Temple

85 Chapel of the Eight Medicine Buddhas (*sman bla bde gshegs brgyad kyi lha khang*)
86 Chapel of the Conqueror Śākyamuni (*rgyal ba shāk ya thub pa'i lha khang*)
87 Chapel of Śākyamuni and Retainers (*ston pa gtso 'khor gsum*)
88 Unrestored Ramp leading to public toilets
89 Chapel of the Eight Stūpas (*bde gshegs brgyad kyi mchod rten*)
90 Chapel of the Great Sage and Retainers (*thub dbang gtso 'khor gyi lha khang*)
91 Chapel Above the Head of Jowo Śākyamuni (*jo bo'i dbu thod lha khang*)
92 Sacristans' Top Floor Office (*rtse mo gnyer pa'i las shag*)
93 Chapel of the Śrīdevī Turret (*dpal lha lcog gi lha khang*)
94 Unrestored Bas Relief of Brahmā Śaṅkapāla (*tshangs pa dung tod can gyi lder sku*)

95 Newāri Doorway
96 Chapel of Peaceful Śrīdevī (*dpal ldan lha mo dung skyong ma'i lha khang*)
97 Chapel of Frog-faced Rematī (*dpal lha sbal gdong ma'i lha khang*)
98 Chapel of the Spiritual Teacher (*bla ma lha khang*)
99 Chapel of the Three-dimensional Maṇḍalas (*blos blangs khang*)
100 Chapel of the Nine Aspects of Amitāyus (*tshe dpag lha dgu*)
101 Chapel of Sixteen Elders (*gnas bcu lha khang*)
102 Double Staircase to Lower Gallery
103 Staircase to gilded roofs
104 Skylight of Main Hall (*dkyil 'khor mthil gyi seng gYab*)
105 Prayer flags (*dar lcog 'dzugs yul*)
106 Incense Burner (*bsang bum*)
107 Staircase to gilded roofs
108 Unrestored "twisted pillar" (*spyan log gis 'chus pa'i ka ba*)

b. Annex

296 Palace Verandah (*bla brang steng gi gzim chung 'gag*)
297 Pinnacle of Ganden" Hall (*dga' ldan yang rtse*)
298 Bay window (*rab gsal rgya phibs can*)
299 Library (*phyag dpe khang*)
300 Bedroom (*mtshan gzim khang*)
301 Back Door
302 Private Toilet
303 Public Toilet
304 Bright Corner Window (*zur 'phyongs rab gsal kun gsal*)
305 Its Inner Chamber (*zur 'phyongs rab gsal sbug gzim chung*)
306 Thousand-spoked Wheel flanked by two deer (*rtsibs stong ldan pa'i 'khor lo dangri dvags pho mo*)
307 Gilded-copper victory banners (*gser zangs kyi rgyal mtshan*)
308 Sacred Threadcross of Sigyalma (*bon lugs srid rgyal ma'i spa mdos*), unrestored
309 Workroom of the Palace Steward (*bla brang khang gnyer*), now demolished
310 Kitchen of the Top Floor (*rtse gsol thab khang*)
311 Corner Verandah (*zur 'phyongs gzim 'gag*), now a residential unit
312 Corner Hermitage (*zur 'phyongs gzim sbug*), now a residential unit
313 Endowment Office (*thebs sbyar las khungs*), formerly the National Mint and now part of a redesigned residential unit
314 Foreign Reception Office (*phyi rgyal las khungs*), now empty
315 Inner Chamber of the Foreign Reception Office (*de'i gzim sbug*)
316 Tax Office for Salt, Wool and Tea (*ja tsha las khungs*), now part of a redesigned residential unit
317 Sacristan' Top Floor Kitchen (*rtse mo'i gnyer pa*), now part of a redesigned residential unit
318 Kitchen of Meru Dratsang (*rme ru grva tshang gi rung khang*), now part of a redesigned residential unit
319 Public Toilet
320 Accounting Bureau (*rtsis zhib zhib khang las khungs*), now part of a redesigned residential unit
321 Office of the Senior Sacristan (*sku gnyer dpon gyi las shag*), now part of a redesigned residential unit
322 Public Toilet
323 Treasury of Offering Sacraments (*chos rdzas sgang*), now part of a redesigned residential unit

Plan of the Rooftop

109 Gilded Roof of the Chapel of Jowo Śākyamuni (*jo bo'i rgya phibs*)
110 Gilded Roof of the Chapel of Four Sibling Maitreya (*byams pa'i rgya phibs*)
111 Gilded Roof of the Chapel of King Songtsen Gampo (*chos rgyal rgya phibs*)
112 Gilded Roof of the Chapel of Mahākāruṇika (*thujs rje rgya phibs*)
113 Southeast Turret, a.k.a. Chapel of Wrathful Mother Śrīdevī (*dpal lha yum dragmo'i shar lho'i lcog*)
114 Small Prayer Flag (*dar chen chung chung*)
115 Southwest Turret, a.k.a. Chapel of the Five Sisters of Longlife (*tshe ring mched lnga'i nub lho lcog*)
116 Northwest Turret (*nub byang gi lcog*)
117 Northeast Turret, a.k.a. Chapel of Sixteen Elders (*gnas bcu'i shar byang gi lcog*)

People gathering sanctified barley grains during the Great Congregation festival. (1986 CB)

Footnotes

1 According to the Tang Annals, King Songtsen Gampo passed away in 649 or 650. Later Tibetan histories claim, however, that he passed away in 698 at the age of eighty-two. See H. E. Richardson, "How Old was Songtsen Gampo" in *High Peaks, Pure Earth*, pp. 3-6.

2 On the edicts of Trisong Detsen (*bka' mchid*) and Senalek Jingyon (*bka'gtsigs*) which proclaim adherence to Buddhism and augment the epigraphic inscriptions of the Samye and Karchung obelisks respectively, see Pawo Tsuklak Trengwa, mKhas pa'i dga' ston, Vol. 1, pp. 373 and 409; and H. E. Richardson, *A Corpus of Early Tibetan Inscriptions*, pp. 28-9 and 76-7; also the latter's article "The First Tibetan Chos-' byung" *in High Peaks, Pure Earth*, pp. 89-99.

3 See Atiśa (disc.), *bKa' chems ka khol ma*, pp. 230ff.; and Drubthob Ngodrub (disc.), *Ma ṇi bka' 'bum*, f. 137b. The extant versions of the former are outlined in Martin (1997), no. 4, pp. 24-25, and the latter is discussed in no. 16, p. 30. On the anachronisms of the Ma ṇi bka' ' bum, see Martin, no. 16; also M. Aris, Bhutan, pp. 8-24, and M. Kapstein, "Remarks on the Maṇi bKa' 'bum and the Cult of Avalokiteśvara in Tibet", in S. D. Goodman and R. M. Davidson (eds), *Tibetan Buddhism: Reason and Revelation*. The *Tang Annals* appear not to cover Tibetan historical events prior to 634, although earlier Tibetan legends and contacts with the Tibetan world are mentioned in the *Old Tibetan Chronicle* from Dunhuang and in older dynastic histories, such as the Sui Annals. See M. Kapstein, *The Tibetans*, pp. 52-55, and R. Vitali, *Early Temples of Central Tibet*, pp. 70-74.

4 On the extant versions of this text, see Martin (1997), no. 18 (pp. 30-31). For a brief biography of Nyangrel, see Dudjom Rinpoche (1991), pp. 755-759, and particularly on his relationship with Drubthob Ngodrub, and the *Ma ṇi bka' 'bum* cycle, *op. cit*, p. 757. Nyangral's history is an important alternative source describing the origins of the Jokhang and the intrigues of Songtsen Gampo's two foreign queens. For Heather Stoddard's appraisal of this account, see below, pp. 160-177.

5 Tibetan accounts give different dates for the inception of the construction of the Great Temple, and for its duration. See R. Vitali, *op. cit*, p. 72. Contemporary scholarship tends to favour the earlier date because Newār influence on the Tibetan court appears to have preceded the arrival of Wencheng in 641. See below, pp. 49-51.

6 See G. Tucci, "The Wives of Srong brtsan Sgam po", in *Oriens Extremus*, ix (1962), pp. 121-6. For the traditional dating, see Pawo Tsuklak Trengwa, *mKhas pa'i dga' ston*, Vol. 1, pp. 204 and 234.

7 See below, pp. 163 ff.; also R. Vitali, *Early Temples of Central Tibet*, pp. 70-75; A. Heller, "The Lhasa gTsug lag khang: Observations on the Ancient Wood Carvings", in Lhasa Valley *Conference Proceedings*, 1997; and H. Stoddard, "Restoration in the Lhasa Tsuglagkhang and the Fate of Its Early Wall Paintings", in *Orientations*, Vol. XX, pp. 69-73.

8 On the comparison with the doorways at Ajanta, see below, p. 222-3; also G. Beguin and P. Caffarrelli, *Demeures des hommes, Sanctuaires des dieux*, pp. 258-60. With regard to the theory that the Great Temple may initially have functioned as a royal residence, see below, pp. 161; also A. Heller, *op.cit.*

9 The lake was in all probability part of the marshland formed by the confluence of the Kyichu its south flowing tributaries in the Lhasa area. Marshland can still be seen north of Damra Rd in Lhasa, while the sand-banks of the Kyichu River are clearly visible to the south. Most of the tributaries have been integrated within a local irrigation system in recent decades. See Dorje (2004a), p. 60. The major geomantic temples are listed in, e.g. *Ma ṇi bka' 'bum* and *rGyal-rabs gsal-ba'i me-long*. One enumeration of these peripheral temples, based on the latter work, is given below, p. 50. For an appraisal of the diverse enumerations found in both early and later chronicles, and their sources, see M. Aris, *Bhutan*, pp. 8-33. Many of the extant geomantic temples are described individually in Dorje (2004a & 2004b)

10 Some historians have doubted this contribution, preferring to associate these activities with Princess Jincheng who reached Tibet in 710. See H. E. Richardson, "The Growth of a Legend", in *High Peaks, Pure Earth*, pp. 39-47; and "Two Chinese Princesses in Tibet," *op.cit.*, pp. 207-15. For a contemporary description of Ramoche, see Dorje (2004a), pp. 88-90.

11 It is unclear to me how the columns would have divided the interior of the hall into thirty-seven sections. For a detailed description of the diffent phase of the building's colonadization, see Ande Alexander's article below, pp. 224-229.

12 An account of these treasures and their concealment is found in Orgyan Lingpa's 14th century revelation, *rGyal po bka' thang*, p. 157.

13 For the original schemata and an appraisal of Tibetan sources referring to it, see R. Vitali, *Early Temples of Central Tibet*, pp. 74-77.

14 See below, p. 84.

15 These texts, listed in the bibliography, are some of the major sources consulted by Zhakabpa while preparing this *Inventory to the Great Temple.* For further information, see Martin (1997) – on Buton's history no. 72, pp. 50-51, on Tshalpa Kunga Dorje's *Red Annals*, no. 77, pp. 52-53, on Sonam Gyaltsen's work no. 94, pp. 60-61, on Go Lotsāwa's *Blue Annals*, no. 141, pp. 78-79, and on Pawo Tsuklak Trengwa's history, no. 168, pp. 88-89.

16 The invasion of Lhasa by Chinese forces following the death of King Songtsen Gampo appears to have been a fabrication of later Tibetan historians. See the discussion in H. E. Richardson, "The Growth of a Legend", in *High Peaks, Pure Earth*, pp. 39-47.

17 See below, p. 71. Zhakabpa attributes this action somewhat anachronistically to Princess Jin-cheng who had already died in 739.

18 See below, pp. 94-95.

19 Contemporary scholarship suggests that the Tibetan empire may have come to an end, partly due to economic implosion as a result of expensive wars and over-extended military logistics, in which case the persecution of the Great Temple in the reign of Lang Darma and its aftermath has been reinterpreted as a casual neglect, rather than a deliberate persecution, as later sources have sought to emphasize. See eg. M. Kapstein (2006), pp. 77-83.

20 See below, p. 75.

21 For a description of the original wall paintings, based on Pawo Tsuklak Trengwa, *mKhas pa'i dga' ston*, Vol. 1, pp. 239, ff., see R. Vitali, *Early Temples of Central Tibet*, pp. 76-8.

22 The ancient murals of the north, north-east and south-east wings of the middle floor were removed recently by Chinese archaeologists. For an account of this deconstruction and the storage of the seventy dismantled panels of the north wing, see H. Stoddard, *op. cit.*, pp. 69-73; and for illustrations prior to their removal, see *The Jokhang*, pp. 76-7; and Liu Lizhong (ed) *Buddhist Art of the Tibetan Plateau*, Plates 271-2. All the murals of the middle floor have now been "renovated" with the exception of the original paintings that survive in the south-east Chapel of the Countenance.

23 For an account of their survival of the Cutural Revolution and subsequent damage inflicted in the name of conservation, see Heather Stoddard's contribution below, pp. 193-6.

24 See the useful note on the sources and background to this contested date in R. Vitali, *Early Temples of Central Tibet*, p. 62, note 1.

25 See below, p. 76.

26 See below, p. 83.

27 On the construction of this Chapel of the Countenance by Zangkar Lotsāwa, see R. Vitali, *Early Temples of Central Tibet*, pp. 78-82.

28 See Pawe Tsuklak Trengwa, *mKhas pa'i dga' ston*, Vol. 1, p. 448.

29 For illustrations, see below, pp. 193-6; also R. Vitali, *Early Temples of Central Tibet*, pp. 80-1, and H. Stoddard, *op. cit.*, pp. 71-2.

30 See below, p. 55; and on the lives of these three figures, see also Dudjom Rinpoche (1991), pp. 653-659, and p. 758.

31 For an account of the kings of this Himalayan enclave, see D. Jackson, *The Mallas of Mustang.*

32 A statue of Gewabum was formerly installed in the Southern Inner Sanctum, on which see below, p. 76.

33 See below, p. 75.

34 See below, p. 56.

35 See below, p. 83.

36 On these developments, see also Troru Khenpo Tsenam, *dPal mnyam med mar pa bka' brgyud kyi grub pa'i mtha' rnam par nge par byed pa mdor bsdus su brjodpa dvags brgyud grub pa'i me long*, p. 80.
37 This account largely follows H. E. Richardson, *Ceremonies of the Lhasa Year*, pp. 110-3.
38 The kingdom of Xixia in present day Ningxia province was annihilated by Genghiz Qan in 1227.
39 See below, p. 68; and for a contemporary description of Gongkar Monastery, see Dorje (2004a), p. 167.
40 The lives of all these five founders of Sakya (*gong ma lnga*) are recounted in Jamgon Amye's 17th century *Sa skya gdung rabs ngo mtshar bang mdzod*, on which see Martin (1997) no. 210, p. 104.
41 On this latter work, see Martin (1997), no. 118, pp. 69-70.
42 For references to recent research on this text and its author, see Martin (1997), no. 65, p. 47.
43 For an illustration of some of these statues, or rather their modern replicas, see below, pp. 12 and 69, and on the yak-horn of Milarepa, see pp. 71-72.
44 A description of this festival is given below, and on the events surrounding the inaugural Great Prayer Festival of 1409, see Heather Stoddard's contribution below, pp. 178-192.
45 The life of Tsongkhapa is recounted in Druk Gyalwang Choje, *rNam thar thub bstan mdzes ba'i rgyan gcig ngo mtshar nor bu'i phreng ba*. On Tsongkhapa's somewhat controversial activities in relation to Jowo Śākyamuni, see below, p. 73; and especially Tashi Tsering's article, pp. 126-27.
46 See below, pp. 92-6 and 102.
47 Nowadays this is a car park.
48 HH Dalai Lama refers to this rivalry in his reminiscences of the Great Temple during the 1940s and 1950s. See below, p. 36.
49 Smuggled video footage documenting the storming of the Great Temple and the maltreatment of monks has been shown in a succession of television documentaries. More recently, in March 2008, a series of demonstrations in front of the Great Temple sparked a period of unrest throughout the Tibetan plateau, during which violent incidents occurred and all signs of dissent were brutally suppressed.
50 One finger of the gilded copper central image is said to contain the actual finger of King Songtsen Gampo. On these images and their chapel, see below, p. 81.
51 The biography of Thangtong Gyalpo, the "Leonardo of Tibet" has recently been translated into English, and thoroughly researched in Cyrus Steans, *King of the Empty Plain*. See also Gyurme Dechen, *Thang stong rnam thar kun gsal nor bu*, and J. Gyatso, "Genre, Authorship, and Transmission in Visionary Buddhism: The Literary Traditions of Thang-stong rGyal-po," in Davidson R. and Goodman, S. (eds), Tibetan Buddhism: Reason and Revelation.
52 Although the line of Phagmodru kings continued from 1478 until 1617, the later *gong ma* had only titular power.
53 Tashi Tsering, director of the Amnye Machen Institute in Dharamsala, drew to my attention the chronicles of Daklha Gampo Monastery, which are preserved in manuscript form at Rumtek Monastery in Sikkim. These early 17th century texts include Trin-le Da'o's *Gangs can 'dir ston pa'i rgyal tshab dpal ldan sgam po pa'i khri gdung 'dzin pa'i dam pa rnams kyi gtam baiḍūrya'i phreng ba*, and Gampopa Mipham Chokyi Wangchuk's *gDan sa che -po dpal dvag -lha sgam po'i ngo mtshar gyi bkod pa dad pa'i me tog*. Further study will reveal whether their accounts serve to balance the partisan Gelug accounts of this period, such as that presented by Sumpa Khenpo in his *Chos'byung dpag bsam ljon bzang*.
54 See below, p. 58.
55 See below, p. 58. Biographical accounts of the lives of the early Dalai Lamas appear in a number of works, including Paṇchen Sonam Drakpa (1478-1554), *bKa'gdams gsar rnying gi chos 'byung*, See also G. Mullin, *The Fourteen Dalai Lamas*.
56 On the varying editions of Fifth Dalai Lama's composition, see Martin (1997) no, 222, pp. 107-8, and on Sangye Gyatso's *Yellow Beryl*, no. 240, pp. 114-5.
57 This image no longer exists. See below, p. 80.
58 On the identification of this mural which is problematic, see below, p. 97, note 225.
59 These activities are mentioned in the three-volume autobiography of the Fifth Dalai Lama, entitled *Ngag dbang blo bzang rgya mtsho'i 'di snang 'khrul pa'i rol rtsad rtogs brjod kyi tshul du bkod pa du ku la'i gos bzang*, The inscription has been copied by Prince Peter of Greece and Denmark, Michael Henss, and André Alexander, among others.
60 This text was republished by Bod ljongs dpe-skrun-khang in 2002, and I have referred to this edition in certain notes.
61 This account follows H. E. Richardson, *Ceremonies of the Lhasa Year*, pp. 60-81.
62 These ceremonies may not have been held publicly during the period when the death of the Fifth Dalai Lama was concealed by the regent Sangye Gyatso. See H. E. Richardson, *Ceremonies of the Lhasa Year*, p. 61.
63 On the Sixth Dalai Lama, see M Aris, *Hidden Teachings and Secret Lives*, pp. 109ff. The detailed biography of his early life is that written by Sangye Gyatso, entitled *Rab gsal gser gyi snye ma*. In general, he is held to have died at Kokonor in 1706. However, according to the *Secret Biography* (*tshangs dbyangs rgya mtsho'i gsang rnam*) by Ngawang Lhundrub Dargye Nomonqan, he died in Amdo in 1746. On the life of Sangye Gyatso, see Gegyepa Tendzin Dorje, "sDe srid sangs rgyas rgya mtsho'i byung ba don bsdus rang bzhin gsong por smras pa'i gtam," in *Bod ljong zhib 'jug*, No. 2 (1985), pp. 31-4. Very brief biographical sketches can also be found in the introductions to Parfianovitch, Dorje & Meyer (1992) and Dorje (2001).
64 See below, p. 74. The slaying of Sangye Gyatso by Lhazang Qan is discussed in M. Aris, *Hidden Teachings and Secret Lives*, pp. 162ff.
65 Richardson, in *High Peaks Pure Earth*, p. 238, suggests that he too may have authored an inventory to the contents of the Great Temple. An important work on the life of this figure is Dokhar Zhabdrung Tsering Wangyal's *dPal mi'i dbang po'i rtogs brjod*, which was written in 1733. See Martin (1997), no. 270, pp. 123-4.
66 See below, p. 104. The biography of the Seventh Dalai Lama entitled *rGyal ba'i dbang po thams cad mkhyen gzigs rdo rje 'chang blo bzang bskal bzang rgya mtsho dpal bzang po'i zhal snga mas kyi rnam thar mdo tsam brjod pa dpag bsam rin po che'i snye ma* was written by Cangkya Rolpei Dorje of Gonlung in Amdo.
67 See below, pp. 60 and 92. A biography of the Eighth Dalai Lama appears in *Gangs can mkhas grub rim byon ming mdzod*, pp. 389-91 and a short account of the life of the regent is also included, *op. cit.*, pp. 490-92.
68 See below, p. 60. A biography of the regent may be found in *Gangs can mkhas grub rim byon ming mdzod*, pp. 486-8, along with a brief biography of the Eleventh Dalai Lama, *op. cit.*, pp. 382-3.
69 See below, pp. 61-2, 99 and 102.
70 See below, pp. 62 and 105.
71 See below, p. 71. A short biography of the Thirteenth Dalai Lama is contained in *Gangs can mkhas grub rim byon ming mdzod*, pp. 393-395.
72 See below, p. 87; and for a contemporary description of Tsurphu Monastery, see Dorje (2004a), pp. 139-141.
73 This aspiration is widely shared by historians such as Tashi Tsering and learned monks, such as Lama Thubten Rinchen.
74 This text is contained in *rGyal chog bcu gsum pa'i gsung 'bum*, Bi, pp. 661-84. I am indebted to Mr Ngawang Tutop Nargyid for locating this important source.
75 Some of these anecdotes have been compiled below by Tashi Tsering. See pp. 138-9. Among them the celebrated story of Jowo Ben of Kongpo is best known through Paltrul Rinpoche, *The Words of My Perfect Teacher* (*Kun bzang bla ma'i zhal lung*), pp. 174-5.
76 On the pilgrimage guide of Jamyang Khyentse Wangpo, see Martin (1997) no. 400, p. 166, and on Katok Situ Chokyi Gyatso's guide, no. 433, p. 176.
77 See S. C. Das, Journey to *Lhasa and Central Tibet;* P. Landon, Lhasa (2 vols); G. T. Tsybikov, "Lhasa and Central Tibet", *Smithsonian Institute Annual Report, 1903, L. A. Waddell, Lhasa and its Mysteries*, and E. H. C. Walsh, "Lhasa" in *Journal of the Royal Asiatic Society*, 1946.
78 See G. Tucci, *To Lhasa and Beyond*, pp. 118-20, H. Harrer, *Seven Years in Tibet*, and Lowell Thomas Jr, *Out of this World*.
79 HH Dalai Lama has made some particularly strong remarks in relation to this incident. See below, p. 33.
80 See V. Sis & J. Vanis, *On the Road Through Tibet*. Spring Books, London.
81 These events in the early life of the Dalai Lama are documented in his official biographies, *My Land and My People*, and *Freedom in Exile*. See also Chapter One of the present work.
82 Oral communication. I interviewed Mrs R. D. Taring, author of *Daughter of Tibet*, at her home in Rajpur in March 2000, shortly before her death. The photographs taken by the father of the contemporary Beijing-based Tibetan writer Whoeser vividly illustrate these events. See p. 24.

83 See below, p. 63.
84 See H. E. Richardson, "The Jo-khang Great Temple of Lhasa", in *High Peaks, Pure Earth*, pp. 237-260.
85 See R. *Vitali, Early Temples of Central Tibet*, pp. 70-75; A. Heller, "The Lhasa gTsug lag khang: Observations on the Ancient Wood Carvings", in *Lhasa Valley Conference Proceedings*, 1997; and H. Stoddard, "Restoration in the Lhasa Tsuglakhang and the Fate of Its Early Wall Paintings", in *Orientations*, Vol. XX, pp. 69-73; also below, pp. 193-6.
86 See *Dazhaosi*, Beijing Publishing House, 1980. The illustrated *Lha sa gtsug lag khang*, published in 2000, has captions and text by Nyima Tsering, one of the most influential of contemporary monks associated with the Great Temple.
87 Formerly, the first offerings on that day would be presented by the Dalai Lama and his government officials. See H. E. Richardson, *Ceremonies of the Lhasa Year*, p. 109.
88 See below, pp. 100-1 and 105.
89 See below, p. 80.
90 See above, p. 11, and below, p. 73.
91 On this chronology, see R. Vitali, *Early Temples of Central Tibet*, pp. 70-74. Since Nepalese records and the earliest Tibetan chronicles appear not to mention this princess or a matrimonial alliance with Nepal, Richardson, Slusser and other scholars have questioned her existence.
92 This princess is known in Tibet under the name Mun-sheng Kon-jo. Richardson and others have speculated that many activities attributed to her were actually the work of the eighth century Tang princess Jin-cheng (Tib. Kim-sheng kon-jo). See above, p. 8 and below pp. 160-177.
93 For a description of the original Potala Palace, see Minyag Chokyi Gyaltsen, "Srong btsan sgam po'i dus kyi pho brang potala'i bzo dyibs dang chags tshul skor rob tsam dpyad pa", in E. Sperling (ed), *Tibetan Studies*, 2000.
94 The role of Wencheng in introducing these scrolls of elemental divination (*'byung rtsis*) is discussed in Dorje (2001).
95 For a detailed account of the various enumerations of these geomantic temples and their disparate identifications, see M. Aris, *Bhutan*, pp. 8-33. Zhakabpa adds that, among them, the location of Tshangpa Lungnon has been disputed. According to the *Biography of Longdol Lama*, it was situated alongside Nyethang Chodzong, whereas Katok Situ Chokyi Gyatso in his *dBus gstang gnas yig* identifies it with Nyetri Namnang Lhakhang in the vicinity of Oyuk Gongon Lhakhang. For contemporary individual descriptions of most of these buildings, see Dorje (2004a & 2004b). The significance of geomantic stones which were affixed to the Great Temple, in order to suppress inimical elemental forces is discussed below, by Heather Stoddard. See pp. 160-177.
96 Many paintings can be found illustrating this geomantic layout, which is still a popular theme for modern artists based in the Barkor and in Norbulingka.
97 See above, p. 7. This date is corroborated in the chronicles of Buton, Tshalpa Kunga Dorje, and Sakya Sonam Gyaltsen.
98 Cf. the passage from the *Scholars Delight*, p. 235, which is reproduced below by André Alexander, p. 229.
99 Some sources such as Nyangrel's *Religious History*, p. 252, claim that Bhṛkuṭīdevī herself built the top floor, but see above, p. 9.
100 On this distinction between the Newar and Indian phases of construction, see Heather Stoddard's contribution below, pp. 163-8.
101 See Nyangrel's *Religious History*, p. 252.
102 The verses and various prophetic injunctions that follow derive from the *Ma ṇi bka' 'bum*, on which see above, note 3.
103 See above, p. 9.
104 As stated above, note 19, there is some evidence suggesting that economic difficulties and military over-extension may have been responsible for the implosion of the Tibetan empire, and the decline of Buddhism may therefore have been due more to neglect in some quarters than to persecution.
105 Zhakabpa mentions an oral tradition referring to Langdarma's edict (*Glang dar khrims 'phog ma*), which claims that there were old bronze images of the buddhas and bodhisattvas which had been pierced by chisels.
106 In Dudjom Rinpoche (1991), p. 605, Lhalung Pelgyi Dorje is known as one of the eight students of Nyak Jñānakumāra, whose names included the affix *dpal*. At the age of seventeen he met Guru Padmasambhava at Paro Taktsang in modern Bhutan, and was accepted as a student by Yeshe Tshogyal. It was predicted by his meditational deity and by his spiritual teacher that he would become a great demon-subduing hero. When he "liberated" the apostate king, he had approximately reached the age of fifty-eight, after which he fled to Kham and Amdo, and remained there in retreat into his eighties. He is said to have sought out two Chinese monks to complete the quorum required for the complete monastic ordination of Lachen Gongpa Rabsel, and subsequently to have given the transmission of the *sMan bla'i mdo chog* to king Nam-de Osung. For descriptions of the sites in Amdo, with which his memory is associated, including Dentik and Achung Namdzong, see Dorje (2004a).
107 According to the *Blue Annals* (*deb sngon*), there were four ḍākinīs among the students of Phadampa Sangye, namely: Labkyi Dronma from Eyul, Jomo Jangchub from Nyel, Zhangmo Gyalthing from Tsang, and Nyonma of Lhasa. Among them, Nyonma of Lhasa promoted Buddhist activities and clearly foresaw that Atiśa would be the discoverer of the *King's Testament* (*rgyal po'i bka' 'chems*). The *Ka khol ma* itself claims that it would be extracted from a place two and a half arm spans from the Vase Pillar (*ka ba bum pa can*), but there are some sources stating that this in fact refers to the Leaf Pillar (*ka ba shing lo can*). On this text, see above, note 3.
108 On this chapel, see above, pp. 79 and 193-6. Zangkar Lotsāwa in 1076 (fire dragon year of the first sexagenary cycle) is said to have translated the *Ornament of Valid Cognition* (*tshad ma rgyan*) and given many exegeses on the outer and inner Yogatantras during a religious festival in Ngari. According to the *Blue Annals (Deb sngon)*, he was in his forty-sixth year when he translated the *Ornament of Valid Cognition* (*tshad ma rgyan*).
109 The "factionalism at Lhasa" (*lha sa sde 'khrug*) refers to the alienation of the descendents of Osung and Yumten, and the schism between the upholders of the Lower Tibetan Vinaya lineage. On this turbulent period, see also R. Vitali, *The Kingdoms of Gu.ge Pu.hrang*.
110 Concerning the involvement of Gompa Tshultrim Nyingpo, see also the passage cited below, pp. 124-6, by Tashi Tsering.
111 On this Tshalpa connection, see above, pp. 11-12.
112 Both *rGya -rabs gsal-ba'i me long* and *rDzogs ldan gzhon nu'i dga' ston* identify this figure as a King of Yartse, which is a synonym for the region of Mustang and Jumla in NW Nepal, as stated in Tshewang Norbu's biography. Zhakabpa adds that, elsewhere, Katok Tsewang Norbu in his *Bod kyi lha btsan po'i gdung rab* refers to this location as "Yartse in Zhang-zhung" (*zhang zhung ya rtse*).
113 Brief biographies of these figures are contained in Dudjom Rinpoche (1991), pp. 653-9, and 758-9.
114 See above, pp. 13-14; also see the *Crystal Mirror Inventory* of the Fifth Dalai Lama (*dKar chag shel dkar*).
115 These events are recorded in Lechen Kunga Gyaltshen, *bKa' gdams chos 'byung gsal ba'i sgron me*, which was composed in 1494. See Martin (1997), no. 148.
116 Zhakabpa notes that a full account of these events is given in Chahar Geshe Lobzang Tshultrim, *rJe rin po che'i rnam thar go sla bar brjod pa dge legs kun byung*, on which see Martin (1997), no. 339, p. 145. This work, composed circa 1800, contains in addition to the biography of Tsongkhapa further historical information on the early development of the Gelugpa school.
117 According to the Fifth Dalai Lama's *rDzogs ldan gzhon nu'i dga'ston*, composed in 1643, a relative of Neu Namka Zangpo, named Neupa Depa Drakpa, replaced the tiled roof (*gyo thog*) of the temple, and erected the pavilion-style roofs of the courtyard and inner walkway. Zhakabpa adds that, according to the late Trijang Rinpoche, the term *gyo thog* is interpreted to mean "slate roof". On this text, see above, note 56.
118 A description of the inaugural Great Prayer Festival is found below, pp. 178-192.
119 On this controversy, see the comments of Tashi Tsering, pp. 126-7.
120 See Druk Gyalwang Choje, *rJe rin po che'i rnam thar thub bstan mdzes rgyan*, f. 298.
121 These events are recounted in Gyurme Dechen, *Thang stong rnam thar kun gsal nor bu*. See the translation in Cyrus Stearns, *King of the Empty Plain*, pp. 283-5.
122 The polemical stance of the Mongolian scholar Sumpa Khenpo Yeshe Peljor (1704-1788) is well kmown. On his *dPag bsam ljon bzang*, which was composed in 1748 and covers the evolution of Buddhism in India, China, Tibet and Mongolia, see Martin (1997), no. 289, pp. 129-30. Less derogatory references to the state of the Great Temple during this period may be found in the early 17th century writings such as Gampopa Mipham Chokyi Wangchuk's *gDan sa chen po dpal dvags lha sgam po'i ngo mtshar gyi bkod pa*

dad pa'i me tog, and Trin-le Da'o 's *Gangs can 'dir ston pa'i rgyal tshab dpal ldan sgam po pa'i khri gdung 'dzin pa'i dam pa rnams kyi gtam baiḍūrya'i phreng ba,* the manuscripts of which are preserved at Rumtek Monastery in Sikkim.

123 Zhakabpa notes that these events are recorded in the biography of Neljor Wangchuk Drakpa Tha-ye, entitled *rNam thar ngo mtshar nor bu.*

124 For further detail, refer to Yangpa Choje, *Biography of rGyal ba dge 'dun rgya mtsho* (*rNam thar dpag bsam ljon bzang*).

125 See the biography of the Third Dalai Lama, Sonam Gyatso, *entitled rNam thar dngo grub rgya mtsho'i shing rta.*

126 These donations are recorded in the Thirteenth Dalai Lama's Inventory to the Great Temple, entitled *dKar chag dad snang 'bum phrag 'char ba'i 'o mtsho'i rdzing bu.*, on which see above, note 74.

127 See the Biography of the Fourth Paṇchen entitled *sPyod tshul gsal bar ston pa nor bu' 'phreng ba*, p. 116 ff.

128 Zhakabpa notes here that according to the *dKar chags skal bzang dad pai'sgo 'byed ngo mtshar rgya mtsho'sde mig* there was a middle ranking servant of the *Tshalpa Tripon* Ganden Zangpo of Trehor, named Dongyal who attended on both the Tshalpa and Zhika Neupa governors. Consequently, he was appointed as administrator of Nyangban Ganden, and given the title Gandenpa. The power and influence of his family increased over several generations, until one of his descendents, General Sonam Gyalpo, received the entire Jeri Taktse estate as a reward for exemplary heroism in battle. When the Fifth Dalai Lama was young he visited this Ganden Khangsar estate at Taktse. His autobiography (*Du ku la go bzang*) clearly recounts that the dilapidated butter lamps of the Great Temple were replaced by the Ganden Khangsar. Subsequently, during the time of the regent Sonam Chopel, the head of Ganden Khangsar appears to have been given a role in government.

129 It is said that several of the pillars used in the construction of the Great Courtyard were removed from the destroyed monastery of Tashi Zilnon in Zhigatse, following the victory of the Gelugpa faction in the Civil War. On this, see André Alexander's article, below, p. 210.

130 The murals are described in the Fifth Dalai Lama's autobiography (*Du ku la'i gos bzang*), ff. 94-100; and the balcony in Sangye Gyatso's *Yellow Beryl* (*Vaiḍūrya ser po*), ff. 74-79.

131 Zhakabpa notes that this phase of restoration is documented in the biography of Ngawang Tshultrim of Tshemonling, entitled *Tshe gling no mi han gyi rnam thar dad pa'i sgo 'byed.*

132 This is recorded in the Thirteenth Dalai Lama's Inventory to the Great Temple (*dKar chags dad snang 'bum phrag 'char ba'i 'o thang mtsho'i rdzing bu*).

133 The source is the same as that mentioned in the previous note.

134 See below, pp. 242-243.

135 Bracketed numbers refer to the plans of the chapels and images within the Great Temple. See below, pp. 108-111.

136 This is indicated in the plan of the Great Temple made by Taring Dzaku. However, Zhakabpa notes that this may requires further research because he had not seen any reference to it in other historical documents.

137 Zhakabpa omits Śākyaketu, and associates the chapel with only the other seven medicine buddhas.

138 A detailed description of the hand-emblems of the thousand arms is given in *rGyal rabs gsal ba'i me long*, ff. 7b.4. Zhakabpa adds that although most historical works do suggest that the original image had one thousand arms, according to the biography of Ngawang Chodrak Gyatso entitled *Tambura'i sgra dbyangs* the thousand arms were added at a later date.

139 This is *the Ma ṇi bka' 'bum* which was reputedly extracted as treasure from below the foot of Hayagrīva by the accomplished master Ngodrub. See above, note 3.

140 These oral instructions are mentioned in the *Ma ṇi bka' 'bum* and the *rGyal rabs gsal ba'i me long.*

141 According to *bKa' gdams chos 'byung gsal ba'i sgron me*, f. 50a.7, Atiśa remarked that there was no more astonishing image of Mahākāruṇika than this one, believing that the image actually was Mahākāruṇika in person. Zhakabpa also notes that, according to the *rNam thar thugs rje chen po'i zlo gar,* at a later date, when no-one was able to straighten the tilt of this image, Drukpa Kunkhyen Pema Karpo entered the chapel and prayed, touching his head to its heart, whereupon the image with a sharp crack naturally straightened its posture.

142 In connection with the origin of the name Rangjon Ngaden, the *dKar chag shel dkar me* long recounts that two lights emerged from the image of Mahākāruṇika. At the end of one of these lights the wrathful deity Amṛtakuṇḍalin appeared, and usurped the abodes of the *ma mo* spirits, encircling them with an indestructible perimeter. At the end of the other ray of light, Hayagrīva appeared and from his mouth a thunderous conflagration emerged, expelling the gods and demons to the furthest periphery of the ocean. These lights were then re-absorbed within this natural image. In addition there was a natural *urāgagarbha* sandalwood image of Mahākāruṇika, which inserted itself within the image as a mantra core, and there were the actual bodies of King Songtsen Gampo and his two queens who subsequently vanished into it. For all these reasons, the image came to be known as Rangjon Ngaden (*rang byon lnga ldan*).

143 A photograph of this remnant was published by the Information Office, Dharamsala, in their newsletter (February, 1967). On this see also H. E. Richardson, "The Jokhang Great Temple of Lhasa" in *High Peaks, Pure Earth,* p. 251.

144 Zhakabpa adds that, according to an uncorroborated report of the late Ling Rinpoche, this image had been sculpted by students of Tsongkhapa, and was originally kept at Tsongkhapa's residence in Lhasa (later known as the residence of Depon Thonpawa). It was here that the master commented on its striking physical resemblance and handled it personally, endowing it with great blessings. Later, Shankhawa Gyurme Sonam Tobgye had it transferred to the Great Temple.

145 See his autobiography, entitled *sNa tshogs stug po'i 'khri shing.*

146 Richardson, *op. cit.*, p. 251, adds that this image was known locally as Gungthang Meshor – "Gung-thang is on fire!" because a finger of its out-stretched hand pointed in that direction. On the account of the Chinese invasion of Lhasa, which never actually occurred, see above, note 16.

147 On this, see the reminiscences of HH Dalai Lama, above, p. 34.

148 Despite the lack of documentary evidence, there is an oral tradition which says that the images of the Four Great Guardian Kings were frolicking at the time when they were installed. At that very moment, the gaze of Dhṛtarāṣṭra and Virūḍhaka caused a pilgrim entering the Jokhang to lose his senses, and the gaze of Virūpākṣa and Vaiśravaṇa caused him to become stupefied. Therefore, even now, the images of the great kings to the left have a harsh expression while those to the right have a jovial expression. The physical demeanours of the great kings will be seen, even nowadays, to accord with that legendary account.

149 Zhakabpa anachronistically attributes these actions to Princess Jin-cheng who had already passed away in 739.

150 It suggests in the *Biography of Atiśa* (*Jo bo'i rnam thar*) that when Atiśa himself sailed from India to Sumatra, he actually encountered this image somewhere on an island near Sumatra.

151 The other is of course the image of Buddha in the form Akṣobhyavajra (*jo bo mi bskyod rdo rje*) which was introduced to Tibet from Nepal.

152 Not identified. Surely this Dharmapāla is considerably earlier that the great king Dharmapāla of the Pāla Dynasty who founded Vikramaśīla Monastery in the 8th century.

153 Not identified.

154 Zhakabpa adds that while the image of Jowo Śākyamuni formerly remained in India, it is said to have occupied a throne in the middle storey of the Mahābodhi Stūpa at Vajrāsana, and similarly while it remained in China, it was placed on a throne in the Temple of Chang'an, the capital of Tang China, in present-day Shanxi Province.

155 This is mentioned in the catalogue of the restoration of Ramoche, entitled *Mu tig do shal 'dzad med phan bde'i rgyan gyur.*

156 On this historical fabrication, see above, note 16.

157 It is recounted that the Jowo image was buried in sand in the early years of Trisong Detsen's life during a period of Bon resurgence (circa 739-779), before he issued a decree proclaiming Buddhism as the state religion. At that time Bon ministers had tried to return the image to China, but three hundred men were unable to move it from the chapel. During that period, the temple was converted to a slaughterhouse. Subsequently, the image was once again buried in sand by Langdarma. Another later tradition (recorded by Tucci) states that the original Jowo image was partially destroyed in 1717 by the Dzungars, the present image being stylistically later. There also appear to be some differences between photographs of the image prior to 1959 and those taken subsequently. For a recent study of the Central Inner Sanctum, see C. Warner (2008).

158 See above, p. 11.

159 On this, see the illustrations on pp. 182-3. The best photographs of Jowo Śākyamuni, prior to the Cultural Revolution, were taken by the Czech travellers Sis and Vanis, *op. cit.*, pl. 66.

160 Another tradition recounts that Dolma told Drogon Chogyal Phakpa not to remove an offering scarf. Zhakabpa adds that there was formerly an image of Kopon Jangchub Sempa in this alcove.
161 This text had been concealed as treasure on the edge of a beam two and a half arm-spans from the Leaf Pillar. Later, in accordance with the prophecy of Nyonma of Lhasa, Atiśa extracted and reproduced it. The original is regarded as the actual manuscript of Thonmi Sambhoṭa, and one fragment of it was kept securely in a government vault. On the variant manuscripts, see note 3.
162 Another tradition associates the stove with Wencheng.
163 Zhakabpa remarks that he had heard this was the skin of the tigress to whom Buddha Śākyamuni donated his body when born in a previous life as a bodhisattva prince, but the late Trijang Rinpoche had then directed him to a reference in the Seventh Dalai Lama Kelzang Gyatso's *rTen gsum dkar chags* (*gSung-'bum*, Vol. Cha, f. 154a), suggesting that this was Songtsen's emanational tiger skin. When preparations were being made for his golden reliquary (named *dGe legs 'dod 'jo*, and contained in the Potala Palace), a fragment of Songtsen's emanational tiger skin was retrieved from the wool mat in the Great Temple and included with the other relics.
164 On this ceremony, see the above account, p. 17, which is based on H. E. Richardson, *Ceremonies of the Lhasa Year*, pp. 52-55.
165 Identified as either the father or royal relative of Princess Bhṛkuṭī, on whom see above, pp. 8 and 160ff.
166 On this figure, see above, p. 12. According to Zhakabpa, the sacristans of the Great Temple used to claim that this image contained the embalmed torso of *Lharje* Gewabum, and that the lower part of his mortal remains were interred within the protective river dyke (*jo bo'i chu rags*).
167 On the geomantic significance of this goat head, see Heather Stoddard's contribution, below, pp. 174-177.
168 Zhakabpa adds that between Chogyal Phakpa and Sonam Gyaltsen there was also a statue of Jamyang Donyo Gyaltsen.
169 The late Trijang Rinpoche informed Zhakabpa that during the reign of the Thirteenth Dalai Lama, there had been a plan to copy and repaint these murals, but no sooner had scaffolding been erected when water overflowed from a well in the Main Hall. For this reason, Tsedrung Yeshe Gyatso advised the artists to postpone their restoration.
170 According to another tradition, the central image of King Songtsen Gampo is flanked (on the left) by: Gar, Bhṛkuṭī, Nyatri Tsenpo, and Trisong Detsen; and (on the right) by: Tri Relpachen, Lhatotori Nyentsen, Wencheng and Thonmi Sambhoṭa. Formerly it also contained images of Mongza Tricham, Gungri Gungtsen, and Zhanglon.
171 The mantra core of this image was offered by Phurchok Ngawang Jampa, and the consecration was performed jointly by Zhok Donyo Khedrub and Ngawang Jampa.
172 See above, p. 33.
173 On this point, see Phurchok Ngawang Jampa's *Jo bo'i smon lam drang srong shing brjod 'dod pa kun 'jo'i mdzas sbyangs*.
174 The late Dardo Rinpoche informed Zhakabpa that this point was explained to him by the Sertri monk Yeshe Nyima, on one occasion when he accompanied his tutor to visit the Great Temple.
175 I.e. the primary mantra of Padmākara: OṂ ĀḤ HŪṂ VAJRA GURU PADMA SIDDHI HŪṂ.
176 See above, p. 11; also see the comments of André Alexander below, pp. 232-3.
177 On these murals and recent restoration efforts since 1991, see p. 24. Heather Stoddard, pp. 193-6 recounts her rediscovery of the murals in the Chapel of the Countenance, and the unnecessdary damage that was subsequently influcted upon them. She also suggests that the Vaiśrāvaṇa mural may predate the others.
178 It is clear from the biography of Zhang Yudrakpa that Lama Zhang himself passed long periods of time in retreat within this chapel.
179 See above, p. 24.
180 It is known from Sumpa Khenpo's *dPag bsam ljon bzang* that Tsongkhapa and Lama Umapa both spent long periods of retreat in this chapel.
181 Sacristans used to say this chapel always smelled of wine because the wine flask (*'khrungs ban*) of King Songtsen Gampo was formerly kept here.
182 This incident is described in Katok Siti Chokyi Gyatso's *dBus gtsang gnas yig*, on which see above, p. 22, note 76.
183 The *dKar chag dvangs shel me long* and Katok Situ Chokyi Gyatso's *dBus gtsang gnas yig* both attribute the sculpting of these images of the religious king and his queens to Dungkar Drukdra, although the Thirteenth Dalai Lama in his later composition *Nyams gso'i dkar chag dad snang 'bum phrag 'char ba'i rdzing bu* claims they were sculpted during the period of Tshalpa guardianship.
184 On these ceremonies, see above, p. 13; also H. E. Richardson, *Ceremonies of the Lhasa Year*, pp. 110-113.
185 Zhakabpa's note adds that here the Six Sages are drawn in accordance with their description in the *Ma ṇi bka' 'bum.*
186 See above, p. 9.
187 See above, p. 24, and the comments of André Alexander, below, p. 232.
188 Zhakabpa notes that according to the *rNam thar thub bstan mdzes rgyan*, both Tsongkhapa and Lama Umapa passed long periods of retreat in this chapel.
189 See pp. 193-6.
190 See above, p. 50.
191 According to some reports the cornice comprises 144 lion-faced figurines.
192 Oral communication by Chung Tsering and Kusho Puntsok.
193 These alterations are described below, p. 106.
194 Zhakabpa's description of the chapels 85, 86, 89 and 90 accords with the account given in Sangye Gyatso's *Yellow Beryl* (*Baiḍūrya ser po*).
195 See above, p. 73.
196 See above, p. 74.
197 Tshultrim Gyaltsen, a monk of Meru recounted to Zhakabpa the tale of a woman from Phabongkha who suddenly arrived there, carrying incense in a wicker basket and the first fruits of ale in a flat clay jar. She entered the presence of the Śrīdevī image and offered the incense and ale (*ljags skyems*), whereupon she promptly vanished into the image, leaving the wicker basket and the flat wine jar on the floor in front! Therefore it was said that Śrīdevī had actually manifested. Subsequently, a single fragment of the wicker basket was said to offer protection from harmful forces. Until recent times a fragment of the wicker basket and the flat clay jar could still be seen here.
198 According to the *Yellow Beryl* (*Baiḍūrya ser po*), the victory banner above this door was donated by Sangye Gyatso in person.
199 The complexion and direction of the face of this image of Śrīdevī are said to change from time to time. There are many accounts of it exuding sweat and nasal blood. This is also mentioned in the biography of the Eighth Dalai Lama Jampal Gyatso entitled *'Dzam gling mtha' gru yangs pa'i rgyan*, f. 198.
200 See the reminiscences of HH Dalai Lama, above, pp. 36-37.
201 This custom was attributed to another maternal injunction imposed on wrathful Śrīdevī.
202 On this ceremony, see above, p. 13.
203 Regarding the rulers of Mustang, see above, note 31.
204 Zhakabpa notes an oral tradition concerning a potentate called Gocha who ruled over the Lower Kyichu valley (*skyid shod*), and who has two sons: the crown prince Dondrub and his younger sibling Donyo.
205 See note 199.
206 Concerning Lhalung Palgyi Dorje, see above, p. 10; and for a description of the Wood Enclosure, see below, p. 94.
207 The late Ling Rinpoche advised Zhakabpa to investigate whether the guidebooks refer to this wooden proturberance. One informant, a monk from Meru Nyingba named Tshultrim Gyaltsen and the Newār Yeshe Gyaltsen both reported that when the faces of the main images of the Great Temple were being regilded, gold paint was also applied to this proturberance. It was also secured by a silver metal sheet which prevented mouse droppings emerging from the ceiling above the heads of the Peaceful and Wrathful Aspects of Śrīdevī. However, they could not discern the shape of a rhino horn, even after carefully inspected the planks and beams.
208 The original image of Tashi Tseringma, foremost of the Five Sisters of Longlife (*tshe ring mched lnga*), was reputedly made by the hand of the Fifteenth Karmapa Thekchok Dorje. The other four sibling deities (*mched gzhan bzhi*) were constructed later, following the advice of the present Dalai Lama. For an account of the life of Chokgyur Dechen Zhigpo Lingpa, see Orgyen Topgyal, *The Life and Teaching of Chokgyur Lingpa.*
209 This area is described below, p. 106.
210 Useful elevational drawings of the building, showing the roof ornaments and the decorations of the external walls, are included below, in André Alexander's article, pp. 218-9.

211 Heather Stoddard draws upon references in Nyangral's history to describe the geomantic stones affixed to the external walls of the building. See below, pp. 160-177.
212 It says in the *dKar chags* of the Fifth Dalai Lama that this large stone had been extracted from a brass object by Tsongkhapa and was initially placed in front of the Central Inner Sanctum, before being moved to its present location in front of the Great Acacia Gate at the time when the floorboards were laid at the entrance to the Central Inner Sanctum.
213 The "daily offerings of the courtyard" (*khyams ra rgyun mchod pa*) would be carried out by a hundred monks who would come in rotation every four months from the estates and monasteries of Taklung in Phenyul and from Ze-chu (=*bZhad rngul chu chos rdzong*).
214 On all these events, see above, p. 63.
215 This account is clearly mentioned in a compilation of historical documents from Drayab, which were written by Drayab Ranub Nyima Dorje, by way of digression from a description of Nyagnyon Sewa Rinchen's construction of the Gongkhul Lagon. It also appears to suggest that the sack and rope he used to carry the earth for making the Tārā image were until recently preserved here within the Dolma Lhakhang. Zhakabpa adds that his mother regarded this Tārā image as the actual embodiment of pristine cognition. Its facial complexion would frequently change, and sometimes the extended right leg would slightly contract, making it impossible for her to touch the image's feet with her head. Then, after a while, the same leg would become slightly extended, enabling her to touch it easily with her head.
216 It is mentioned in the *Yellow Beryl* (*Baiḍūrya ser po*) that these stūpas were constructed by the Fifth Dalai Lama, during the funeral of his regent Sonam Chopel.
217 One of six temples built by King Tri Relpachen during the ninth century, Meru Nyingba was constructed on the site of an earlier chapel where Thonmi Sambhoṭa reputedly finalized the Tibetan alphabet. It was destroyed by Langdarma and subsequently rebuilt by Atisa. The oldest existing structure there is the Jambhala Lhakhang, and the main building, dedicated to aspects of Pehar, is of 20th century reconstruction. For a contemporary description, see Dorje (2004a), pp. 84-85.
218 It states in the inventory to the reliquary of the Fifth Dalai Lama entitled ' *Dzam gling rgyan dkar chag*, p. 295. na. 5, that the images of the first four of these chapels had been commissioned by the regent Sangye Gyatso in person.
219 The throne and its canopy were damaged during the Cultural Revolution, when a three-storied playground, known euphemistically as the "Children's Palace" was constructed there to obscure the beautiful south façade of the Great Temple.
220 As stated above, p. 101, the hand-turned Maṇi Wheels originally had the Six-Syllable Mantra embossed with gold foil on a cotton base. However, in 1941 (iron snake year of the sixteenth cycle), forty-one wheels of gilded brass with ornate jewel pendants and the Six Syllables embossed in Rañjanā script were newly constructed. These were all subsequently destroyed and the present wheels are functional replicas.
221 See below, p. 101.
222 The history of the flagpoles in the Barkor is recounted by Tridrung Lobzang Thubten, "Bar skor byang chub byon lam gyi dar chen rnams kyi lo rgyus", in *Bod kyi shes rig zhib ched rtsom bdam bsgrigs* (2, 1991).
223 On this rite, see above, p. 20; also H. E. Richardson, *Ceremonies of the Lhasa Year*, pp. 61 ff.
224 See H. Harrer, *Seven Years in Tibet*, pp. 23-24.
225 Zhakabpa adds that this appears to require further research because there is some doubt as to whether Sangye Gyatso and not Sonam Chopel held the rank of *sde-srid* during the lifetime of Gushi Qan Tendzin Chogyal. Nonetheless, the previous Dalai Lama in his *Nyams gso'i dkar chag dad snang 'bum phrag 'char ba'i 'o mtsho'i rdzing bu* asserts that the reference applies to Sangye Gyatso.
226 According to the *Du ku la*, it was planned to execute scenes illustrating the hundred deeds of the buddhas from the *Avadānakalpalatā* on the walls of the Great Courtyard to fulfil the last wishes of the Fifth Dalai Lama, but the regent Sonam Chopel (on whom see above p. 59) decreed that the thousand buddhas should be depicted. The task was completed easily and swiftly by the artist Umdze Tsunchung.
227 Tib. *Gu ru nas rdog ma.*
228 These murals of the Hundred Deeds according to the *Avadānakalpalatā* which adorn the outer walls of the inner walkway, according to the *dKar chag dad snang 'bum phrag*, were commissioned during the lifetime of the Fifth Dalai Lama, and later renovated during the lifetime of the Eighth Dalai Lama Jampal Gyatso and the first regent of Tshegaling, as stated in the *rNam thar dad pa'i sgo 'byed*. However, in the biography of the Eighth Dalai Lama Jampal Gyatso, entitled *mTha' gru yangs pa'i rgyan*, it states that there previously were no murals on the inner walls and that the murals depicting the hundred deeds of the great aeon (*bskal chen mdzad brgya*) and so forth were newly commissioned at that time, to fulfil the earlier wishes of the Fifth Dalai Lama.
229 Tib. *'jigs brgyad nas rdog ma.*
230 This is explained to suggest that he has never been tamed.
231 See pp. 59-60.
232 According to the plan of Jigme Taring, p. 25, this room formerly contained the wool supplies of the Palace Treasury (*bla phyag bal khang*).
233 Here a group of four monks from Nechung Drayangling would perform the ritual service and means for attainment of *Phur pa yang snying spu gri*, a treasure-doctrine revealed by Orgyan Lerab Lingpa.
234 Only two of these are indicated on Zhakabpa's plan, but see Jigme Taring Dzaku, p. 26, who describes the south room as that of the regent, the middle room as a hermitage of the Dalai Lama, and the north room as a chapel.
235 It was in this room on the eighteenth day of the sixth month of 1727 (fire sheep year of the twelfth cycle), that the chief minister Khangchen-ne Daching Badur Sonam Gyalpo was assassinated by the ministers Pe-se Ngaphodpa, Gunglumpawa and Thaji Jarwa.
236 According to the plan of Jigme Taring Dzaku, p. 20, this storeroom held herbs (*smankhrog khang*).
237 This description accords with Jigme Taring's plan of the middle floor, p. 20. Zhakabpa omits any mention of the function of this chamber. Some sources suggest that this room once served as a jail, affiliated to the notorious Nangtseshak Jail of the Barkor.
238 According to the plan of Jigme Taring Dzaku, p. 21, this room is described as a "pay office" (*phogs khang las khung*).
239 These are unindentified on Zhakabpa's plan, but see Jigme Taring Dzaku, p. 28.
240 Shown on Jigme Taring Dzaku's plan, p. 28.
241 On Jigme Taring Dzaku's plan, p. 28, this is described as a prayer room or meditation cell (*gzim sbug*).

The Great Prayer Festival. (1986 CB)

The revered image of Jowo Śākyamuni within the Central Inner Sanctum (Jokhang). (1999 HS)

Part 2

Jowo Śākyamuni

The Central Figure of the Great Temple of Magical Emanation at Rasa: A Representative Image Conferring Liberation through Sight, which is [recognised as] one of the Six Modes of Liberation[1]

Compiled by Tashi Tsering

Translated by Gyurme Dorje and Sonam Tsering

Face-gilding ceremony in the Central Inner Sanctum. (2000 JS)

Introduction

In Tibet, both from geographical and Buddhist perspectives, the land occupying the upper, middle and lower reaches of the Yarlung and Kyichu Rivers is considered to be the central part of the country (U). Specifically, from the geographical perspective, this region lies at the heart of [the three traditional provinces]: [A]mdo, U[tsang] and Kham; and from the Buddhist perspective, it is [also regarded as central] because it is where the three [original] Buddhist institutions [of Tradruk, Lhasa, and Samye] are located, and above all where Jowo Śākyamuni is installed within the Great Temple of Magical Emanation at Rasa. For, this image [resembles] a wish-conferring gemstone, granting all that is desired when prayers are offered in its presence.

According to the tradition of the New Translation Schools, Jowo Śākyamuni is the most important representative image conferring liberation through sight, which is recognised as one of the six [possible] modes of liberation (*grol-ba drug*). The statue, which had been revered as a most sacred representative image by the Tang emperors of China, was transported to Tibet, in 641, as part of the dowry of the Chinese princess [Wencheng] Konjo during the reign of the thirty-third Tibetan king Songtsen Gampo (617-650), himself revered as a master of miraculous abilities. At first, Ramoche was built to house this image of Jowo Rinpoche, and later the image was transferred to the Great Temple of Magical Emanation at Rasa.

According to all the royal dynastic histories of Tibet, before the construction of Ramoche and the Great Temple of Magical Emanation at Rasa, more than a hundred stūpas and temples, including the Border Taming temples (*mtha'-'dul*), Further Taming temples (*yang-'dul*), and District Controlling temples (*ru-gnon*), were constructed throughout the lands that were then controlled by Tibet; and it was only subsequently that the Great Temple of Magical Emanation at Rasa and the great temple of Ramoche were reportedly built.

The image of Jowo Śākyamuni depicts our [historical] Teacher, Śākyamuni [Buddha] at the age of twelve, and it is held to have been personally consecrated by the Teacher himself. Later it was kept as a sacred representative image at the palace of the Tang emperors of China. Then, following the death of King Songtsen Gampo in 650, a rumour of imminent Chinese invasion into Tibet is thought to have precipitated the interchanging of the two Jowo images then held in the Great Temple of Magical Emanation at Rasa and in Ramoche. [Therefore], at the present day, it is Jowo Miyko Dorje (Akṣobhayavajra), the image brought [to Tibet] by the Nepalese princess [Bhṛkuṭī] that is installed within Ramoche. Furthermore, it is recorded in the royal dynastic chronicles of Tibet that during the early part of King Trisong Detsen's lifespan (742-797), when a minister named Zhanglon Mazhang Trompakye planned to return the image of Jowo [Śākyamuni] to China, [other] ministers who were sympathetic to Buddhism arranged for it to be [securely] held at Kyirong in the Mangyul region of Tibet, near the Nepalese border, for fourteen years.

Around 1153, having reached the age of thirty, a student and nephew of Dakpo Lharje named Gompa Tsultrim Nyingpo (1116-1169) is said to have intervened: Influenced by malignant spirits and ogres, dissension arose within the monastic community, so that the mātaraḥ protectors of the Buddhist teaching completely burnt and destroyed the Great Temple of Magical Emanation at Rasa. At that time, the female protectress Rematī and Dribkyi Dzongtsen made an entreaty that the razed building should be restored. The elder Sherab Drak, while considering whether he should go [to assist with the rebuilding], said, "We are referred to as yogins, and officialdom has no regard for us, so don't go!" Rinpoche [Gompa Tsultrim Nyingpo] replied, "You have doubts, thinking I'll make a mistake, but I won't be mistaken. In addition, I'll forge a reconciliation, restore the temple, reclaim all the land that has been lost, and make the four [disputing] monastic communities of Lhasa adhere to the laws of the state." So saying, he went [to offer his assistance]. He was received at the entrance to his cave [hermitage] by the goddess Marīcī, and the moment he appeared before Jowo [Śākyamuni], all those who were present saw the image shed tears and emanate rays of light from its heart, which then vanished into his own heart. The image then instructed him to summon all the leaders and forge some reconciliation, but he was unable to settle their differences because they were extremely undisciplined. He intended to leave the next morning, when, in a dream, his precious spiritual teacher appeared and said, "How dare you leave me alone!" Therefore, he remained for a while and offered his services [to the image of

Preparing the offering lamps. (2000 JS)

Jowo Śākyamuni], but his heart was saddened by the extensive destruction [of the building] and the utterly depraved behaviour [of the monastic communities].
At that time, [abandoning all hope of reconciliation], he decided to leave, but as he stood in front of Jowo Rinpoche, the the image said, "If you cannot reconcile this strife, who else can! If you leave, I too shall leave!" So then the thought arose in his mind that he had no choice but to stay, and that if he did not successfully reconcile the discord, the Buddha's teaching might not survive [in Tibet].
Then he prayed to the Three Precious Jewels, made *torma*-offerings to suppress spirits and ogres, and swore a powerful declaration of truth (*bden-tshig*). Jowo [Rinpoche] then made a prophetic declaration, saying, "Reconciliation will be made tomorrow!" The next morning, he again summoned the leaders, and they [unexpectedly] accepted his advice, so that he was able to bring about reconciliation among the four dissenting factions. He then reestablished the monastic community. In the service of the Jowo, he restored the middle storey [of the building] and its railings, he whitewashed the [outer] walls, fitted a decorative architrave of potentilla wood, and crafted an iron gate with lattices. He then built the white-coloured eastern dyke [that warded off the flooding waters of the Kyichu], and established the custom of making offerings to ordained monks and donating alms to beggars. He enforced strict observance of the ten modes of doctrinal conduct (*chos-spyod bcu*) among the monastic community and the ten modes of virtuous action (*dge-ba bcu*) among householders. Restraining even those of reckless and negative disposition from their evil acts, he took them into the fold of the Three Precious Jewels, and made the Buddhist teaching shine as bright as the sun. Even at the present day it is customary, whenever the post of chief sacristan [of the Great Temple] in Lhasa rotates, to read aloud the legal decrees that extensively describe his actions on that occasion, as well as the guidelines he imparted for future ritual observances and the appropriate regulations. These [documents] should be [carefully] studied.

Jowo Śākyamuni. (1999 HS)

At that time, he said,

Unable to bear the decline.
Of this precious teaching of the Sage,
I shall persevere for the sake of the teaching and for all beings.
Having reconciled this unbearably harsh strife,
I restored the Great Temple
And caused the teaching to spread and flourish.
O my followers of posterity!
Without being dispirited, you should engage in powerful actions.

Thus the line of his enlightened actions [in the service of Jowo Śākyamuni] was transmitted to the spiritual teacher Zhang Yudrakpa.[2]

Another text states,

Initially the Chinese-style roofs of the Great Temple were made of terracotta tiles, and it was Ri'u Malla (fl. 1213), the king of Guge in Ngari, who first erected a Chinese-style roof of gilded copper above the chapel of Jowo Śākyamuni.[3]

Tsongkhapa's Transformation of Jowo Śākyamuni

From the time of the religious king Songtsen Gampo until the epoch of Je Tsongkhapa Lobzang Drakpa, the image of Jowo Rinpoche had the appearance of the supreme buddha-body of emanation (*mchog-gi sprul-sku*), with its right hand in the earth-suppressing gesture, the left in the gesture of meditative equipoise, and its torso draped in the three sacred robes [ie. the upper and lower robes and *saṃghāṭī* of a Buddhist monk]. However, in 1409, Je Tsongkhapa instituted the Great Prayer Festival during the Tibetan [month] of miracles, which commemorates the anniversary of the Buddha's performance of miracles at Śrāvastī. On that occasion, he altered the appearance of the image of Jowo Śākyamuni stylistically from a representation of the supreme buddha-body of emanation to one depicting the buddha-body of perfect resource (*longs-spyod rdzogs-pa'i sku*). [In this new form], the image was bedecked in the thirteen ornaments of the buddha-body of perfect resource, comprising the eight ornaments made of precious gemstones and five silken garments. The eight ornaments are enumerated as the crown, earrings, neck-band, mid-length necklace, long necklace, shoulder-straps, bracelets, and anklets. The girdle with its pendants and half-pendants is also included. The five garments are the silken tiara, jacket, veils, belt and skirt. In addition, the image came to be endowed with the following nine peaceful attributes: suppleness, slenderness, handsomeness, uprightness, youthfulness, radiance, lustre, magnificence and charisma.

This transformation of the image of Jowo Śākyamuni into one representing the buddha-body of perfect resource was criticized by many revered individuals of the Sakya, Kagyu and Nyingma schools, including Gyelwang Karmapa VII Chodrak Gyatso (1454-1506), Pema Lingpa (1450-1521), the treasure-finder from Bumthang, and Śākya Chokden (1428-1507), the great paṇḍita of Serdog. However, on this the learned Dodrak Gendun Chopel (1903-1951) has written,

Images like the Jowo of Lhasa, which has the right arm exposed, and at the same time is bedecked with the crown and throat-ornament, are ubiquitously found among the ancient stone sculptures of India, and they are also found among old bronze images. Sometimes, I feel that the ancient custom of adorning buddha images with a crown, which was quite widespread in India, is non-existent nowadays in Tibet. In Burma and Thailand the custom of fashioning Buddha images with crowns has been widely followed until the present day. Furthermore, a small band of gems and even a miniature statue may be inset between the eyebrows of the image. If an image were to lack such ornaments, it would be considered incomplete! Therefore, those who deemed the teacher Je [Tsongkhapa] to have established a new precedent when adorning the image of Jowo Śākyamuni with a crown were quite ill-informed.

Some have said, in response [to this criticism] that though the image did not have a crown when it was introduced to Tibet, it previously did when it was brought to Oḍḍiyāna, but this point is, in reality, just suppositional. [Such attempts to prove something that cannot be proven] are akin to the parable of "the oracle pig-head". Instead of first examining the reasons why no buddha images were constructed during the reign of the Emperor Aśoka and so forth, it is quite fanciful to insist upon one's personal speculations, rolling one's head [thoughtlessly], in the manner of a *ḍāmaru*. On the contrary, if a statement is made with a modicum of sincere

intellectual effort, based on close study and research, no one can disprove it.
A great many stūpas and shrines were built [in the time of Aśoka], but in all likelihood none were engraved with scenes depicting the life of the Buddha. Since the physical stature of the Teacher is apparent [only] to the Teacher himself, it could not have been [fully] grasped, even though one might think that it was perceived in such and such a form, in one specific ephemeral location. These two Jowo images [of Ramoche and the Great Temple of Magical Emanation at Rasa] are said respectively to represent [the Buddha] the size of an eight year old and the size of a twelve year old, and therefore it seems that they should [rightly] assume the form of a bodhisattva because they illustrate the period during which [the Buddha] was [in fact] a bodhisattva.[4]

Legendary Origins of the Image of Jowo Śākyamuni and the Geomantic Temples

Although there are many extant records describing the origins and history of Jowo Rinpoche, I have extracted the following passage from the writings of Chahar Geshe Lobzang Tsultrim (1740-1810):

Initially, the reason for the construction of this image of Jowo Śākyamuni was as follows: Once when the Teacher, the Transcendent Lord [Buddha], was dwelling at Jetavana, the venerable Mañjughoṣa repeatedly implored him to create a representative image that would enable any sentient beings to acquire merit. Subsequently, rays of light emanated from the visage of the Transcendent Lord [Buddha] and touched the four gods – Brahmā, Viṣṇu, Śakra and Viśvakarman. They, inspired by the power of the Buddha, appeared before the Teacher, and pledged to build a representative image that would engender extensive spiritual and temporal well-being for themselves and for others. Then, Brahmā gathered a diverse collection of gemstones from the god realms, which Viśvakarman pounded and melted. They then constructed a stūpa symbolising the buddha-body of reality (*chos-sku*) of the Teacher, the Transcendent Lord. This stūpa is presently preserved in Oḍḍiyāna as an object to which the ḍākinīs make offerings. Then Viṣṇu collected a mass of jewels from the realm of serpentine water spirits; and Viśvakarman made a representative image of the Teacher in the form of the buddha-body of perfect resource, called Himamahāsāgara (*gangs-can mtsho*). This was kept in the great outer ocean as an object to which non-human beings, including the planets and stars would make offerings. Then Śakra collected sapphire, azure and other gems from the god realms, and other precious stones and metals such as gold, silver, coral and pearls from the human world, which Viśvakarman used to fashion three representative images of the Teacher, in the form of the buddha-body of emanation: large, medium and small. Among them, the large one which represented the Teacher at the age of twenty-five, is now preserved in the Realm of Thirty-three Gods (Trāyatriṃśa). The medium-sized image represented the Teacher as a twelve year old, and was initially taken to the god realms by Śakra, and later brought to Oḍḍiyāna, and then, in turn, to India and China. Nowadays it is known as the larger Jowo of Lhasa, [preserved in the Great Temple of Magical Emanation at Rasa]. The smallest image, representing the Teacher at the age of eight, is nowadays the one known as the smaller Jowo of Lhasa, [preserved in Ramoche]. These representative images were personally consecrated and blessed by the Teacher, king of the Śākyas, for which reason they hold an extremely great blessing, indistinguishable from that of the actual Buddha.

Let us now look at how the two images of Jowo Śākyamuni were brought to Tibet. In the earth ox year, the 1544th year following the birth of our teacher, Munīndra [Śākyamuni] in the fire horse year, a son was born to the Tibetan king Namri Songtsen. An image of the Buddha Amitābha manifested on the crown of the child's head, and he was endowed with the excellent major and minor marks. At the time of his birth, there were many [other] wondrous signs that appeared. The son was given the name Tride Songtsen, and enthroned in his thirteenth year. During the coronation, all the buddhas and bodhisattvas are said to have appeared in the sky and anointed him with water from a vase fashioned of precious gems. They offered a benediction, and caused a shower of flowers to fall. This location [where the coronation took place] is the site of present-day Ganden Monastery. The king sent his minister Thonmi Sambhṭāa to India, where he became learned, and

Jowo Śākyamuni and offerings. (2000 GD)

Decorative pillars and offering lamps of the Central Inner Sanctum. (1993 HMS, 1985 HM)

invented the Tibetan capital letter script (*gzab-yig*) and the cursive scipt (*gshar-yig*). He also translated into Tibetan the *Sūtra of the Rites of Renunciation and Fulfillment* (*sPang-skong phyag-rgya-pa'i mdo*, T. 267) and other discourses.

Then the king urged all his subjects to establish the noble customs of practicing the ten virtuous actions, offering ritual service to the Three Precious Jewels, and reciting the Six Syllable Mantra [of Avalokitesvara]. It was for these reasons that he became known as the "religious king" Songtsen Gampo. It was then that Bhṛkuṭī, an emanation of the goddess Bhṛkuṭī and daughter of King Aṃśuvarman of Nepal, was brought [to Tibet] as a royal consort for Songtsen Gampo. When she traveled to Tibet, she carried with her the aforementioned lesser image of Śākyamuni Buddha, as well as images of Maitreyanātha and Tārā, a monk's begging bowl fashioned of beryl, and many other sacraments of precious gems which her father offered to the king [as a dowry]. This image of our Teacher, Buddha Śākyamuni, is the smallest of the three images that had been crafted by Śakra, and is [today] known by the name: Jowo Mikyo Dorje (Akṣobhyavajra). However, there are those who maintain that this lesser Jowo image was not made by Śakra at all, but rather at a much later date.

And [from the same source]:

... Then [the king] took Princess Wengcheng Kongjo, an emanation of the venerable Tārā and daughter of the Chinese emperor Tang Tai Zong, as his queen. When this princess traveled [to Tibet], she brought the image of Jowo Śākyamuni along with countless other precious gems and material resources.

Also,

This Jowo was the medium-sized image of the Teacher, commissioned, as explained above, by Śakra. It is presently known as the Jowo Rinpoche of Lhasa.

[The same text] further recounts that:

Then Bhṛkuṭī laid the foundations of a temple at Ladong Neutab but it was completely obliterated by [malign] non-human spirits during the night. She reported this to the king, who then escorted the two queens to the shore of the Milk Plain Lake. The king asked them to throw a ring into the air, and when it alighted in the lake, a stūpa was seen by all [onlookers], emanating rays of light from the midst of the lake. Then the king uttered some auspicious verses, while his ministers and subjects threw many stones into the lake, making an extremely firm foundation of stone. Efforts were made to construct a temple there, but it too was destroyed by [malign] gods and spirits. The queen Wengcheng Konjo then examined the site in accordance with the tradition of Chinese elemental divination, and reported to the king that the terrain of Tibet resembled the form of a supine ogress, with the lake being located at her heart. She suggested a series of remedial acts whereby temples should be constructed upon her limbs. The king greatly rejoiced, and all three of them – the king with his two queens – proceeded to Phabongkha where they practised ritual service and means for attainment over a seven day period. The Lords of the Three Enlightened Families (Avalokiteśvara, Mañjughoṣa and Vajrapāṇi) then actually manifested, and consecrated the terrain [of Tibet]. Subsequently, to subdue hostile forces that possessed the land, they built the temple of Katsel on the site resembling the right shoulder of the ogress, and similarly they built Tradruk on the left shoulder, Tsangdram on the right foot, and Drompa Gyang on the left foot. These constitute the four "district controlling temples" (*ru-gnon-gyi lha-khang bzhi*). Then, they constructed the four "border taming temples" (*mtha'-'dul-gyi lha-khang bzhi*), namely: Buchu on the right elbow, Lhodrak on the left elbow, Kadrak on the right knee, and Traduntse on the left knee. [Finally] they constructed the four "further taming temples" (*yang-'dul-gyi lha-khang bzhi*), namely: Lungnon on the right palm, [Lang]-tang Dron[ma] on the left palm, Jamtrin on the right heel and Mon [Bumthang] on the left heel. Subsequently, they secured the great foundation stones upon the Milk Plain Lake [in Lhasa], they laid out juniper logs and plastered them with mud [offered by] serpentine water spirits. Upon this [base], they built a firm and solid foundation, filling it in with earth that was transported by an [emanational] white goat. Upon this they built the Great Temple of Magical Emanation, with its entrance facing southwest. Nowadays this building is also known as the "Great Temple of the Larger Jowo".

Thereafter, Queen Wengcheng Konjo constructed Ramoche Temple, to the left side of the [Great Temple of Magical Emanation]. To suppress hostile geomantic spirits, she had lions carved of stone and positioned [below the gallery]. Initially the larger

Jowo was installed in Ramoche, and the smaller Jowo in the Great Temple of Magical Emanation. Later, when King Songtsen Gampo was in his eighty-second year, at the time of his own passing into final nirvāṇa, he and his two queens made extensive offerings to the two images of Jowo Śākyamuni, along with aspirational prayers. He proceeded [to the area] in front of the chapel of "naturally produced" Mahākāruṇika, and offered his advice and many prophecies regarding the future to the princes, ministers and subjects. The two queens also offered many aspirational prayers, and imparted their advice, and so forth. Once they had decreed that the Greater Jowo should be installed in the Great Temple of Magical Emanation, and her Lesser Jowo in Ramoche, the king and the two queens vanished into the Mahākāruṇika image.

Also [he adds],

The year in which the religious king Songtsen Gampo built the Great Temple of Lhasa was the water ox year, the 1568th year following the fire horse year when Munīndra [Śākyamuni Buddha] was born. This was the ox year (653) coinciding with Songtsen Gampo's twenty-fifth year. Je Rinpoche [Tsongkhapa] was born in the fire bird year, the seven hundred and fifth year following the temple's construction.[5]

Head and crown of Jowo Śākyamuni. (1994 HMS)

Desi Sangye Gyatso on the Importance of Circumambulation

Among the [diverse] customs of the Tibetan people, there exists a tradition that [pilgrims] should circumambulate sacred power places – whether these are categorized as major, associated, minor, ostensible, subsidiary or substitute power places, as well as temples housing important representative images of buddha-body, speech and mind, monasteries, sacred mountains and sacred lakes. Just as all such sacred places have their distinctive circumambulatory routes, so the two images of Jowo [Śākyamuni] in Lhasa are also known to have their intermediate circumambulation (*bar-bskor*) and outer circumambulation (*gling-bskor*), and the like. On this subject Sangye Gyatso(1653-1705), regent of the Fifth Dalai Lama, writes:

Although I have not previously seen any references to the [requisite] number of such circumambulations in the sūtras and tantras, it is said in the *Means for Attainment derived from the Tantra of Vairocana*, according to the bodhisattva Chodwang (*byang-chub sems-dpa'spyod-dbang-gi rnam-par sang-mdzad rgyud-kyi sgrub-thabs*), which belongs to the Northern Treasures (*byang-gter*), that "one should circumambulate stūpas and their relics. One should perform one hundred and eight circumambulations to fulfill one's purpose; and one should make one hundred thousand circumambulations to benefit others. The advantage of this [practice] is that it will develop the roots for virtuous action in respect of the Tathāgatas who are as numerous as the hundred thousand million grains of sand on the River Ganges".

Nowadays, the number one hundred thousand is well known in common parlance, as in the phrase 'one hundred thousand circumambulations and one hundred thousand prostrations'. Accordingly I arranged for Chakarwa Pema Sonam to measure the circumferences of the [various] shrines, and for the [distances of] the circumambulations around [Marpo]ri Hill. I also had the outer circumambulatory walkway [of Lhasa] (*gling-skor*) measured, once by Peljor Gyatso and Gyasargang Konchok who were both monastic secretaries at the Potala (*rtse-drung*), and a second time by Sonam Rabten of Chikhang chak village and Pema Tseten of the Zhol estate, who were both lay secretaries (*shod-drung*). Minor differences that were found between the two sets of measurements were studied, and an average reading was established for the distance of these circumambulations.

Although there [previously] had been no custom of circumambulating this life-sustaining [Marpo]ri Hill, [abode] of sublime Lokeśvara, which resembles an elephant tied to its trough and where the Potala Palace is located, I gradually made this practice widespread, in the interests of our [conjoined] spiritual and temporal affairs. Accordingly, the route [that I sanctioned] extended from Drakgo Kakni, to the west of the Zhol Gate, and ran behind [the hill], to the East Gate. It therefore avoided the need to circumambulate the Drak Genmo pile of boulders and the stone marked with the three naturally arisen syllables, on the east side. I also took into account the difference in distance on the section that runs from the corner of the Ngozo Gubukhang to the West Gate between the normal straight path and the slightly circuitous path that has to be followed whenever flooding occurs. Overall, I estimated the distance of one actual circumambulation of the hill at 1,032 double

Chest embellishments of Jowo Śākyamuni. (1985 HM)

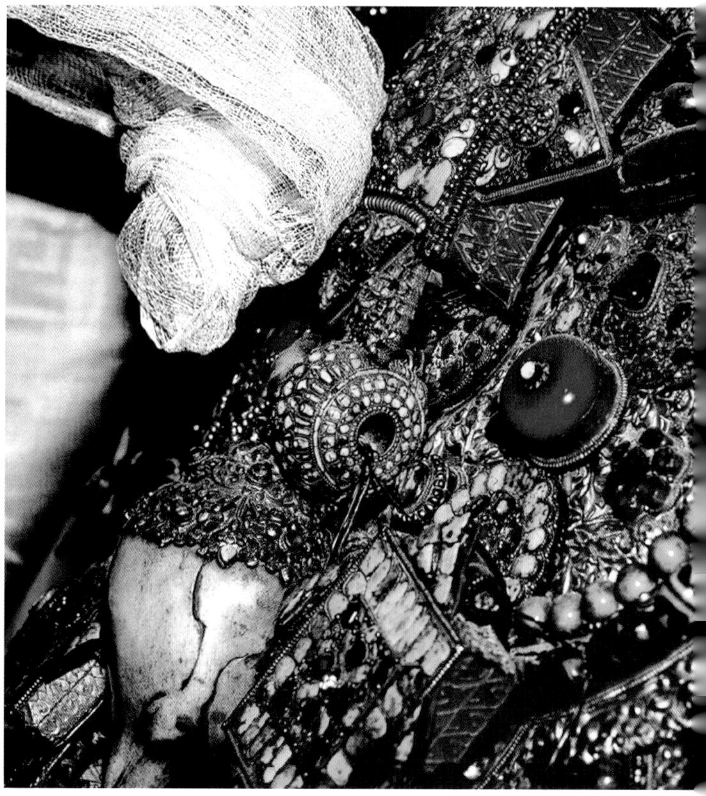

Attending to Jowo Śākyamuni. (1993 HMS)

Decorative features of the throne. (1985 HM)

arm-spans (*'dom*), using the [traditional] scale of relative finger-widths.

The precious five-storied golden reliquary [of the Fifth Dalai Lama], known as the Unique Ornament of the World (*'dzam-gling rgyan-gcig*), which is made of refined gold, has a circumference of one hundred and forty relative finger-spans (*mtho*) and four finger-widths (*sor*). One must therefore circumambulate the entire hill 1,700 times, to complete 100,000 circumambulations of the reliquary. The circumference of the [adjacent] eight silver stūpas that commemorate the deeds of Buddha Śākyamuni is 307.50 relative finger-spans, so that one must circumambulate the hill 3,725 times in order to complete the tally of 'one hundred thousand'. The foremost image in the Chapel of Past Emanations (*'khrungs-rabs lha-khang*) depicts our teacher Śākyamuni, the size of a twelve-year-old, and is made of solid gold. The circumference of its lotus plinth is twenty-two relative finger-spans, and so one must circumambulate the hill 267 times in order to complete the tally of one hundred thousand. The foremost image of the Chapel of the Graduated Path (*lam-rim lha-khang*) depicts Tsongkhapa the Great, [emanation of] Lord Mañjughoṣa, king of the sacred teachings, and the circumference of its lotus plinth is twenty relative finger-spans, so that one will have to circumambulate the hill 243 times in order to complete the tally of one hundred thousand. The foremost image of the Chapel of the Awareness Holders (*rig-'dzin lha-khang*) depicts Orgyan [Guru Padmākara], the second buddha. The circumference of its lotus plinth is twenty relative finger-spans and one finger-width, and so it will require 144 circumambulations of the hill to complete the tally of one hundred thousand. The entire reliquary chapel containing the stūpa known as the Unique Ornament of the World, which is painted with red and yellow mineral pigments requires 11,822 circumambulations of the hill to make up the tally of one hundred thousand. The illustrious image of Sublime Lokeśvara and its cavernous chapel require 180 circumambulations of the hill to complete the tally of one hundred thousand. And, in the future, those wishing to [honour] my great spiritual teacher [the Fifth Dalai Lama] will have to circumambulate the hill 310 times to complete the tally of one hundred thousand. This is what one should be aware of when circumambulating the precious reliquary stūpa of our venerable spiritual teacher.

The great spiritual [master] Dīpaṃkara [Atiśa], in his travelogue, tells of how, in India, people would attain spiritual accomplishment by circumambulating the major towns and temples. He also recounts how a patient suffering from podagra was cured and attained spiritual accomplishment by [merely] circumambulating the Chapel of Khasarpaṇi. People [generally] believe that when they make offerings for the sake of accumulating [merit], there are greater advantages if they circumambulate places where very large numbers of monks congregate. This is why is has become an established tradition to undertake the outer circumambulation (*gling-skor*) which encompasses all the sacred objects and shrines of the [Great Temple of] Lhasa, Ramoche, Meru, Zhide, and the three hills: Marpori, Chakpori and Bangpori. These sacred places have a circumference of 4,523 relative arm-spans. The lotus plinth of Jowo Rinpoche Śākyamuni, foremost image in the Great Temple of Magical Emanation at Rasa, has a circumference of twenty relative finger-spans and five finger- widths, requiring 57 outer circumambulations (*gling-skor*) to complete the tally of one hundred thousand. The lotus plinth of Jowo Mikyo Dorje, the central image of Ramoche, has a circumference of 18 relative finger-spans and four finger-widths, thus requiring 51 outer circumambulations to complete the tally of one hundred thousand. The lotus plinth of the self-arisen image of Sublime Lokesvara [in the Potala] has a circumference of six relative finger-spans and six finger-widths, requiring 18 outer circumambulations to complete the tally of one hundred thousand. The golden reliquary known as Unique Ornament of the World requires 388 outer circumambulations to complete the tally of one hundred thousand, while the eight [adjacent] silver stūpas together require 850 outer circumambulations to complete the tally of one hundred thousand. In the case of the likeness of Jo[wo Śākyamuni in the Potala], it will require 61 outer circumambulations to complete the tally of one hundred thousand; and for the images of venerable Tsongkhapa and the great master [Guru Padmākara], it will require 56 outer circumambulations in each case. So, on this basis, individuals can estimate the number of circumambulations that they privately target, with regard to the sacred images or shrines of their preference.

In brief, there are established to be three modes of outer circumambulation:

extensive, medium and short. Among them, the extensive outer circumambulation encompasses the Jowo and the golden reliquary known as the Unique Ornament of the World, so that it will require 445 outer circumambulations to complete the tally of one hundred thousand. The medium one encompasses only the golden reliquary, so it will require 388 circumambulations, and the short one encompasses only the image of Jowo Śākyamuni, so that it will require 557.
Incidentally, each intermediate circumambulation of Ramoche, which was built by the Chinese princess, is thirty-two times the circumference of the lotus plinth of Jowo Mikyo Dorje. It therefore undoubtedly requires 3,025 rounds to complete the tally of one hundred thousand. However, our great venerable master himself asserted with regard to the distance of the Ramoche circumambulation, that if one were to circumambulate [the temple] 3,300 times, one would make up for any miscalculations and complete the tally without [fear of] omission. Then, with regard to the intermediate circumambulatory path (*bar-skor*) and the outer circumambulatory path (*phyi-skor*), which presently encompass the lotus plinth of the image of our teacher [Jowo Śākyamuni], the size of a twelve-year-old, situated in the Great Temple of Magical Emanation that brings forth the four joys, it will require 2,408 rounds of the intermediate path to complete the tally of one hundred thousand, and 564 rounds of the outer path. Thus, nine circuits of the intermediate path are [roughly] equivalent to two of the outer path.
In the travelogue of Jowo[je Atiśa], which is included among those documents that concern the measurements of the circumambulation around Lhasa, it is stated that in order to [accumulate] the roots of the virtues that are not yet free from corruption, nothing surpasses the inner circumambulation (*nang-skor*) [of the Jokhang chapel]. When visiting the Great Temple of Magical Emanation, Atiśa saw many wondrous signs. He saw a multitude of yoginīs, and there was even an arhat [within the temple]. He also identified the temple as the location of a sacred charnel ground that had been said to exist in Tibet.

There is also an authentic oral tradition, not mentioned in that source, to the effect that Jowo [Atiśa] would look upon the young men of Lhasa as spiritual heroes, and the young women as spiritual heroines, and that he established the standard number of circumambulations at twenty centuries. Later, Paṇchen IV Lobzang Chokyi Gyeltshan increased the number to twenty-seven centuries, in order to purify the obscurations arising from the human carnage inflicted by the Mongolian banner of the Tsangpa forces at Chakpori. Thereafter, the Regent Sonam Rabten and [Gushi Qan] Tendzin Chogyal, ruler of heaven and earth, each raised the number by a further century, making a total of 29; but as the number nine is inauspicious [according to Tibetan numerology], they finally raised the number to 30. Some, however, maintain that it was Jowo Dīpaṃkara [Atiśa] himself who set the number at 20 centuries on behalf of his own mother, and then increased it by eight, in recognition of his eight siblings. Paṇchen Lobzang Chokyi Gyeltshan then increased the number by one century, and then it was eventually raised to 30. Such [comments] suggest that there are diverse, uncorroborated sources attributed to former spiritual teachers and officials in Tibet, as well as to Jowo [Atiśa], concerning the [requisite] tally of 27, 28 or even 30 centuries.

[Elsewhere], it is said that one outer circuit (*phyi-skor*) of the temple is equivalent to four circuits of the intermediate path (*bar-skor*), while [the sacristans] Lharje Gewabum and Sangye Chamo asserted that if one were to carry stones to [repair] the stone dykes on special occasions [deemed] suitable for accumulating the one hundred thousand circumambulations, then the merit [of those who carry the stones] would equal that derived from offering butter lamps weighing as much as the stones themselves. This is how the custom of [carrying] stones for the dykes became widespread, and it is clear that as the city wall later expanded from the inner circuit, between the intermediate and outer circuits, the extent of the outer circuit gradually increased. I wonder if these approximate measurements for the one hundred thousand circumambulations do not just encompass the image of our teacher [Jowo Śākyamuni], the size of a twelve-year-old, but also most of the other ancient sacred representative images, such as Mahākāruṇika in the form Rangjon Ngaden, Jampa Chezhi, [Jampa] Truze and so on.

I also feel that my venerable spiritual teacher [Dalai Lama V], while focusing his body, speech and mind [specifically] on the physical acts of accumulating merit and purification, which are commonly accepted as the provisional meaning [of the teach-

Throne supporting Jowo Śākyamuni. (1985 HM)

ings], recognized that when he had previously undertaken one hundred thousand intermediate circuits [of the temple] in order to complete the physical activities of accumulation and purification, four intermediate circuits were [in fact] equivalent to one outer circuit, and that however certain one might be with regard to the accuracy of the number of outer circuits [one had accumulated], 28 centuries would be required to complete the one hundred thousand circumambulations.[6]

Attendant applying gold to Jowo Śākyamuni's body. (1993 HMS)

The Visionary Experiences of Yutok Yonten Gonpo

Starting from the time when the image of Jowo Rinpoche was installed in the Great Temple of Lhasa, there have been reports of many learned and accomplished spiritual teachers from the various Tibetan traditions having experienced pure visions [in its presence] – these are for the most part documented in all the [relevant] biographies. For now, let us examine the following example, taken from the *Biography of Yutok the Elder*, Yonten Gonpo (708-833), who was the father of [Tibetan] medicine:

> Then Yutok the Great traveled to Lhasa. He completed one hundred thousand circumambulations of Jowo Rinpoche within seven days. Then, as he stood saying his prayers, a woman wearing bone ornaments and a yogin wielding a brass trumpet appeared before him and said, "O most learned Yutok, if you want to receive particularly profound instructions on ways to cure rabies and dog bites, there is a ḍākinī dwelling in that shed, over yonder!" So saying, they disappeared. Then Yutok the Great awoke from his dream, and after praying fervently to Bhaiṣajyaguru and the awareness holders, he set forth in search of the ḍākinī. In a shed he found a Monpa woman, ugly, malodorous, lame, scarred and blind in one eye. Yutok the Great requested her to impart the instruction, to which she gesticulated, saying, "Instruction, Instruction!" Yutok the Great had the thought that he should seek out another [ḍākinī] elsewhere, but at that very moment a group of five ḍākinīs appeared and sang the following [verses] in unison:
>
> O ignorant beings,
> The deep sleep of ignorance and mistaken views
> Is the main cause of your roaming through cyclic existence.
> O Yutokpa, you who have found a precious treasure,
> And at the same time returned empty-handed,
> In this life you should certainly attain buddhahood,
> But you have not reached [that goal]. How wretched! How pitiful!
> Even now if you wish to receive instruction,
> Discard mistaken views, and search for the instructions!
>
> So saying, they became invisible. Yutok the great, while absorbed by the melodious tone of the ḍākinīs, stood completely oblivious of the old woman. Then, he [immediately] recollected the following verses from the *Twofold Recension of the Hevajra Tantra:*
>
> Since pleasant and unpleasant things are all conceptual thoughts
> Do not cling to them in any respect whatsoever.
>
> Since he had not understood the meaning of these verses, and had harbored mistaken views, he resolved to go in search of the [appropriate] instructions, even if the Monpa woman had gone to India. He went in search of her, but was unable to find her. So at that juncture he approached the image of Jowo Śākyamuni [in the Great Temple of Lhasa]. [To his amazement], he saw the Monpa woman seated next to the image. Then, when Yutokpa requested that she give him instruction right then, she vanished into light and dissolved into the heart of Jowo [Śākyamuni]. Yutok the Great, having failed to meet the Monpa woman, then prayed one-pointedly to Jowo Rinpoche, revealing his purpose and thoughts. Thereupon Jowo Rinpoche smiled and spoke as follows:
>
> Since you are unable to understand your own mind
> How could you find this ḍākinī, even by searching for her?
> Since you do not know that whatever appears is the instruction,
> How could you find this instruction, even by searching for it?
> Since you do not recognize conceptual thought as the buddha-body of reality,
> How could you find this Monpa woman, even by searching for her?
> Since you have clung to the subject-object dichotomy,
> How could you be introduced to blessings?
> Since you are unable to generate faith in something repulsive,

How could your prayers be fulfilled?
Since you have not abandoned self-centred bias,
How could you engage in activities which benefit others?
If you can understand these points, you will be learned!
If you search now for the Monpa woman, you will find her!
I will confer blessings on the lineage-holders of Yutok, father and son,
So that they might devoutly act for the sake of all sentient beings!

Then, as Yutok the Great set forth in search of the Monpa woman, he reached Kongpo, where he approached the daughter of Donyo Dorje, who was endowed with the signs of a ḍākinī, and he requested her for instructions, there and then. The ḍākinī replied, "I have healing instructions for rabies and other diseases caused by dog bites. They are secret, effective, and particularly profound. Since you are without fear and trepidation even when confronted by a barking dog, I will impart them through the aural lineage to you my son, a worthy receptacle for this instruction. So rejoice!" So saying, she offered the healing instruction on dog bites known as *Bye-ma reg-gcod* and other techniques.

Yutok the Great, the supremely learned scholar, then traveled to Lhasa, where the sacred teachings had been taught. He offered two rolls of *ta-hun* brocade, each eight arm-spans in length, to Jowo Rinpoche, who is endowed with the major marks [of an enlightened being], and to the self-arisen image of sublime [Mahākāruṇika], known as Rangjon Ngaden. He also offered them one hundred and eighty-eight turquoise stones, the largest being as big as the hoof of a pig, and a bushel of pearls, arranged in the shapes of the eight auspicious symbols. Consecrating the five meats and five nectars, he then made offerings to the ḍākinī and her entourage, who in return bestowed a particularly profound teaching known as the *Natural Liberation of Clinging to the Three Poisons* (*Dug-gsum 'ching-ba rang-grol*), which contains general and specific instructions on the treatment of diseases.

Then, [on another occasion], having reached Lhasa, Yutok the Great and his students performed the *Medicinal Garland of Nectar (bDud-rtsis sman-'phreng)* and compounded sacred medicine (*sman-sgrub*) over a twenty-five day period in the presence of Jowo Śākyamuni. On the morning of the fifteenth day, Jowo Chenpo, assuming the appearance of the buddha-body of perfect resource, said, "Yutokpa, come with me if you want to see the [paradise of] blue beryl in the east!" Yutokpa then prayed as follows:

O most excellent of teachers, clarifying the sacred teachings,
Buddha-body of emanation, exquisitely manifesting as the buddha-body of perfect resource,
Through your compassion, may your resplendent luminosity, and charismatic radiance
Transport this corporeal form of mine
To the [buddha] field of blue beryl!
May I see the face of the King of Medicine (Bhaiṣajyaguru)
And receive instructions from him!
Grant your blessings that my mind may merge inseparably with his!

Thereupon, a women clad in bone ornaments [appeared and] said, "Yutokpa, come forth to the pure land!" A white beam of rainbow light then extended outwards and Yutokpa traveled along it. Everyone [present there] saw the firmament filled with offerings of sound, rainbow light and divine flowers, and the sky filled with silken drapes, banners, and so forth. Some people said Jowo Chenpo has gone to a pure land!" Some said, "Yutokpa has gone!". Others said, "Both of them have gone!" Since everyone was incredulous, King Mutri Tsenpo himself went to inspect [the temple]. Since the throne of Jowo Śākyamuni was empty and the bed of Yutokpa was also empty, everyone was confused as to what had happened. Some cried, some laughed, while others prayed. The king and all his subjects prayed for ten days, whereupon Jowo Śākya Chenpo and Yutokpa the Great returned to their respective abodes, riding on the rays of the sun. Everyone was astonished. The king offered a maṇḍala of one thousand gold coins to Jowo Chenpo, and a basin full of turquoise to Yutok the Great. Yutok exclaimed, "Is it not very amazing that the great Jowo Śākyamuni extended this vision to me!" The king replied, "It is to our sheer amazement that Jowo and Yutok, two supreme beings, left for the pure land, but returned to benefit me and my Tibetan subjects!"

Jowo Śākyamuni during the body-gilding ceremony. (1993 HMS)

The monk accompanying Josef Vaniš in 1954 allowed the rays of the sun to enter for a few moments so that he could see further riches of the temple that were normally shrouded in darkness.

The bell left in the 18th century by the Italian Capuchins bearing the inscription *TE DEUM LAUDAMUS* was still hanging from the ceiling in 1954. (JV)

Then again when en route for Lato in Tsang, Yutokpa and his entourage of disciples reached Lhasa and offered gold paint for the face of Jowo Rinpoche, using fifty gold coins. He also offered three gold coins as a maṇḍala, and prayed as follows,

> O, golden-hued resplendent image, adorned with all major and minor marks,
> Your great compassion permeates all living beings.
> You are victorious over all malignant forces of disharmony.
> May you protect all beings afflicted by disease through your compassion!
> Grant your blessings that I may act on behalf living beings,
> And bestow the accomplishment through which medicines are transformed into nectar!

Thereupon he presented gifts to the temple caretakers, pleasing them all. He then prayed in the presence of Jowo Rinpoche, night and day, without distraction, and without uttering a single word. At dawn on the fifth day, he felt exhilarated and heard Jowo Rinpoche speak as follows:

> Sublime Mañjuśrī was the speech-emanation of Bhaiṣajyaguru,
> And his emanation, in turn, was Kumārajīvaka.
> Yutok Yonten Gon is the emanation of Kumāra[jīvaka].
> Inspired by the compassionate spirituality of the buddhas of the three times,
> You will propagate the teaching of medical science in Tibet.
> Among all the discourses, treatises and instructions on medical science,
> There is not a single text that you will not understand.
> Your talents resemble the expanse of the oceans,
> While the talents of others resemble a clay vase filled with water taken from the oceans.
> Even if [this assertion] were disputed owing to the rivalry of proud scholars,
> Though they might dispute this, [you] Yutokpa, are unrivalled.
> You shall remain in Tibet for one hundred and twenty-five [years],
> As the foremost of all practitioners of medicine, curing the ailments of living beings,
> And then, in the splendid palace of Bhaiṣajyaguru,
> You shall become a sacred master of the peerless assembly!

Yutokpa the Great then again made the following aspirational prayer:

> Immutable lord of the sacred teachings, endowed with charismatic golden radiance,
> Emanating immeasurable lights and rays of light throughout the ten directions,
> O sole father of all [beings], endowed with the eye of knowledge and without objective qualification,
> You are the source of the eighty-four thousand components of the sacred teaching.
> O my spiritual teacher, unfailing lord of refuge for all beings,
> We have faith in you!
> Grant your blessings that I become unerringly steadfast
> In realization of selflessness and the abiding nature of reality!

Yutok then asked, "Virtuous actions that are free from corruption have a great benefit resulting from inexpressible meditation, beyond the intellect. But what are the great benefits associated with [virtuous actions] that are not [yet] free from corruption?" Jowo Rinpoche replied, "For one who would accumulate those virtuous actions that are not [yet] free from corruption, the act of saving the lives of sentient beings brings the greatest benefit. Moreover, there is no [benefit] higher than that which comes from protecting the lives of beings who are unprotected, weak, without clothing, and without food, whether they are objects of our compassion or obstacles to the practice of the sacred teachings. This [benefit] is unsurpassed, incomparable, and the best of all the excellent attributes that are particularly sublime. It is the root of all spiritual paths, the highest of all spiritual vehicles, the actual cause for the attainment of buddhahood, and it resembles a seed that will yield [most excellent] shoots. The man [who engages in such conduct] will be a spiritual teacher, belonging to the enlightened family of bodhisattvas. What more need one say! There are also inestimable benefits for one who would save the lives of the great mass of living beings who are obscured, evil, hard to train, and violators of commitments, generating [rebirth] in the lower realms of cyclic existence and obstructing [rebirth] in the higher realms and [the path to] liberation. He is one who will have renounced shamelessness, arrogance, anger, miserliness, jealousy, and inappropriate livelihood. If, grounded in loving kindness and compassion, he dons the robes of modesty, wears the ornaments of strong perseverance and altruism, wields the tools of effective instruction, relies on excellent surgical instruments, and esteems the correct view, then the benefits that accrue will be immeasurable, inexpressible and hard to fathom. This [act of saving lives] is the offering that will please your spiritual teacher! This is the sacrament that will please your meditational deities! This is the feast-offering that will please the ḍākinīs! This oral teaching, that is easy [to comprehend], devoid of difficulties, purposeful, inestimable, and swiftly attainable, will facilitate your attainment of enlightenment without having to meditate, and enable you to traverse the [bodhisattva] levels and paths without having to move [along them], and reach the end of your spiritual path without engaging in [distracting] activities. Endowed with the nine great attributes of [Bhaiṣajya]guru, [king of] Blue Beryl [light], along with seven reasons for confidence, and four appendages, it is the practical instruction of the Buddha!"

In the *Treasury of the Abidharma* (Ch. 4, v. 118) it is said:

> Even though they are not sublime beings,
> Offerings made to one's father and mother,
> To invalids, teachers of religion, and the Bodhisattva in his last birth
> Are worthy beyond measure.

Nāgārjuna has also said:

> The benefits that arise are beyond comparison
> [When one helps] those who are weak and without protection,
> Those who are impoverished and afflicted by pain,
> And those who roam aimlessly, without friends.

And in the words of Śāntideva:

> Until all beings are cured of their sickness,
> However many they are,
> May I become their medicine, their physician,
> And their attending nurse.

In the transmissions of the Vinaya *('Dul-ba lung)* it is stated;

> King Zimigchen (*gZi-mig-can*), while engaged in the spiritual paths of learning, focused entirely on acts of benefit to the sick and did not accumulate any other provisions [of merit]. As a result, in this life he is happy, joyous and prosperous. In the future, he will transcend all the spiritual levels and paths and attain manifest enlightenment – this will all be due to his past actions and long-term aspirational prayers; and to the fact that he perceived that it was important to act on behalf of invalids.

It is also said in a sūtra from the *Pagoda of Precious Gems* (*Ratnakūṭasūtra*):

> O Vajrapramāthin, furthermore, if any bodhisattva, in a dream, cognizes himself or herself as curing sentient beings who are afflicted by ailments, that bodhisattva will come to perceive any of the [bodhisattva] levels, from the first as far as the eighth, whichever is appropriate. Since their obscuration due to past actions will have weakened and the actions associated with malignant forces will have increased, they shall be able to purify all [such malign forces] completely through their great compassion. In this way, they should persevere in altruistic acts, without hope for any return. Thereby, their obscurations will be purified and they will be fully renunciate on the path to enlightenment.
> As for the types of invalid [they treat]: if they cure a child, they will reach the first [bodhisattva] level. If they cure an infant, they will reach the second bodhisattva level. If they cure an adult male, they will reach the third, if they cure a woman and her child, the fourth, if they cure a spiritual teacher or spiritual friend who upholds the monastic vows, they will reach the fifth level, if they cure someone afflicted by a contagious disease, they will reach the sixth, if they cure the ailments of morbid pallor, oedema or dropsy, they will reach the seventh level, if they cure dermatitis and related ailments caused by the spirit lords of the soil of the *gNyan-sha bkra-glang-zhu* class they will reach the eighth, if they cure weight loss, amenorrhea and leprosy they will reach the ninth level, if they cure ailments caused by elementals and malignant forces of the upper atmosphere, they will reach the tenth level; if they cure the brown phlegm type of combined humoral disorder they will reach the eleventh level; if they cure ailments caused by the malignant spirit Bya-'don putra, they will reach the

A large statue of Bodhisattva Maitreya in the Main Hall. (1954 JV)

Carved capital of a pillar in the Main Hall. (1954 JV)

The "Wheel of Doctrine" stands between two gazelles on the facade of the Annexe, the Potala is in the background. (1954 JV)

twelfth level; and if they cure illness caused by rabies, they will reach the thirteenth level, which is known as Vajradhara.

Moreover, in the *Sūtra of the Curing of Ailments (Nad rab-tu zhi-ba'i mdo)* it states:

Whoever takes one step to help a patient shall find abundant food, drink, bedding, medicine, clothes, ornaments, and wealth. Whoever offers a patient one dose of medicine or a set of clothes shall be freed from past actions due to malign forces. If these actions are undertaken out of compassion, one shall not be tied to [future] rebirth in the inferior realms, one will be purified of obscurations associated with past actions, and become a bodhisattva who abides on one of the [successive] spiritual levels.

It also states in the *Sūtra of the Foundation of Mindfulness* (*Smṛtyupasthānasūtra*):

Whether one succeeds in curing a major disease or one of its sub-types, one who is considerate, without being intemperate, and who acts with self-control will have [an inheritance of] positive actions and reach the first level, which is unsusceptible to degeneration.

Then, [having received this vision], Yutok the Great remained for two days in Lhasa, praying to Jowo [Śākyamuni].[7]

Nomadic Enthusiasm for Pilgrimage to the Great Temple

Throughout the three districts of Tibet, there were [in the past] relatively few people who had an opportunity to actually see Jowo Rinpoche. For this reason, it is stated in some sources that "There is hardly anyone who has not been on pilgrimage to [Central] Tibet who will not fold their hands respectfully when the very names of the Jokhang, Potala and the great monastic seats are mentioned. Similarly, when elderly men and women who have visited Central Tibet meet together, it is said they will sometimes visualize the Jokhang in their minds, starting from the entrance portico of the Great Courtyard and proceeding through the Great Acacia Gate (also known as the Lion Gate), as far as the bellows-shaped stone, after which they enumerate the successive [chapels]. When they reach the entrance to the Mahākāruṇika chapel, they all recite aspirational prayers with their eyes closed. Then, when they reach the area in front of Jowo [Śākyamuni], they recite their aspirational prayers in silence, without uttering a single word for a while, so that it is as if they were actually present [in the Jokhang]. During their meditations it even seems that they can recall accurately the number of butter lamps that were offered in front of each of the pillars! But sometimes they also have strong disagreements, disputing the exact order in which the chapels are visited; and then they will invite monks or learned scholar-monks (*dge-bshes*) who have spent a lot of time in Central Tibet to bear witness."[8]

The Great Courtyard. (1954 JV)

Offerings of Immolation in the Great Temple

There is a tradition in Tibet, the land of snows, that any man will consider it an important spiritual action to see Jo[wo Rinpoche] at least once in the course of his life; and in lower Dokham it is customary for large groups of people who are enthusiastic for the Buddhist teachings to make their way to Lhasa, prostrating along the road. And it is even customary for some of them to bind the base of one of their fingers with string, causing it to wither by the time they reach Lhasa after more than a year on the road. They would then offer this [withered] finger as a butter lamp, while confessing their negative past actions and reciting aspirational prayers in the presence of Jowo [Śākyamuni].

In the 11th century, it was reported that [an unusual event] occurred in the Great Temple of Magical Emanation at Rasa. At that time, it is said, "Dolchung Korpon wrapped his body in an oiled cloth, and immolated himself, from the crown of the head downwards, as an offering in the presence of Jowo [Śākyamuni]. As his body burned, he recited the *Aspirational Prayer of Good Conduct* (*Bhadracaryāpraṇidhānarāja*) twice, and during the third recitation, as he reached the verse 'I die in the presence of all lordly [ones]!' he became elated and passed away. At that very moment a great light emerged from the crown of his head, in the place where his skull had caved in, and vanished into the sky. Immediately thereafter, there was an earthquake and a great shower of flowers."[9]

In the seventeenth century, the learned and accomplished master Karma Chag-me (1610-1678) also recounted an event from his own life, in the following verses:

Going to Lhasa and appearing before [Jowo] Śākyamuni,
I offered one of my left fingers as an offering lamp,

And I took the extensive vow to cultivate the mind of enlightenment.
At that moment, an old monk who was very biased said
"Wasn't his recitation of the *Aspirational Prayer of Good Conduct* interrupted before?"
"But now he is reciting it nine times, not [once]!"
The Newars, *atsaras*, Mongols and others looked on with great amazement.[10]

Aspirational Prayers Offered in the Great Temple

All sorts of Tibetans, including those from Lhasa and visitors, as well as peoples of Tibetan ethnic origin, Mongols and others have recited aspirational prayers one-pointedly and with fervent devotion in the presence of Jowo Rinpoche. I have included here one anecdote concerning the different types of aspirational prayers that Tibetans make on these occasions: One day, as usual, when a large crowd of devotees who had come to pay their respects to Jowo [Śākyamuni], were prostrating in front of the Great Temple and circumambulating it, there were a couple of "Apho Hor" nomads from the north who joined them. As they finished making their prostrations and before they could start reciting their aspirational prayers, a loquacious old lady from Lhasa barged in front of them, with her hands folded and loudly recited the following prayer:

By the power of the virtuous actions I have undertaken through my positive higher aspiration and sincere altruistic motivation, may the negative obscurations caused by non-virtuous actions and all the sufferings endured by all sentient beings who have been my kind parents throughout cyclic existence, from beginningless time until the present, be refined and purified!

Transforming [these sufferings] into the roots and branches of spiritual and temporal well-being, may the precious teaching of the Conquerors, which resembles molten gold, flourish and thrive in all directions and at all times, illuminating all corners of Jambudvīpa, from east to west, as if by the light of the sun!

May all the saintly learned and accomplished upholders of the Buddhist teachings, headed by my root spiritual teacher, who is endowed with kindness, have a long and steadfast life, wherever they reside! May all their heart-felt aspirations for the flourishing of the teachings and the happiness of living beings be effortlessly fulfilled, without impediment. May those who uphold the teachings develop the enlightened attributes associated with scriptural transmissions and realizations! May the venerable communities of monks and nuns who are without bias, live in harmony, without transgressing their monastic codes, even in their dreams! May they raise the victory banners of exegesis through teaching, debate and composition, and of spiritual attainment, higher and higher!

May the stains of misunderstanding and wrong understanding afflicting the mass of humanity whose eyes of discriminative awareness that may engage in virtuous actions are blinded, and who do not guard against the pitfalls of negative actions, be purified! May they attain the eyes of intelligence that correctly recognize things to be adopted and things to be renounced! May this era of strife, war and weapons which maims sentient beings and deprives them of their precious lives be ended!

May the course of all serious and incurable diseases be interrupted!

May fears of debilitating poverty and of famine which brings hunger and thirst be assuaged!

Generally speaking, may all living creatures, submerged in the swamp of the ocean of suffering throughout cyclic existence, through their obdurate past actions and dissonant mental states, lacking even a moment of tranquility, due to the fierce waves of the three types of suffering, [eventually find release]! And in particular, may all the negative acts amassed over hundreds of aeons by those wretched Tibetan citizens who are unprotected in all ways and on all sides, without a secure domicile, their own land having fallen to an alien power, and being forced into exile in alien lands where they have no control, be purified! May the truth and conclusions of the unfailing laws of past actions and their results swiftly become transparent!

May we be freed from this oppression which resembles a sky obscured by dark clouds!

May we be freed from this affliction of hunger and thirst, which resembles a flame reaching its zenith! May we be released from the snares of danger and fear, as if falling into a bottomless abyss!

May all our compatriots living in exile be reunited with their relatives!

May this beloved country in which we rejoice fall into our own hands!

May the sun of freedom, happiness and prosperity that we always cherish rise up!

May all the temporary afflictions of this life that torment myself and all sentient beings who are my mother be alleviated!

Officials in the administrative wing of the Great Temple. (1954 JV)

Officials and monks in The Great Temple. (1954 JV)

When [consciousness] is transferred to another world from this one, at the time of death, may we not have to endure severe sufferings of affliction!
Passing from one happy state to another, may we increase our understanding of the [bodhisattva] levels and paths, and finally attain the state of omniscience, with ease!"[11]
When she had completed this prayer, it is said that the Apho Hor [nomads], intoned the following prayer, "We too pray for the very same things that this old lady from Lhasa is praying for!"
Once there was a group of pilgrims from Golok who came to see Jowo Rinpoche. They presented their offering scarves, made offerings to express their refuge [in the Buddhist teachings] and presented other offerings as a dedication of merit [on behalf of deceased persons]. Then, after filling the butter lamp, they were overheard reciting the following prayer:

> I dedicate this for the well-being of all sentient beings of the six classes, who have been my mother, their number equaling the limits of space. I dedicate this for the sake of my most gracious parents and my grandparents to whom we are indebted. I dedicate this for my travelling companions on the three peaks of the highlands and for my thieving friends in the three valleys of the lowlands. I dedicate this for those whose lives have been cut short through killing, and to the many who suffer from various afflictions and diseases. I dedicate this to all beings, who have been killed knowingly by our own hands and trampled unknowingly underfoot. I dedicate this to all beings whose minds have entertained thoughts of murder. I dedicate this to those who have tasted slain flesh. I dedicate this for those friends with whom I have sworn an oath. I dedicate this for cattle and horses that breed well. I dedicate this for those whom I have cursed or threatened. I dedicate this for our [female] dependents who work with thread and needles. I dedicate this for domestic cattle and guard dogs. I dedicate this for our [sedentary] compatriots, who make use of doors and pillars, and for nomads who make use of hearths and ropes. I dedicate this for my immediate and distant relatives![12]

Popular Songs Eulogizing Jowo Śākyamuni

Jowo [Śākyamuni] is also eulogized in Tibetan folk songs, such as the following:

> In Lhasa, park of precious jewels,
> Never say, "There aren't any jewels!"
> If Jo Śāk, the wish-fulfilling Jewel,
> Is not a jewel, then what is it?

And:

> Outside it is encircled by a perimeter wall.
> The perimeter wall is encircled by mountain willows.
> Inside there is seated a precious jewel,
> Jo Śāk, the wish-fulfilling jewel!

Also:

> O Jo Śāk, wish-fulfilling jewel,
> Seated under a gilded copper roof,
> In the past, there were no changes.
> At this time, too, do not permit any changes!

And:

> As for happiness, my own land is a happy one,
> But I have been forced abroad by dint of past actions.
> O Jo Śāk, wish-fulfilling jewel,
> Bring me to my homeland!

There are numerous songs such as these, but the selection given above will suffice as examples of the genre.

The Offerings and Visions of Kongpo Ben

Tibetans have great faith in Jowo Rinpoche of Lhasa, and there is one particular story, handed down through an oral tradition, which goes as follows:

Once there was a simple-minded fellow from Kongpo who [later] became known as Jowo Ben. He made a journey to Central Tibet to see the image of Jowo Rinpoche. When he first arrived in front of the image, there was no caretaker or anyone else about. Seeing the food offerings and the butter lamps in front of it, he imagined that Jowo Rinpoche must dip pieces of the offering cakes in the melted butter of the lamps and eat them. The wicks were burning in the lamps, he supposed, to keep the butter from solidifying. "I think I'd better eat some, like Jowo Rinpoche does," he thought to himself, and dunking a piece of dough from the offering cakes into the butter, he ate it. He looked up at the face of Jowo. "What a nice spiritual teacher you are," he said. "Even when dogs come and steal the food you've been offered, you smile. When the draught makes your lamps splutter, you still keep smiling. Here, I'll leave you my boots. Please look after them for me while I walk around you!" He took off his boots and put them up in front of the image. While he was circumambulating the middle pathway that circles the chapel, the caretaker returned and was about to throw the boots out, when Jowo Rinpoche said, "Don't take those boots away! Kongpo Ben has entrusted them to me!" Ben eventually came back and took the boots. "You really are what they call a good spiritual teacher!" he said to image. "Next year, why don't you come and visit us. I'll slaughter an old pig and cook it for you and brew you up some nice old barley beer. I'll be waiting!" "I'll come!" said Jowo Rinpoche.

Ben went back home and told his wife, "I've invited Jowo Rinpoche. I'm not sure exactly when he's coming, though – so don't forget to keep an eye out for him." One day, the following year, as she was drawing water from the river, Ben's wife clearly saw a reflection of Jowo Rinpoche in the water. Straight away she ran home and told her husband, "There's something down there, in the river… I wonder if it's the guest you invited?"

Ben rushed down to the river and saw Jowo Rinpoche shining in the water. Thinking that he must have fallen into the river, Ben jumped in after him. As he grabbed at the image, he found that he could actually catch hold of it and bring it along with him. As they were proceeding towards Ben's house, they arrived in front of a huge rock by the side of the road. The Jowo did not want to go any further. "I do not enter lay-peoples' homes," he said, and disappeared into the rock.

This place, to which the Jowo himself was seen coming, is called Jowo Rock (*rdo-le jo-bo*) and the spot in the river where the image appeared bears the name of Chu Jowo. Even nowadays, it is said that this place confers the same blessing as the Jowo in Lhasa, and everyone does prostrations and makes offerings there.[13]

The Swearing of Oaths in the Name of Jowo Śākyamuni

According to a Tibetan saying, "Men cannot consume their oaths! Dogs cannot eat iron!" There is a custom among Tibetans that the act of swearing an oath in the name of someone or something should refer either to an extremly holy or extremly sinful entity. For example, younger people in Lhasa, when swearing an oath, will say, "Jowo knows!" or "Precious Jowo!" The Apha Horpa nomads of the North and the Khampas will say, "Jowo, wish-fulfilling Jewel!" while Khampas and Amdowas might say, "By the Lhasa highlands!", "By sunlit Lhasa", or "By the Utsang Highlands!" During the Cultural Revolution (1966-76), it was considered anachronistic to swear an oath by Jowo Rinpoche, so people would swear "By Chairman Mao!"

The Obscured Vision of the Unfortunate

To illustrate the uncertainty of subjective perceptions, which is an esoteric instruction of the spiritual teachers of the gradual path (*lam-rim*) in Tibet, it is customarily recounted that:

Once a bandit chief from Upper A-rig in Golok made a journey to see the image of Jowo [Śākyamuni] in Lhasa, but he couldn't see even the butter lamps or the other [offerings] arrayed in front of Jowo, let alone the image itself! The previous Gyalsey Rinpoche of On (*'on rgyal-sras gong-ma*) advised him to purify his past actions and obscurations, so he then made ten thousand offerings, along with prostrations and circumambulations. Finally, he was able to see the butter lamps, but not the Jowo![14]

Side elevation with bearing joists of the temple roof. (1954 JV)

The carved heads of the bearing joists of the temple roof. (1954 JV)

Detail of a fresco from the wall of the temple with repeated motif of Amitāyus, the Buddha of Infinite Life. (1954 JV)

Tangtong Gyalpo's Aspirational Prayer

Near the end of the fourteenth century, when fear of famine arose in Utsang, the great accomplished master Tangtong Gyalpo prayed to Jowo Rinpoche, and dispelled the fear of famine. This incident is recounted in all recensions of his biography, in the following verses:

Herein is contained a prayer for the alleviation of the fear of famine, uttered by the great accomplished master Tangtong Gyelpo

To save infinite numbers of living beings, O Compassionate Conqueror,
You who have cultivated the supreme unsurpassed enlightenment
And perfected the two provisions [of merit and pristine cognition]!
O guides, bodhisattvas, pious attendants, and hermit buddhas of the ten directions!
O host of spiritual teachers, meditational deities, ḍākinīs and protectors of the sacred teachings!
[From this point the recitation of verses should be completed three times!]
May the sylvan spirits, wealth deities and treasure lords, with their retinues,
Look upon the defenseless beings of this degenerate era with loving kindness!
To save these corporeal beings afflicted by the sufferings of hunger, thirst, and poverty.
May they yield in this Jambudvīpa, land of snows,
A downpour of jewels, food, wealth, grain, bedding
And all other useful resources that are pleasing!
May they pacify harmful afflictions caused by the four elements,
Such as untimely winds, fires, bad omens, and floods!
May grains, nutritious foods, fruits and crops
Ripen fully, as in the Perfect Age!
Through the power of this extensive aspirational prayer,
Encouraged by loving kindness and compassion,
May aeons of diseases, strife and famines cease,
And may beings possess long life, free from illness,
And endowed with happiness and joy!
By the power of the compassion of all the Conquerors and their spiritual sons.
And the unfailing truth of past actions and their results,
May the teachings of the Conquerors flourish and thrive,
And may all beings swiftly attain unsurpassed enlightenment!

At a time, when there was great fear of hoarfrost and hail afflicting the harvest in Utsang, the venerable and great accomplished master Tangtong Gyelpo presented a gold begging bowl filled with grain on the altar in front of the image of Jowo Rinpoche in Lhasa, and he made this aspirational prayer. Consequently, worthy individuals saw the sublime Avalokiteśvara shower a downpour of grain upon Tibet from the heavens. So this prayer, possessing the blessings of indestructible buddha-speech, has the power to liberate all living beings from the sufferings of hunger and thirst.[15]

A Listing of Inventories of Offerings and Renovations Made in the Great Temple

Whenever the succession of omniscient Dalai Lamas, the successive Paṇchen Lamas or Karmapas, and other genuine spiritual teachers went to see the image of Jowo [Śākyamuni] in Lhasa, they would offer gold for face-painting ceremonies, as well as gold butter lamps, crown ornaments, and robes. As such times, it was customary to make a record [of the details of their offerings]. Also at intervals there were rulers of Tibet, aristocrats, wealthy merchants and the like who also made donations, out of faith, in the above manner; and it was customary for them to record all the offerings that they entrusted [for this purpose] to the spiritual teachers that they respectively venerated with devotion. Here I have prepared a rough list of these records, by way of illustration:

rGyal ba lnga pa'i gsung 'bum. Vol. DZA
"Lha ldan sprul pa'i gtsug lag khang gi dkar chag shel dkar me long". 21 folios.
rGyal ba sku phreng bcu gsum pa'i gsung 'bum, Vol. 5, Sec. BI
"Lha ldan sprul pa'i gan dho la chen por nyams gso mdzad pa'i dkar chag." 12 folios.
Paṇ chen blo bzang chos rgyan gyi gsung 'bum. Vol. CA (middle part)
"Jo bo rin po che'i shākya'i rgyal po'i zhabs drung du mchod pa'i rnam grangs 'ga' zhig phul ba'i kha byang." 3 folios.

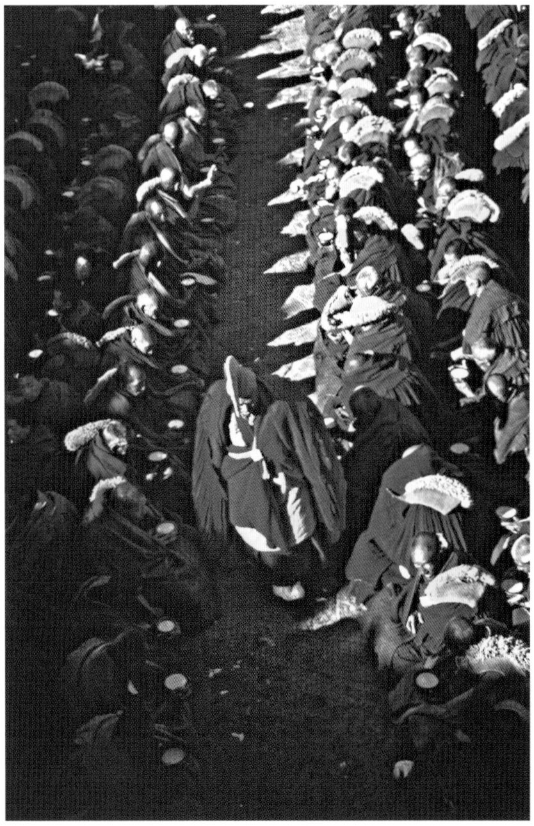

Monlam Chenmo. Proctor monk processing through the monks during the Wet Ceremony. (1986 CB)

Monlam Chenmo. Monks unloading barley flower donated by pilgrims in the Wood Enclosure. (1986 CB)

Monlam Chenmo. Monks debating in the Great Courtyard. (1986 CB)

Stag brag ngag dbang gsung rab mthu stobs kyi gsung 'bum, Vol. 2
  "Rab byung bcu drug pa'i shing bya lo gzhung sa mchog nas lha ldan jo bo chen po'i dbus rten gtso khag la dbu rgyan snyan rgyan na bza' sogs 'bul gnang mdzad pa'i smon tshig." 18 folios.
gTer ston sangs rgyas gling pa'i gter chos. Bris ma. Vol. 4
  "Pho brang ra sa dang bsam yas gso tshul." 11 folios.
sDe khri 'jam dbyangs thub bstan nyi ma'm gsang mtshan ratna badzra'i gsung 'bum, Vol. 1
  "Jo bo'i lo rgyus rin chen za ma tog," 6 folios.
'Jam mgon a myes zhabs gsung 'bum, Vol. KA
  "Lha sa'i jo bo rin po che la snyan zhal mdzes byed phul ba'i kha yig." 2 folios.
rGyal dbang lnga pa chen po'i gsung 'bum, Vol. MA

1 Chu log smon lam thog khar kha er ti ni hong tha'i jis rin po cher dngul gyi maṇḍala phul ba'i kha yig sku gsum rgyal mtshan rtser mzes. f. 8b.2
2 Lha sa sogs kyi 'phros don rin chen phreng ba. f. 12b.1
3 rGyal ba tsong kha pa chen pos jo bo śākya mu ni la gser sbyangs kyi dbu rgyan 'bul ba gnang ba'i ngo bo bcos bslad med pa la lhan thabs kyi tshul du o rod kho shod kyi da las kun ci rgyal mos gser zho nyis brgya nyis shu dang rin po che sna tshogs kyi khras spras te dpangs tshad mtho bar byas nas phul ba'i kha yig phan bde'i 'dod 'jo. f. 16b.5
4 Shing bya se chen chos rgyal ba'i 'phrin las pas jo bo rin po cher gser gyi mchod rkong phul ba'i kha yig gtan bde'i mun sel snang. f. 18a.2
Sa phag sa skyong bsod nams rab brtan gyi legs byas spel ba'i ched du jo shāk yid bzhin nor bur gser srang nyis brgya brgal ba las bskrun pa'i maṇḍala phul ba'i kha yig byang chub mchog la legs sbyor. f. 129a.1
5 Sa skyong bsod nams rab brtan gyi dgongs pa rdzogs bayed du lha sa byang gling pa bsam grub rgyal pos g.yas g.yon gyi rna rgyan gnyis jo shāk dang rang byon lnga ldan la phul dus kyi kha byang. f. 130a.5
6 lCags glang hor zla bdun par jo bo rin po cher dbu rgyan snyan rgyan dar dpyangs dang bcas phul ba'i kha byang tshigs bcad lhug snyan rgyan g.yas g.yon. f. 136a.4
7 Bod yul gyi rdo rje gdan ra sa 'phrul snang gi gtsug lag khang du jo shāk yid bzhin nor bu'i thog drangs pa'i mchod yul dam pa rnams kyi spyan sngar gser dngul las grub pa'i maṇḍala ri rab mngon pa lugs su byas pa'i gsar bzos lcags glang hor zla bdun pa nyis brtsegs kyi tshes bcu gsum la las gra btsugs chu stag nag pa zla ba'i nang du legs par grub nas phul ba'i mu ran stod smad kyi kha yig tshigs bcad lhug zhing khams rgya mtshor spungs pa'i legs byas. f. 139b.6
8 Khro mo'i lo mkha' 'gro blo bzang bstan skyong gis jo shāk yid bzhin nor bu la dngul kong phul ba'i kha yig char nub spangs pa'i nyi ma. f. 167a.5
9 Jo bo shākya mu nir rgyun mchod gtsugs pa'i kong gi zhal byang. f. 227b.4

rGyal dbang lnga pa chen po'i gsung 'bum, Vol. TSHA

1 lCags 'brug cho 'phrul mchod pa'i dus jo bo rin po cher snyan shal phul ba'i kha yig byang chub snying por 'bab pa'i nyal 'gro. ff. 228-230
2 Shing bya nyan yod mchod pa'i dus jo bo śākya mu nir phul ba'i snyan shal kha yig phan bde'i lo 'bras khur dud. ff. 250-251
3 Me phag smon lam chen mo'i dus jo bo śākya mu nir phul ba'i snyan dar kha yig ma 'dris kun gyi mdza' bshes. ff. 265-266
4 Shing rta ra sa 'phrul snang du gser chab mchod pa 'phar ma phul skabs jo bo śākya mu ni'i snyan shal kha yig nges legs rin can them skas. f. 307

Gong sa sku phreng bcu gsum pa chen po'i bka' 'bum, Vol. NYI

1 Lha ldan jo bo rin po cher mdun sgrig gser gyi 'khor lo rtsibs stong dang ra che jo bor rin chen gnyis kyi 'khor lo rtsibs stong bcas phul ba'i smon tshig. ff. 5b.2-6a.1
2 Yab gzhis lha klu dga' tshal ba nas lha ldan jo bo chen por rin dang las grub pa'i dbu rgyan rin chen srid nor khyad 'phags du ma'i khras gtams pa gsar bzhengs dad 'bul gyi 'dod gsol smon tshig dge. ff. 54b.2-55a.5

A List of Eulogies Offered to Jowo Śākyamuni

There are also many eulogies that have been offered to Jowo Rinpoche, in the form of one-pointed devotional prayers. Among them there are some eulogising the magnificence of the image's major and minor marks, while others are written as poignant laments, calling for Jowo [Śākyamuni's] attention to problems of social unrest. They include, for example:

1 *Sa skya bka' 'bum*, "Chos rje sa pan gyi gsung"
Lha sa'i bde gshegs rnams la bstod pa
ba karma pa mi bskyod rdo rje" gsung 'bum. Vol. GA
2 Lha sa'i jo bo la phul ba'i zhu yig 15 folios
rGyal dbang lnga pa'i gsung. Vol. BA
3 Phan bde'i rtsa lag jo shāk rnam gnyis kyi brtan bzhugs la. 8 folios
bKras lhun sman ri ba blo bzang rnam rgyal gyi gsung 'bum. (Bris ma).
4 Lha ldan gtsug lag khang gi rten gtso jo bo śākya mu ni la bstod pa
rdzogs ldan sprin gyi rnga sgra. 4 folios
5 *Ngag dbang ye shes thub bstan rab 'byams pa'i gsung 'bum* Vol. KHA
Jo mjal smon tshig 'dod dgu'i dpal ster. 1 folio.

Monlam Chenmo. The statue of Maitreya emerging from the Main Gate of the Jokhang during the Maitreya procession on the last day of the festival. (1986 CB)

Monlam Chenmo. Procession during festival in 1943. (TS)

Sangye Gyatso on the Iconometric Proportions of Jowo Śākyamuni

Following the establishment of the Ganden Phodrang administration in the 17th century, the regent Sangye Gyatso commissioned, both publicly and privately, [many] sacred representative images, and to this end he wrote a monograph on the ideal iconometric proportions for Tibetan-style paintings and sculpture. The piece is contained in the *Removal of Rust* (*gYa'-sel*), a series of comments and answers to various questions that arose in connection with the publication of his *White Beryl* (*Baiḍūrya dkar-po*) in 1688. Accordingly, it says:

> Vertically, the iconometric proportions [of buddha images] are set at one hundred and twenty-five relative finger-widths according to the *Tantra of the Wheel of Time* (*Kālacakratantra*), and at one hundred and twenty relative finger-widths according to the *Tantra of Cakrasaṃvara* (*Saṃvarodayatantra*). Although I initially had some doubt owing to the different [measurements] presented in these two texts, when I investigated further, it seemed that they both conform to the ideal iconometric proportions laid down by Menthangpa, and the annotations of Tulku Trengkhawa, because the standard of one hundred and twenty-five [relative finger-widths] presented in the *Tantra of the Wheel of Time* is given with reference to sculpted images, and the standard of one hundred and twenty [relative finger-widths] presented in the *Tantra of Cakrasaævara* is given with reference to painted images. So, if there is such a distinction between the [iconometric proportions] of sculptures and paintings, i.e. if there is a distinction owing to three-dimensionality, the doubt would arise that one should have to calculate a difference of one twenty-fourth for each relative finger-width in all cases, whereas a standard iconometric measurement for paintings of one hundred and twenty-five [relative finger-widths] is also found to be different. But, I understand that this image of Jowo Rinpoche [in Lhasa], which represents Munīndra the size of a twelve-year-old, and was commissioned by Śakra, sculpted by the emanational artisan [Viśvakarman], and consecrated by the Buddha himself, conforms to the standard iconometric proportions. When one investigates this in detail, the measurements from the hair line to the hair ringlet [between the eyebrows] and between the hair ringlet and the tip of the nose are exactly four relative finger-widths, in accordance with Menthangpa's system; and the measurement from the tip of the nose to the chin increases this by one-half [to four and a half relative finger-widths], and so on. This increase can mostly [be seen] in bell metalwork. Moreover, in the case of all images, slight differences can be observed in the measurement of relative finger-widths for the lower part of the body, the length of the fingers and toes, and even in the distance from the heart to the armpit which should be one face-measure (*zhal-tshad*), but [in some cases] does not quite reach twelve relative finger-widths! I think [these discrepancies] have arisen due to differences in artistic style, and that they are compatible, on a par with the aforementioned distinction between the iconometry of painting and sculpture. Here, my understanding of these matters is based on extensive sources, such as the *Tantra of the Wheel of Time*, the *Tantra of Cakrasaṃvara*, and the *Tantra of Black Yamāri*, as well as the iconometric proportions of the *Lag-len dmar-'chang*, which rejects the criticisms of other traditions.[16]

In brief, it is clear that the iconometric measurements of Jowo Yizhin Norbu in the Great Temple of Magical Emanation at Lhasa were calculated excluding the drapery.

Offerings Made to Jowo Śākyamuni by Newly-appointed Officials

In Tibetan history, from the later part of the life of the Seventh Dalai Lama onwards, it has been customary to observe an inaugural day for ministers of the Tibetan government, and other [important appointees]. On such occasions, "In accordance with past custom, one is first escorted by a cavalry procession to make offerings and see [the image of Jowo Śākyamuni] in the Great Temple"[17] Then the new minister should be introduced, and "he should donate robes and extensive offerings of five sorts to the foremost images housed in the Potala and the Great Temple. In this context, the offerings that he prepares should include a golden wheel which he should present to Jowo Śākyamuni. The size of the golden wheel depends on the financial status of its sponsor. In my case, I offered a wheel made from thirty gold coins."[18] Burmiok Jedrung Karma Palden Chogyal (1871-1942) of Sikkim prepared a list of expenses he had incurred in performing a Thousand-fold Offering Ceremony in the Jokhang on the 19th day of the 9th month of the fire dragon year (1916). The accounts are presented as follows:

81.2 *srang* for purchasing 203 [14 kg] loads of roasted barley flour for ritual offerings at the rate of 0.4 *srang* per load
186.1 *srang* for purchasing 131 loads of butter for consumption and ceremonial use [in sculpture and lamps]
0.9 *srang* for six packets of 100 incense sticks
0.15 *srang* for flowers
0.11 *srang* for curd, milk and crystalised sugar
0.51 *srang* for medicinal powders and Kashmiri saffron
4.5 *srang* as a stipend and food allowance for those who prepared the offerings
0.3 srang as a stipend for those attending to the hundredfold offering lamps
4.53 *srang* for purchasing gold [for the face-painting ceremony]
2.5 *srang* for the artists who applied the gold [used in the face-painting ceremony]
24.05 *srang* as a stipend for the one hundred and fifteen monastic officials and assistants
3 *srang* for one set of *ashi* ceremonial offering scarves
3 *srang* for four sets of *zubshi* offering scarves
0.75 *srang* for three sets of *dri-phyi* offering scarves (?)
2.3 *srang* for hiring golden butter lamps
0.45 *srang* for three squares of cotton offering cloth
67.6 *srang* for purchasing 52 [14 kg] loads of offering grain at the rate of 1.3 *srang* per load
4.35 *srang* for purchasing two compressed bricks of good quality (*'bru-gnyis*) tea
2.4 *srang* for purchasing grain and wheat flour
1.31 *srang* for three *rgya-ma* (= 1.5 kg) of sugar
0.45 *srang* for five measures (= 3.5 kg) of cheese
0.9 *srang* for [dried] grapes
0.9 *srang* for four part-time caretakers
1.2 *srang* for the two sacristans
1.5 *srang* for eighteen handymen
4.8 *srang* for purchasing firewood and hiring utensils for melting butter
4.5 *srang* for purchasing additional firewood at Meru Temple
0.3 *srang* for those who offered the salt
0.3 *srang* for the supervisors, cleaners, janitors and watchmen
3.5 *srang* for food served to the guests
12 *srang* for purchasing two sacks of rice
0.75 *srang* as alms for the undertakers
1.5 *srang* as alms for beggars
Grand total: 463 *srang*.[19]

The following official petition was prepared towards the end of the 1930s in connection with an extensive thousand-fold offering ceremony to be held in the Great Temple of Magical Emanation at Lhasa where Jowo Rinpoche resides:

> To the lotus feet and golden throne of the Ocean [of Wisdom], combining all unsurpassed objects of refuge, the supreme field of merit for gods and other sentient beings!
> I, [so and so], taking refuge in you, sincerely and one-pointedly pray with body, speech and mind!

Monlam Chenmo. Ganden Tripa on the throne in the Southern Debating Courtyard. (1986 CB)

Monlam Chenmo. The Maitreya procession moving off. (1986 CB)

That the precious teaching of the omniscient Conqueror, which is the source of spiritual and temporal well-being for the world in general, and particularly this essence of the teaching of the Yellow Hats, combining the sūtras and the tantras, like refined gold, which was reformed by Tsongkhapa the Great, king of the sacred teachings throughout the three world-systems, might flourish in all directions, times and circumstances, and long remain [powerful]!

That the crown ornament of all upholders of the teachings, the incomparably gracious lord of refuges, HH Dalai Lama XIV, [embodiment of] Vajradhara the Great, [known as] the venerable Jampal Ngawang Lobzang Yeshe Tendzin Gyatso, who is glorious, noble and peerless in his authority throughout the three levels of existence; and the precious reincarnation and supreme emanation of the omniscient and all-seeing Paṇchen [Rinpoche IX], the lord of Sukhāvatī, might have long lives, untainted by even the slightest signs of misfortune with respect to the mysteries of buddha-body, speech and mind. Before long, may they be permitted to enjoy the auspicious festivals of their respective enthronements!

That all the revered and saintly incarnations of Central Tibet, wherever and whoever they are, headed by the regent of the Dalai Lama, the life-support of the spiritual and temporal well-being of the teaching and all living beings throughout the Land of Snows, Nomihan the Great, *qutuktu* of Reting Monastery, might have an indestructibly long life. May their blessed enlightened activities bring to maturity glory and good fortune for the sake of the teachings and all living beings!

That the impartial monastic communities, exemplified by the three great monastic institutions [of Ganden, Drepung, and Sera] and the two Tantric Colleges for the study of the most secret [mantras], might pass their time in harmony, maintaining purity of monastic discipline, and pursuing the threefold wheels of exegesis, practice and study!

That all sorts of [environmental] disaster, such as diseases, famines, wars and conflicts, which cause the five degenerations (*snyigs-ma lnga*) to flourish, wherever they arise throughout the length and breadth of the land, may be pacified, and that the rainy season is timely, crops and livestock thrive, and that all beings continuously experience the glory of spiritual happiness, and in particular that, on account of their big-hearted aspirational prayers that the precious Buddhist teachings might spread throughout the country, they might all aim to fulfill their wishes!

And that while we continue this day to offer service to the assembled monks of the Upper Tantric College who are actually making the offerings in connection with this extensive thousand-fold offering ceremony, in the presence of all the supreme sacred images within the Great Temple of Lhasa, a silver coin (*zho*) should be offered to each [participating] monk for roasted barley flour! In addition the articles of offering [for each monk] will include five silver coins, a silk (*ashi*) scarf as a token of respect and a *zub-phyi* scarf as a token of gratitude. A silk scarf will also be offered to the painted scroll in the Protector Chapel!

With these offerings, I earnestly implore the esteemed assembly to pray for the fulfillment of the prayers, expressed above, in connection with the formal recitation of the *Rite of Vijayā* (*rNam-rgyal-ma'i cho-ga*)![20]

Nomads from Amdo in front of the Great Temple. (1986 CB)

Political Strategies Invoking Jowo Śākyamuni

In Tibetan history, shrewd rulers and chieftains have misused the name and honor of Jowo Rinpoche in order to overpower their enemies or to incite rebellion. In the autobiography of the Fifth Dalai Lama, for example, it is written that:

> On the 29th day of the twelfth lunar month (*dgu-gtor*) [which is a day for exorcising negative forces] in the earth hare year (1639), [Donyo Dorje, king of Beri] sent prayer flags to the encampment for hoisting on the sacred mountain (*lha-ri*), and he dispatched a message through a merchant named Dralhachen, saying: "Since our [Chokthu] Mongol forces have been unsuccessful, next year I will come to Utsang with my own army. Since the copper statue called Jowo Rinpoche leads the enemy forces [of Gushri Qan], it should be drowned in the river. Sera, Drepung and Ganden should be destroyed, and a stūpa should be erected in each of these places". He went on to say that the Tsangpa [king of Tibet] and he should form an alliance, and pay their respects to all the [other] Buddhist and Bon communities of Utsang and Kham. When this message [was intercepted and] publicized, the Tsangpa king and his ministers were unable [to act] because the matter concerned the copper

image of Jo-[wo Śākyamuni]. So although he was unable to do anything, good or bad, it became transparent that this [King of] Beri was a [deserving] object for the practice of ritual murder (*las-sbyor*) because he certainly possessed all the [negative] attributes that characterize the ten [types of beings who can be violently dispatched to the [buddha]fields.[21]

Similarly, in the mid-19th century, Nya-ke Agon [= Gonpo Namgyal of Nyarong] schemed to bring the Jowo from Lhasa to Nyarong by force. Later when he boasted that he would tie his mount to the Lhasa Obelisk, this was a crucial point that prompted the Tibetan Government to send an invasion force [into Nyarong]. Regarding this, it is said:

> Gonpo Namgyal was never accustomed to addressing the Tibetan Government with its formal name. Instead he would offensively allude to it as the "Dung Beetle Serdreu Nyaguma." He incessantly bragged that "The Indian king of the highlands is a man, the Chinese king of the lowlands is a man, and I, the ruler of Nya-ke, am also a man!" Astonishingly, he is also said to have remarked that, "Those who go to Lhasa [on pilgrimage] invite difficulties. They will be drenched by rain, smitten by icy winds, panged by hunger, and forced to endure great hardships. Instead, if I bring the Lhasa Jowo here to Nyarong, all elderly people will have an opportunity to see it!" Also he once said, "If monks no longer like to travel to Lhasa, why will they not be able to practice the sacred teachings here, in their native land? Is it that they will not attain buddhahood if they do not join a centrally located monastery? When fat monks go hustling and bustling, it seems they are heading for happy Lhasa, sun of the highlands!" Akhyok Lu-u-ma understood the deep animosity of Gonpo Namgyal. Since Lu-u-ma was acting as the governor of Derge [on behalf of Gonpo Namgyal], Chago Pema Lekdrub dispatched false letters between Nyarong and Tibet, causing much dissension between the two sides. The letter he sent up to Tibet contained the words, "I am going to occupy Tibet and Kham. So, be prepared to surrender!" The reply that he sent down to Nyarong read, "This is a dispatch for the chieftain of Nyarong! The kingdom of Derge, the plains of Batang, Litang and Gyeltang, and the five districts of Hor supply monks to the three central monasteries and sponsor the teaching [tradition] of the Ganden Palace. So we will not permit them to be forcefully occupied. Go back to your former abode immediately!" Lu-u-ma thought that the letters were genuine, and he dispatched a letter to the secretariat of the Tibetan Government in the Potala Palace of the Dalai Lamas, saying, "The two Jowos are the common property of [Greater] Tibet, the land of snows. They are not privately owned by your Tibet alone. We shall bring them down here to Nyarong. All monastic and lay government officials, of all ranks, should be prepared to surrender to Nya-ke! If you do not do so, I'll turn the Jokhang into a stable and the obelisk into a tethering pole! The troops of Nyarong are more numerous than mustard seeds, and their weapons are sharper than needle points. The king of India should tremble! The king of China should shake with fear; and, you dung beetles, if I cannot turn you into grooms for the horses of Chief Nya-ke, I Lu-u-ma will be a dog, not a man!" This letter was sent numerous times, and the packages were filled with mustard seeds, needles, dog's dung, and so forth. However, the chieftains and nobility of Litang and the Hor districts sided with Tibet. Tashi Gelek, the palace chamberlain of Derge, Kunga Yonten, treasurer [of Derge], and the caretaker Gyangkhang, among others, requested support from Tibet; as did the thirteen ministers of the Da-ge chieftain who had formerly fled to China through Mongol Branak territory during the Nyarong civil war, and later traveled on to Lhasa. Nyarong's dominion over Do-me, one of the three traditional provinces of Tibet, caused much displeasure to the Tibetan Government. So the government carried out divinations, made astrological calculations, and sought prophetic declarations from the protectors of the sacred teachings. They instructed the monasteries of Sera, Drepung and Ganden to practice sorcery, and Kongpo magicians to spin the wheels of Yama. An army was mustered from all areas of Utsang in Tibet, and the troops were guided by scouts who had fled Kham for Tibet. The Tibetan forces prevailed, and in the wood mouse year, they reached Derge.[22]

Monlam Chenmo. Nomads watching ceremonies from the balconies above the Great Courtyard. (1986 CB)

Treasures Associated with Ling Gesar

There were many government offices along the right and left wings of the Great Temple. Also, to one side, there was a basement treasury where it was customary to store offering scarves that had been presented to Jowo Rinpoche to sustain the living, as well as dedication offerings for the deceased, offerings made during oath-taking ceremonies,

and offerings made while performing the confession of negativity. Among the items which were carefully conserved here, according to the epics of *Lingje Gesar*, were the helmet of the slain prince Nangu Yutak and the final testament of Shenpa at Drugu, which were presented as offerings in connection with the confession of negativity.
On this subject, *tsipon* Zhakabpa Wangchuk Deden (1908-1989), the one of the most prominent of Tibetan historians, wrote (1976), "Gesar Norbu Dradul, the lord of Ling and most excellent of beings, was strong and possessed miraculous powers. The diverse and astonishing objects associated with him, including his armor, arrows, spears, and swords are not only mentioned in inventories – I myself have seen so many of them."[23] Also, in his *Inventory to the Great Temple* (*gtsug-lag-khang-gi dkar–chag*, 1982), he writes, "Near the door of the Chapel of Bathing Maitreya there is "a copy of the *Prajñāpāramitā in One Hundred Thousand Sections* which had been commissioned by Shenpa Marutse, as a means of confessing his negativity".[24] Also, he adds that within a sealed chest filled with artifacts that had been presented by the cabinet of Tibetan government, and placed within the enclosure of the Main Hall, "there were many relic boxes, the most important of which contained the blood-stained helmet and armor of Nangu, the general's son, who had been slain by the forces of Hor during the war between Hor and Ling".[25]

The State Astrologer Drakton Jampa Gyaltshan also confirmed, in a letter addressed to me and dated 23rd June, 1990, that the bloodstained helmet and armor of Nangu Yutak, the younger son of the chief commander of Ling, was preserved in the Jokhang. The letter states:

> The bloodstained armor and helmet of Nangu Yutak, the younger son of the chief commander Rongtsha Tragen, who was the paternal uncle of Gesar Norbu Dradul, lord of Ling, whose life had been lost in battle during the war between Hor and Ling, were offered as a dedication of merit [on behalf of the deceased] to Jowo [Sākyamuni], in Lhasa, and kept in the storeroom for artifacts that had been offered to the Jowo, underneath the Chapel of the Likeness of Tsongkhapa on the ground level of the Great Temple of Lhasa, along with [other] sacramental substances that had been offered to the Milk Plain Lake. Prior to 1959, it had been customary for the Prime Minister, the Chief Sacristan and other dignitaries to go there on the morning of the 15th day of the fourth lunar month. The caretakers would enter first, holding burning lamps, and usher the way, after which the Prime Minister himself would enter and place offerings into the [subterranean] lake, below the feet of Jowo [Śākyamuni], all the while making aspirational prayers as he stood before the offering scarves and sacraments of the lake. Then, incidentally, on some occasions, it seems that he would even inspect the sealed relic boxes of Jowo [Śākyamuni]. My late father Draktongpa Chogyal Dorje (1913-1964), a lay aristocrat, related to me his first hand experience of being in the basement. Following his recruitment in 1935 as a civil servant and personal bodyguard of the Prime Minister Bondrong Shopa Tseten Dorje (1889-1945), when the prime minister went to make offerings to the sacraments of the lake in the fourth lunar month of that year, the bodyguards were also asked to follow him, and so my late father also went along. He related that, "At first, in order to place our offering sacraments in the lake, we had to proceed through the darkness of the basement, carrying torches to light the way, and at that time, although we could not clearly discern the form of the lake, we could constantly feel a cool breeze and hear the rippling sound of waves. Then, further on, we had to walk on wooden planks that had been placed over the lake, as we proceeded towards the place immediately below the feet of Jowo [Śākyamuni]. We halted when the caretaker said we should go no further, and when the prime minister threw the sacraments of the lake, wrapped in silk, we could [actually] see the lapping water. As the sacraments of the lake reached the surface of the water, we could see them sink down into the weedy lake. [On way back], Bon Shopa relaxed somewhat, and inspected the artifacts and [stored] costumes of Jowo [Śākyamuni]. Among them was a matching helmet and set of armor, which he picked up and examined. There was an inscription saying it had been offered on behalf of the deceased Nangu Yutak of Ling, to Jowo Rinpoche. Bonsho then fitted the helmet on my head and exclaimed, 'Look! See the difference in size between the men of the past and the men of today! Although Nangu was only thirteen when he wore the helmet, even now it is too big for one of Draktong La's stature!' (My father was 6 feet and 3 inches tall). In fact, it was about one finger-width larger than my head, and it reached my eyebrows. Taking it off, Bonsho looked closely [at the objects]. He observed that both the helmet and body armor were of high

Monlam Chenmo. Monks playing conch shell horns on the roof of the Great Temple. (1986 CB)

Monlam Chenmo. Pilgrims and Lhasa residents watching the ceremonies from the balconies above the Great Courtyard. (1986 CB)

quality and that there were some dry blood stains on them, adding that, 'They say this is the body armor of Nangu!' I didn't think it at the time, but now I wonder whether, if I had scraped some of the blessing [i.e. the dry blood] from the body armor of Nangu, it would have been suitable for making protection amulets now!" My father narrated this to me in 1958, a year when our homeland was pillaged and our countrymen enlisted in the national volunteer army. From this, I can deduce that the offering of Nangu's helmet and armor, which is recounted in the first part of the *Epic of Hor and Ling* is indeed true.

Now, the last will and testament of Nangu Yutak, the young prince of Ling, declaring that his armor and helmet were to be offered as a dedication to Jowo [Śākyamuni] in Lhasa, Central Tibet, after he had been slain on the battlefield, is described in the following verses from the *Garland of Wondrous Tales Concerning the Battle between Hor and Ling* (*Hor-gling g.yul-'gyed ngo-mtshar gtam-gyi phreng-ba*):

Then, Older and Younger Bothers of Ling!
I, Nangu, as my personal heirlooms
Have three [valuables]:
A helmet that is white and protected by the gods,
Armor that is also white, bequeathed by a garuḍa,
And a silken plume that shines the sun.
Offer these, with gold paint,
To the pure face of Jowo [Śākyamuni].
Do not forget this son, Nangu, but keep me in your hearts,
Save my father Tragen from the swamp of cyclic existence,
And keep my mother Amen in your thoughts!
Please dedicate [these offerings] for the sake of the profound sacred teachings,
And request Jowo to look upon the whole of Tibet with compassionate spirituality.[26]

Also,

Never forget to pray
To Jowo [Śākyamuni] of Lhasa![27]

Restorations of the Great Temple during the Later Phase of Buddhist Propagation

In conclusion, I would like to discuss the events surrounding the destruction of sacred temples and images, especially those of the Great Temple of Lhasa and their subsequent restoration, starting from the popular rebellion of 869 (earth ox) and the looting of the royal tombs in 877 (fire bird), when the royal dynasty of Tibet came to an end and the later disintegration took place, and continuing through to the end of the fifteenth century.

It says in the *Scholars' Feast of Doctrinal History* (*Chos-'byung mkhas-pa'i dga'-ston*):

Saintly beings subsequently appeared and performed acts of service in Rasa and Samye. In this regard, after the popular rebellion, both [the main shrines] of Rasa were left unattended, and occupied by beggars. Kitchen stoves were installed in all the temples, which were, for a while, blackened by smoke. Around that time, Zangkar Lotsāwa Phakpa Sherab and Dolchung Korpon built separate accommodation for the beggars. Concealing their troops, they arranged a grand feast [for the beggars] in a certain place, and immediately occupied the temples that had been vacated by the assembled beggars. In this way the beggars were expelled. Since the images of the Central Inner Sanctum were too small, they appeared to be unsuitable, so they were installed in the [main chapel of] the top floor. However, the [central] image of Dīpaṃkara in the form Acala was heard to proclaim, "I will not move from here!" For this reason it became known by the epithet, "the one which proclaimed it would not move from the presence of the Jowo" (*jo-bo mi-'gro gsung-byon*). Then, they commissioned an image of Vairocana Hīmamahāsāgara, flanked by [twelve] male and female bodhisattvas, and the [two] gatekeepers. They also repaired [the temple] and performed great acts of service.

Later, Dolchung Korpon wrapped his body with an oily cloth and immolated himself, from the head downwards as an offering to Jowo [Śākyamuni], while sitting upright and reciting the *Aspirational Prayer of Good Conduct* (*Bhadracaryāpraṇidhānarāja*). After making two full recitations, during the third, as he reached the verse, "'I die in the presence of all lordly [ones]!" he became elated and passed away. At that very

Songtsen Gampo flanked by his queens. (1954 JV)

Thonmi Sambhota, minister to King Songtsen Gampo. (1954 JV)

Entrance to the Vestibule of the Central Inner Sanctum. (1954 JV)

moment a great light emerged from the crown of his head, in the place where his skull imploded, and vanished into the sky. Immediately thereafter, there was an earthquake and a great shower of flowers.

Also it was in Rasa that Lu-me established the four schools of the Lower Tibetan Vinaya lineage (*smad-'dul-gyi sde-bzhi*), known as rBa-rag 'bring-tsho, and propagated the exegesis and study [of the sacred teachings]. Later, when conflict broke out between the rBa and 'Bring schools, the whole of the Great Temple was damaged by warfare. During that phase of destruction, following a prophetic declaration of Dharmarāja, the venerable Gompa Tsultrim Nyingpo was invited [to Lhasa] by the mother monastery and the civil authorities. He tried to reconcile the dispute, but found it very difficult, and so he started to leave. But, at that time, Jowo [Śākyamuni] shed tears, and was heard to exclaim, along with his retinue, "If you do not reconcile this dispute, who will do so?" Later, when he again thought it would be very hard [to resolve], he had a vision of his spiritual teacher [Dakpo] Lharje himself, who arrived and said, "How can you dare leave me alone?" He said that it was then that he realized the Jowo [Śākyamuni] and Gampopa were no different, and immediately thereafter, he succeeded in reconciling the dispute.

Thereafter, he began to renovate all the ceilings, walls and murals of the inner courtyard and the circumambulatory pathway. The Jowo image was transported from the Southern Inner Sanctum to the Central Inner Sanctum, in accordance with an earlier prophecy. He also made inestimable offerings, and restored the teaching. The glorious Khacho Wangpo remarked that he considered the prophetic declaration found in the *Sūtra of the White Lotus of Compassion (Karuṇāpuṇḍarikasūtra)* that "After five years, this monk physician will, besides other things, decorate my stūpa with gold." to refer to the venerable Gompa Tsultrim who followed in the footsteps of Gampopa, five years on.

Then, he entrusted the two great temples of Rasa to his student, the saintly Zhang Rinpoche. Their successors, including the latter's attendant, Tshalpon Darma Zhonu, and the descendents of Tshalpon Sangye Ngodrub who themselves claimed descent from the familial line of Lonpo Gar, commissioned the images of the religious king [Songtsen Gampo] and his queens [which grace the middle storey], and they added the outer vestibule with its images of the gatekeepers and acacia gate. They also constructed the great dyke and carried out inestimable other acts of service. There were many other persons who attended to the dykes and performed acts of service, including Lharje Gewa Bum, his sister Yeshe Chok, and Zhikpo Dudtsi. Re'u Mal, the king of Yartse, then dispatched the learned and talented master Rindor and his chancellor Ardzu, among others [to Lhasa]. Utilizing five hundred gold coins and one hundred and four measures of copper, each weighing as much as eighteen [14 kg] loads of copper, in 1310 (iron male dog), they constructed a gilded roof above the head of Jowo [Śākyamuni]. With the remainder, they fashioned a smaller gilded roof, which was positioned above the head of eleven-faced Mahākāruṇika – later it was enlarged by king Puna Mal of Yartse. In the years that followed, restorations and new commissions were undertaken by many [important] figures, such as Drogon Dungtso Repa, the accomplished master Gon Yeshe, and Nelpa Yoncho. The venerable Karmapa IV Rolpei Dorje and venerable Karmapa V Dezhin Shekpa both made many extraordinary offerings [to Jowo Rinpoche], including priceless robes made from pearls.

With regard to the great temple at glorious Samye, it later times it was Lama Dampa [Sonam Gyeltsan], the illustrious spiritual teacher of Sakya, alone who, with great kindness, restored [the chapels] and performed infinite acts of service.

Prophetic Declarations from Revealed Teachings

The spiritual practices which were formerly the meditative commitments of the religious king Songtsen Gampo comprise three cycles: the sūtra cycle (*mdo-skor*), the cycle of means for attainment (*sgrub-skor*) and the cycle of oral teachings (*zhal-gdams-kyi skor*). Among them, the king entrusted his nephew and son with the task of propagating the twenty-one sūtra and tantra-texts forming the sūtra cycle. The emanational king [Songtsen Gampo] himself taught many works on the legend of the Buddha's deeds, and tales of past lives, as well as the thirteen major and minor texts forming the cycle of means for attainment, and the cycle of oral teachings. The latter comprises eighty-five major oral teachings including scrolls pertaining to the first, intermediate and final promulgations, which are classified as "extensive" instructions, taught for the sake of others, and seventy-four minor oral teachings which are classified as "profound" instructions, taught for his own purposes. These were written down by Thonmi Sambhoṭa and concealed under the feet of the image of Hayagrīva, in the Northern Inner sanctum, on the beams, and in the chapel of the Yakṣas. Later, the great master Padma-[sambhava] opened these treasure-troves and revealed them to the religious king Trisong Detsen, before resealing them. Later still, they were discovered by the accomplished master Ngodrub who imparted them to Nyima Ozer, an emanation of the religious king Trisong Detsen. Another five texts, including the *Descriptive Basis of Mahākāruṇika, King of Space* (*Thugs-rje chen-po nam-mkha' rgyal-po'i mngon-rtogs*) and the *Revelation of the Hidden (Gab-pa mngon- du phyung)* which had been separately sealed and hidden under the silken robe covering the right thigh of the image of Kubera in the Yakṣa Chapel were later revealed by the treasure-finder Śākya Zangpo who imparted then to Lharje Gewabum. All these teachings were gradually propagated among many worthy recipients, and came to form the basis for [a cycle of] maturational [empowerments] and liberating [guidance]. [In this regard, it has been prophesied that]:

In this way, the people of Tibet, worthy recipients [of these teachings],
Will be established in enlightenment – directly and indirectly.
In some future time, from now,
In order to reverse the concept that living beings are permanent,
And disclose the pure perfection stage [of meditation],
The emanational chapels and the contents
Of the emanational palace of the Great Temple of Rasa.
Will also be absorbed into the expanse of quiescent reality's expanse,
Just as the supreme buddha-body of emanation [Śākyamuni] disclosed the act of final nirvāṇa. Escorted by the ḍākinīs of that era,
[The chapels and their contents] will be seen passing away into the expanse of Akaniṣṭha Ghanavyūha,
Enveloped by a canopy of rainbow light, visible to all in common,
While all the gods and serpentine water spirits make offerings.
[This vision] will appear to travel from the river's mid-stream to the ocean,
Dispelling all the darkness underground!
The emanational [chapels] of the great palace at Samye, too,
Will be consumed, burnt by the fire of pristine cognition!
Therefore, whoever strives to save these great temples
From [destruction due to] fire and water,
Will accrue merits surpassing the extent of space!
Although supreme indestructible seats cannot be destroyed by nature's forces,
This revelation will conform to the mundane common perceptions of childish beings,
And in order to encourage our Tibetan subjects to purify negativity and cultivate virtue,
This act of skillful means will be compassionately revealed!

Given that both the Great Temple of Magical Emanation at Rasa and the Great Temple of Unchanging Spontaneous Presence at Samye comprise actual emanational chapels and images, like the Sukhāvatī buddhafield, in the end, just as the supreme emanational teacher [Śākyamuni Buddha] demonstrated the way to pass into final nirvāṇa, they too will demonstrate the way in which the buddha-body of emanation passes away. Accordingly, the great master Padma [sambhava] made the following prophetic declaration, which was revealed among the treasures discovered at Khomting Temple:

The master declared,
"When great temples are constructed
Sentient beings possess increasing merits.
When great temples are circumambulated
The merits of living beings are mediocre.
When great temples are destroyed,
The merits of living beings are diminishing.
After the third generation of your descendents [O King],
The kingdom will become desolate and its royal laws infringed.
Gods and ogres will be agitated by the conflicts among the Tibetan people,
And through this agitation of gods and ogres, the elemental spirits will be disturbed.

The renowned Mahākāruṇika of the Northern Inner Sanctum. (1954 JV)

Maitreya within the Main Hall. (1954 JV)

Devotees in front of Jowo Śākyamuni. (1999 HS)

When the end of this period is reached,
Lhasa will be devastated by water,
And Samye will be destroyed by fire.
However, sentient beings will [still] be meritorious,
And they can postpone these events somewhat, through their skillful means."
The king [Trisong Detsen] replied,
"In general, Samye and Lhasa, receptacles of offering,
Are the life-sustaining pillars of Tibet.
By what means can they be destroyed?
Alas, how needing of compassion are the Tibetan people!
A great temple which brings satisfaction just by hearing of it!
A great temple which brings satisfaction just by recollection of it!
By what means can they be destroyed?
Alas, how deluded are the Tibetan people!
Being like the sun and the moon in the sky,
What darkness can remove this [illumination]?
I pray that they may be protected from water and fire,
Enemies resembling a sword-wielding assassin!

To this, the master replied,

"O religious king, do not be depressed!
You should know that cyclic existence resembles an illusion.
You should know that adverse conditions are [the results of] past actions.
All things of the phenomenal world
Are not eternal, so abandon your worries!
Nor are they subject to nihilism, so not be disillusioned!
For individuals endowed with pure vision
The conquerors do not pass into final nirvāṇa,
The buddha-fields are never emptied,
Sentient beings do not roam through cyclic existence,
And cyclic existence does not really have inherent existence.
Disturbances of the four elements do not arise.
Hence Samye and Lhasa can never be destroyed.
Since sentient beings who are bewildered and obscured
Do not see the great temples of Samye and Lhasa
Even though they are born nearby,
In order that they might accumulate the provision of merit and purify obscurations,
Fire and water will become natural expressions of Mahākāruṇika,
The deity who embodies perseverance.
These are not enemies, so abandon misconceptions!
O great religious king, relax your mind!
I, the king of skillful means, will now teach!"

Making the hand-gesture of the hook, he summoned Takṣaka, king of serpentine water spirits, who offered [the king] a precious crystal. The master then said:

Place this crystal alongside the life-supporting axial pillar of Samye, and as long as it remains in that position, the Great Temple will not be burnt by fire. Whenever the Great Temple becomes dilapidated due to the residual confusion of the elements, at such times you should persevere to repair it! At such times, the acts of service, offering and circumambulation, and all acts of restoration, starting with the application of even a little plaster to mend the slightest crack [in the walls of the Great Temple] are in fact actions made out of respect to all the Conquerors of the three times. [Thereby] all the sacred teachings will be attained, all the Sugatas will be venerated, and you will acquire the merit to restore the Great Temple! At that time, you will transmigrate and be reborn on a lotus stalk in Sukhāvatī!

So saying, [Padmasambhava] concealed a large amount of riches to be used for the restoration of the Great Temple. He then also said:

The ancient king Songtsen Gampo, actual embodiment of Mahākāruṇika, endowed with supernormal cognitive powers, constructed this Great Temple near the banks of the river. This river flows so close to the Great Temple that the people of the future will have to construct dykes to avert it. So it was that the emanation of Mahākāruṇika revealed that [the temple should be built] purposefully close to this river, enabling living beings to purify their obscurations of body, speech and mind, and plant the seeds of enlightenment. Those beings who, at that [future] time, dedicate their bodies to the task of barricading the river, and protecting the Great Temple, will attain the buddha-body of emanation. Those who offer verbal advice will attain the buddha-body of perfect resource, [symbolic of] buddha-speech; and those who mentally express their concern, wishing to protect the Great Temple, will attain the buddha-body of reality, [symbolic of] buddha-mind. At that time there is no doubt that those who strive physically, verbally and mentally, building the dykes, making circumambulations and offerings, and rejoicing at heart, will all purify the obscurations of their [mundane] body, speech and mind; and attain [the goals of] the Greater Vehicle.

These advantages [arising from service to the Great Temple] are also found in the *Testament (bKa'chems)* of the religious king [Songtsen Gampo] himself, and they appear to be identical. The master further stated:

This Great Temple of Lhasa
Outwardly leads living beings to faith,
Inwardly reverses ordinary attachments,
And secretly it is the expressive power of naturally manifesting awareness.
This river water that threatens to destroy the temple
Outwardly [appears] as serpentine spirits, carrying off its images, books and stūpas,
Inwardly, its waters purify the obscurations of living beings,
And secretly, it is a naturally arising, pure ablution.
Then, as for the offering lamps that protect the images of the Great Temple,
Outwardly, they embody perseverance on the path,
Inwardly, they represent actual emanations of sublime beings,
And secretly, they represent the attainment of enlightenment. How Wonderful!
All fortunate living beings of the future,
Listen, as I explain the supreme skillful means!
When, at the end of this half-millennium, Anavatapta, king of serpentine spirits,
Comes to carry off the image of Śākyamuni,
The river waters will cut off the land:
As the right fork of the river spreads out,
Resembling a stone placed in a slingshot,
That is the time when Śaṅkagrīva, king of serpentine spirits, will make his request [for the image].
At that time, not only should the demonic battle-force of the lower realms of cyclic existence.
Be averted by the building of dykes and all acts of service,
But also the right fork of the river should be barricaded,
And a stūpa with multiple chapels should be built upon the dyke.
Thereby Śaṅkagrīva, king of serpentine spirits, will be averted!
When the river waters divide into two halves,
And the Elephant-nosed King of serpentine spirits comes to escort [the image],
Resembling a dry-measure box placed upon a wet hide,
At that time, all those who rebuild the dykes of the Great Temple
Will be purified of the ripening effect of their past actions, and attain great bliss.
Circular dykes should be built,
And if a powerful triangular obstacle remover
Is built upon the dyke, the Elephant-nosed one will be averted!
When the river waters swirl around,
Resembling a mill stone placed upon a shield,
This means that Anavatapta, king of serpentine spirits, will have come to carry off [the image].
At that time, all human beings who make offerings and circumambulate the Great Temple, and rebuild its dyke,
Will fulfill whatever aspirational prayers they make.
A square dyke should be built with a cairn at each corner,
And the four wrathful [gatekeepers]: Yamāntaka, Hayagrīva,
Amṛtakuṇḍalin and Mahābala should be installed.
If this is done, it will help to some extent.

Losar. Pilgrims making offerings of incense outside the main gate of the Great Temple. (1986 CB)

Monlam Chenmo. Monks leaving the Great Courtyard at the end of the ceremony. (1986 CB)

When the king of serpentine spirits comes to escort [the image],
Resembling a coracle sinking into a lake,
Offerings and prayers should be made from a distance,
And inestimable extensive aspirations will be fulfilled!
All the living beings who gather at that time
Will be embodiments of the Great Compassionate One,
And their varying degrees of perception, high and low,
Will be determined by their respective degrees of purity or impurity:
Those endowed with pure vision may perceive the Great Temple
Departing for the Akaniṣṭha realm,
While those of ordinary perception,
Will perceive the Great Temple entwined by a snake,
And carried off into the river, along with a canopy of rainbow light!
For some, all things that are seen, heard, or touched
Are focal points for the attainment of liberation!

So saying, [Padmasambhava] escorted the king through his miraculous powers and actually revealed to him all the treasure-texts of Lhasa. It is reported that some of them, including the *Disclosure of the Hidden* (*Gab-pa mngon-phyung*) were copied and presented as an offering into the hands of [the image of] Vairocana at Samye, and this version concurs with the prophetic declaration of the religious king himself, in stating that:

"When the water level rises between the flowing right fork of the river and the city of Lhasa, the sandbank will resemble a fish, or an oblong object, reminiscent of the main part of a sling, and at that time when the serpentine spirit Śaṅkagrīva comes to carry off [the image of Jowo Śākyamuni], it is said that "an incisive ritual summons should be undertaken when [the sandbank] resembles a fish". Then, the right fork should be barricaded with a dyke, and on top of the dyke a stūpa with multiple chapels should be erected.

When the river waters divide into two halves, the sandbank will resemble a tapering triangle, and it is said that "the dykes should be worn as a hat", as the waters swirl from the neck downwards in a triangular formation. Then, a triangular shaped obstacle remover should be built in the Great Temple, and this will avert the invitation of the Elephant-nose king of serpentine spirits.

Then, when the sandbank forms a square depression and the water flows around it, the king of serpentine spirits Anavatapta himself will come to carry off [the image], and at that time it is said "the dykes should be spread out like a mat". A square [dyke] like a perimeter wall should be built with a cairn or a stūpa at each corner. Then if the four wrathful [gatekeepers] are visualized and installed there, there should be some slight benefit. Afterwards, when the corners of the sandbank have diminished, it will become circular in shape, like a drum, and then come to resemble a brush. At that time, fine offerings should be arrayed, and if the people pray fervently, [the image of Jowo Rinpoche] may well remain [in Lhasa] for a short time.

In general, it is said that these different [forces of nature] each have their respective remedial prayers.

Then, when the phenomenon resembling a coracle sinking into a lake arises, that is the time when [the image] itself will depart. Many different visions will appear, and the people, looking on from the mountainsides, should recite aspirational prayers.

I have heard a legend stating that once the great temples of Rasa, Samye and other sites have mostly been devastated, the treasure-store of precious gems at Tradruk will be opened, the tomb of Songtsen Gampo [at Chongye] will be opened, and men will make offerings to and circumambulate the five temples it contains, while some naturally originated images will newly appear.

Henceforth, in the future, O faithful creatures!
Lhasa and Samye and other sites which are the life-sustaining channels of the teaching
Will be restored, and those that have not been damaged will thrive.
You should make offerings devotedly in all the chapels,
And to all the images which were the meditative commitments of the King, his ministers and emanations!
You should make prostrations, circumambulations and maṇḍala offerings!
You should offer flowers, incense, butter lamps, and the like.

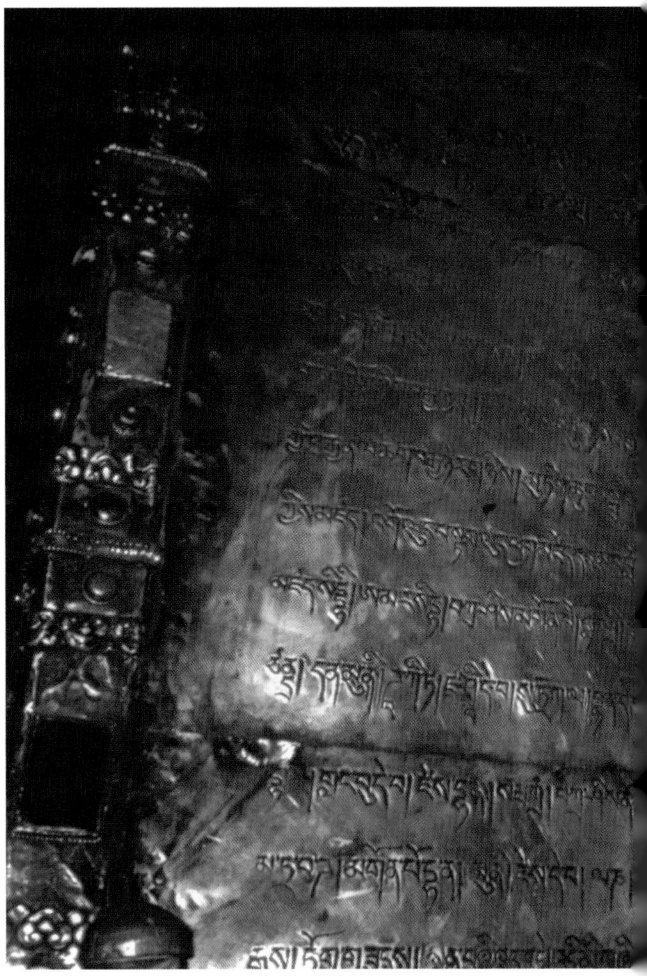

Inscription on the back of Jowo Śākyamuni's plinth. (1991 HMS)

The lantern-bearer for Joseph Vaniš in the Jokhang. (1954)

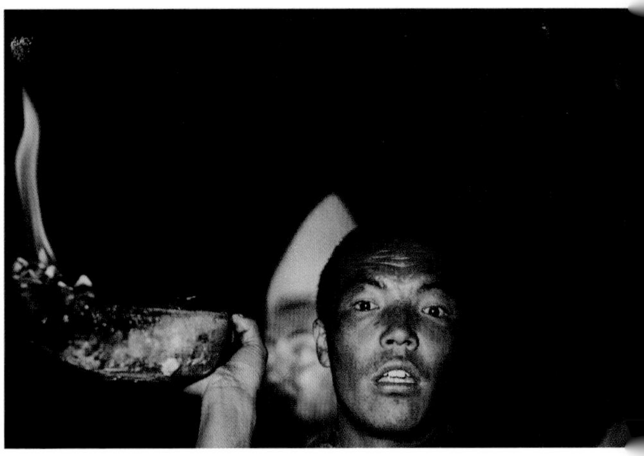

The inconceivable advantages of such actions are explained in the sūtras.
If your body, speech and mind are not directed towards virtuous actions,
Even though you might have a human form,
You would resemble those born in an aeon of darkness.
If you do not strive to make offerings and donations to the Precious Jewels,
Even though you possess resources and wealth,
You will resemble a guard dog at the treasury.
If you do not really know the results of positive and negative past actions,
Even though you may appear to be learned,
You will resemble a monkey.
If you do not cultivate the essential sacred teachings,
Even though you have obtained a human body,
You will be empty-handed and meaningless.
This is an age when we constantly strive to amass
The resources and property of living beings, which is illusory!
Now is the age when we take as the essence this body
Which is without essence and impure, [fragile] as a bubble.
Deceived by the dream-like appearances of this life,
Let our steadfast aspirations focus on the sacred teachings,
And as liberation comes solely from our spiritual friends,
Let us find a qualified tutor, and serve him with our lives!
This is an age when essentials are deceived by verbiage,
Let us focus on the essential nature of mind, nucleus of the oral instructions!
Death approaches those who delay until tomorrow or the next day,
So persevere with experiential cultivation, from now, this very moment!
Whatever one does, be virtuous and do not be entwined by selfishness.
Act solely in the interest of [sentient beings] who have been one's parents,
Their number filling the expanse of space.
Exaggerating [the dichotomies] of self and others, cyclic existence and nirvāṇa,
One does not remain in the presence of immaculate discriminative awareness.
These living beings who have been our mother,
Bewildered, in their dreamlike world, without knowing this,
Are the prime objects of our compassion.
Combining in a common savour
The discriminative awareness that realizes emptiness
And the limitless compassion for living beings who lack realization,
May we cultivate the ten perfections for the sake of perfection, maturation and purification.
Seeing all phenomena as completely perfect enlightenment
From the beginning and in all respects,
And not discriminating between existence and quiescence, or self and others, and the like,
May we not interrupt the infinite enlightened activities for the sake of those to be trained.
May all sufferings be dispelled, just by [mentioning] your name,
O you who are endowed with enlightened activities surpassing those of all the conquerors!
Recollecting your kindness, most sublime Avalokiteśvara,
May [all beings] attain your level!

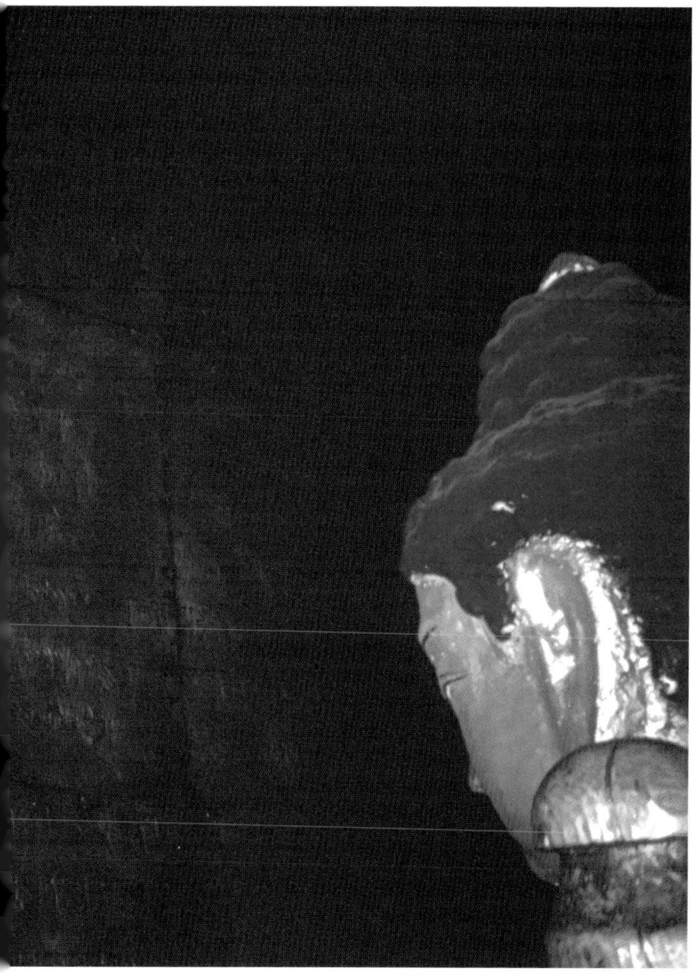

The Interdependence of the Great Temple with Yerpa

Accordingly, all intelligent persons should strive to ensure that the Great Temple is preserved. They should strive to restore the deities within it and the dykes outside it; and in particular, since Yerpa is [considered to be] the life-supporting axis of Lhasa, it will be important to maintain that auspicious connection too. It says in the *Earlier Inventory of Yerpa* (*Yer-pa'i dkar-chag snga-ma)*:

> The emanational king said, "Those who have striven to make offerings to my hermitages and representative images have outdone the Conquerors in performing acts of service to the Conquerors. They have performed acts of service and veneration on behalf of all the buddhas. To make or restore a votive terracotta imprint at Yerpa is more powerful than the act of building all the stūpas that fill the trichiliocosm. To meditate for a single day at Yerpa

Monlam Chenmo. Proctor processing through the monks assembled in the Great Courtyard. (1986 CB)

is more powerful than meditating for a hundred years elsewhere.
Lhasa is the life-sustaining axis of Tibet.
Yerpa is the life-sustaining axis of Lhasa.
If the stūpa at Yerpa is not destroyed,
The teaching will survive in Lhasa,
And Lhasa will be unharmed
By earthquakes, vermin, fire, water, and wind.
If Yerpa is not destroyed, restorers will continuously come to Lhasa. These restorers too will outdo the Conqueror in their service to the Conquerors. As long as Yerpa is not destroyed, there is no risk of Lhasa's prospects being damaged. If the restorers and sacristans at Lhasa wish to enjoy a long life, they should mend the sacred representations, cracks, and walls at Yerpa. It is important to insert plaster into the cracks and [damaged] walls. Henceforth, Lhasa and Yerpa will be interconnected. If their prospects are damaged fill the cracks with barley flour and straighten the crooked pillars. If there is an earthquake, tap the maṇḍala offering with a precious gemstone. If there is damage caused by fire, repair the waterspouts and bind any holes with blue silk. If there is damage caused by wind, repair the doors and fill in any cracks in the doors with the five red substances. If there is an epidemic among the populace, restore the maṇḍala offerings, using sacramental substances and the five nectars. If there is an epidemic afflicting cattle, perform ablutions and sprinkle water at Drak Lha[lupuk]. If there are fears due to an invading army or weapons, renovate the sacred offering receptacles, secure flags to their poles and affix long-life arrows. If there is a risk of subsidence and flooding, restore the offering chapels, the incense chapels and the butter lamp chapels. If kings try to carry off Jowo [Śākyamuni], restore the plinths and thrones of the deities and stūpas. If royal penalties or taxes are imposed, repair the bells, drums and other ritual instruments. If there is social unrest, repair the door latches and apply glue or resin to them. If there are psychotic people or rabid dogs, repair the roofs with birch and juniper wood. If there is famine, repair the kitchens and fix the outer walls of the granary. If there is damage caused by robbers, thieves or savages, repair the heads and hands of figures on the murals. If the crops fail to ripen properly, repair the natural springs and offer ritual tormas made of the three white and the three sweet ingredients. If there is a shortage of grain, repair the thrones and torma containers, and offer tormas made of grain. If there is drought, refurbish the chapels of the serpentine water spirits and offer tormas to them. If the lifespan becomes short, repair the life-sustaining poles of juniper wood inside the stūpas and bind them with silk and coloured threads along with the five precious metals, medicines, grains, sandalwood, eaglewood, and so forth. If wealth does not increase, repair the walls of the treasury, fill the cracks with gemstone, and hold a feast-offering ceremony. If there is no economic restraint, repair the chimneys and conduct burnt offering rites using precious gems and various foods. If there is a shortage of clothing or bedding, renew the whitewash and drapes, and attach [new] silk and cotton or woolen textiles to the walls. If there is a risk of bees swarming, re-adjust the door hinges and the locks. If there are dangers due to spiders, scorpions, frogs or snakes, restore the thresholds, so that they are not cracked or broken. If there are dangers due to lice, nits and moths, replace the old book straps with new ones. If there is a risk of infectious eye diseases, restore the white walls and windows, and apply fresh paint. If there are dangers due to serpentine water spirits or the spirit lords of the soil, restore the bells and remove all dirt and rust. If there are dangers due to [malignant] male and female spirits, secure the dangerous narrow pathways. If there are spirits causing paediatric disorders, restore the staircases and carpets without patching them. If the observance of the Vinaya discipline deteriorates, establish a community of four pure monks, who are without deceit. If the course of study and exegesis is interrupted, establish a Buddhist college for those who are learned, venerable, and pure in their commitments. If the people become rough mannered, establish a meditation hermitage where they can inspect their minds without distraction. If circumstances are inauspicious, establish a rite of spiritual attainment conducted by mantrins with pure commitments. If there

are dangers due to [the inferior output] of the restorers, let the repairs be undertaken by those who are hardworking and patient. If [the Great Temple of] Lhasa runs short of sacristans, arrange for the scriptures to be recited at Yerpa. This point should be clearly and correctly noted. All that is wished for in Lhasa comes about through restorations undertaken at Yerpa. However, inspired by the compassion of the two Jowo [images] in Lhasa, there are many ways to restore [the complex at] Yerpa. Such actions will outdo the Conqueror in their service of the Conquerors.

These remarks of the king [Songtsen Gampo] were documented by Princess Wencheng Kongjo.

It is therefore important to restore all the geomantic temples of the border-taming, further taming and district controlling classes, including these; but all those which remain undamaged should not be demolished or relocated. Unless there is a definite need to restore them and [in so doing] remove their spiritual treasures, their general treasures and particular hidden wealth and riches should not be unearthed. The obstructive forces and oath-breaking spirits that have been suppressed underneath should not be removed. [Positive] actions such as these should be accomplished if the people know how to pray to the Compassionate One, and unimpededly engage in offerings and gathering merit. It is important only to act on behalf of the teachings and sentient beings, and, besides that, not to indulge the selfish whims of this life in order to foster one's own ambitions or acquire territory.[28]

Concluding remarks:

The foregoing accounts refer exclusively to perspectives based on devotion and sacred outlook, a mode of Tibetan perception that is widely circulated in the extant legends. However, the reliable, authentic and starkly factual historical accounts, such as the New and Old Chronicles of the Tang Dynasty (*Thang hru'u deb gsar rnying*), written in Chinese, the Old Chronicles of the Dunhuang grottoes (*tun hong brag phug gi yig rnying*), and the epigraphic records of the obelisks dating from the Pugyal Dynasty in Tibet, make no clear reference to the legend which states that Jowo Śākyamuni, the central image of the Great Temple of Lhasa, was brought to Tibet as the dowry of the earlier Chinese princess Wencheng (?-680). It is essential that everyone should know these important facts.

Leaving aside the [fascinating] claims that the Chinese princess commissioned sacred relief carvings and images on rock cliffs at Rala, Bikhog and Bom, it remains a most fertile field for future research to investigate whether the Great Temple of Lhasa was completed by the Newāri stone masons and carpenters before the princess even reached Tibet in 641; and whether or not she was the one who recognized Tibet as a geomantic abode of the supine ogress (*srin mo gan rkyal*), and whether or not very expression "geomantic supine ogress" (*sa dpyad srin mo gan rkyal*) had antecedents in India, China, and Nepal, and so forth.

Yet, with regard to the emergence of the aforementioned perspectives which are based on historical narratives inspired by devotion and sacred outlook, it is the case that they gradually evolved from two sources: 1) the revelation the *Testament of King Songtsen Gampo (rgyal po'i bka' chems bka'khol ma)*, which was extracted from the Vase-shaped Pillar within the confines of the Great Temple in 1048 by Jowoje Palden Atiśa, in accordance with a prophetic declaration of the so-called "mad woman of Lhasa" (*lha sa'i smnyon ma*). The various extant versions of the *Testament of the King (rgyal po bka' chem)* are clearly adulterated with many later interpolations, derived from Buddhist and Vedic narratives, as well as with tales from the Bon tradition and the aforementioned *Cycle of Mahākāruṇika (Thugs rje chen po'i chos skor)*, 2) the revelation of the *Ma ṇi bka' 'bum*, which occurred consequent on the dissemination of the *Doctrinal Cycle of Mahākāraruṇika: A Gemstone Ornament (Thugs rje chen po nor bu rgyan pa'i chos skor)*[29] in Tibet after the 12th century; and this has resulted, incidentally, in a hybrid narrative that is "neither sheep nor goat". Even nowadays, this text is extant in various renditions, extensive and concise, of diverse length.

Concerning these interpolations, there is even an extant thirteen-folio work [in Tibetan] which was composed at the start of the 17th century by Drago Rabjampa Phuntsok Gyeltsan of Meru in Lhasa, entitled *Genuine Signs of Interpolation and Adulteration in the Maṇi bka' 'bum of King Songtsen (rgyal po srong btsan bka' 'bum bsre lhad yod tshul lhag bsam brda btang)*.

Monlam Chenmo. Butter sculpture being made to be set up around the Barkor for the 'Offerings of the Fifteenth Day'. (1987 CB)

These oral traditions are in accord with an enlightened intention transcending the direct perception of worldly folk. Indeed, they exclusively adhere to [the genre of] inconceivably secret hagiographies based on devotion and sacred outlook, replete with wondrous, marvelous, and miraculous events, that transcend [even] the conceptions and expressions familiar to idealists. According to those whose perspectives conform with the statements and tradition ascribed to this view, the earlier Chinese princess {Wencheng] was not a mundane human lady, constituted of flesh, blood and bones, as is well-known in the world or commonly perceived, but rather, it is believed that she came as an emanation of Blue Tārā, bringing from China as her dowry [the sacred statue of] Jowo Śākyamuni, the size of a twelve-year-old, that she personally set foot in various places in Kham and Amdo, and that she carved many images and *dhāraṇī* mantras on rock cliffs. Indeed it became commonplace to treat the earlier princess with the devotion and reverence associated with the sublime [female bodhisattva] Tārā, so much so that the many astonishing and popular legends around her seem to [be farfetched], having [in the words of a Tibetan proverb] "used the design of a hat to cover a shoe" (*zhva dpe lham 'gebs*).

At the behest of my friend Hansjorg Mayer, I, Tashi Tsering, compiled the first draft of this article and gifted it to my friend at the Tenth Conference of the International Association for Tibetan Studies held at the Oxford University, England, on 10th September 2003. With added information, this article was duly completed on 18th January 2005.

Jowo Śākyamuni photographed by Josef Vaniš in 1954 prior to the Cultural Revolution (note the heavy layer of gold on the face and different throne design).

1 Tib. *Grol-ba drug-ldan-gyi nang-nas mthong-grol sku-rten-gyi gtso-mchog ra-sa 'phrul-snang gtsug-lag- khang-gi jo-bo shā-kya mu-ne//*
2 This quotation derives from Śākyei Gelong Zangpo, *Gangs-can 'dir ston-pa'i rgyal-tshab dpal sgam-po pa'i khri-gdung 'dzin-pa'i dam-pa-rnams-kyi gtam baiḍūrya'i phreng-ba zhes-bya-ba bzhugs*, Dwags lha sgam po edition, ff.16a.3-17b.6. The author was himself appointed to lion teaching throne of Gampopa the Great in 1640.
3 Tshalpa Kunga Dorje, *Deb-ther dmar-po-rnams-kyi dang-po hu-lan deb-ther 'di bzhugs-so*, annotated by Dungkar Lobzang Trinle, Pe cing mi rigs dpe skrun khang, 1981, pp. 49-255.
4 Gendun Chopel, "rGyal-khams rig-pas bskor-ba'i gtam-rgyud gser-gyi thang-ma zhes-bya-ba bzhugs-so," in *dGe 'dun chos-'phel-gyi gsung-rtsom dang-po*, Vol. 1, *Gangs-can rig-mdzod*, No. 10, Bod ljongs bod yig dpe rnying dpe skrun, 1990. pp. 67-8.
5 These passages are quoted from Chahar Geshe, "rJe thams-cad mkhyen-pa tsong-kha-pa chen-po'i rnam- thar le'u drug-pa bzhugs-so," p. 377, contained in *The Collected Works of Cha-Har dGe-bshes*, Vol. 2, New Delhi, 1972.
6 Quoted from Desi Sangye Gyatso, *mChod-sdong 'dzam-gling rgyan-gcig gtso-bor gyur-pa'i lha-sa ra-mo- che rigs gsum bla ri dang bcas-pa spyi bye-brag-gi sko- tshad byang-chen bgrod-pa'i myur-lam bzhugs*, pp. 99b.5-102b.4. These lines are quoted from a partly undecipherable manuscript, and hence will require closer study based on a more comprehensible text.
7 This passage is quoted from Darmo Menrampa Lobzang Chodrak, *g.Yu-thog gsar-rnying-gi rnam-thar*, Pe cing mi rigs dpe skrun khang, 1982, pp. 230-278.
8 This quotation is derived from Tethong Rakra Tubten Chodar, *dGe-'dun chos-'phel-gyi lo-rgyus*, Library of Tibetan Works & Archives, 1980. p. 175.
9 Pawo Tsuklak Trengwa, *Chos-'byung mkhas-pa'i dga'-ston*, Pe cing mi rigs dpe skrun khang, Vol. 1, 1985, p. 447.
10 Quoted in "Rigs-rus-dang 'brel-zhing sangs-rgyas-kyi bstan-pa'i 'jug-sasyo-dang mthun-pa'i spy'i rnam- thar", which is contained in *dGe slong Ra'g arye'i rnam thar* (*The Autobiographical Writings of Karma-Chags-med* [RA-GA-ASYA]), Published by Tana Lama, Kollegal, Volume I, p. 134. This reference was provided by Chamdo Lobzang Sherab.
11 This source was provided by Zhewo Lobzang Dargye, a former minister of Central Tibetan Administration of the Tibetan government-in-exile.
12 This source was provided by Golok Damcho Pelzang of the Library of Tibetan Works & Archives, Dharamsala.
13 Quoted in Patrul Rinpoche, *The Words of My Perfect Teacher* (*Kun-bzang bla-ma'i zhal-lung*), Padmakara Translation Committee, Harper Collins, 1994, pp. 174-5; and also quoted in secondary sources such as *gZhi-rim 'dzin-grva drug-pa'i slob-deb rig-pa'i nyin-byed las dang-po snyan-sum*, Department of Education, Dharamsala, 1965. pp. 2-4.
14 Quoted in a compilation made in 1957 by Trijang Losang Yeshe, the junior tutor to His Holiness the Dalai Lama, entitled *rNam-grol lag-bcangs-su gtod-pa'i man-ngag zab-mo tshang-la ma nor-ba mtshungs-med chos-kyi rgyal-po'i thugs-bcud byang-chub lam-gyi rim-pa'i nyams-khrid-kyi zin-bris gsung-rab kun-gyi bcud-bsdus gdams-ngag bdud-rtsi snying-po zhes-bya-ba bzhugs-so*, Ganden Shartse Norling Monastery Publications, Karnataka, pp. 142b. The source was provided by Geshe Beri Jigme Wangyal.
15 Quoted in *sTag-lung ma-thang ri-bo-che'i bsang-yig dang gser-skyems skor, Rituals for the Propitiation of the local and mountain deities of Ri-bo-che Monastery*, Reproduced from a rare collection of manuscripts from Khams, Published by Pema Gyaltsen, Nangchen Division, T. K. I. S., Bir, Kangra, H. P. 1979. pp. 549-553.
16 Quoted in Desi Sangye Gyatso, *Va-ḍūrya G-Ya'- Sel*, Published by T. Tsepal Taikhang, Volume II, New Delhi, 1971, pp. 676-7.
17 Quoted in Tren Lhalu Tsewang Dorje's "Rough Personal History" (*phran (lha-klu) tshe-dbang rdo-rje rang-nyid-kyi byung-ba rags-rim brjod-pa*), which is contained in *Bod-kyi lo-rgyus rig-gnas dpyad-gzhi'i rgyu-cha bdams-bsgrigs*, Issue No. 16, edited by Bod rang-skyong-ljongs srid-gros lo-rgyus rig-gnas dpyad-gzhi'i rgyu-cha u-yon lhan-khang, Pe cing mi rigs dpe skrun khang, 1993, p. 172.
18 Ibid., p. 171.
19 See Monumenta Tibetica Historica, Abteilung III-Band 3, Dieter Schuh und L. S. Dagyab, *Urkunden, Erlasse und Sendsschreiben, aus dem Besitz sikkimesischer, Adelshauser und des Kloster Phodang*, VGH Wissenschaftsverlag, St. Augustin, 1978, Dokument XXXVIII, linke Hälfte, Zeile 1-7.
20 Quoted in H. E. Kalon Shadra & Kadrung Nornang, *Letter-Writers, Yig-bskur rnam-gzhag*. Edited and published by G. Tharchin, Tibet Mirror Press, Kalimpong 1956, pp. 170-171.
21 Quoted in Ngawang Lobzang Gyatso, *Du- ku-la'i gos-bzang*, Vol. 1. 'Bras spungs dga' ldan pho brang edition, Vol. KA ff. 98b.4-99a.1. See also Tsipon Zhakabpa Wangchuk Deden, *Bod-kyi srid-don rgyal-rabs*, Kalimpong Shakabpa House. 1976. p. 412.
22 Quoted in Nyaga Sherab Ozer, *lCags-bdud nyag-sked- kyi lo-rgyus dpa'gtum stag-mo'i nga-ro.*
23 Tsipon Zhakabpa Wangchuk Deden, op. cit., p. 256.
24 See Tsipon Zhakabpa Wangchuk Deden, *lHa-ldan ra sa 'phrul-snang gtsug-lag-khang-gi dkar-chag gser- dang ra-gan rnam-dbye gsal por byed-pa nor-bu ni-ka-sha zhes bya-ba bzhugs-so.* Kalimpong. Zhakabpa House, 1982, pp. 44-45.
25 *ibid.*, p. 59.
26 See 'Dzam-gling ge-sar rgyal-po'i rtogs-brjod hor-gling g.yul-'gyed ngo-mtshar gtam-gyi phreng-ba-las stod-cha bzhugs-so, Vol. 3, p. 260. As manuscripts referred were partly illegible, see other manuscripts).
27 Ibid., p. 261.
28 This long passage derives from Pawo Tsuklak Trengwa, *Chos-'byung mkhas-pa'i dga'-ston*, Vol.1, pp. 447-459.
29 This includes the sūtra cycle (*mdo skor*), which was discovered by Jetsun Śākya Zangpo, as well as the cycle of means for attainment (*sgrub skor*) and the cycle of oral instructions (*zhal gdams skor*), which were revealed respectively by Drubtob Ngodrub and Ngadag Nyangrel Nyima Ozer (1124-1204).

Altar figurines and butter lamps. (1954 JV)

The stone phallus, West outer wall, second floor, Main Hall, intended to subdue the restless 'Supine Demoness' of Tibet. (1998 AA)

Part 3

From Rasa to Lhasa

The Geomantic Stones of the Jokhang
The First Monlam Chenmo
The Early Wall Paintings in the Jokhang

Heather Stoddard

The Geomantic Stones of the Jokhang

The Jokhang Temple was built on a marsh called 'Milk Lake Plain', Otsho-thang[2], near the Kyichu River in Central Tibet, a few years after Tibet's first great emperor, *tsenpo* Songtsen Gampo (ca 617-649), established his new capital there, in 633 CE.[3] The valley was much wider and had better communications in all directions, as compared to the well protected 'cradle of Tibetan civilisation' in the Yarlung-Chongye valleys, south of the Tsangpo River. Furthermore, Tri Songtsen, as he is known in the early texts, had fond memories of the region from his childhood, when he used to go there hunting with his father, and one source says that their ancestor, Lhathothori, had already built a palace on the Red Hill, long, long ago.

Known initially as Rasa 'Place of the Goats', or 'Walled Place' it became Lhasa, 'Place of the Gods' once the first Buddhist statues brought to Tibet were consecrated inside its chapels, following construction of the temple. Tibetan narratives going back to between the 12th and 14th century CE., some half a millenium after the events, have taken on a legendary tinge, but they provide fascinating details on the circumstances of its foundation. This 21st century version is based essentially upon a hitherto sparingly used 12th century literary source composed by the famed Tibetan yogin and 'treasure-finder', Nyangral Nyima Ozer (1124/36-1192).[4] Echoing the rich pages of his *'History of the Dharma. The Essence of Flower Nectar'* (henceforth Nyangral), we shall weave a new narrative, exploring the interaction between Songtsen Gampo and his two most important foreign spouses, the Nepalese princess Brikhuti-devi, and the Chinese princess Wencheng *gongzhu,* during the building of the Jokhang Temple.[5] This narrative stands in contrast to the more well known *Pillar Testament of Songtsen Gampo,* still sometimes attributed to the mid-11th century, since it is said to be a 'treasure text' taken out of its hiding place in the Jokhang by the Bengali pandit, Atisha (982-1054). However, the version we have today is certainly a later more structured re-write, as compared to Nyangral, and although it is not clear whether the 'author' of the *Pillar Testament* actually saw or knew about Nyangral's Essence of *Flower Nectar,* both narratives follow essentialy the same plot with occasional parts that clearly have the same source. *The Pillar Testament* is the more pious and magical version, akin to the 13th-14th century 'biography' of Songtsen Gampo, the *Maṇi Bka' 'bum,* as was shown long ago.[6] Indeed, sometimes it seems as if the author of the *Pillar Testament* is trying to 'improve' or 'correct' Nyangral's text, giving a richer, more coherent narrative. But on other occasions he paints quite a different scene, or proposes a radically opposite point of view. Probably both versions depended upon early written materials, that were more or less clear or incomplete, as well as the colorful, romanticised oral tradition.[7]

At the same time, we shall try to link up a small group of modest stone symbols found in the Jokhang today, with the original geomantic layout of the temple and the surrounding valley.[8] The Jokhang is said to lie directly over the heart of the restive, pre-Buddhist "Supine Ogress of Tibet" (*bod gan rkyel srin mo*), and it is, indeed, matters of the heart that shall be outlined below. It might even be said that the founding of the Jokhang Temple is also Tibet's first love story – a triangular, cosmopolitan one at that.[9]

The Jokhang roofs with the Potala in the background. (1996 HMS)

The skyline at dusk. (1991 OK)

The early written sources of the Second Diffusion of Buddhism in Tibet make elaborate use of dialogue and narrative to provide a lively human background to historical events.[10] Nyangral's text, written in alternating prose-and-poetry, is full of satire, humour and magic. Whether the story-teller is the great 'treasure-finder' rewriting ancient'treasure-texts' that he found in Khomthing and other places in southern Tibet, or whether he is weaving old manuscript sources from his library with the oral tradition, he takes tangible and even mischievous delight in the whole range of human emotion and weakness. Yet, at the same time he introduces serious reporting on all sorts of technical, philosophical and religious aspects present in the process of the introduction of Buddhism, and of foreign cultures, into the Land of Snows.

With regard to the manner of inviting the two Buddhist princesses to Tibet, and the building of new palaces and temples, Nyangral gives an emotionally charged and suggestive account of the confrontation between the foreign pair. This appears in a more explicit and coherent form in the *Pillar Testament,* but both versions agree on two basic points of contention, for which Brikhuti insists upon her rights of precedence – firstly, in the building of the main temple, and secondly with regard to access to her spouse, the emperor. Songtsen Gampo, for his part, appears to be more interested in the acquisition of a second palace (*pho brang*) built by his Nepalese bride, than with the founding of a temple, let alone '108', and it is the new triangular dynamic created when Wencheng arrives, over the Gola Pass, that brings the question of temple building into the marshy foreground.

Here it may be suggested that the various terms used for buildings that are established during this period might to a certain extent be interchangeable, or to have had a dual purpose. The main terms are *pho brang* (palace), *gtsug lag khang* (house of branches of knowledge/science, ie. the Indian vihara); *lha khang* (temple or chapel), and perhaps the first Buddhist temples or chapels were built inside the palaces. This certainly appears to be the case for Brikhuti, for she was living in a palace when Wencheng arrived, and her image of Shakyamuni must have been with her, in a chapel specially reserved for it.

Scholars place the princesses on two distinct levels of historicity, based on the two groups of written sources that are available. The chronological gap is of four or more centuries[11] and the difference in the historical outlook of the available documents is huge. The first texts were written by chroniclers living in Tibetan-controlled Central Asia, during or just after the collapse of the Pugyal empire, ca 9th-10th centuries and they are minimalist to the extreme.[12] The second group bears witness to a veritable literary phenomenon – rich, eloquent and expressive – they date to the early Second Diffusion of Buddhism, from the 12th century onwards, and as mentioned above both written and oral traditions are no doubt fused within this fine 'new' literary tradition. The linguistic, cultural and conceptual leap between the two remains somewhat of an enigma, although other early sources, such as the Chronicle of Ba (*Dba' bzhed*), and the *namthars* of Bairotsana, Atisha and Rinchen Zangpo, all of which date to ca 11th century – do help bridge the gap.[13]

Wencheng's journey to Tibet, ca 640-641 CE, is attested in the Tibetan Annals (PT1288 and in S0750) from Dunhuang, dating to ca mid-9th century[14], two hundred years after the events. However, only three lines mention her presence, as *'Mun c(h)ang kong co'.* Firstly, we learn that 'Minister Gar invited her to Tibet'. No date is visible but it can be deduced from the neigbhouring entries. Secondly, just after this first mention of her name, comes the announcement of Songtsen Gampo's death, and the notification that 'he united with her for three years'. The date of his demise must also be deduced from the entry in the following year of the Dog, 650 CE, when his body is 'laid out in the funerary chamber (*ring khang*) at Chingwa castle', the ancient family seat of the Pugyal dynasty, in Chongye. Thirdly, the date of her death, in ca 680 CE, is again only infered by the mention of the final ritual ceremony of reburial (*mdad btang ba*) that took place in the winter of 683 CE, in the year of the Sheep, normally three years after her passing away, according to Tibetan custom.[15] In Chinese sources, her departure from Chang'an is mentioned in the *Tang Annals* which, according to the Chinese historiographical tradition, would have been compiled at the end of that dynasty (618-907 CE), ie. ca early 10th century.[16]

There is a strong oral tradition that has kept alive memories of the princess's passage through numerous localities in Eastern and Central Tibet. However, inspite of the present day legend that nourishes a Wencheng connection with sites in Kham, the inscriptions that accompany two groups of early Tibetan Buddhist bas-relief stone sculpture indicate that both sites date to one and a half centuries later. The inscription at the Bimdo Namnang Temple, or what is famously promoted by the present regime as the "Wencheng Temple", near Jyekundo, dates most probably to 806 CE, to the reign of Emperor Tri Desongtsen or Senalek (776-ca 815). The other important site, at Denmatrak, appears to belong to the same reign period.

Indeed, material evidenceof the passage of both Wencheng and the second Chinese princess, Jincheng, is exremly rare. The Rmoche temple that Wencheng is said to have built in Rasa does not appear to have kept any trace of Chinese influence at all, in its architecture or decorative motifs, apart from the fact that the main door faces East, towards the Middle Kingdom. Indeed, the recently published bas-relief sculpture of a '*yaksha*', that must be one of the earliest elements found in Ramoche today, is in what appears to be a naive Tibetan rendering of the 'Indian style', more sophisticated examples of which can be seen in the *yakshas* at the base of the earliest Jokhang pillars.[17]

Brikhuti-devi's case is rather different. No serious scholar doubts the Newari origin of the Jokhang Temple, but her arrival is not attested in written sources dating to the Pugyal empire, the earliest known narratives about her being the 12th-14th century texts of Second Diffusion of Buddhism, such as Nyangral's *History of the Dharma,* used here. Other texts, notably the *Pillar Testament (bka 'chems ka khol ma)*;[18] and the *Mirror Illuminating the Royal Genealogies (rgyal rabs gsal ba'i me long)*; as well as the later *Feast of the Scholars (mkhas pa'i dga' ston)*; include rich details on her life in Tibet.[19] It should also be noted that although Brikhuti's name is not specifically mentioned in the *Tibetan Chronicle* from far-away Dunhuang, there is an entry, immediately following the one attesting to Wencheng's invitation to Tibet in 641, informing of the 'death of the Nepalese Yunakukti and the enthroning of Naribaba as king'. Naribaba is no doubt Narendra, who received Chinese ambassaders ca 646 CE, and who succeded King Viradeva (Yunakukti?), who himself succeeded Brikhuti's father, Amshuvarman, founder of the Thakuri dynasty ca 602.[20] The manuscript goes on to note that three years later, Zhangzhung submited to Songtsen Gampo, and six years later, the emperor passed away.[21] In any case, the absence of written data does not prove the *in-existence* of an historic personnage, and there is strong circumstantial evidence of Nepalese presence in Tibet during the 7th century. Furthermore, it is said that the entire royal court of Nepal sojourned in Tibet around this time, during a critical period in their political history.[22]

Short columns of the Main Hall, looking south towards the Svastika Alcove. (1996 AA)

The two early styles of wooden doorways in the most ancient part of the Great Temple:
'Newar style, with a horseshoe archway entrance. (1999 HS)

'Indian' or 'Ajanta' style doorway, with a rectangular entrance, with typical Indian, or 'Ajanta style' motifs, such as pillars and lotus motif to each side. (1999 HS)

The 'Two Phases' of Construction of the Inner Sanctuary

Here we would like to propose, somewhat in accord with textual sources, that there are two early phases in the construction in the inner sanctuary of the Jokhang. They are found as two distinct styles, visible in the structure and in the ornamental carvings of the nine main doorways, as well as in the decorative motifs of the pillars, beams and ceilings. If this hypothesis is well-founded, the original building, belonging to the 'Nepalese' or Licchavi style (Phase I), would have been a rectangular two (or three) storey structure with five or seven chambers, and a veranda running along the building at the front, as can be seen even today in many old Newari buildings.[23] When the temple was extended sometime afterwards (Phase II), this smaller building would have been incorporated into the east wing of the new courtyard, designed to follow closely the prevailing Indian Buddhist vihara style. This second phase can be clearly seen today on the south, west and north sides of the courtyard, in the doorways, pillars, and ceilings, and it also appears on the east side, in the main pillars, but especially in the large classical Indian-style portal that leads into the Jowo chapel. Visible remains of the older building are to be seen in the smaller, simpler pillars that stand closely aligned with the large 'Ajanta-style' pillars near the Jowo chapel, and in the four unpainted 'Nepalese' style doorways on either side.

These two phases – originating from the same Indian cultural matrix – merge well together, but the visible point of juncture is in the complex arrangement immediately in front of the Jowo chapel, where double pillars, multiple brackets and complex beams form an unusual and somewhat bizarre architectural arrangement that does not look as if it were conceived as part of one single coherent plan. Furthermore, André Alexander discovered what he calls a 'second skin', enveloping what must have been the original wall, even with the remains of windows, indicating that there must indeed have been two distinct periods of construction.[24] The possible explanations that emerge from the textual sources are again two.

Firstly, the above-mentioned complex structure immediately in front of the Jowo chapel may perhaps be read as proof of problems of subsidence reported by Brikhuti, and by the 8th century emperor, Tri Songdetsen, when he was trying to build the Samye vihara. Perhaps the original foundations over the marsh were not sufficiently stable, so they had to prop up the building, at one point, to save it from collapsing over the Jowo chapel. This could explain the complex structure in front. However, the author has not found this eventuality mentioned in the texts concerning the Jokhang. Secondly, and this is a preferable argument, in my view: There were indeed two early phases of construction during the Pugyal empire, as described above. Firstly, the small two (or three) storey 'palace' built by Brikhuti for Songtsen Gampo, over the marsh, facing west towards Nepal, and secondly, an extension built to the front, in classical 'Indian vihara-style', creating a large courtyard with the main doorway still facing west.[25]

The most convincing and widely accepted archeological evidence of Nepalese presence, during Phase I, is to be seen in the four ancient horseshoe-shaped doorways on both stories, on either side of the central Jokhang chapel.[26] The door-jambs have a slight incline towards the top (also widely found in Tibetan architecture), and art historians agree that the bas-relief motifs adorning the lintels must date closely to the 7th century. They are unpainted and carved in fine Licchavi or 'Nepalese style', presenting charming lively scenes from the Jataka stories, entirely absent from the doorways and other sculpted features of Phase II.[27] These four

The late Tenth Panchen Lama alongside Mahakarunika in the Main Hall. (1996 HMS)

Peripheral figures in the Central Inner Sanctum. (1996 HMS)

'original doorways' stand in contrast to the second series of five upright square section doorways, belonging to Phase II, that are found on both floors of the 'Indian style' vihara extension. There are two on the ground floor and two on the first floor, in the centre of the south and north galleries. The fifth one in this style is the elaborate main portal into the Jowo chapel, above which towers a sculpted canopy or ceiling, raised aloft on tall composite pillars, protecting the approach to the Jowo chapel.[28] These five doors, the canopy, and the impressive lotus flower motif on the ceiling, to the right of the canopy just in front of the south Zhalray Lhakhang, are all sculpted and painted in the same style, identical to that found all around the vihara extension. It is this 'second phase' that follows closely the layout and style of classical Indian Buddhist viharas, as seen, for example, in Ajanta and Nalanda during the same period, 7th-9th centuries.[29]

From this constat, as mentioned above, it may be that the original Jokhang was a symmetrical rectangular structure built by Newar architects, at the behest of Brikhuti, over the Milk Lake Plain, facing west towards Nepal. It had a central chamber and either four or six smaller ones, distributed on each side over two storeys, making five or seven chambers altogether. There must have been a gallery or a veranda in front, on both stories, including the two Zhalray Lhakhang, reached via the adjoining stairway to the right. The smaller, simpler pillars in the complex arrangement at the front of the Jowo chapel, would have been the original ones. This would be the second 'palace' (*pho brang*) built for Songtsen Gampo by Brikhuti, and even today, there is a special wooden funnel situated on the ground floor, just near the stairway, through which pilgrims can listen to the sound of the water of the lake below.

However, according to other versions of the story, the whole vihara was built by Songtsen Gampo himself, scattering out magical emanations in true Mahayana fashion, doing all the work alone, to please Brikhuti, who was the only person permitted to bring him his meals. He even spread out a mist to keep it a secret from the city folk. But one day, just as he was finishing off the lion beam ends on the balcony, his army of carpenters (ie. himself), working in unison, cut the noses off all the lions in one fell swoop. This was done in a moment of distraction, when a servant girl came in un-announced, instead of Brikhuti, bringing him his sustenance.[30]

However – as has been suggested above – the original structure may have been added to, thus forming a courtyard, well-protected from the elements and from human aggression. Some texts say that embellishment or enlargement took place about one hundred and fifty years later, during the reign of *tsenpo* Tri Desongtsen Senalek (ca.799/804-815).[31] He was one of the most ardent defenders of Buddhism among the Pugyal emperors, and it was his father, the great emperor Tri Songdetsen (r. 745-797), who built the first fully-fledged Tibetan vihara in Samye, completing it, ca 779. By that time, the empire had out spread out in all directions around the Tibetan plateau, and if we are to rely on our 12th-14th century sources, a cosmopolitan taste in art and architecture had impregnated the Tibetan court to such a degree that when they built their palaces and temples the styles of the neighboring lands were incorporated on different floors and extensions of the buildings. Basically, the ground floor would be in Tibetan style, with an assortment of Chinese, Khotanese and Indian floors higher up. Thus, according to the *dBa' bzhed,* the main Utse temple in Samye was built in three styles, Tibetan (ground floor), Chinese (middle floor) and Indian (top floor). At the same time, a Sankrit Translation College (*Rgya gar sgra 'gyur gling*) was established within the walls of the vihara, where numbers of Indian, Kashmiri and Nepalese pandits lived and worked for years in partnership with the Tibetan *lotsawa*-translators. They worked in teams, and together they set in motion one of the great translation programmes in Buddhist history. It was a time of discovery and exchange with the neighboring lands,[32] and given this special context, it would not be surprising if the Indian vihara-style extension to the Jokhang Temple does date to the latter period of the Pugyal empire.[33] Furthermore, as Alexander mentions, large reddish fired bricks were used in the building, pointing again to Indian or Newari origins.[34]

To come back to the two princesses, with archeological evidence adding weight to the rich literary tradition, it becomes clear that neither can be discarded off-hand. As will be seen below, several of the geomantic devices alluded to in Nyangral, are to be found as stones embedded in the outer walls of the three-storey Jokhang chapel, as it stands today. Thus, we are faced with a question. If this three-storey tower belongs to Phase I of the Jokhang temple, then the geomantic stones that will be presented below may well go back to the period of foundation. But if the tower belongs to Phase II of the building, and if Phase II dates to the reign of Senalek, then this must clearly add a new and more complex dimension to the geomantic history of the site.

These observations having been made, we shall return to our main source in order to try and trace the links between the well-developed but unpolished 12th-century narrative presented by Nyangral, and the geomantic stones that can be seen today on and around the three-storey chapel. According to all Tibetan sources, the main reason why Wencheng enters into the story is precisely because of her expert knowledge of geomancy. Brikhuti had architects at her disposal, for when Wencheng arrived she had already built two palaces, one for her lord and one for herself on the Red Hill promontory, where the Potala Palace stands today.[35] They were joined together by an iron bridge, with a thousand tinkling bells that tinkled as the two spouses went to and fro. However, she was facing a real challenge in trying to build '108' Buddhist temples. Whatever was put up during the day collapsed or was pulled down at night. The Nepalese princess was at her wits end.

It might be remembered that the same scenario was to repeat itself one hundred and thirty years later when Tri Songdetsen (742-797) was trying to build Samye. Perhaps a partial or more 'rational' way of explaining this phenomenon is that until the unification of Tibet and the expansion of the Pugyal empire (7th-9th c. EC), which led to wide scale contact with all the surrounding civilisations, the important structures of Tibetan architecture were built on rocky promontories, rather than on the marshy or sandy valley floors. Villages clustered in the lea of the mountain, while the nomads had their own prefered sites for pitching tents, on high grassy meadows. Therefore, perhaps the techniques for laying solid foundations on flat low-lying, potentially unstable ground had not yet been properly developed. Furthermore, the conditions and materials for construction in Tibet, with its high altitude, extreme climate and seismic terrain, were certainly different from those found in Nepal and China, so the 'Lords of the Earth' were not pleased, and some sections of the population too.

The last straw came for Brikhuti when she saw princess Wencheng arriving, after considerable delay, dressed in her finery, knocking at the east gate of Songtsen Gampo's palace. Like Brikhuti, the new foreign bride had

A scene from a Jataka story, on the lintel of a Phase I doorway, in Newar style. (1993 HMS)

Lion beam ends on the first storey, inner courtyard, of the Great Temple, often attributed to Songtsen Gampo. (1993 HMS)

The double outer wall of the original Great Temple building, showing evidence of an extension made during the Pugyal empire. (1996 AA)

Clearing snow off the roof of the main entrance, which often ignites bouts of snowball fights on the Barkor street below. (1996 LH)

The main entrance during winter. (1996 LH)

brought a golden statue of the Jowo, 'Lord' Buddha Shakyamuni, as part of her dowry. It is traditionally believed to represent the Awakened One and to have been made in India during his lifetime, the 'size of a twelve year-old boy'.[36] It was only after considerable peregrinations that it had come by sea to China, before being carried overland in a chariot to the Land of Snows. Its Indian origin, and especially the tradition that says it is contemporary with the Lord Buddha, is the reason why it is considered to be particularly holy. Indeed, it is the most sacred image in all of Tibet and far beyond. Brikhuti's Jowo Shakyamuni statue was similar, but is said to have been smaller, the size of a boy aged eight, and we must surmise that she had built a special chapel to house it inside one of the palaces, while waiting for its final installation in one of the temples she was trying to build.

Brikhuti could see from her window that her rival had set up a make-shift shrine to protect her statue, made of four pillars and some diaphanous silk curtains, up at the spring of Ne'uchung,[37] for the Buddha and its chariot had sunk into the mud and refused to move, getting heavier and heavier, in spite of vigorous attempts at dislodging it by Wencheng's Chinese 'athletes' (with very Tibetan names), Lhaga and Luga.[38] This was taken as a sign that the image wanted to stay exactly where it was. Leaving two bodyguards to watch over it, Wencheng went to see her lord. It looked ominously to Brikhuti as if a permanent shrine was going to be built before she would be able to construct even one of her temples, let alone 108. Songtsen Gampo had asked her to build a second palace, and Brikhuti was trying to comply. She was in love with her splendid spouse and the sight of Wencheng filled her heart with jealousy.

Quite apart from the wonderful descriptions of the trials and tribulations that the clever Minister Gar had to go through, at the courts of Nepal and Tang China, in order to win two foreign brides for his emperor, it is the lengthy narrative that follows this part of the story that is worthy of interrogation here. It concerns Wencheng's journey, after leaving China and eastern Tibet, and her approach to the Lhasa valley. Nyangral describes the progress of the princess and her entourage in the summer, 'sixteen days' of joyful picnics in the meadows, accompanied by music,and offerings made to the Buddha image, as well as the more laborious stage by stage progress of the baggage caravan, led by her bodyguards. She is not in a hurry for she is waiting for minister Gar to catch up with her. He has been detained in Chang'an as a hostage against her safe arrival in Tibet. Escaping by means of elaborate subterfuge, the kind of thing at which he is past master, Gar reaches the party at Nagsho[39] where a welcome feast is prepared for him.

Here Nyangral provides an interesting sub-plot to the story. It appears briefly in the *Pillar Testament*, but has been dropped from the 14th century *Mirror illuminating the Royal Genealogies*.[40] Nyangral affirms that Wencheng was carrying minister Gar's child, and that this is the reason why she tarried through the highlands, 'mending the pathways'. It may also explain why the direction and the time of her coming was kept such a secret.[41]

This rumour is considered to be politically incorrect in China today, and in this regard, the affront to traditonal Confucianist morality is compounded by a certain puritanism inherent to the Maoist regime, and by the present day capitalist illusion, according to which Tibet is destined to become a vast income-producing tourist paradise. The principal symbol of this latest long-term plan is the well-worn image of Songtsen Gampo-and-princess Wencheng, as a symbol of Tibet-China harmony. In spite of everything, the story is well-loved by the more open-minded Tibetans and Mongols. It was

Barkor Square. (2009 GG)

incorporated long ago into their popular mythology, and a Tibetan Ache Lhamo opera, *Gyaza Belza*, was written about it, over half a century ago, telling the story of the two princesses and their wise husband Songtsen Gampo.[42] Indeed the tolerance of the Tibetans with regard to sexual matters, *and* the success of PRC propaganda with regard to princess Wencheng is shown by the fact that in spite of the scandal, she is still highly respected in Tibet *and* is held to be a true daughter of the emperor Tang Taizong.

From a strictly scientific point of view, Wencheng's family status was questioned long ago by the distinguished French sinologist, Paul Demiéville, in his *Concile de Lhasa*, where he traces her lineage in Tang dynasty sources to show that she was not a daughter of the emperor, but more probably one of his nieces, or a well-born demoiselle at the court.[43] Whatever the real situation is, today, her story serves both political and touristic ends, being used on the one hand as propaganda to imprint her image on Tibetan minds and on the landscape, everwhere. On the other, the flattering image is counterpoised by an ancient and deep-seated Chinese principle found in Sunzi, *The Art of War*, and originally pronounced by the unifier of the Xiongnu nomad tribes, Mo Tun, and which may be resumed as follows 'Give women and young boys to the enemy, but not one inch of land'.[44]

Gar Tongtsen's brilliance as a tactician is noted by all and sundry, and while Nyangral's narrative goes into intricate detail on both visits to Nepal and China, it dwells more especially on his long sojourn in Chang'an. Gar, the skillful diplomat who had succeeded in bringing the temperamental Nepalese princess up to Rasa in spite of stiff opposition from her Buddhist father, King Anshuvarman; Gar the clever negociator who had gone through all sorts of subtle, imaginative tests at the Tang court in Chang'an, in order to win a second beautiful foreign bride for his emperor.

When his skill in pleasing women,[45] and his ambition to rule over Tibet are taken into consideration, this rumour appears somewhat less of a 12th century Tibetan fantasy. It might help explain his absence (in Nyangral) at the time of the arrival of the Chinese delegation in Rasa, as well as the statement in the Tibetan Chronicle from Dunhuang that it was *'Minister Gar who invited Mun chang kong co to Tibet'*.[46] Indeed he succeeded extremely well in his ambition, for just nine years later, immediately after the demise of Songtsen Gampo, he and his clan took over the reigns of power *de facto*, instigating a new legal system and continuing the expansion of the territories of the Pugyal empire for half a century (650-699). The only way for *tsenpo* Dusong (r. ca 677-704), rightful heir to the throne of Pugyal, to get rid of them was to organise a great hunting party during which the entire Gar clan fell into the trap and became the hunter's prey. They were surrounded and massacred altogether on the spot, in 699.[47]

A more honorable and pleasing explanation of Wencheng's long journey is that she was an adventurous Han princess exploring the high plateau of Tibet, traveling from the Sun-Moon Pass, in the far north near Yellow River,[48] down through eastern Tibet as far as Tsawarong, before turning west towards Central Tibet. In this way she allowed the Buddha Shakyamuni to 'set foot' all over Tibetan territory,[49] and at the same time, the well-educated, studious princess was able to analyse the geomantic layout of what was going to be her homeland for the next forty years. So that is why the journey took rather longer than expected.

In any case, it was not known in Lhasa from which direction she was coming. This lack of information appears odd for such an important delegation, especially when the high mobility of the horse-riding *tsenpo*, his court and his army, is taken into consideration.[50] It may be best understood in an allegorical manner, suggesting the ubiquitousness of Lord Buddha, represented by the image that Wencheng was bringing to Tibet. In any case, Nyangral appears to maintain a certain mischievous ambiguity with regard to the 'Chinese lady' and her gallant minister.[51] Thus the 'city people' were ordered to go out East, South, West and North 'to improve the pathways', beginning in the east at Gar Nadong – which appears to be rather a suggestive location, 'Gar's Nose-Face'!.[52]

In the end, she and her party approached from the North across the Gola Pass, coming from Nagshö and Phenpo, but just as her caravan reached a spring in the upper part of Ne'uchung,[53] the chariot carrying the image of Lord Shakyamuni got stuck in the mud.

Pilgrims leaving through the snow-covered South Debating Courtyard. (1996 LH)

Wencheng makes Geomantic Calculations

'Kongjo wondered,' Why is this? What sign is this ?' and she spread out a divination chart with trigrams in 300 sections (*spor thang sum brgyai gab rtse*), in order to make calculations using the *jushag* threads.[54] She understood that the territory, the realm of Tibet, the Land of Snows, was *like* an ogress lying on her back. She understood the Milk Lake of Lhasa, as being the heart blood of the ogress. She understood this territory as being over her heart. She understood the two prominent hills (*ri bog chad*) in the centre of the plain as her 'heart bones' that had the evil intention of consuming the lives of all living beings'. The follow-up to this episode is resumed or partially translated below.

She saw further that there were two rows of mountains surrounding the valley in all four directions. The first four, the inner circle, embodied conflictual, opposing forces facing each other, East v. West, South v. North, and vice-versa. This explained why 'the people were ill-mannered', and why 'the land was full of bandits'. Calculating more broadly:

'She looked and saw to the east of the valley that there was a mountain *like* a pile of red lotuses; to the south was a mountain *like* a heap of jewels; to the west was a mountain *like* an offering stand (*mchod sdong*) planted there; to the north was a mountain on Manjika, *like* a conch shell, placed there and filled with 'Dharma water' (*chos chab*). She understood these as a prophecy (*lung*) that many people full of faith would come and gather there, and that the qualities of each one of them would emerge. She also understood that (the emperor Songtsen Gampo) was thinking of building a vihara, so that 'appropriate activities would naturally develop and increase, based upon a foundation of quality'. As she performed the geomantic analysis (*dpyad mdzad pa*), she found 360 different aspects in the land (*sa'i dbye ba*); 73 separate geomantic riches (*sa'i dpyad nor re re*); 90 points of recognition (*ngos bzung ba*); as well as the (manner of) rebuffing faults in their recognition; and the means to not waste the results. Gathering all this data together, it was to be resumed under four headings, and in this way, it emerged that the valley would become:

1) A place where many people would gather.

2) A permanent location for the emperor's capital, and a place where 'noble ones' (ie. monks) would be ordained.

3) A permanent location for a vihara and a place where many lay practitionners (*drang srong*) who uphold their vows would gather; it would become a permanent location for monasteries and a place where (people) would enjoy (performing felicitous actions).

Pilgrims from Amdo in the Barkor Square. (1996 LH)

4) A permanent location for ordinary people.

Out of these, the first two were already established. Furthermore, a site with eight qualities was required, and that site would also have approximately five faults.

The eight qualities (actually only five appear to be present in the text) are:

1) The sky forming an eight-spoked wheel.
2) The earth (thus) being like an eight-petalled lotus.
3) The median space between 1 and 2 being adorned with the eight auspicious symbols.
4) There being a pure temple of *juyag* (ie. divination ?).[55]
5) It being a place with five different precious substances.

In order to reveal the strength (of the eight qualities) she understood that the five faults needed to be cleared away. The five faults were:

1) The palace of the water spirits *(klu'i pho brang)*.
2) A place where ghosts gather to discuss *('dre'i 'dun phung)*.
3) The sleeping place of the mamo female spirits *(ma mo'i nyal sa)*.
4) An alleyway where the red gods of the rocks run *(btsan gyi rgyu srang)*.
5) Opposing forces from the earth element *('byung ba'i sa dgra)*.

In order to gradually repulse *(bzlog)* these five, she understood that the Jowo Shakyamuni (image) was (already) performing the act of 'pressing down' over the palace of the water spirits (fault # 1). It was at this moment, that she planted four pillars around her statue in the four directions and adorned them with silk curtains, leaving her two *gyad* strongmen to guard the make-shift temple, and going off with her entourage to the east gate of the emperor's palace.[56]

At this point in the text, a description of the preparations that were to be undertaken so that the *tsenpo* and Wencheng could meet in an appropriate manner is given. The Chinese party (or according to KChK, minister Gar)[57] sends a written message announcing her arrival and that of the 'Golden God Shakyamuni', ie. the statue, asking for a banquet to be prepared. Songtsen Gampo gives out orders and when the feasting drum is beaten, the townspeople are delighted. They dress up in their finest attire and walk noisily up and down the lanes. Brikhuti in her palace, hears the noise and wonders what is going on. She sees that Wencheng has arrived with her suite at the east door of the tsenpo's palace. She sees the golden image of Shakyamuni at the source of the spring, at 'Lhasa Sand Island', and immediately decides that she must build a temple for her statue first.[58]

The next episode in the tale consists of a series of lengthy dialogues between the two princesses, in which Brikhuti appears as a somewhat extravagant, bossy, jealous elder queen, wishing to prevent contact between her beloved spouse and the newcomer. Wencheng is presented as a gentle, knowledgeable, generous lady, with Buddhist values. But the tables keep on being turned, as Nyangral, in collusion with both the oral tradition and earlier texts, appears to enjoy creating tension, and even psycho-drama, between the two protagonists.[59]

The dialogues are couched in a classical vernacular, alternating between direct confrontational language and subtle manipulation. The first meeting takes place between the two princesses after Wencheng's visit to the east gate of Songtsen Gampo's palace. Brikhuti is seriously worried and calls her rival, addressing her 'insistently', ' Ye! Princess! You are here with your god, but I too have a god. I am the eldest and I have built a palace such as this. What I have achieved is greater. Until I have built my temple, do not build yours!'

She goes on, 'Alas, princess, you have come with servants and a large entourage. The go-between (Minister Gar) managed to invite you with considerable difficulty. Then you came to Tibet without any hitch.[60]
But it is I who crossed the threshhold first. I, the elder (queen) am greater. The elder is more venerable and should be treated with greater respect. The elder one is more fierce and should be treated as such. If the elder greater one is not venerated, if the earlier one is not treated in virtuous manner and with deference,[61] then the proper way of the world will decline. Even more than this, since my hearth was established before yours, and since I saw the lord's body first, you must respect me as the one who has prescedence.'

Brikhuti continues her lengthy tirade, underscoring their future rivalry in all aspects of Buddhist activity, including the building of viharas, and in effacing the 'earth elemental opposing forces' (*sa'i dgra*), demonstrating that she too has some notion of geomancy, no doubt helped by her recent unpleasent experiences. She ends up, however, by coming back to what was perhaps her main point, ' If you cannot compete with me, do not hope for the king !'.[62]

Wencheng agrees with Brikhuti, expressing herself in a considerate, distinctly Buddhist manner. At the same time, she insists that in order to build the temple, her rival must wipe out the marshland of the Milk Plain Lake. Brikhuti listens but finds it a daunting task, and continues to block access to the *tsenpo*. Then the ministers intervene and manage to arrange a distinctly Tibetan mariage ceremony between Songtsen Gampo and princess Wencheng, with Bonpo priests performing 'all kinds of (*ritual*) actions', and the newly-weds being 'seated on the same couch, tying together their hair, and exchanging little cups (*skyu brje ba*) of *tsampa* dough filled with liquid butter'.[63]

Immediately in the next paragraph, Brikhuti appears again, crossing the silver bridge with its tinkling bells, between her palace and the *tsenpo*'s. She appeals to him, asking for another site on which to found her temple, since he is the 'Lord of the Land'. He agrees to give her an excellent site, saying 'Build!' So off she goes accompanied by a large mounted escort, and surrounded by numerous *yaksha*, to explore possible building sites. It is true that she is extravagent, since they lay the foundations of not one but '108 temples' in all the delightful places (*yul dga' ba*), such as Dol, Yarlung and Sogkha. However, once again, at each place, what is built during the daytime gets destroyed at night. So Brikhuti comes to the conclusion that it is high time to consult with Wencheng (once again) since 'she is clever at Chinese analysis and calculations'.[64]

So a servant girl is sent off with 'a full measure of gold coins', to Ne'uchung spring at Lhasa Sand Island, to visit the white silk tent where Wencheng is making offerings to her statue of Jowo Shakyamuni. Wencheng repeats the same observations that she had made previously on the eight qualities of the valley, but this time she adds more detail on the specific aspects of each mountain. The place-names and symbolism of the vantage points are quite close to later accounts. However Nyangral's version includes variant readings and specific allusions to the geomantic stones that are the subject of this chapter, as well as a more subtle view of the actual geomantic procedure, and the roles that each of the three main protagonists play.

Barkor Square at different times of the day. (1998 AA)

The Eight Qualities, Five Faults and the Elemental Opposing Forces[65]

'Kongjo shows (the servant girl) some good land and sends back the following message (to Brikhuti). 'In this place where many people gather there are eight qualilties. In order to bring out their beneficial aspects, the five faults must be repelled. The eight qualities are (the fact that) the valley is adorned with the 'eight auspicious symbols'. Below the 'eight spokes of the sky wheel' and above the 'eight petals of the earth lotus', on the mountain of Phenkar, there is (a formation) like a parasol. On the Raka Rock there is (a formation like) a fish with three eyes. On the Dzongtsen Rock, there is (a formation like) a vase. The entire dagger (*phur*) of Drib Sedrom (South) is (a formation like) a left-turning conch shell; on the corner of Drib Dayugma there is (a formation like) a heart, an eternal knot *(dpal be'u)*. On the Shun Rock there is (a formation like) a banner of victory. In the East, on Mount Tsib, a tongue of a mountain, is an open lotus.[66]

The five faults are as follows: to the south in the Deer Park, there is a place where the *dre* ghosts gather to parley. This should be scattered (*gtor*). To the south-west there is the runway of the *tsen* mountain deities. This must be obstructed (*khog*). To the north-west, in the cave that faces southwards, there is the sleeping place of the mamo female spirits. This should be captured (*phrogs*). To the north, is the palace of the water spirits in Sand Island. That place is (already) being pressed down (*mnan*) by Lord Shakyamuni.[67]

Then come the earth elemental opposing forces *('byung ba'i dgra)*.[68] It is these that involve the geomantic stones that are to be seen inserted in the outer walls of the Jowo tower. Nyangral's text follows in almost perfect symmetry the modest stone symbols that were shown to the author in October 1996.

To the east, in the Empty Valley of Sand Island, there is an 'earth elemental opposing force' (*sa dgra*), like a demoness holding her genitals up in receptive fashion (*srin mo 'doms bzed pa*).[69] Plant a phallus of great Ishvara in there (*dbang phyug chen po'i ling ga tshugs*). To the south, on Mount Yugma, there is a (formation like a) black tortoise concentrating on its food *(gzan la gzhungs pa)*. Display the face of a *khyung* garuda bird towards it *(bya khyung ga ru da kha ston)*. To the west, on Shun Rock, there is an 'earth opposing force' like a black demon on the lookout (*bdud nag po bya ra byed pa*). Build a *seru* stupa in that direction. To the north, on Mount Nyangdren, there is a (formation like a) powerful elephant charging into battle *(g.yul la zhugs pa)*. Set up a white stone lion against it (*rdo'i seng ge dkar mo tshugs*). Having done all this, in the middle, in Milk Plain Lake, the billy goat (*ra skyes*) shall transport earth and efface the lake.[70] Once the temple is built, the strength of the 'blue turquoise dragon' to the south and the *'red bya phu* bird to the north-west, the 'black vajra tortoise' to the north, and the 'pale tiger of the Sandhill' to the east will be brought out.[71]

Mines

Wencheng then brings up the question of mines. She is perhaps the first foreigner to have cast an observant eye upon the mineral wealth of Tibet, exploited by Tibetans themselves in a conservative manner right down the centuries, so as not to derange the ' Lords of the Land' (*sa bdag*). However, as noted in the *Tang Annals,* Tibet was already famous for its impenetrable iron-ringed armour that left only holes for the eyes, and for the fine production of animal style artwork in precious metals, especially silver and gold. They would need a lot of metal to make images and to embellish the temple.[72]

'The iron of the Inner Gate, Gophuk; the copper of Raga;[73] the silver of Latok; the gold of 'Iron Mountain', Chakari, will at last become available.[74] You too will be able, at last, to build your temple.[75] All the nine excellent qualities of the kingdom of the Land of Snows shall at last appear, and it shall be possible to carry out actions that will erase all faults'.

'The servant girl gets the message back to front. She hears that the lake should be effaced by goats bringing earth from Phenyul, and when they do this, the lake becomes troubled. So Brikhuti imagines that Wencheng is jealous of her and thinks she should tell the king. She goes to the Peak Fortress.'

The following episode finds Brikhuti and Songtsen Gampo in friendly collusion once again. After explaining to her spouse the trouble that she is having building '108 temples', he replies that he will consult 'someone'. This 'someone' is his tutelary deity, represented by the sandalwood image of the Great Compassionate One, Avalokiteshvara, the very first Buddhist statue to be brought to Tibet, according to tradition, from Sri Lanka in the early 7th century, by the monk Akaramatishila.[76] In this passage, it is the tutelary deity who helps the pair decide where to build the temple and with what materials. When they go out riding together near Milk Plain Lake, the emperor uses a traditional Tibetan divination method to decide on the exact spot for laying the foundations. This is far simpler than Chinese geomancy, and consists of throwing or casting and object, or shooting an arrow, in the desired direction. Songtsen Gampo casts his ring into the sky and it lands 'beyond Brikhuti's saddle', right in the middle of Milk Plain Lake! (ie. back to square one...).[77]

The Nepalese princess is in despair again, thinking that the emperor has had words with Wencheng, and tears well up in her eyes. But Songtsen Gampo reassures her by saying that he will actually help her build the temple. She is delighted and decides to follow orders. However, he then tells her to build a palace in the lake. She complies, and builds one in 'three storeys', and she invites ten chaplains (*mchod gnas*) inside.[78]

The detailed narrative goes on, and it is not until several pages later that the last 'earth opposing force' has been repulsed, and the time has come for the actual construction of the Jokhang Temple to begin. There are no more obstacles. All 'nine good things' are spreading in Tibet, and all 'nine faults' have been eliminated (nine being a number meaning 'a lot'). The emperor transforms himself into '5,000' artisans, and builds the temple, working alone in secret, emanating a multitude of physical forms, including a whole battalion of carpenters.[79]

The building of the Jokhang over the heart of the 'Prone Ogress' appears, from the majority of sources, to be the final, rather than the initial stage, in the larger geomantic scheme that spreads out pinning down her whole body. These are the territories of southern, western and eastern Tibet that Songtsen Gampo had brought under his dominion at the beginning of the expansion of the military empire of Pugyal. The Jokhang is, as it were, the crowning glory.

Barkor Square from Mentsikhang Lam soon after construction. (1985 CB)

Pilgrims circumambulating the Barkor, juniper smoke billowing from incense burners in front of the Great Temple. (1985 CB)

Dates

Nyangral does not propose any dates for these events, but the *Mirror* suggests 635 CE, for 'laying the foundations stones (*mkhar las kyi rmang 'ding*), in the year of the Female Wood Sheep. Since princess Wencheng arrived ca 641 CE, there would have been a gap of six years or so between the start of the building projects by the Nepalese in Rasa, and the arrival of Chinese techniques of geomancy.

One question that does not get asked in Nyangral, but which is explicitly present in the more full-some structured narrative of the *Pillar Testament*, is why Wencheng should propose the somewhat zany idea of building a temple on a marsh in the middle of Milk Plain Lake, when Brikuti is looking elsewhere for land to build her temple? Especially when archeological evidence shows that in pre- or proto-historic Tibet, the Tibetans built their forts on high rocky promonteries, and the villages in the lea of the mountainside, in places that were safe from flooding and wild beasts, and had a good clear view. This is precisely the case of the recently excavated neolithic village of Chugong, behind Sera monastery.

Was it the arrival of foreign cultural influences in Tibet during the early period of imperial expansion that brought new architectural concepts from the more settled peoples who lived on the plains, like the Chinese, or on flat valley floors, like the Newars? Indeed, the latter are said to have formed one of the most exclusive urban communities in human history. It was Brikhuti's father, Anshuvarman who founded the city of Kathmandu in the early 7th century on the valley floor.

Other archeological evidence supporting a certain historicity of the attempts at taming the 'Prone Ogress' is to be seen in several of the surviving temples that figure amongst those planted on strategic points of her body, including two in present day Bhutan. As suggested above, these appear to represent an early stage of the unification of Tibetan territory. However, as several scholars have pointed out, the chronology still remains uncertain, because the available literary sources refer to somewhat later stages in the historical coming together of the Land of Snows.[80]

Perhaps the finest visual tribute to the original restive Srinmo Ogress of Tibet is the beautiful annotated painting of her made under orders from the regent, Desi Sangye Gyatso (1653-1705), with the Jokhang placed right over her heart. He and the Fifth Dalai Lama were in the process of building the Potala Palace and re-uniting Tibetan territory. They were looking back, like Tai Situ Changchub Gyaltsen, and Amdo Gedun Chompel in the 20th century, to the glorious age of the Pugyel Empire of Great Tibet.

Thus, in spite of Brikhuti's misgivings, the reason why Wencheng was invited to help choose the site for the temple was because she was the recognised expert in geomancy. It was not only a question of the right spot, but of protective devices that were needed to ward off negative influences or to increase positive ones, in order to facilitate the building of Buddhist temples in the Land of Snows. The 'obstacles' and 'favorable aspects' were for the most part natural formations, interpreted as resembling various creatures with qualities or defects. Or else they were perceived as elemental dieties of earth and water, irrascible in the face of invadors of another kind who were bent on taking over their ancestral territory.[81]

No doubt the legendary instability of the 'Prone Ogress' is partly due to the special topography and environment of the high Tibetan plateau, its vast and wild natural landscapes, and the threat of earthquakes and tremors due to the continual rising of the Himalayas, the youngest chain of mountains in

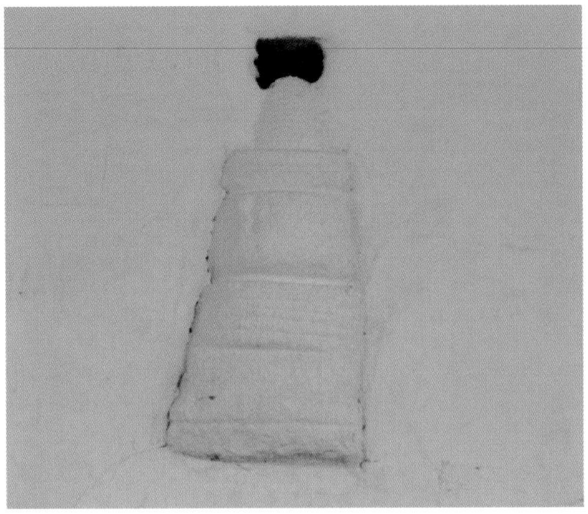

Archaic stone chorten or stupa, West outer wall, second storey, Main Hall, thickley whitewashed. (1997 HMS)

Archaic stone garuda, outer South wall, second storey, Main Hall, thick new multi-coloured paint. (1997 HMS)

Archaic stone lion beam end, North outer wall, second storey, Main Hall, traces of red paint on lips and eyes. (1997 HMS)

the world. The constant movement of the tectonic plates and as well as the noxious vapours that escape from time to time from the depths of the earth, may have given rise to this personification of the body of Tibet. On the other hand, the destroyers of the temple walls may also have been human beings who were displeased at the arrival of a new religion on their ancestral territory. In a pre-televion and media society is easy enough to demonize a living person, or group of human beings, and even more so when they are long dead. '*Dre*'! As they say in Amdo, of a nasty obstructive person.[82]

The Jowo + Nine Stones + The Goat

The nine geomantic stones are at present divided into two groups, the first five being embedded in the upper, outer walls of the Jokhang tower. They included a 3-D carved stone phallus (East), a painted garuda-face in bas-relief (South), a stupa in bas-relief, now heavily white-washed (West), a 3-D bust of a lion (North), and a small humanoid or monkey face (North). The last two are essentially unpainted, with some touches of red or other colours.

The second group of four are free-standing, 3-D, carved and unpainted stones on the top-most terraces, presented on wooden frames. They include a conch shell (East), a stupa (South-West), a garuda and a lion (North). Since the garuda to the south in the first group is hidden from sight by a prayer-flag, and the second group is placed on the high inaccessible terraces, it would be hard for anyone without a guide, without knowledge of the early Tibetan sources, or without close familiarity with the Jokhang, to take note of their collective existence.[83]

A tenth stone, well-known and beloved by Tibetan pilgrims may be added to the list. It is mentioned immediately after the elemental opposing forces in Nyangral, and takes the form of a small goat. It is to be seen in one of the ground floor chapels of the 'vihara', on the south side, towards the south-west corner. A few years ago it was just a simple well-worn 3-D half natural, half man-made stone sculpture of the head of a goat, similar in its archaic manner to the conch and stupa on the terraces, or the lion on the north wall. But now it is thickly painted with gold, like the Jowo image itself. According to the well-loved legend, it represents the goat, or rather herd of goats, that are supposed to have bravely transported stones to fill in the marsh of Milk Plain Lake, before construction on the temple could begin.

The eleventh or rather the first 'geomantic' device for which we still have physical evidence today is the Jowo statue itself, mentioned by Nyangral as being responsable for 'pressing down' the fifth of the faults, ie. the 'Palace of the Naga Kings' in Lhasa Sand Island to the north. Indeed, the Jowo is mentioned immediately before the enumeration of the 'elemental opposing forces'. Thus in the table below, I have included both the Jowo Shakyamuni, and the goat, together with the stones, since Nyangral associates them in immediate proximity in his text.

Archaic-style stone bas-relief pouncing lion, free-standing, Easterly exterior terrace, above second storey of Main Hall (NB. Perhaps a recent copy, in yellow sandstone). (1997 HMS)

Archaic stone 3-D stupa, free-standing, Easterly exterior terrace above second storey of Main Hall. (1997 HMS)

Archaic stone garuda clasping snake in talon and beak, free-standing bas-relief, Easterly exterior terrace above second storey of Main Hall. (1997 HMS)

Conclusions

If these stones do indeed belong either to the first (mid-7th c.), or to the second (early 9th c.), period of construction of the Jokhang – as proposed here – their presence provides tangible and fascinating archeological confirmation of the use of geomantic principles in Tibet during the early historic period. Until now, as already mentioned, we have only had written sources that recount the legend, dating to several centuries after the events. The stones complete and support the Jowo image, seen in this context as the first agent in the stabilisation of the territory, in both its potentially good and bad aspects, pressing down the watery 'Palace of the Nagas', immediately below the temple. Here we are faced with a sliding geographic location for the Jowo Shakyamuni image, who moves, or so it seems, from its original stopping place in the lush meadow at the Ne'uchung spring, high up in the valley near the Gola Pass, where the image first sunk into the mud, then down to the site of the 'Chinese Tiger' or Ramoche Temple, down on the valley floor, apparently within the area of Milk Plain Lake, and finally into the Jowo Chapel in the Jokhang itself.

Whatever the date of the stones – and the author considers them to be of considerable antiquity – they support the founding narrative of the Jokhang, its intimate links with questions of geomancy, and the 'taming' of what 'resemble' both negative and positive forces inhabiting the surrounding landscape. The widely-known legend that speaks of the 'Prone Ogress of Tibet', the bod *srin mo gan rkyal,* makes her, the restive body of Tibet, the main heroine of the drama. However, in the case of these modest stone symbols, especially the four main ones that are embedded in the structure, they are directed against entities in the immediate neighbourhood of the Lhasa valley. They are in the region of her heart, forming the innermost ring of a series of concentric energy patterns that were laid over the pre-Buddhist geomorphic body of Tibet.

The spatial distribution of the stones as given in the table below is based upon their actual presence in the Jokhang, as well as on Nyangral's text. There is a surprisingly close correlation between the two, and indeed they follow the geomantic layout of the valley as provided in Wencheng gongzhu's analysis. As Mills has pointed out in his recent article, they include but are not exclusively dedicated to the 'suppression' (*kha snon*) of negative elements in the landscape, Furthermore, the geomantic elements to be 'suppressed' or 'developed' do not refer specifically to any pre-Buddhist Bon deities, but are expressed rather as configurations in the landscape that are 'similar to' certain animals or mythical creatures, or to inanimate symbolic forms.[85] It might be noted, on the other hand, that the evocation of elements such as the 'Naga Palace', the 'Elephant charging into Battle', the 'Garuda Bird' and the 'Phallus', are not adequate to Chinese geomancy, and point rather to an Indian cultural matrix.

Thus, at least four key questions remain. Firstly, if the hypothesis of the two phases in the early building of the Jokhang is acceptable, then to which one do the stones actually belong? They appear at present to be solidly integrated into the structure of Phase II. But they could, of course, have been removed from the first structure and replaced on the outer walls of the larger three-storey tower belonging to the 'Indian-style' vihara extension. This should have been done for the sake of visibility, in order to maintain the geomantic efficiency with regard to the surrounding land formations. In this case the stones would still go back to the original Newar building, and thus to the time of Songtsen Gampo, and the princesses Brikhuti and Wencheng.

Secondly, if after all they belong to the second phase, then are we witnessing – as many scholars might suspect – a shifting, overlapping mythology with regard to the history of the introduction of Buddhism to Tibet. If this is the case, then the founding date of the Jokhang Temple, as well as the Songtsen Gampo-Brikhuti-Wencheng legend, may be in need of reviewal. There is for example, the second Chinese princess Jincheng (in Tibet ca. 710-730), and the Buddhist emperor, *tsenpo* Senalek (ca.799/804-815), to whom we have tentatively attributed Phase II of the Jokhang vihara structure. Perhaps it was one of these later personalities who introducted temple building and geomancy into Tibet? This argument, however, goes against the considerable mass of information, both in archeological and written form, dating to between the 7th and 14th centuries with regard to Songtsen Gampo's reign, and the Pugyal empire, in general.[84]

Thirdly, with regard to textual sources, the knotty question of how to evaluate them remains. The first group is made up of manuscripts from Dunhuang and stone stele or rock inscriptions dating to the Pugyal empire. These provide the historical 'skeleton' of that period. Then there is a major rupture of approximately 130 years, before the second group provides the 'flesh and blood' of an historical romance. Amongst the later sources it is the 'treasure texts' that predominate, ie. ancient written documents that are held to date back to earlier times, but which are often as not rewritten in the language of the century in which they were 'discovered'. They contain hitherto unknown rich and complex narratives, in which several genres are inextricably entwined – history, philosophy, literature, various other 'sciences' or fields of knowledge, as well as prophecy, and Mahayana or Tantric magico-realism. They strongly suggest a flowing together of ancient oral and literary traditions, as well as more latter-day attempts at getting to grips with the glorious past. Nyangral's *History of the Dharma* is an excellent case in point, and in the view of this author, it represents the earliest overview that is available today, on the Pugyal Empire. Nyangral, like the later scribes or scholars, are no longer secretaries on the hoof employed by an expansive military empire, in contact with peoples from the main Asian civilisations, but Buddhist yogins and clerics whose views on the universe, on history and human society, on the very foundations of existence, are radically different from those of their predecessors.

Fourthly, there is the second major rupture in Tibetan history, the Cultural Revolution (1966-1978). During that decade and its aftermath, the destruction, pillaging and displacement of objects – not to mention the exportation of thousands of art works onto the international market – has left a gaping ravine in our knowledge that will never be filled. Luckily there remains a wealth of written documents, but the historic fabric and material culture, the art and architecture of Tibet have very largely been destroyed. The Jokhang Temple itself is but a shell in comparison to what it was before 1966. Yet, a certain mystery remains. It is the Lhasa Trulnang, 'House of the Gods of Magical Emanation' that survives today at the centre of Tibetan civilisation, pressing down the heart of the Prone Ogress. It commands our attention as no other building in Tibet will ever do, and it is far more alive than the splendid Potala Palace.

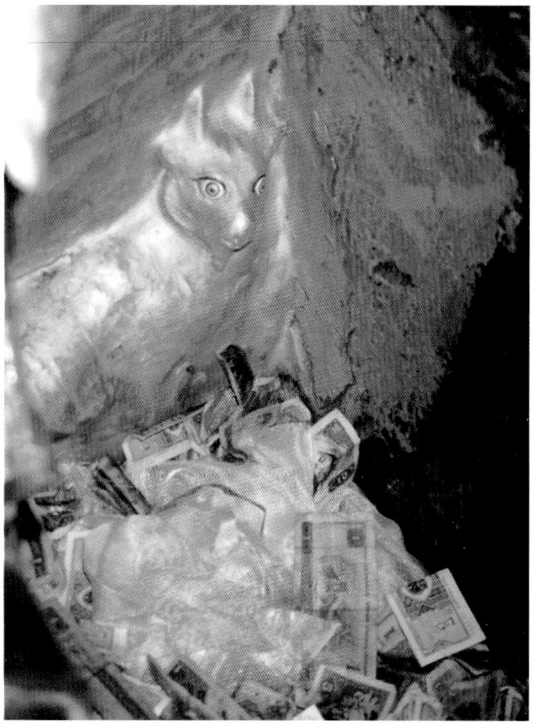

Archaic stone goat, ground floor, last but one chapel on South side, Main Hall, thick new gold paint, and pilgrims' offerings. (1997 AA)

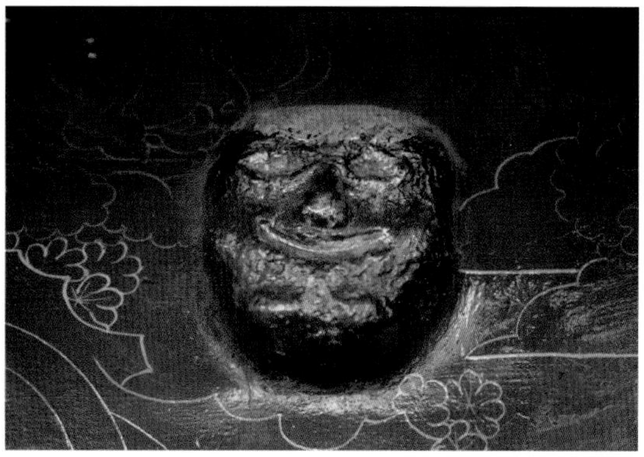

Archaic stone human or monkey face, North outer wall, second storey, Main Hall, traces of paint. (1997 HMS)

Archaic stone lion, outer South wall, second storey, Main Hall, thick new multi-coloured paint. (1997 AA)

TABLE OF THE GEOMANTIC STONES OF THE JOKHANG DIVIDED INTO THREE GROUPS (Nyangral, 234-240)

Directions N E S W C	NNO pp.	I. **THE JOWO STATUE & THE INSERTED STONES**	ELEMENTS TO BE 'SUPPRESSED' OR QUALITIES TO BE BROUGHT OUT *sa dgra gnon 'am nus ba gdod*
North Bye ma'igling	234, 239-40	**Jowo Shakyamuni** 'pressing down' the Naga palace	Klu'i pho brang yod pa
East Bye ma'i lung stong	234, 239	**Phallus** / dbang phyug chen po'i ling ga tshugs	'byung pa'i dgra: Srin mo 'doms bzed pa 'dra ba'i sa dgra yod
East	240	**Stupa** / mchod rten	Shar srin mo'i kha gnon: To protect ordained monks
South-East		**White conch** / dung dkar	Srin mo ri
South Yug ma'i ri	234, 239	**Garuda bird** / bya khyung ga ru da kha ston	Rus sbal nag po gzan la gzhungs pa 'dra ba yod
West Shun gyi brag	235, 239	**Seru Stupa** / mchod rten bse ru rtsigs	Bdud nag po bya ra byed pa 'dra'i sa dgra yod
North Nya ran(Nyang bran) gi ri	235, 239	**White stone lion** / rdo'i seng ge dkar mo tshugs	Glang po stobs can g.yul la zhugs pa 'dra ba yod
Centre 'O thang gi mtsho	235	**Goat(s)** or a place name Rakye (?) Ra skyes las sa bskyal nas mtshob srubs te/ lha khang byas na.../ NB. Two readings of the text in Nyangral are possible, thus Ra skyes may refer here to the goats, or is it a place name.	S. g.yu 'brug sngon mo N.W. bya phu'i bya dmar po N. rdo rje'i rus sbal nag po E. bye ma ri'i stag skya bo rnams la nus pa gdod byung/Sgo phu'i lcags dang Raga'i zangs dang La rtog gi dngul dang lcags kha ri'i gser kyang gdod byung/
Inside Jo bo temple	237-239	**The Eleven-headed image of Avalokiteshvara**/ Spyan ras gzigs dbang phyug zhal bcu gcig pa	The first Buddhist image of the Land of Snows, which is also a life-size portrait of Songtsen Gampo.
North	No mention	II. **A HUMAN OR MONKEY FACE**	My guide to the stones said it may recall the monkey bodhisattva and brag srin mo story of the origin of the Tibetan people.
		III. **FREE-STANDING STONES ON WOODEN FRAMES**	
South-west of klu'i pho brang (Jo bo)	239-240	**Keru Stupa** / mchod rten ke ru (upper east terrace)	Btsan gyi rgyu srang bcad par bya ba'iphyir...kha ba can gyi sgrub pa po & rab tu byung ba la btsan gyi gnod pa mi'byung ba'i phyir/
East	234	**White conch** / dung dkar (upper east terrace)	Grib bse sgrom gyi phur Dung dkar.g.yas su 'khyil ba.'dra ba yod
North	234, 239	**Garuda** (upper north terrace) NB. opposite position to Garuda facing South, towards Yukmari. (new?)	
North	235, 239	**Lion** (new?) white stone bas relief in archaic style, (upper north terrace)	

The First Monlam Chenmo

The 'Great Prayer' of the Land of Snows held in the Jokhang New Year 1409 by Lord Tsongkhapa

In 1373, as the armies of the Mongol Empire were retreating from their vast domains across the Eurasian continent, a young Tibetan monk, Lobsang Drakpa (1357-1419), was on his way to Central Tibet from Amdo, the north-eastern province of the Land of Snows.[85] He was traveling with a group of companions, including two maternal uncles and a benefactor from the Kagyu monastery of Drigung Thil, not far from Lhasa. They were well aware of the precocious talent of their fifteen-year-old protegee.

Instead of taking the 'northern route' across the vast and silent Changthang desert, they traveled via the (slightly) more populated 'southern route', that led them through Amdo and Kham, across the broad rich pastures of Dzorge, to Barkham in Gyalmorong, and from there to Chamdo where the Dzachu and Ngomchu Rivers flow into one. Continuing their way slowly upwards and westwards they arrived at the monastery of Drigung Thil, in CentralTibet.[86]

Like many of those who have become leading figures in Tibetan history, Lobsang Drakpa knew the Land of Snows because he himself had travelled across much of its vast territory. The journey must have taken several months as they crossed the pasturelands and precipitous passes of Eastern Tibet, visiting hermitages and monasteries on their way. His homeland of Tsongkha, in the north-east, had been part of Tibet since the 7th century, when the first *tsenpo*, emperor Songtsen Gampo (r. 617-649), founded a military empire that would last two hundred years, first uniting the scattered principalities of Central Tibet, then expanding across the plateau and far beyond into Central Asia.

Tsongkha, or 'Onion Land', is mentioned in the earliest Tibetan manuscripts from Dunhuang (8th-10th c.), and even today its people celebrate the annual Luröl festival, recalling the courage of their heroe's who defended the northern frontiers of Great Tibet, over a thousand years ago.

Reknowned as one of Tibet's most outstanding scholar-yogins, Lord Tsongkhapa's life is recorded in 'seven biographies' that provide much detail on his activities as a student and teacher, yogin and reformer, and as a strong confederator of lay and religious leaders in Tibet. After reaching Drigung Thil at the age of sixteen, he never returned to Amdo, but spent the rest of his life traveling throughout Central Tibet, studying at the feet of over forty masters from the various traditions of Tibetan Buddhism, before becoming reknowned as a 'Lord of the Dharma'. He taught widely, gathered a huge following of disciples, and was closely linked with the Drigung Kagyu, Sakyapa, Jonangpa and Kadampa traditions, as well as the Shalupa or Bulug of Shalu Monastery, which followed a non-sectarian, all-embracing current established by the great scholar-yogin, Butön Rinchendrub (1290-1364).

The first thing Tsongkhapa did upon arrival in Drigung-thil, in 1373-34, was to learn the *Six Yogas of Naropa*.[87] After that he returned there several times, and enjoyed continuous support throughout his life from donors of the famous hermit monastery.[88] The next step, when he still only seventeen years of age, was to go and study medicine in Tshal Gungthang, near Lhasa, where he is said to have rapidly become an excellent physician. From that time on, he traveled back and forth through Central Tibet, studying and teaching in all the major centres of learning, in Sakya, Narthang, Shalu, Rinpung, Dewachen, Ngurmig, Nenying, Ngamring, Densathil, Drigung,

Monlam Chenmo. Ceremonies in the South Debating Courtyard presided over by the Ganden Tripa on the Sungchöra throne. (1986 CB)

and last but not least, Tsechen where he met Rendawa Shonnu Lodrö (1349-1412), a Sakyapa master, who made a decisive contribution to the development of studies in logic in Tibet, and who taught the three main founders of the Gelukpa order, Tsongkhapa, and his two disciples, Khedrup-jey and Gyaltsab-jey. Tsongkhapa was impressed with Rendawa`s 'utterly impartial and direct teachings on the *Abhidharmakosa'*, and he went on to study *Madhyamaka* and dialectics at his feet, as well as an abundance of other teachings.[89]

Although the Gelukpas have long had a reputation as dry, hair-splitting dialecticians, it is clear that their founding master was both a great practitioner and a philospher, and that he embodies, as do most other major figures of Tibetan religious history, the dual Vajrayana ideal of the 'scholar-yogin' (*mkhas-grub*). His biographers record that he was constantly having 'clear visions' of deities and pandits, as well as astonishing dreams and that in his early twenties when travelling between Ü and Tsang he stayed for a while in Kyormolung Monastery. During the *mangcha* or tea assemblies, when the entire community of monks would gather in the Assembly Hall ro recite the Prainaparamita on the practice of Emptiness, he would spontaneosly fall into the deep *samadhi*, oblivious of all ythat was around him, remaining one-pointedly in 'none-grasping clarity-emptiness' in accordance with the meaning of the teaching, and he would remain in that state right through the session from beginning to end.[90]

However, by the time he reached the age of thirty-five, he had come to the following conclusion with regard to the state of Buddhism in Tibet, no doubt based upon personal observation and experience. 'The ultimate view of the noble Nagarjuna and his 'sons' (ie. rational, analytical study according to the Middle Way philosophy); and the Five Stage Path of the *Guhyasamaja* (ie. techniques of yoga and meditation) and within the latter five, the Illusiory Body (*rgyu lus*) – these are particularly difficult to grasp. If one does attain realization in them, it is of great import. But if one practices and does not attain realization, then the gaping ravine into which one might fall is so huge, that this is the reason why meditation on the 'true essence', and the search for 'Enlightenment' based upon the 'unsurpassable path' of Mantrayana, have become mere words'.[91]

Not long afterwards with his eight close disciples, Tshongkhapa went into a four-year retreat at Olkha Chölung hermitage, just below the sacred mountain of Odegung-gyal. Each of them completed an awesome 'thirty-five sets of 100,000 prostrations, each set being dedicated to one of the thirty-five Buddhas of Confession (ie. 3.5 million), and eighteen sets of the 100,000 mandala offerings (ie. 1.8 million)'.[92] Tsongkhapa applied himself so diligently to these ascetic practices that even when his toes split (during the prostrations) and his forearm bled (during the stone mandala offering), he kept up the rhythm without stopping. Indeed, it is said in Olkha Chölung today that the wooden planks with deeply worn toe imprints, in the small chapel upstairs, are Tsongkhapa's own.[93]

Thus, Tsongkhapa came to understand the philosophical views of Buddhism in all their profundity, as well as the varied practices of yoga and meditation that had been developing in Tibet since the 7th century CE. At the same time, he observed, all over Central Tibet, what appeared to him to be a certain disarray in the transmission and practice of Buddhism. So he launched a reform of the basic system of religious training, teaching his own *Lamrim Chenmo 'Gradual Path'* as a renewed approach to Buddhist practice, re-emphasizing the importance of the *Vinaya* monastic discipline, and pure adherence to vows.

Torma exorcism during the Great Prayer Festival. (film stills 1940 JG)

Monastic policemen preparing for crowd control.

One of his favorite hermitages near Lhasa was at Chöding, perched on a rocky outcrop high above the valley floor to the north, just above the site where the second of his 'three great seats' of learning, Sera monastery, would be established in 1419, the year in which he passed away. He studied logic and later on taught the same subject in the 'Potala', which in those days must have been a smaller structure standing on the same Red Hill,[94] for tradition says that Songtsen Gampo had already built a palace there in the 7th c. CE. This was not far from the Jokhang, where in Tsongkhapa's day a thriving market town filled with throngs of pilgrims, and merchants who bartered the goods they brought from afar, while visiting the holy of holies of Tibetan Buddhism.

The collapse of the Pugyal Empire in the mid-9th century was followed by a 'Period of Fragmentation' when a series of petty dynasties ruled over the central Tibetan provinces of Ü and Tsang, as well as territories all around the peripheral zones of the high plateau. These included the kingdom of Tsongkha, founded by a prince descended from the imperial clan. He had been invited from Chang Latse, in Central Tibet, to Amdo, in the 10th century, in order to re-unite the frontier territories on the north-eastern periphery of the Land of Snows. Little by little, these widely scattered principalities forged links with the new orders of Tibetan Buddhism and by the second half of the 14th c. – when Tsongkhapa appeared on the scene – the political centre had moved several times and was still oscillating between Sakya and the cradle of Tibetan civilization at Ne'udong, in the Yarlung valley. Rivalry between the two central provinces of Ü and Tsang is endemic to Tibetan history to this very day, largely due to the topographical layout, and although the great monastery of Sakya in Tsang had ruled Tibet all through the Mongol empire, by the time Tsongkhapa arrived the balance of power had shifted over to Ne'udong, and the ruling house of Phagmodru, founded by the famed myriarch, Changchub Gyaltsen (1302-1364). Tsongkhapa was to forge a close and long-lasting friendship with his most illustrious successor, Drakpa Gyaltsen (1374-1432), the ruling Neu'dong *gongma* of his time.

Tsongkhapa was born just before the collapse of the Mongol Empire, and as a youth it is almost certain that he knew of the passage through his home territory of the great Sakyapa hierarchs – imperial preceptors at the court of the Mongol Khans of the Yuan dynasty from 1260-1368. They traveled through Tsongkha on regular missions between Sakya and Beijing, and indeed it was just to the north of the old Tsongkha kingdom that the meeting between Sakya Pandita and Godan Khan had taken place in 1247. The site, known as Chang-ngö or 'North Face' in Tibetan,[95] was Godan Khan's headquarters, Sakya pandita lived there until his death in 1251, and his funerary stupa still stands there today.

Here it is important for the background history, and for the immediate political and religious context of the Monlam Chenmo, to make a detour and take a closer look at Tibet's international relations during the preceding period and especially in the early 15th century.

Although it was Sakya Pandita's nephew, Phakpa, who was chosen by Kublai Khan, in 1260, as the first of a long series of Sakyapa imperial preceptors in permanent residence at the Mongol court, there had been an initial period of Drigung Kagyu ascendency and rivalry with Sakya, with regard to the Mongol khans and the winning of their favors, as donors and benefactors of the Buddhist church in Tibet. This first period of contact had led to the founding of a multiple Mongol-Tibet alliance, when four of Jenghis Khan's great-grandsons, Mongor, Kubilai, Hulahu and Arigbhoke, all joined in to become donors and protectors of the Drigung, Tsalpa, Phagdru and Taglung branches of the Kagyu order in Tibet.[96] The Karma Kagyu were also favored, but like the Drigung, they seem to have lost out on a political level, when the second Black Hat Karmapa, Karma Pakshi (1206-83), left the Mongol court in the mid-13th century in the wake of violent conflict, traveling westwards to found a monastery in the Tangut Kingdom of Minia (Chin. Dangxiang, or Xixia). This was in 1256, just five years after Sakya Pandita's demise in Chang-ngö, and three decades after Jenghis Khan's attempt to annihilate the entire Tangut population.[97]

Although each tradition, including the Gelukpa, tends to emphasize its own role at the courts of the Tangut and Mongol khans, and later on at the court of the Ming emperor Yongle, historical evidence suggests that contact and exchange between the various parties took place over long periods, somewhat intermittently, due to the immense distances and difficult terrain. The Tibetans vied with each other for the favors of their powerful neighbors as donors and benefactors, while the princes and emperors at the Tangut, Mongol, and to a lesser extent the Ming Chinese court, cultivated the Tibetan lamas to a remarkable degree. This was not the usual relationship of sovereign to vassal, but a special alliance as 'priest-and-patron' (*mchod-yon, or yon-mchod*) in the Buddhist sense, no doubt with somewhat differing objectives and points of view, but acknowledged clearly on both sides. Indeed, it was partly thanks to the generosity of the great khans that the various orders of Tibetan Buddhism were able to stabilize and flourish during the important period of consolidation and expansion from the 13th through to the 15th centuries.[98] On the other side of the coin, the 20th century Gelukpa scholar, Tseten Shabdrung, affirms that 'it was due to the 'skillful means' (*thabs mkhas*) of the *yon-mchod* alliance that the Riwo Galdenpa order (ie. Gelukpa) flourished more than the others, even in the 'Degenerate Age'. He was of course referring not to Tsongkhapa's time, but to the Manchu dynasty and the era of the Dalai Lamas, when a line of Gelukpa hierarchs, including the great Changkya Hutuktu, served as imperial preceptors at the Manchu court in Beijing. In this they were following the original pattern established in the 13th century between the Tibetans and the Mongols. With the Manchus it was to last for two hundred and fifty years (1642-1911).

It is probable that Tsongkhapa himself, or older members of his family in Amdo, had vibrant memories of maurauding Mongol armies surging from the vast emptiness of the Gobi Desert, or the Changthang, 'Northern Plain' of Tibet. He must have heard of the massacre of hundreds of monks at the monastery of Drigung Thil, in Central Tibet, a century earlier in 1290, and he was surely aware of the mongolization of the Sakyapa hierarchs that many Tibetans disapproved of deeply. His intimate knowledge of the vast territory of Tibet as well as of regional and sectarian tension no doubt played a role in the strong re-centralising effort he achieved through the Monlam Chenmo, just four decades after the fall of Mongol and Sakyapa power. He certainly triumphed in his purpose.

During Tsongkhapa's childhood, as the Mongol empire imploded, it was a Chinese Buddhist monk-turned-soldier, Zhu Yuanshang (or Hongwu), who ousted the descendants of Kublai Khan from China, and founded the Ming dynasty. Establishing the new capital in Nanjing, he and his army set out to destroy as much as they could of Khanbalic, the northern capital of the Mongolian 'barbarians' (actual Beijing). One of the main targets of attack was what the Chinese considered to be their corrupt practice of Buddhism in its Tibetan form.[99]

Senior monks, cavalry commanders (yaso) and aristocrats at the Great Prayer Festival.

Cavalry commanders (yaso) and monastic policemen.

Gathering of the cavalry commanders (yaso) and nobility, dressed in their finery.

Monlam Chenmo. Torma offerings depicting Songtsen Gampo and his wives for the 'Offerings of the Fifteenth Day'. (1986 CB)

Monlam Chenmo. Torma offerings fashioned of butter set up along the Barkor during the 'Offerings of the Fifteenth Day'. (1986 CB)

The third Ming emperor, Chengzu, commonly known as Yongle (r. 1403-1424), had immense vision and a more tolerant view with regard to the outside world. He spent much of his youth riding with the princes of the Mongolian banners to the north of Beijing, and had a soft spot for Central Asia. Indeed there is an ongoing debate in scholarly and less scholarly circles in Asia, and on the www, as to whether he was a full-blood Mongol, or partly Korean, with the main discussion being centered on the question as to whether he might have been the son of the last Mongol emperor and his consort.[100]

Although during his reign China turned her attention towards the rising sun, to become the greatest seafaring nation in the world, at the same time Yongle made vigorous attempts to re-establish a 'priest-and-patron' relationship with the Tibetans, following the example of the Tanguts and Mongols before him, to such a degree that his adulation of the Tibetan lamas was criticized at court.[101] His approach followed the pattern of the initial relationship between Jenghis's grandsons and the lamas of diverse lineages. This might be interpreted as partaking of the traditional Chinese policy of 'divide and rule' amongst their Central Asian neighbors, but in any case, like the rulers of other Han dynasties, he laid no territorial claims to the Land of Snows,[102] and made no attempt at establishing any sort of administrative system there. On the other hand, he did send nine diplomatic missions to Tibet between 1402 and 1419, loaded with rich offerings for the religious masters, and the one that arrived in 1408, with an invitation for Tsongkhapa, numbered several hundred men.[103]

This was contrary to the political theory and practice of the Middle Kingdom, according to which a true emperor – he who had the 'mandate of heaven' (*tian ming*) – ruled through 'human righteousness and virtue' (*ren and yi*), thus attracting to his august presence 'all under heaven' (*tianxia,* ie. *the* empire), including not only the Han Chinese, but all the 'barbarian' nations beyond. There was no need for him to spread physically outwards in an undignified manner to court the 'cooked barbarians', let alone the 'uncooked barbarians' far on the other side of the Great Wall,[104] for they would come to pay tribute of their own accord. The unshakable belief in this centripetal concept is amply illustrated as late as the 18th century, during the Macartney Embassy, sent by George III of Great Britain to the Manchu court in Beijing, in 1793. The great Manchu emperor, Qianlong, was 80 at the time and he considered that the white, blue-eyed, long-nosed strangers were coming as vassals to pay tribute to his person.[105]

Tsongkapa, Deshinshekpa and Yongle

To come back to Yongle, he was a dynamic, enterprising cosmopolitan figure who was very much a 'product' of both the Mongolian empire and the Chinese world system. He built up the greatest library in the world, sent out numerous maritime expeditions, and ambassadors throughout Asia, and personally led ten expeditions to the northern frontiers. The beginning of his reign coincides precisely with the last period of Tsongkhapa's life, when the great monk was reaching his fifties, and had risen to a peak of religious authority and pre-eminence in Central Tibet. His followers were known as the new Galdenpa, but as yet could barely be called a 'order'.

The other Tibetan lamas who received envoys from the emperor included leading figures of the Phagdru Kagyu orders, the Lingtsang, Drigung and Taktsang (1402); as well as the Karma Kagyu (1403); Sakyapa (1406 and 1410); the lastly Tsongkhapa (1408 and 1413). From the Tibetan point of view, when Yongle's emissaries arrived on their doorstep from far distant China, this must have been interpreted as a sign of great respect. They would have understood the overtures as a continuation of the priest-and-patron (*mchod-yon*) legacy, and would have accepted the fine gilt bronze Buddhist statues, woven *kesi* thangkas and exquisite ritual instruments with particular pleasure, since they were made in a style that would please them, reflecting closely the major Tibeto-Nepalese style of art that was prevalent in Central Tibet at the time.[106] In return, eight missions from Tibet to Nanjing are recorded,[107] but only three lamas actually made the long journey. They were, respectively, leading spiritual figures from three of the four major orders of Tibetan Buddhism, Deshinshekpa, the Fifth Black Hat Karmapa (1384-1415, mission 1406-1408), head of the Karma Kagyu order; secondly, Kunga Tashi, chief abbot of Sakya (b. 1349, mission 1412-1414); and thirdly, Shakya Yeshe (1354/7-1435, mission 1414-1415), a disciple of Tsongkhapa, and future founder of Sera. None of them had any eminent political status in Tibet, and when they arrived at the Ming court, they were given sumptuous honorific religious titles as 'Kings of the Dharma', (Tib. *chos kyi rgyal po;* Skt. *dharmaraja;* Chin. *fawang*), as well as rich presents, following the custom established by the Mongols. The other five lamas received less grand titles, including the denomination 'prince', *rgyal bu,* in Tibetan, or *wang;* 'king' (in Chinese). These were carried by Yongle's ambassadors to their monastic seats in Tibet.[108]

Monlam Chenmo. The main torma offering on the Barkor at night during the 'Offerings of the Fifteenth Day'. (1986 CB)

Deshinshekpa visit to Nanjing

The first of the 'Kings of the Dharma' to be welcomed by Yongle was the youngest. Deshinshekpa, the Fifth Black Hat Karmapa, was just twenty years of age, and was following an established tradition, for three of his previous incarnations had been in close alliance with the Mongol khans.[109] Yongle had no doubt heard about the great lamas of Tshurphu through his Mongolian friends. The next was an elderly Sakyapa abbot, and lastly, Tsongkhapa's disciple, Shakya Yeshe, who was over sixty years of age.

When Deshinshekpa received the invitation in 1403 – in the first year of Yongle's reign – it was to perform funeral rites for the emperor's parents. This once again clearly indicates the deep respect that the emperor felt for Tibetan Buddhism and its hierarchs. A splendid long scroll (4968 x 66 cm) with forty-nine panels, each one identified by inscriptions in five languages, was painted to commemorate the occasion. It depicts the miracles that occurred on twenty-two days during the second and third months of 1408, when Deshinshekpa was staying in Nanjing, at the Lingtu Temple, performing the funerary rites. The polyglot inscriptions reflect the cosmopolitan cultural milieu inherited from the Mongol empire, in contrast to the monolithic ethic of Confucianist China, according to which there is only one true civilization, that of the Middle Kingdom, with its centralized state organization, and unique script and language.

Thus, following in the footsteps of his pre-incarnations,[110] the Karmapa undertook a three-to-four year journey, between 1406 and 1409, traveling thousands of kilometers across Tibet and China to the Ming capital in Nanjing,[113] and then making a large detour via Mongolia and the Tangut Kingdom, before descending south through Eastern Tibet to Yunnan, then returning to Kham and Karma Gön, the mother monastery of his order, and finally to Central Tibet in 1409.

Monlam Chenmo. Monk sculpting torma from butter and barley flour in the Great Temple for the 'Offerings of the Fifteenth Day'. (1986 CB)

On his arrival in Nanjing, he was hosted in the Huagai Palace, before moving to the Linggu-si monastery from where he performed the funerary

Procession of the cavalry. (film stills 1943 TS)

Military regalia on display during the Great Prayer Festival.

rituals.[112] Amongst the rich presents he received on several official occasions was a newly made crown of woven black silk, a copy of the original legendary one made from the hairs of 'one hundred thousand dakini', that the founder of the Karma Kagyu lineage, Dusum Khyenpa (1110-1193) had first received in a vision. A fine early portrait statue of Deshinshekpa shows him wearing this crown. It appears to be a taller and more ornate version of the original, very similar to the one used by the Sixteenth Karmapa when he performed the 'Black Hat Ceremony' all over the world in the second half of the 20th century.[113]

Upon Deshinshekpa's return to Central Tibet in 1409, leading lamas of Sakya, Drigung, and the royal monastery of Densathil came to greet him, but Tsongkhapa excused himself, sending an image of the Buddha with a message to say that he hoped very much to meet the Karmapa later on. Indeed, all the way through, Tsongkhapa keeps a distance from worldly activities, especially those of Tibetan-Mongolian-Chinese Dharma politics. Yet ultimately, by sending his own disciple, Shakya Yeshe, to visit Yongle in 1414, he too allowed his nascent order to take part in the reaping of material wealth from the great donors in traditional Buddhist manner, for the benefit of his monks and their education. In this way, he also created a karmic link, one that would mature, two and a half centuries later, when the 5th Dalai Lama established a new 'priest-and-patron' relationship with the first Manchu emperor, Shunzhi, in 1642, two years *before* the founding of the Manchu dynasty. This was to have incalculable long-term consequences, including the creation of a new lineage of Gelukpa 'imperial preceptors' at the Manchu court, continuing right through two and a half centuries, to the end of the dynasty in 1911. As Tseten Shabdrung writes, in his version of Tsongkhapa's life story, giving the Tibetan point of view, 'It is thanks to the power of skillful means in the creation of the alliance of patron-and-priest that, at the end of this degenerate age, the Riwo Gelukpa order has spread and remained for a long period as the most prominent order in comparison the others'.[114]

Tsongkhapa declines Yongle's invitation

Thus the third of Yongle's 'Kings of the Dharma' ought to have been Tsongkhapa himself. He was fifty-two when a large Chinese delegation, numbering 'hundreds of men', reached Central Tibet to invite him to Nanjing. This was in the sixth month of 1408,[115] not long after the Karmapa had set off from the Ming capital in the direction of Mongolia, and two years after another delegation had arrived in Tibet, in 1406, offering a letter and a seal to Drakpa Gyaltsen, ruling hierarch of the Phagmodru dynasty.

It was to Drakpa Gyaltsen and his chief minister, Namkha Zangpo, in Ne'udong, that Yongle's emissary, Ta Shingbzhi (Chin. Da Xingxi?)[116] and his escort went first of all with their invitation. The visitors were told that Tsongkhapa was in retreat and could not be seen. The emissary wept tears and insisted, so it was agreed that he would be allowed to go up to Sera Chöding to make his plea. But the great monk firmly refused to receive them, declining the invitation and sending some Buddhist images as presents for Yongle, instead, insisting that there would be large obstacles and little use if he did make the long journey to China.[117] During the whole of the summer, as he had done for nearly two years already, Tsongkhapa stayed in strict isolation in his hermitage and as soon as he came out, he sent a message out telling of his wish to hold a Great Prayer festival, in the coming new year.[118]

It might be noted here that neither Tsongkhapa's name, nor that of his disciple, Chamchen Chöje appear in the *Mingshilü* records, until many years later. This was no doubt due to Tsongkhapa's refusal to go and meet the emperor Yongle.[119] However, when his disciple, Chamchen Chöje did finally go to Nanjing in 1415-1416, at Tsongkhapa's behest, he was well received. A portrait thangka made during his visit shows a somewhat elderly lama, around sixty years of age, wearing a black lotus-petal crown of a style different from the Karmapa's, adorned with the Buddhas of the five Tathagata families, instead of a yellow pandit's hat, as might have been imagined.[120]

This busy exchange over the two decades of Yongle's reign – coinciding with the last two decades of Tsongkhapa's life – is an exceptional period in the history of Tibet-China relations. Let us take for example, the presents that were sent between the Tibetan Buddhist hierarchs and Yongle. On at least eight occasions, between 1406 and 1417, Tibetan lamas, beginning with the Karmapa, sent Buddhist sculptures and paintings to Yongle, and in return, the Chinese 'king' sent or gave images and texts on nine occasions to Tibetan lamas, between 1408 and 1419.

It is clear that the now famous Yongle 'bronzes', and other religious offerings of superb quality, produced in the imperial workshops, were made to please the lamas in an appropriate fashion. The emperor, and his successor, Xuande (r. 1425-1435), no doubt revived the century-old school of Vajrayana Buddhist art that had flourished in the Mongol capital from 1273 through to 1368, under the direction of the Nepalese artist, Arniko (Chin. Anige) and his successsors.[121] The artists who produced Buddhist imagery for Yongle must have inherited this tradition, but it is interesting to note that their production is directly inspired by the contemporary Tibeto-Newari style of Central Tibet. Indeed, the first complete xylographic edition of the Tibetan canon, known as the 1410 *Kanjur,* made under orders from Yongle, was adorned with illustrations in the distinct Tibetan style of that period, and when it is said in the *Mingshilü* that Buddhist texts were given to the abbot of Sakya, Kunga Tashi, in 1413 and 1414, and to Tsongkhapa's own disciple, Chamchen Chöje Shakya Yeshe, in 1416, it was no doubt copies of this important edition of the Tibetan canon that they received.[122]

Moreover, the inscriptions that mark the statues and thangkas made during Yongle's reign do not follow the usual official court language. The verb used in Chinese is *shi,* not meaning 'bestowed' in imperial fashion, but rather 'offered', or 'donated' in a Buddhist sense, by a benefactor to his teacher, or to the Sangha. This usage is considered by certain Chinese scholars to be significant with regard to Yongle's and Xuande's respect for their Tibetan Buddhist preceptors. It also confirms the point of view of the Tibetan sources with regard to the special *mchod-yon* relationship, as a classic Buddhist exchange of services between the spiritual guide and his or her lay donor.

Tsongkhapa decides to hold the first Monlam Chenmo

With this politico-religious background in mind, Tsongkhapa decided, in the autumn of 1408, that the time was ripe to rally the population of Tibet and re-establish the centre of their world in the heart of Rasa Trulnang, ie. the Jokhang Temple. In spite of the extreme discretion with regard to politics in his *namthars,* perhaps we may put two and two together and propose that the overtures made to the Karmapa by the Ming court had some influence on his decision. As an Amdowa, he was fully aware of the extent of Tibetan

Procession of the cavalry commanders (yaso).

Obeissance of the cavalry commanders.

Proctor of Drepung monastery carrying a heavy silver mace.

territory, and of the threat of outside military intervention. He would certainly have been sensitive to recent violence in Central Tibet, which had been seen as a most unwelcome departure from the hitherto peaceful Phagmodru dynasty, ruling from Ne'udong.[125] He may also have apprehended a renewed and inappropriate politicization of the Buddhist teachings, and a rising of tension between the major Tibetan lineages. Indeed, there appears to be some kind of urgency about Tsongkhapa's decision. No doubt he also saw the potential of the Lhasa valley as a major centre for the development of Tibetan Buddhism. Furthermore, although several monastic communities took part in the Great Prayer, these appear mostly to be linked with Ne'udong and the royal dynasty of Phagmodru, and there are noticeable lacunae, including representatives of the Karmapa from Tshuphu (the Fifth Karmapa, Deshinshekpa, as mentioned above, was traveling in Mongolia), and the great hierarchs of Sakya (they had been defeated and relieved of their century-old position as rulers of Tibet by Changchub Gyaltsen, fifty-nine years previously). There do not appear to be any Nyingmapa dignitaries either.

Whatever the case may be, Tsongkhapa decided to perform a great symbolic act for the New Year festival of 1409. Consulting with the *gongma* of Ne'udong, Drakpa Gyaltsen (1373-1432) and his minister Namkha Zangpo, in the autumn of 1408, he first set in motion an extensive restoration of the 'Lhasa Mandala' (*Lha sai dkyil 'khor*), ie. the Jokhang, especially the top floor and the balconies (*seng dang yab*) that protect the upper stories of the main chapels. According to the descriptions given in his *namthar*, the Jokhang had fallen into a sorry state of disrepair.

The fact that Drakpa Gyaltsen was his chief supporter is not surprising. He was myriarch or 'emperor' (*gongma*)[124] of the house of Phagmodru, and as such was ruler of Tibet and had direct links with the royal monastery of Densathil, as well as with Drigungthil, one of the monastic communities with whom Tsongkhapa had closest ties.[125] The Phagmodru dynasty had been founded by Changchub Gyaltsen in 1350, when he ousted the Sakyapas and what was considered by many Tibetans to be invasive Mongol influence at the Sakya court – Mongolian language, dress, customs and food. Together with his court at Ne'udong, in Tsethang, he forged a Tibetan national revival, putting value on the ancient heritage of the empire of Great Tibet, creating new-old state ceremonies to reinforce Tibetan identity, including a parade of officials, in the ancient robes of the tsenpo of Pugyel, that was still celebrated until 1951.[126] He re-organised the territory into *dzongs*, prefectures, with a three-yearly term of office for the prefects, and his rule ushered in a period of peace and prosperity that continued right across Tibet for several generations after his passing away. The well-structured legal system he established may be considered as complementary to, though earlier than Tsongkhapa's re-organisation of the monastic community, based on proper respect of monastic rule, the *Vinaya*, and on strict adherence to vows and moral discipline.[127]

Parallel to his announcement, Tsongkhapa began to make contact with other lay leaders, and monastic communities across Tibetan territory, notably with Tshal Gungthang, Gyama Rinchen-gang, and Drehor in Kham. The aim was to gather materials for the Great Prayer. He had been in retreat for two years in Sera, but after coming out, began to travel again and while he was in Drumbulung, 'he sent out messages and made great efforts to encourage the monasteries, lay dignitaries and donors, as well as his own disciples, from Drigung and Reting, and up to the high valley of Olkha, to make offerings for the festival'. Once everyone, including Drakpa Gyaltsen,

The Panchen Lama addressing pilgrims and Lhasa residents from the roof of the Great Temple during the Monlam Chenmo in 1986. (CB)

was convinced of the desirability of organizing the Monlam Chenmo, an 'astonishing quantity of offerings came pouring in, thanks to the power of his compassion'. Furthermore, he and his disciples 'dedicated almost everything that they owned, and all that came into their hands', to the festival.[128]

A contemporary account of the first Monlam Chenmo is found in the short biography of Tsongkhapa written by Khedrup Jey (1385-1438), one of his two chief disciples. It shows that Lhasa and the surrounding region was, in the early 15th c., an important religious, cultural and administrative centre, capable of providing large numbers of skilled artists and quantities of rich materials. It was to became, at short notice, a gathering place for thousands of monks.

A resumé of Khedrup Jey's description of the preparations and daily events of the Monlam Chenmo is given below.

'First of all, Tsongkhapa went and held council with the minister, Namkha Zangpo. They made a sumptuous restoration of the upper storey and the balconies of the Lhasa Mandala (*Lha sai dkyil 'khor*), and prepared well all the ritual necessities for the Great Prayer.

'He went and held council with Lord Drakpa Gyaltsen in Ne'udong. He held council in Lhasa too, gathering together many artists as well as vast quantities of paint, gold and paper. The painted images and sculptures in the Jokhang were dirty and it was hard even to distinguish their colours. He had them cleaned and washed with sweet smelling water, and their original colors restored. He had them adorned with gold leaf, so they looked as if they were made anew. He gathered together many artisans and had quantities of robes made for the statues, as well as temple banners and other decorations sewn in silk and brocade that had been offered by the faithful. In that same year of the Rat (1408), towards the end of the 12th month, he went to the Lhasa Temple, the 'Place of the Gods'... Over eight thousand monks were gathered. Each of the Masters of Studies offered provisions. Each monk was given four *nyag* measures[129] of a Lhasa *srang* of butter, and sixty silver *srang* worth of tea was distributed for the monks to drink.

'From the first day of the first month of the year of the Bull (1409), through to the fifteenth, taking the period of the'Miraculous Events' in the life of the Buddha as the basis, fine offerings were made to Jowo Shakyamuni. On the first day, Tsongkhapa offered to the Jowo a crown of the Five Tathagata made of fine pure gold mounted on silk and felt, beautifully decorated with precious *nal,* river pearls and turquoise, etc. He also offered superb silver crowns to the (statues of) Lord Akshobhya and the Eleven-headed Avalokiteshvara. A large silver begging bowl was placed before the Jowo image, together with a silver mandala of about the same size. On each day throughout the festival, the two Jowo statues (in the Jokhang and Ramoche) and the Eleven-headed Avalokiteshvara had their faces 'washed' with gold. On the eighth and fifteenth days their whole bodies were washed with gold... All the other statues were draped with new upper and lower garments made of silk brocade. Furthermore, the *tog* finials and *bya 'dabs* parapets of the large and small temples of the Jokhang and Ramoche were gorgeously festooned with strings of banners, flying canopies and bells, from the pinnacles to the corners of the roofs. On the outside of the Great Outer Circumambulation Route (*phyi'i 'khor lam chen mo*) (*ie. the present Barkor*) extremely tall planks of wood were adorned with terrific banners of the fifteen protectors of the directions, each painted in appropriate colors, each with its own mantra written on the cloth. Every evening, sacrificial cakes were offered in front of each one, and at the foot of

View of Lhasa from the roof of the Jokhang. (1991 US)

each banner. In the intervals between, white parasols and other appropriate symbols were placed according to the rituals for each deity. These wooden structures were linked up by festoons of flags, flying canopies and bells, until the sky was filled with rainbow colors. Furthermore, in the daytime, all around the Innermost Circuit (*yang khyam nang ma,* inside the Jokhang), four hundred butter lamps were kept burning. On the Middle Circuit (*bar skor*) there were over one hundred. On the Outer Circuit (*phyi skor,* ie. the actual Barkor), beside the stone stele (that records the peace treaty between Tibet and China, dated 822 CE), in direct line with the Jowo's face, great square receptacles, one span *('dom)* in width, three in each direction, were filled to the top with butter, making blazing tongues of fire all around the outer rims, so that the sky was blotted out by the golden flames. There were tall clay lamps, thick as a large man's arm, filled with butter, burning in lines as long as an arrow shot, around the Outer Circuit.

'Also in Ramoche, Luphuk, the Potala, and in Gungthang, many lamps were burning, and at night, all around the circuit of the Barkor walls, and by the *ka tshar* of the pillars of the Outer Courtyard (*khyams grva phyi ma*), rosaries of butter lamps burned so brightly that it hurt the eyes to behold. Thus in this 'great place', the light rays from each and every burning flame on the rosaries of lamps, *phya,* rivalled the spangled stars in the heavens, defeating the dark hordes of the night, who abashed, withdrew below the earth, to be seen no more. Thus, the young willow saplings ranged between Ramoche and the Potala cast shadows on the ground as if in bright sunlight, and there was no difference between night and day. Not even one amongst the masses of stars in the sky could not be seen, as when hundreds of suns rise simultaneously over the horizon... Moreover, each day, over one hundred water offerings were made, each perfumed with Kashmiri saffron, so that the air was filled with the scent. Even more than this, there were victory banners and parasols, and other vessels filled with burning incense, so that the whole environment, inside and outside, day and night, was filled with smoke rising and billowing in clouds, creating tall spirals in the sky.

'Finally, the pathways of the Outer Circuit were planted with fresh bundles of incense, and of course, over the length of an arrow's shot, each day, the one hundred and eight charming adornments of the Seven Precious Possessions of the Dharmaraja etc., that were made of butter, would be renewed. On stands, to the right and left of the giant butter lamps were sacrificial cakes well adorned, each made of four hundred loads of tsampa, distributed freely to the needy. So that the beggars, freed from the pangs of hunger, were fully satisfied in both food and drink and wanted to eat no more. Indeed, the variety of offerings was without end, and the Lord Lama himself blessed the charming arrangement of offerings of the Seven Precious Possessions of a Dharmaraja, by means of Tantra, Mahamudra and Samadhi. He made pure ritual offerings from the Sutra Pitaka and the Tantra Pitaka, and each day taught widely and with great energy on the 'unique intention' towards the Buddha's teachings, and towards living beings. He prayed each day for the sake of all beings, and each day he taught the assembled monks one session of the Jataka Stories written by Master Pawo.[130] At that time, both gods and men were fully satisfied by the offerings, and the artists were fully recompensed. Over the period of sixteen days, meals and tea were offered three times a day to the assembly of monks, by the faithful from Drigung etc.

'At the same time, tens of thousands of the black-headed lay people gathered together, and by the power of his compassion, in spite of the great number, not one sign of a bad word nor any fighting was to be seen. Not

Torma exorcism during the Great Congregation – a rare image taken pre-1956. (Photographer unknown)

only that, unlike other great gatherings of this kind there was no singing or dancing, no drinking, nor any other immodest behavior. On the contrary, everyone became gentle, delighting in faith and virtue. Day and night, they did nothing but listen to the Dharma. They made prostrations, did circumambulations, recited prayers and mantras, and at midnight, although those making circumambulations around the Outer Circle might reduce a little in number, the general flow of people continued without ceasing all through the day and the night....'[131]

Day by day donors at the Monlam Chenmo

Another version of the events, together with the names of donors who took part on each day of the Monlam Chenmo, is given in a recent Tsongkhapa *namthar*, compiled by the well-known orthodox Gelukpa scholar of the mid-20th century, Tseten Shabdrung, who was also born in Amdo.[132]

Tseten Shabdrung reports that when the restoration of the Jokhang was complete, Tsongkhapa prepared the main offerings for the festival of 'Great Miracles' from the first to the fifteenth day of the month, in the same way as long ago in India, during the life-time of Buddha Shakyamuni, it is said that King Selgyal organized a series of donors to provide offerings on each of the fifteen days of his performance of Miracles at Shravasti.[133] Thus, in a similar spirit, Tsongkhapa called upon important lay leaders of Central Tibet, many of whom he already knew well from his constant journeying throughout the region, over the previous thirty-five years. He invited them, as well as representatives from the eastern Tibetan provinces of Kham and Amdo, to join in and support the celebration held in honor of the Buddha. This was to be the first Mönlam Chenmo, the 'Great Prayer' of the Land of Snows, held in the newly refurbished Jokhang and attended by leading figures and well-to-do persons from all over the land.[134] To judge from the names of religious dignitaries who attended, they were essentially the chief hierarchs of Densathil and Drigung, with whom Tsongkhapa been closely associated since his arrival in Central Tibet as an adolescent. Those from the royal monastery of Densathil were the religious hierarchs of the Phamodru dynasty who ruled the thirteen myriarchies of Central Tibet from Ne'udong, in Tsethang. There were also leading religious figures from the Kagyu monastery of Tshal Gungthang, and from the Kadampa monastery of Gyama Rinchengang,[135] as well as Trehor (in Kham?). On the other hand, although several names off the donors are unknown (to the author), representatives of the great Sakyapa monastic establishment in Tsang that had ruled over Tibet, under Mongol overlordship, for over a century; as well as members of the Nyingmapa order, seem to be noticably absent.

The 'Miracles of Shravasti', count as one of the 'Twelve Acts' of the life of Shakyamuni, and commemorate his defeat – through a series of magical displays – of the 'heretical' non-Buddhist Tirthaka of India. Thus, for fifteen days in succession, during the Monlam Chenmo of Tibet, a new prodigy was celebrated based on the original event in Shravasti. The names of the orginal patrons and the magical displays are given by Tseten Shabdrung, while the parallel events that took place in Tibet are said to 'proceed' from each original moment, two millennia previously. The names of the donors and details of the rich presents that they offered, as well as descriptions of the festivities and rituals that were enacted, are also given. From these it is clear that Tsongkhapa had the backing of many of the main political players of his day. He sought to bring together representatives not only from all over Tibet, but also (to judge from some of the names) to gain the support of some friendly foreigners.[136]

Pageantry of monastic musicians from the Namgyal Monastry. (film stills 1943 TS)

A resumé of the fifteen days is given below, with only the main donors mentioned.

1) On the first day of the New Year, 1409, it was Tsongkhapa himself and his entourage of monks who acted as donors, providing the funds for the Jowo's new five-petalled crown, as well as crowns for other main images, and numerous rich offerings. The head lama of Densathil, the royal monastery of the Phagmodru dynasty, Chenga Rinpoche Sonam Zangpo and his community, were also there as principal donors.

A long description of the different offerings is given for each day, as is customary during Buddhist events. This acts both as recognition for the donors, and as a register for the monastic community, for the offerings become part of the collective wealth of the monastery. The first item mentioned is 368 golden *zho* that were offered for the making of the golden crown and for gilding of the main images.[137]

2) On the second day, the Ne'udong *gongma*, the ruler of Tibet, Drakpa Gyaltsen, acted as chief donor, participating in the offerings of gold and silver for the making of the various crowns, for the Jowo etc., and for the gold 'washing' ceremonies.[138]

3) On the third day, Gyanbu Lhundrup Gyaltsen,[139] his siblings and their mother, provided the main offerings.

4) On the fourth day, the Prefect of Drakar was chief donor, offering precious silk *taa-hun* robes for the Jowo, etc.[140]

5) On the fifth day, the donor chief Dzepa, father and son, made special offerings in memory of the passing away of chief Drakpa Zangpo.[141]

6) On the sixth day, the donors were Jowo Sala, father and son, as well as Drangphuda, and Nön Sanggyal, who made special offerings for (Changchub Gyaltsen's nephew) Jamyang Gushri,[142] and the glorious Drakpa Zangpo, to commemorate their passing away. The people of Drib also contributed.[143]

7) On the seventh day, Tashi Cha'u Da'o performed a general ritual in favour or the teachings, and another 'life affirming ritual for the great emperor and his chaplain(s)'. (In view of the Tibetan-Chinese hybrid name, it would appear that the emperor in question is Ming Yongle, but the meagre sum of seven *zho* of gold offered by Tashi Cha'u Da'o for the Jowo's crown and for the 'washing' of his face with gold dust, is a very humble offering, not one that would have any connection with the emperor or his court, so we may rather presume that *gongma* refers to Drakpa Zangpo, ruler over the thirteen myriachies of Tibet from Ne'udong).[144]

8) On the eighth day (the 1st, 8th and 15th are especially sacred days in the Buddhist calendar), minister Namkha Zangpo,[145] husband and wife, were the chief donors. They made special offerings in honor of *chenga rinpoche* Drakpa Gyaltsen, (and in memory of) *drung rinpoche* Tai Situ Changchub Gyaltsen, his nephews etc. An especially rich and detailed description of events and presents is given here.[146]

9) On the ninth day, the Chamberlain (*gzims g.yog* of Ne'udong) and other local groups acted as donors.[147]

10) On the tenth day, the Treasurers, with Sonam-Phel at the head, were donors. They too remembered the minister Drakpa Zangpo.

11) On the eleventh day, the Great Treasurer, Gedunpel, was donor. He performed a long life ceremony for *gongma* Drakpa Jungnay,[148] and in order to thank Lhatsun Lhawang Lodrö, and the Great Treasurer, Chokyab.[149]

12) On the twelfth day, the people and/or the chief of Kyormolung[150] were donors. On the same day, the community of monks of Tshal Gungthang

made offerings for the passing away of *chenga rinpoche* Lekpa Gyaltsen, etc. etc.[151]

13) On the thirteenth day, the people of Trehor (in Kham?) made offerings to commemorate the passing away of Trehor Paljor Zangpo. Also minister Tshulgyal of Trachi made offerings, etc etc.[152]

14) On the fourteenth day, Butshalwa and Lechen Dorgyal were the donors, etc etc.[153]

15) On the last and fifteenth day, various other donors made contributions, including those from the monastery of Gyama Rinchengang. In this way, Lord Tsongkhapa and the Lord of Men, Drakpa Gyaltsen, together with the Sangha, the Lord of the Dharma of Drigung, Drakpa Gyaltsen (ie. the ruler of Tibet),[154] all the great and small communities of the Highlands and the Lowlands (*stod smad*, ie. all of Tibet?), all the prefects (*nang so*), high, middling or low, motivated by faith and great generosity, united in respectful offerings made to gods and men, each in accordance with his or her means'.[155]

There were 'tens of thousands' of the black-headed lay people gathered together, and thanks to the compassion of the 'Lord', there were none who spoke to each other with rough words, or who confronted others with violence, they were all joyful and relaxed, and unlike other such gatherings, they naturally abandoned all immodest behavior, like singing, dancing and drinking beer. They were all spontaneously gentle, coming under the influence of others, full of faith and taking pleasure in virtue. They listened to the Dharma and made prostrations, circumambulations and prayers, and recited mantras, day and night.[156]

At that time Tsongkhapa had a dream, 'a good manifestation of his own tutelary diety', a large woman who was holding the Tsuklakhang Temple in her arms. He asked what she was doing and she replied that she was protecting it against fire. Just after that, on the following evening, a large lamp had almost run out of butter and before it was refilled, bits of cotton at the bottom, all impregnated with butter, caught alight and made a huge fire. Everyone was terrified. The Lord went immediately to his room and sat in meditation on his tutelary deity. No wind arose, and with skillful means it was easy to put a stop to it. Immediately the fire died down and no harm was done at all.[157]

A general account of expenses for the Great Prayer is given as follows: 9,215 golden *sho*; 500 *sho* of silver; 37,060 loads of butter; 18,211 loads of *tsampa;* 416 *sho* of white tea; 163 *(sho)* of black *nag sig* tea; 18 *ltang* of black *buram* sugar; 2,172 carcases of dried meat; 33 large *'phen* banners(?) and victory banners; 30 brocade robes; 290 robes in fine silk, *dar yug;* 731 cotton robes; 51 rolled carpets(?); over sixty lumps of 'old turquoise', large and small; milch yak (*mdzo*), horses etc., estimated at a price of 2,073 *smar sho*; 14 *ther* of tea to offer to each Thousand District; 21 loads of white incense *spod dkar*; 3 *bla bre tsems ma* (?); and 33,270 sticks of arrow-length incense. Numerous other small items were used. For the details see the annexe to the Great Catalogue (*dkar chag chen mo*). Further descriptions of the daily offerings over the whole period of the Monlam are given in the 20th century version of Tsongkhapa's *namthar,* complied and edited by Tseten Shabdrung.[158]

At the end of the Great Prayer, Tsongkhapa had another dream in which an uncountable number of human beings from the region of Lhasa had come out and were rising into the sky. He asked them what this meant and they replied that since they had made such offerings to the Jowo they were

Procession of the Ging – acolytes of the protector deities in pursuit of the Lugong scapegoat during the Great Congregation.

Monastic musicians in their full regalia.

going to the world of Brahma. Others said: A long time ago, Songtsen Gampo hid the scroll catalogue in the 'tree leaf pillar' (in the Jokhang) and Lord Atisha, following an oral prophecy, took it out as treasure, three scrolls in all. The one by the ministers was called Dawai Öjo (*Zla ba'i 'od 'jo, 'Milking the Moonlight'*). The one by the queens was called Darkar Selwa (*Dar dkar gsal ba, Clarifiying White Silk*); and the one by the king himself was called the 'Great Testament of the Pillar' (*bKa' 'chems chen mo bka' khol ma*). This manuscript contains many prophecies on Songtsen Gampo, Rinchen Zangpo, the great translator Ngog and his nephew Legpa'i Sherab; a prophecy on the restoration and rehabilitation of Lhasa by Dvagpo Lharje, uncle and nephew. There is an ambiguous prophecy concerning "an ordained monk bodhisattva, from the east, who would 'change the face' and make sublime offerings".[159] This is often read by Gelukpas as a prophecy of Tsongkhapa's restoration of the Jokhang and the gilding and crowning of not only the Jowo, but of many statues of the temple, as seen in the above mentioned preparations for the first Monlam Chenmo. However, in 'scientific terms' this would make the text date to the 15th century, at the earliesr and there is one detail in *The Pillar Testament* that suggests identification rather with an earlier Sakyapa master, Kunga Nyingpo (1099-1158). Indeed, he would fit in much better with the other figures of the early Second Diffusion of Buddhism already mentioned in the text, and his life span is not too far away from the date 1048/1049 CE, given for the finding of the hidden text in the Jokhang.

Whatever the case may be, at the conclusion of the Great Prayer, Tsongkhapa appears as the fulcrum in a new historic, geographic, political and religious dynamic that would lead Tibet along a new path. One of his closest disciples, Gedun-drup would be recognised, retrospectively, as the 1st Dalai Lama. Like Songtsen Gampo, the unifier of Tibet, Tsongkhapa is present in both Yarlung and Lhasa, for he is hand-in-glove with the ruling dynasty in Ne'udong, and has renovated the most sacred temple of Tibetan Buddhism in Lhasa. Like the Phagmodru dynasty who renewed and reinforced the code of law, bringing peace to Tibet from one end of the plateau to the other, and pride in the ancient institutions of the Pugyel empire, so Tsongkhapa brought order and discipline into the monastic community, reasserting purity of conduct and vows, creating a new and well-structured 'non-sectarian' (*ris med*) system of education. Politically – no doubt backed by Ne'udong – he is said to have brought together, at the Monlam Chenmo, all the lay prefects, 'high, middling and low of the Highlands and Lowlands of Tibet', and religiously, he united many ofthe monastic communities (ten thousand monks were fed breakfast, lunch and tea, all through the fifteen days of the Monlam). Through his restoration of the Jokhang, the crowning of the Jowo, and through prophecies, dreams and 'pure visions', he was recognised as a true benefactor and protector of the holy site, along with Songtsen Gampo and Dvagpo Lharjey. At the same time, through prophecy, he appears to some, to be included in the lineage of the 'New Translation School', beginning with Atisha, Rinchen Zangpo, Ngog Loden Sherab, and his nephew, Ngog Legpai Sherab, pointing towards the Kadampa school. This would, at the time of Tsongkhapa, evolve into the Galdenpa or Gelukpa order. In a political sense, the Sakyapas were out of the runnning, but confrontation with the Kagyupa order was only just beginning. The centuries-old struggle for political and religious power over Tibet would culminate, two and a half centuries later, in 1642, with the foundation of the Ganden Phodrang government by the Fifth Dalai Lama, in Drepung, the largest of Tsongkhapa's great 'seats' of learning. The destiny of Tibet, until the mid-20th century, was sealed.

Early extant murals in the Chapel of the Countenance. (1993 AA)

The early Wall Paintings

Since its foundation ca. 1375 years ago, the Jokhang has grown from the original small two-storey 'palace', into a large multi-functional religious-and-political complex. It has survived factional and regional rivalry, sectarian conflict, invasion and diverse political regimes, because it is the pivot of a living religion. It has weathered expansion and restoration, as well as neglect and decay. During the time of the 'Fragmentation' of the Pugyal empire, through to the early 'Second Diffusion' (mid-9th-end 11th c.), it became the regular haunt of beggars, and this seems to have happened again before Tsongkhapa's restoration in 1408, when the images were 'so dusty their colors could no longer be seen'. But it was the Cultural Revolution (1966-1978) and its aftermath that caused the greatest damage. Ancient treasures were plundered, statues destroyed and wall paintings defaced. The temple was turned into a pigsty and slaughterhouse, and it became the site of an infamous massacre of Tibetan students.

From the end of the 1970s, several official restoration projects were undertaken in order to re-furbish the building. It appears that the temple's most intimate treasures were exposed at this time. Marxist historians had heard or read the stories of auspicious substances hidden at the time of construction, or described in early Tibetan texts. The opportunity of historical materialism was used to search in the floors and walls of the sacred temple. Rumor has it, for example, that a large rectangular pond filled with mercury was found, beneath the main entrance in the early 1980s. The precious quicksilver was syphoned out and taken away. This and other important research findings, concerning the most ancient surviving wooden temple in Tibet, have not yet been published. The author witnessed two other major phases of excavation and restoration in the 1980s and early 1990s, when the roofs were taken off, the walls entirely brought down, and the floors dug up, leaving only the timber structures in standing position.

Thus, today, apart from the wooden structure, the stone floors and some of the roofs, very little of the original fabric of the temple, and few of the treasures have survived. Yet the building itself still breathes an awe-inspiring, mysterious presence. Furthermore, rich and detailed textual sources are available. They describe the entire edifice, its legends and stories, its builders and donors, as well as the contents and the numerous roles and functions that the great temple played though history at the centre of the Tibetan world. Several of these texts have been elegantly and faithfully translated for this book, by Gyurme Dorje.

In 1982, when I visited Lhasa for the first time, the Panchen Lama had just returned after eighteen years in prison in China. He was in the Jokhang giving the *chakwang* 'hand blessing', to all those who wished to receive it, and it seemed as if the entire population of Tibet had converged on the holy city. The Barkor was thronging densely with nomads, farmers and monks, and the Jokhang palpitated with the presence of thousands of pilgrims, who had arrived from every corner of the Tibetan plateau to salute a long-lost spiritual leader.

At that time, the inner sanctum was still a fine mediaeval wooden temple, although it was said that almost all the statues had been remade. The juniper wooden steps of the main stairway and the thresholds of the early chapels were beautifully worn and polished by 1350 years of pilgrims' feet. The air was dense with the smoke of butterlamps, the murmur of prayers, and the tangible suffering of the people.

Faded murals from the Chapel of the Countenance. (1993 HMS)

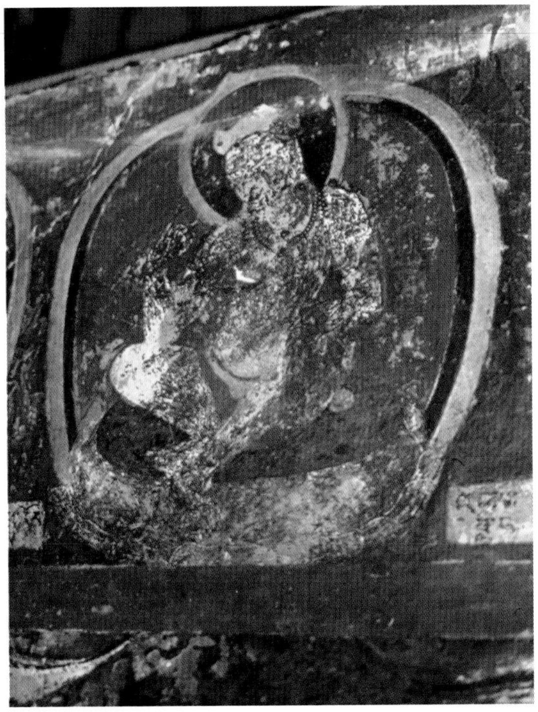

Figure of a lineage-holder. (1993 HMS)

Mandala mural in the Chapel of the Countenance. (1993 HMS)

It was dark inside and packed with human bodies, pressed tighly queuing in all directions, so although one strained, in the role of a 'scientific researcher', to catch a glimpse of the wall paintings beneath the soot – those that might have survived the holocaust – it was difficult to make out more than a few that seemed to be 'early'. Later visits revealed more panels, and soon afterwards, photos of murals dating back to the 12th or 13th centuries or even earlier were published by a group of young Chinese artists whose task it was to copy them, with a view to their future restoration. Thus in spite of the traumas of recent history, it looked as if there was some hope in the future of seeing some really fine early paintings in the temple.

Then a couple of years later, several keen observers of Tibetan art saw that meters and meters of the most ancient murals had been cut off the walls, in thick wedges, and laid on wooden frames. It was said that they were to be taken away for restoration purposes. When the monks were asked about this, they said that in any case the specialists had said that they were not 'old', since a coin had been found in a wall in a corridor, and it dated to the Ming dynasty.

In 1990, Roberto Vitali published his important book, *Early Temples of Central Tibet,* based on several years of extensive fieldwork in Tibet, and on the newly available historical texts, many of which were published for the first time in the PRC. He included one chapter on the Jokhang, discussing the historical background to the early period and the wall paintings from the Zhelray Lhakhang, the 'Temple of the Countenance', on both north and south sides.

It was after these revelations that, in early November 1991, I went with a Tibetan friend, and a Swiss researcher with a similar destination whom we happened to meet at the entrance to the Jokhang, to visit the Chapel of the Countenance. To our great disappointment, the unwalled north aspect with the earliest paintings – estimated by Vitali to be 'possibly 7th century' and so extremely important – was quite bare. A newly prepared mud surface was all that remained. It had not long ago been adorned with two fine panels showing a six-armed female diety surrounded by the smaller figures of her entourage, and a crowned Tathagata with his four bodhisattva attendants. They were undoubtedly the oldest murals in the Jokhang about which we have some visual record.[160]

The murals in the well protected south chapel were still there, however. The Jowo's old silk robes were stacked in a couple of large trunks in this small chamber and it was pitch black inside. We only had one torch. As Vitali had described, there were three panels on the eastern wall, divided by two dark wooden pillars that were engaged in the wall. Each pillar bore deeply carved parallel ridges, descending in a straight line from the top of the pillars down to midway, where they turned inwards and upwards at an angle, to form a simple hook pointing towards the central panel.[161] Vitali's photos were from the lower sections of all three panels. The rest was covered in dust.

We had two cameras and began to take photos in the dark. As usual I was particularly attracted by an inscription that was to be seen in a long band across the bottom of the central panel. With permission from the monks, I took a silk khatak from one of the chests and began gently to wipe the inscription to try and get a better reading. It was not easy. I thought it would be better to wait until the next visit when I would be better equiped and not so short of time. Then I moved slowly upwards towards the top half where the dust lay in a thick even layer. It came away easily in the perfectly dry conditions of the temple. I felt nervous and looked at my companions. With their assent, I continued very gently to wipe the dust away. The murals grew and grew, until they filled completely the three panels, from top to bottom. There were three new scenes in the top halves of each panel, and the colors were vibrant. The central one showed a portly and sumptuously dressed Vaishravana, adorned with a heavy gold crown and jewels, holding a gilt scepter and a mongoose. He was surrounded by a dense and lively gathering of his minions, or bodhisattvas of many hues, all wearing the same rich ornaments. They had long curly black hair, large Indian features and gentle expressions. Each face was set alight by beautiful wide inward-staring eyes. They looked very Indian, but it was in a style that I had never seen before. It could have been 11th century, or even earlier, perhaps 9th-10th century. A feeling of awe spread around the small group of those present. There was a sense of wonder at just being there.

The left and right panels were more damaged with pigment loss and overpainting, perhaps. Slim vertical cracks zig-zagged down, especially on the right panel. But the situation was not serious and only light restoration would be needed to reveal the full splendour of these unique paintings. There appeared to be at least two if not three different styles. The top right panel had a series of Nepalese or Indian monks dressed in simple robes, both shoulders covered, wearing pandits' hats. Each one was identified by inscription in Tibetan. The photos would reveal all, at least that is what we thought.

The long inscription at the foot of the central panel, below the elephant and a frieze of intertwined flowers was difficult to read, especially since we only had one torchlight and this was needed for taking photos. There were no windows and it was pitch dark in the chapel. The monks guarding the door, while my Tibetan friend stood quietly by. Evening was approaching and it was time to close the temple. We worked as fast as we could, thinking that in any case there was no desperate hurry since it would be possible to come back and study the whole chapel at leisure, next time.

The next morning I left for Kathmandu on my way back to Paris, and it was not until the 17th of May 1993 that I was able to return to Lhasa. I went straight to the Jokhang. A tragic scene came before my eyes. The monks said that the information about the discovery had got out to the administration in Lhasa, so they decided to send in two carpenters (sic!) to 'clean up' the paintings and fill in the cracks. They must have used some abrasive cloth or a brush to scrub down the precious murals, especially on the central panel. The pigment on the faces of Vaishravana and the bodhisattvs gathered around him had been wiped so clean, almost down to the underpaint, that the life had gone out of them. The wide eyes of the splendid young Indian princes – the bodhisattva hosts – were blind, and Vaishravana's face was all but illegible. The cracks on the right panel and the lower central panel had been so well filled in with a 'clay-based binder', that half of the delicate paintings had disappeared, together with all the inscriptions. This was in 1993, fifteen years after the end of the Cultural Revolution. What had been done was no doubt well-meaning. But it seemed even more tragic than the hysterical iconoclasm of the Red Guards.

Two weeks later (31.5.1993), I returned to the Jokhang and was invited to inspect the storage chambers on the ground floor, totally unknown to the general public. The monks knew of my enquiry of several years on the whereabouts of the early murals that had been cut off the walls in the early 1980s. There they were, all stacked up, dusty and higgeldy-piggeldy, in the long narrow chambers that formed part of the supporting structure of one

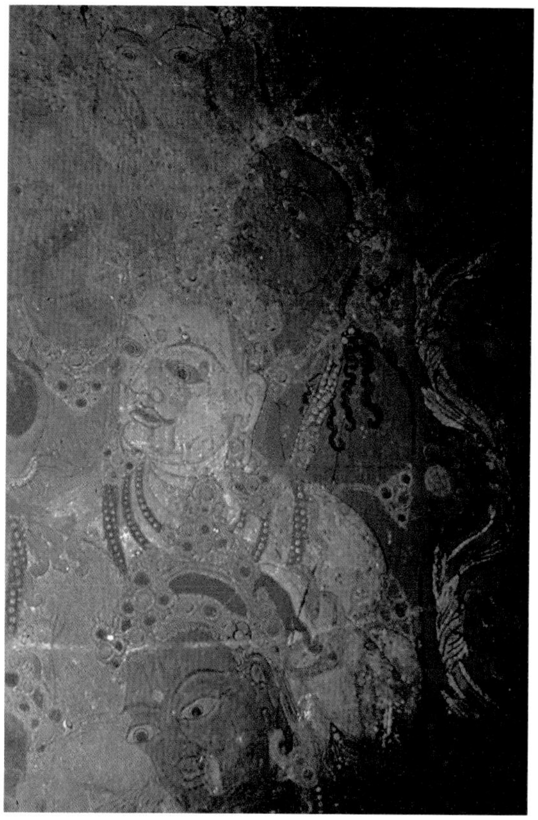

Standing bodhisattvas and decorative motifs depicted in the murals of the Chapel of the Countenance. (1993 HMS)

Fragment of the oldest surviving murals in the Great Temple today: the very Indian-inspired images in the Zhalrey Lhakhang. (1993 AA)

wing of the temple complex. There were several dozen rectangular blocks of different sizes, all about ten centimeters thick, and they were severely cracked. Amongst them could be seen the earliest murals from the north Zhalray Lhakhang, as well as others dating to the 11th and 12th century, and a later series, dating according to their style to ca. 15th century. This last group includes several large mandalas of yidam deities, including the Yamantaka cycle, painted in predominantly red, blue and yellow. It seemed then, as now, that they may well go back to the time of the restoration carried out by Tsongkhapa, in 1408, before the first Monlam Chenmo, for this yidam deity is particularly favored by the Gelukpa order.

Furthermore, at that time, there was one other mandala still hanging on the ceiling at the entrance to the main corridor that leads into the inner sanctuary. Smaller and less striking than the Yamantaka group, it was held, by the monk guardians of the Jokhang, to date back to the time of the great 'Man from Onion Land'.

It was during my next visit to the Jokhang in the following year, that the monks invited me, with evident satisfaction, to see all the panels of the early murals neatly stacked in rows in a chamber that had been specially allotted to them, on the north side of the temple. The Shalu Association gave a small donation for curtains to be put up at the windows to protect them from sunlight, and it is to be hoped that one day these extremely precious early wall paintings will be properly restored and re-hung, as was originally intended, in the Jokhang Temple.

Three key periods in the history of the Jokhang have been presented in this chapter. First of all the founding of the original Jokhang temple, ca. 636; secondly the founding of the Great Prayer Festival in 1409, and thirdly, the destruction of the images in the Jokhang during the Cultural Revolution by the Red Guards from 1966 onwards, and the fate of the early paintings.

Large sections of murals were destroyed to give access to the walls behind during the government-sponsored 'renovations' between 1990-1993. (1993 AA)

Footnotes

1 Thanks to the kind monk friend who invited me on a tour of the geomantic stones, one day in the autumn of 1996; as well as to Samten Karmay (SGK) and Tenzin Nyima (TN) for useful corrections and remarks with regard to the Tibetan texts. However, the conclusions presented here are my own, and the mistakes are mine.

2 Nyang ral Nyi ma 'od zer, Chos 'byung me tog snying po sbrang rtsi'i bcud (NNO), Lhasa 1988, 235; bKa' 'chems ka khol ma (KChK), Gansu 1989, 214.

3 *btsan po* means literally 'Mighty One' and is the term used for the emperors of the Pugyal military empire of Great Tibet and their dynasty (7th-9th c. CE). The term, 'Yarlung dynasty' that is often used in Western sources appears to have been created by European Tibetologists. It is either not found at all, or very rarely found in Tibetan texts, and would refer to the princely line before 633 CE, when Songtsen Gampo is held to have moved his 'capital' to Rasa/Lhasa.

4 A group of historians working on collective projects over the last ten to fifteen years, in Tibet and in the texts, have made good use of Nyangral, as well as the other rich early sources that have become available since the mid-1980s, in the TAR & the PRC. See notably P. Sorensen, G. Hazod and Tsering Gyalpo, in bibliography below.

5 NNO, See other recent studies based on the early accounts of the 'Supine Ogress', in relation to the founding of the Jokhang temple, see bibliography, notably, M. Aris 1979, J. Gyatso 1987, A. Miller 1998, M. Akster 1999, A. Marko 2003, M. A. MIlls 2007. Songtsen Gampo is recorded as having had five queens, one Nepalese, one Chinese, one from Zhangzhung and two Tibetan. The senior Tibetan queen Mongza Tricham, is the only one to have given him a child, see KChK 208, for one list.

6 See for example, Vostrikov, *Tibetan Historical Literature*, New Dehli, 1970, 28-32.

7 We shall indicate in the notes some key points of comparison. The recent in depth article on the 'Prone Ogress', by Mills, is based on a comparison between the *Pillar Testament*, that he appears to accept as belonging to the 11th c., and the 14th c. *Mirrior Illuminating the Royal Genealogies,* translated with detailed annotations by P. Sorenson, 1994.

8 So far, in Western sources, only A. Alexander 2009, 55, has mentioned the existence, of three of the stones, the stone lingam that points at the demoness in Chemalung to the east, one of the stupa; and the lions. He is preparing a new publication with P. Sorensen, on the temples that pin down the body of the 'supine ogress', in which he mentions these three, see site 1, Lhasa Jokhang, founded 639 CE.

9 A love story, as will be seen in the resumé given here, that is full of rivalry, jealousy, ambition and tender attention. The saga is narrated in great detail in the Tibetan texts, first between the Nepalese princess Brikhuti and the Tibetan *tsenpo* Songtsen Gampo, then the triangular drama that emerges when the Chinese princess Wencheng arrives on the scene, several years later. Only rarely are the other queens mentioned, see no. 5 *supra.*

10 *Choix de documents tibétains a la Bibliothèque national.* Corpus syllabique, (CDT) ed. Imaeda and T. Takeuchi, 1990, vol. III, Paris, PT 1287, l.0454, *Bod kyi chos kyi gzhung bzang po kun/ btsan po Khri Srong brtsan gyi ring las byung ngo//*

11 Counting from the mid-7th c., when the actual events took place through to the well-polished versions of the legend as given in the the *Bka' 'chems ka khol ma,* and the *rGyal rabs gsal ba'i me long,* dating to the 14th century.

12 See CDT vol. III, in which important Tibetan historical texts from Dunhuang are presented together with a syllabic corpus. See also www.otdo, the web site concerning Old Tibetan Documents from Dunhuang, and IDP, International Dunhuang Project, www.idp.bl.uk and www.idp.bnf.fr.

13 *dBa'bzed,* translation with commentary by Pasang Wangdu and H. Diemberger, 2000, *The Royal Narrative Concerning the Bringing of the Buddha's Doctrine to Tibet,* Wien; *Bairoi rnam thar 'dra 'bag chen mo,* 1995, Sucguan Mi rigs dpe skrun khang; *Gu ge Khyi rang pa Dznya-na-shri, Byang chub sems dpa' Lo tstsha ba Rin chen bzang poi 'khrungs rabs dka' spyad sgron ma rnam thar shel gyi phreng ba lu gu rgyud,* pp. 51-128, in *Collected Biographical Material about Lo-chen Rin-chen bzang po and his subsequent reembodiments, from dKyil Monastery,* Spiti, Dehli 1977; Nag mtsho lotsawa Tshul khrims rgyal ba, *Jo bo rje dpal ldan Mar me mdzad ye shes kyi rnam thar rgyas pa,* Varanasi 1970.

14 See above no. 12.

15 CDT vol. III, PT 1288, 1.0010, l.0014-15, *btsan po Khri Srong brtsan dgung du gshegs so/btsan mo Mun cang Kong co dang dgung lo gsum gshos so//*; PT 0750, l.0034, *dgun btsan mo Mun cang kong co'i mdad btang bar/.*

16 Demiéville 1952, *Le concile de Lhasa,* Paris, PUF, 356.

17 On the 806 CE dating of the inscription at 'Bis mdo rnam snang or Wencheng temple, see S. G. Karmay, 1998, *Arrow & Spindle,* Mandala Book Point, Katmandu, 'Inscriptions dating from the reign of btsan po Khri lDe srong btsan', 55-68, 62. See A. Heller, 1988, 'Ninth Century Buddhist Images Caeved at Gdan ma brag to commemorate Tibeto-Chinese Negociations', ed. P. Kvaerne, *Tibetan Studies,* Oslo, vol. I, 335-49; A. Heller. 1999, *Tibetan Art,* Jaca Book, 49. On the other hand, in KChK 185-6, a clear association between the gDan ma brag sculptures, Srong btsan sgam po and Wencheng is made, perhaps based on a latter day an-historic confusion?

18 The author has visited Ramoche on several occasions since 1982, including the period of extensive renovation in the early 1990s, with the express intention of finding evidence of the early structure. This is almost entirely absent. See A. Alexander 2005, 48, *yaksha* image. This judgement is made from the photo. It needs checking out, *in situ.*

19 The author is not convinced of this early dating, at least if judgement is made based on the version published inthe PRC, *bKa' 'chems ka khol ma,* Gansu 1989. This text appears to be post-Nyangral, perhaps a 13th or 14th century rewrite.

20 See bibliography.

21 Sylvain Levi, *Le Népal,* Paris, Le toit du monde, vol. I, 60. The dates given for the founding of Kathmandu, vary considerably according to the source. S. Levy, idem, 52, gives 724 CE., but confirms that Amshuvarman founded the Thakuri dynasty, and appears to have been enthroned in 625 CE.

22 CDT vol. III, PT 1288, line 0011-14, *Bal po Yu sna kug ti bkum/Na ri ba ba rgyal phor bchug//*

23 S. Levi, ibid, 280-281, who does not mention the exile, but suggests a period of serious upheaval.

24 Some sources say that she built a three-storey 'palace', others that her intention was to build one in three-storeys, but ended up only with two.

25 A. Alexander 2005, 38, 40, level 2, 13.

26 Ibid. 38-41

27 A. Alexander 2005, 47, however, from the photo, the 'Od dpag med gtso 'khor lha khang, to the left of the Jowo chapel, on the ground floor, does not seem to have the horseshoe surround.

28 A. Heller, 2005, "The Lhasa gtsug lag khang: Observations on the Ancient Wood Carvings," The Tibet Journal, vol. xxix, no. 3, pp. 3-24.

29 A. Alexander 2005, 50-53.

30 Ibid. 36, for comparative floorplans.

31 Ibid. 54-55, a C14 test done on four segments of juniper wood from the inner sanctuary, including a paw of one of the lions, comes up with a ca 7th century date for the timbers.

32 A. Alexander 205, 53, 'balustrade resting on four raised pillar, added in the 9th c.'. See G. Dorje, supra p.5, however, he notes that Shakapa (= Zhakabpa) attributes the building of the *vihara* to the period of the second Chinese princess, Jincheng (in Tibet 710-739), ie. to the reign of her spouse, Mes Agtsom (ca 712-755).

33 From the first half of the 7th through to the mid 9th century, the expanding Tibetan empire came face to face with all the great civilizations around the periphery, and adopted techniques of various kinds, architectual and artistic styles and motifs, political ideas, medical diagnoses and treatment etc., from the neighbours. In this case it is quite clear that the Indian stone architecture in Buddhist *viharas* was the direct model for the inner courtyard of the Jokhang.

34 A. Alexander 2005, 35-56; G. Dorje, supra p. 5.

35 Ibid. 38-40; 45, bottom left and right. See KChKh 144-146, Brikhuti uses bricks etc., to build Songtsen Gampo's fort on the Red Hill. The text goes on to say that an image of the fortress, or palace, is painted on the west wall of the Rasa *vihara.* Later copies are still visible today.

36 NNO 207, a "Sogpo (Sogdian?) palace of nine storeys, and a Peak Fortress for the king, of equal size, linked by (an) iron chain (bridge) with a silver and copper canopy and a thousand bells attached"; also NNO 236-237, 3a *mkar bu* (small fortess) was built in the Milk Lake, by Nepalese stone masons.

37 There are two Tibetan versions with regard to the two Jowo statues. One version holds that the images represent the Buddha aged 12, and aged 8. The second that the size of the statues were like those of boys aged 12 and 8. This second version is more coherent. Since the images – at least the Jowo in the Jokhang, shows Buddha Shakyamuni seated in lotus posture at the moment of Enlightenment, with his hand in earth-touching gesture. When Shakyamuni was 8 and 12 he was a young prince at the court of his father, in Kapilavastu, and would certainly not have been wearing the robes of a monk.

38 NNO 228. Ne'u chung is not the site just below 'Bras spung monastery of the same name, where the temple of the state oracle still stands, and which has a long history going back according to traditional historiogrpahy, to the imperial period, to the 8th-9th century.

39 NNO 228.

40 Perhaps 'Lower' Nagchu, north of Lhasa, near Namtsho Lake, or else a location in Kham, according to KChK 186.

41 GSM chapter 13; *Mirror* 240-241.

42 NNO 226-227.
43 *Mirror*, 242, n. 704.
44 P. Demiéville 1952, note 2, p. 7, paragraph 2.
45 S. B. Griffith 2005, *The Illustrated Art of War. The Definate English Translation*, chapter I, 'Estimates', pp. 97-98, paragraph 23.
46 NNO 214-215, KChK 167, he is also said to have pleased (or even seduced?) the lady who was taking care of the residence of the foreign ministers and ambassadors who had come to win the hand of the princess, in order to obtain more precise information.
47 See above no. 15.
48 T. Kerihual 2005, *Essai sur l'histoire du clan Mgar, des origines jusqu'à l'a 700*, MA thesis, INALCO, Paris.
49 Today there is an imposing tourist monument recording her passage, on the top of the Sun-Moon pass, seen at a distance by the author, in 2006.
50 NNO 227, at the same.
51 See CDT vol. III, for numerous references to the summer and winter councils of the ministers and generals, *dbyar 'dun/ dgun 'dun/ 'dun ma/*.
52 NNO 227-228.
53 NNO 227.
54 NNO 228. Note the Buddhist distribution of space E, S, W, N, according to the correct reading of a mandala, or of the world system around Mt Meru. It is tempting to see Ne'u chung as the site of the oracle temple below the monastery of 'Bras spung. However see the sketch map, it is probably further over to the east, and higher up the valley than the present Ramoche temple. Ne'u can mean a 'rich wet meadow', and it would appear to fit here.
55 S. G. Karmay (email dated 24.09.08) gives the following information on the *ju zhag*, or *ju thig* Bonpo system of divination alluded to here: 'The main text is called *Zhang zhung ju thig rgyud 'bum*, but unfortunately it seem to have been lost. There is a big volume in the *Bon Katen* collection, written by sKyang sprul Nam mkha' rgyal mtshan in the 19th century, explaining the *ju thigs* system of divination, according to the six strings are cast onto the ground or a table. The prediction is made according to the figures or patterns of the falling strings. The book has a section with drawings of the figures.'
56 See no. 55, *supra*
57 NNO 228-230.
58 KChK 197.
59 NNO 230-231.
60 NNO 230-237.
61 Note the opposite information given in KChK 205, *tshegs chen*, although ultimately the main outline of the story remains the same through both texts.
62 TN. *Gnyan*, violent, threatening, like a powerful Tantrika, or a mountain god, who can be dangerous if ruffled, but benevolent and kindly if well treated. A dog is not described as *gnyen*, but as *btsan*. Here *gnyan* is also used for the attitude of the entourage with regard to the powerful person, so in this case it is translated as 'deference'.
63 NNO 230-231. The Dunhuang annals note that Srong btsan sgam po and Wencheng 'were united for three years', appartently not long before he passed away in 649. Thus it seems that Brikhuti may have been rather successful in her strategy of preventing commerce between Wencheng and the emperor.
64 Cf. KChK 210.
65 NNO 232-233.
66 SGK suggests 'opposing force' for *dgra*, instead of 'enemy' which is the usual translation in English.
67 NNO 234. There only seem to be seven of the eight auspicious symbols here. The reading of certain passages in NNO is tentative.
68 NNO 234-235. The terms in bold correspond to the geomantic elements present in the Jokhang today, including the four principal stones, the Jowo image itself, and the goat, all mentioned one after the other in Nyangral's text.
69 TN. The *sa dgra, chu dgra* etc., refering often to natural calamities, or potentially dangerous configurations in the landscape, that would often be noted and eliminated during the construction of a monastery etc.
70 *'doms bzed pa* means 'raising her genitals in order to receive (the appropriate filling)', ie. a phallus.
71 TN. This part of the text may be read quite differently, with the 'billy goat' being a place name, rather than the goat(s) that tradition has taking part in filling up the lake.
72 Note the typically Buddhist organisation of the earth elemental opposing forces, ESWNC.
73 NNO 235, and supra p. 26, 'Songtsen Gampo's wine pot', still in the Jokhang today.
74 TN. Perhaps Ragashar, place name and family name in Lhasa valley, until 20th c.
75 KChK 213-214.
76 *gdod, da gdod* cf. *da gzod, gzhi gnas* = only from the present moment.
77 NNO 235-236. See also GSM, chap. 11, 78-84.
78 Note that in the 14th c., GSM version, Wencheng accompanies the two.
79 NNO 236-237.
80 NNO 235-246.
81 Cf. M. Aris 1979, *Bhutan: The Early History of a Himalayan Kingdom*, Warminster: M. A. Mills, 2007. 'Re-Assessing thr Supine Demoness: Royal Buddhist Geomancy in the Srong btsan sgam po Mythology', *JIATS*, no. 3, December; Ramble, C., *The Navel of the Demoness. Tibetan Buddhism and the Civil Relegion in Highland Nepal*, Oxford.
82 See in particular M. A. Mills 2007.
83 See H. Stoddard 1996, 'Nine Brothers of the White High' on the gradual demonisation process of an old woman, in the context of the founding of the Byang Mi nyag or Xixia Empire, according to Tibetan sources.
84 Unfortunately the author has not been able to return to check the free-standing stones, nor to take better photos of the ensemble.
85 Mills 2007, 17-18.
86 S. G. Karmay. 1998. *The Arrow and the Spindle. Studies in History, Myths, Rituals and Beliefs in Tibet.* Mandala Book Point, 'Amdo. One of the Three Traditional Provinces of Tibet', 523-531.
87 'Tshe tan zhabs drung 1981, ed., *'Jam mgon chos kyi rgyal po Tsong kha pa chen poi rnam thar*, mTsho sngon, 122-123. Two Tsong kha pa *rnam thar* have been used as sources here, the early one being by one of the two chief discibles, mkas grub rje (1385-1438),*rje btsun bla ma Tsong kha pa chen poi ngo mtshar rmad du byung bai rnam par thar pa dad pai 'jug ngogs*, mTsho sngon 1982. The second cited here, is prehaps by a younger contempor 'Brug rGyal dbang chos rie, ca. mid-15th c. (d. 1476?), 13th abbot of Rva lung. It was edited and published in modern format from a Lhasa xylograph by the 20th c. gelukpa scholar, Tseten Shabdrung, in 1981 (henceforth abbreviated to "Tshe tan zhabs drung 1981", however see p. 3 for the authors name). This is a much more extensive compilation, and includes significant detail on the succession of events of the 15 days of the *smon lam chen mo*, notably giving the names of the donors for each day.
88 Glenn Mullin 1996, *Tsongkhapa's Six Yogas of Naropa*, Snow Lion. Several times afterwards in his life he underwent training in this and other systems of yoga that were present in Tibet, notable the *sbyor drug*, closely linked to the *Kalacakra* teachings.
89 mKhas grub rje 1982, 18.
90 Tshe tan zhabs drung 1981, 128.
91 Ibid. 131-133; mKas grub rie 1982, 27-29. The latter contemporary source notes that he became severely ill in the upper part of the body, not long after this episode, due to the intensity of his various practices, as well as the extreme cold, and fatigue, and that it was not until he went to receive the Lam 'bras teachings in Sakya, over a period of eleven months, that an old mantrin was able to heal him completely, by reciting a special mantra.
92 Ibid. 204-205.
93 Ibid. 206, where neither these numbers, nor the length of their retreat are clearly stated. However see www.Berzinarchives.com, 'A Short Biography of Tsongkhapa'.
94 Ibid. 206. The author has a photo of the toe imprints taken during a visit there in 1988, with Robert Thurman and his group. The local monk said that the plank had been saved from another hermitage close by, also below Mt 'OIde gung rgyal. Perhaps both sites were damaged or destroyed during the Cultural Revolution, and so the plank may have been placed there recently following some reconstruction.
95 mKhas grub rje 1982, 43, 76.
96 Tib. Byang ngos; Chin. Liangzhou, modern Wuwei. This frontier region changed hands on several occasions through history, belonging alternately to Tibetans, Tanguts, Mongols, Manchus and Han & Hui Chinese. It is known to Tibetans as Byang ngos, especially as a Buddhist pilgrimage site, with its 'Four communities' (*sde bzhi*). Of these four holy sites of Tibetan Vajrayana Buddhism, three survived to some extent the destruction of the Cultural Revolution, and have been rehabilitated. The author visited there in 2006.
97 See G. Tucci, 1949, *Tibetan Painted Scrolls*, vol. II; 629.
98 Tangut. Minia, Tib. Mi nyag, Chin. Dangxiang or Xixia.
99 Tshe tan zhabs drung 1981, 303.
100 See www.chinahistoryforum.com/index.php?showtopic=23930&st=15&start=15.
101 ESTA 2008, 50.
102 Indeed, Chinese maps of Ming China show their territory as covering exclusively the agrarian zone of traditional Han Chinese civilisation.
103 According to the official Ming dynasty records, *Mingshilü*, references given in ESTA, chap. 5, 65-97.
104 The wall was joined up and rebuilt during the Ming dynasty, precisely to keep the Mongols out.
105 Bickers, Robert 1993 (ed.). *Ritual & diplomacy: The Macartney Mission to China, 1792-1794.* London, British Association for Chinese Studies. Ko'ssau Tapestry:

A poem by the Emperor reads: 'Formerly Portugal presented tribute; now England is paying homage. They have out-travelled Shu-hai and Heng-chang. My Ancestors' merit and virtue must have reached their distant shores. Though their tribute is commonplace, my heart approves sincerely. Curios and the boasted ingenuity of their devices I prize not. Though what they bring is meagre, yet, in my kindness to men from afar I make generous return, wanting to preserve my prestige and power'.

106 Today the Yongle bronzes are highly prized in China, and the world over, for their fine quality, see *ESTA* 2008, chap. 5.

107 Cf. note 103, *supra*.

108 *ESTA* 2008, chap. 5.

109 www.Berzin Archives.com, 'A short Biography of Tsongkhapa'.

110 Douglas & White 1976. *Karmapa*, part 2, on the 2nd, 3rd and 4th Karmapas and their visits to China, Mongolia and Tangutia.

111 In 1418, he moved the Ming capital from Nanjing to Beijing, the site of the former capital of the Mongol empire, Khanbalic.

112 See *ESTA* 2008, ch. 5; *Baozang. Zhongguo Xizang lishi wen wu*, Beijing 2000, vol. III, p. 148, 94-137, for numerous photos of the magnificent illustrated scroll with explanations of the scenes in five script.

113 *Portraits of the Masters, ed. Dinwiddie, Serindia* 2003, 166-169. See also *ESTA* 2008, p. 16, pl. 7; *Lost Empire of the Silk Route*, Milan, Electa, 82 & pl. 7, 120-121, for a contemporary portrait of the second holder of the Black Hat lineage, Karma Pakshi (1204-1283), from Kharakhoto, dating to ca 1256, when he was building a monastery in the Tangut Kingdom. He wears the more simple form of the crown that is still in use today, see www.kendrabodhi.com, 17th Karmapa Thinley Thaye.

114 'Tshe tan zhabs drung 1981, 303. *yon mchod zung du 'brel bai thabs mkhas kyi mdzad pai mthu' las/...*

115 *ESTA* 2008, 71-72, for an English translation of Tsongkhapa's letter declining the invitation. It is found in his *Collected Works*, and is dated 19th day of 6th month of the Rat year (1408). Thus the ambassadors must have arrived a little while before this.

116 There is an ambiguity in the reading of the Ming emissary's name.

117 mKhas grub rje 1982, 84, 'Tshe tan zhabs drung 1981, 302; *ESTA* 2008, 72. Some sources affirm that he did not receive the emissary on the first visit, only on the second, others say that he did finally accept to talk to 'Ta Shing bzhi'.

118 Tsongkhapa's message about organizing the *smon lan chen mo*, mKhas grub rje 1982, 85; Tshe tan zhabs drung 1981, 304-305.

119 *ESTA* 2008, 72.

120 See *Baozang*, vol. III, pl. 55-56, for a woven kesi portrait thangka of Byams chen chos rje, with inscriptions in Chinese and Tibetan. However, this black hat seems to disappear, while other forms of Tibetan style yellow hats came to dominate the portrait images of Tsongkhapa and his followers, from the 15th century right down to the present day, see 'Jam 158, on the original yellow hat given to Klu mes by Bla chen dGongs pa rab gsal.

121 Arniko created a cosmopolitan school of art employing people of different ethnic origin that would continue to influence the Chinese, Mongolian and Tibetan artistic traditions for many years, and even centuries to come. See Anning Jing, Artibus Asiae... It was Pakpa (1235-80), Sakya Pandita's learned nephew and successor, who had brought Arniko to the attention of Kublai Khan. Mongolia's greatest artist, Zanabazar, who was also the first Bogd Khan, is said, for example, to have been inspired by Arniko's tradition.

122 *ESTA* 98-99.

123 See Shakabpa. *A Political History of Tibet*, Potala, 1982-83, on the murder of Zingchen Drakrin, a relative of the ruling clan.

124 This title, *gong ma*, is the same used by Tibetan historians for the emperors of China.

125 The 'Bri gung pa order was very close to the Phag mo gru, being an offshoot of the original order, founded at Dan sa mthil, in 1158 by Phag mo gru rDo rje rgyal po (1110-1170).

126 See H. E. Richardson 1993, *Ceremonies of the Lhasa Year*, Serindia, 14-20.

127 See M. Kapstein 2006, *The Tibetans*, Blackwell, 116-123.

128 'Tshe tan zhabs drung 1981, 304-309; mKhas grub rje 1982, 85-86.

129 *Nyag* is a unitary measure of weight or size(?), *srang* is a measure of money.

130 Ie. the Indian master Asvaghosa, and his version of the *Jataka Stories*, the previous lives of Buddha Sakyamuni, translated into Tibetan.

131 mKhas grub rje 1982, 86-92.

132 Tshe tan zhabs drung 1981, 304-351.

133 There are different versions of this event.

134 Tshe tan zhabs drung 1981, 346-347.

135 A *dge lugs pa* monastery located in *rGya ma* Mal gro gung dkar rdzong founded in 1119 as a *bka' gdams pa* monastery, the seat of the *rGya ma* myriarchy.

136 Tshe tan zhabs drung 1981, 329.

137 TPS 28, the title of *gongma*, 'superior' or 'emeror' was adopted by Phag gru dynasty, after Grags pa rgyal mtshan's reign.

138 See Tshe tan zhabs drung 1981, 320-321, 336-337, *TPS* 26, 28. It appears from this entry and the following one on the 15th day, that Grags pa rgyal mtshan was both gong ma of Ne'udong and myriarch of 'Bri gung mthil. However, the author has not been able to verify the list of myriarchs of 'Bri gung mthil. This remains to be done.

139 Ibid. 322-323. Place names and personal names of several lay donors are not known to the author, see days 3, 4, 5, 6,7, 10, 11 & 14.

140 Ibid. 323-324.

141 Ibid. 326 *dpon* Grags pa bzang po; *TPS* 635, 73b.

142 TPS 24-26, 'Jam dbyangs *gushri* was 'grandson' or rather grand-nephew of Byang chub rgyal mtshan, who maintained strict abstenance from women, alcohol and meat during his whole life. He succeded his great uncle on the throne in 1372, and organised the final ousting of the decaying Sa skya pa regime, following the collapse of the Mongol empire. His father was bSod nams bzang po.

143 Tshe tan zhabs drung 1981, 327.

144 Tshe tan zhabs drung 1981, 329. When it is first considered that Tsongkhapa and hid disciples, not to speak of all the other donors, gave 368 *zho* of gold on the first day of sMon lam, this is a meager offering indeed. Also the fact it is the seventh day, puts Tashi Cha'u Da'o in a hierarchical position of reduced importance.

145 Nam mkha' bzang po, Grags pa rgyal mtshan's chief minister, who also took part in the restoration of the 'Dzing phyi Maitreya temple by Tsongkhapa, TPS 160.

146 Tshe tan zhabs drung 1981, 331-334.

147 Ibid. 335-336.

148 TPS 28, grags pa 'byung gnas was the son of Grags pa rgyal mtshan's younger brother, and he was made *gongma* of Ne'u sdong by *spyan snga* bSod nams rgyal mtshan, perhaps after Grags pa rgyal mtshan's passing away, thus establishing the passing of religious or political control from uncle to nephew, as in many Tibetan lineages, including the Sa skya pa.

149 Ibid. 337-338.

150 Probably what was to become the *dge lugs pa* monastery of Ga' ldan chos 'khor gling, in sTod lung bde chen rdzong.

151 Ibid. 339-341. Legs pa rgyal mtshan was perhaps the head lama of Tshal Gung thang(?).

152 Ibid. 341-343, Tre hor.

153 Ibid. 343-344.

154 There do not appear to be two leading figures with the name of Grags pa rgyal mtshan, one in sNe'u sdong and the other in 'Bri gung mthil, as this paragraph suggests, but rather one and the same person, who originated from 'Bri gung (?), see above, notes 126 and 139.

155 Tshe tan zhabs drung 345-350; 347.

156 Ibid. 315-316. mKhas grub rje 1982, 92.

157 mKhas grub rje 1982, 92.

158 Tshe tan zhabs drung 1981, 309-348.

159 KChK 287, cf. NNO 261. In KChK the direction given for the birth of the master is 'south', where as it is 'south-east' in the earlier NNO. The last part of the monks name, snying po, given in KChK, is ansent from the earlier NNO. This might be due to different sources for the two texts or to an evolution, a creative or dynamic use of prophecy, either intentional or unintentional, in the terms of an ancient written text. Recently the author witnessed a re-interpretation or re-actualisation of an ambiguous Guru Rimpoche prophecy, by a distinguished person in Tibet, who thus was deliberately re-enacting the words, allowing them to fulfil present day expectations, hopes and fears.

160 Perhaps three like the southern chamber, but photos of only two panels have survived.

161 Later on, the author discovered examples of this motif in ancient Nepalese temples.

Celebration of the Monlam festival on the first full moon of the Tibetan New Year 1992.

Part 4

The Lhasa Jokhang

An Indian Vihāra in Tibet

André Alexander

Monlam 1992 was a very subdued affair. Only once since 1959 was the celebration of Monlam Chenmo allowed in Lhasa, in 1986/87 under the auspices of the Panchen Lama.

Site introduction

'The Jokhang became the symbol of Tibetan culture in its role as a gallery of Tibetan Buddhism that transcended sectarian divisions. It had, therefore, taken on the character of an anomalous royal temple; when the long royal period came to an end, the care imparted by the kings was continued by the leading religious masters and the spiritual lineages which succeeded one another in controlling the country. In this respect, the Jokhang constitutes a peculiar dynastic temple, where the dynastic role from the time of [the later diffusion of Buddhism] onwards was exercised not by a succession of ruling kings, but by lineages of religious masters, who celebrated their spiritual and temporal impact by taking charge of the Jokhang. Though considered a plague by Western art historians, the successive renovations are the essence of the temple. The history of the Jokhang is imbued in them, and as such so is the history of Tibet itself.'

Roberto Vitali [1]

The list of historic dignitaries responsible for restoration of the Lhasa Jokhang reads indeed like a roll-call of Tibetan history. Therefore, the following description can by no means offer a complete discussion of the temple's history and significance.

For the Tibet Heritage Fund's Lhasa Old City Conservation Project (see www.tibetheritagefund.org), detailed surveys of the Jokhang temple were conducted, led by the present author. In order to present and discuss the findings made during these surveys, the major construction phases are briefly summarized. It is hoped that the comparative analysis of the building plan and details help us appreciate the larger architectural idiom which the Jokhang represents, contributing to our understanding of the early development of Tibetan monastic architecture. The findings confirm much of what Tibetan source texts tell us about the genesis.

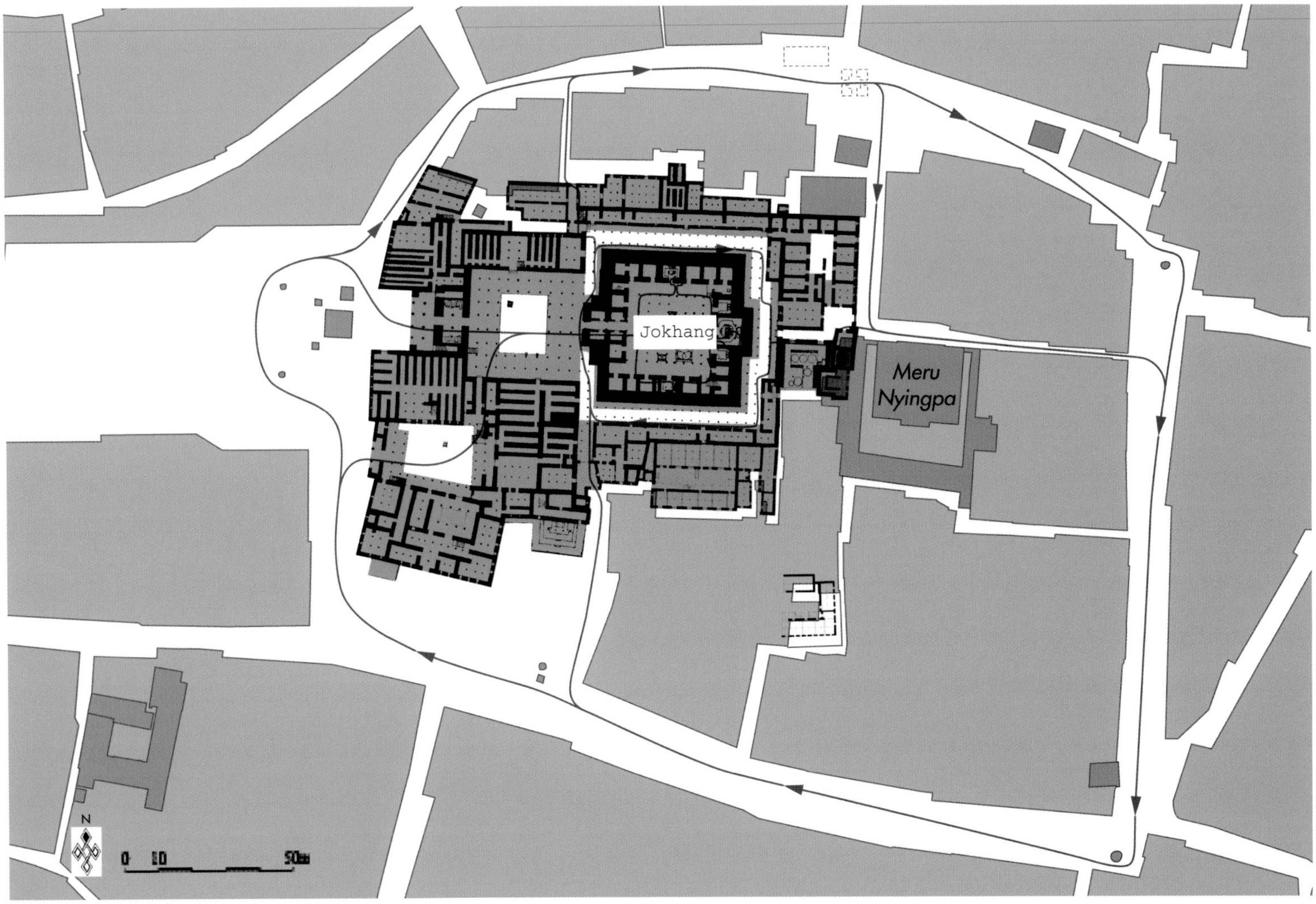

Before 1959, the Great Temple could be entered and departed freely through any of the four cardinal doors. This made it possible to combine daily circumambulation with a short-cut to the way home for the people of Lhasa.

Site description

The Lhasa Jokhang is known to many Tibetans as the Lhasa Jokhang (the Lhasa cathedral). Jokhang ('house of the Jowo') is originally a generic Tibetan term referring to a chapel with a "precious" image, i.e. usually an image of the historic Buddha Śākyamuni.[2] In Western literature about Tibet, the name Jokhang has become synonymous with the Lhasa Jokhang.

The temple gave the city its name – in Tibetan traditional accounts, Lhasa ('place of the gods') explicitly refers to the temple itself. Even in recent times, for local Tibetans, the geographic term Lhasa referred only to the immediate surroundings of the Jokhang, excluding Ramoché, other residential quarters and the Potala Palace area. The Jokhang has been a religious centre for many centuries, and its presence has shaped the urban development of Lhasa city. Processional routes lead clockwise around the temple like concentric circles. These include the Barkor, the outer Barkor and the Lingkor. Eight ancient protector chapels were positioned in the alleyways surrounding the Jokhang at the cardinal and intermediate directions. The present square to the west of the shrine was created only in 1985, and formerly the now somewhat neglected Sung-chöra square to the south was used for large assemblies and public gatherings.

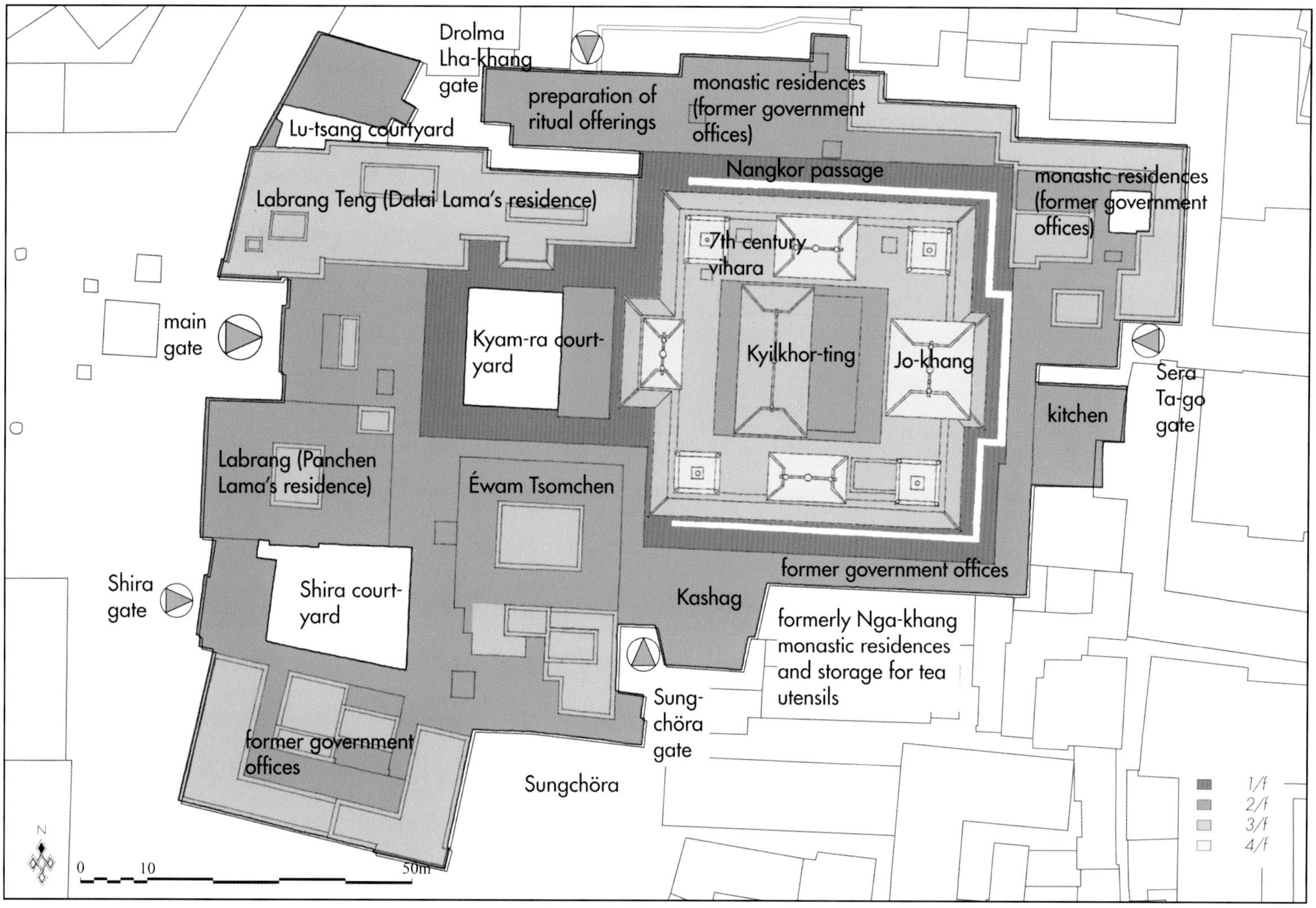

The Great Temple and its component spaces in 2000, before the demolition of the Nga-khang building (south-east corner).

The Jokhang itself is a sprawling complex of chapels, courtyards and residential and service buildings. The temple's gilded canopy roofs have historically constituted the height limit within the central city area.[3]

The central building within the complex, measuring 44.5 meters square, is considered the original 7th century foundation. Many Lhasa people refer to this building when they talk about the Jokhang.[4]

This temple is separated from the surrounding structures by a processional corridor, today known as the Nangkor. The surrounding structures include courtyards, residences of the Dalai and Panchen Lama-s, service wings, monks' dormitories, kitchens, storage rooms and government offices, including the meeting room of the Tibetan cabinet (Ka-shag), which have been added over the centuries. Four doors in the four directions enabled visitors to enter and perform parikrama (devotional circumambulation) around the Nangkor corridor.

A series of wall-paintings with Tibetan inscriptions in the Norbulingka's Takten Migyur Po-trang, 1956, illustrating the founding of the Lhasa Tsuklakhang (1994 AA).

1 'Tri-tsun's [Brikuti] maid delivered the message [concerning Wen-cheng's geomantic instructions] confusedly. [Brikuti tried] to fill up the lake [of O-tang] and failed wherefore she thought that this was due to the wicked instructions of the Chinese Princess [and so she] consulted with the King [Songtsen Gampo]. The King responded: 'I have a source where we can seek advice'. He made prayers to his tutelary deity. [Then] from the heart [of the statue] a ray of light emanated that was absorbed into the lake, and [the King] realized the necessity of building the temple upon the filled-in lake. The next morning the King and the Queen both went to the grassland by the side of the lake. 'Tri-tsun throw your ring into the sky. Where it falls down onto the plain there the temple shall be built', [the King] said.'

Illustrations of the founding narrative of the Jokhang, taken in the Jokhang (1), Norbulinka (2, 3) and in the Potala (4).

2. 'The King made prayers to the stupa of bright light [that miraculously appeared] in the center of the lake. Accompanied by the sound of the six-syllable prayer [Om Mani Padme Hum] uttered by the ministers, stones were deposited into the lake. In the center of the lake a square stupa out of stone raised itself, miraculously self-manifest. The entire length of [the stupa] [was spanned] by 16 very broad tree trunks [by implication shug pa wood]. At their root ends they rested firmly on huge boulder stones at the edges [of the lake]. At their top ends they rested firmly on the self-manifest stupa in the centre of the lake. Thereupon the trunks of la-ba wood [were placed so that] a chequerboard pattern was formed. From a manifestation of a Naga spirit adamantine clay was received with [which] the wood was impregnated in its entirety. Until the end of the present age [it] will not rot. And fire cannot destroy [it]. There on top bricks were laid [which] were then fastened with molten bronze, and then the lake was [finally] filled up.

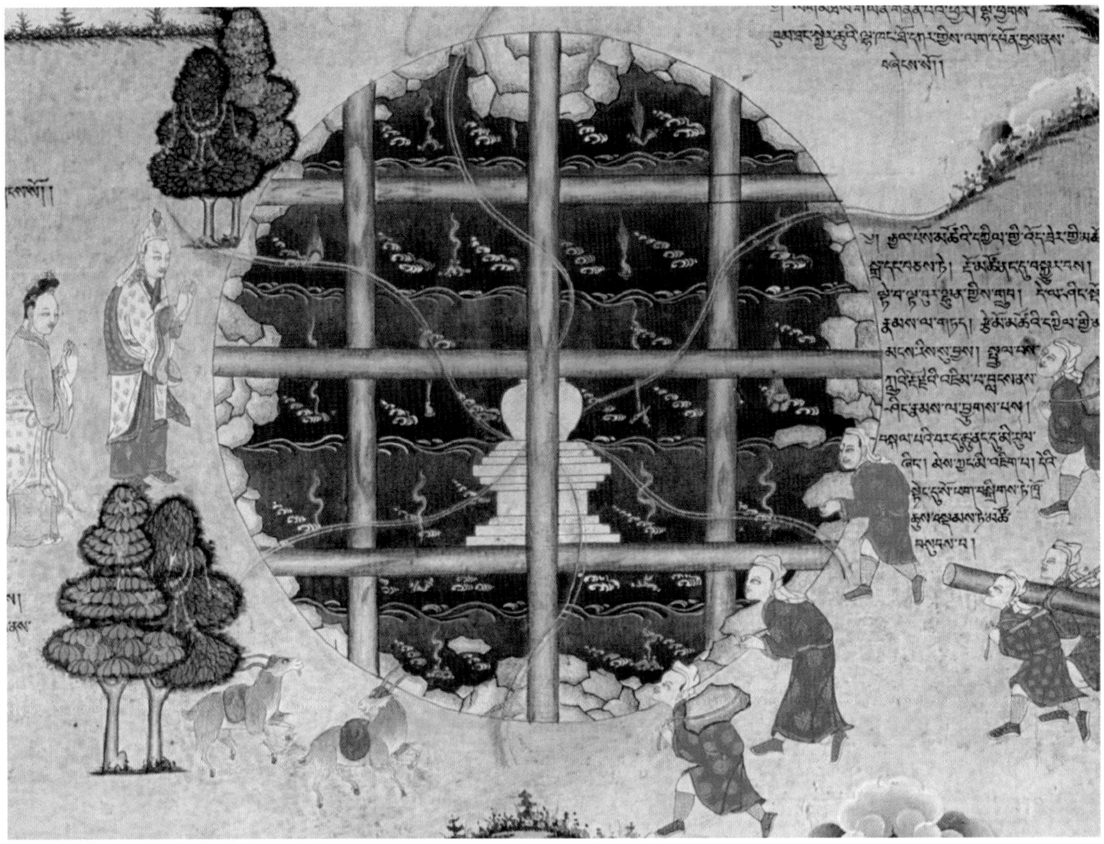

3 'Thereafter [the King] concluded that there was no hindrance left for the construction of the temple. He blessed the site and drew the lines for the foundations [on it]. The King miraculously generated 108 emanations from his body. They guarded the door [to the temple]. Inside 108 carpenter emanations [created by the king] secretly did the carpentry work. Later the Nepali [Queen] went to call for some provisions. The servant [of the Queen] [opened] the door a crack wide and so saw all the emanations. She was laughing 'he-he'. The King was distracted whereby accidentally all those [emanational carpenters] cut off the noses from a hundred of the lions [they were just making]. The King's emanations completed the work. Since [the temple] was made in the shape of a four-doored mandala the [Buddhist] lamas rejoiced. Since the pillars were made in the shape of a ritual dagger *[phur ba]* the Tantric adepts rejoiced. Since the four corners [of the foundation] were arranged in the shape of a swastika, the followers of Bön rejoiced. Since the [basic room arrangement] was in chequerboard pattern, the Tibetan population rejoiced. The entrance to this Miraculous Temple of Fourfold Happiness *(dga' bzhi 'phrul kyi lha khang)* faced west in the direction of Nepal.'

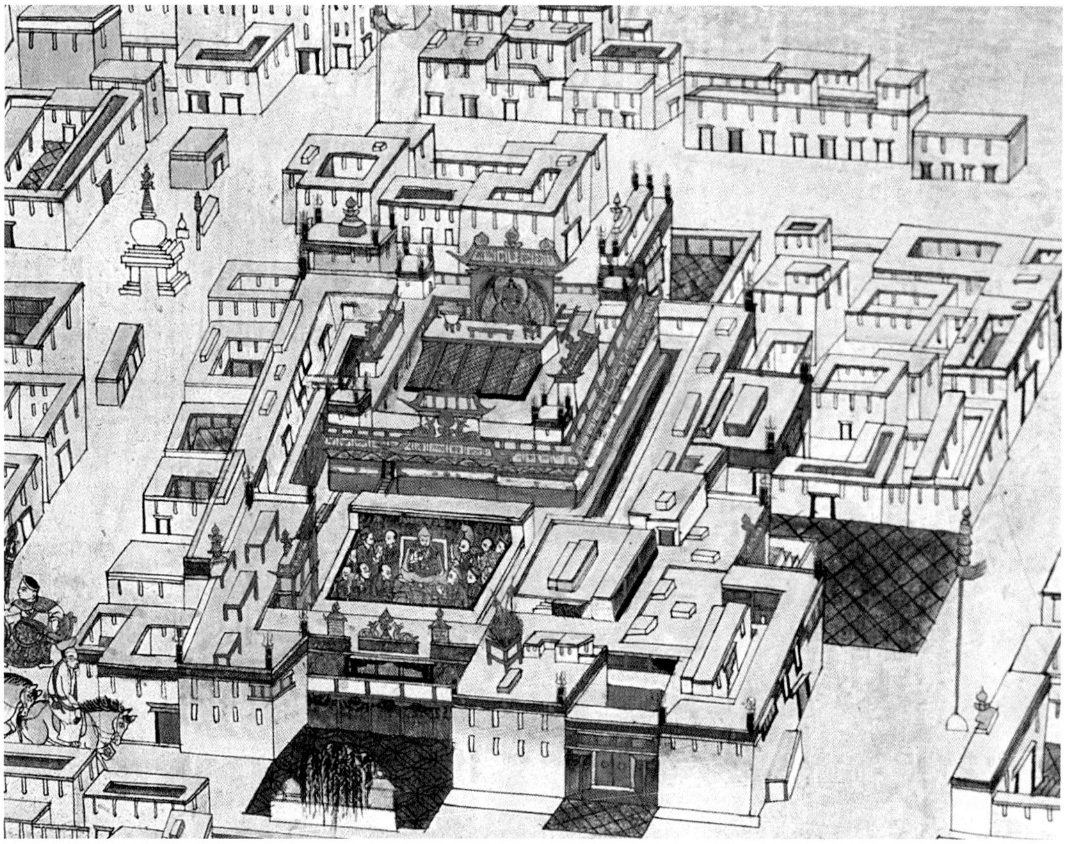

4 The completed Lhasa Tsuklakhang, of the 1950s rather than 7th century, centre left the Nga-khang complex with red penbey frieze.

Note: the Tibetan inscriptions accompanying these pictures are a condensed rendering of the story as it is told in the texts rGyal rabs gsal ba'i me long and bKa' chems ka khol ma. Prof. Sørensen (whom I thank for critical advice on my translation of these three inscriptions) has pointed out that this founding legend closely resembles the origin of the Svayambhucaitya in Nepal (Sørensen forthcoming). In the case of the Lhasa Tsuklakhang, this was certainly built on marshy wetlands if not a lake. Much of the surroundings of the city remained marshland until the early 1990s, and a large remaining tract to the north of the Potala Palace has recently been declared a nature preserve. When THF installed new water supply lines in the Barkor area in the late 1990s, we found that the level of ground-water was unusually high, especially in the north-eastern Barkor area. Tibetans maintain that until 1959, the subterranean O-tang lake could still be accessed from a secret (no longer existing) door in the Tsuklakhang. The inscription also mentions the swastika form inherent in the groundplan and the arrangement of the rooms according to a squaregrid, both common features in early Indian temple architecture.

Sungchöra Square was for centuries Lhasa's principal public square, used for religious and lay ceremonies, including public performances of Tibetan Opera. During the Monlam festival in the first Tibetan month it was used for public teachings attended by thousands.
(1940s, courtesy Hugh Richardson)

Site history

Tibetan historical sources unanimously attribute the Jokhang to emperor Songtsen Gampo (d. ca. 649). It is often said to have been built in the Pig Year 639.[5] The impetus for the construction came from his first wife, the Nepali princess Bhrikuti. She had brought Buddha images with her from Nepal, and Newar artisans accompanying her had completed a royal residence at Marpori. Songtsen Gampo personally collected more religious images and took part in the construction of one of Tibet's first Buddhist temples.[6]

It was originally called the Ra-sa Trulnang ('Miraculously self-apparent temple of Rasa'), Rasa being the original name for Lhasa.[7] The craftsmen are generally described as Nepali in the sources (bal bo'i lha bzo),[8] and Vitali has convincingly shown that Lhasa provided asylum for the exiled Licchavi court at that time.[9] According to Tibetan beliefs, Songtsen Gampo himself built most of the ground floor structures, while a Tibetan workforce assisted by Nepali artisans built the second floor.[10]

In later histories the Chinese wife Wen-cheng is credited with having provided geomantic planning for the temple, but since she only arrived in Lhasa in 641 (when the Newar royalty are believed to have departed), it would appear that she was not involved the architectural design of the temple. As we shall see below, the architectural model for the original Jokhang is without doubt Indian.

Over the following two centuries, several of Songtsen Gampo's successors celebrated the founding of the Jokhang as instrumental to the introduction of Buddhism to Tibet, and used it to legitimize their religious policies.

This is known from surviving royal edicts and contemporary inscriptions on stone steles (known in Tibet as *do-ring*, 'long stones'). One of them, the 9th century Kar-chung inscription, reads:

'*In the time of the miraculously divine Tsenpo* [*title of the emperor*], *the ancestor Tri Songtsen* [*Gampo*], *in practising the religion of the Buddha, shrines of the Three Jewels* [*i.e. Buddhism*] *were established by building the Jokhang of Ra-sa and so on...*'[11]

Sungchöra square during the anti-Lin-Biao campaign, early 1970s (photographer unknown).

A brief suppression of Buddhism preceding the collapse of the Yarlung empire in the mid-9th century was followed more than a century later by the Tenpa Chidar, or 'later diffusion of Buddhism' in Tibet. Significantly, one of the important protagonists of Tenpa Chidar, the Bengali Buddhist master commonly known as Jowo-jé Atisha, visited the Lhasa Jokhang and discovered Songtsen Gampo's testament underneath one of the old wooden pillars on the ground floor.[12]

Subsequently, the restoration of the Jokhang became an important *leitmotif* in the history of Tibet. Influential Buddhist teachers and local rulers established their credentials partly by their restoration activities.

New rulers, especially since the settling of regional and sectarian rivalries in favour of Lhasa, regularly began their rule with a restoration of the Jokhang and a handful of other significant monasteries.

Since the 18th century, offices of the Tibetan government were established within the growing Jokhang complex. Following the death of Tibet's last Mongolian ruler, Lhazang Khan, the Tibetan council of lay ministers convened in the Labrang-teng rooms. When the government was reformed in the mid-18th century under the suzerain Qing dynasty, the offices of the cabinet known as Ka-shag were reestablished above the southern gate of the temple.[13]

Fortunately for the art historian, while the Jokhang grew and absorbed new functions, the lower two floors of the Trlnang temple retained much of their early shape and detailing.

The main building phases can be discerned as follows:[14]

7th century (ca. 639): foundation, building of a two-storied, square *vihara*.

9th century: Repachen (r. 815-36) adds balustrade and four tall 'sky-bearing' pillars. Temple is vandalized during Langdarma's persecution of Buddhism.

For the Tibetan New Year celebrations, the Tsuklakhang entrance is regularly decorated with colourful flags and appliqués. In 1994 the Tibetan national flag was hoisted here. People queued to present white khata scarves. (1994 AA)

11th century (last quarter): modification of the central chapel by Zangskar Lotsawa, creation of Shey-ré Lha-khang.

12th century (third quarter): temple falls into disrepair because of sectarian strife, restoration after 1160, and Drolma Lha-khang added.

13th-14th century (last half 13th to last quarter 14th): further modification of the Jowo chapel and the upper floors, the Nepali artist Arniko builds throne for the Jowo image. Creation of the Chö-gyel and Pel-lha Chok chapels. Creation and decoration of Nangkor (at that time called Barkor) by Tri-pön Mönlam Dorjé and his successor, Kunga Dorjé. Two canopy roofs are placed above the northern and central chapels (RTF bookmark start:) (*gtsang khang byang ma, gtsang khang dbus ma).*

Part of the central courtyard is roofed with the addition of 12 'sky-bearing' pillars. These works were completed by the time Jé Tsongka-pa arrived in Lhasa at the end of the 14th century. Tsongka-pa established the first teaching throne on Sung-chöra square (which assumed its modern proportions under the Seventh Dalai Lama).

17th century: the Ganden Po-trang government extends the courtyard soon after 1642 (with pillars carried off from the sack of Tashi Zilnon monastery in Shiga-tsé Zilnon), and adds two more canopy roofs. Building of Labrang Teng. Chapels established around the Nangkor.

18th century: restoration after the Dzungar raid (1718-1721); subsequently the Tibetan government moves into the Jokhang. Government offices established on four different sides of the temple: judiciary – north, finance department – east, Kashag cabinet, agricultural department and finance department – south, finance department – west. Under the Seventh Dalai Lama, the Jokhang is extended to its present size; no more extensions or major changes until the events of 1959 and demolition of the Nga-khang in 2002.

In 1961 the Jokhang was listed as a Nationally-Protected Monument by China's State Council. It was desecrated and ransacked in 1966, occupied by armed Red Guard factions, and the by the Chinese army (PLA), who used the temple as a pigsty (see appended translation of Rimbur Rinpoché's account). An initial restoration took place in 1972, when the main building was cleaned and paintings were restored by some of the last surviving master painters.[15]

Full rehabilitation and further restoration took place after 1978 and continued until the early 1990s. During this period, most of the oldest wall-paintings that had survived the Cultural Revolution, dating to the 10th-13th centuries, were removed. Most suffered irreparable damage. The quality of subsequent restorations improved dramatically, traditional techniques and methods were used, and historic paintings in other sections have been retained (for example, the 1920s murals in the Nangkor corridor were recently cleaned). In 2000, the Jokhang was listed under the name 'Jokhang Temple Monastery' by the UNESCO as a World Heritage Site, as an extension of the 1994 listing for the Potala Palace.[16]

In 2002, the Nga-khang wing of the Jokhang (formerly used to store ritual utensils) was demolished by the Lhasa Construction Department and the site built up with private residential housing.

The entrance to the Tsuklakhang's main building. The gate known as Sengden Gomo was added in the 14th century. Over the stone-paved passage hangs a wooden canopy of unknown date, covered with finely carved and gilded flowers (1993 AA).

Site survey, Jokhang

Ground level, plan

The historic core of the Jokhang is laid out to a square plan. The entrance faces west. The centre of the square is a courtyard space, originally open, known as Kyil-khor-ting (*dkyil 'khor sdings* or *dkyil 'khor mthil*). This is lined by seven rooms or niches on each side (except on the entrance side: six rooms and the entrance space). Roofed passages in front of the chapels are supported by rows of eight wooden pillars. The lay-out of the corner rooms is varied so that the arrangement takes on the shape of a swastika (see map section).

The three rooms at cardinal points are the largest, and according to tradition, the principal original chapels, decorated with intricately-carved wooden doorframes. Two minor chapels with carved doorframes flanking the central chapel also belong to the earliest temple. The other rooms have much plainer doorframes and were turned into chapels much later on. We have no sources of information for their early usage, but according to established practice in Indian *vihara* design, we can presume that these rooms were originally intended as monastic cells and resting places for pilgrims. Our survey in 2000 discovered that the building has a double skin, a second wall layer which so far we have been unable to date.[17]

It is not original, as completed outward-facing wooden window and doorframes in the inner wall can be discerned, which have been made obsolete by the outer wall. It is likely that the outer wall encasing the original building was built at a later time to provide structural support. This is reminiscent of the common Tibetan architectural practice of erecting external support walls for structurally weakened historic buildings, examples of which can be found at U-ru Ka-tsel and Ön Ké-ru.[18]

The second wall layer was certainly the most mysterious of our findings. According to the sources, the outward-protruding extension (*glo 'bur*) of the Jowo chapel at the eastern side was built by Zangskar Lotsawa in the 11th century. If we look at comparable ground plans of Indian vihara buildings of the same period, we find already similar examples of sanctum chapels protruding beyond the basic square on which the plans are generally based. Therefore the degree of modifcation by Zangskar Lotsawa to the Jowo chapel cannot be ascertained. The Tsel-pa rulers Mönlam Dorjé and Kunga Dorjë added the outward-protruding extension of the entrance area.[19]

They sponsored a major restoration in the 14th century, which was continued by the rulers of Ne'u-dong on behalf of Tsongka-pa. During that time, a skylight was added over the eastern part of the Kyil-khor-ting courtyard, supported by 12 raised pillars.

The Jokhang's plan is identical to the early Indian Buddhist monastery type known as *vihara*. Contemporary *vihara* buildings across the sphere of Indian civilization are similar to the Lhasa Jokhang in scale, room arrangement and architectural detailing. The important early post-imperial sources all confirm this information, stating unanimously that the Rasa Jokhang is based on an Indian *vihara* (in Tibetan rendered variously as *bi har, bi ha ra* and *dpe dkar*). Songtsen Gampo's alleged testament states that it was built modelled on the 'best contemporary Indian temple'.[20]

The earliest known vihara structures belong to the Gandhara civilization and can be dated to the 1st and 2nd centuries AD, the monasteries Jaulian 2 and y (see illustration in map section). The Lhasa Jokhang plan is also comparable to monastery 1a of Nalanda, currently dated by the Archaeological Survey of India to the 6th century, and an as yet undated temple in the vicinity of the Sanchi *stupa*. Only foundations of these sites still exist. They were built with burnt bricks and interior timber frame, and excavated fragments tell of their detailing. Well-preserved are the central Indian cave monasteries of Ajanta, Ellora and Aurangabad, *viharas* carved out of stone in a style imitating brick and timber architecture.[21]

Some of their ground plans closely match the Jokhang, for example Ajanta 1 (6th century), and here we also find closely corresponding colonadization and arrangement of images.

We can conclude that the Jokhang's building plan followed an established pattern that was used by Indian civilizations for over six centuries as a blueprint for constructing *vihara* temples. In Lhasa, this blueprint was closely followed by Nepali artisans with no apparent local modifications.

Early vihara buildings
The arrangement of chapels in these monasteries (except Ajanta) gives the access corridor the form of a clockwise-turning swastika.
This feature is sometimes described in Tibetan sources as linked to the Bön religion, but the comparison shows that it is in fact a feature of *vihara* architecture whose origin must be searched for in India.

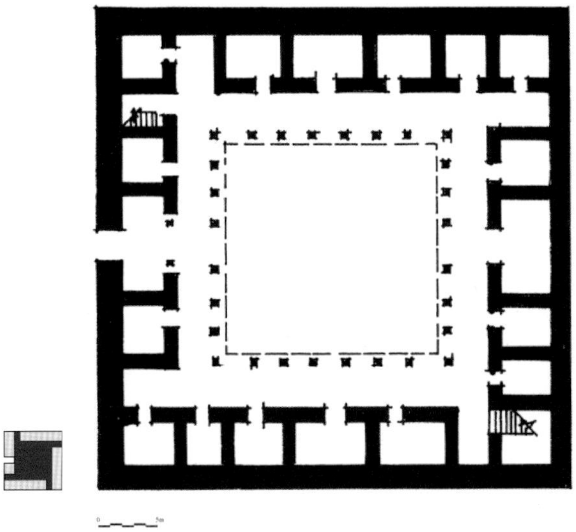

Lhasa Trül-nang, 7th century (CRB).

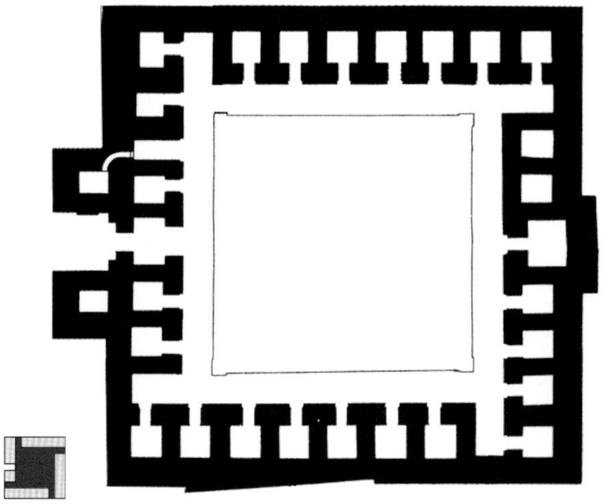

Jaulian (Gandhara civilization), monastery 2, 1st century (ASI).

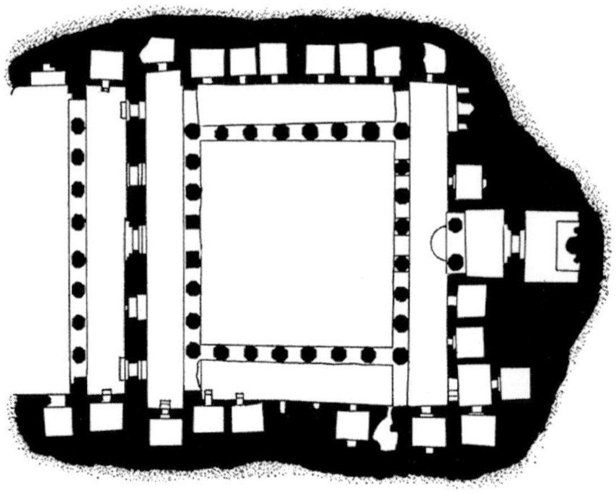

Ajanta, cave 4, second half of 5th century (ASI).

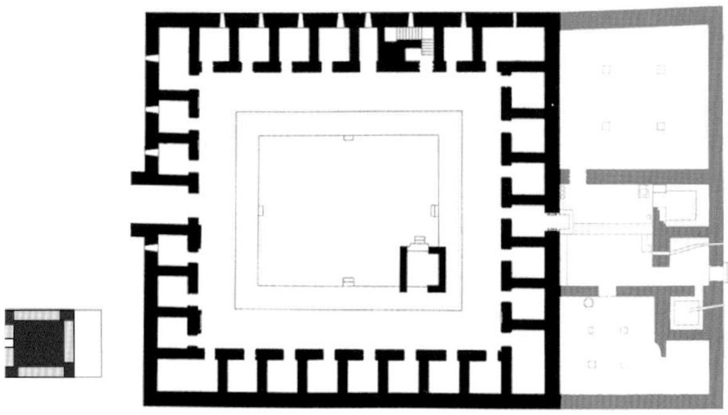

Nalanda, monastery 1a, 6th century (ASI).

Top Left: Jowo Rinpoché (2004 JM).

Top Right: Tsangkhang Ü-ma, the chapel housing the Jowo image on a throne created by the famed Newar artist Arniko, (1244-1306). The wooden door frame is one of nine very early frames preserved in the Tsuklakhang, all based on Indian designs (1995 AA).

Left: The bodhisattva images installed by Zanskar Lotsawa in the 11th century in the Jowo chapel, lining the innermost circumambulation passage (1995 AA).

Above: Modern two-storey tall image of Guru Rinpoché (1992 AA).

Second level

Tibetan historical sources agree that a second floor was part of the Jokhang's original design.[22]

This is compatible with the vihara design; among the Ajanta and Ellora complexes, two- and even three-storied *vihara-s* have survived (Ajanta 6, late 5th century; Ellora 11 and 12, 8th century). The Jokhang's second floor was modified during the 11th and 13th century restorations, when more chapels were added. The designs of four historic doorframes, two flanking the Jowo chapel area and two on the southern and northern sides, appear contemporary with the original ground floor chapels. The Chögyel chapel above the entrance was added in the 14th century.[23] The famous silver image of the king has been lost, but an ancient silver jug is still preserved.[24]

The murals showing a series of mandala-s were painted during the 1972 restoration. Behind this chapel is an inaccessible two-pillar room filled with precious objects as an auspicious offering.

Over the entrance area of the Jowo chapel is an extended wooden balustrade, rich in detail. This structure is again entirely traceable to Indian origins.

On the northern section of this floor the second 'skin', an outer wall enclosing the building, is most clearly discernible. Windows and doorways of the inner wall are matched by the outer one, and a narrow gap between the two walls is visible (on the floor below, the gap is partly filled with rubble).

Several sections of the second floor, including the south-eastern chapel with ancient doorframe, were completely rebuilt in 1993 (see accompanying illustrations). The only area on this floor that has retained historic painting fragments is a room directly to the south of the Jowo chapel, identified by Vitali as the remains of the 11th century Shey-ré Lha-khang.[25]

Today, this area is in disarray. Large pieces of plywood have been used to seal the open area above the Jowo chapel. Plywood hardly seems an adequate material in this context. Fragmented historic beams indicate that the area has undergone some recent changes that have resulted in the removal of historic fabric. Fragments of an ancient wooden Torana (see photo section) partly covered by bookshelves add to the mystery. We do not fully understand the pre-1959 lay-out of this area, and even if one were to remove the bookshelves and plywood walls, it would be very difficult to find out.

Third level

Most of the rooms on this level were added in the 17th century. They suffered considerable damage during the 1960s, and underwent a very lengthy and slow restoration during the 1990s. The most interesting room on the third floor, containing fragments of historic art, is the hall directly over the Jowo chapel *(Jo bo'i dbu'i thog lha khang)*. Until 1967 this room housed the original eight Bodhisattva retinue statues and two door protectors from the Jowo chapel, moved here during Zangskar Lotsawa's 11th century restoration.[26]

From an opening in the centre of this room it is possible to look directly onto the roof over the Jowo's throne. On the walls, especially on the western wall, are fragments of wall-paintings. These have been overpainted and the cleaning was only partly successful. Water damage may have added to the problem. The fragments show unidentified protector deities.

The important Pel-lha Chok chapel dating to the 14th century is located between the second and third levels, and it is connected to an important 9-pillar assembly room leading to the roof. This assembly room, the Pel-chok Dukhang, has a two-winged gate ornamented with gilded brass sheets in the Newar fashion.[27]

On the second floor level above the entrance is the 14th century Chögyel chapel dedicated to Songtsen Gampo, with a new image of the king and his two principal consorts. On the back wall are mandalas painted during the 1972 restoration by some of Lhasa's last remaining master painters at the time. (1992 AA)

Detail of the gap between the two walls, wooden window frames with pema-chudzö carvings are discernible. (2000 AA)

The gilded canopy roof over the Jowo chapel, first added in the 13th century and restored in the 17th, is flanked by two chapels with flat roofs and penbey frieze. The gilded canopy roofs over the northern and southern main chapels can be seen in the back. The entire *vihara* building has a white plaster frieze, decorated with gilded medallions; the cornice consists of a gilded canopy-style balustrade. (View from east, 2000 AA)

The important Pel-lha Chok chapel is situated between the second and third roof levels, seen through the gilded doors of the Pel-lha Du-khang. (1995 AA)

Fourth level

The four chapels on this floor are open usually in the early morning; three protector chapels (*gön-khang*) and one 16-arhat chapel. They have been extensively restored in the 1980s and 90s. The gilded canopy roofs are said to have survived the Cultural Revolution. In 1990, the government added a canopy roof of good workmanship over the hitherto open western section of the Kyil-khor-ting. Before that, only the traditional thick curtains made from woven yak-hair were used to cover the assembly space in the case of rain or cold at night. The *melong* gilded brass decorations on the *penbey* frieze of the top floor and of the four roof chapels were taken from the several plane-loads of Tibetan metal images shipped to Beijing to be melted down but returned in the 1980s. Their origin could no longer be ascertained, and many of these art works were simply divided between the major surviving monasteries.

Plan, level 1

(all: JH, EK, BU, AA, MA)

1 Sengden Gomang door
2 two raksha chapels (Kubera Lha-khang and Mahakala Lha-khang, both closed)
3 two naga chapels
4 closed stairway
5 Tsangkhang Jangma, northern principal chapel, aka. Tukjé Chenpo Lha-khang
6 Jampa Tru-dze chapel
7 Öpa-mé Tsokhor Lha-khang
8 Tsangkhang Ü-ma, aka. Jowo Shakyamuni chapel
9 Jampa Chökhor Lha-khang
10 access to upper floors
11 Yungdrung-puk
12 Tsangkhang Lhoma, aka. Jampa Cheshi Tsokhor Lha-khang with Rama Gyelmo image
13 space where Jowo image was purportedly hidden in the 8th century
14 Kyilkhor-ting area (roofed courtyard)
15 Guru Rinpoché image
16 Gashi-wa's Tukjé Chenpo image
17 Barshi-wa's Jampa, now replaced by Jam-khang Jampa 1
18 Pola Miwang's Jampa
19 Jampa originally donated by Lhazang Khan (now replaced)

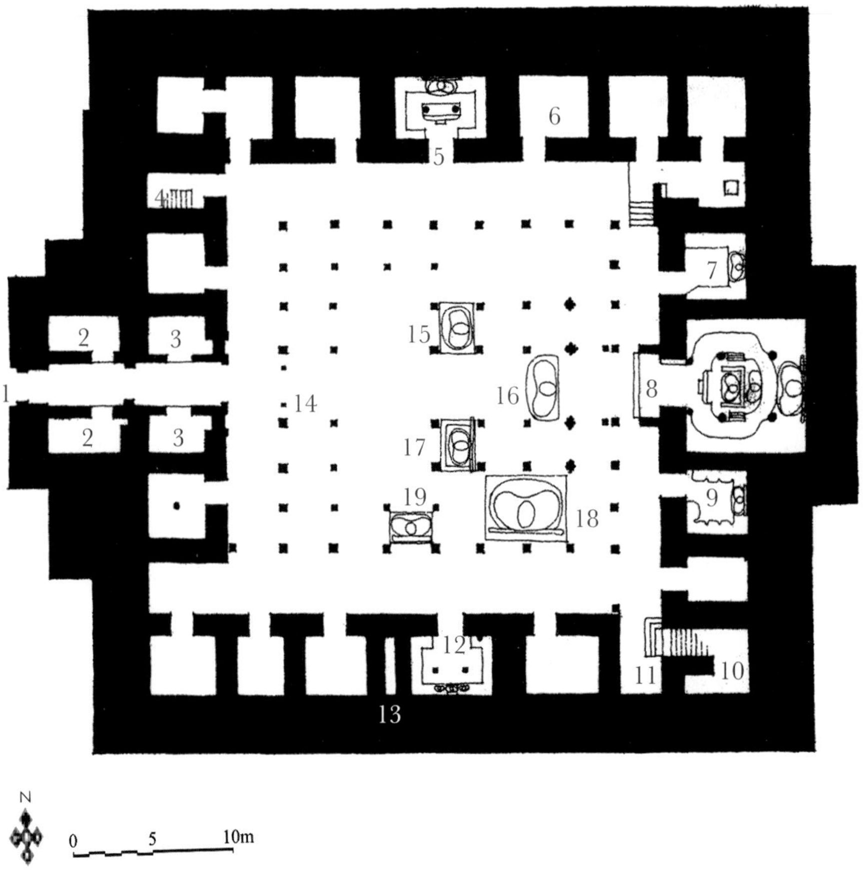

Level 2

1 secret chamber flled with auspicious objects
2 Chögyel Lha-khang (Songtsen Gampo chapel)
3 access gallery
4 second gallery added in 14th century
5 closed stairway
6 empty, formerly apparently Jigjé Lha-khang
7 Chögyel Zimpuk Lha-khang
8 Jowo Rinpoché chapel
9 Shey-ré Lha-khang with early mural fragments
10 Guru Tsokyé Dorjé Tsokhor Lha-khang
11 staircase, access to Pel-lha chok
12 Tub-pa Tsokhor Lha-khang
13 second wall-layer

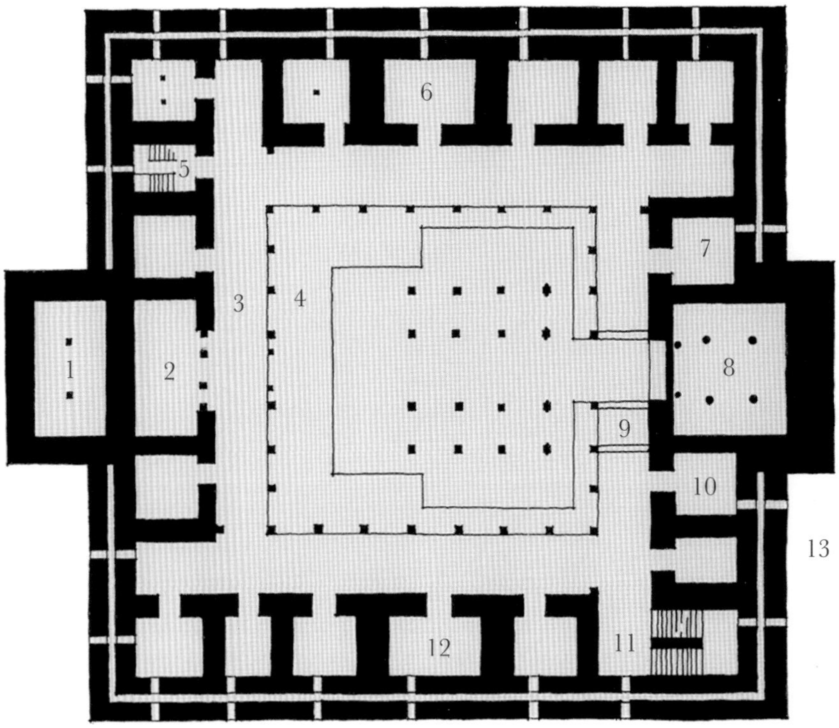

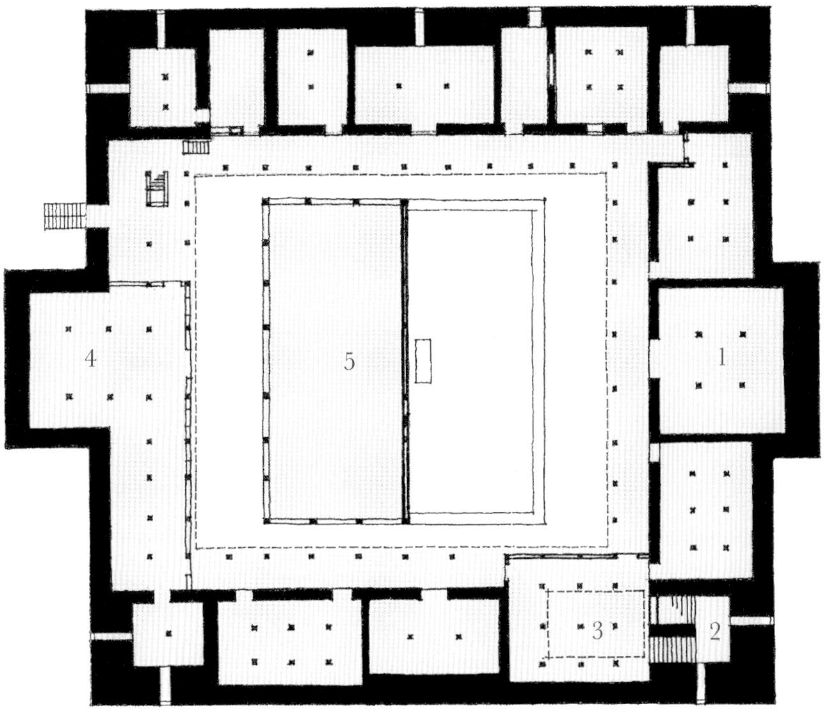

Level 3

1 Jowo Ü-tog Lha-khang
2 Pel-lha Chok
3 Pel-lha Du-khang
4 Tashi Tri-go Lha-khang
5 new roof added in 1990

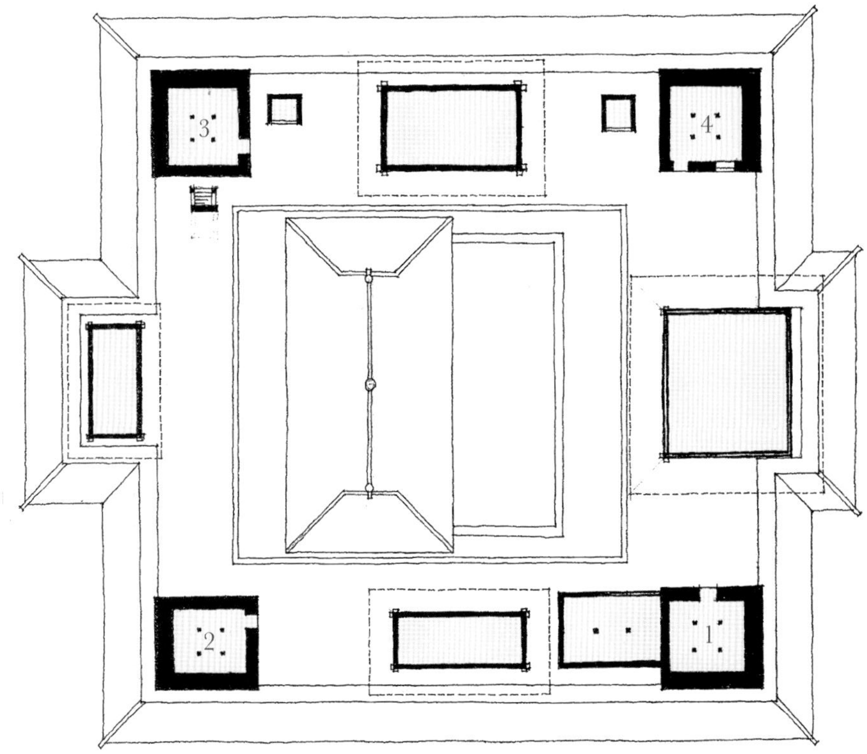

Level 4

1 Pel-lha Drakmo Gön-khang
2 Tsering Che-nga Gön-khang
3 Lhabum Lubum chapel
4 Ne-chu Lha-khang (arhat chapel)

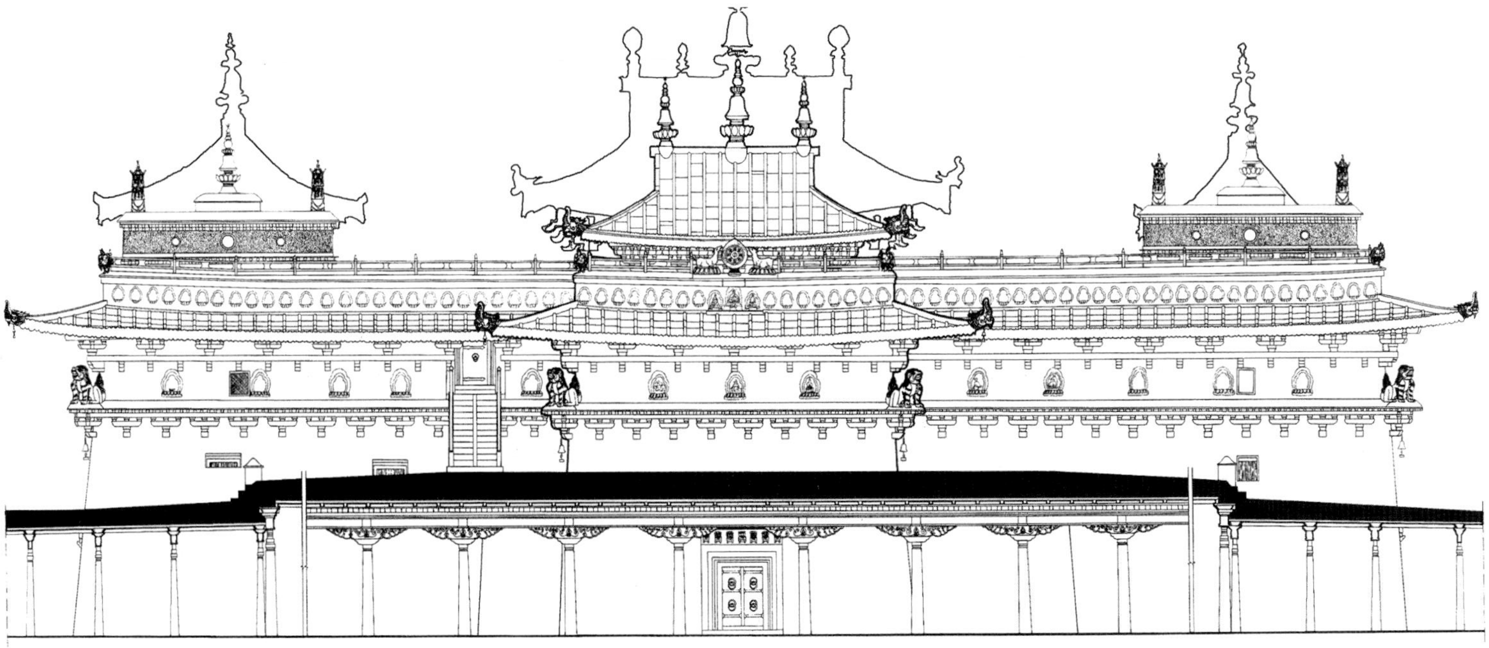

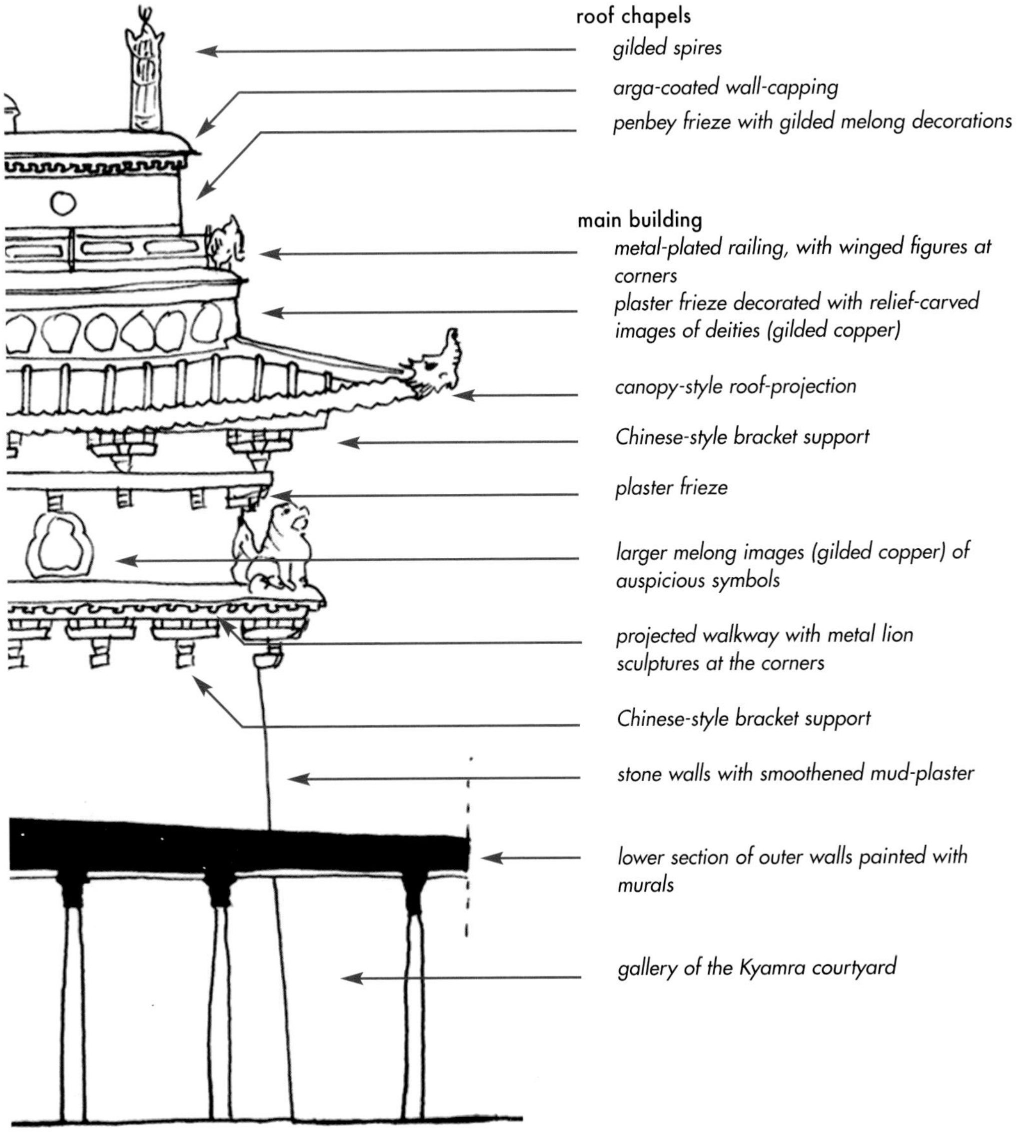

Lhasa Tsuklakhang, west elevation of main building. Until obscured by the Fifth Dalai Lama's extension and partial roofing of the Kyamra courtyard, the original temple building stood out visibly as a separate structure to visitors. Unusual in Tibetan architecture, the outer walls have a smooth plaster finish.
(AL based on CRB, BU, EK, AA surveys)

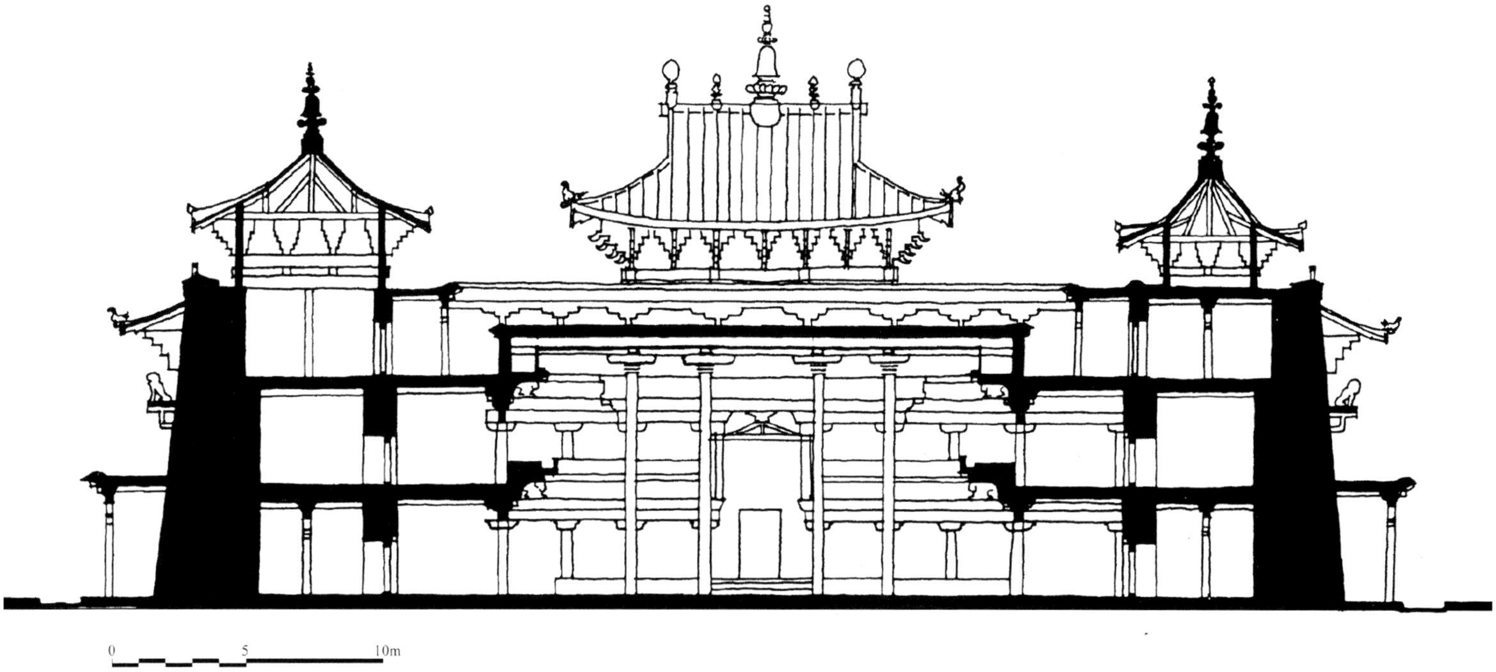

North-south section

showing the sky-bearing pillars added in the 14th century. (JH/BU/EK)

West-east section
(courtesy Minyak Chökyi Gyentsen, revised by JH after BU, EK).

1 entrance with raksha chapel
2 naga chapel
3 original colonaded corridor
4 Kyilkhor-ting with pillars added in the 13th-14th centuries
5 raised pillars added in the 14th century
6 9th century raised pillars for balustrade
7 Jowo chapel

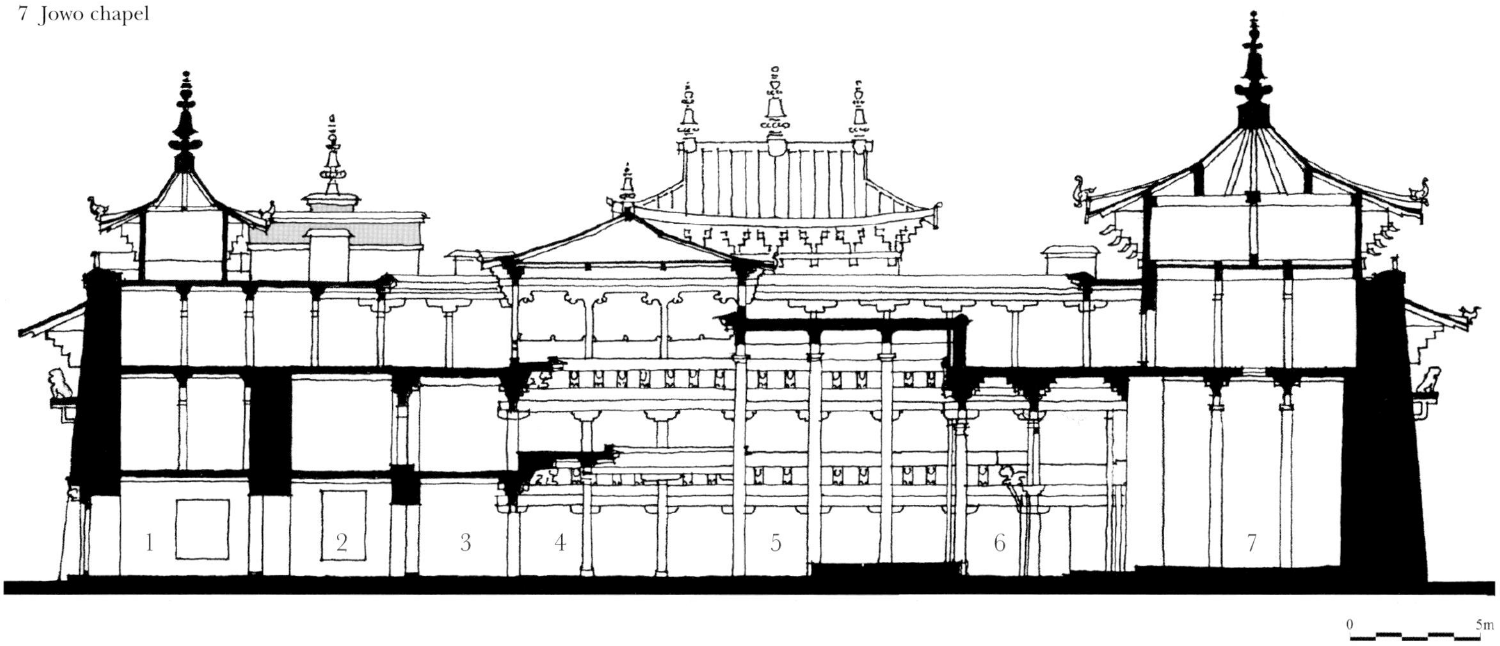

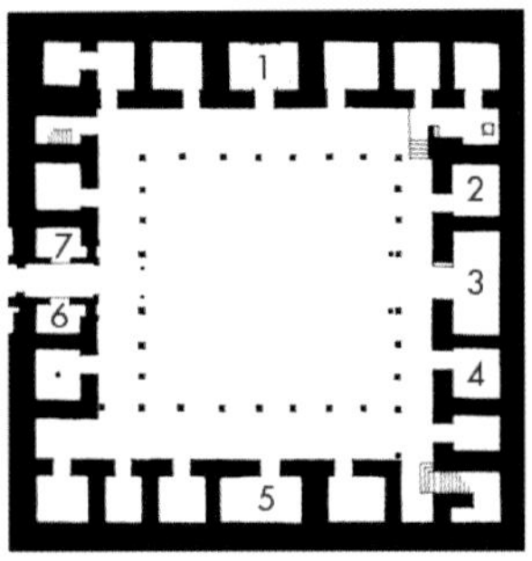

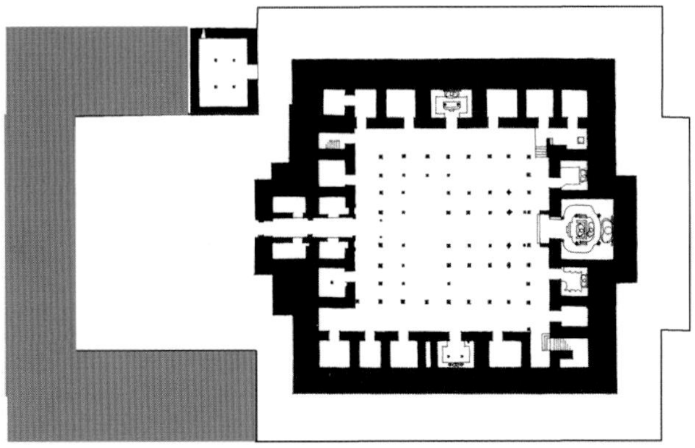

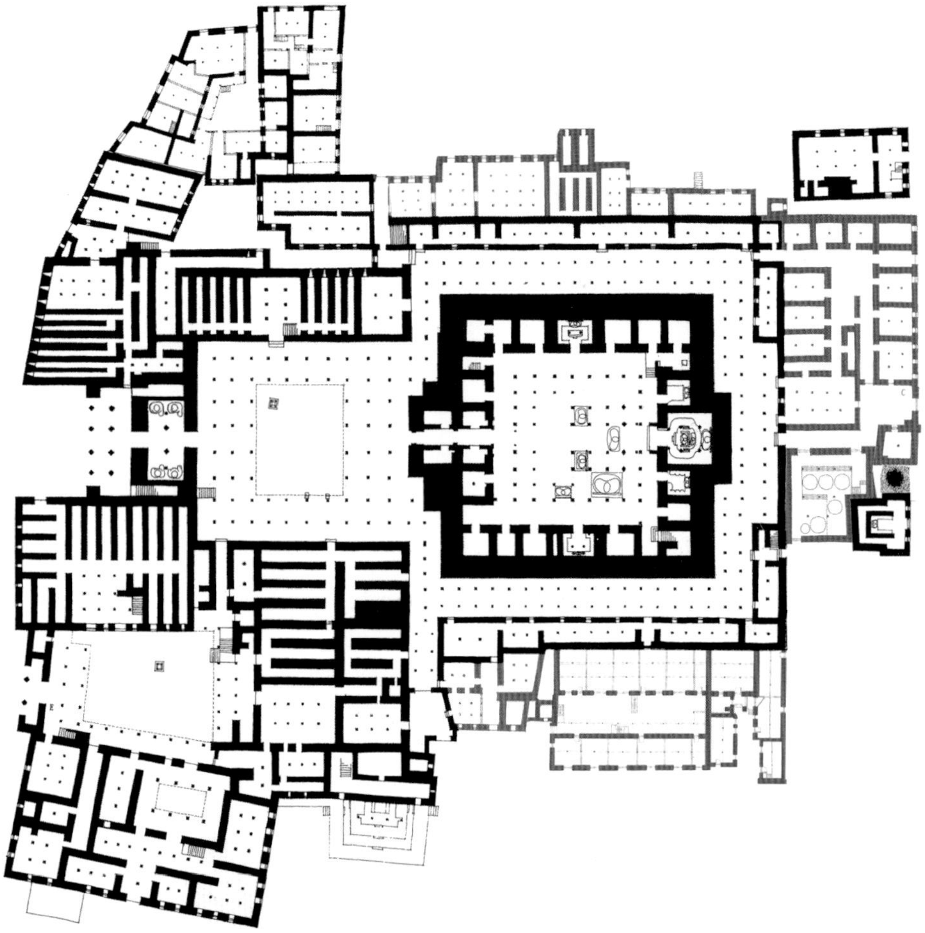

Lhasa Tsukla-khang building history

Early phase

Imperial period, Songtsen Gampo's reign after 629. The original chapels and main images according to historical sources:

1 Tsang-khang Jangma with Tukjé Chenpo as main image
2 Tsang-khang Yena with Ö-pamé image
3 Tsang-khang Ü-ma with Mi-trukpa, a retinue of eight and two door guardians
4 Tsang-khang Yöna with Jampa image
5 Tsang-khang Lhoma with Mikyö Dorjé as main image
6, 7 Yaksha and Raksha chapels

The boulder to the right of the temple was deemed an auspicious site by Songtsen Gampo. In the 9th century, the Meru chapel was built next to it. During that time, four pillars were added in front of the Tsukla-khang's eastern gallery to support a balustrade.

Middle phase

In the late 11th century, the Tsang-khang Ü-ma was extended in the form of a 'lobur' protrusion. By the 14th century, the entrance had been extended, and 12 raised pillars added in the centre of the Kyilkhorting to support a skylight. 10 pillars added on the western side support a second gallery. The Drolma Lha-khang and the Nangkor had been established, and the Khyamra courtyard defined.

Late Phase

Early Ganden Po-trang 1642-1750, the Tsuklakhang complex was expanded under the Fifth Dalai Lama and particularly his regents Dési Losang Tutob and Dési Sangyé Gyatso. Available sources (including the wall-paintings in the Potala's Red Palace) tell us that the western part of the Tsuklakhang, including the entrance, the Shira courtyard and the Labrang Teng, have come into being during that time. We lack specific information to know whether the grey-coloured sections were finalized already during that time, but do know of the existence of the Labrang Nyingpa building (not shown) and the Trapchi-sha house (upper left). By the mid-18th century under the Seventh Dalai Lama, the Tsuklakhang reached its present dimensions, when the Sungchöra teaching throne, the chapels around the Nangkor and government offices on the upper floor were finalized.

Construction materials and methods

From the outside, the Jokhang conforms to standard Tibetan architectural practice – white-washed stone walls lined with a maroon *penbey* frieze. The central building is white-washed on polished plaster, decorated with several cornices and gilded brass images, including lions placed at the four corners. The outer wall is built from stone. The 1993 restoration revealed that the walls of some (perhaps all) of the interior chapels at least are built from baked bricks, hidden beneath mud-plaster.[28]

This conforms with the standard practice in India during the Buddhist period (i.e. 2nd century BC-ca. 1200 AD), and suggests that foreign craftsmen where at work. In Tibet, with an abundance of high-quality stone, building with baked bricks has never caught on. So far, the Trül-nang is the only historic Tibetan temple built with baked bricks identified so far (and the wide-scale destruction during the 1960s has revealed far more wall interiors than anyone could wish to investigate). The central ambulatory of the 9th century Meru Nyingpa chapel is built with stone, according to the 1999 investigation. It remains to be seen whether future archaeological investigation of imperial period sites in Tibet will find further usage of burnt bricks.

Regarding the timber elements, Tibetan sources mention juniper (shing shug pa) as the building material,[29] as well as 'la' wood (gla, tentatively identified as seabuckthorn).[30]

We investigated a small number of historic timber elements, four pillars and two beam ends carved in the shape of lions, and all were identified as juniper.

The fragments of the Shey-ré Lha-khang are behind this plywood wall erected during the 1993 restoration. (2000 AA)

View of the Jowo chapel ceiling, with an open screen in the centre. (1995 AA)

View of the roof of the Jowo's throne seen from the Jowo U-tok chapel. (2000 AA)

Left: Burnt red brick found in the Jowo chapel entrance during the 1993 restoration, modern in appearance but no record exists.

Right: Burnt brick found in the Tsuklakhang interior chapel walls south of the Jowo chapel during the 1991-1993 restoration; it appears to be moulded in Indo-Newar fashion and can be reasonably presumed to be of very early date. (1994/2000 AA)

The nine ancient doorways of the Lhasa Tsuklakhang.

1 Tsangkhang Jangma, aka. Tukjé Chenpo Lha-khang.

2 Öpa-mé Tsokhor Lha-khang.

3 Tsangkhang Ü-ma, aka. Jowo Shakyamuni Tsokhor Lha-khang (doorway shown elsewhere).

5 Tsangkhang Lhoma, aka. Jampa Tsé-shi Tsokhor Lha-khang.

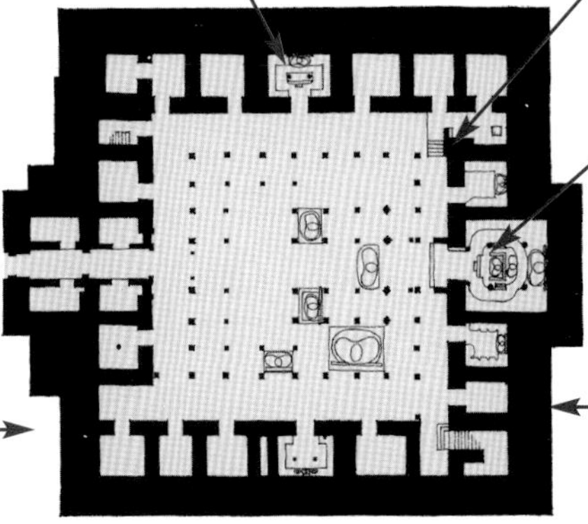

4 Jampa Chökhor Lha-khang.

6 Kangyur-Tangyur Lha-khang.

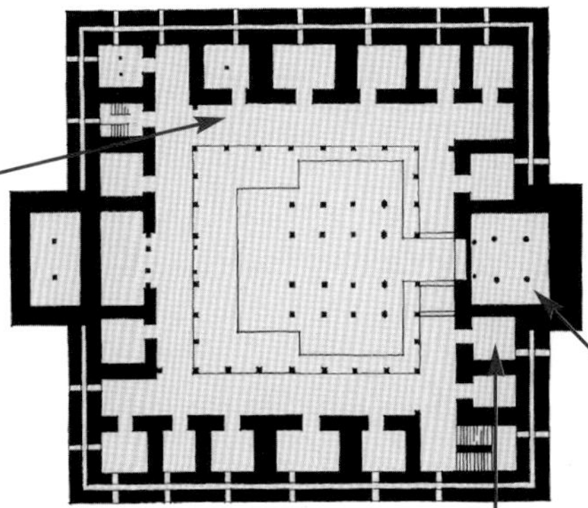

7 Chögyel Zimpuk Lha-khang.

9 Tub-pa Tsokhor Lha-khang.

8 Guru Tsokyé Dorjé Tsokhor Lha-khang, with early murals on adjacent walls lost in 1993. (1991 AA)

Detailing

'For the benefit of the king's lineal descendants and those taking Buddhist ordination in future, the beams were painted with figures from the Abhidharma teachings, figures from the Sutra-s on the beam-ends, and illustrations from the Vinaya on the pillars. In order that future generations should understand the canons of knowledge, images from the (pre-Buddhist) 'narratives' (sgrung), 'codes' (lde'u) and 'rites' (bon), such as the 'sky-going deer', were painted on doorways [door lintels] (gag spang), pillar capitals (ka gzhu), lesser beams (gdung phran) and so on.

' Pa-wo Tsuk-lak Trengwa [31]

On the ground floor, three major and two minor wooden doorways stand out (doorways 1-5 on the detail map). The doorways concur with those pointed out in Tibetan sources as the principal original chapels. The structure of these doorways is classically Indian, based on an established pattern refined over centuries, shared by both Hindu and Buddhist shrines, which reached its maturity during the early Gupta period. It consists of multiple, progressively recessed jambs, decorated with carved images of narrative scenes, door protectors, deities, decorative friezes and occasionally pilasters. The doorway to the Jowo chapel is flanked by two pilasters, with squatting figures at the base, which frame three sets of jambs. The innermost is covered by brass sheets, apparently covering old carvings. The middle jamb is carved in the form of a snake. The outer jamb set consists of a series of panels with carved single figures, appearing to be Bodhisattva-s, Tara-s or *apsaras,* one of which holds a lotus flower. Several panels are covered by brass sheets. On each side are six panels with such images, and above the doorway are five panels with one larger central panel containing two figures. Above is a lintel that has six panels with paired images and a central panel with a representation of the wheel of Dharma. On the bottom of the jambs are carved images of the Indian fertility goddesses Ganga and Jamuna (representing the twin rivers that water the northern Indian plains), another indication that an established foreign pattern has been re-created here without modification. The doorway closely matches the doorways of Ajanta 1, 5 and 24.

The doorways of the two flanking chapels are smaller, but similarly decorated by three sets of jambs and one lintel decorated with carved frames, illustrating events from the life of the historic Buddha Sakyamuni.[32]

The doorway of the southern sanctum chapel has two pilasters and only one set of jambs, surrounded by a T-shaped decorative frame. T-shaped doorways are a common feature in ancient Indian temple architecture. The carvings on the jambs are eroded. The lintel has five panels with carved figures. Carved lion heads flank the lintel, above which are two pilasters and two panels with *apsara* images, and a row of ten protruding yaksha or *apsara* figures. The doorway of the northern sanctum chapel, the Tuk-jé Chenpo Lha-khang, closely matches the design of its direct opposite, except that the carved lions flanking the lintel are shown with their entire bodies.

On the upper floor are four matching ancient doorways. On the eastern side, they decorate the Guru Tso-kyé Dorjé Tso-khor (s) and Chögyel Zimpuk (n) chapels.[33] The northernmost has been hollowed out and placed on a modern wooden frame, while the other is well-preserved despite the reconstruction of its entire surroundings. Both are of very similar design, forming curved archways, flanked by *apsaras.* The jambs have carved Indian patterns, foliage and lotus flowers. Two rather massive lintels are carved with figurative panels. The three panels on the lower one illustrate *Jataka* tales, the five panels on the upper one show deities.[34]

The original pillar bases on the first and second floor levels are decorated with carved yaksha images according to early Indian preferences. (1991 AA)

Ground floor eastern gallery with some of the best-preserved original pillars, protected by a thick coat of butter against any undue repainting attempts. (1998 AA)

Pillar in front of Tsang-khang Lhoma, type B (photo 2003 NT, drawing AA survey EK).

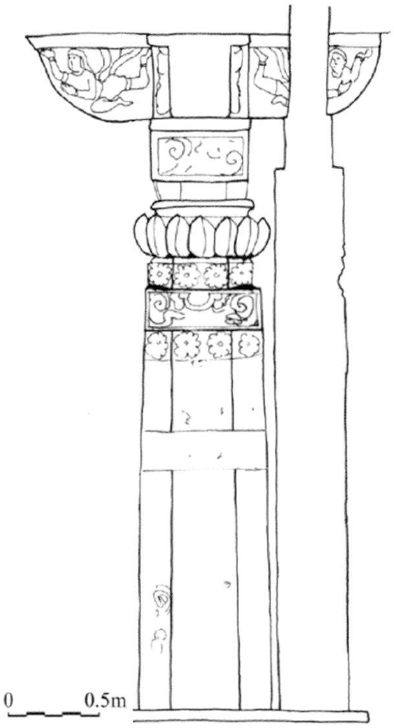

Tsuklakhang, pillar p5 in front of the Jowo chapel, type A with support pillar type C. (photo and survey 2000 AA with EK)

Left: Example of the Indian 'cushion'-type pillar, Aurangabad, ca. 5th century. (2003 AA)

Right: Ajanta, cave 1, 6th century pillars in eastern gallery. (2003 AA)

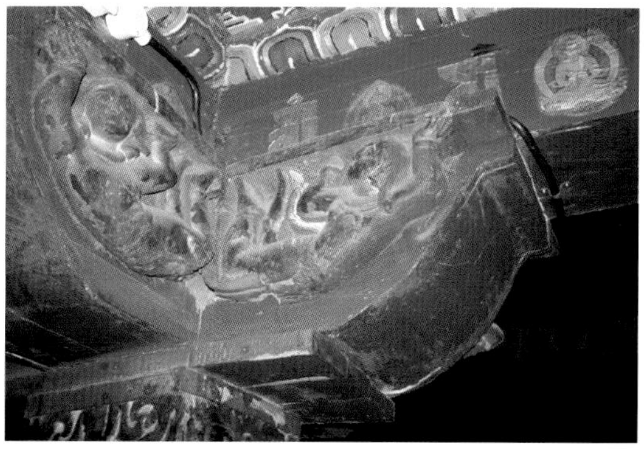

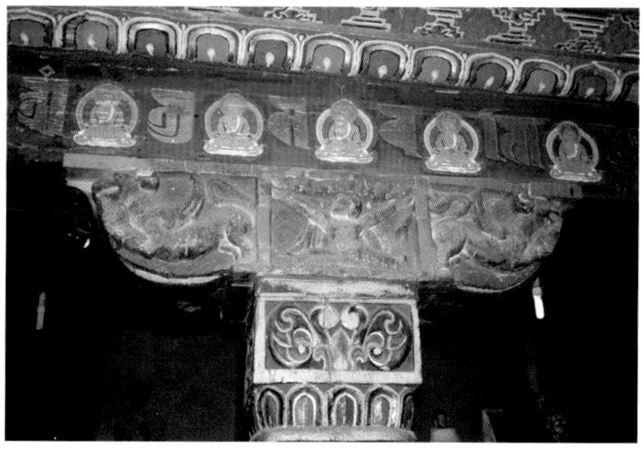

Pillar bracket designs in eastern gallery on ground floor: apsara P1, elephant P2, gryph P3, duck P7. (1995 AA)

On the southern and northern sides are doorways matching those of the northern and southern sanctum chapels, decorating here the chapel of 'Buddha and his disciples' (s) and an empty, presently unused chapel (n).[35]

The southern doorway is flanked by two pilasters and a T-shaped frame. The inner jambs are decorated with carved foliage, the outer jambs are carved in lotus pattern. The T-frame is carved in diamond pattern, and flanked by two lion figures facing outwards. Above the lintel is a central panel with a *yaksha* image, and a row of ten protruding *yaksha* or *apsara* images. The southern doorway is well-preserved, except for two missing panels in the outer corners of the T-frame. The northern doorway is decorated correspondingly, but the images flanking the T-frame here are winged gryphs. This doorway has been restored, with missing elements replaced by matching designs executed in modern craftsmanship.

The nine 'ancient' doorways described here are closely related in their design and match the Indian-modelled building plan, and so can be associated with the Jokhang's founding period. Their iconography is archaic by classical Tibetan Buddhist standards, because of the inclusion of Hindu deities and *yaksha-s*. The 14th century Chögyel chapel on the western side of the second floor level has a notably different doorway design. The Sengden Gomo main door *(seng ldeng sgo mo)*, which dates to the same period, exemplifies the preferred gate design of later Tibetan temples, with pema-chudzö frame, an upper lintel with lion heads and the door panel covered with canvas painted in geometric patterns.[36]

Colonadization

The pillars on the Jokhang's ground and second floor levels carrying the upper galleries differ widely in proportion and design from any other pillars known in Tibet.

Two separate but related styles can be identified. Type A is distinguished by its very prominent adaption of the Indian *ghata* or cushion-type moulding (here similar to a pumpkin), situated between a square capital and an octagonal shaft. The overall design closely resembles the stone pillars of Ajanta 1, 2 and 21 (all 6th century).

Type B has a much more simplified adaption of the *ghata* moulding, and while the upper part of the shaft is shaped octagonally, the larger lower part is square. Many have images of squatting deities or *yaksha*-s carved on their bases. This exemplifies a common early Indian design type, the *purna-kalasha* pillar. Almost identical pillars in stone can be found at Aurangabad III (late 5th century), Ajanta I portico (early 6th) and Ellora II (mid-5th).

Type A only occurs on the ground floor at the four corners and in front of the Jowo chapel, all examples appear to be of very early date. Most pillars of type B appear to have been repaired, replaced or repainted many times. Stylistically, the carving on later B types is stiffer and less artistically successful.

The row of pillars P1-P8 on the eastern side of the Kyil-khor-ting are most readily recognizable as ancient. Pillars P2 and P3 are replacements, but the brackets are ancient. P6 and P7 are ancient but have been repaired. P8 has been cast in plaster. Two support pillars (C) next to P4 and P5, probably added during the 11th century modification of this area, have some stylistic similarities to the ancient pillars, but are of different proportions.

All the pillars in this row, except for the two replacements, are unpainted, and polished by the hands of pilgrims and butter from the ubiquitous butter lamps. Some detailing has been lost long ago through abrasion, but the coat of butter is probably the best possible protection against repair and repainting.

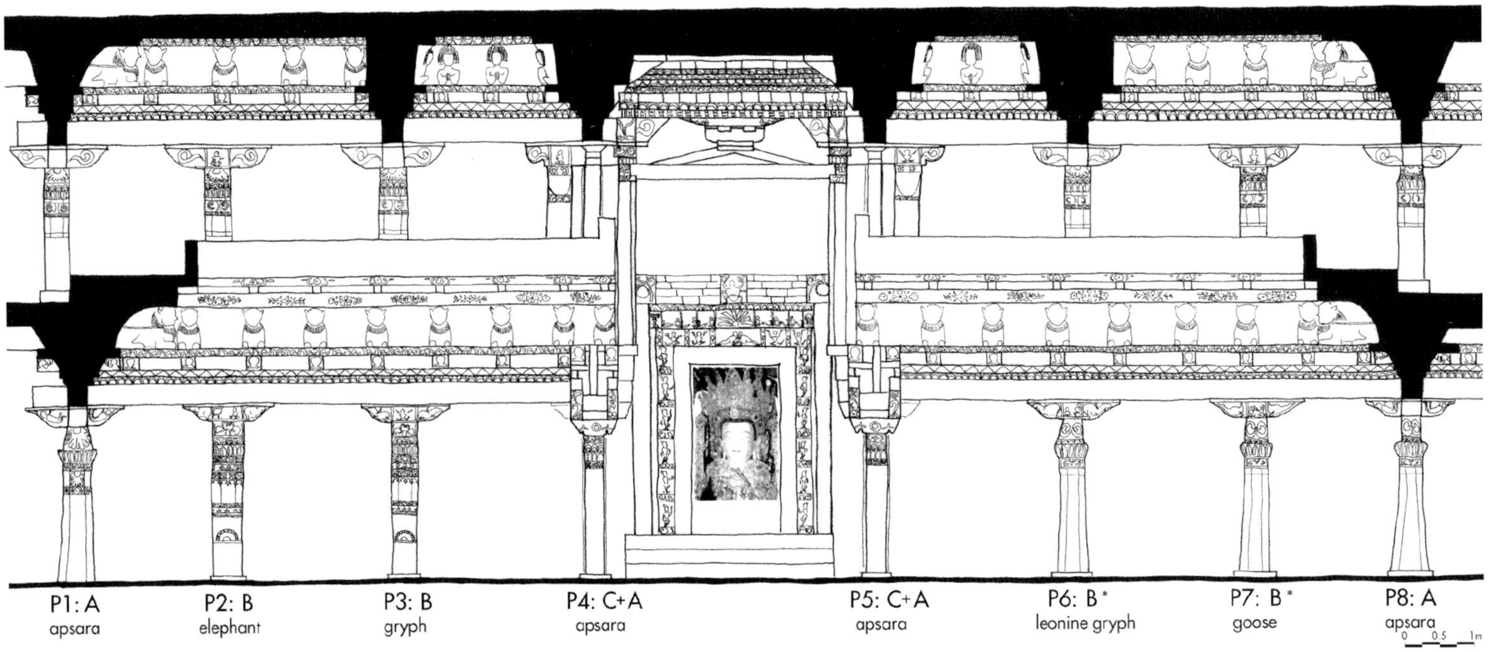

Lhasa Tsuklakhang, north-west section showing eastern gallery and sanctum. (2000 BU with EK, AA)

Ajanta 4, second half of 5th century, sanctum and gallery. (2003 AA)

A ninth ancient-looking pillar has been added for structural reasons close to the southern swastika recess.

The brackets in the row of the eight original pillars are of uniform design, a central square medallion with Indian figures flanked by animals or *apsara*-s (see map section for illustrations); from north to south the flanking bracket images are, respectively, *apsara*-s, elephants, gryphs, *apsara*-s, *apsara*-s, gryphs, geese and *apsara*-s.

The pillars found elsewhere in the Tsuglakhang, including those on the third and fourth floor levels of the central *vihara*, are of standard Tibetan design and proportions. The raised pillars carrying the rooflight and balustrade appear to have no design features traceable to Indian prototypes.

We can conclude that pillar designs A and B match the Jokhang's groundplan, and so the designs (and some of the actual pillars) are contemporary with the founding. Nowhere else in Tibet have similar pillars survived, which serves to re-enforce the interpretation that the Jokhang was one of the earliest forays into temple-building on Tibetan soil. Later restorations have attempted, not always successfully, to maintain the early styles when pillars had to be replaced, constituting an important tradition of historic preservation.

Four tall pillars in front of the eastern section carry a balustrade (*seng g.yab*), richly decorated in the Indian mould. It contains wooden ceiling panels decorated with carved figures. A row of 24 Bodhisattva-like figures, similar to those above the Jowo-chapel gaze out of blind windows along the eastern rail of this balustrade. The design of both window frames and figures is entirely comparable to common Indian decorative features, occurring in some of the earliest known reliefs at Barhut (2nd century BC),

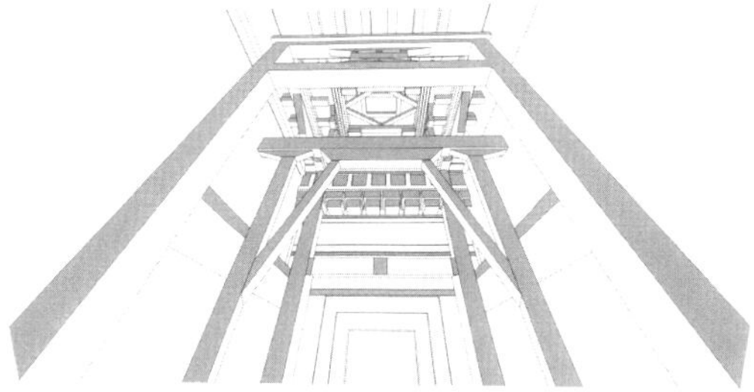

Ceiling construction above entrance to Jowo chapel (BU).

Triangular arch above entrance corridor to Jowo chapel (2000 AA+EK).

and particularly resembling the balustrade above the entrance to Ajanta cave 1. The row of figures along the Jokhang's balustrade, decorated like royalty with crowns and jewelry, implies that the upper area of the Jokhang at the time was designated as a celestial mansion, the realm of the gods, following an early Indian architectural concept. The centrepiece on the lower side of the balustrade is a richly decorated panel that forms the canopy which in Indian temples is typically placed in front or above a central image.

The existence of the balustrade has been literally overshadowed, even made somewhat superfluous both structurally and decoratively, by the 14th century roofing of this area and the 12 raised pillars. The balustrade also appears to have been modified in the area above the entrance to the Jowo chapel, where the ceiling panels closest to the entrance are different in design. This area was modified in the 11th century when the Shey-ré Lha-khang was created, but our understanding of this no longer extant chapel is limited. This suggests that the balustrade pre-dates the 11th century. The detailing generally matches early Indian preferences and particularly the decorative art at Ajanta and Ellora. Tibetan sources tell us that king Repachen erected four 'sky-bearing' pillars (*gnam yangs ka ba*) 'bedecked with precious objects'[37] in the Jokhang, i.e. the extra-long pillars that typically support a skylight, portico or other structures added to ceiling constructions. The balustrade is indeed supported by four pillars higher than those supporting the ground and second floor levels, so we can tentatively place the balustrade to the 820s. The row of five blind-windows with Bodhisattva-like images high above the entrance to the Jowo chapel is stylistically identical and must date from the same period.

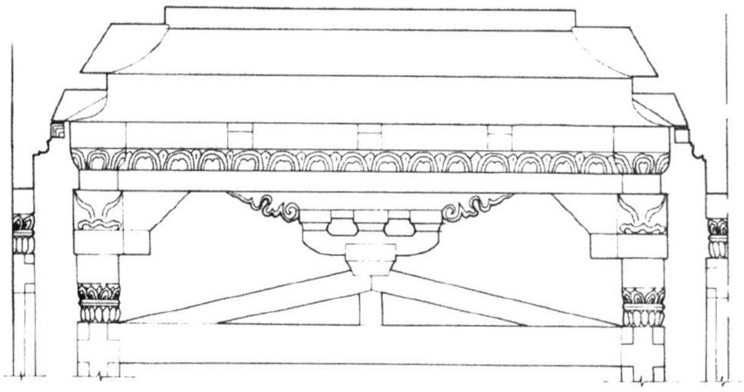

West-facing arch detail. (After CRB)

Trifoliated arch, entrance to Wanla temple, Ladakh. (2004 AA)

Ceiling of the vajra enclosure, turn of the 15th century. (2003 JM)

Sixth blind window with face on the hidden end of the frame above the Jowo chapel's entrance. (2000 AA)

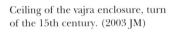

Vyala (Indian gryph with rider) on the southern end of the wooden *prabha-mandala* above Jowo chapel entrance. (2000 AA)

Jowo chapel entrance with early Indian door frame. (EK)

The 12 raised pillars that provide structural support for the roofing over the eastern section of the Kyil-khor-ting, forming the so-called *vajra* enclosure, were added in their present form in the 14th century.[38]

The wooden ceiling construction differs quite sharply in design from the carved ceiling panels of the 9th century balustrade. The panels are simple squares, decorated with mantra-s painted in lotus-shapes. Ten long pillars along the western half of the Kyil-khor-ting were added during the same period, creating an additional gallery space on the second floor level.

The area in front of the Jowo chapel, including the Shey-ré Lha-khang fragments, is not so easy to understand. The 1990s restoration has left this area in disarray, plywood boards screen the second floor galleries from the chapel's entrance and historic timber elements appear structurally abandoned where the workforce could not make sense of them. Plywood walls also screen the timber and mural fragments preserved in the rump Shey-ré Lha-khang.

High above the door of the Jowo chapel is a row of five Bodhisattva images looking out of blind windows, closely resembling the row of 24 on the edge of Repachen's balustrade. A sixth image is found to the right of the corner pillar and beam construction that defines the entrance corridor of the Jowo chapel, making it likely that a seventh image exists at the other end of the row of images. A modern shelf with religious clay images obscures the area between these Bodhisattva-s and the doorframe below. We found a large wooden *prabha-mandala*, the traditional torana or throne back of a Buddha image, located behind the shelf. To the right of the shelf a *vyala* image can be seen (gryph with a rider). A winged *garuda* with flanking *chu-srin* (*makara-s*), which constitute the top of a throne back, rises above the shelf. This throne back is likely another important fragment of the 11th century Shey-ré Lha-khang, indicating that at one time, a large Buddha image was placed here.

A wooden triangular arch spans the gap between the northern and southern second floor galleries above the Jowo entrance corridor. The construction seems vaguely based on a well-known decorative element in Indian temple architecture, intricately decorated triangular arches placed in the entrance area. There are well-known examples at the monasteries of Alchi and Wanla in Ladakh. The Jokhang arches are much simpler in design. It is possible that the triangular arch came to Lhasa via Kashmir and western Tibet with Zangskar Lotsawa in the 11th century, and that the triangular arch we see today has replaced an earlier (and much more decorated) one. The entrance area to the Jowo chapel has been continuously re-arranged over centuries, starting with the addition of the 9th century balustrade, and ending only recently with the placement of two plywood walls sealing the upper sections of this area.

The lions

'The pillars (ka), pillar capitals (gzhu), beams (gdung) and beam-ends (gdung khebs) were beautifully laid and made in various forms. All the projecting beam-ends (phyam sna) in the upper and lower galleries were made in the form of 108 rampant white lions with turquoise manes.

Pa-wo Tsuk-lak Trengwa [39]

The beam ends facing the Kyil-khor-ting on the ground and second floors are carved in the shape of crouching male lions, except for one on the upper western side carved as a human face. These lion figures exemplify an ancient building tradition of early pan-Indian Buddhist civilizations, with the earliest examples found in Gandhara.[40]

We find no identical examples in other Tibetan temples. The Ramochè temple preserves a row of carved lion heads on a much smaller scale, decorating a beamline in the assembly hall (see Chapter 2). These are similar to the rows of carved lion heads commonly placed on lintels above the main doors of Tibetan monasteries, based on another Indian decorative tradition. Several Jokhang beam end lions were investigated; all were carved from juniper wood. Some years ago I was given as a present a paw of one such lion that was replaced during the 1993 restoration. The paw is juniper wood, 21 cm long, 9 cm high and 11 cm wide. It has five claws. Two separate carbon datings place it with very high probability into Songtsen Gampo's time. Professor Richard Ernst, who was awarded the Nobel prize for Chemistry in 1991, kindly facilitated a Carbon-14 analysis in Switzerland's renowned ETH.[41]

A second test facilitated by Dr. Achim Bräuning of Stuttgart University confirmed the results. In 1999, Dr. Bräuning collected further samples in the Jokhang for testing, with matching results:

'From one of the oldest buildings in Lhasa, the Jokhang temple, four pieces of juniper wood could be investigated. One rectangular beam had a width of 34.5 cm and showed 555 growth rings. One edge of the beam is shaped in the form of a lion's head [...]. A high-precision[14] C-sample from the outermost 10 rings of this beam (sample No. Hd-21765 LJo9 2C) yielded a date of 1633±17 BP which leads to an absolute calendar date of 409-428 AD (1 sigma). However, the outermost rings under the bark of the tree had been cut away, so the last preserved ring does not represent the felling date of the tree. Since the growth rates of this wood sample range from 0.1-0.5 mm only, the cutting of about 3 cm of wood could have removed more than 200 growth rings. Thus, it is very probable that the beam originates from the first construction period of the Jokhang temple in the 7th century. The tree germinated around 136(±10) BC and was probably cut for the construction of the Jokhang temple in the 7th century AD.'[42]

On the upper wall sections and the roof of the Jokhang are a number of stone images which are locally claimed to have been placed by Songtsen Gampo as protective devices.

1: One of an identical pair of ceiling panels flank-ing the central Indian-style ceiling panel. (2000 AA)

2: Balustrade above Jowo chapel entrance, north-west corner. (2000 AA)

3: Ceiling structure above Jowo chapel entrance platform; the blend of different styles reflects the modification of this area since the 11th century. (2000 AA)

4: Ceiling above entrance area to Jowo chapel. (1996 AA)

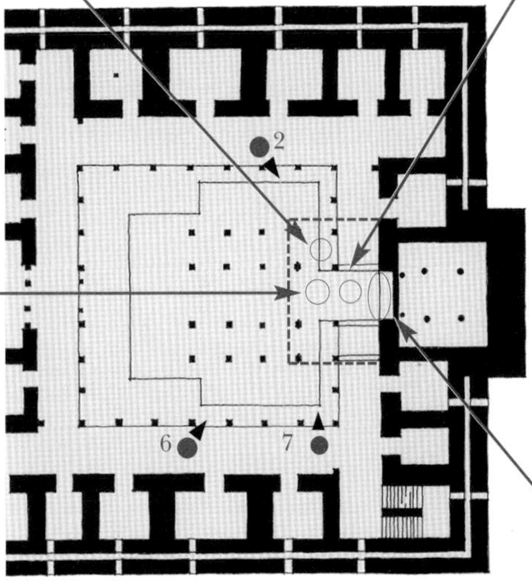

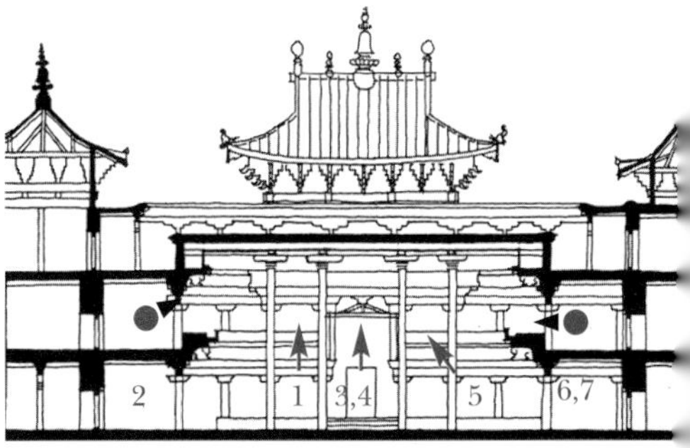

5: Entablature above Jowo chapel entrance – row of five blind windows with pilasters and faces in royal attire similar to (but larger than) those on the balustrade. (2000 AA)

6: Balustrade resting on four raised pillars added in the 9th century, with Indian-style decorations of Bodhisattva-s in royal attire gazing out of blind windows, in identical style to the row of faces above the Jowo chapel door. (2000 AA)

7: Entrance to Shey-ré Lha-khang on second floor level. (1994 courtesy Katia Buffetrille)

The 1993 restoration has allowed us to understand the construction – the bodies of the lions are carved from the ends of massive juniper beams. According to the carbon dating, some of these beams have rested here for 1,300 years. The heads of the lions were detached during the repair work but have been re-attached again afterwards. (1993 AA)

Their actual antiquity is difficult to assess, but the sources associate them with 7th century geomancy. The most prominent is the stone lingam on the eastern side, pointing towards Jema-lung, where Princess Wen-cheng's geomantic investigation identified the manifestation of a female demoness (*srin mo*) baring her pubic hair.[43]

The throne of the Jowo

A significant iconographic shift has taken place in the Jokhang between the imperial period and the time of Tsongkapa. However, a discussion of the iconographic program of the Jokhang, past and present, would fill a book on its own (for the authoritative description of the temple's pre-1959 iconography, see Zhva sgab pa 1982). For a discussion of the Jowo chapel, it is sufficiently to note that the general set-up still corresponds to imperial Tibetan preferences – two door protectors, and a central image surrounded by a group of standing *bodhisattva*-s. There is a circumambulation path around the central Jowo image, and the back area of the chapel appears to have been filled with additional images at a later stage. There is another Buddha image placed directly at the back of the Jowo's throne, facing a lengthy inscription on a sheet of brass.

According to the most authoritative source that we have, the Fifth Dalai Lama's Guide to the Lhasa Jokhang, the present throne of the Jowo image was offered by the first Sakya Ponchen Shakya Zangpo (*Sa skya dpon chen Shalya bzang po*) who summoned the Newar artist Arniko (1244-1396) for the task.

The inscription on the back was copied by myself in 1996 and shared with the late Hugh Richardson. Richardson, in the middle of editing the publication of his collected works, High peaks, Pure Earth, was unable to work in much detail on the inscription. But he immediately recalled some details about the life of the regent who had commissioned the inscription in a series of letters to me written in the late summer of 1996, starting on 15 September.

The inscription on the back of the Jowo image commemorates the restoration of the Jowo throne carried out by the Fifth Dalai Lama's regent Lobsang Tutob (Blo bzang mthu stobs, r. 1669-1674).

The beam ends of the interior galleries of the temple's first two floors are decorated with lion figures. One has a human face, here decorated with a khata scarf. (2000 AA)

Detail of a lion on the lower gallery. All the lions are male. Only one has a human face (seen in the centre of the picture on the top of this page, often explained as the result of a distraction by Songtsen Gampo. This is related to the episode reported in the sources, whereafter a maid of the Nepali princess distracts the king while his emanations are engaged in carpentry work inside the Tsuklakhang. (2000 and 2005 AA)

Fragments of murals removed during the 1993 restoration and discarded. Some came from the southern and eastern galleries of the second floor level. The large piece in the center came from the skylight of the Kyamra courtyard in the Tsuklakhang. Judging from the style, it seems to have dated to the Thirteenth Dalai Lama's 1920s renovation of the Kyamra. (AA 1993)

The text describes in detail offerings of gold and precious stone for a new canopy roof above the Jowo image and the backside of the throne, as well for the image of the Medicine Buddha placed at the back of the Jowo's throne, and images of Dorje Chang with two attendants made from amber. The works took place during the entire water-ox year of 1673 (*chu glang lo*). Under the supervision of the Talung steward Lobsang Ngawang Paljor, and a great number of Tibetan Newar artisans, 2,937 gold pieces, 7,259 ounces of silver and amounts of turquoises, corals and pieces of amber were used.

Mural paintings

'Then the king summoned the Newar artists, who made ready their paints and brushes and so on alongside the pillar with the leaf design, and next day the king and his ministers came to the temple to discuss which images should be painted. On the south wall they painted Lokesvara-khasarpani protecting against the eight fears in one panel, and demonstrating the various means of converting beings to Dharma in another, and once both were finished, even more colours appeared by themselves, and all were amazed, and bowed and worshipped before them. Then the emanated artists did the rest of the paintings.'[44]

Until quite recently, the Jokhang preserved a significant amount of early wall-paintings. Located on the second floor level, in the area between the Shey-ré Lha-khang, the Panden Lhamo chapel and the stairway, they depicted Boddhisattva images in a style reminiscent of Indian Pala period paintings. Professor Heather Stoddard believes these to have been the earliest wall-paintings in Central Tibet. Most of these paintings were removed during renovation work between 1985-1993. Surviving panels are now stored in a former chapel room on the northern section of the Nangkor corridor. Still preserved *in situ* and enclosed by plywood walls is a single wall with early paintings, divided by a wooden frame into three panels. They are believed to be the remains of the Shey-ré Lha-khang (discussed in detail by Vitali 1990). Their art seems directly derived from Indian styles, and differs from known Tibetan mural paintings dating to the 11th-13th centuries preserved elsewhere. These three panels constitute the oldest surviving murals in the Jokhang today. Together with those murals found by our survey in the chapel above the Jowo; they also constitute the only historic paintings remaining inside the temple.[45]

Survival image in the Jowo Ü-tog chapel. The history of this room starts with the 11th century renovation of Zangskar Lotsawa. He moved the original retinue images of the Tsangkhang Ü-ma to here, and they may have survived in this room until 1967. During the Tselpa supremacy, the Yartse kings placed canopy roofs above the Tsuklakhang's eastern and northern main chapels, and modification of the Jowo Ü-tog chapel took place. The mural fragment could not be dated. (2000 AA)

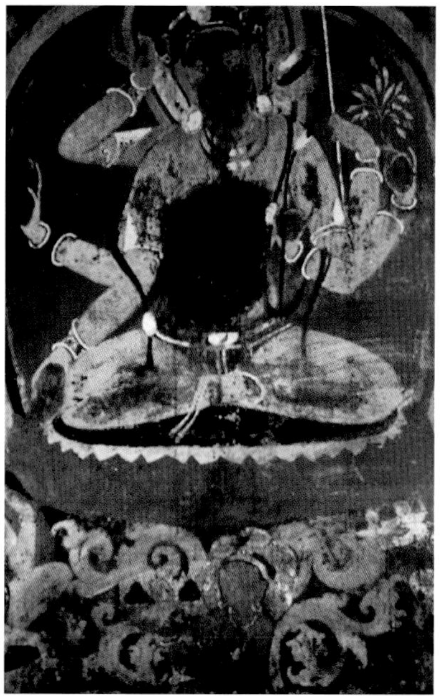

Cherchez le Vasudhara... photographed outside the Shey-ré Lha-khang in 1985; today the fragmented remains are kept in a store-room. (Courtesy H. Stoddard)

The Shey-ré Lha-khang preserves traces of a remarkable but long forgotten early painting style that survived on the upper floor of the Tsuklakhang undisturbed for many centuries. The last remaining paintings are on the east wall of the chapel, about 2x2 metres and in stable condition, divided into three sections by a wooden arch. The south wall of the chapel has been rebuilt and newly plastered in 1993. The northern and western walls are modern, built largely out of plywood. (1996, 1997, 2000 AA)

Site survey, surrounding complex

The Labrang-teng was first created during the Fifth Dalai Lama's reign as his residence in the Jokhang. In the 18th century it was used by the Tibetan council of ministers. It was completely rebuilt in 1950 on the occasion of the enthronement of the Fourteenth Dalai Lama. On the ground floor there is a recently restored chapel room, on the middle floor are mainly service and storage rooms, and on the upper floor a long monastic assembly room and private quarters for the Dalai Lama. The craftsmanship is superb, including fine carving work and detailed mural paintings.

The 12th century Drolma Lha-khang was rebuilt at same the time; no ancient architectural details remain.

The Nangkor paintings were restored by the Thirteenth Dalai Lama's government in 1920-1922; they are generally in good condition and were recently (2002) cleaned.

The Nangkor chapels have lost all their historic decorations and images. After lengthy preparations on site in the early 1990s, one of them has been reopened as a Guru Rinpoché chapel (east side). A former chapel on the north side now contains the deteriorating fragments of the old wall-paintings removed during the 1990s restoration. The kitchen to the east still contains an old shrine, the old mud hearth where previously butter tea for hundreds of monks was prepared, and four raised pillars made out of stone slabs (a common practice in monastic kitchen rooms because of the danger of fire).

The Kashag offices were completely rebuilt during the 1986-1993 restoration, nothing old remains.

The upstairs É-wam Tsomchen assembly hall still preserves old pillars and painting fragments. It has been used in recent times for the consecration of new religious images and re-consecration of restored historic images.

Labrang Teng (orange colour) overlooking the Kyamra Chenmo courtyard. (1992 SW)

Detail of the canopy-roof structure above the Jowo chapel, in the background the skylight of the eastern kitchen and the Ta-go Khang-sar residential courtyard. (2000 AA)

Geomancy

Early Indian Buddhist architecture is largely based on the concepts of vastu-shastra, the Hindu science of architecture. The main concerns of priest-architects of both religions lay in providing clearly-defined sanctum space and ambulatory passages, with cloister halls added in later and larger projects. According to the vastu-purusha-mandala, the Hindu formula for sacred building, rectangular cloister halls are ideally planned based either on the Mandukamandala, an underlying division of 8 by 8 squares, or on the Paramayikamandala of 9 by 9 squares. The resulting checkerboard pattern is used to identify underlying energy forces and corresponding placements of protective devices and auspicious placement of chapels and doorways. In Tibet, as standard practice for the erection of both temples and residential buildings, similar grid patterns are drawn on the ground prior to construction. Early Chinese builders used a somewhat comparable practice for city planning, dividing a designated area into squares for the placement of shrines, royal residences and gates.

Songtsen Gampo's Chinese bride Wen-cheng drew on her native cosmological traditions to devise a scheme that related the Lhasa Jokhang to her husband's growing empire by linking it with three quartets of temples located across Tibet.

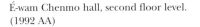

É-wam Chenmo hall, second floor level. (1992 AA)

For centuries, the Lhasa Tsuklakhang was, in typical Tibetan fashion, surrounded by residential buildings inhabited by Tibet's upper strata. These included the 18th century house of the prominent Do-ring family (on the left), and Peljor Rabten, belonging to the Panchen Lama's estate. (After Schäfer 1939)

In 1981 the Barkor was a paved motorable road, here the south-western corner. (1981 FM)

In 1985 an open plaza was created in front of the western main entrance, since then decorated with European-style fin-de-siècle street lamps, fountains and shrubberies. (2000 KO)

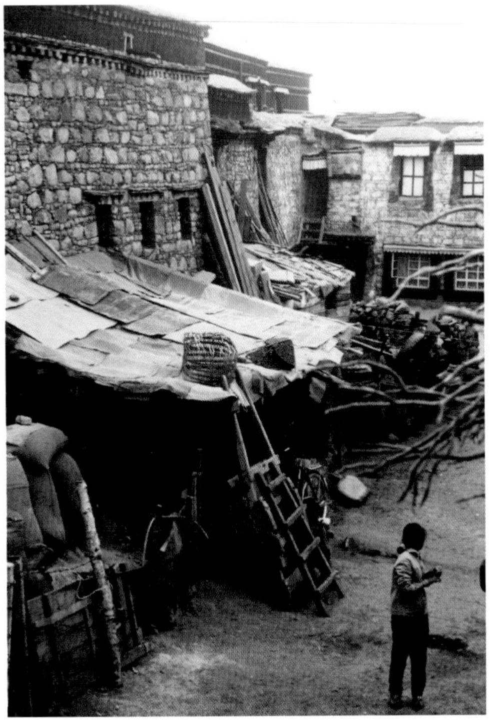

North: The Drolma Lha-khang gate; in the mid-1990s' restoration, the old stone walls, dating in all likelihood to the Fifth Dalai Lama's time, were rebuilt. In the process, the original penbey frieze was replaced by plaster. The gate is on the far right side. (1981 FM and 1998 AA)

East: The Sera Ta-go gate, next to Meru Nyingpa monastery. (1998 AA)

West: The building with the imposing battered corner is part of the Labrang Teng, the residential complex within the Tsuklakhang reserved for the Dalai Lama lineage. The upper door, with a balcony facing the Tsukla-khang's entrance, contains a large reception hall and private residential rooms, last restored in 1950 for the Fourteenth Dalai Lama. (2001 YH)

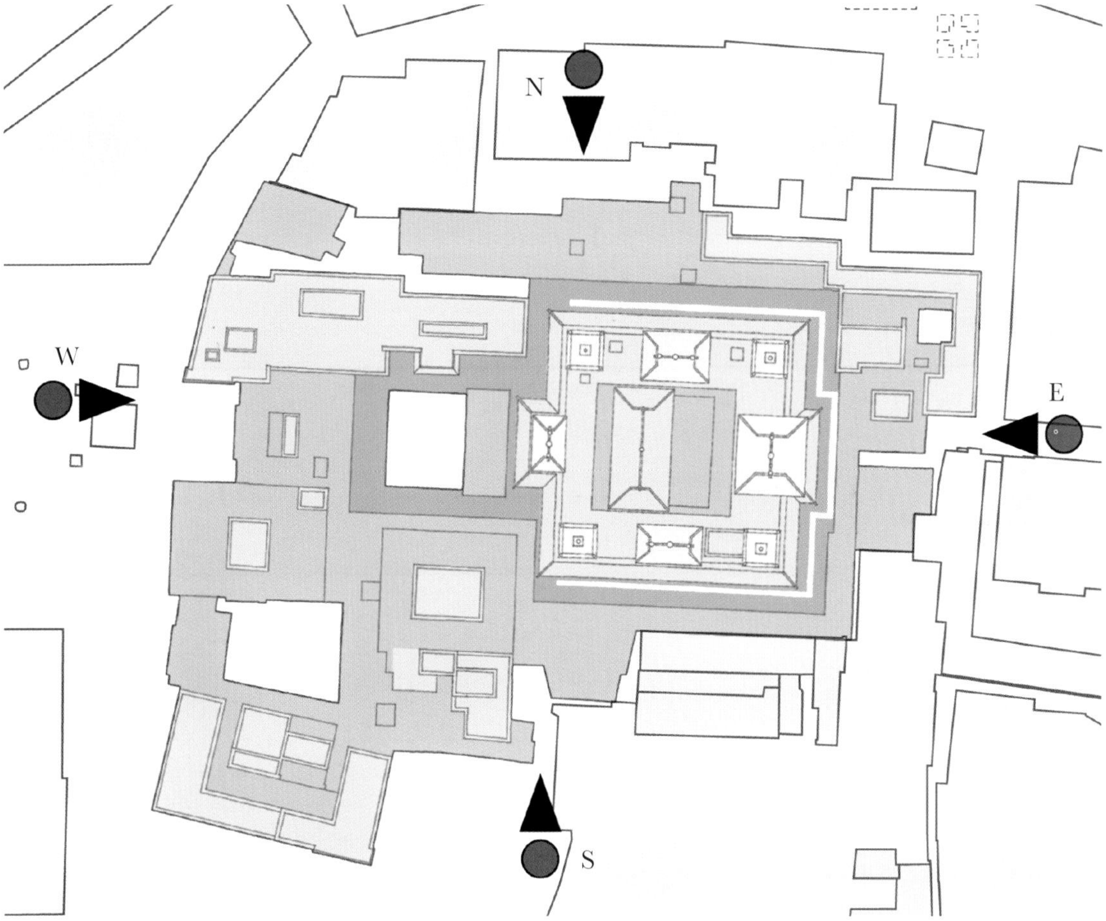

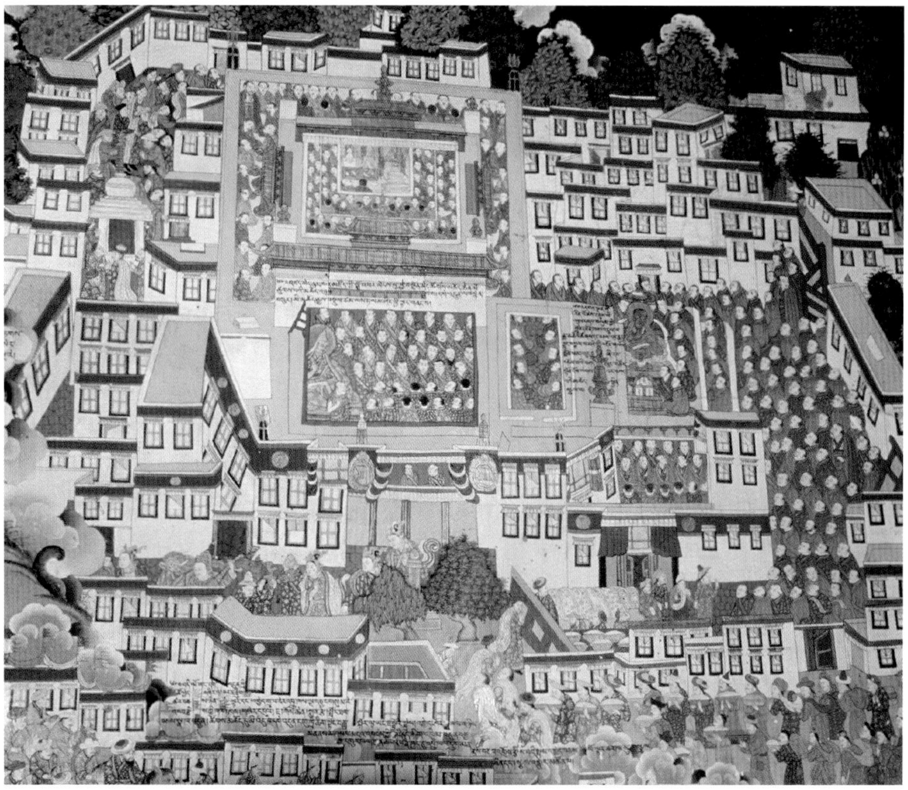

Wall-painting, Potala Palace, late 17th century, showing the Tsukla-khang during the Mönlam festival. The Fifth Dalai Lama is leading prayers inside the temple, while the Ganden throne holder is giving teachings in Sungchöra square.
To the left of the temple's main gate are the Lütsang gate and Trapchi-sha house. To the right are the Shira gate and the Shira courtyard, and facing Sungchöra square is the western gate of the Nga-khang complex. (2002 AA)

South: The Sungchöra gate, above which was the main meeting room of the Tibetan cabinet known as Kashag. (1981 FM)

Tsuklakhang, plan level 1

1 main gate
2 Kyamra Chenmo courtyard
3 Namtar Gosum Lha-khang
4 Lutsang courtyard
5 Lutsang gate
6 Chötrikhang
7 Drolma Lha-khang gate
8 Drolma Lha-khang
9 Nangkor (for a list of the chapels around the Nang-kor before 1959 see Zhwa sgab pa 1982)
10 Sera Tago Khang-sar
11 Sera Tago gate
12 kitchen
13 Ö-de-pug gate
14 Nga-khang gate
15 Nga-khang complex
16 Sungchöra gate
17 Sungchöra throne
18 Shira courtyard
19 kitchen
20 storage
21 Shira gate
22 willow tree planted by princess Wen-cheng
23 9th century stele with Sino Tibetan peace treaty
24 garage
25 Meru Nyingpa

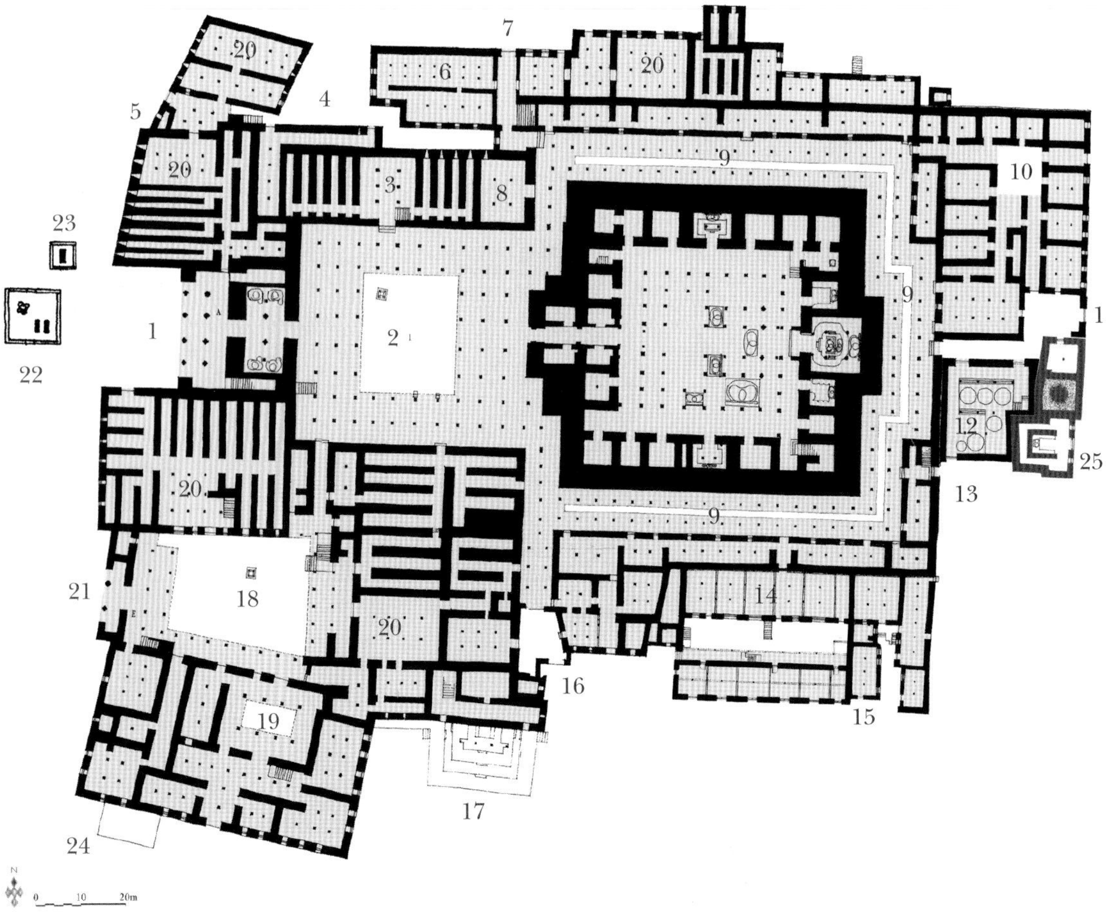

Level 2

1 Simchung Khamsum Zilnonreception room
2 former government dept, (paymaster)
3 'Lower Labrang' quarters for the Panchen Lama lineage
4 É-wam Chenmo hall
5 former govt. dept. (social security)
6 former govt. dept. (agriculture)
7 former govt. dept. (judiciary)
8 former govt. dept. (treasury)
9 former primary school
10 former rooms of the Tibetan cabinet (Kashag)
11 former govt. dept. (treasury)

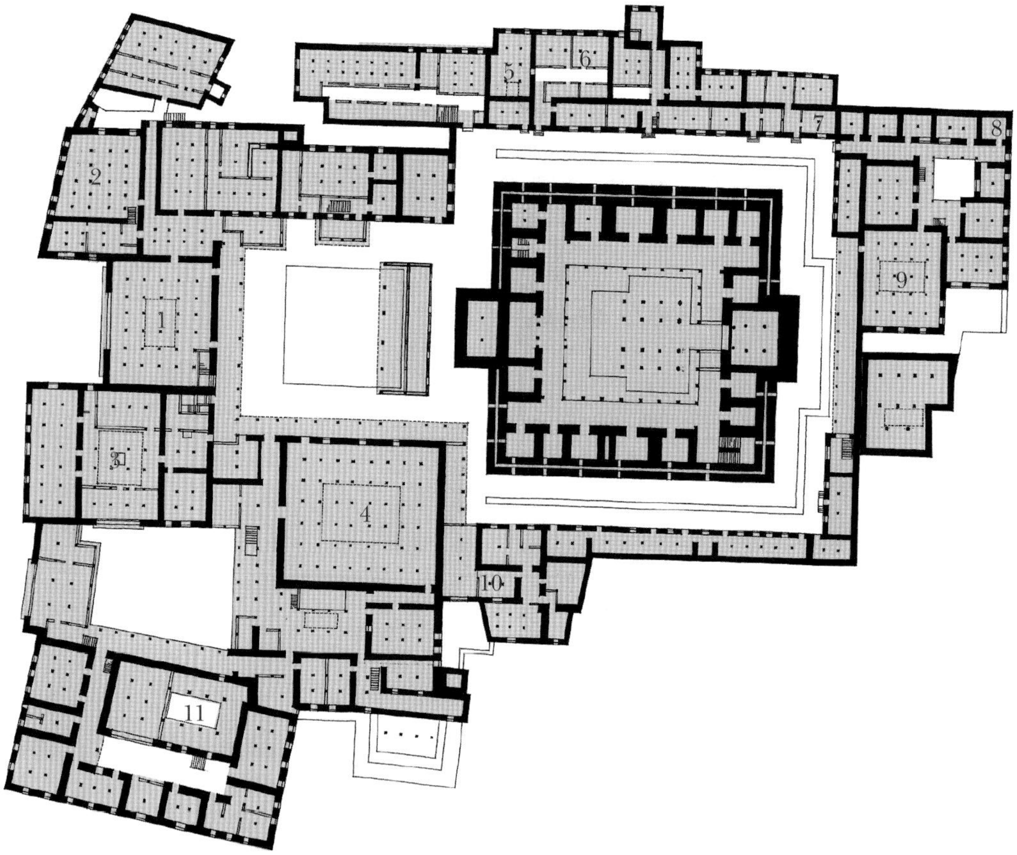

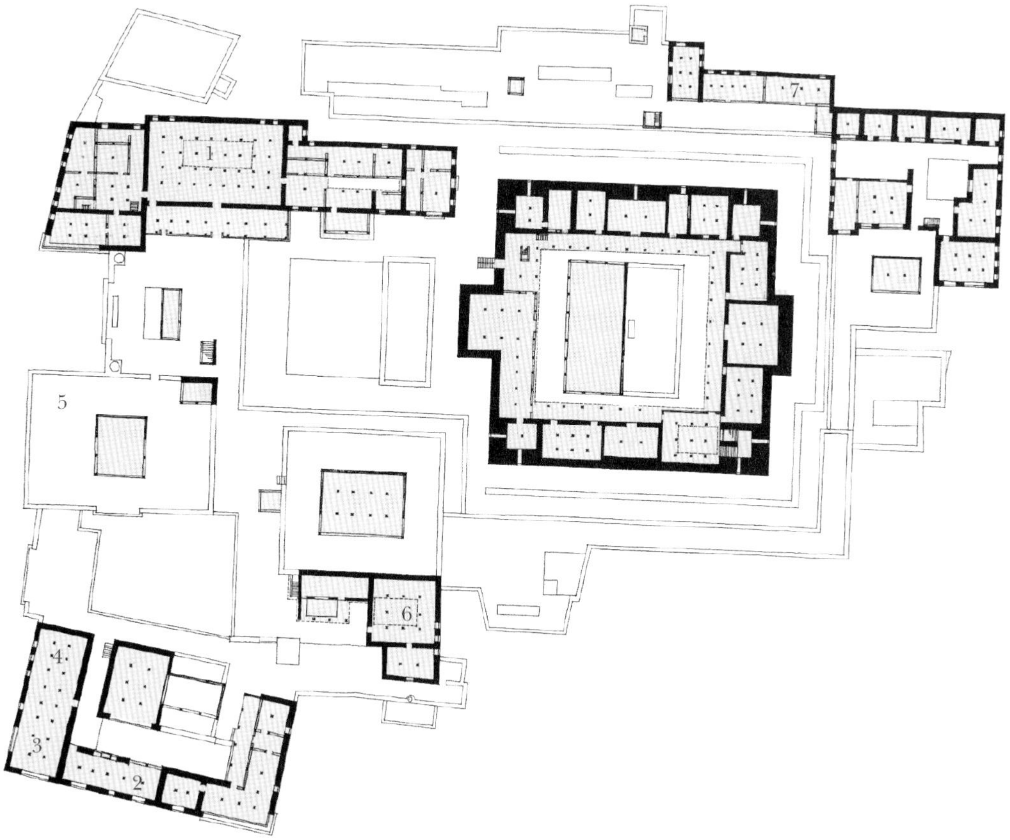

Level 3

1 Labrang Teng – quarters for the Dalai Lama
2 former govt. dept., 'salt and tea tax' (revenue collection)
3 former govt. dept. (Foreign Affairs)
4 former govt. dept., Teptsa Läkhung (to raise and account for funds for the Mönlam Chenmo festival)
5 Bön cross
6 kitchen serving the Dalai Lama
7 storage for religious objects

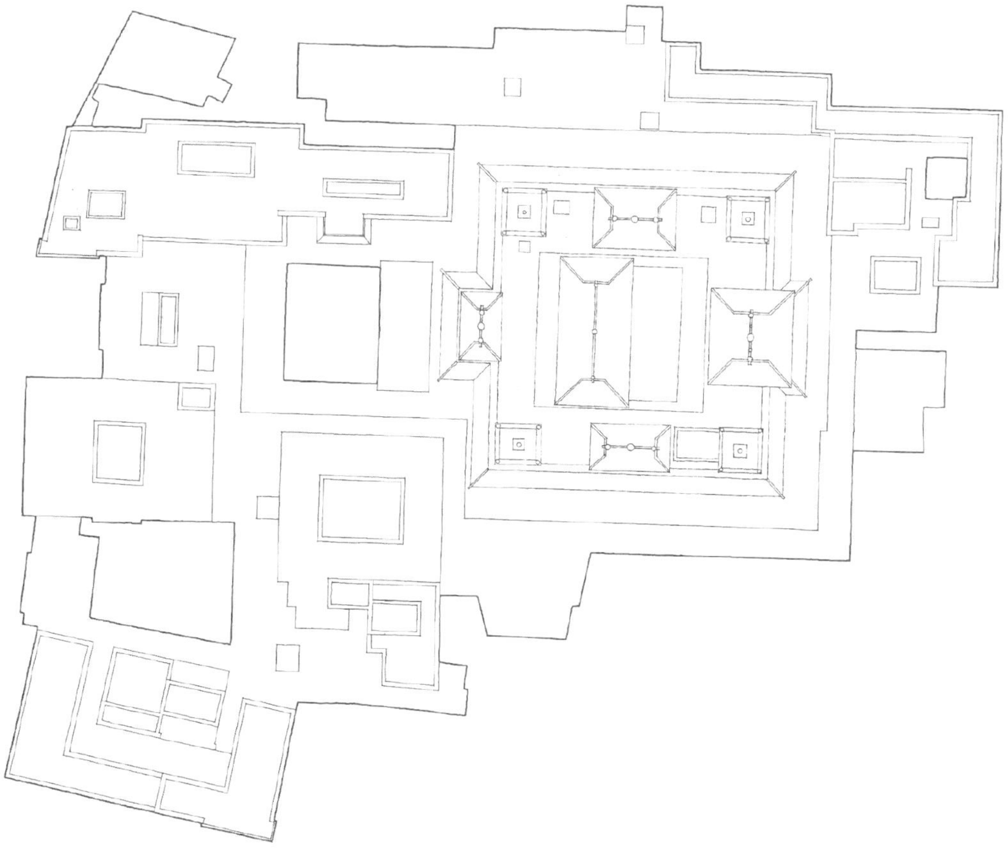

Roof plan

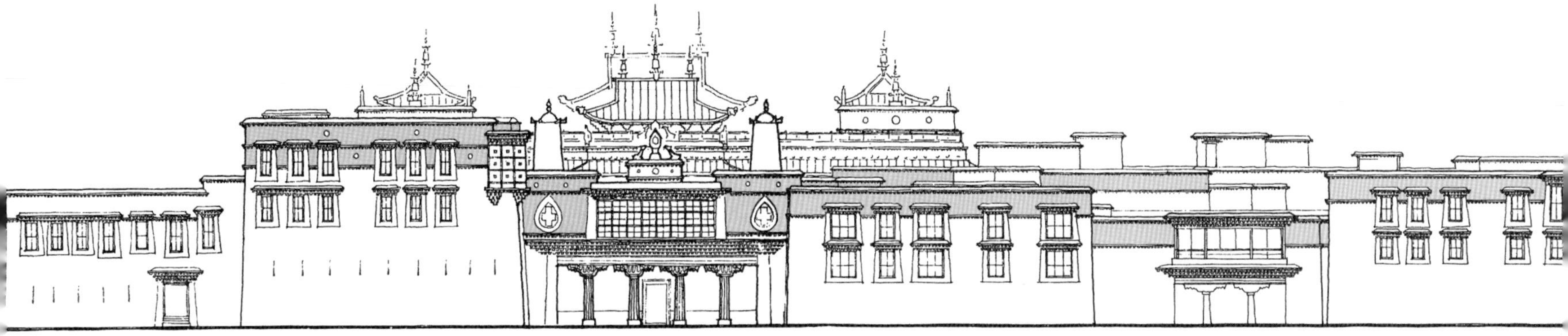

Tsuklakhang west elevation (CRO).

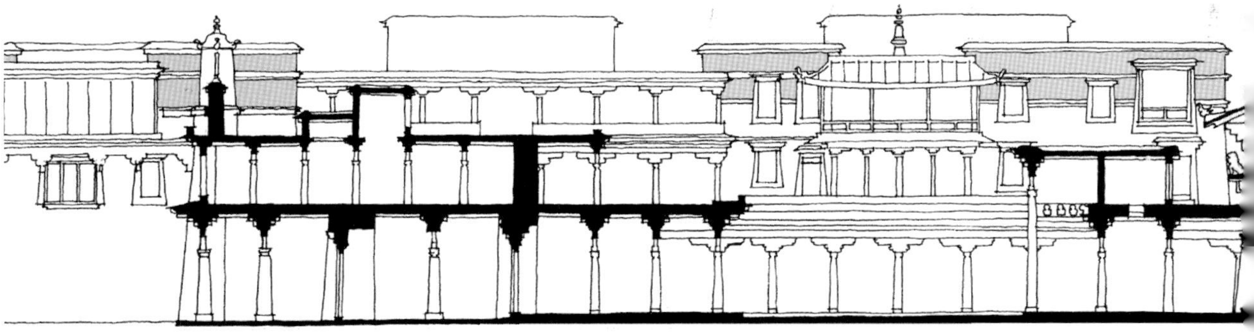

West-east section. (Minyak Chökyi Gyentsen and JH with BU, EK, AA)

Kyamra Chenmo courtyard, built by the Fifth Dalai Lama in part with pillars taken from the sacked Shigatse palace monastery. The entablature is typical Ganden Po-trang architecture. (2003 JM)

On most days, one can see people performing ritual prostation in front of the Tsukla-khang's main gate, seen here decorated for Tibetan New Year. (1993 AA)

South elevation (JH).

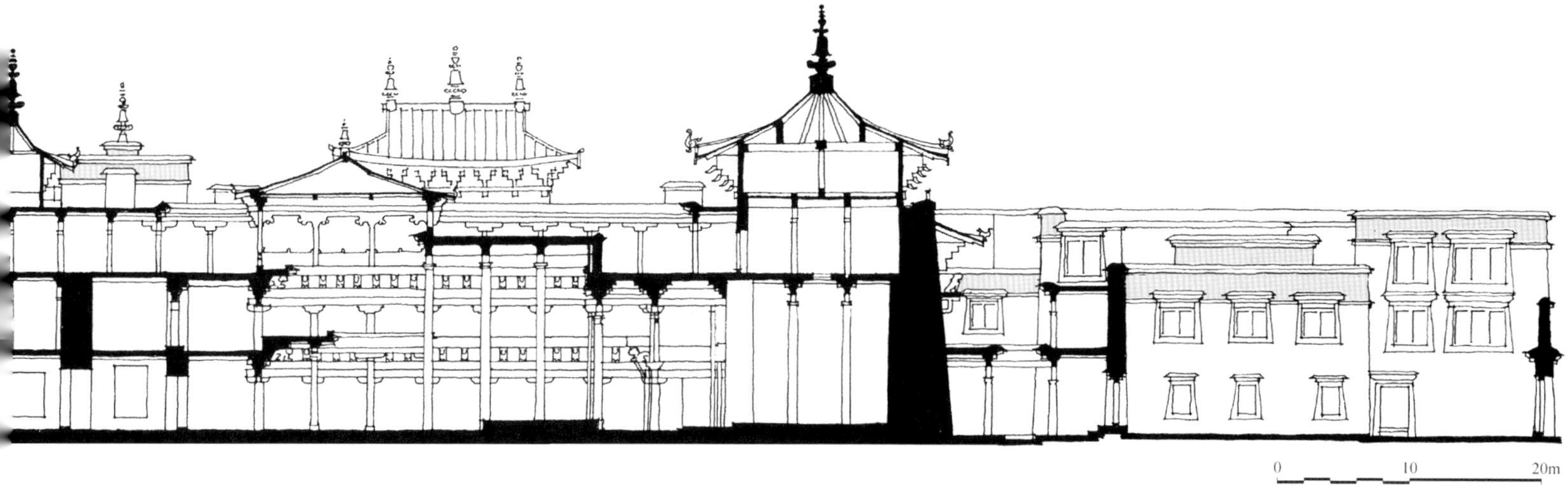

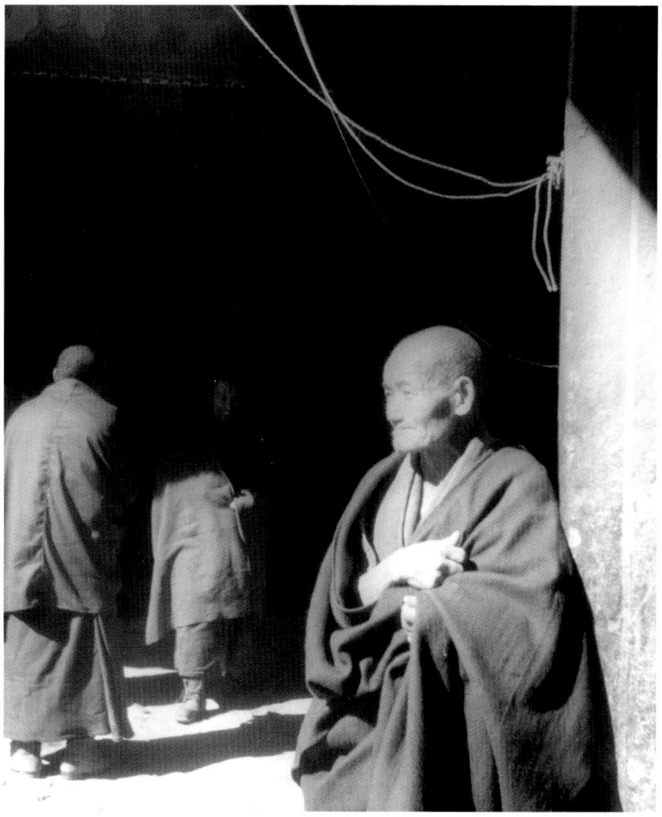

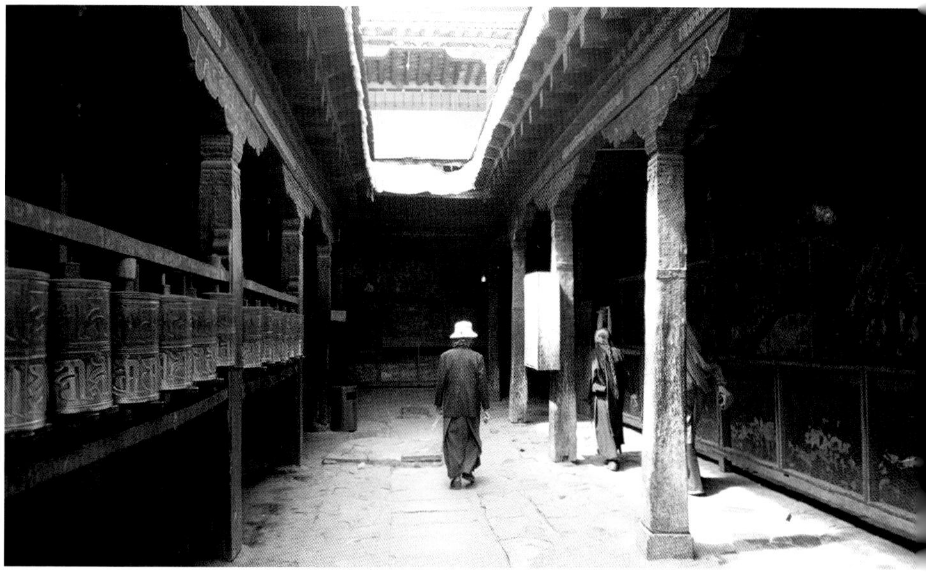

Nangkor, in existence since the 14th century and last renovated and repainted under the Thirteenth Dalai Lama. (2003 AA)

Monks in the Kyamra courtyard. (1987 AA)

The Nga-khang complex was built as an extension of the Tsukla-khang, linked to the Nangkor corridor via a two-winged gate. (Date unknown, courtesy Siddharta Man tuladhar)

Below right: The square on the southern side of the Tsuklakhang, known as Sungchöra, has been used to give Buddhist teachings in public since the time of Jé Tsong-kapa. On the eastern side of the square Drepung monastery had established an important satellite around the Nga-khang complex. (detail of wall-painting in the Norbulingka showing monks in Sungchöra during the Monlam festival, 1994 AA)

Nga-khang

The Lhasa Jokhang is associated with the Mo2nlam Chenmo festival, since its inception by Tsongkapa in 1409. For the duration of the festival, two weeks starting from the 15th day of the first Tibetan lunar month, the city authorities ceded control of the city to the monks of the 'Three Seats' (Drépung, Séra and Ganden). These monasteries established satellites around the Jokhang to be used during that period. During the Fifth Dalai Lama's time, the Nga-khang, a southern annex to the Jokhang owned by Drépung's Tantric College *(sNgags pa grva tshang)*, took its final shape. Precious tea utensils such as silver pots and copper cauldrons were stored here. The southern wing, two storeys with penbey frieze, had a large gate leading via an alley to the Barkor. From the northern wing, a door led directly into the Nangkor courtyard. The southern and western wings of the Nga-khang complex were destroyed during the Cultural Revolution, and lay in ruins until the early 1980s. The Lhasa Construction Department then erected a three-storey traditional building to be used as public housing. Two wings of the historic Nga-khang remained in sound condition, Ten-khang shar *(bsTan khang shar)* and Nga-khang Pu *(sNgags khang sbug)*, the innermost wing physically adjoining the Jokhang.

In 1996, the Lhasa Construction Department floated the proposal to strip the Nga-khang complex off the Jokhang, and build exclusive residential housing on the site as part of the government's housing privatisation drive. However, at the time, this proposal was rejected by the municipality. In 2002, two years after the Jokhang was officially inscribed on the UNESCO World Heritage List, the remains of the Nga-khang complex was demolished and replaced by concrete-frame housing blocks.

THF surveyed the Nga-khang complex in 1998. Ten-khang-shar, two storeys, had a classical facade onto the depug alleyway. The courtyard galleries had preserved historic wooden railings. The western wing of Nga-khang Pu had an old ground floor and modern second floor; the eastern wing was the best-preserved of all.

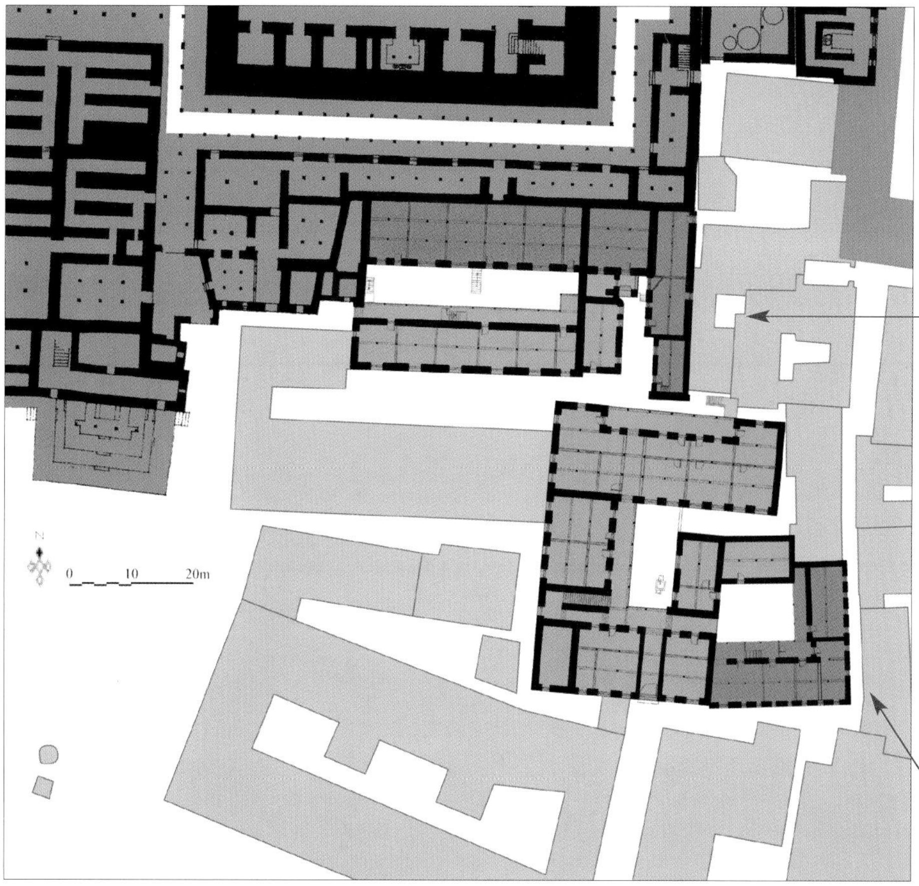

In 2002, the entire Nga-khang complex was stripped from the Tsuklakhang, and replaced by an expensive housing project. The eastern facade of the Tenkhang-shar wing of the Nga-khang, 18th century. (1999 AA)

Location map Nga-khang complex, condition in 1999 (KO+AA). bright orange: historic building pale orange: rebuilt in early 1980s after severe damage in the Cultural Revolution.

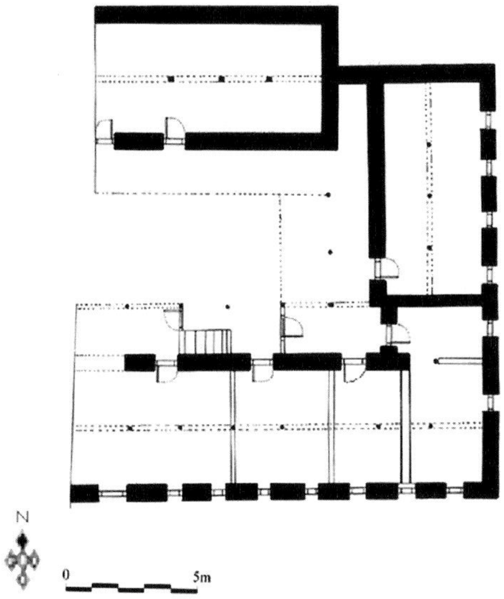

Tenkhang-shar was surveyed and drawn by the first group of Tibetan draftsmentrained by THF, Dakar and Loden. Plan level 1. (DK/L)

The south-eastern part of the Nga-khang complex was known as Tenkhang-shar house. (1998 PdA)

Below: Tenkhang-shar, south elevation (DK/L). The large window on the left was part of the entrance gate arrangement (no longer extant at the time of the survey).

Tenkhang-shar, east elevation. (DK/L)

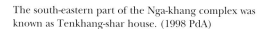

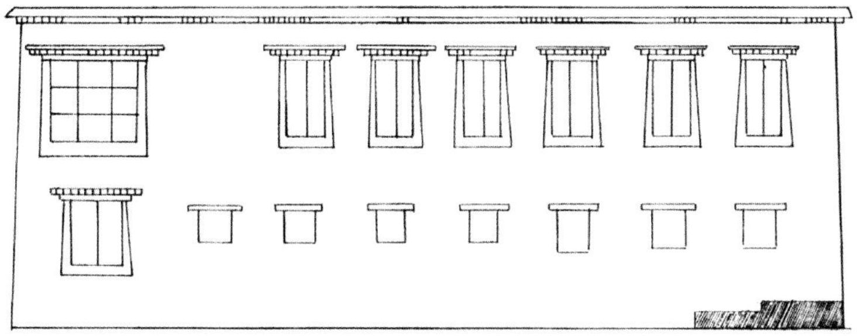

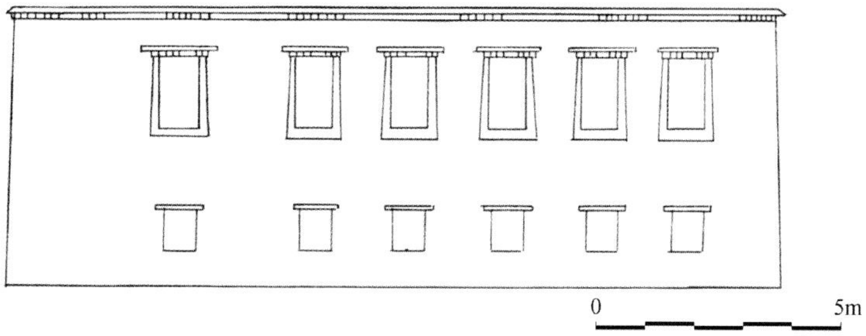

Site evaluation

Art historians and archaeologists have for some time pointed out Indian influences in the Jokhang's decorations and carvings, while the monument is often described as representing Newar craftsmanship. As we have shown above, the Lhasa Jokhang in fact belongs to a larger, pan-Indian idiom of temple building. This idiom can be traced to the Gandhara civilization of the 1st and 2nd centuries BC. It reached its maturity during the 5th and 6th centuries, and the best surviving examples are among the Ajanta and Ellora caves. It seems only natural that Indian architecture should have influenced early Tibetan temples, much like the Indian canonical works and treatises that were translated and copied for the organization of religious practice in Tibet.

Because the Jokhang matches this well-documented architectural idiom so perfectly, it is unlikely that it was turned into an Indian *vihara* through later modification. The *vihara* was clearly built at one time, apparently encouraged by the presence in Lhasa of a large contingent of Newar royalty. Their Licchavi kingdom was exposed to central Indian cultural achievements since a 3rd century matrimonial alliance with the Gupta dynasty. Later restorations and modifications of the Lhasa Jokhang preserved the square form, the central courtyard and the cell structure we see today. Since the later part of the royal period, the Tibetans built very different temples, sometimes based on Indian models but increasingly adapted for the needs and conditions prevalent in Tibet. No surviving building from any later period matches the Indian pattern in either plan or detailing.[46]

All this makes an early date highly probable. Combined with the stylistic evidence and the carbon-datings, we have little doubt confirming Songtsen Gampo's reign as the date of construction, with the workforce consisting of Nepali artisans, immersed in the latest pan-Indian temple building technologies.

The traditional story that the founding of the Lhasa Jokhang involved Chinese geomancy assisting Indian construction technology may be seen as applicable to the entire period of the 'early diffusion' of Buddhism, during which Indian and Chinese elements were absorbed and blended with indigenous ones to create an architectural style for Tibetan Buddhist civilization. The Samyé and Ramoché temples illustrate this principle graphically. The Lhasa Jokhang ignited this process, as recorded in empire-period inscriptions, but its architectural conception pre-dates the fusion of elements. The contribution of Wen-cheng's geomancy was to 'Tibetanize' the foreign Jokhang (and thus the foreign Buddhist religion) by linking it with a cosmologic scheme that helped to define ideology and territory of the Tibetan empire.

The Lhasa Jokhang is the oldest surviving Buddhist monument in Tibet, indeed the only imperial temple to survive in a comparable state of preservation into the 21st century, and a major repository of early Buddhist decorative art. During successive renovations undertaken by rulers and great Lamas over the long course of history, the building was expanded, modified and ornamented, naturally in the style of the day, but the original core of the temple was preserved throughout with remarkable efficiency. This 7th century vihara on the plain of Lhasa is also the earliest functioning Indian-style brick-and-timber temple, and one of the oldest timber frame buildings in the world.[47]

THF water and sanitation work 1999-2000: sewage piping underneath Sungchöra square, restoring the historic ground level in the Lu-tsang courtyard and subsequent paving with traditional slate stone. (all 1999-2000 AA)

In 2000, the Tsukla-khang officially became part of mankind's cultural heritage when it was listed by UNESCO as part of the Potala Palace inscription (2001 PU).

Part of the arga roof team trained by THF was hired by the Tsukla-khang for extensive restoration of the roofs and galleries (2002 AA).

Lhasa Tsukla-khang; celebration of the anniversary of Jé Tsongkapa's death on the 25th day of the 10th lunar month. (1996 AA)

Visitors with butter lamps in the early morning of the first day of the Tibetan New Year. (1992 AA)

Visitors with butter lamps on the upper floor. In the foreground is the huge Guru Rinpoché statue in the Kyilkhor-ting area, added in 1984. (1992 AA)

Footnotes

1 Vitali 1990, p. 69.
2 The architectural survey was carried out as part of the Tibet Heritage Fund (THF) Lhasa Old City Conservation project 1996-2000. Britta Uhlig, Esther Kehrer and André Alexander surveyed the central Tsukla-khang building. John Harrison surveyed the surrounding complex. Minyak Chökyi Gyentsen kindly provided us with a section drawing based on his 1983-84 survey. André Alexander and Pimpim de Azevedo undertook additional room-by-room inspection in the entire complex, and planned and supervised the Lu-tsang and Sung-chöra project activities. Engineer John Niewoehner and Lundrup Dorjé provided detail planning and implementation of the water and sanitation improvement works. Financial support for the THF project was provided by the embassies of Germany, Holland and Canada, MISEREOR and Trace Foundation, see also www.tibetheritagefund.org.
3 In 2000 China's State Administration for Cultural Relics famously reenforced the height limitation by ordering the demolition of the upper floor of the Surkhang department store.
4 Technically, the term refers only to the chapel in which the jo bo image is installed, i.e. the gtsang khang dbus ma.
5 'When [king Songtsen Gampo] was 22, in the Earth Dog year (638), the lake on the 'plain of milk' was drained. When he was 23, in the Earth Pig year (639), the foundations were laid. Then the king issued orders that his Tibetan subjects all had to help in building his temple, and people gathered from each region and held a conference on the building of a temple. At that time, the king marshalled 5,000 emanations and founded (a temple) the size of a medium sea-going vessel, modelled on the Henkang Vihara.' mKhas pa'i dga' ston p. 234, translated by Matthew Akester.
6 Vitali 1990 chapter 3 and Soerensen 1994 chapters 12-14 discuss in detail the more fantastic aspects of the founding, involving prophecies, miracles and apparitions.
7 See for example the Karchung inscription quoted elsewhere. In the Dunhuang Annals, (PT.252, & IO.103, Bacot 1940 p.20/42) for the year 710 we find: btsan mo kim shang khong co ra sa'i sha tsal du gshegs. Thanks to Professor Toni Huber for this reference.
8 bKa' chems ka khol ma p. 218, also Gyal rabs gsal ba'i me long translation Soerensen 1994 p. 274: 'In order to continue [the construction] Khri-btsun summoned many artists *(bzo bo)* from Nepal well-versed in crafts (rig byed), whereafter the upper construction was erected.'
9 See Vitali 1990 pp. 70-73 for a discussion of the founding in historical perspective.
10 'The king ordered that the Tibetan subjects should cut wood for his temple on the morrow, and when it was not carried out, the 5,000 emanations [of himself] filled the temple with wood by the evening of the same day. The next day, he marshalled 300 artist-emanations, and while they were doing the carpentry, queen Bhrikuti sent a maid to deliver the midday meal, a silver platter of meat and butter, thirteen cooked dishes, rice beer, wine and so on, because she was washing her hair and had no time to go herself. The maid saw 300 artisans at work whom she had never seen before and being unable to recognise the king, she came back. Then Bhrikuti took the meal herself, entered [the temple] as her maid had just done, and got past the emanated artisans to deliver the meal to the king, who was standing over the central Mandala wearing a black cape and a red headscarf, and holding a measuring line. When the meal was brought, he let the measuring line drop, and the 300 artisans slipped and the movement of their tools went awry. Seeing that the artisans were all emanations of the king, the maid laughed out loud and as he lost his concentration, a hatchet slipped, a chisel slipped, a saw slipped, and 100 workers cut the noses of 100 lions, bored 100 holes and sheared a corner off 100 pillars.' Excerpted from mKhas pa'i dga' ston II p. 235, translated by Matthew Akester.
11 'Phrul gyi lha btsan po. myes. khri srong brtsan gyi ring la. sangs rgyas kyi chos mdzod de. ra sa'i gtsug lag khang las stsogs pa brtsigs shing. dkon mchog gsum gyi rten btsugs pa dang, transcript kindly sent to Lhasa by the late Hugh Richardson in 1997, when THF assisted the Rama-gang villagers to re-assemble the pieces of the Kar-chung stele, blown to pieces in the late 1960s. The inscription is also published with translation in Richardson 1952 and Tucci 1950.
12 This was later published as bKa' chems ka khol ma, but its authenticity, even when taken as a source compiled (rather than discovered) during Atisha's time, at least in the available versions, is generally doubted. The pillar is believed to be Pillar 3 on the map in the map section, the second to the north of the Jowo chapel.
13 In the eyes of the Qing dynasty, this location may have appeared to lend legitimacy to a quartet of mostly lay ministers governing a self-declared Buddhist state.
14 Based on bKa' chems ka khol ma, mKhas pa'i dga' ston, Sørensen 1994, the Fifth Dalai Lama's Guide, lHa ldan rwa sa 'phrul snang gtsug lag khang gi dkar chag, Vitali 1990, Qiao Yu 1985, Su Bai 1996, Matthew Akester, and research on site including oral information supplied by monks and Lhasa residents.
15 This restoration may have been related to the resumption of Chinese-Nepalese ties and the visit to Lhasa and to the Tsukla-khang by the then king of Nepal in 1974. The Tsukla-khang remained closed to the public until the end of the 1970s.
16 Report of the 24th Session of the World Heritage Committee: 'The Jokhang Temple Monastery is an exceptional Buddhist religious complex, founded in the 7th century. Its buildings and decoration reflect the high quality of Tibetan art in the 7th century and again in the 15th-16th centuries, and also demonstrate cultural interchange between Tibet and its neighbouring countries', taken from http://whc.unesco.org/sites/707bis.htm.
17 The Fifth Dalai Lama's Guide mentions that lHa rje dGe ba 'bum rebuilt the outer walls, p. 33, see appendix. The Thirteenth Dalai Lama writes in his inventory of the Tsukla-khang (Lhasa blockprint edition, f5b, translation Matthew Akester): 'In the Water Hare year of the 13th cycle (1783), the temple was extensively restored by rGyal dbang 'Jam dpal rgya mtsho and the regent Tshe smon gling Ngag dbang tshul khrims, acting as preceptor and sponsor. Damaged mural paintings and woodwork around the Bar skor were replaced, the chapels were given new doors and iron grilles, and partitioning [walls] where needed, making a secondary enclosure around the main temple [...]'.
18 U-ru Ka-tsel lies on the outskirts of Me-tro Gungkar town, 80 km to the east of Lhasa at n29ō49' e91ō43'. Ké-ru, in the Ön valley to the east of Samyé, has been discussed by Vitali 1990 under the name of Ka-chu; the external wall supports are on the eastern side of the temple. Ké-ru is also discussed by Suo lang Wang dui and Zhang 1986: 17-29.
19 Gung thang dkar chag Everding 2000 p. 127.
20 rGya gar gyi lha khang legs, bKa' chems ka khol ma p. 222. The other sources offer a range of Indian monasteries as model, mKhas pa'i dga' ston p. 21 f.41b says the Tsuklakhang is based on the rGya'i hen khang bi har; bKa' thang sde lnga p.116 names the 'great Indian gTsug lag khang Ka ma la' as a model; Soerensen 1994 p. 274 lists additional examples. In the absence of a single, clearly identifiable model, we have argued that the Lhasa Tsukla-khang is based on a generic format, which Songtsen Gampo's alleged testament seems to confirm.
21 Ajanta caves 16 and 20 prove that these vihara-s are stone adaptations of contemporary timber architecture: their ceiling structure is cut to imitate wooden roof beams, boards and eaves.
22 bKa' chems ka khol ma reports that it took 13 years to build the second floor, p. 264; Soerensen 1994 p. 274 quotes a gloss in the rGyal rabs gsal ba'i me long saying '[The erection] of the upper construction (steng khang) of the lHa sa temple and Ra mo che, these two, lasted for two months before they were completed together', but notes that this is contradicted by the majority of sources that say the upper floor took 12 or 13 years to complete.
23 By the two Tshal pa khri dpon-s sMon lam rdo rje and Kun dga' rdo rje, Everding 2000 p. 127.
24 This jug has been discussed in detail by Amy Heller, see www.asianart.com/articles/heller/index.html.
25 Vitali 1990 chapter 3, see also graphic on p. 79.
26 These eight Bodhisattva-s originally formed the retinue of the principal chapel's Mi 'khrugs pa image, see the Fifth Dalai Lama's Guide, p.30 in the Tibetan version, and lHa ldan rwa sa 'phrul snang gtsug lag khang gi dkar chag p. 68.

27 Similar brass decorations can be found, for example, at the Golden Temple in Pathan in the Kathmandu valley.
28 Tibetan sources mention bricks in their description of the building and its foundation, Ka chem ka khol ma p. 218 has pha gu, which could mean baked brick, Soerensen 1994 p. 266 has so phag.
29 Soerensen 1994 p. 273.
30 Ka chem ka khol ma p. 218 and Soerensen 1994 p. 265 both describe gla wood as having been used to lay the temple's foundations in the o-tang lake. Tibetan carpenters have confirmed in interviews that gla ba wood is exceptionally durable and water resistant, but that it occurs mostly as a shrub or bush and that it was almost impossible these days to find a full-grown specimen.
31 Excerpted from mKhas pa'i dga' ston II p. 239, translated by Matthew Akester.
32 These doorways and their iconography have been discussed in detail by von Schroeder 2001 pp. 406-431. He describes the doors further as being made from acacia wood, but we were unable to confirm the species of the wood used. Tibetans popularly describe them as being carved from sandalwood or juniper, but that may be due to a vague assumption that these were the woods preferably used during Songtsen Gampo's time, and sandalwood does not occur in Tibet. See also note 32.
33 Gu ru mtsho skye rdo rje gtso 'khor and Chos rgyal gzim phug.
34 These two are also discussed in detail by von Schroeder 2001 p. 409. He identifies the images on the upper lintel of the northern-most doorway as Bhrikuti, Sri Potalak-Lokanatha, Indra, Maitreya or Kubera, Lakshmi; and on the southern-most as Sarasvati or Tara, Avalokitesvara, Maitreya.
35 Thub pa gtso 'khor (s); for (n) according to Zhwa sgab pa 1982 bKa' bstan sogs bzhugs pa'i lha khang, according to Taring 1980 'Jigs byed lha khang. The Tsuklakhang monks generally regard Shakapa as reliable. The chapels on the northern side were closed and empty during the investigation, and their original names and usage could not be ascertained in all cases. Vitali 1990 p. 76 has a diagram illustrating the original placement of sculptures based on mKhas pa'i dga' ston, for (n) we find yaksha (gNod sbyin pho), for (s) yaksha (gNod sbyin pho) and 'two wrathful king kang'.
36 Gung thang dkar chag, see Everding 2001 p. 127; the creation of the seng ldeng sgo glegs must be placed before 1346. Tibetans often translate seng ldeng as sandalwood (for which the term tsan dan stands more frequently). Sandalwood does not occur in Tibet and the term is usually a euphemism for the equally fragrant but locally-available juniper wood.
37 Sørensen 1994 p. 415.
38 gNam g.yengs rdo rje'i rva ra, the 'vajra enclosure [supported by] sky-bearing [pillars]', was provided by the sNe'u rdzong ruler Grags pa rgyal mtshan following a request from Tsongkha-pa, see the Fifth Dalai Lama's Guide. However, the same source also mentions that the Tsel-pa ruler Gadé Zangpo (ca. 1396-1410, i.e. a contemporary of Tsongka-pa's time in Lhasa) extended 12 pillars, which can only apply to the same pillars and so would appear to be a confusion.
39 Excerpted from mKhas pa'i dga' ston II p. 238, translated by Matthew Akester.
40 Gandharan influences have already been noted by Vergara and Beguin 1987.
41 The results were presented at the 8th seminar of the International Association of Tibetan Studies in Bloomington, Indiana (the proceedings are still unpublished).
42 Dr. Achim Bräuning, Christine Roth and Peter Wittmann kindly contributed this paragraph to the present publication. Dr. Bräuning has also published a number of papers on his findings, including Dendrochronologia 19 (1): 127-137.
43 bKa' chems ka khol ma p. 215.
44 Excerpted from mKhas pa'i dga' ston II p. 238, translated by Matthew Akester.
45 Discussed in detail by Vitali 1990 chapter 3. Vitali (ibid.) and Soerensen 1994 chapter 15 also offer descriptions of wall-paintings in the Tsuklakhang during Songtsen Gampo's time according to later sources. Professor Heather Stoddard, Michael Henss and Lionel Fournier have kindly shared their photographs of these paintings.
46 The southern monastery of Tan-druk (Khra 'brug), attributed to Songtsen Gampo, located at n29ŏ08' e91ŏ47' near the town of Tsé-tang in Lhoka prefecture, must be mentioned for comparison. The arrangment of six surviving cells on the ground floor leaves room for speculation that the original structure might have been based on a comparable vihara structure. Tan-druk was rebuilt several times, and the Chinese archaeologist Su Bai (1998: 74-76) claims no imperial period structures remain. Sonam Wangdu and the present author undertook research and survey work in Tan-druk, which we will present under separate cover. Tan-druk is discussed by Wang Yi 1961, Suo lang Wang dui and Zhang Zhong li 1986, and Su Bai 1998. Sørensen and Hezod have published a lengthy discussion of this important monument with the Österreichische Akademie der Wissenschaften (Thundering Falcon, Vienna 2005).
47 Japan's Horyu-ji temple founded 607 in Nara is generally considered to be the world's oldest functioning timber frame building.

Standing bodhisattvas and the gatekeeper Vajrapāṇi within the Central Inner Sanctum.

Part 5

108 Bronzes from the Jokhang Repository

Contained within the Great Temple of Lhasa there are some 800 portable metal sculptures and thousands of painted scrolls. Approximately 500 of the former were photographed and documented by Ulrich von Schroeder between 1992 and 1997. These are of diverse provenance – originating from Kashmir, Northern India, Nepal, Tibet and China. Among them, 311 have been published in his *Buddhist Sculptures in Tibet* (2001). A further selection of 108 bronzes are published here for the first time. Many of the portable metal sculptures were offered to the Great Temple by the populace for safekeeping in the aftermath of the Cultural Revolution, and are housed in the former Kungarawa Chapel (see p. opp.) of the Middle Storey (see p. 82, no. 83).

24D (See p. 273).

1A

1B

1C

1A **Avalokiteśvara Padmapāṇi**
North-Eastern India: Late Pāla Style; 12th C.
Brass; cast in two parts. Ht: 20 cm.
Inv. no. 517.

1B **Buddhaḍākinī**
North-Eastern India: Late Pāla Style; 12th C.
Brass; hollow cast in two piece. Ht: 14.5 cm.
Inv. no. 752.

1C **Unidentied Tārā**
North-Eastern India: Late Pāla Style; 12th C.
Brass; hollow cast in one piece. Ht: 15.2 cm.
Inv. no. 232.

1D **Avalokiteśvara**
North-Eastern India: Late Pāla Style; 12th C.
Gilt copper; hollow cast in one piece.
Ht: 12.2 cm. *Inv. no. 420.*

1E **Pīta-Jambhala**
North-Eastern India: Late Pāla Style; 12th C.
Brass; hollow cast in one piece. Ht: 9.6 cm.
Inv. no. 295[A].

1D

1E

2A

2B

2C

2A **Buddha Maitreya or Buddha Sākyamuni (?)**
Western Tibet (mNga' ris); circa 11th C.
Buddha hollow cast of brownish brass; nimbus solid cast of yellowish brass. Ht: (total) 25.1 cm; (Buddha) 17.2 cm. *Inv. no. 396.*

2B **Vajrasattva**
Western Tibet (mNga' ris); 11th/12th C.
Brass; hollow cast in two parts. Ht: 19.6 cm.
Inv. no. 548.

2C **Sthiracakra Mañjuśrī**
Western Tibet (mNga' ris); 11th/12th C.
Brass; hollow cast in one piece. Ht: 18.7 cm.
Inv. no. 979.

2D **Avalokiteśvara Padmapāṇi**
Tibetan Brass Traditions; 12th/13th C.
Brass; hollow cast in one piece. Ht: 37.5 cm.
Inv. no. 359.

2E **Mañjuśrī**
Western Tibet (mNga' ris); 12th C.
Brass; cast in two parts. Ht: 21.5 cm.
Inv. no. 305[B].

2D

2E

3A

3B

3C

3D

3E

3A **Vairocana**
Tibetan Brass Traditions; circa 13th C.
Brass; hollow cast in two parts, with the crown separately cast. Ht: 50.5 cm.
Inv. no. 986.

3B **Akṣobhya**
Tibetan Brass Traditions; circa 13th C.
Brass; hollow cast in one piece. Ht: 26.7 cm.
Inv. no. 297.

3C **Amoghasiddhi**
Tibetan Brass Traditions; circa 13th C.
Brass; hollow cast in one piece. Ht: 32 cm.
Inv. no. 180[B].

3D **Vairocana**
Tibetan Brass Traditions; circa 13th C.
Brass; hollow cast in one piece. Ht: 41 cm.
Inv. no. 284[B].

3E **Amoghasiddhi**
Tibetan Brass Traditions; circa 13th C.
Brass; hollow cast in one piece. Ht: 37.2 cm.

4A

4B

4C

Inv. no. 161.

4A **Akṣobhya**
Tibetan Brass Traditions; circa 13th C.
Brass; hollow cast in one piece. Ht: 37.3 cm.
Inv. no. 785.

4B **Maitreya**
Tibetan Brass Traditions; 14th C.
Brass; hollow cast in one piece. Ht: 23.3 cm.
Inv. no. 255.

4C **Vairocana**
Tibetan Brass Traditions; 13th C.
Brass; hollow cast in one piece. Ht: 41.6 cm.
Inv. no. 274.

4D **Maitreya**
Tibetan Brass Traditions; 14th C.
Brass; hollow cast in one piece. Ht: 42.1 cm.
Inv. no. 11[B].

4E **Vajrasattva**
Tibetan Brass Traditions; 14th C.
Brass; hollow cast in one piece. Ht: 24 cm (?)
Inv. no. 321.

4D

4E

5A

5B

5C

5D

5E

5A **Buddha Śākyamuni**
Tibetan Brass Traditions; 12th/13th C.
Brass; hollow cast in one piece. Ht: 27.2 cm.
Inv. no. 990.

5B **Buddha Śākyamuni**
Tibetan Brass Traditions; 12th/13th C.
Brass; hollow cast in one piece. Ht: 22.7 cm.
Inv. no. 787.

5C **Buddha Śākyamuni**
Tibetan Brass Traditions; 12th/13th C.
Brass; hollow cast in one piece. Ht: 28.5 cm.
Inv. no. 211.

5D **Buddha Śākyamuni**
Tibetan Brass Traditions; 13th/14th C.
Brass; hollow cast in one piece. Ht: 25.2 cm.
Inv. no. 292.

5E **Buddha Śākyamuni**
Tibetan Brass Tradition; 13th/14th C.
Brass; hollow cast in one piece. Ht: 26.8 cm.
Inv. no. 261[B].

6A

6B

6C

6D

6E

6A **Buddha Vajrāsana**
Tibetan Brass Traditions; circa 14th C.
Brass; hollow cast in piece. Ht: 37 cm.
Inv. no. 23[A].

6B **Buddha Śākyamuni**
Tibetan Brass Traditions; circa 14th C.
Brass; hollow cast in one piece. Ht: 16.8 cm.
Inv. no. 209[A].

6C **Buddha Śākyamuni**
Tibetan Brass Traditions; 12th C.
Partly copper and partly brass; hollow cast in one piece. Ht: 16.4 cm.
Inv. no. 271[A].

6D **Buddha Śākyamuni**
Tibetan Brass Traditions; circa 13th C.
Brass; hollow cast in one piece. Ht: 44.2 cm.
Inv. no. 786[B].

6E **Buddha Śākyamuni**
Tibetan Brass Traditions; circa 13th C.
Brass, hollow cast in one piece. Ht: 37 cm.
Iinv. no. 419[B].

7A

7C

7D

7A **Vajradhara** (B not ill.)
Tibetan Brass Traditions; 14th C.
Brass; hollow cast in four parts, with the lower arms and lotus pedestal separately. Ht: 28.8 cm. *Inv. no. 162[C].*

7C **Buddha Śākyamuni**
Tibetan Brass Traditions; 12th C.
Brass; hollow cast in one piece. The bottom of the pedestal is not sealed. Ht: 26.8 cm. *Inv. no. 850.*

7D **Buddha Śākyamuni**
Tibetan Brass Traditions; 13th C.
Brass; hollow cast in one piece. Ht: 34.1 cm. *Inv.no. 970.*

7E **Buddha Maitreya**
Tibetan Brass Traditions; 13th C.
Brass; hollow cast in one piece. Ht: 35 cm. *Inv. no. 956.*

7F **Buddha Śākyamuni**
Tibetan Brass Traditions; 12th/13th C.
Brass; hollow cast in one piece. Ht: 34.5 cm. *Inv. no. 18.*

7E

7F

8A

8B

8C

8A **Vajradhara and Consort**
Nepal (Three Malla Kingdoms); 16th/17th C.
Gilt copper; hollow cast in three parts.
Ht: 11.5 cm. *Inv. no. 522.*

8B **Indra**
Nepal (Early Malla Period); 14th/15th C.
Gilt copper; hollow cast in one piece.
Ht: 13 cm. *Inv. no. 980.*

8C **Śyāma-Tārā ("Green Tārā")**
Nepal (Early Malla Period); 14th/15th C.
Gilt copper; hollow cast in one piece.
Ht: 24 cm. *Inv. no. 206[A].*

8D **Amitāyus**
Nepal (Early Malla Period); 14th/15th C.
Copper alloy partly gilt; hollow cast in one piece. Ht: 37.8 cm. *Inv. no. 229.*

8E **Maitreya**
Nepalese Schools in Tibet; circa 16th C. (?)
Gilt copper; hollow cast in two parts.
Ht: 25.1 cm. *Inv. no. 403.*

8D

8E

9A

9B

9A **Vajradhara**
Tibetan Gilt Copper Traditions; circa 16th C.
Gilt copper; hollow cast in two parts. Ht: 24 cm.
Inv. no. 45.

9B **Vajrasattva**
Tibetan Gilt Copper Traditions; 16th/17th C.
Gilt copper; hollow cast in one piece. Ht: 25 cm.
Inv. no. 19[A].

10A–B **Mañjughoṣa**
Tibetan Gilt Copper Traditions; circa 16th C.
Gilt copper; hollow cast in one piece. Ht: 36.4 cm. *Inv. no. 37[A].*

10C **Vajrasattva**
Tibetan Gilt Copper Traditions; 16th C.
Gilt copper; hollow cast in two parts. Ht: 44 cm. *Inv. no. 348[B].*

10D **Vajrasattva**
Tibetan Gilt Copper Traditions; 15th/16th C.
Gilt copper; hollow cast in one piece. Ht: 22.7 cm. *Inv. no. 312[B].*

10E **Amitāyus**
China (Ming Dynasty: Xuande Period); 1426–1435 AD
Gilt brass; hollow cast in one piece. Ht: 15.9 cm. *Inv. no. 579.*

10F **Amitāyus**
Tibetan Gilt Copper Traditions; 15th/16th C.
Gilt copper; hollow cast in one piece. Ht: 15.1 cm. *Inv. no. 320.*

10A

10B

10C

10D

10E

10F

11A

11C

11D

11A **Crowned Buddha Śākyamuni** (B not ill.)
Tibetan Gilt Copper Traditions; 14th/15th C.
Gilt copper; hollow cast in one piece.
Ht: 20.5 cm. *Inv. no. 837[A].*

11C **Crowned Buddha Maitreya or Śākyamuni (?)**
Tibetan Gilt Copper Traditions; 16th/17th C.
Gilt copper; hollow cast in one piece. Ht: 19.1 cm.
Inv. no. 220.

11D **Buddha Śākyamuni**
Tibetan Gilt Copper Traditions; circa 17th C.
Gilt copper; hollow cast in two parts. Ht: 34.5 cm.
Inv. no. 284[A].

11E **Maitreya**
Tibetan Gilt Copper Traditions; 16th/17th C.
Gilt copper; hollow cast in two parts. Ht: 28 cm.
Inv. no. 167[A].

11F **Maitreya**
Tibetan Gilt Copper Traditions; 19th C.
Gilt copper; hollow cast in three parts. Ht: 29 cm.
Inv. no. 163.

11E

11F

12A

12B

12C

12A **Buddha Śākyamuni**
Tibetan Gilt Copper Traditions; circa 13th C.
Gilt copper; hollow cast in three parts, with the head and lower right arm, which is lost, separately. Ht: 63 cm. *Inv. no. 987.*

12B **Buddha Vajrāsana**
Tibetan Gilt Copper Traditions; 14th C.
Gilt copper, hollow cast in two parts.
Ht: 40.6 cm. *Inv. no. 75[B].*

12C **Buddha Śākyamuni**
Tibetan Gilt Copper Traditions; circa 16th C.
Gilt copper; hollow cast in two parts.
Ht: 44.8 cm. *Inv. no. 136.*

12D **Buddha Śākyamuni**
Tibetan Gilt Copper Traditions; 15th C.
Ht: 45 cm. *Inv. no. 91.*

12E **Buddha Śākyamuni**
Tibetan Gilt Copper Traditions; 14th/15th C.
Gilt copper, hollow cast in two parts.
Ht: 45.2 cm. *Inv. no. 339.*

12D

12E

13A

13B

13A **Nirmāṇakāya Amitāyus**
Tibetan Gilt Copper Traditions; 14th/15th C.
Gilt copper; hollow cast in two parts.
Ht: 37 cm. *Inv. no. 21.*

13B **Buddha Śākyamuni**
Tibetan Gilt Copper Traditions; 14th/15th C.
Hollow cast in two parts: Buddha gilt copper, pedestal ungilt brass.
Ht: 42 cm. *Inv. no. 72.*

14A

14B

14C

14D

14E

14A **Buddha Śākyamuni**
Tibetan Gilt Copper Traditions; 13th C.
Gilt copper; hollow cast in two parts.
Ht: 55.2 cm. *Inv. no. 985.*

14B **Akṣobhya**
Tibetan Gilt Copper Traditions; circa 16th C.
Gilt copper; hollow cast in two parts.
Ht: 26.8 cm. *Inv. no. 12.*

14C **Nirmāṇakāya Amitāyus**
Tibetan Gilt Copper Traditions; 14th/15th C.
Gilt copper; hollow cast in two parts.
Ht: 45.7 cm. *Inv. no. 19[C].*

14D **Buddha Vajrāsana**
Tibetan Gilt Copper Traditions; 15th/16th C.
Gilt copper; hollow cast in two parts.
Ht: 41.8 cm. *Inv. no. 46[B].*

14E **Buddha Śākyamuni**
Tibetan Gilt Copper Traditions; 16th/17th C.
Gilt copper; hollow cast in two parts.
Ht: 33 cm. *Inv. no. 39[B].*

15A

15C

15D

15A **Pañjara Mahākāla** (B not ill.)
Indian Schools in Tibet: Pāla Style; circa 16th C. Brass; hollow cast in two parts.
Ht: 16.8 cm. *Inv. no. 735.*

15C **Mahākāla**
Indian Schools in Tibet: Pāla Style; 13th C.
Brass; hollow cast in one piece.
Ht: 11.3 cm. *Inv. no. 351.*

15D **Acala**
Tibetan Pāla Style; circa 12th C.
Brass; hollow cast in two parts.
Ht: 12.9 cm. *Inv. no. 159[B].*

15E **Acala**
Tibetan Pāla Style; circa 13th C.
Brass; hollow cast in one piece.
Ht: 36.8 cm. *Inv. no. 593.*

15F **Acala**
Tibetan Brass Traditions; 13th C.
Brass; hollow cast in one piece.
Ht: 19.6 cm. *Inv. no. 356.*

15E

15F

16A

16B

16C

16A-B **Pañjara Mahākāla**
Tibetan Gilt Copper Traditions;
14th/15th C.
Gilt copper; hollow cast in two parts.
Ht: 20.2 cm. *Inv. no. 37[B].*

16C **Kālacakra** (D not ill.)
Tibetan Gilt Copper Traditions;
14th/15th C.
Gilt copper; hollow cast in two parts.
Ht: (without modern pedestal) 30 cm.
Inv. no. 16[A].

16E **Saṃvara and Vajravārāhī**
Tibetan Gilt Copper Traditions;
16th/17th C.
Gilt copper; hollow cast in two parts.
Ht: c. 20 cm. *Inv. no. 14[C].*

16F **Saṃvara and Vajravārāhī**
Tibetan Gilt Copper Traditions; 16th C.
Gilt copper; hollow cast in one piece.
Ht: 19.7 cm. *Inv. no. 15[A].*

16E

16F

17A

17B

17C

17E

17A **Caṇḍa-Vajrapāṇi**
Tibetan Gilt Copper Traditions; 14th/15th C.
Gilt copper; hollow cast in one piece. Ht: 27 cm.
Inv. no. 27[A].

17B **Caṇḍa-Vajrapāṇi**
Tibetan Gilt Copper Traditions; 15th/16th C.
Gilt copper; hollow cast in one piece. Ht: 17.7 cm.
Inv. no. 245.

17C **Caṇḍa-Vajrapāṇi** (D not ill.)
Tibetan Gilt Copper Traditions; 15th/16th C.
Gilt copper image on a blackened brass pedestal; hollow cast in two parts. Ht: 14.2 cm.
Inv. no. 11[C].

17E **Acala** (F not ill.)
Tibetan Gilt Copper Traditions; 15th/16th C.
Gilt copper; hollow cast in one piece. Ht: 18.3 cm.
Inv. no. 354.

17G **Acala** (H not ill.)
Tibetan Gilt Copper Traditions; 15th C.
Gilt copper; hollow cast in one piece. Ht: 26.5 cm.
Inv. no. 192.

17G

18A

18B

18C

18E

18G

18A **Uṣṇīṣavijayā**
Tibetan Brass Traditions; 16th/17th C.
Brass; hollow cast in one piece. Ht: 15.1 cm.
Inv.no. 215.

18B **Uṣṇīṣavijayā**
Tibetan Gilt Copper Traditions; 18th C.
Gilt copper; hollow cast in one piece. Ht: 20.7 cm.
Inv. no. 186.

18C **Uṣṇīṣavijayā** (D not ill.)
Tibetan Gilt Copper Traditions; 15th/16th C.
Gilt copper; hollow cast in one piece. Ht: 18.9 cm.
Inv. no. 635[A].

18E **Guhyasamāja Akṣobhya with Sparśavajra**
(F not ill.) Tibetan Gilt Copper Traditions; 16th C.
Gilt copper; hollow cast in two parts. Ht: 22 cm.
Inv. no. 123.

18G **Guhyasamāja Akṣobhya with Sparśavajra**
(H not ill.) Tibetan Gilt Copper Traditions; 16th C.
Gilt copper; hollow cast in two parts. Ht: 25.5 cm.
Inv. no. 19[B].

19A

19B

19C

19D

19A **Phag mo gru pa (?)**
Tibetan Brass Traditions; circa 13th C.
Brass; hollow cast in one piece.
Ht: 19.2 cm. *Inv. no. 832.*

19B **Unidentified *Phag gru bKa' brgyud* Monk (?)**
Tibetan Brass Traditions; circa 13th C.
Brass; hollow cast in one piece.
Ht: 13.7 cm. *Inv. no. 536[B].*

19C **Unidentified *Phag gru bKa' brgyud* Monk (?)**
Tibetan Brass Traditions; circa 13th C.
Brass; hollow cast in one piece.
Ht: 22.1 cm. *Inv. no. 866.*

19D **Unidentified *Phag gru bKa' brgyud* Monk (?)**
Tibetan Brass Traditions; 13th/14th C.
Brass; hollow cast in one piece.
Ht: 15.4 cm. *Inv. no. 741.*

20B

20C

20A

20D

20E

20A **Unidentified *Phag gru bKa' brgyud* Monk (?)**
Tibetan Brass Traditions; 12th/13th C.
Brass; hollow cast in one piece.
Ht: 19.2 cm. *Inv. no. 571.*

20B–C **Phag mo gru pa (?)**
Tibetan Gilt Copper Traditions; 13th C.
Gilt copper; heavy hollow cast in one piece.
Ht: estimate 10 cm. *Inv. no. 840.*

20D–E **Unidentified *Phag gru bKa' brgyud* Monk (?)**
Tibetan Brass Traditions; 13th C.
Brass; hollow cast in one piece.
Ht: 13.9 cm. *Inv. no. 452.*

20F **Unidentified Monk**
Tibetan Brass Traditions; circa 12th C.
Brass; hollow cast in one piece.
Ht: 11.1 cm. *Inv. no. 150.*

20G **Hva shang**
Tibetan Brass Traditions; 14th/16th C.
Brass; hollow cast in one piece.
Ht: 9 cm. *Inv. no. 137.*

20F

20G

21A

21C

21D

21E

21F

21A **Unidentified *bKa' brgyud* Monk** (B not ill.)
Tibetan Brass Traditions; circa 14th C.
Brass; hollow cast in one piece.
Ht: 17.1 cm. *Inv. no. 410.*

21C **Unidentified *bKa' brgyud* Monk**
Tibetan Brass Traditions; circa 16th C.
Brass; hollow cast in one piece.
Ht: 14 cm. *Inv. no. 42[A].*

21D **Portrait Statue Inscribed as Mar pa (?)**
Tibetan Gilt Copper Traditions; circa 15th C.
Gilt copper; hollow cast in one piece.
Ht: 12.4 cm. *Inv. no. 81[A].*

21E **Karma Pakshi**
Tibetan Brass Traditions; 16th/17th C.
"Silver" alloy; hollow cast in one piece.
Ht: 19.8 cm. *Inv. no. 247.*

21F **Unidentified Karma pa**
Tibetan Gilt Copper Traditions; 16th/17th C.
Gilt copper; hollow cast in one piece.
Ht: 23.5 cm. *Inv. no. 4[A].*

22A

22B

22C

22D

22A–B Unidentified *bKa' brgyud* Monk
Tibetan Brass Traditions; 15th/16th C.
Brass; hollow cast in one piece.
Ht: 15.7 cm. *Inv. no. 214[B].*

22C rGyal sras spom brag pa bsod nams rdo rje
Tibetan Gilt Copper Traditions; circa 16th C.
Gilt copper; hollow cast in one piece.
Ht: 22.8 cm. *Inv no. 162[A].*

22D Unidentified *bKa' brgyud* Monk
Tibetan Gilt Copper Traditions; 14th/15th C.
Gilt copper; hollow cast in one piece.
Ht: 26.5 cm. *Inv. no. 978.*

22E sPyan snga Grags pa 'byung gnas
Tibetan Gilt Copper Traditions; 15th C.
Gilt copper; hollow cast in one piece.
Ht: 15.4 cm. *Inv. no. 299.*

22F 'Brom ston rGyal ba'i 'byung gnas (?)
Tibetan Gilt Copper Traditions; circa 16th C.
Gilt copper, hollow cast in one piece.
Ht: 18.1 cm. *Inv. no. 78.*

22E

22F

23A

23B

23C

23A–B **Mahāsiddha Tilopa**
Tibetan Gilt Copper Traditions;
circa 18th C.
Gilt copper; hollow cast in one piece.
Ht: 25.2 cm. *Inv. no. 85[A].*

23C–D **Mi la ras pa**
Tibetan Gilt Copper Traditions;
16th/17th C.
Gilt copper; hollow cast in one piece.
Ht: 10.9 cm. *Inv. no. 704.*

23E **Mi la ras pa**
Tibetan Brass Traditions; 16th/17th C.
Brass; hollow cast in one piece.
Ht: 11.8 cm. *Inv. no. 510[B].*

23F **gYu thog pa Yon tan mgon po**
Tibetan Brass Traditions; circa 16th C.
Brass; hollow cast in one piece.
Ht: 10.6 cm. *Inv.no. 125.*

23E

23F

24A

24B

24A–B **Virūpa as Teacher of the "Path with the Goal"**
Tibetan Gilt Copper Traditions; 15th C.
Gilt copper; image hollow cast in one piece with the pedestal separately made of an embossed sheet of copper.
Ht: 15.7 cm. *Inv. no. 626.*

24C–D **Virūpa "Arresting the Sun in its Course"**
Tibetan Gilt Copper Traditions; 15th C.
Gilt copper; hollow cast in one piece.
Ht: 27.7 cm. *Inv. no. 977.*

24C

24D ill. p. 249

Bibliography

Works in Tibetan

Anon, *Tun hong brag phug gi yig rnying [= Old Tibetan Chronicles of Dunhuang]*

Atiśa (disc.), *bKa' chems ka khol ma [= Pillar Testament]*. Gansu mi rigs dpe skrun khang (1989). See also Martin (1997), no. 4, pp. 24-25.

Buton Rinchendrub (1290-1364), *Chos 'byung [= Doctrinal History]*. Bod kyi shes rig dpe skrun khang. (1988) See also Martin (1997) no. 72, pp. 50-51.

Chahar Geshe Lobzang Tsultrim (1740-1810), *rJe rin po che'i rnam thar go sla bar brjod pa dge legs kun byung, also entitled rJe thams cad mkhyen pa tsong kha pa chen po'i rnam thar le'u drug pa*, contained in *The Collected Works of Cha Har dGe bshes*, Vol. 2, New Delhi (1972). See also Martin (1997), no. 339, p. 145.

Cangkya Rolpei Dorje (1717-86), *rGyal ba'i dbang po thams cad mkhyen gzigs rdo rje 'chang blo bzang bskal bzang rgya mtsho dpal bzang po'i zhal snga mas kyi rnam thar mdo tsam brjod pa dpag bsam rin po che'i snye ma [= Biography of Dalai Lama VII Kelzang Gyatso]*.

Chapel, "Lha sa gtsug lag khang gi lo rgyus rags bshad", in *Bod ljongs zhib 'jug*, pp. 10-44 (1982).

Dalai Lama V, Ngawang Lobzang Gyatso (1617-82), *Lha ldan gtsug lag khang gi dkar chag shel dkar me long. [= Inventory to the Great Temple of Lhasa]*, republished by Bod ljongs dpe-skrun-khang (2002).

—— *[rGyal rabs rdzogs ldan gzhon nu'i dga' ston] dpyid kyi rgyal mo'i glu dbyangs [=Song of the Queen of Spring]*. See Martin (1997) no. 222, pp. 107-8.

—— *Ngag dbang blo bzang rgya mtsho'i 'di snang 'khrul pa'i rol rtsad rtogs brjod kyi tshul du bkod pa du ku la'i gos bzang [Three-volume Autobiography of the Fifth Dalai Lama]*. Bod ljongs dpe-skrun-khang (1989).

Dalai Lama VII, Kelzang Gyatso (1708-57), *rTen gsum dkar chags*. In *gSung-'bum*, Vol. Cha.

Dalai Lama XIII Thubten Gyatso (1876-1933), *Lha ldan sprul pa'i gandola chen por nyams gsos bgyis ba'i dkar chag smon tshig dang 'brel ba phan bde'i bkod pa char du dngar pa dad snang 'bum phrag 'char ba'i 'o mtsho'i rdzing bu*. In *rGyal chog bcu gsum pa'i gsung 'bum*, Bi, pp. 661-84.

—— *bSam yas nyams gso'i dkar chag dad pa'i sgo 'byed.*

—— *rGyas gtab ra mo che'i nyams gso'i dkar chag mu tig do shal 'dzad med phan bde'i rgyan.*

Darmo Menrampa Lobzang Chodrak, *g.Yu thog gsar rnying gi rnam thar.* Beijing mi rigs dpe skrun khang (1982).

Depa Khenpo Lobzang Tu-je (1770-c 1835), *Tshe gling rgyal thog ngag dbang tshul khrims kyi rnam thar dad pa'i sgo ' byed* [= *Biography of Tseling Ngawang Tsultrim*]. See Martin (1997), no. 329, p. 143.

Desi Sangye Gyatso (1653-1705), *Baiḍūrya dkar po* [= *White Beryl*]. 2 vols. Krung go'i bod kyi shes rig dpe skrun khang (1996).

—— *dGa' ldan chos 'byung baiḍūrya ser po* [= *Yellow Beryl*]). Krung go'i bod kyi shes rig dpe skrun khang (1989). See also Martin no. 240, pp. 114-5.

—— *Baiḍūrya gYa' sel* [=Beryl: *Removal of Tarnish*]. 2 vols. published by Krung go'i bod kyi shes rig dpe skrun khang (2002); also by T. Tsepal Taikhang, New Delhi (1971).

—— *mChod sdong 'dzam gling rgyan gcig dkar chag thar gling rgya mtshor bsgrod pa'i gru rdzing.[= Inventory to the Great Golden Reliquary of Dalai Lama V; Unique Ornament of the World]*. Bod ljongs mi dmangs dpe skrun khang (1990).

—— *Rab gsal gser gyi snye ma* [= *Life of Dalai Lama VI*]. Bod ljongs mi dmangs dpe skrun khang (1989).

Dokhar Zhabdrung Tsering Wangyal (1697-1763), dPal mi'i dbang po'i rtogs brjod. See Martin (1997), no. 270, pp. 123-4.

Drakgon Tulku Jamyang Tenpa Gyatso, *dBus gtsang gnas yig mi brjed dran pa'i gsol 'debs gzur gnas mkhas pa'i rna rgyan.*

Drubthob Ngodrub (fl. 12th c, disc), *Ma ṇi bka' 'bum.* On this work, which may not have reached its final form until the 15th century, see Martin no. 16, p. 30.

Druk Gyalwang Choje, *rJe rin po che'i rnam thar thub bstan mdzes rgyan gcig ngo mtshar nor bu'i phreng ba [= Biography of Tsongkhapa]*. mTsho sngon mi rigs dpe skrun khang (1981).

Dudjom Rinpoche [Jigdrel Yeshe Dorje, 1904-87], *sNga ' gyur rnying ma'i chos 'byung lha dbang gYul las rgyal ba'i rnga bo che'i sgra dbyangs [= History of the Nyingma School of Tibetan Buddhism]*. Trans. Gyurme Dorje & Matthew Kapstein, London & Boston, Wisdom Publications. 1991. See also Martin (1997), no. 471, p. 186.

Gampopa Mipham Chokyi Wangchuk (fl. 1617), *gDan sa chen po dpal dvags lha sgam po'i ngo mtshar gyi bkod pa dad pa'i me tog*, ff. 26 (sGam-spar dpe-ring).

Gegyepa Tendzin Dorje, "sDe srid sangs rgyas rgya mtsho'i byung ba don bsdus rang bzhin gsong por smras pa'i gtam," in *Bod ljong zhib 'jug*, No. 2, pp. 31-4 (1985).

Gendun Chopel, "rGyal khams rig pas bskor ba'i gtam rgyud gser gyi thang ma zhes bya ba bzhugs so," *in dGe 'dun chos 'phel gyi gsung rtsom dang po*, Vol. 1, *Gangs can rig mdzod*, No. 10, Bod ljongs bod yig dpe rnying dpe skrun (1990).

Go Lotsäwa Zhonupel (1392-1481), *Deb ther sngon po* [= *Blue Annals*]. 2 vols. Sichuan mi rigs dpe skrun khang (1984). See also Martin no. 141, pp. 78-79.

Gyurme Dechen (1540-1615), *Thang stong rnam thar kun gsal nor bu* [*Biography of Thangtong Gyalpo*]. Sichuan mi rigs dpe skrun khang (1982). Trans. C. Stearns, King of the Empty Plain (Snowlion, 2007).

Jamgon Amyezhab (1597-1662), *Sa skya gdung rabs ngo mtshar bang mdzod.* Mi rigs dpe skrun khang (1986). See also Martin (1997) no. 210, p. 104.

Jamyang Khyentse Wangpo, (1820-92), *dBus gstang gnas yig ngo mtshar lung ston me long.* In *'Jam dbyangs mkhyen brtse'i dbang po'i gsung rtsom gces sgrig*, pp. 273-311. Si khron mi rigs dpe skrun khang (1989). See also Martin (1997) no. 400, p. 166.

Kalon Shadra & Kadrung Nornang, *Yig bskur rnam gzhag* [= *Letter Writers*], edited and published by G. Tharchin, Kalimpong, Tibet Mirror Press (1956).

Karma Chagme [aka. Raga-asya, c. 1605-70], "Rigs rus dang 'brel zhing sangs rgyas kyi bstan pa'i 'jug sgo dang mthun pa'i spyi'i rnam thar", in *dGe slong Ragasya'i rnam thar [= The Autobiographical Writings of Karma Chags med]*, published by Tana Lama, Kollegal.

Katok Situ Chokyi Gyatso (1880-1925), *dBus gstang gnas yig nor bu zla shel sen mo do. Gangs can rig mdzod*, Vol. 33. Bod ljongs bod yig dpe rnying dpe skrun khang (1999). See also Martin no. 433, p. 176.

Katok Tsewang Norbu (1698-1755), *Bod kyi lha btsan po'i gdung rabs tshig nyung don gsal. Contained in Kaë thog rig 'dzin tshe dbang nor bu'i bka' 'bum.* Vol. 3, pp. 45-60. Krung go bos rigs dpe skrun khang (2006). See also Martin (1997), no. 284, p. 128.

Khedrubje Gelek Pelzang (1385-1483), *rJe btsun bla ma tsong kha pa chen po'i ngo mtshar rmad du byung ba'i rnam par thar pa dad pa'i 'jug ngogs* [= Biography of Tsongkhapa], Qinghai (1982).

Koshul Drakpa Jungne and **Gyalwa Lobzang Khedrub** (eds), *Gangs can mkhas grub rim byon ming mdzod.* mTsho sngon mi rigs dpe skrun khang (1992). See Martin, no. 602, p. 218.

Kunkhyen Pema Karpo (1527-92), *rNam thar thugs rje chen po'i zlo gar* [= *Autobiography of Pema Karpo*].

Lechen Kunga Gyaltsen (fl. 1494), *bKa' gdams chos 'byung gsal ba'i sgron me.* See Martin (1997), no. 148.

Lhalu Tsewang Dorje, "Rang nyid kyi byung ba rags rim brjod pa" [= *Rough Personal History*], in *Bod kyi lo rgyus rig gnas dpyad gzh'i rgyu cha bdams bsgrigs*, Issue No. 16, edited by Bod rang skyong ljongs srid gros lo rgyus rig gnas dpyad gzhi'i rgyu cha u yon lhan khang, Pe cing mi rigs dpe skrun khang (1993).

Longdol Ngawang Lobzang (1719-94), *bsTan pa'i sbyin bdag byung tshul ming gi rnam grangs, in Gangs can rig mdzod*, Vol. 21, pp. 419-459. Bod 'jongs bod yig dpe rnying dpe skrung khang (1991). See also Martin (1997), no. 321, p. 140.

Minyag Chokyi Gyaltsen, "Srong btsan sgam po'i dus kyi pho brang potala'i bzo dyibs dang chags tshul skor rob tsam dpyad pa", in E. Sperling (ed), *Tibetan Studies*, 2000.

Ngawang Lhundrub Dargye Nomonqan, *Tshangs dbyangs rgya mtsho'i gsang rnam [= Secret Biography of Dalai Lama VI].* Bod ljongs mi dmangs dpe skrun khang (1981).

Ngor Khenchen Palden Chokyong Zangpo (1702-59), *Rang rnam sna tshogs stug po'i 'khri shing.*

Nyala Sherab Ozer, *lCags bdud nyag sked kyi lo rgyus dpa' gtum stag mo'i nga ro.*

Nyangral Nyima Ozer (1136-1204), *Chos 'byung me tog snying po sbrang tsi'i bcud [= Doctrinal History entitled Honey Essence of Flower Nectar].* See Martin (1997), no. 18, pp. 30-31.

Nyima Tsering, *Lha sa gtsug lag khang*, illustrated with captions and text. Beijing, (2000).

Orgyan Lingpa (c. 1323-1360, disc.), *rGyal po bka' thang.* In *bKa' thang sde lnag.* Mi rigs dpe skrun khang (1986). See also Martin (1997), no, 78, p. 53.

Orgyan Lerab Lingpa (1856-1926, disc.), *Phur pa yang snying spu gri.* In the *Collected Visionary Revelations and Textual Discoveries of Las rab gling pa.* Byalakuppe, Pema Norbu Rinpoche (1985+).

Paôchen IV Lobzang Chogyen, *Rang rnam spyod tshul gsal ba'i ston pa nor bu'i 'phreng ba.*

Paôchen Sonam Drakpa (1478-1554), *bKa' gdams gsar rnying gi chos 'byung.* See Martin (1997) no. 164, p. 87.

Patrul Orgyan Jigme Chokyi Wangpo (1808-1887), *Kun bzang bla ma'i zhal lung [= The Words of My Perfect Teacher].* In *dPal sprul gsung 'bum.* Vol.

Pawo Tsuklak Trengwa (1504-66), *Chos 'byung mkhas pa'i dga' ston [= Doctrinal History: Feast of the Scholars].* Pe cing mi rigs dpe skrun khang, Vols.1-2, 1985. See also Martin no. 168, pp. 88-89.

Phurchok Ngawang Jampa (1682-1762), *Jo bo'i smon lam drang srong shis brjod 'dod pa kun 'ja'i mdzas sbyangs.*

Riwoche Pontsang (1446-1451), *Lho rong chos 'byung [= Religious History of Lhorong].* Bod ljongs bod yig dpe rnying dpe skrung khang, Vol. 26 (1994). See also Martin (1997), no. 118, pp. 69-70.

Säkyei Gelong Zangpo, *Gangs can 'dir ston pa'i rgyal tshab dpal sgam po pa'i khri gdung 'dzin pa'i dam pa rnams kyi gtam baiḍūrya'i phreng ba*, Dwags lha sgam po edition.

Säkya Zangpo *(disc.)*, *Thugs rje chen po nam mkha' rgyal po'i mngon rtogs [= Descriptive Basis of Mahākāruôika, King of Space].*

Säkya Zangpo (disc.), *Gab pa mngon du phyung [= Revelation of the Hidden].*

Shenyen Tsultrim (ed), *Lha sa'i dgon tho rin chen spungs rgyan.* Bod jlong mi rigs dpe skrun khang (2001).

Sonam Gyaltsen (1312-75), *rGyal rabs gsal ba'i me long [= Mirror Illuminating Royal Genealogies].* See also Martin (1997) no. 94, pp. 60-61, and P. Sorensen (1994).

Sumpa Khenpo (1704-88), *Chos 'byung dpag bsam ljon bzang.* Gansu mi rigs dpe skrun khang (1992). See also Martin (1997), no. 289, pp. 129-30.

Tai Situ Jangchub Gyaltsen (1302-64), *bKa' chems mthong ba don ldan [Meaningful to Behold].* Bod ljongs mi rigs dpe skrun khang ((1989). See also Martin (1997), no. 65, p. 47.

Taring Dzaku, Zasak J, *Lha sa gtsug lag khang gi sa bkra dang dkar chag.* Rajpur, Taring House, nd.

Tethong Rakra Tubten Chodar, *dGe 'dun chos 'phel gyi lo rgyus.* Dharamsala, Library of Tibetan Works & Archives, 1980.

Tridrung Lobzang Thubten, "Bar skor byang chub byon lam gyi dar chen rnams kyi lo rgyus", in *Bod kyi shes rig zhib ched rtsom bdam bsgrigs* (2, 1991).

Trijang Losang Yeshe (1901-1981), *rNam grol lag bcangs su gtod pa'i man ngag zab mo tshang la ma nor ba mtshungs med chos kyi rgyal po'i thugs bcud byang chub lam gyi rim pa'i nyams khrid kyi zin bris gsung rab kun gyi bcud bsdus gdams ngag bdud rtsi snying po.* Ganden Shartse Norling Monastery Publications, Karnataka.

Trinle Da'o (fl. 1640), *Gangs can 'dir ston pa'i rgyal tshab dpal ldan sgam po pa'i khri gdung 'dzin pa'i dam pa rnams kyi gtam bai durya'i phreng ba.* sGam-par dpe-'bring, nd.

Troru Khenpo Tsenam, *dPal mnyam med mar pa bka' brgyud kyi grub pa'i mtha' rnam par nge par byed pa mdor bsdus su brjod pa dvags brgyud grub pa'i me long, Gangs can rig brgya'i sgo 'byed lde mig.* Mi rigs dpe skun khang (1989).

Tsetan Zhabdrung (1910-85), *'Jam mgon chos kyi rgyal po tsdong kha pa chen po'i rnam thar [= Biography of Tsongkhapa].* Qinghai (1981).

Tshalpa Kunga Dorje (1309-64), *Deb ther dmar po [= Red Annals].* Annotated by Dungkar Lobzang Trinle, Pe cing mi rigs dpe skrun khang, 1981, Martin no. 77, pp. 52-53.

Tsenpo Nomonhan (1789-1838), *'Dzam gling rgyas bshad snod bcud kun gsal me long.* See also Martin (1997), no. 367, pp. 154-5.

Tsongkhapa (1357-1419), *Byang chub lam rim chenmo.* mTsho sngon mi rigs dpe skrun khang (1985).

Yangpa Choje, *rNam thar dpag bsam ljon bzang [= Biography of Dalai Lama II, Gendun Gyatso]* Zhakabpa Wangchuk Deden (1908-89), *Lha ldan rva sa'phrul snang gtsug lag khag gi dkar chag gser dang rag an rnam dbye gsal por byed pa nor bun i ka sha*, Shakabpa House, Kalimpong (1982)

—— *Bod kyi srid don rgyal rabs*, [=Tibet: A Political History]. Shakabpa House, Kalimpong (1976). See also Martin (1997), no. 498, p. 193.

Indic Sources

i Kangyur Sūtras & Tantras

Karuṇapuṇḍarikasūtra [= Sūtra of the White Lotus of Compassion] T. 112.
Kälacakratantra [= Tantra of the Wheel of Time] T. 362.
Bhadracaryäpraṇidhänaräja [= Aspirational Prayer of Good Conduct] T. 44, T. 1095.
Ratnaküṭasūtra [= Anthology of the Pagoda of Precious Gems] T. 45-93.
Śatasāhasrikä-prajñäpäramitä [= Perfection of Discriminative Awareness in One Hundred Thousand Sections] T. 8.
Saṃvarodayatantra [= Tantra of the Origin of Cakrasaṃvara] T. 373.
Smṛtyupasthānasūtra [= Sūtra of the Foundation of Mindfulness] T. 287.
Hevajra Tantra [= Twofold Recension of the Hevajra Tantra] T. 417-8.

ii) Tangyur Commentaries

Kṣemendra, *Avadānakalpalatä* [= Narrative of the Bodhisattva's Lives] T. 4155.
Tilopā, *Ṣadharmopadeśa* [= Six Yogas of Näropä] T. 2330.
Prajñäkaragupta, *Pramāṇavārtkālaṃkāra* [= Ornament of the Exposition of Valid Cognition] T. 4221.
Vasubandhu, *Abidharmakośa* [Treasury of the Abhidharma] T. 4089.

Chinese Sources

Dazhaosi, Beijing Publishing House, 1980.

Mengzi (c. 372-289 BCE), *Mengzi [= The Book of Mencius]* trans. J. Legge. Clarendon Press (1895).

Mingshilu [= *Record of the Annals of the Ming Dynasty*].
sPang skong phyag rgya pa'i mdo [Sütra of the Rites of Renunciation and Fulfillment] T. 267.

Suishi [= *Annals of the Sui Dynasty*]

Su bai, *Zang chuan fu jiao si yuan kao gu [= Archaeological Studies on the Monasteries of Tibetan Buddhism]*, pp. 1-20. Beijing, Cultural Relics Publishing House (1996).

Jiutangshu [= *Old Chronicles of the Tang Dynasty*]. Tib. trans. in *Thang hru'u Deb gsar rnying* [= *New and Old Chronicles of the Tang Dynasty*] by Dondrub Gyal and Khrin-chin dbyin. See Martin (1997), no. 533, p. 202.

Xintangshu [= *New Chronicles of the Tang Dynasty*]. Tib. trans. in *Thang hru'u Deb gsar rnying* [= *New and Old Chronicles of the Tang Dynasty*] by Dondrub Gyal and Khrin-chin dbyin. See Martin (1997), no. 533, p. 202.

Works in Other Languages

Ahmad, Z, (revised trans.), *The Song of the Queen of Spring or A History of Tibet.* New Delhi, International Academy of Indian Culture and Aditya Prakashan (2007).

Aris, M, *Bhutan.* Warminster, Aris & Phillips (1979).

—— *Hidden Teachings and Secret Lives.* London & New York, Kegan Paul International (1989).

Batchelor, S, *The Tibet Guide,* London, Wisdom Publications (1987).

Bacot, J, Thomas, F, and **Toussaint, C,** *Documents de Touen-houang relatifs a l'histoire du Tibet.* Paris, Libraire orientaliste Paul Geuthner (1940).

R. Bickers, *Ritual and diplomacy: The Macartney Mission to China, 1782-4.* London, (1993).

Brauning, A, "Dendrochronologia 19 (1), pp. 127-137.

Caffarrelli, P & Beguin, G, *Demueres des hommes, Sanctuaires des dieux.* Rome, Universita da Roma (1987).

Chen, V, *Tibet Handbook.* Chico, CA, Moon Publications (1994).

Dalai Lama XIV, *My Land and My People: Memoires of the Dalai Lama of Tibet.* New York, McGraw Hill (1962).

—— *Freedom in Exile: Autobiography of the Fourteenth Dalai Lama.* Abacus (1998).

Das, S. C., *Journey to Lhasa and Central Tibet.* Delhi, Cosmo Publications (1902).

Demieville, P, *Le Concile de Lhasa.* Bibliotheque de l'Institut des Hautes Etudes Chinoises, vol. VII, Paris, Imprimerie Nationale de France (1952).

Dorje, G, *Tibetan Elemental Divination Paintings.* London, Eskenazi & Fogg (2001).

—— *Tibet Handbook.* Bath, Footprint (4th ed. 2009, 3rd ed, 2004a).

—— *Bhutan Handbook* (2004b).

Douglas, N & White, M, Karmapa, *The Black Hat Lama of Tibet.* London, Luzac (1976).

Dowman, K, *The Power Places of Central Tibet.* London, RKP (1988).

Dudjom Rinpoche, *The Nyingma School of Tibetan Buddhism.* Translated by Gyurme Dorje & Matthew Kapstein, Boston and London, Wisdom Publications (1991).

Gyalbo, T, Hazod, G and **Sorensen, P,** *Civilization at the Foot of Mount Sham-po: The Royal House of lHa Bug-pa-can and the History of g.Ya'–bzang.* Vienna, Verlag der Osterreichische Akademie der Wissenschraften (2000).

Gyatso, J, "Genre, Authorship, and Transmission in Visionary Buddhism: The Literary Traditions of Thang-stong rGyal-po," in S. D. Goodman and R. M. Davidson (eds), *Tibetan Buddhism: Reason and Revelation.* Albany, SUNY Press (1992).

Harrer, H, *Seven Years in Tibet.* London, Rupert Hart-Davis (1953).

Heller, A, "The Lhasa gTsug lag khang: observations on the ancient wood carvings". Lhasa Valley Conference Proceedings, 1997.

Hazod, G, Sorensen, P & Sensen, P, *Thundering Falcon.* Vienna, Oestereichische Akademie der Wissenschaften (2005).

Imaeda & Spanien, Vol. 111, Choix de documents (1990).

Jackson, D, *The Mallas of Mustang: Historical, religious and Oratorial Traditions of the Nepalese-Tibetan Borderland.* Dharamsala, (1984).

Kapstein, M, "Remarks on the Maôi bKa' 'bum and the Cult of Avalokiteśvara in Tibet", in S. D. Goodman and R. M. Davidson (eds), *Tibetan Buddhism: Reason and Revelation.* Albany, SUNY Press (1992).

—— *The Tibetans.* Oxford, Blackwell Publishing (2006).

Karmay, S. G, The Arrow and the Spindle. Studies in History, Myths. Rituals and Beliefs in Tibet. Kathmandu, Mandala Book Point (1998).

Kerihual, T, "Essai sur l'histoire du clan Mgar, des origins jusqu'a l'an 700", MA thesis, INALCO, Paris (2005).

Landon, P, *Lhasa.* 2 vols. London, Hurst & Blackett (1905).

Larsen, K & Sinding-Larsen, A (eds), *The Lhasa Atlas: Traditional Tibetan Architecture and Townscape.* London, Serindia (2001).

Levi, S, *Le Nepal, Le toit du monde,* 1985.

Liu, L (ed), *Buddhist Art of the Tibetan Plateau,* San Francisco, China Books and Periodicals, 1988.

Martin, D, *Tibetan Histories.* London, Serindia Publications (1997).

Mills, A, *Identity, Ritual and State in Tibetan Buddhism.: The Foundation of Authority in Gelukpa Monasticism.* London, Routledge/Curzon (2003).

—— *"Re-assessing the Supine Demoness: Royal Buddhist Geomancy in the Srong btsan sgampo Mythology",* JIATS, no. 3, Dec. 2007.

Mullin, G, *Tsongkhapa's Six Yogas of Naropa.* Ithaca, Snowlion (1996)

Parfianovitch Y, Dorje G & Meyer F, *Tibetan Medical Paintings.* London, Serindia Publications (1992).

Orgyen Topgyal, *The Life and Teaching of Chokgyur Lingpa.* Kathmandu, Rangjung Yeshe Publications (1982).

Paltrul Rinpoche (transl. Padmakara Translation Committee), *The Words of My Perfect Teacher.* San Francisco, Harper Collins (1994).

Ramble, C, *The Navel of the Demoness: Tibetan Buddhism and Civil religion in Highland Nepal.* Oxford, OUP (2007).

Richardson, H. E, *A Corpus of Early Tibetan Inscriptions.* London, Royal Asiatic Society (1985).

—— *Ceremonies of the Lhasa Year.* London, Serindia Publications (1993).

—— *High Peaks, Pure Earth: Collected Writings on Tibetan History and Culture.* London, Serindia Publications (1998).

—— "How Old was Songtsen Gampo" in *High Peaks, Pure Earth,* pp. 3-6.

—— "The First Tibetan Chos-' byung" in *High Peaks, Pure Earth,* pp. 89-99.

—— "The Jo-khang Great Temple of Lhasa", first published in A. Macdonald & Y. Imaeda, eds, *Essais sur l'art du Tibet,* Maisonneuve, Paris, 1977, pp. 157-188; republished in *High Peaks, Pure Earth,* pp. 237.260.

—— "Mun Sheng Kong Co and Kim Sheng Kong Co, Two Chinese Princesses in Tibet", first published in *Tibet Journal,* 22/1: 3-11, 1997; republished in *High Peaks, Pure Earth,* pp. 207-15.

—— "The Growth of a Legend", in *High Peaks, Pure Earth,* pp. 39-47.

Roerich, G, (trans.), *The Blue Annals.* Delhi, Motilal Banarsidas (1976).

Schuh, S & Dagyab, L. S., *Urkunden, Erlasse und Sendsschreiben, aus dem Besitz sikkimesischer, Adelshäuser und des Kloster Phodang,* Monumenta Tibetica Historica, Abteilung III-Band 3, VGH Wissenschaftsverlag, St. Augustin (1978).

Shakabpa, T. W. D., *Tibet: A Political History.* New Haven/London, Yale University Press (1967).

Stearns, C, *King of the Empty Plain.* Ithaca, Snowlion Publications (2007).

Sis, V & Vanis, J, *On the Road Through Tibet.* London, Spring Books, 1956.

—— with **Kolmas,** J, *Recalling Tibet,* Institute for Comparative Research in Human Culture, Olso, 1997.

Sorensen, P. K., *Tibetan Buddhist Historiography: The Mirror Illuminating the Royal Genealogies.* Wiesbaden, Harrassowitz Verlag (1994).

Stoddard, H, "Restoration in the Lhasa Tsuglagkhang and the Fate of Its Early Wall Paintings", in *Orientations,* Vol. XX, pp. 69-73.

Taring, R. D., *Daughter of Tibet.* London, Murray (1970).

Thomas, L. Jr, *Out of this World: Across the Himalayas to Tibet.* London, (1951).

Tsybikov, G. T., "Lhasa and Central Tibet", *Smithsonian Institute Annual Report* (1903).

Tucci, G, *Tibetan Painted Scrolls,* 13 vols. Rome, Libreria dello Stato (1949).

—— "The Wives of Srong brtsan Sgam po", in *Oriens Extremus,* ix (1962), pp. 121-6.

—— *To Lhasa and Beyond.* Ithaca, Snowlion Publications (1983).

Vitali, R, *Early Temples of Central Tibet.* London, Serindia Publications (1990).

—— *The Kingdoms of Gu.ge Pu.hrang.* Dharamsala, Tho ling dpe med lhun gyis grub pa'i gsug lag khang lo 1000 'khor ba'i rjes dran mdzad sgo'i sgrig tshogs chung (1996).

Von Schroeder, U, *Buddhist Sculptures in Tibet*, Vols I-II. Hong Kong, Visual Dharma Publications (2001).

— *108 Buddhist Statues in Tibet.* Chicago, Serindia Publications (2008).

Vostrikov, A. I, *Tibetan Historical Literature.* Trans. from Russian by Harish Chandra Gupta. K. *The Hidden History of the Sino-Indian Frontier,* Calcutta, Indian Studies Past and Present (1974).

Waddell, L. A, *Lhasa and its Mysteries,* London (1905).

Walsh, E. H. C, "Lhasa" in *Journal of the Royal Asiatic Society,* 1946.

Warner, C. D, "The Precious Lord: The History Practice of the Cult of the Jowo Śākyamuni in Lhasa, Tibet." Ph.D Dissertation, Department of Sanskrit and Indian Studies, Harvard University, 2008.

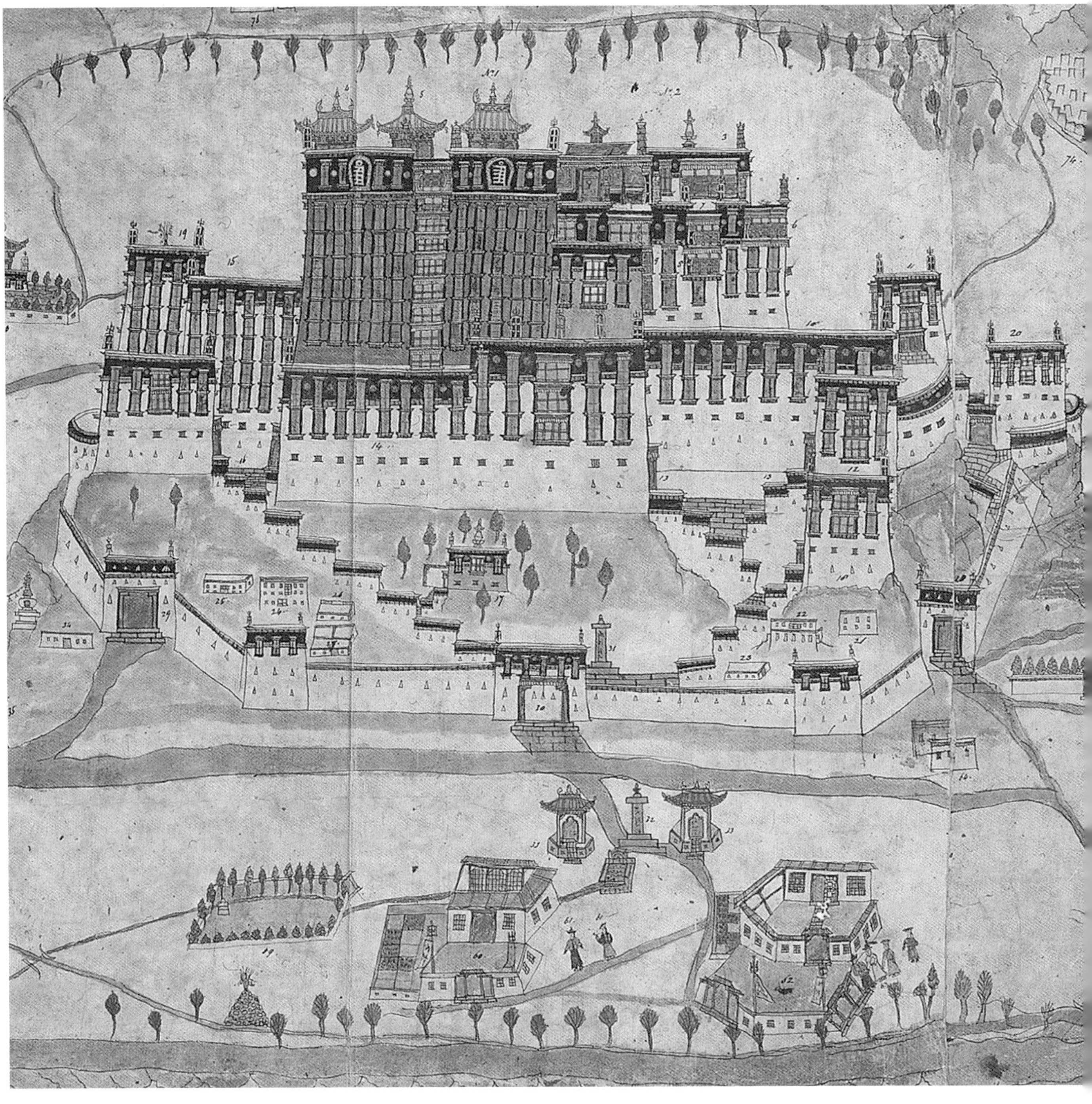

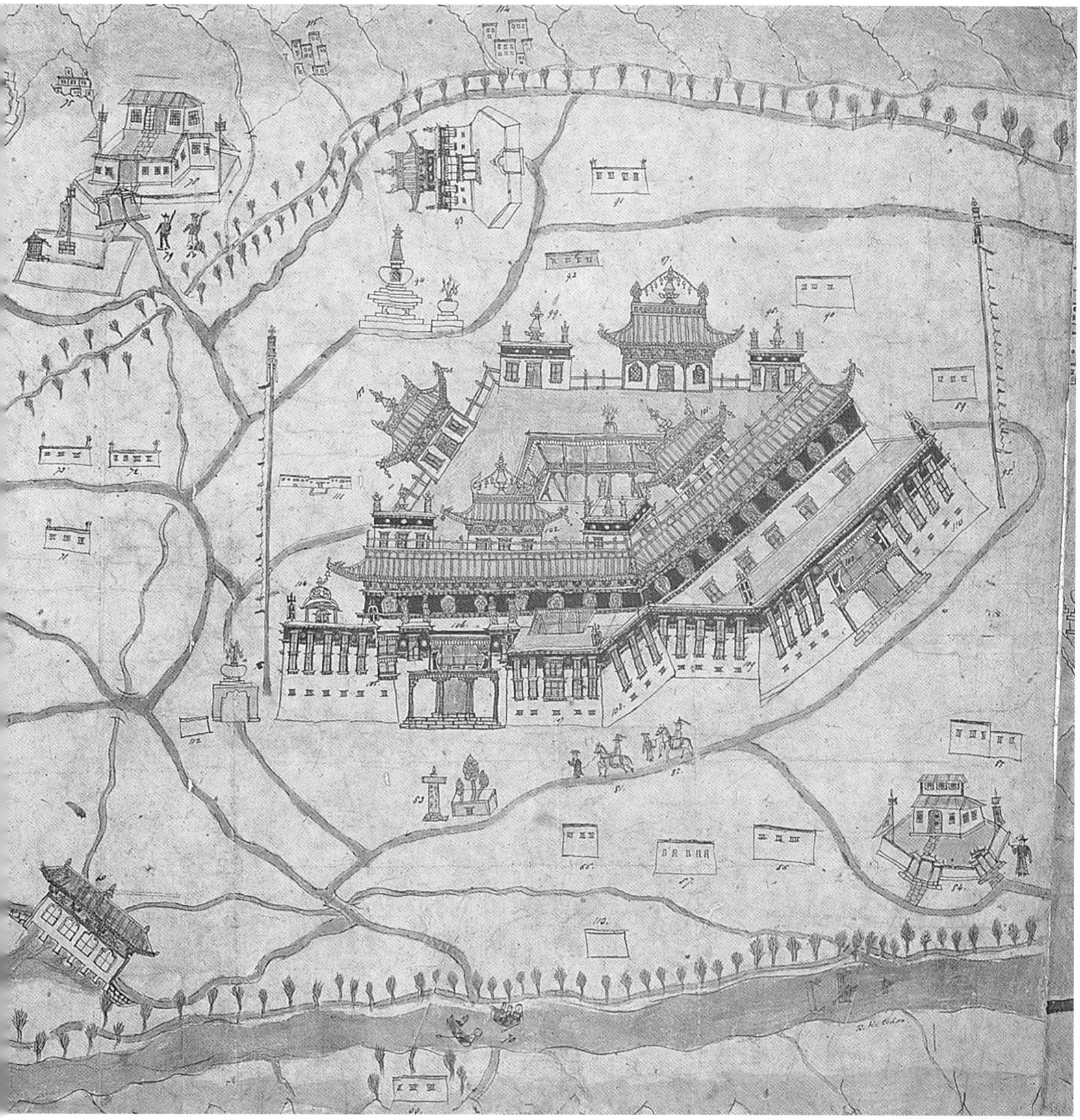

A drawing of Lhasa, circa 1860, by a Tibetan lama,
showing the Potala on the left and the Jokhang on the right.

Index

Photo credits

The publisher wishes to acknowledge his gratitude to all the following who generously contributed photographic material:

AA – André Alexander
CB – Catriona Bass
GD – Gyurme Dorje
TD – Tsering Dorje
MF – Michael Freeman
LG – LeRoy Griggs
GG – Gonkar Gyatso
OK – Ozer Karmay
LH – Lhala
HM – Hansjorg Mayer
JM – Josef Müller
KO – Ken Okura
HS – Heini Schneebeli
US – Ulrich von Schroeder
JS – John Stanley
HMS – Heather Stoddard
JV – Josef Vanis

Clare Harris and Philip Grover for historical photographs from the *Tibet Album* of the Pitt Rivers Museum, Oxford, British Photography in Central Tibet 1920-1950; www.tibet.prm.ox.ac.uk,
SC – Frederik Spencer Chapman, (p. 42, *1998.131.571*, p. 43, *-575*)
RL – Rabden Lecha, (p. 30a, *1998.285.213*, p. 31, *1998.285.212.2 + 215*)
HR – Hugh Richardson, (p. 32, *2001.59.1.55.1*, p. 33a, *-9.17.1*, p. 33b, *-60.1*, p. 34, *-51.1*, p. 35, *-20.1*, p. 37, *-67.1*, p. 38, *-50.1*, p. 39a, *-17.1*, p. 40, *-54.1*, p. 41, *-73.1*, p. 45, *-43.1*,
WR – Willoughby Patrick Rosemeyer, (p. 30b, *1998.285.542*, p. 46, *-286.41.1*)
HSt – Harry Staunton, (p. 39b, *1999.23.1.39.3*)

Jan Faull for film stills from material held in the *Tibet Collection* at the British Film Institute, National Archive, London; www.bfi.org.uk
BG – Basil Gould
JG – James Guthrie
GS – George Sheriff
TS – Tsieu-lien Shen